3rd Workshop on Deep Learning Approaches for Low-Resource Natural Language Processing (DeepLo 2022)

Online
14 July 2022

ISBN: 978-1-7138-5628-3

Printed from e-media with permission by:

Curran Associates, Inc.
57 Morehouse Lane
Red Hook, NY 12571

Some format issues inherent in the e-media version may also appear in this print version.

Association for Computational Linguistics
209 N. Eighth Street
Stroudsburg, Pennsylvania 18360

Phone: 1-570-476-8006
Fax: 1-570-476-0860

acl@aclweb.org

Additional copies of this publication are available from:

Curran Associates, Inc.
57 Morehouse Lane
Red Hook, NY 12571 USA
Phone: 845-758-0400
Fax: 845-758-2633
Email: curran@proceedings.com
Web: www.proceedings.com

DeepLo 2022

The 3rd Workshop on Deep Learning Approaches for Low-Resource NLP

Proceedings of the DeepLo Workshop

July 14, 2022

The DeepLo organizers gratefully acknowledge the support from the following sponsors.

Gold

Order copies of this and other ACL proceedings from:

Association for Computational Linguistics (ACL)
209 N. Eighth Street
Stroudsburg, PA 18360
USA
Tel: +1-570-476-8006
Fax: +1-570-476-0860
acl@aclweb.org

Introduction

The NAACL 2022 Workshop on Deep Learning Approaches for Low-Resource Natural Language Processing (DeepLo) takes place on Thursday, July 22, in Seattle Washington, USA, immediately after the main conference.

Natural Language Processing is being revolutionized by deep learning. However, deep learning requires large amounts of annotated data, and its advantage over traditional statistical methods typically diminishes when such data is not available. Large amounts of annotated data simply do not exist for many low-resource languages. Even for high-resource languages it can be difficult to find linguistically annotated data of sufficient size and quality to allow neural methods to excel; this remains true even as few-shot learning approaches have gained popularity in recent years.

This workshop aims to bring together researchers from the NLP and ML communities who work on learning with neural methods when there is not enough data for those methods to succeed out-of-the-box. Specifically, it will provide attendees with an overview of new and existing approaches from various disciplines, and enable them to distill principles that can be more generally applicable. We will also discuss the main challenges arising in this setting, and outline potential directions for future progress.

Our program covers a broad spectrum of applications and techniques. It is augmented by invited talks from Yulia Tsvetkov, Sebastian Ruder, Graham Neubig, and David Ifeoluwa Adelani.

We would like to thank the members of our Program Committee for their timely and thoughtful reviews.

Colin Cherry, Angela Fan, George Foster, Gholamreza (Reza) Haffari, Shahram Khadivi, anyun (Violet) Peng, Xiang Ren, Ehsan Shareghi, Swabha Swayamdipta

Organizing Committee

Organizing Committee Members

Colin Cherry, Google Research
Angela Fan, Facebook AI Research
George Foster, Google Research
Gholamreza (Reza) Haffari, Monash University
Shahram Khadivi, eBay
Nanyun (Violet) Peng, UCLA
Xiang Ren, USC/ISI
Ehsan Shareghi, Monash University
Swabha Swayamdipta, Allen Institute for AI

Program Committee

Invited Speakers

Yulia Tsvetkov, University of Washington
Sebastian Ruder, Google
Graham Neubig, Carnegie Mellon University
David Ifeoluwa Adelani, Saarland University

Reviewers

David Adelani, Saarland University
Emily Allaway, Columbia University
Parnia Bahar, AppTek
Marco Basaldella, Amazon
Leonard Dahlmann, eBay
Haim Dubossarsky, Queen Mary University of London
Kevin Duh, Johns Hopkins University
Markus Freitag, Google
Yingbo Gao, RWTH Aachen University
Thamme Gowda, University of Southern California
Xuanli He, Monash University
Yacine Jernite, Hugging Face
Robin Jia, University of Southern California
Jonathan K., University of Michigan
Zhuang Li, Monash University
Manuel Mager, University of Stuttgart
Evgeny Matusov, AppTek
Zaiqiao Meng, University of Glasgow
Phoebe Mulcaire, University of Washington
Benjamin Muller, INRIA Paris
Arturo Oncevay, University of Edinburgh
Pavel Petrushkov, eBay
Victor Prokhorov, University of Edinburgh
Roi Reichart, Technion
Sebastian Ruder, Google
Partha Talukdar, Google Research India
David Thulke, RWTH Aachen University
Nicola Ueffing, eBay
Thuy-Trang Vu, Monash University
Ivan Vulić, University of Cambridge
Sarah Wiegreffe, Georgia Tech
Zhaofeng Wu, AI2
Minghao Wu, Monash University
Poorya Zaremoodi, Oracle Labs
Jinming Zhao, Monash University
Mengjie Zhao, LMU
Yanpeng Zhao, University of Edinburgh
Wenxuan Zhou, University of Southern California

Table of Contents

Program

Thursday, July 14, 2022

08:50 - 09:00	*Opening Remarks*
10:00 - 09:45	*Invited talk - Sebastian Ruder (Virtual)*
10:00 - 10:30	*Coffee Break*
10:30 - 11:15	*Invited talk - David Ifeoluwa Adelani (In-person)*
11:15 - 12:15	*Poster session I (Virtual)*
13:30 - 12:15	*Lunch Break*
13:30 - 14:15	*Invited talk - Yulia Tsvetkov (In-person)*
14:15 - 15:15	*Poster session II (In-person) and Poster session III (Virtual)*
15:15 - 15:30	*Coffee Break*
15:30 - 16:15	*Invited talk - Graham Neubig (In-person)*
16:15 - 16:30	*Closing remark*

Introducing QuBERT: A Large Monolingual Corpus and BERT Model for Southern Quechua

Rodolfo Zevallos[◇] **John E. Ortega**[§] **William Chen**[▽] **Richard Castro**[Ω] **Nuria Bel**[◇]
Cesar Yoshikawa[ψ] **Renzo Ventura**[ψ] **Hilario Aradiel**[ψ] **Nelsi Melgarejo**[α]
[◇]Universitat Pompeu Fabra [§]Universidade de Santiago de Compostela (CITIUS)
[▽]University of Central Florida [Ω]Universidad Nacional de San Antonio Abad
[ψ]Universidad Nacional del Callao [α]Pontificia Universidad Católica del Perú
{rodolfojoel.zevallos, nuria.bel}@upf.edu, john.ortega@usc.gal, wchen6255@knights.ucf.edu,
rcastro@hinant.in, {ctyoshikawaa, rventuras, haradielc}@unac.edu.pe, nelsi.melgarejo@pucp.edu.pe

Abstract

The lack of resources for languages in the Americas has proven to be a problem for the creation of digital systems such as machine translation, search engines, chat bots, and more. The scarceness of digital resources for a language causes a higher impact on populations where the language is spoken by millions of people. We introduce the first official large combined corpus for deep learning of an indigenous South American low-resource language spoken by millions called *Quechua*. Specifically, our curated corpus is created from text gathered from the southern region of Peru where a dialect of Quechua is spoken that has not traditionally been used for digital systems as a target dialect in the past. In order to make our work repeatable by others, we also offer a public, pre-trained, BERT model called *QuBERT* which is the largest linguistic model ever trained for any Quechua type, not just the southern region dialect. We furthermore test our corpus and its corresponding BERT model on two major tasks: (1) named-entity recognition (NER) and (2) part-of-speech (POS) tagging by using state-of-the-art techniques where we achieve results comparable to other work on higher-resource languages. In this article, we describe the methodology, challenges, and results from the creation of QuBERT which is on on par with other state-of-the-art multilingual models for natural language processing achieving between 71 and 74% F1 score on NER and 84–87% on POS tasks.

1 Introduction

With the availability of online digital resources for computation and data storage, the capability for executing natural language processing (NLP) tasks such as named-entity recognition (NER), part-of-speech (POS) tagging, and machine translation (MT) on low-resource languages, languages with few digital resources available, has increased. The processing power and data available for experimentation are unsurpassed in history and research (Edwards, 2021) has shown that in the current decade we are on track to overcome previous methods, such as Moore's law (Schaller, 1997), for predicting computing time of experiments. This finding is better observed on high-resources languages like English and French where the amount of data that exists is more than enough to take advantage of the latest computing architectures. Unfortunately, for other low-resource languages like Quechua, an indigenous language spoken by millions in Peru, South America, it is more difficult to create statistically significant NLP models due to the amount of data needed (typically on the order of millions of sentences). Therefore, it is critical to create public-facing mechanisms for low-resource languages like Quechua to help provide research collaboration which will improve the quality for low-resource language NLP systems. We aim to improve the digital resources available for Quechua by curating a large monolingual corpus for southern Quechua, a dialect of Quechua spoken in the southern region of Peru not commonly found in most literature.

The initiative we present in this article can be considered a major contribution and advancement as means to improve the quality of NLP tasks for the Quechua language. We outline the multiple innovations and contributions provided below.

1. A considerably large, curated, monolingual corpus of southern Quechua consisting of nearly 450K segments.

2. A normalization technique applied to the corpus based on finite-state transducers (FSTs) (Rios, 2015; Rios and Göhring, 2016; Ortega et al., 2020a).

Proceedings of the Third Workshop on Deep Learning for Low-Resource Natural Language Processing, pages 1 - 13
July 14, 2022 ©2022 Association for Computational Linguistics

3. Several tokenization techniques applied to the corpus, each made available for download, including byte-pair encoding (BPE) (Sennrich et al., 2015), BPE-Guided (Ortega et al., 2020a), and Prefix-Root-Postfix-Encoding (PRPE) (Chen and Fazio, 2021; Zuters et al., 2018).

4. A pre-trained transformer model based on RoBERTa (Liu et al., 2019) called *QuBERT* that uses the corpus along with the best performing normalization and tokenization techniques from items 2 and 3 above.

5. A comparison of the performance of the techniques introduced in items 2 and 3 above on a NER classification task.

6. A comparison of the performance of the techniques introduced in items 2 and 3 above on a POS classification task.

In order to cover our innovations and contributions, we highlight the details in several sections. First, in Section 2, we describe the latest work on Quechua and other techniques related to low-resource NLP tasks such as the ones we introduce on NER and POS. Next in Section 3, we provide more background on the Quechua language by covering morphological, phonological, and other important grammatical details. Then, we describe how we curated our corpus in Section 4. In Section 5, we provide details on the parameters and configuration for our models and tokenization techniques which leads way to the experimental evaluation and results from the NER and POS tasks in Section 6. Finally, we wrap up with a few proposed lines of future work and a conclusion in Section 7.

2 Related work

In this section we present several works that can be considered state-of-the-art at this time for Quechua. Since we are introducing several new contributions, we briefly cover the most recent work and how it related to each contribution mentioned.

First, concerning the introduction of the corpus, we discuss work where corpora have been introduced for public use. Like many low-resource NLP projects, one of the several corpora that is often used is the Opus[1] (Tiedemann, 2012) corpus. It contains text similar to ours in southern Quechua (Quechua II, see more details on Quechua variants in Section 3); however, it contains biblical text only. Other work (Ortega et al., 2020a) introduced the JW300 corpus (Agić and Vulić, 2019); their corpus was for one domain also. The corpus we present contains entries from several diverse sources while at the same time including Opus and the JW300. Ortega et. al (Ortega et al., 2020a) also presented a magazine selection known as *Hinantin* which contained 250 non-biblical Quechua—Spanish sentences found on-line[2]. While the Hinantin magazine was a more diverse domain than other Quechua corpora previously introduced, our corpus is the largest and most diverse compiled currently available.

Our second contribution consists of a normalization technique used in previous work (Rios, 2015; Rios and Göhring, 2016; Ortega et al., 2020a). The work presented in this article uses the same normalization technique (described further in Section 5) but, to our knowledge, this is the first time that the normalization technique has been used on a corpus of this size for southern Quechua.

Thirdly, for Quechua, there has not been a tokenization comparison similar to the one presented here. There are two works (Chen and Fazio, 2021; Ortega et al., 2020a) that present approaches called *BPE-Guided* and *PRPE* separately but their work did not compare on such a varied corpus for named-entity recognition or part-of-speech tasks, both of their works for the machine translation task only.

The fourth, fifth, and sixth contributions are all related to the first-time presentation of a deep learning transformer model for Quechua that is used for NER and POS classification tasks. One of the works that presented deep learning approaches for Quechua is a shared task (Mager et al., 2021a) from the first workshop on NLP for indigenous languages of the America (Mager et al., 2021b). Another work called *indt5* (Nagoudi et al., 2021) used an encoder-decoder model transformers based on T5 (Raffel et al., 2020). Both models were mainly used for translation and the data did not contain nearly as much Quechua–Spanish text as ours. (Ortega et al., 2020a) applied a deep learning approach where quality was low due to the use of the Opus corpus for training and Hinantin for test – their deep learning approach was for machine translation also. Other work (Zheng et al., 2021; Liu et al., 2020) has presented large corpora with trans-

[1] `http://opus.nlpl.eu`

[2] `http://hinant.in`

former architectures but did not include Quechua as one of the low-resource languages. The one work that can be considered closest to ours in size and technique is the work by Wongso et. al (Wongso et al., 2021), they pre-trained mono-lingual models on GPT-2 (Radford et al., 2019), BERT (Devlin et al., 2019), and RoBERTa (Liu et al., 2019). Like our work, they used a monolingual corpus which consisted of a variety of text and evaluated the models on a sentiment classification task for Sudanese. The main difference between their work and our work is that our tasks are slightly different and are based on Quechua. In order to better understand why NLP tasks for Quechua can be more complex than for other languages, we present more details in the next section on the language.

3 Quechua language

Quechua is an indigenous language native to several regions in South America, mainly Peru, Ecuador, and Bolivia, and is spoken by nearly 8 million people. It is known (Pinnis et al., 2017; Kann, 2019; Karakanta et al., 2018) to be a highly inflective language based on its suffixes which agglutinate. Due to its morphology, Quechua has been found to be similar to other languages like Finnish (Ortega et al., 2021, 2020b; Ortega and Pillaipakkamnatt, 2018).

Linguistically, Quechua can be considered a unique and even complex language due to the highly polysynthetic nature and phonology. Slight changes in morphemes (small sub-word units) can modify a word's meaning drastically. Since Quechua is the South American language with the highest amount of native speakers and those speakers tend to introduce diverse accentuated tones on different words depending on the locality, one can assume that the combination of morphological and tonal rules that cause inflection can make tasks like the ones presented in this article (NER and POS) difficult due to the high likelihood of non-common meanings for sub-words and letters. For example, by adding an accent to the letter 'o' in Quechua, words become plural.

Quechua synthesis, or the *synthetic index* (Greenberg, 1963) – the average number of morphemes per word, is about two times larger than English. English typically has around 1.5 morphemes per word and Quechua has about 3 morphemes per word. This high morphological complexity has been described in detail in the past (Muysken, 1988); few have been able to overcome the challenges that low-resource languages like Quechua present for digital processing. Quechua's phonology uses three vowels for the most part: *a*, *i*, and *u*. Consonants, on the other hand, are numerous and depending on the region where it is spoken, Quechua can have up to 14 constants (Ortega et al., 2020a). Generally speaking, lexemes are monosyllabic or bi-syllabic having two vowels (VV) or two consonants (CC) that do not concur in the same syllable. From a phonological perspective, the scheme of any Quechua root is: (C)V(C)-CV(C) (Cerrón-Palomino, 1994).

The region where Quechua is spoken can be considered important. Alfredo Torero (Torero, 1964) reported that there are two main divisions of the language (Quechua I and Quechua II). Quechua II is mostly spoken in regions such as Ayacucho, Peru and is considered a "southern" language. There are several more dialects spoken and others (Adelaar, 2004) report several divisions for Quechua II; but, in this article we focus specifically on the southern version at a high-level.

A lot of the Quechua morphology has been documented in previous works (Rios et al., 2008; Rios, 2015; Muysken, 1988; Monson et al., 2006; Torero, 1964); however, there is not a clear consensus to resolve all morphology issues that may arise. In order to statistically determine which branch of morphemes a verb phrases falls under can be difficult with Quechua since there are so few resources. A short example sentence of how complex morpheme determination can be is depicted in Table 1. In some cases, there are hundreds of options to choose from when choosing which suffix to use for a given Quechua word.

4 Corpus details

4.1 Monolingual

We consider the introduction of our monolingual corpus on southern Quechua the largest corpus of its kind to date. Table 4 gives a precise overview of all of the corpora that we have combined in October 2021 in order to present our corpus publicly online[3]. We have created the corpus from several sources. The majority of corpora combined to create the final corpus is a compilation of 50 monolingual corpora from different sources on the web including OSCAR (Suárez et al., 2019), JW300 (Agić and

[3] `https://huggingface.co/datasets/Llamacha/monolingual-quechua-iic`

Test sentence: Chantapis **Bibli**anejta **qotucha**kuynejta **ima yanapalla**wanchejtaj

Stemmed Morpheme	Potential Suffixes
Chanta	–pis –s
Biblia	–niq –ta
qutachu	–ku –y –niq –ta
ima	
yanapa	–lla –wa –nchik –ta
yanapalla	–wa –nchik –ta

Table 1: The sub-segment suffix choices of a short sentence for a Quechua sentence. (Ortega et al., 2020a)

Vulić, 2019), and CC-100 (Conneau et al., 2020; Wenzek et al., 2020). To our knowledge, these corpora have not yet been introduced as one southern Quechua corpus to the wider research community. Additionally, our corpus contains other corpora mentioned below (see Table 4 for a complete list) that are not easily found on-line.

The introduction of our corpus is part of a larger project called *Llamacha*[4] focused on helping under-resourced communities . In Llamacha, the authors have begun to use the corpus directly as a form of creating software tools able to help teachers in regions of southern Peru where Quechua II is spoken. Llamacha tools cover several use cases such as government documents, children's internet tools, and more. This demand constitutes the main reason we distribute this corpus for public use – it is our hope that others from the research community will get involved to help develop more tools that can use our corpus.

With such a high demand for diverse performance, we compiled our corpus to cover the domains mentioned and more. Our compilation spans across several domains including religion, economics, health, social, political, justice and culture. We consulted several sources such as books and stories from Andean narratives and the Peruvian Ministry of Education[5] to collect data. Table 4 illustrates the entire data set which consists of 4,408,953 tokens and 384,184 sentences, including what are known as "Chanka" and "Collao" variants, variants specific to the Quechua II branch. In effect, we have created a corpus that is nearly ten times larger than most widely used Quechua corpus (Rios, 2015) until now which has eight combined corpora, 47,547 tokens, and 3,614 sentences.

4.2 Named-entity recognition and part-of-speech

Both the NER and POS corpora were created using the corpus introduced and are made publicly available online[6]. There are slight differences, nonetheless, between the amount of examples used that we note in this section.

In order to create the NER and POS corpora a team of ten annotators were selected. The annotators were university students and 7 of 10 of them were native Quechua speakers. Nonetheless, they were all students of what is known as a "Intercultural Bilingual Education" in Peru where students are taught coursework in both Quechua and Spanish. Annotation was performed using Label-Studio[7] to annotate sentences for NER and POS.

The NER corpus was built using 5,450 sentences using the CoNLL2003 (Sang and De Meulder, 2003) format. Work was reviewed to ensure that annotations were standardized and using an BIO format annotating only the following tags: Person (PER), Location (LOC) and Organization (ORG). The POS corpus was built using 4,229 sentences and annotated identical to previous work on POS Rios (2015) for Quechua. Additionally, as a way of having a more precise tagging strategy, we used official dictionaries of "Chanka" and "Collao" Quechua from the Peruvian Ministry of Education to identify POS tag correctness.

5 Experimental settings

5.1 Tokenization

Our tokenization strategy is to include the state-of-the-art techniques currently being used for Quechua, regardless if it is Quechua I or II (Torero, 1964). We do this as a mechanism to show that

[4]https://llamacha.pe
[5]http://www.minedu.gob.pe/
[6]https://github.com/Llamacha/QuBERT
[7]https://labelstud.io

Text	Ismael Montes Hatun Yachay Wasi Yachachiqkunap
BPE	Ismael Montes H@@atun Yachay Wasi Yachachiqkuna@@p
PRPE	Ismael Monte@@s Hatun Ya@@chay Wasi Yach@@achiq@@kuna@@p
BPE-Guided	Is@@m@@a@@el Mon@@t@@es Hatun Yachay Wasi Yach@@achiq@@kunap

Table 2: The use of four word-tokenization techniques for Quechua.

the corpus presented in Section 4 can be used to achieve high performance (around 80–90% accuracy) for tasks similar to high-resource languages as a recent survey (Li et al., 2020) has shown.

We use the latest tokenization techniques which focus on sub-word segmentation. (Haddow et al., 2021; Chen and Fazio, 2021; Ortega et al., 2020a; Sennrich et al., 2015) Byte-pair encoding (BPE) (Sennrich et al., 2015) can be considered one of the most widely-used approaches and a fundamental technique that has served as a baseline for previous research (Ortega et al., 2021, 2020a,b) on Quechua. The BPE approach is considered the de-facto standard tokenization algorithm for agglutinative languages (Chimalamarri and Sitaram, 2021). BPE represents text at the character-level and then merges the most frequent pairs iteratively until a pre-determined number of merge operations have been reached. Our BPE tokenizer was trained on the entire collective corpus from Section 4 with a vocabulary size of 52,000.

Alternatively, we additionally experiment with a popular extension of the BPE technique called *BPE-Guided* (Ortega et al., 2020a), used for increasing performance on Quechua machine translation. BPE-Guided is similar to the BPE approach in that it iteratively "discovers" sub-word segmentation by jointly learning a vocabulary and character-level segmentation. The extension offered by BPE-Guided is that it introduces Quechua knowledge in a *a-priori* manner by using the BPE algorithm for excluding common suffixes found on Wikimedia[8] before learning a vocabulary or segmentation. In our experiments, we use the list of Quechua suffixes introduced previously (Ortega et al., 2020a).

Another tokenization technique that has been shown to perform better than BPE and BPE-Guided on Quechua texts (Chen and Fazio, 2021) is known as the Prefix-Root-Postfix-Encoding (PRPE) (Zuters et al., 2018) technique. The PRPE algorithm separates words into three main divisions: (1) a prefix, (2) a root, and (3) a postfix. It completes this separation by first learning a sub-word vocabulary through detecting potential prefixes and post-fixes based on a heuristic. It then aligns the prefixes and post-fixes into sub-strings of a word to find potential roots. Once the roots have been located, the text is segmented into sub-words according to their statistical probability. Table 2 shows an example southern Quechua sentence tokenized by the three approaches mentioned.

Lastly, all text with exception of one experiment (Text and BPE in Table 3) is normalized with the Quechua toolkit (Rios, 2015) that uses finite-state transducers (Mohri, 1997) to determine if words belong to the same category and can be merged into one. Rios (2015)[Section 2.5] describe their normalization methodology which contains four models that are based on morphology, the "normalization" technique used in our experiments follows their work which includes all four models.

5.2 Model Architecture

We call our model **QuBERT** because it is a transformer model based on BERT (Devlin et al., 2019). More specifically, our model has been trained using the RoBERTa (Devlin et al., 2018) enhancement to BERT which can be considered higher-performing for NER and POS tasks (Li et al., 2020). An example of the model architecture is shown in Figure 1 which shows how our model produces NER classifications given a Quechua sentence.

Our model has been first pre-trained with southern Quechua text on 384,184 sentences. Then, we fine tuned the model with 4,360 sentences for the NER task and 3,383 sentences for the POS task. For the training process, we used 6 hidden layers. Each layer was 768 dimensions, giving us a total of 84 million parameters. For optimization, we used the Adam optimizer with hyper-parameter values of β_1=0.9 and β_2 = 0.99 along with a learning rate of 2.7e-06. Lastly, we incorporated a weight

[8] `https://en.wiktionary.org/wiki/Category:Quechua_suffixes`

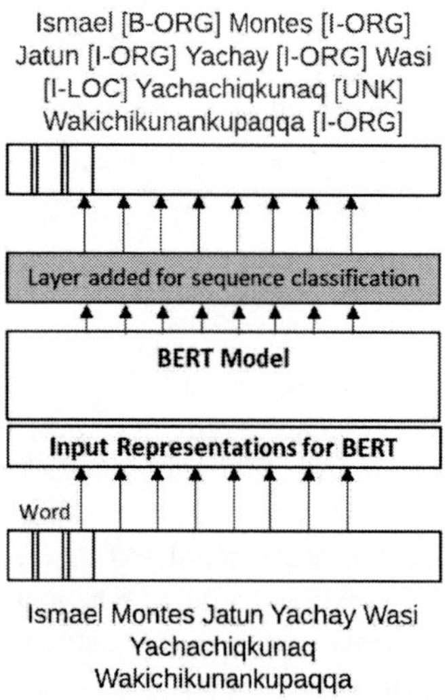

Figure 1: Model architecture based on Bert (Devlin et al., 2019).

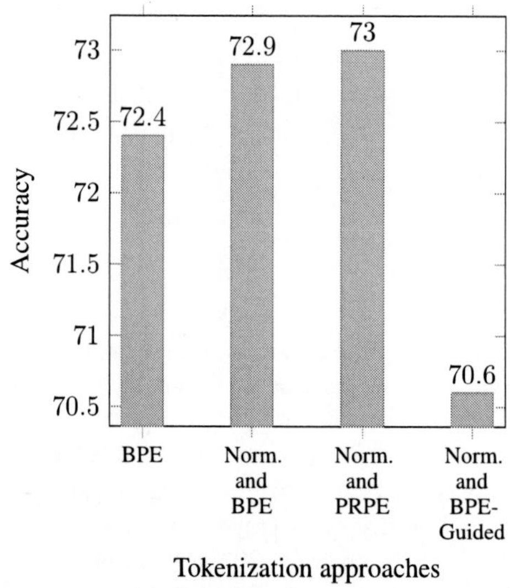

Figure 2: An accuracy comparison of tokenization techniques on southern Quechua (Quechua II) using a RoBERTa (Liu et al., 2019) model for named-entity recognition (NER).

decay factor of 0.1 to prevent overfitting. The pre-training was for two epochs and a batch size of 64 with 12k iterations, before being fine-tuned on the downstream task for 10 epochs and a batch size of 32. Initial development was done on a Google Colab[9] notebook, while models used for final testing were pre-trained and fine-tuned on a single 16GB NVIDIA Tesla V100 GPU.

6 Results

The results presented in this section show how well **QuBERT** performs on two main tasks: NER and POS. We feel that the contributions presented in Section 1 are sufficient to warrant wider use of our work; however, it is our intention to show that the corpus, model, and experiments could provide easy access for future work. We cover each task (NER and POS) as separate sections below in order to provide better insight into how the model performs in different scenarios, specifically for the different tokenization and normalization (called "norm." in Table 3) techniques mentioned in Section 5. Nonetheless, we provide precision, recall, and F1 scores in Table 3 for both tasks as an aggregate to get an overall sense of how well our base model performs on both tasks.

6.1 Named Entity Recognition

Figure 2 illustrates the accuracy from our model on the NER task. We note that the accuracy scores are somewhat lower than the state-of-the-art for high-resource languages on the NER task (Li et al., 2020). However, our F1 scores seems to be inline with other newly published work on low resources (Bouabdallaoui et al., 2022) (69–70%) for various deep learning models). In future work, we plan on adapting our model to more complex architectures such as those found in SemEval-2022 Task 11 (Malmasi et al., 2022).

To further investigate the findings we report the following findings[10] based on these NER tags: B-LOC, B-ORG, B-PER, I-LOC, I-ORG, I-PER, O. When text was normalized and then tokenized with BPE we noticed that I-ORG and I-PER were the highest amount of true positives (227 and 196 respectively) when compared to other tokenization techniques. However, BPE without normalization performed worse than other techniques on I-PER classification, mainly classifying them as B-LOC. BPE-Guided generally scored similar to BPE on NER with a trend of being slightly lower than BPE. PRPE scored better on I-LOC and I-ORG (306 and 227 respectively) than other techniques and was able to achieve the highest accuracy of all techniques.

From the illustration in Figure 2, we believe that

[9]https://colab.research.google.com

[10]For a complete confusion matrix, please refer to Appendix Table 5.

Tokenization Approach	NER			POS		
	F1	Prec	Recall	F1	Prec	Recall
Text and BPE	0.736	0.749	0.724	0.860	0.859	0.862
Text with norm. and BPE	0.741	0.753	0.729	0.861	0.861	0.862
Text with norm. and PRPE	0.741	0.753	0.730	0.867	0.866	0.868
Text with norm. and BPE-Guided	0.716	0.726	0.707	0.843	0.843	0.843

Table 3: A comparison of tokenization techniques on southern Quechua (Quechua II) using a RoBERTa (Liu et al., 2019) model for classification. Normalization (norm.) is applied using the Quechua toolkit (Rios, 2015). Scores are calculated at the token level and weighted-averaged by class.

the different techniques are closely related but it is clear that the BPE-Guided approach was not as successful for the NER task as it has been in the past for machine translation (Ortega et al., 2020a). We feel that this is probably due to the amount of data introduced in our corpus which did not contain as many matching suffixes as was done in the previous work (Ortega et al., 2020a). Since this is a first-time introduction of a deep learning model for NER in Quechua, we believe that this can serve as a baseline for future work.

6.2 POS tagging

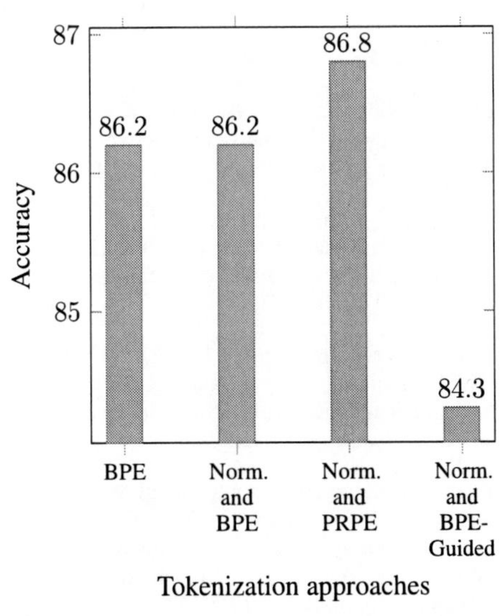

Figure 3: An accuracy comparison of tokenization techniques on southern Quechua (Quechua II) using a RoBERTa (Liu et al., 2019) model for part-of-speech (POS) tagging.

The part-of-speech task seems to be more fitted for our model since we are able to achieve accuracy in the high 80% range as shown in Figure 3, similar to other high-resource tasks(Li et al., 2020). We feel that for POS tagging our model is optimal given the current state-of-the-art. Also, our annotations, while completed by a near-native speaker were somewhat easier to complete due to the more rigid classification of vocabulary-based words in Quechua, essentially the annotator could look up words and parts of speech when there was doubt. In the future, as with the NER task, we fill that we can achieve higher quality with professional translators/annotators.

For POS tagging, unlike the NER task, we were able to discern performance from our analysis based on terms that could be found in a dictionary.[11] Adjectives, verbs and adverbs were mostly correct by all tokenization techniques. Particularly, PRPE outperformed other techniques with the correct classification of 262 adjectives when compared to BPE (259) and BPE-Guided (235). PRPE also performed slightly better on POS verb identification than other techniques. BPE-Guided, on the other hand, performed better with determinant detection finding 43 true positives as opposed to 39 by PRPE and BPE.

7 Conclusion and future work

In this article, we have introduced a novel monolingual corpus, curated and compiled for southern Quechua. We have shown that the corpus can be used for downstream tasks such as NER and POS tagging by creating and releasing a deep learning model based on BERT (Devlin et al., 2019) called **QuBERT**. Additionally, we experimented with the state-of-the-art tokenization techniques for preprocessing and normalization in order to achieve results similar to those found on high-resource languages.

[11] For a complete confusion matrix, please refer to Appendix Table 6.

In the future, we would like to experiment with other model architectures for more complex NER tasks such as those presented at SemEval-2022 (Malmasi et al., 2022), of particular interest is the work from Wang et al. (2022). We would like to include more native Quechua speaking annotators in order to improve the data set even more. The introduction of two or more annotators will allows us to introduce models for tasks such as machine translation, question-answering, and topic modeling where the reference data is even more important. We believe that our work can serve as a baseline for future work and invite other researchers to use the contributions presented here for further investigative lines such as the ones we are considering: online tools for native Quechua speakers and human interaction.

Acknowledgments

This work was partially funded by Project PID2019-104512GB-I00 of the Spanish Ministerio de Ciencia, Innovación and Universidades and Agencia Estatal de Investigación.

References

Willem FH Adelaar. 2004. *The languages of the Andes*. Cambridge University Press.

Željko Agić and Ivan Vulić. 2019. JW300: A wide-coverage parallel corpus for low-resource languages. In *Proceedings of the 57th Annual Meeting of the Association for Computational Linguistics*, pages 3204–3210, Florence, Italy. Association for Computational Linguistics.

Ibrahim Bouabdallaoui, Fatima Guerouate, Samya Bouhaddour, Chaimae Saadi, and Mohamed Sbihi. 2022. Named entity recognition applied on moroccan tourism corpus. *Procedia Computer Science*, 198:373–378.

Rodolfo Cerrón-Palomino. 1994. Quechua sureño. diccionario unificado. *Biblioteca Básica Perúana, Biblioteca Nacionál del Peru*.

William Chen and Brett Fazio. 2021. Morphologically-guided segmentation for translation of agglutinative low-resource languages. In *Proceedings of the 4th Workshop on Technologies for MT of Low Resource Languages (LoResMT2021)*, pages 20–31.

Santwana Chimalamarri and Dinkar Sitaram. 2021. Linguistically enhanced word segmentation for better neural machine translation of low resource agglutinative languages. *International Journal of Speech Technology*, pages 1–7.

Alexis Conneau, Kartikay Khandelwal, Naman Goyal, Vishrav Chaudhary, Guillaume Wenzek, Francisco Guzmán, Edouard Grave, Myle Ott, Luke Zettlemoyer, and Veselin Stoyanov. 2020. Unsupervised cross-lingual representation learning at scale. In *Proceedings of the 58th Annual Meeting of the Association for Computational Linguistics*, pages 8440–8451, Online. Association for Computational Linguistics.

Jacob Devlin, Ming-Wei Chang, Kenton Lee, and Kristina Toutanova. 2018. BERT: pre-training of deep bidirectional transformers for language understanding. *CoRR*, abs/1810.04805.

Jacob Devlin, Ming-Wei Chang, Kenton Lee, and Kristina Toutanova. 2019. BERT: Pre-training of deep bidirectional transformers for language understanding. In *Proceedings of the 2019 Conference of the North American Chapter of the Association for Computational Linguistics: Human Language Technologies, Volume 1 (Long and Short Papers)*, pages 4171–4186, Minneapolis, Minnesota. Association for Computational Linguistics.

Chris Edwards. 2021. Moore's law: what comes next? *Communications of the ACM*, 64(2):12–14.

Joseph Harold Greenberg. 1963. Universals of language.

Barry Haddow, Rachel Bawden, Antonio Valerio Miceli Barone, Jindřich Helcl, and Alexandra Birch. 2021. Survey of low-resource machine translation. *arXiv preprint arXiv:2109.00486*.

Katharina Kann. 2019. Acquisition of inflectional morphology in artificial neural networks with prior knowledge. *arXiv preprint arXiv:1910.05456*.

Alina Karakanta, Jon Dehdari, and Josef van Genabith. 2018. Neural machine translation for low-resource languages without parallel corpora. *Machine Translation*, 32(1-2):167–189.

Jing Li, Aixin Sun, Jianglei Han, and Chenliang Li. 2020. A survey on deep learning for named entity recognition. *IEEE Transactions on Knowledge and Data Engineering*, 34(1):50–70.

Yinhan Liu, Jiatao Gu, Naman Goyal, Xian Li, Sergey Edunov, Marjan Ghazvininejad, Mike Lewis, and Luke Zettlemoyer. 2020. Multilingual denoising pre-training for neural machine translation. *Trans. Assoc. Comput. Linguistics*, 8:726–742.

Yinhan Liu, Myle Ott, Naman Goyal, Jingfei Du, Mandar Joshi, Danqi Chen, Omer Levy, Mike Lewis, Luke Zettlemoyer, and Veselin Stoyanov. 2019. Roberta: A robustly optimized bert pretraining approach. *arXiv preprint arXiv:1907.11692*.

Manuel Mager, Arturo Oncevay, Abteen Ebrahimi, John Ortega, Annette Rios Gonzales, Angela Fan, Ximena Gutierrez-Vasques, Luis Chiruzzo, Gustavo Giménez-Lugo, Ricardo Ramos, et al. 2021a. Findings of the americasnlp 2021 shared task on open machine translation for indigenous languages of the americas. In *Proceedings of the First Workshop on Natural Language Processing for Indigenous Languages of the Americas*, pages 202–217.

Manuel Mager, Arturo Oncevay, Annette Rios, Ivan Vladimir Meza Ruiz, Alexis Palmer, Graham Neubig, and Katharina Kann. 2021b. Proceedings of the first workshop on natural language processing for indigenous languages of the americas. Association for Computational Linguistics.

Shervin Malmasi, Anjie Fang, Besnik Fetahu, Sudipta Kar, and Oleg Rokhlenko. 2022. Semeval-2022 task 11: Multilingual complex named entity recognition (multiconer). In *Proceedings of the 16th International Workshop on Semantic Evaluation (SemEval-2022). Association for Computational Linguistics.*

Mehryar Mohri. 1997. Finite-state transducers in language and speech processing. *Computational linguistics*, 23(2):269–311.

Christian Monson, Ariadna Font Llitjós, Roberto Aranovich, Lori Levin, Ralf Brown, Eric Peterson, Jaime Carbonell, and Alon Lavie. 2006. Building nlp systems for two resource-scarce indigenous languages: mapudungun and quechua. *Strategies for developing machine translation for minority languages*, page 15.

PC Muysken. 1988. Affix order and interpretation: Quechua.

El Moatez Billah Nagoudi, Wei-Rui Chen, Muhammad Abdul-Mageed, and Hasan Cavusoglu. 2021. IndT5: A text-to-text transformer for 10 indigenous languages. In *Proceedings of the First Workshop on Natural Language Processing for Indigenous Languages of the Americas*, pages 265–271, Online. Association for Computational Linguistics.

John Ortega and Krishnan Pillaipakkamnatt. 2018. Using morphemes from agglutinative languages like quechua and finnish to aid in low-resource translation. In *Proceedings of the AMTA 2018 Workshop on Technologies for MT of Low Resource Languages (LoResMT 2018)*, pages 1–11.

John E Ortega, Richard Castro Mamani, and Kyunghyun Cho. 2020a. Neural machine translation with a polysynthetic low resource language. *Machine Translation*, 34(4):325–346.

John E Ortega, Richard Alexander Castro-Mamani, and Jaime Rafael Montoya Samame. 2021. Love thy neighbor: Combining two neighboring low-resource languages for translation. In *Proceedings of the 4th Workshop on Technologies for MT of Low Resource Languages (LoResMT2021)*, pages 44–51.

John E Ortega, Richard Alexander Castro Mamani, and Jaime Rafael Montoya Samame. 2020b. Overcoming resistance: The normalization of an amazonian tribal language. In *Proceedings of the 3rd Workshop on Technologies for MT of Low Resource Languages*, pages 1–13.

Mārcis Pinnis, Rihards Krišlauks, Daiga Deksne, and Toms Miks. 2017. Neural machine translation for morphologically rich languages with improved subword units and synthetic data. In *International Conference on Text, Speech, and Dialogue*, pages 237–245. Springer.

Alec Radford, Jeffrey Wu, Rewon Child, David Luan, Dario Amodei, Ilya Sutskever, et al. 2019. Language models are unsupervised multitask learners. *OpenAI blog*, 1(8):9.

Colin Raffel, Noam Shazeer, Adam Roberts, Katherine Lee, Sharan Narang, Michael Matena, Yanqi Zhou, Wei Li, and Peter J. Liu. 2020. Exploring the limits of transfer learning with a unified text-to-text transformer. *Journal of Machine Learning Research*, 21(140):1–67.

Annette Rios. 2015. *A basic language technology toolkit for Quechua.* Ph.D. thesis, University of Zurich.

Annette Rios and Anne Göhring. 2016. Machine learning applied to rule-based machine translation. In *Hybrid Approaches to Machine Translation*, pages 111–129. Springer.

Annette Rios, Anne Göhring, and Martin Volk. 2008. A quechua-spanish parallel treebank. *LOT Occasional Series*, 12:53–64.

Erik F Sang and Fien De Meulder. 2003. Introduction to the conll-2003 shared task: Language-independent named entity recognition. *arXiv preprint cs/0306050.*

Robert R Schaller. 1997. Moore's law: past, present and future. *IEEE spectrum*, 34(6):52–59.

Rico Sennrich, Barry Haddow, and Alexandra Birch. 2015. Neural machine translation of rare words with subword units. *arXiv preprint arXiv:1508.07909.*

Pedro Javier Ortiz Suárez, Benoît Sagot, and Laurent Romary. 2019. Asynchronous pipeline for processing huge corpora on medium to low resource infrastructures. In *7th Workshop on the Challenges in the Management of Large Corpora (CMLC-7)*. Leibniz-Institut für Deutsche Sprache.

Jörg Tiedemann. 2012. Parallel data, tools and interfaces in opus. In *Lrec*, volume 2012, pages 2214–2218.

Alfredo Torero. 1964. *Los dialectos quechuas*. Univ. Agraria.

Xinyu Wang, Yongliang Shen, Jiong Cai, Tao Wang, Xiaobin Wang, Pengjun Xie, Fei Huang, Weiming Lu, Yueting Zhuang, Kewei Tu, et al. 2022. Damo-nlp at semeval-2022 task 11: A knowledge-based system for multilingual named entity recognition. *arXiv preprint arXiv:2203.00545.*

Guillaume Wenzek, Marie-Anne Lachaux, Alexis Conneau, Vishrav Chaudhary, Francisco Guzmán, Armand Joulin, and Edouard Grave. 2020. CCNet: Extracting high quality monolingual datasets from web crawl data. In *Proceedings of the 12th Language Resources and Evaluation Conference*, pages 4003–4012, Marseille, France. European Language Resources Association.

Wilson Wongso, Henry Lucky, and Derwin Suhartono. 2021. Pre-trained transformer-based language models for sundanese.

Francis Zheng, Machel Reid, Edison Marrese-Taylor, and Yutaka Matsuo. 2021. Low-resource machine translation using cross-lingual language model pretraining. In *Proceedings of the First Workshop on Natural Language Processing for Indigenous Languages of the Americas*, pages 234–240, Online. Association for Computational Linguistics.

Jānis Zuters, Gus Strazds, and Kārlis Immers. 2018. Semi-automatic quasi-morphological word segmentation for neural machine translation. In *International Baltic conference on databases and information systems*, pages 289–301. Springer.

A Appendix

The figures below represent several of the individual differences between corpora and their corresponding language in Table 4 and tokenization approaches for NER and POS in Tables 5 and 6 respectively.

Corpus	# Sentences	# Tokens	Dialect	Year	Dominio
jw300_2013	124,038	1,465,494	Chanka	2013	Religion
wikipedia_2021	96,560	1,009,631	Collao	2021	Miscellaneous
cc100-quechua	86,250	1,206,770	Collao	2018	Miscellaneous
jw300_2017	25,585	294,473	Collao	2017	Religion
microsoft	5,018	60,847	Collao	2021	Norma
que_community_2017	21,139	38,570	Collao	2017	Miscellaneous
tribunal_constitucional	1,148	32,974	Chanka	2021	Justice
tierra_vive	4,731	27,768	Collao	2013	Religion
conectamef	433	20,683	Collao	2016	Economy
unesco	937	16,933	Collao	2020	Program
oscar_quz	491	12,717	Collao	2020	Miscellaneous
constitucion_simplified_quz	999	12,217	Collao	1993	Norma
libro_quechua	781	11,476	Chanka	2002	Agreement
handbook_quy	2,297	11,350	Chanka	2019	Education
dw_quz	325	11,079	Collao	2009	Social
yaku_unumanta	283	10,787	Chanka	2013	Norma
uywaymanta	683	9,231	Collao	2015	Education
maria_mamani	987	9,179	Chanka	2011	Education
anta	451	8,839	Collao	2010	Education
Agreement _nacional_2014	356	8,355	Chanka	2014	Agreement
omnilife	336	8,184	Collao	2017	Health
pasado_violencia	373	8,001	Chanka	2008	Social
cosude_2009-2011_qu	536	7,959	Collao	2011	Social
fondo_monetario_internacional	291	7,227	Collao	2010	Economy
peru_suyupi	449	6,420	Chanka	2014	Education
fundacion_quz	440	5,776	Collao	2008	Social
greg_quz	185	5,505	Collao	2010	Narrative
imayna	250	5,425	Chanka	2008	Social
ahk_1968-2008_quz	391	5,186	Collao	2008	Economy
directiva	355	4,988	Chanka	2014	Resolution
achka	256	4,844	Chanka	2015	Education
cartillas	870	4,674	Chanka	2006	Education
lectura-favorita-chanka-2019	781	4,363	Chanka	2019	Education
lectura-favorita-cusco-2019	769	4,351	Collao	2019	Education
amerindia	321	4,280	Chanka	2000	Education
yachay_qipikuna	464	4,174	Collao	2009	Education
reglamento_simplified_quz	287	4,053	Collao	2008	Norma
focus_2008_quz	243	3,797	Collao	2008	Narrative
poder_judicial	154	3,347	Chanka	2021	Justice
focus_2007_quz	220	3,238	Collao	2007	Narrative
literatura	190	2,930	Chanka	1999	Culture
guia_collao	288	2,824	Collao	2015	Education
wikimedia	163	2,712	Collao	2021	Miscellaneous
docente	286	2,550	Chanka	2015	Education
convencion	115	2,548	Collao	1994	Agreement
yupaychaqa_ley	129	2,484	Chanka	2014	Norma
mikhunanchiskunamanta	127	1,925	Collao	2013	Social
tatoeba	428	1,778	Collao	2021	Miscellaneous
nanoquechua	92	1,431	Collao	2016	Culture
kallpa_qu	100	968	Collao	2019	Narrative
defensoria	60	882	Chanka	2021	Justice
yachay	62	756	Collao	2015	Culture
Total	**384,184**	**4,408,953**	-	-	-

Table 4: Details of each corpus included in the Southern Quechua corpus introduced.

Tokenization Approach		NER Class						
		B-LOC	B-ORG	B-PER	I-LOC	I-ORG	I-PER	O
BPE	True Positive	453	81	189	300	226	162	477
	False Positive	319	11	150	71	51	87	31
	False Negative	64	37	79	171	80	207	82
Norm. and BPE	True Positive	451	70	187	302	227	196	470
	False Positive	299	8	138	83	51	94	32
	False Negative	66	48	81	169	79	173	89
Norm. and PRPE	True Positive	449	79	187	306	227	186	471
	False Positive	304	14	135	95	53	74	28
	False Negative	68	39	81	165	79	183	88
Norm. and BPE-Guided	True Positive	453	71	176	299	222	156	466
	False Positive	294	16	164	93	57	113	28
	False Negative	64	47	92	172	84	213	93

Table 5: Breakdown of prediction results used to calculate weighted precision, recall, and F1 for the NER task .

POS Class		Algorithm			
		BPE	Norm. and BPE	Norm. and PRPE	Norm. and BPE-Guided
adj.	True Positive	253	259	262	235
	False Positive	98	106	92	96
	False Negative	143	137	134	160
verb	True Positive	764	760	761	744
	False Positive	77	86	72	98
	False Negative	78	82	81	72
pron.	True Positive	36	36	37	34
	False Positive	14	13	13	18
	False Negative	7	7	6	9
prep.	True Positive	0	0	0	0
	False Positive	0	1	0	0
	False Negative	1	1	1	1
adv.	True Positive	183	184	188	161
	False Positive	57	53	56	51
	False Negative	50	49	46	73
pron. indef.	True Positive	0	1	1	1
	False Positive	0	0	0	0
	False Negative	2	1	1	1
adv. interr.	True Positive	1	1	1	1
	False Positive	0	0	0	0
	False Negative	0	0	0	0
pron. interrog.	True Positive	8	7	8	7
	False Positive	5	2	5	2
	False Negative	2	3	2	3
num.	True Positive	0	0	0	0
	False Positive	0	0	2	3
	False Negative	5	5	5	5
conj.	True Positive	7	8	8	8
	False Positive	6	6	6	8
	False Negative	5	4	4	4
det.	True Positive	39	39	39	43
	False Positive	33	36	33	38
	False Negative	20	20	20	16
subj.	True Positive	1380	1376	1386	1380
	False Positive	138	124	131	193
	False Negative	112	115	107	113
interj.	True Positive	0	0	0	0
	False Positive	0	0	0	5
	False Negative	3	3	3	3

Table 6: Breakdown of prediction results used to calculate weighted precision, recall, and F1 for the POS task .

Improving Distantly Supervised Document-Level Relation Extraction Through Natural Language Inference

Clara Vania **Grace E. Lee*** **Andrea Pierleoni**
Amazon Alexa
{vaniclar, apierleoni}@amazon.co.uk
grace.lee2@thomsonreuters.com

Abstract

The distant supervision (DS) paradigm has been widely used for relation extraction (RE) to alleviate the need for expensive annotations. However, it suffers from noisy labels, which leads to worse performance than models trained on human-annotated data, even when trained using hundreds of times more data. We present a systematic study on the use of natural language inference (NLI) to improve distantly supervised document-level RE. We apply NLI in three scenarios: (i) as a filter for denoising DS labels, (ii) as a filter for model prediction, and (iii) as a standalone RE model. Our results show that NLI filtering consistently improves performance, reducing the performance gap with a model trained on human-annotated data by 2.3 F1.

1 Introduction

Relation extraction (RE) is the task of identifying relations between two entities in natural language text. It has an important role in many NLP applications, such as knowledge base population and question answering. Existing work on RE has been focused mostly on extraction within a sentence (Mintz et al., 2009; Zhang et al., 2017; Han et al., 2018). However, sentence-level RE has one major limitation: it is not designed to extract relational facts expressed in multiple sentences.[1] To address this, recent work has explored models which use document-level context to extract both intra- and inter-sentence relations from text (Li et al., 2020; Xu et al., 2021; Eberts and Ulges, 2021)

Currently, high-performance RE models require large-scale human-annotated data, which is expensive and does not scale to a large number of relations or new domains. To reduce the reliance on human-annotated data, Mintz et al. (2009) introduce the distant supervision (DS) approach, which assumes that if two entities are connected through a relation in a knowledge base, sentences that mention the two entities express that relation. While this assumption allows the creation of large-scale training data without expensive human annotation, it also produces many noisy labels (Riedel et al., 2010).[2] As a result, the performance of models trained on DS datasets is considerably lower (~5%) than models trained on human-annotated datasets.

This paper aims to reduce the performance gap between models trained on DS versus annotated data through natural language inference (NLI). NLI, also known as *textual entailment*, is the task of determining whether a premise entails a hypothesis. Recently, Sainz et al. (2021) used an NLI model as a standalone RE model and demonstrated its effectiveness for zero-shot and few-shot sentence-level RE. In line with their work, we investigate if NLI can also benefit document-level RE in this paper. Specifically, we apply NLI for document-level RE in three scenarios: (i) as a filter for denoising DS labels, (ii) as a filter for model prediction, and (iii) as a standalone RE model.

We experiment with DocRED (Yao et al., 2019), the largest document-level RE dataset to date. It consists of both DS and human-annotated datasets, which is ideal for our study. Across all scenarios, we find that NLI is especially effective when it is used as a filter; we observe improvement up to 2.3 F1, reducing the gap with a model trained on annotated data from 5.3 to 3.0 F1. However, the gains are less significant when the model has access to human-annotated data. Finally, we highlight the importance of having high-quality entity type information when using NLI as a standalone RE model.

* Work completed at Amazon Alexa. The author now works at Thomson Reuters.

[1] According to Yao et al. (2019), at least 40.7% facts in Wikipedia can only be extracted from multiple sentences.

[2] For document-level RE, Yao et al. (2019) report 41% and 61% incorrect labels for intra- and inter-sentence relations in DS, respectively.

Proceedings of the Third Workshop on Deep Learning for Low-Resource Natural Language Processing, pages 14 - 20
July 14, 2022 ©2022 Association for Computational Linguistics

2 NLI for RE

We first describe the approach by Sainz et al. (2021), which uses an NLI model as a standalone model for sentence-level RE.

Let p be an input text containing two entity mentions m_1 and m_2. We take p as the premise and generate the hypothesis h by verbalizing each relation r using a template t, m_1, and m_2. For example, the relation "*capital of*" can be verbalized using the template "$\{m_1\}$ is the capital of $\{m_2\}$". One relation can be verbalized using multiple templates, leading to multiple hypotheses. To avoid mismatch between the entity types and the relation, a set of allowed types for the first and the second entities is created for each relation, e.g., the relation "*date of birth*" should involve a PERSON and a DATE entities. We use a function f_r to determine whether a relation $r \in R$ matches the given entity types, e_1 and e_2:

$$f_r(e_1, e_2) = \begin{cases} 1 & e_1 \in E_{r1} \wedge e_2 \in E_{r2} \\ 0 & \text{otherwise} \end{cases} \quad (1)$$

where E_{r1} and E_{r2} are the set of allowed types for the first and the second entities in r. We then compute the probability of each relation r as:

$$P_r(p, m_1, m_2) = f(e_1, e_2) \max_{t \in T_r} P_{NLI}(p, h|t, m_1, m_2) \quad (2)$$

where P_{NLI} is the entailment probability of (p, h) given by the NLI model, and T_r is the set of templates for relation r, and h is the hypothesis generated using a template t and the two entity mentions, m_1 and m_2. In practice, we only need to run NLI inference for relation with $f_r(e_1, e_2) = 1$. To identify cases when no relation exists between m_1 and m_2, we apply a threshold $\mathcal{T}$ to Eq. 2. If none of the relations surpasses $\mathcal{T}$, then we assume there is no relation between the two mentions, otherwise we return the relation with the highest entailment probability:

$$\hat{r} = \arg\max_{r \in R} P_r(p, m_1, m_2). \quad (3)$$

Adapting to Document-Level RE For our experiments with document-level RE, we adapt the same setup as Sainz et al. (2021) by treating the whole document context as the premise. We apply NLI in three scenarios: (i) as a filter to for denoising DS labels (**pre-filter**), (ii) as a filter for model predictions (**post-filter**), and (iii) as a standalone RE model. In the pre-filtering scenario, we verbalize the labels (relations) identified using the DS assumption and remove all labels that do not surpass the threshold $\mathcal{T}$ from the DS dataset. Similarly, in the post-filtering scenario, we verbalize the relations predicted by an RE model and remove those which do not surpass $\mathcal{T}$. In both scenarios, we do not need to generate candidate relations (Eq. 1) since they are provided by the DS labels or the RE model predictions. Unlike Sainz et al. (2021) which chooses *one* relation label that maximizes the probability of the hypothesis (Eq. 3), we use *all* relation labels that have entailment probability above $\mathcal{T}$.[3] In our experiments, we set $\mathcal{T} = 0.5$, i.e., taking all relations that the NLI model predicts as entailment. Additionally, since the DS dataset is known to be noisy, for the pre-filtering scenario, we also experiment with higher thresholds to study the effect of using more strict filters on the RE performance.

We experiment with two types of NLI models: a model that is not trained specifically for RE (zero-shot NLI) and a model that is fine-tuned using a small number of human-annotated RE examples (few-shot NLI). The zero-shot NLI model simulates a case when we do not have any annotations, while the few-shot NLI model simulates a case when we have a small budget for annotations. We fine-tune the NLI model for a binary entailment task (*entail* or *not entail*). Since DocRED annotations do not contain negative examples (*no-relation* label), we generate the non-entail examples for NLI as follows. First, we train a model using the DS dataset and generate predictions for the human-annotated training data. We then use the model's incorrect predictions as the non-entail examples. We use a maximum $N = \{10, 100\}$ examples per relation.

3 Experiments

Dataset We experiment with DocRED (Yao et al., 2019), a document-level RE dataset created from Wikipedia articles aligned with Wikidata. It covers six entity types (ORG, LOC, PER, TIME, NUM, MISC) and 96 relation types. DocRED contains $101,873$ DS training documents and $5,051$ human-annotated documents, split into training $(3,053)$,

[3] The setup of Sainz et al. (2021) most likely influenced by their experimental dataset, TACRED (Zhang et al., 2017), which only allows one relation per mention pair. On the other hand, DocRED annotations may have multiple relations per entity pair.

development (998), and testing (1,000). [4]

RE Model For our document-level RE model, we use JEREX (Eberts and Ulges, 2021) which obtains comparable performance with the state-of-the-art SSAN (Xu et al., 2021) model when using `bert-base-case` encoder. The model has four main components (entity mention localization, coreference resolution, entity classification, relation classification), which share the same encoder and mention representations, and are trained jointly. For the relation classifier module, we use the multi-instance version, which predicts relation on the mention-level. JEREX is originally designed for end-to-end RE without the need for entity information. However, since our main focus is on the RE side, we use its standard RE pipeline, which assumes that entity clusters are given.

NLI Model We use a pretrained document-level NLI model based on DeBERTaV3 (He et al., 2021)[5], which was trained on 1.3M premise-hypothesis pairs from 8 datasets: MNLI (Williams et al., 2018), FEVER-NLI (Nie et al., 2019), NLI dataset from Parrish et al. (2021), and DocNLI (Yin et al., 2021) (which is curated from ANLI (Nie et al., 2020), SQuAD (Rajpurkar et al., 2016), DUC2001[6], CNN/DailyMail (Nallapati et al., 2016), and Curation (Curation, 2020)). The model was trained for a binary entailment task.

Training and Optimization For training JEREX models, we use the default hyperparameters of Eberts and Ulges (2021). We use a maximum of 10 epochs for training with the DS dataset and 40 epochs for training with the human-annotated dataset. For NLI fine-tuning, we use a maximum of 10 epochs for the few-shot setting and one epoch when using the full annotated data. We tune the learning rate $\in \{1e{-}5, 2e{-}5, 3e{-}5\}$, with a batch size of 8 and gradient accumulation steps of 4. Each model is trained using a single V100 GPU with 16GB memory. We train each model with three random restarts and report the average performance.

[4]We use the revised version of DocRED development set with 998 documents after two documents were removed because they overlap with the annotated training data.

[5]https://huggingface.co/MoritzLaurer/DeBERTa-v3-base-mnli-fever-docnli-ling-2c

[6]https://www-nlpir.nist.gov/projects/duc/guidelines/2001.html

Threshold	zero-shot	10-shot	100-shot	full
low (0.5)	73.4	71.1	66.0	65.1
med (0.95)	68.6	70.1	56.4	48.4
high (0.99)	59.0	69.1	38.8	12.3

Table 1: Percentages of triples left in the DS data after pre-filtering with NLI.

Model	Precision	Recall	F1	IgnF1
Training with annotated data only (supervised)				
BERT Base†	-	-	58.6	56.3
SSAN Biaffine†	-	-	59.2	57.0
JEREX	64.5	54.8	59.2	57.4
Training with DS data only (weakly supervised)				
JEREX	51.5	**56.5**	53.9	51.0
+ pre-filter (low)	61.3	51.8	56.1	54.0
+ pre-filter (med)	62.4	50.3	55.7	53.7
+ pre-filter (high)	**65.7**	46.2	54.3	52.6
+ post-filter	60.8	52.3	**56.2**	**54.1**
+ double-filter	64.0	50.0	56.1	54.2

Table 2: Results on DocRED development set when using zero-shot NLI models. Results with † are from Xu et al. (2021). IgnF1: F1 score that ignores triples occur in the annotated training data.

4 Results and Analysis

Zero-shot NLI Table 1 shows the percentages of triples left in the DS dataset (out of ~1.5M instances) after pre-filtering with different thresholds $\mathcal{T}$ (for other thresholds, see Appendix A). For the zero-shot NLI, setting $\mathcal{T}$ to the lowest value (0.5) leaves us with 73.4% of the original DS triples, while setting it to the maximum value (0.99) leaves us with 59.0% of the original DS triples.

Table 2 reports our main RE results. Our baseline is a JEREX model trained with the DS dataset. To understand how far NLI can help in reducing the gap between models trained using the DS (*weakly supervised*) vs. human-annotated (*supervised*) datasets, we also provide results of supervised models using BERT base, JEREX, SSAN (Xu et al., 2021). All of the models use the same BERT base encoder (Devlin et al., 2019).

We find that NLI improves RE performance in both pre-filter and post-filter scenarios. Post-filtering with NLI achieves the best performance with 56.2 F1, reducing the gap with the supervised model by 2.3 F1. Looking into the other metrics, it is evident that NLI filtering yields RE models with higher precision but lower recall. We observe that our most aggressive pre-filtering (*high*) outper-

Model	Precision	Recall	F1	IgnF1
10-shot NLI				
JEREX	65.5	56.2	60.5	58.6
+ pre-filter (low)	64.3	58.5	**61.2**	**59.7**
+ pre-filter (high)	61.9	**59.6**	60.7	58.6
+ post-filter	**69.0**	52.7	59.8	58.2
+ double-filter	66.1	55.8	60.5	58.8
100-shot NLI				
JEREX	66.3	57.8	61.7	59.8
+ pre-filter (low)	65.5	**59.3**	**62.2**	**60.4**
+ pre-filter (med)	66.2	56.9	61.2	59.4
+ pre-filter (high)	67.3	54.6	60.3	58.7
+ post-filter	**70.3**	53.3	60.6	59.1
+ double-filter	69.9	53.9	60.8	59.3
Training with DS + full annotated data				
JEREX	68.0	**58.3**	62.7	60.9
+ pre-filter (low)	71.3	57.8	**63.8**	**62.3**
+ pre-filter (med)	70.5	56.7	62.9	61.4
+ pre-filter (high)	64.4	46.7	54.2	52.5
+ post-filter	71.0	54.1	61.4	59.9
+ double-filter	**73.4**	54.0	62.2	60.9

Table 3: Results on DocRED development set when using fine-tuned RE and NLI models.

forms the precision of the supervised model. This result suggests that pre-filtering is especially useful for applications where having high precision is preferable to recall. We also experiment with the *double-filter* scenario, where we apply both our best pre-filter (low) and post-filter. We find it has minimal effect on the model performance.

Few-shot NLI This scenario assumes that a small human-annotated dataset is available, so in the next set of experiments, all RE models are trained using the DS dataset and then fine-tuned using the small annotated dataset.[7] Unlike NLI fine-tuning, where we limit the maximum number of examples per relation when fine-tuning the RE models, we use all annotations in the document since we want the model to learn all and not just the subset of correct triples. We fine-tune the RE models using 427 and 1,761 annotated documents for the 10-shot and the 100-shot NLI settings, respectively.

As shown in Table 3, in the few-shot settings, we can still see improvement by using NLI as a pre-filter. However, the improvements are not as large as in the DS-only training.[8] We also see 1.2

[7]The DS training followed by fine-tuning setup yields the best model performance on DocRED (Xu et al., 2021).

[8]We only experiment with *low* and *high* for the 10-shot experiments since the *medium* filtering yield very similar training data distribution (Table 1).

NLI Model	Precision	Recall	F1	IgnF1
Coarse-grained types				
Zero-shot	3.1	68.0	5.9	5.2
10-shot	2.5	68.4	4.8	4.2
100-shot	2.3	66.6	4.4	3.8
Full-data	2.4	68.2	4.7	4.1
Fine-grained types				
Zero-shot	20.4	27.8	23.5	20.5
10-shot	15.4	28.4	20.0	16.9
100-shot	15.3	26.5	19.4	16.5
Full-data	16.6	27.6	20.7	17.7

Table 4: Results on DocRED development set when using NLI as a standalone RE model.

F1 improvements when using the full annotated data (~3k documents) for fine-tuning the NLI and RE model.

NLI as a standalone RE model We utilize the entity type information in the DocRED annotated training data to create the list of allowed entity types for each relation. However, we find that this strategy still leads us to mismatch types between the relation and entity, which might be due to several reasons. First, DocRED entities are annotated with coarse-grained types (Section 3), which might confuse the model when learning about relations that exist between entities. For instance, frequent location relations such as P17 (*country*) require the tail entity to be a country. However, with the generic LOC type and sometimes similar NLI template (e.g. "$\{m_1\}$ is located in $\{m_2\}$"), other types of locations, such as cities, can also fit the slot for m_2 and be inferred as correct by the NLI model. We also find that the MISC type is especially ambiguous since it is allowed in almost all relations. Second, DocRED relations are annotated on entity-level, where one entity can have multiple mentions with different types, e.g., the entity *Finland* has mentions *Finland* (LOC) as well as *Finnish* (MISC). To alleviate this, we only add entity types to a relation if they co-occur more than 100 times in the data. In addition, we also experiment using ~500 fine-grained entity types using ReFinED (Ayoola et al., 2022), which currently obtain state-of-the-art performance on several entity linking datasets.

Table 4 presents our results. We observe that using coarse-grained entity type information leads to poor model performance. In particular, we find that the model overpredicts the relations, as shown by the high recall. Using finer-grained types improves performance up to 23.5 F1, but it is still

NLI Model	Training	F1	IgnF1
Zero-shot	Annotated only	59.5	57.5
	DS only	52.9	49.8
	DS + NLI	55.6	53.4
Few-shot	10-shot	59.3	57.4
	10-shot + NLI	61.1	58.8
	100-shot	61.7	59.7
	100-shot + NLI	61.8	59.9
Full-data	DS + Annotated	62.0	60.0
	DS + Annotated + NLI	**63.4**	**61.5**

Table 5: Results on DocRED test set.

far below the performance of a model specifically trained for RE. This result suggests that when the NLI model is provided with a set of noisy candidate relations, it predicts many of them as correct. On the other hand, when the set of candidate relations is less noisy (given by the DS labels or RE model predictions), the NLI model performs well and can improve RE performance.

Results on Test Set We validate our result by running our overall best strategy, pre-filtering by NLI ($\mathcal{T} = 0.5$) on the test set. Table 5 shows a similar pattern as observed in the development data: NLI filtering consistently improves performance in all settings. We only report F1 and IgnF1 since DocRED CodaLab output does not provide precision and recall numbers.

5 Conclusion

In this paper, we presented a systematic study on the use of NLI for distantly supervised document-level RE, focusing on the case when human-annotated data is not available. Our results demonstrate that NLI is most effective when used as a pre-filter to denoise DS labels. In the absence of human annotations, we show that NLI filtering reduces the gap with a model trained on human-annotated data by 2.3 F1. We also show that NLI filtering still benefits the RE model (+1.1 F1) when we have small human-annotated data. Our experiment on using NLI as a standalone model for document-level RE leads to worse performance than using it as a pre-filter, suggesting that using NLI directly as an RE model for document-level is more challenging than sentence-level RE.

For future work, we plan to explore other strategies to better leverage the entity type information for RE with NLI and investigate if document-level NLI is also more challenging than sentence-level NLI. Another potential direction is to experiment with other DS techniques, such as integrating a denoising module to the RE model (Xiao et al., 2020) or using DS-trained models as a DS filter (Zhou and Chen, 2021).

Acknowledgements

We thank Tom Ayoola, Shubhi Tyagi, Siffi Singh, Marco Damonte, and the anonymous reviewers for helpful discussion of this work and comments on previous drafts of this paper.

References

Tom Ayoola, Shubhi Tyagi, Joseph Fisher, Christos Christodoulopoulos, and Andrea Pierleoni. 2022. ReFinED: An Efficient Zero-shot-capable Approach to End-to-End Entity Linking. In *Proceedings of the 2022 Conference of the North American Chapter of the Association for Computational Linguistics: Human Language Technologies: Industry Papers*, Seattle, Washington. Association for Computational Linguistics.

Curation. 2020. Curation corpus base.

Jacob Devlin, Ming-Wei Chang, Kenton Lee, and Kristina Toutanova. 2019. BERT: Pre-training of deep bidirectional transformers for language understanding. In *Proceedings of the 2019 Conference of the North American Chapter of the Association for Computational Linguistics: Human Language Technologies, Volume 1 (Long and Short Papers)*, pages 4171–4186, Minneapolis, Minnesota. Association for Computational Linguistics.

Markus Eberts and Adrian Ulges. 2021. An end-to-end model for entity-level relation extraction using multi-instance learning. In *Proceedings of the 16th Conference of the European Chapter of the Association for Computational Linguistics: Main Volume*, pages 3650–3660, Online. Association for Computational Linguistics.

Xu Han, Hao Zhu, Pengfei Yu, Ziyun Wang, Yuan Yao, Zhiyuan Liu, and Maosong Sun. 2018. FewRel: A large-scale supervised few-shot relation classification dataset with state-of-the-art evaluation. In *Proceedings of the 2018 Conference on Empirical Methods in Natural Language Processing*, pages 4803–4809, Brussels, Belgium. Association for Computational Linguistics.

Pengcheng He, Jianfeng Gao, and Weizhu Chen. 2021. Debertav3: Improving deberta using electra-style pre-training with gradient-disentangled embedding sharing.

Bo Li, Wei Ye, Zhonghao Sheng, Rui Xie, Xiangyu Xi, and Shikun Zhang. 2020. Graph enhanced dual attention network for document-level relation extraction. In *Proceedings of the 28th International Conference on Computational Linguistics*, pages 1551–1560, Barcelona, Spain (Online). International Committee on Computational Linguistics.

Mike Mintz, Steven Bills, Rion Snow, and Daniel Jurafsky. 2009. Distant supervision for relation extraction without labeled data. In *Proceedings of the Joint Conference of the 47th Annual Meeting of the ACL and the 4th International Joint Conference on Natural Language Processing of the AFNLP*, pages 1003–1011, Suntec, Singapore. Association for Computational Linguistics.

Ramesh Nallapati, Bowen Zhou, Cicero dos Santos, Çağlar Gulçehre, and Bing Xiang. 2016. Abstractive text summarization using sequence-to-sequence RNNs and beyond. In *Proceedings of The 20th SIGNLL Conference on Computational Natural Language Learning*, pages 280–290, Berlin, Germany. Association for Computational Linguistics.

Yixin Nie, Haonan Chen, and Mohit Bansal. 2019. Combining fact extraction and verification with neural semantic matching networks. In *Association for the Advancement of Artificial Intelligence (AAAI)*.

Yixin Nie, Adina Williams, Emily Dinan, Mohit Bansal, Jason Weston, and Douwe Kiela. 2020. Adversarial NLI: A new benchmark for natural language understanding. In *Proceedings of the 58th Annual Meeting of the Association for Computational Linguistics*, pages 4885–4901, Online. Association for Computational Linguistics.

Alicia Parrish, William Huang, Omar Agha, Soo-Hwan Lee, Nikita Nangia, Alexia Warstadt, Karmanya Aggarwal, Emily Allaway, Tal Linzen, and Samuel R. Bowman. 2021. Does putting a linguist in the loop improve NLU data collection? In *Findings of the Association for Computational Linguistics: EMNLP 2021*, pages 4886–4901, Punta Cana, Dominican Republic. Association for Computational Linguistics.

Pranav Rajpurkar, Jian Zhang, Konstantin Lopyrev, and Percy Liang. 2016. SQuAD: 100,000+ questions for machine comprehension of text. In *Proceedings of the 2016 Conference on Empirical Methods in Natural Language Processing*, pages 2383–2392, Austin, Texas. Association for Computational Linguistics.

Sebastian Riedel, Limin Yao, and Andrew McCallum. 2010. Modeling relations and their mentions without labeled text. In *Machine Learning and Knowledge Discovery in Databases*, pages 148–163, Berlin, Heidelberg. Springer Berlin Heidelberg.

Oscar Sainz, Oier Lopez de Lacalle, Gorka Labaka, Ander Barrena, and Eneko Agirre. 2021. Label verbalization and entailment for effective zero and few-shot relation extraction. In *Proceedings of the 2021 Conference on Empirical Methods in Natural Language Processing*, pages 1199–1212, Online and Punta Cana, Dominican Republic. Association for Computational Linguistics.

Adina Williams, Nikita Nangia, and Samuel Bowman. 2018. A broad-coverage challenge corpus for sentence understanding through inference. In *Proceedings of the 2018 Conference of the North American Chapter of the Association for Computational Linguistics: Human Language Technologies, Volume 1 (Long Papers)*, pages 1112–1122, New Orleans, Louisiana. Association for Computational Linguistics.

Chaojun Xiao, Yuan Yao, Ruobing Xie, Xu Han, Zhiyuan Liu, Maosong Sun, Fen Lin, and Leyu Lin. 2020. Denoising relation extraction from document-level distant supervision. In *Proceedings of the 2020 Conference on Empirical Methods in Natural Language Processing (EMNLP)*, pages 3683–3688, Online. Association for Computational Linguistics.

Benfeng Xu, Quan Wang, Yajuan Lyu, Yong Zhu, and Zhendong Mao. 2021. Entity structure within and throughout: Modeling mention dependencies for document-level relation extraction. In *AAAI*.

Yuan Yao, Deming Ye, Peng Li, Xu Han, Yankai Lin, Zhenghao Liu, Zhiyuan Liu, Lixin Huang, Jie Zhou, and Maosong Sun. 2019. DocRED: A large-scale document-level relation extraction dataset. In *Proceedings of the 57th Annual Meeting of the Association for Computational Linguistics*, pages 764–777, Florence, Italy. Association for Computational Linguistics.

Wenpeng Yin, Dragomir Radev, and Caiming Xiong. 2021. DocNLI: A large-scale dataset for document-level natural language inference. In *Findings of the Association for Computational Linguistics: ACL-IJCNLP 2021*, pages 4913–4922, Online. Association for Computational Linguistics.

Yuhao Zhang, Victor Zhong, Danqi Chen, Gabor Angeli, and Christopher D. Manning. 2017. Position-aware attention and supervised data improve slot filling. In *Proceedings of the 2017 Conference on Empirical Methods in Natural Language Processing*, pages 35–45, Copenhagen, Denmark. Association for Computational Linguistics.

Wenxuan Zhou and Muhao Chen. 2021. Learning from noisy labels for entity-centric information extraction. In *Proceedings of the 2021 Conference on Empirical Methods in Natural Language Processing*, pages 5381–5392, Online and Punta Cana, Dominican Republic. Association for Computational Linguistics.

A Pre-filtering with NLI

Threshold	zero-shot	10-shot	100-shot	full
0.5	73.4	71.1	66.0	65.1
0.7	72.6	70.8	64.9	63.7
0.9	70.8	70.4	60.9	56.2
0.95	68.6	70.1	56.4	48.4
0.97	66.1	69.9	52.4	40.0
0.99	59.0	69.1	38.8	12.3

Table 6: Percentages of triples left in the DS data after pre-filtering with NLI with different threshold values.

B DocRED NLI Templates

Relation	Templates
applies to jurisdiction	{head} rules {tail}. {head} represents {tail}. {head} works for the {tail} government.
author	{head} is written by {tail}. {head} is a story by {tail}. {tail} is the author of {head}. {tail} wrote {head}.
award received	{head} received {tail}. {head} won {tail}. {head} was a recipient of {tail}. {head} was awarded {tail}.
basin country	{head} is located near {tail}. {tail} is located in {head}.
capital of	{head} is the capital of {tail}. {tail}'s capital is {head}.
capital	{head}'s capital is {tail}. {tail} is the capital of {head}.
cast member	{head}'s cast includes {tail}. {tail} starred in {head}. {tail} appeared in {head}.
continent	{head} is located in {tail}.
country of citizenship	{head} country of citizenship is {tail}. {head} is from {tail}.
country	{head} is located in {tail}.
creator	{head} is created by {tail}. {tail} is the creator of {tail}.
date of birth	{head} was born {tail}.
date of death	{head} died {tail}.
director	{head} is a movie directed by {tail}. {head} is a game directed by {tail}. {tail} is the director of {head}.

Table 7: Examples of DocRED NLI Templates. Full templates can be found in the supplementary materials.

IDANI: Inference-time Domain Adaptation via Neuron-level Interventions

Omer Antverg and **Eyal Ben-David** and **Yonatan Belinkov**[*]
Technion - Israel Institute of Technology
{omer.antverg@cs.|eyalbd12@campus.|belinkov@}technion.ac.il

Abstract

Large pre-trained models are usually fine-tuned on downstream task data, and tested on unseen data. When the train and test data come from different domains, the model is likely to struggle, as it is not adapted to the test domain. We propose a new approach for domain adaptation (DA), using neuron-level interventions: We modify the representation of each test example in specific neurons, resulting in a counterfactual example from the source domain, which the model is more familiar with. The modified example is then fed back into the model. While most other DA methods are applied during training time, ours is applied during inference only, making it more efficient and applicable. Our experiments show that our method improves performance on unseen domains. [1]

1 Introduction

A common assumption in NLP, and in machine learning in general, is that the training set and the test set are sampled from the same underlying distribution. However, this assumption does not always hold in real-world applications since test data may arrive from many (target) domains, often not seen during training. Indeed, when applied to such unseen target domains, the trained model typically encounters significant degradation in performance.

DA algorithms aim to address this challenge by improving models' generalization to new domains, and algorithms for various DA scenarios have been developed (Daume III and Marcu, 2006; Reichart and Rappoport, 2007; Ben-David et al., 2007; Schnabel and Schütze, 2014). This work focuses on unsupervised domain adaptation (UDA), the most explored DA setup in recent years, which assumes access to labeled data from the source domain and unlabeled data from both source and target domains. Algorithms for this setup typically use the target domain knowledge during *training*, attempting to bridge the gap between domains through representation learning (Blitzer et al., 2007; Ganin et al., 2016; Ziser and Reichart, 2018; Han and Eisenstein, 2019; David et al., 2020). Recently, Ben-David et al. (2021) and Volk et al. (2022) introduced an approach for *inference*-time DA, assuming no prior knowledge regarding the test domains but still modifying the training process to their gain.

In contrast to this line of work, we assume a more realistic scenario, in which the model was already trained on a source domain, and encounters unlabeled data from the target domain during inference time.

Given an example from a target domain, we would have liked to change it to a source domain example, so that the model would be more likely to perform well on it. Since this is difficult to achieve, we aim to change its representation in a fine-grained manner, such that we modify only information about the domain of the representation, without hurting other information. To do so, we take inspiration from work analyzing language models, which showed that linguistic properties are localized in certain neurons (dimensions in model representations) (Dalvi et al., 2019; Durrani et al., 2020; Torroba Hennigen et al., 2020; Antverg and Belinkov, 2022; Sajjad et al., 2021). We first rank the neurons by their importance for identifying the domain (source or target) of each example. Then, we modify target-domain representations only in the highest-ranked neurons, to change their domain to the source domain. Since the model was trained on examples from the source domain, we expect it to perform better on the modified representations. We name this method as Inference-time Domain Adaptation via Neuron-level Interventions (IDANI).

We follow a large body of previous work, testing

[*] Supported by the Viterbi Fellowship in the Center for Computer Engineering at the Technion.

[1] Our code is available at `https://github.com/technion-cs-nlp/idani`.

Proceedings of the Third Workshop on Deep Learning for Low-Resource Natural Language Processing, pages 21 - 29
July 14, 2022

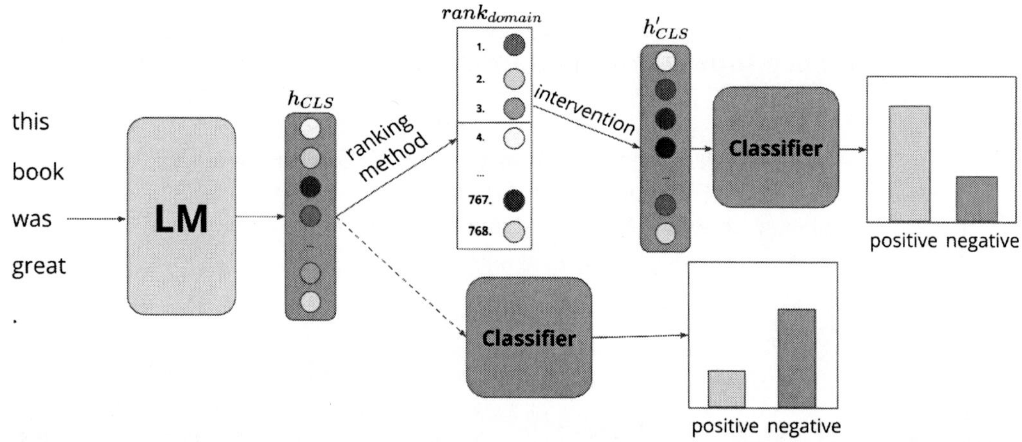

Figure 1: The language model—which was trained on some source domain, e.g., airline—creates a representation (CLS) for the review. Since the review is from a domain on which it was not trained, the model's classifier mistakenly classifies it as negative (bottom). In IDANI (top), the representation is fed into a neuron-ranking method. The k-highest ranked neurons are modified by an intervention, to change the domain of the review, and the new representation is fed into the classifier, which correctly classifies it as positive.

IDANI on a variety of well known DA benchmarks, for a total of two text classification tasks (sentiment analysis, natural language inference) and one sequence tagging task (aspect identification), across 52 source–target domain pairs. We demonstrate that IDANI can improve results in many of these cases, with some significant gains.

2 Method

Given a model M with a classification module f and hidden dimensionality d, which was fine-tuned on data from a source domain $D_s = \{X_s\}$, we receive unlabeled task data $D_t = \{X_t\}$ from a target domain for inference. As $s \neq t$, M's performance is likely to deteriorate when processing X_t compared to X_s. Thus, we would like to make the representation of X_t more similar to that of X_s (regardless of the labels). To do so, we apply the IDANI intervention method:

1. We process X_s and X_t through M, producing representations $H^s, H^t \subseteq \mathbb{R}^d$. We also compute $\bar{v}^s$ and $\bar{v}^t$, the element-wise mean representations of X_s and X_t.

2. We apply existing ranking methods to rank the representation's neurons by their relevance for domain information, i.e., the highest-ranked neuron holds the most information about the representation's domain (§ 2.1).[2]

3. For each $h^t \in H^t$, we would ideally like to have h^s, its source domain counterpart. Since h^s is impossible to get, we create a counterfactual $\tilde{h}^s$ that simulates it by modifying h^t only in the k-highest ranked neurons $\{n_1, ..., n_k\}$, such that $\forall i \in \{1, ..., k\}$,

$$\tilde{h}^s_{n_i} = h^t_{n_i} + \alpha_{n_i}(\bar{v}^s_{n_i} - \bar{v}^t_{n_i}) \quad (1)$$

   To allow stronger intervention on neurons that are ranked higher, we scale the intervention with $\alpha \in \mathbb{R}^d$, a log-scaled sorted coefficients vector in the range $[0, \beta]$ such that $\alpha_{n_1} = \beta$ and $\alpha_{n_d} = 0$, where β is a hyperparameter (Antverg and Belinkov, 2022). We denote the new set of representations as $\tilde{H}^s$.

4. Representations from $\tilde{H}^s$ are fed into the classifier f—without re-training f—to predict the labels. Since $\tilde{H}^s$ is more similar to H^s than H^t is to H^s, we expect performance to improve. That is, for some scoring metric γ, we expect to have $\gamma(f(\tilde{H}^s)) > \gamma(f(H^t))$.

The process is illustrated in Fig. 1.

2.1 Ranking Methods

We consider two ranking methods for ranking the representations' neurons (step 2):

[2] Following previous work (Antverg and Belinkov, 2022), our method assumes that neurons with the same index carry similar information. While this is not necessarily true, we perform extrinsic (Table 1) and intrinsic evaluations (Table 2) that support this assumption.

LINEAR (Dalvi et al., 2019) This method trains a linear classifier on H^s and H^t to learn to predict the domain, using standard cross-entropy loss regularized by elastic net regularization (Zou and Hastie, 2005). Then, it uses the classifier's weights to rank the neurons according to their importance for domain information. Intuitively, neurons with a higher magnitude of absolute weights should be more important for predicting the domain.

PROBELESS The second ranking method is a simple one and does not rely on an external probe, and thus is very fast to obtain: it only depends on computing the mean representation of each domain ($\bar{v}^s$ and $\bar{v}^t$), and sorting the difference between them. For each neuron $i \in \{1, ..., d\}$, we calculate the absolute difference between the means:

$$r_i = |\bar{v}_i^s - \bar{v}_i^t| \quad (2)$$

and obtain a ranking by arg-sorting r, i.e., the first neuron in the ranking corresponds to the highest value in r. Antverg and Belinkov (2022) showed that for interventions for morphology information, this method outperforms LINEAR and another ranking method (Torroba Hennigen et al., 2020).

3 Experiments

3.1 Datasets

We experiment with two text classification tasks: sentiment analysis (classifying reviews to positive or negative (Blitzer et al., 2007)) and natural language inference (NLI; classifying whether two sentences entail or contradict each other (Bowman et al., 2015)), and a sequence tagging task: aspect prediction (identifying aspect terms within reviews (Hu and Liu, 2004; Toprak et al., 2010; Pontiki et al., 2014)). For each task, the model is trained on a single source domain and tested on different target domains. We explore a low-resource scenario, thus we use 2000–3000 examples from the source domain to form the training set.[3] For test, we use equivalent size data from the corresponding target domain. Further data details are in Appendix A.

3.2 Experiments

For each task and pair of source and target domains, we fine-tune a pre-trained BERT-base-cased model (Devlin et al., 2019) on the training set of the source domain and evaluate its in-domain performance on the dev set of the source domain.[4] We intervene on representations from the last layer of the model: word representations for the aspect prediction task, and CLS token representation for the other tasks. We then test the model's out-of-distribution (OOD) performance on the test set of the target domain, for different k (number of modified neurons) and β (magnitude of the intervention) values: We perform grid search where k is in the range $[0, d]$ ($d = 768$) and β is in the range $[1, 10]$. We experiment with both ranking methods described in § 2.1.

We consider the model's performance at $k = 0$ as its initial (unchanged) OOD performance (INIT), and report the difference between initial performance and performance using IDANI, with either PROBELESS (Δ^P) or LINEAR (Δ^L) rankings. A limitation of IDANI (which we further discuss later) is the inability to choose the best β and k for each domain pair. Following Antverg and Belinkov (2022) we report results for $\beta = 8, k = 50$ ($\Delta_{8,50}$), as well as oracle results (the best performance across all values, Δ_O). We consider the model's performance when fine-tuned on the target domain as an upper bound (UB). For all pairs, we repeat experiments using 5 different random seeds, and report mean INIT, $\Delta_{8,50}$, Δ_O and UB across seeds, alongside the standard error of the mean.

Since we assume that the model is exposed to target domain data only during inference, we cannot experiment with UDA methods, as they require access to the data during training. Furthermore, experimenting with *inference-time DA* approaches (Ben-David et al., 2021; Volk et al., 2022) is also not possible since they assume multiple source domains for training.

4 Results

Overall, we have 52 source to target domain adaptation experiments. Table 1 aggregates results across all experiments in three different categories: experiments where we can be confident that we improved the initial performance (i.e., the mean result across seeds is greater than the standard error), damaged it (mean lower than the negative standard error) or did not significantly affect it. Detailed results per each source–target domain pair are in Appendix B.

[3]For development data we split our training set in a ratio of 80:20, where the smaller portion is used for development.

[4]For all experimented models, we define a maximum sequence length value of 256 and use a training batch size of 16.

	Improved	Damaged	Neither	AVG Δ
$\Delta^P_{8,50}$	21	9	22	0.25
$\Delta^L_{8,50}$	23	7	22	0.25
Δ^P_O	51	0	1	1.77
Δ^L_O	50	0	2	0.93

Table 1: Number of experiments in which IDANI improved, damaged, or did not significantly affect the initial performance. Δ^P and Δ^L refer to PROBELESS and LINEAR respectively, while $\Delta_{8,50}$ and Δ_O refer to $\beta = 8, k = 50$ and oracle values.

As seen, IDANI provides decent performance, improving results much more than damaging even with default hyperparameters ($\Delta^P_{8,50}$ and $\Delta^L_{8,50}$). With oracle hyperparameters (Δ^P_O and Δ^L_O) it improves performance in almost all experiments.

Some of these gains are quite impressive: In the aspect prediction task, we gain 18.8 and 14.4 F1 points when adapting the Restaurants source domain to the target domains Laptops and Service, respectively. In other domain pairs, the gain is marginal. On average we gain 4 points with Δ^P_O.

In sentiment analysis, the airline domain (A) is quite different from the others, leading to lower INIT (initial performance) scores when it is the source domain. Adapting from A using IDANI results in a gain of up to 4.9 accuracy points. When other domains are used as source domains, we see mostly marginal gains, as the upper bound is closer to the initial performance, leaving less room for improvement in this task (UB − INIT is low).

In NLI, it seems harder to improve: the room for improvement is lower (3.3 F1 points on average), which may imply that domain information is not crucial for this task. Still, we do see some significant gains, e.g., an improvement of 2 F1 points when adapting from Slate to the Telephone domain.

Generally, across all tasks and domain pairs, PROBELESS provides better performance than LINEAR as $\Delta^P_O > \Delta^L_O$ in 47 of the 52 experiments (Appendix B). This is in line with the insights from Antverg and Belinkov (2022), who observed that PROBELESS was better than LINEAR when used for intervening on morphological attributes.

4.1 Qualitative Analysis

To analyze the benefits of IDANI, for each word in the dataset we record the change in results when classifying sentences containing the word (sentiment analysis) or when classifying the word itself (aspect prediction). We report the words with the greatest improvement in Table 2. When switching from the Airline domain to the DVD domain in the sentiment analysis task, those are mostly words that sound negative in an airline context, but may not imply a sentiment towards a movie (*terrorist, kidnapped*). In the aspect prediction task, those are mostly target domain related terms that are not likely to appear in the source domain.

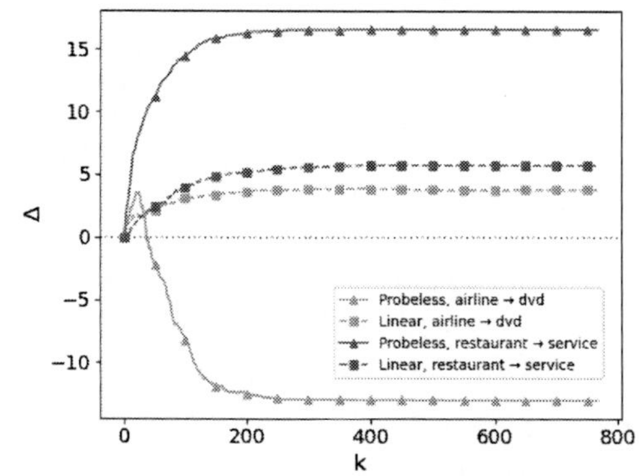

Figure 2: Results for different k values, using $\beta = 8$.

4.2 Default β and k are Not Optimal

While the potential for performance improvement with PROBELESS is high, the selection of $\beta = 8, k = 50$ turns out as non optimal, as $\Delta^P_{8,50}$ is well below Δ^P_O across our experiments. This is also true for $\Delta^L_{8,50}$ compared to Δ^L_O, but to a lesser degree.

Fig. 2 shows that a milder intervention—lower k value—would have been more ideal for the Airline $\rightarrow$ DVD scenario. Modifying too many neurons probably affects other encoded information—besides domain information—damaging the task performance. Thus, we might lean towards smaller k values. However, this is not always the case: Fig. 2 also shows that for the Restaurant $\rightarrow$ Service scenario in the aspect prediction task, PROBELESS' performance reaches a saturation point around the value of $k = 100$ neurons. Thus there is no ideal value of k across all domain pairs. A similar phenomenon with β is shown in Appendix C.

Therefore, hyperparameters should be task- and domain-dependent, but it is unclear how to define them for each domain pair. Yet, in most real-world cases some labeled data should be available or could be manually created. In such cases, the best approach would be to grid-search over the hyperparameters on the available labeled data, and use the selected values for the (unlabeled) test data.

Airline → DVD (Sentiment)	*immortal, insanely, terrorist, crossing, obsessive, buzz, kidnapped*
Laptops → Restaurant (Aspect)	*Food, soup, selection, sushi, food, atmosphere, menu, staff*
Restaurant → Laptops (Aspect)	*time, user, slot, speed, MAC, Acer, system, size, SSD, design*

Table 2: Words that are part of sentences for which accuracy has improved the most (sentiment analysis), and words for which F1 score has improved the most (aspect prediction), using IDANI.

5 Conclusion

In this work, we demonstrated the ability to leverage neuron-intervention methods to improve OOD performance. We showed that in some cases, IDANI can significantly help models to adapt to new domains. IDANI performs best with oracle hyperparameters, but even with the default ones we see overall positive results. We showed that IDANI indeed focuses on domain-related information, as the gains come mostly from domain-related information, such as domain-specific aspect terms. Importantly, IDANI is applied only during inference, unlike most other DA methods.

Acknowledgements

This research was supported by the ISRAEL SCIENCE FOUNDATION (grant No. 448/20) and by an Azrieli Foundation Early Career Faculty Fellowship. We also thank the anonymous reviewers for their insightful comments and suggestions.

References

Omer Antverg and Yonatan Belinkov. 2022. On the pitfalls of analyzing individual neurons in language models. In *International Conference on Learning Representations*.

Eyal Ben-David, Nadav Oved, and Roi Reichart. 2021. Pada: A prompt-based autoregressive approach for adaptation to unseen domains. *arXiv preprint arXiv:2102.12206*.

Shai Ben-David, John Blitzer, Koby Crammer, Fernando Pereira, et al. 2007. Analysis of representations for domain adaptation. *Advances in neural information processing systems*, 19:137.

John Blitzer, Mark Dredze, and Fernando Pereira. 2007. Biographies, bollywood, boom-boxes and blenders: Domain adaptation for sentiment classification. In *ACL 2007, Proceedings of the 45th Annual Meeting of the Association for Computational Linguistics, June 23-30, 2007, Prague, Czech Republic*. The Association for Computational Linguistics.

Samuel R. Bowman, Gabor Angeli, Christopher Potts, and Christopher D. Manning. 2015. A large annotated corpus for learning natural language inference. In *Proceedings of the 2015 Conference on Empirical Methods in Natural Language Processing*, pages 632–642, Lisbon, Portugal. Association for Computational Linguistics.

Fahim Dalvi, Nadir Durrani, Hassan Sajjad, Yonatan Belinkov, Anthony Bau, and James R. Glass. 2019. What is one grain of sand in the desert? analyzing individual neurons in deep NLP models. In *The Thirty-Third AAAI Conference on Artificial Intelligence, AAAI 2019, The Thirty-First Innovative Applications of Artificial Intelligence Conference, IAAI 2019, The Ninth AAAI Symposium on Educational Advances in Artificial Intelligence, EAAI 2019, Honolulu, Hawaii, USA, January 27 - February 1, 2019*, pages 6309–6317. AAAI Press.

Hal Daume III and Daniel Marcu. 2006. Domain adaptation for statistical classifiers. *Journal of artificial Intelligence research*, 26:101–126.

Eyal Ben David, Carmel Rabinovitz, and Roi Reichart. 2020. Perl: Pivot-based domain adaptation for pre-trained deep contextualized embedding models. *Transactions of the Association for Computational Linguistics*, 8(0):504–521.

Jacob Devlin, Ming-Wei Chang, Kenton Lee, and Kristina Toutanova. 2019. BERT: Pre-training of deep bidirectional transformers for language understanding. In *Proceedings of the 2019 Conference of the North American Chapter of the Association for Computational Linguistics: Human Language Technologies, Volume 1 (Long and Short Papers)*, pages 4171–4186, Minneapolis, Minnesota. Association for Computational Linguistics.

Nadir Durrani, Hassan Sajjad, Fahim Dalvi, and Yonatan Belinkov. 2020. Analyzing individual neurons in pre-trained language models. In *Proceedings of the 2020 Conference on Empirical Methods in Natural Language Processing (EMNLP)*, pages 4865–4880, Online. Association for Computational Linguistics.

Yaroslav Ganin, Evgeniya Ustinova, Hana Ajakan, Pascal Germain, Hugo Larochelle, François Laviolette, Mario March, and Victor Lempitsky. 2016. Domain-adversarial training of neural networks. *Journal of Machine Learning Research*, 17(59):1–35.

Chenggong Gong, Jianfei Yu, and Rui Xia. 2020. Unified feature and instance based domain adaptation for aspect-based sentiment analysis. In *Proceedings of the 2020 Conference on Empirical Methods in Natural Language Processing, EMNLP 2020, Online,*

November 16-20, 2020, pages 7035–7045. Association for Computational Linguistics.

Xiaochuang Han and Jacob Eisenstein. 2019. Unsupervised domain adaptation of contextualized embeddings for sequence labeling. In *Proceedings of the 2019 Conference on Empirical Methods in Natural Language Processing and the 9th International Joint Conference on Natural Language Processing, EMNLP-IJCNLP 2019, Hong Kong, China, November 3-7, 2019*, pages 4237–4247. Association for Computational Linguistics.

Minqing Hu and Bing Liu. 2004. Mining and summarizing customer reviews. In *Proceedings of the Tenth ACM SIGKDD International Conference on Knowledge Discovery and Data Mining, Seattle, Washington, USA, August 22-25, 2004*, pages 168–177. ACM.

Quang Nguyen. 2015. The airline review dataset.

Maria Pontiki, Dimitris Galanis, John Pavlopoulos, Harris Papageorgiou, Ion Androutsopoulos, and Suresh Manandhar. 2014. Semeval-2014 task 4: Aspect based sentiment analysis. In *Proceedings of the 8th International Workshop on Semantic Evaluation, SemEval@COLING 2014, Dublin, Ireland, August 23-24, 2014*, pages 27–35. The Association for Computer Linguistics.

Roi Reichart and Ari Rappoport. 2007. Self-training for enhancement and domain adaptation of statistical parsers trained on small datasets. In *Proceedings of the 45th Annual Meeting of the Association of Computational Linguistics*, pages 616–623, Prague, Czech Republic. Association for Computational Linguistics.

Hassan Sajjad, Nadir Durrani, and Fahim Dalvi. 2021. Neuron-level interpretation of deep nlp models: A survey. *ArXiv*, abs/2108.13138.

Tobias Schnabel and Hinrich Schütze. 2014. Flors: Fast and simple domain adaptation for part-of-speech tagging. *Transactions of the Association for Computational Linguistics*, 2(0):15–26.

Cigdem Toprak, Niklas Jakob, and Iryna Gurevych. 2010. Sentence and expression level annotation of opinions in user-generated discourse. In *ACL 2010, Proceedings of the 48th Annual Meeting of the Association for Computational Linguistics, July 11-16, 2010, Uppsala, Sweden*, pages 575–584. The Association for Computer Linguistics.

Lucas Torroba Hennigen, Adina Williams, and Ryan Cotterell. 2020. Intrinsic probing through dimension selection. In *Proceedings of the 2020 Conference on Empirical Methods in Natural Language Processing (EMNLP)*, pages 197–216, Online. Association for Computational Linguistics.

Tomer Volk, Eyal Ben-David, Ohad Amosy, Gal Chechik, and Roi Reichart. 2022. Example-based hypernetworks for out-of-distribution generalization. *arXiv preprint arXiv:2203.14276*.

Adina Williams, Nikita Nangia, and Samuel R Bowman. 2018. A broad-coverage challenge corpus for sentence understanding through inference. In *2018 Conference of the North American Chapter of the Association for Computational Linguistics: Human Language Technologies, NAACL HLT 2018*, pages 1112–1122.

Yftah Ziser and Roi Reichart. 2018. Pivot based language modeling for improved neural domain adaptation. In *Proceedings of the 2018 Conference of the North American Chapter of the Association for Computational Linguistics: Human Language Technologies, Volume 1 (Long Papers)*, pages 1241–1251, New Orleans, Louisiana. Association for Computational Linguistics.

Hui Zou and Trevor Hastie. 2005. Regularization and variable selection via the elastic net. *Journal of the royal statistical society: series B (statistical methodology)*, 67(2):301–320.

A Data Details

We test IDANI on three different tasks: sentiment analysis, natural language inference, and aspect prediction. Further details of the training, development, and test sets of each domain are provided in Table 3.

Sentiment Analysis We follow a large body of prior DA work to focus on the task of binary sentiment classification. We experiment with the four legacy product review domains of Blitzer et al. (2007): Books (B), DVDs (D), Electronic items (E) and Kitchen appliances (K). We also experiment in a more challenging setup, considering an airline review dataset (A) (Nguyen, 2015; Ziser and Reichart, 2018). This setup is more challenging because of the differences between the product and service domains.

Natural Language Inference (Williams et al., 2018) This corpus is an extension of the SNLI dataset (Bowman et al., 2015). Each example consists of a pair of sentences, a premise and a hypothesis. The relationship between the two may be entailment, contradiction, or neutral. The corpus includes data from 10 domains: 5 are matched, with training, development and test sets, and 5 are mismatched, without a training set. Following Ben-David et al. (2021), we experiment only with the five matched domains: Fiction (F), Government (G), Slate (SL), Telephone (TL) and Travel (TR).

Since the test sets of the MNLI dataset are not publicly available, we use the original development sets as our test sets for each target domain, while source domains use these sets for development. Following prior work (Ben-David et al., 2021; Volk et al., 2022) we explore a low-resource supervised scenario, which emphasizes the need for a DA algorithm. Thus, we randomly downsample each of the training sets by a factor of 30, resulting in 2,000–3,000 examples per set.

Aspect Prediction The aspect prediction dataset is based on aspect-based sentiment analysis (ABSA) corpora from four domains: Device (D), Laptops (L), Restaurant (R), and Service (SE). The D data consists of reviews from Toprak et al. (2010), the SE data includes web service reviews (Hu and Liu, 2004), and the L and R domains consist of reviews from the SemEval-2014 ABSA challenge (Pontiki et al., 2014). The task is to identify aspect terms within reviews. For example, given a sentence "The price is reasonable, although the service is poor", both "price" and "service" should be identified as aspect terms.

Sentiment Classification			
Domain	**Training (src)**	**Dev (src)**	**Test (trg)**
Airline (A)	$1,700$	300	$2,000$
Books (B)	$1,700$	300	$2,000$
DVD (D)	$1,700$	300	$2,000$
Electronics (E)	$1,700$	300	$2,000$
Kitchen (K)	$1,700$	300	$2,000$
MNLI			
Domain	**Training (src)**	**Dev (src)**	**Test (trg)**
Fiction (F)	$2,547$	$1,972$	$1,972$
Government (G)	$2,541$	$1,944$	$1,944$
Slate (SL)	$2,605$	$1,954$	$1,954$
Telephone(TL)	$2,754$	$1,965$	$1,965$
Travel (TR)	$2,541$	$1,975$	$1,975$
Aspect			
Domain	**Training (src)**	**Dev (src)**	**Test (trg)**
Device (D)	$2,302$	255	$1,279$
Laptops (L)	$2,726$	303	800
Restaurants (R)	$3,487$	388	800
Service(SE)	$1,343$	149	747

Table 3: The number of examples in each domain of our four tasks. We denote the examples used when a domain is the source domain (src), and when it is the target domain (trg).

We follow the training and test splits defined by Gong et al. (2020) for the D and SE domains, while the splits for the L and R domains are taken from the SemEval-2014 ABSA challenge. To establish our development set, we randomly sample 10% out of the training data.

B Detailed Results

Results for all domain pairs are shown in Tables 4, 5 and 6. As described in § 4, IDANI can potentially significantly improve performance, shown by the results of Δ_O^P. Current hyperparameter values do not fulfill this entire potential, but still improve performance in most cases ($\Delta_{8,50}^P$).

C Performance for different β

While our default hyperparameter values, $\beta = 8$ and $k = 50$ improve performance in most cases, they are not optimal for all cases. Fig. 3 shows that when $k = 50$, the optimal β value for the Airline $\rightarrow$ DVD case is 5, whereas for Restaurants $\rightarrow$ Service it is actually better to use a greater β. Thus, it is not possible to find one value that would be optimal for all cases.

	A → B	A → D	A → E	A → K	B → A	B → D	B → E
INIT	77.4 ± 1.3	75.5 ± 2.2	85.2 ± 1.0	84.9 ± 0.9	83.7 ± 0.7	87.9 ± 0.3	90.4 ± 0.2
UB	88.0 ± 0.5	89.2 ± 0.5	92.4 ± 0.4	92.4 ± 0.2	88.0 ± 0.1	89.2 ± 0.5	92.4 ± 0.4
$\Delta^P_{8,50}$	-4.4 ± 4.8	-2.2 ± 5.4	-1.2 ± 2.4	-1.5 ± 1.9	0.5 ± 0.1	0.1 ± 0.1	-0.0 ± 0.0
$\Delta^L_{8,50}$	2.0 ± 1.0	2.1 ± 1.0	1.3 ± 0.4	1.1 ± 0.5	0.2 ± 0.1	0.1 ± 0.0	-0.0 ± 0.0
Δ^P_O	3.0 ± 1.3	4.9 ± 1.8	2.3 ± 0.8	2.3 ± 1.0	0.9 ± 0.2	0.3 ± 0.1	0.1 ± 0.0
Δ^L_O	2.9 ± 1.3	4.2 ± 1.8	2.3 ± 0.8	2.2 ± 0.9	0.3 ± 0.1	0.1 ± 0.0	0.0 ± 0.0

	B → K	D → A	D → B	D → E	D → K	E → A	E → B
INIT	87.8 ± 0.4	81.5 ± 0.3	89.4 ± 0.3	90.3 ± 0.2	88.1 ± 0.5	86.3 ± 0.4	86.8 ± 0.4
UB	92.4 ± 0.2	88.0 ± 0.1	88.0 ± 0.5	92.4 ± 0.4	92.4 ± 0.2	88.0 ± 0.1	88.0 ± 0.5
$\Delta^P_{8,50}$	0.1 ± 0.0	0.8 ± 0.2	0.1 ± 0.1	-0.0 ± 0.1	0.8 ± 0.3	0.0 ± 0.0	0.6 ± 0.2
$\Delta^L_{8,50}$	0.1 ± 0.0	0.5 ± 0.1	0.1 ± 0.0	0.1 ± 0.0	0.2 ± 0.1	0.0 ± 0.0	0.1 ± 0.1
Δ^P_O	0.4 ± 0.1	1.4 ± 0.3	0.3 ± 0.1	0.3 ± 0.1	1.4 ± 0.5	0.2 ± 0.0	1.0 ± 0.3
Δ^L_O	0.2 ± 0.0	0.8 ± 0.1	0.2 ± 0.1	0.1 ± 0.0	0.5 ± 0.2	0.1 ± 0.0	0.3 ± 0.1

	E → D	E → K	K → A	K → B	K → D	K → E	AVG
INIT	86.5 ± 0.2	93.2 ± 0.3	83.9 ± 0.4	87.0 ± 0.2	86.4 ± 0.1	92.2 ± 0.2	86.2 ± 0.7
UB	89.2 ± 0.5	92.4 ± 0.4	88.0 ± 0.1	88.0 ± 0.5	89.2 ± 0.5	92.4 ± 0.2	90.0 ± 0.4
$\Delta^P_{8,50}$	0.2 ± 0.1	0.2 ± 0.2	0.7 ± 0.2	0.1 ± 0.1	0.2 ± 0.1	0.1 ± 0.0	-0.2 ± 1.7
$\Delta^L_{8,50}$	-0.1 ± 0.1	-0.0 ± 0.0	0.1 ± 0.1	0.1 ± 0.0	0.0 ± 0.0	0.0 ± 0.0	0.4 ± 0.4
Δ^P_O	0.4 ± 0.1	0.4 ± 0.2	1.2 ± 0.3	0.2 ± 0.0	0.5 ± 0.0	0.2 ± 0.0	1.1 ± 0.6
Δ^L_O	0.1 ± 0.0	0.2 ± 0.1	0.5 ± 0.2	0.1 ± 0.0	0.2 ± 0.0	0.0 ± 0.0	0.8 ± 0.6

Table 4: Sentiment analysis results (accuracy).

	F → G	F → SL	F → TL	F → TR	G → F	G → SL	G → TL
INIT	70.2 ± 0.8	63.7 ± 0.8	67.4 ± 1.3	65.6 ± 0.8	59.9 ± 0.8	62.1 ± 0.5	64.9 ± 0.9
UB	73.8 ± 0.4	62.6 ± 0.9	68.3 ± 0.4	69.9 ± 0.3	67.6 ± 0.9	62.6 ± 0.9	68.3 ± 0.4
$\Delta^P_{8,50}$	0.5 ± 0.5	0.4 ± 0.4	0.1 ± 0.4	-0.2 ± 0.4	0.8 ± 0.2	-0.2 ± 0.2	0.4 ± 0.3
$\Delta^L_{8,50}$	0.1 ± 0.2	0.0 ± 0.1	0.3 ± 0.2	0.1 ± 0.1	0.7 ± 0.4	-0.2 ± 0.1	0.1 ± 0.1
Δ^P_O	1.2 ± 0.4	0.9 ± 0.3	0.9 ± 0.3	0.7 ± 0.2	1.8 ± 0.6	0.4 ± 0.1	1.2 ± 0.2
Δ^L_O	0.6 ± 0.2	0.6 ± 0.2	0.8 ± 0.3	0.5 ± 0.2	1.5 ± 0.5	0.2 ± 0.0	0.9 ± 0.2

	G → TR	SL → F	SL → G	SL → TL	SL → TR	TL → F	TL → G
INIT	68.8 ± 0.2	62.0 ± 1.6	71.1 ± 1.4	63.7 ± 1.2	67.0 ± 1.2	63.6 ± 0.5	69.7 ± 0.4
UB	69.9 ± 0.3	67.6 ± 0.9	73.8 ± 0.4	68.3 ± 0.4	69.9 ± 0.3	67.6 ± 0.9	73.8 ± 0.4
$\Delta^P_{8,50}$	-0.0 ± 0.1	0.8 ± 0.4	-0.5 ± 0.2	1.1 ± 0.4	-0.1 ± 0.1	-0.6 ± 0.3	-1.1 ± 0.6
$\Delta^L_{8,50}$	-0.1 ± 0.1	0.4 ± 0.2	0.1 ± 0.1	0.7 ± 0.1	0.1 ± 0.2	0.2 ± 0.1	-0.2 ± 0.1
Δ^P_O	0.5 ± 0.1	1.5 ± 0.4	0.3 ± 0.1	2.0 ± 0.5	0.5 ± 0.1	0.7 ± 0.2	0.7 ± 0.2
Δ^L_O	0.2 ± 0.1	1.4 ± 0.4	0.3 ± 0.1	1.4 ± 0.2	0.6 ± 0.1	0.6 ± 0.1	0.3 ± 0.0

	TL → SL	TL → TR	TR → F	TR → G	TR → SL	TR → TL	AVG
INIT	61.6 ± 0.5	64.9 ± 0.5	60.0 ± 1.0	71.5 ± 0.7	61.3 ± 0.6	63.3 ± 1.1	65.1 ± 0.9
UB	62.6 ± 0.9	69.9 ± 0.3	67.6 ± 0.9	73.8 ± 0.4	62.6 ± 0.9	68.3 ± 0.4	68.4 ± 0.7
$\Delta^P_{8,50}$	-0.3 ± 0.4	-0.5 ± 0.4	-0.1 ± 0.5	-0.1 ± 0.2	0.1 ± 0.2	0.4 ± 0.3	0.0 ± 0.4
$\Delta^L_{8,50}$	0.5 ± 0.2	-0.4 ± 0.3	0.3 ± 0.5	0.3 ± 0.3	0.0 ± 0.1	0.3 ± 0.3	0.2 ± 0.2
Δ^P_O	1.2 ± 0.1	0.7 ± 0.1	1.7 ± 0.4	0.7 ± 0.2	0.8 ± 0.2	1.2 ± 0.3	1.0 ± 0.3
Δ^L_O	1.1 ± 0.2	0.6 ± 0.1	1.0 ± 0.4	0.7 ± 0.2	0.6 ± 0.2	0.8 ± 0.3	0.7 ± 0.2

Table 5: MNLI results (macro-F1).

	D → L	D → R	D → S	L → D	L → R	L → S	R → D
INIT	50.9 ± 0.8	36.9 ± 1.1	40.5 ± 0.9	47.6 ± 0.2	35.3 ± 0.8	36.3 ± 0.5	46.2 ± 0.9
UB	85.5 ± 0.3	83.4 ± 0.2	81.2 ± 0.2	67.1 ± 0.5	83.4 ± 0.2	81.2 ± 0.2	67.1 ± 0.5
$\Delta^P_{8,50}$	-1.2 ± 0.6	-3.0 ± 1.2	-2.2 ± 1.0	0.9 ± 0.1	3.6 ± 0.7	1.0 ± 0.3	1.3 ± 0.3
$\Delta^L_{8,50}$	-0.2 ± 0.1	-0.4 ± 0.3	-0.1 ± 0.2	0.2 ± 0.1	0.3 ± 0.2	0.2 ± 0.1	0.1 ± 0.1
Δ^P_O	0.3 ± 0.2	0.6 ± 0.3	0.2 ± 0.2	1.4 ± 0.1	6.7 ± 1.0	1.9 ± 0.4	2.1 ± 0.5
Δ^L_O	0.2 ± 0.1	0.3 ± 0.2	0.4 ± 0.1	0.7 ± 0.0	1.5 ± 0.3	0.5 ± 0.2	0.7 ± 0.2

	R → L	R → S	S → D	S → L	S → R	AVG
INIT	44.1 ± 1.1	33.2 ± 0.9	49.1 ± 0.3	44.9 ± 0.5	55.6 ± 0.6	43.4 ± 0.8
UB	85.5 ± 0.3	81.2 ± 0.2	67.1 ± 0.5	85.5 ± 0.3	83.4 ± 0.2	79.3 ± 0.4
$\Delta^P_{8,50}$	9.5 ± 0.8	11.2 ± 0.7	0.6 ± 0.2	-2.1 ± 0.4	-4.2 ± 0.7	1.3 ± 0.7
$\Delta^L_{8,50}$	2.2 ± 0.5	2.4 ± 0.6	0.0 ± 0.1	-0.5 ± 0.2	-0.7 ± 0.4	0.3 ± 0.3
Δ^P_O	14.4 ± 0.9	18.8 ± 0.9	0.9 ± 0.2	0.3 ± 0.2	0.3 ± 0.2	4.0 ± 0.5
Δ^L_O	5.7 ± 0.9	6.8 ± 0.7	0.3 ± 0.1	0.2 ± 0.1	0.2 ± 0.1	1.5 ± 0.4

Table 6: Aspect prediction results (binary-F1).

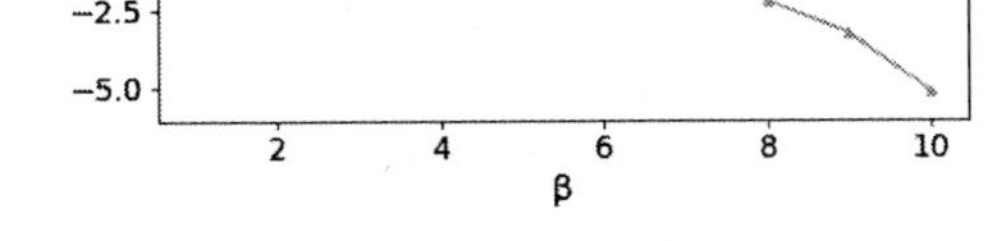

Figure 3: Results for different β values, using $k = 50$.

Generating unlabelled data for a tri-training approach in a low resourced NER task

Hugo Boulanger, Thomas Lavergne, Sophie Rosset
Université Paris-Saclay, CNRS,
Laboratoire Interdisciplinaire des Sciences du Numérique, 91400, Orsay, France
first-name.last-name@lisn.upsaclay.fr

Abstract

Training a tagger for Named Entity Recognition (NER) requires a substantial amount of labeled data in the task domain. Manual labeling is a tedious and complicated task. Semi-supervised learning methods can reduce the quantity of labeled data necessary to train a model. However, these methods require large quantities of unlabeled data, which remains an issue in many cases.

We address this problem by generating unlabeled data. Large language models have proven to be powerful tools for text generation. We use their generative capacity to produce new sentences and variations of the sentences of our available data. This generation method, combined with a semi-supervised method, is evaluated on CoNLL and I2B2. We prepare both of these corpora to simulate a low resource setting. We obtain significant improvements for semi-supervised learning with synthetic data against supervised learning on natural data.

1 Introduction

Training models to solve NER tasks requires a considerable amount of labeled data. In most NLP tasks, this data needs to be related to the task domain and must be in the targeted language. While English is a well-covered language, corpora are still being built to cover new domains or expand existing ones. For any other languages, corpora cover fewer domains. Data in the private sector is rarely shareable due to privacy reasons. It is also the case in domains such as the medical domain.

Recent approaches tackle the issue of the absence of resources by leveraging knowledge or data from other sources. Zero-shot learning is a learning paradigm trying to solve a target task without any labeled data. It uses the knowledge of how to predict labels of an adjacent task and applies it to predict the unseen labels of the target task (Wang et al., 2019). We do not aim to solve the NER problem in a situation with such strict data restrictions. Labeling a few examples is almost always possible. Few-shot learning provides training methods to generalize from a few labeled examples. These methods use the labeled examples to build representations of the class, which serve as comparison points for inference (Dopierre et al., 2021). Transfer learning leverages the knowledge learned on tasks of the domain to improve the performance on a specific task (Ruder, 2019). It is quite common to see cross-lingual transfer from higher-resourced languages where the task exists. However, the most prominent use case of transfer learning in NLP is the use of language models for data representation. We use this type of transfer learning to build high-performing taggers from BERT models. Semi-supervised learning is a paradigm where unlabeled data is widely available. The unlabeled data is used to improve the model's performance by giving a better topology of the data space.

We propose to use a semi-supervised learning method in a context where data is scarce enough to be fully labeled. We aim to achieve this by using large language models to generate the necessary unlabeled data. We test whether large language models can generate data that make tri-training a viable option in a low-resource context. The performances of our baseline models are compared against the performances of the ensembles of models trained with tri-training on CoNLL (Sang and De Meulder, 2003) and I2B2 (Uzuner et al., 2011). Significant improvements are observed using our method on the reduced datasets.

Language modeling has already been used as an augmentation method to generate labeled and unlabeled examples for NER in DAGA (Ding et al., 2020). However, our taggers overperform the taggers presented on the gold standard by 30 points at size 1000 and 9 points at full size. The semi-supervised method used in DAGA, self-training, is also prone to errors due to reinforcement of early mistakes. In our case, we generate unlabeled sen-

Proceedings of the Third Workshop on Deep Learning for Low-Resource Natural Language Processing, pages 30 - 37
July 14, 2022

tences using pre-trained large language models. We test this method with subsets of data ranging from 50 examples to 1000 examples vs. over 1000 in DAGA.

Thus, our main contribution is using out-of-the-box large language models as tools to obtain unlabeled data for semi-supervised learning in NER in a low-resource setting. The code relative to the experiment will be available in a public repository[1].

Section 2 presents state of the art related to data augmentation, semi-supervised learning in NER, and language modeling. Section 3 presents tri-training (Zhou and Li, 2005), and how we fit generation into it. Section 4 touches on the technical details of the experiments. Section 5 and 6 are the discussion and the conclusion of the article.

2 Related Works

Learning models in a low-resource setting require extracting every possible information from the available data. Data augmentation is a common technique that creates synthetic data from available data. In Natural Language Processing, augmentation is used across various tasks to help achieve better performances. In classification, techniques such as back-translation (Sennrich et al., 2016) or Easy Data Augmentation (Wei and Zou, 2019) are used. However, in tagging, paraphrasing using back-translation (Neuraz et al., 2018) is not bringing significant improvements. Recent works show that using language models learned on the training data to generate labeled and unlabeled examples can bring improvements (Ding et al., 2020).

Inductive semi-supervised learning (Van Engelen and Hoos, 2020) aims at improving the performances of models through the addition of unlabeled data. For Named Entity Recognition, *pseudo-labeling* is a method that has been used (Chen et al., 2019). *Pseudo-labeling* is one of the semi-supervised learning methods. The unlabeled data receives pseudo-labels from the models trained. This pseudo-labeled data is then used alongside labeled data to train the models. Variants of the method exists (Yarowsky, 1995) (McClosky et al., 2006) (Blum and Mitchell, 1998) with varying quantities of models trained. The separation of the data between the different models trained and how the models are used to produce pseudo-labels also creates variants to this method. In our case, we use tri-training (Zhou and Li, 2005), which uses three models. This method has been used to solve Clinical Concept Extraction in the medical domain (Chen et al., 2019) on new data.

Semi-supervised learning methods still require a significant amount of unlabeled data. However, with current advances in language modeling, this method could be improved. Transformer-based models (Vaswani et al., 2017) have been a revolution in the language modeling landscape. From their first iterations like GPT (Radford et al., 2018) to their more recent ones like T5 (Raffel et al., 2020) and GPT-3 (Brown et al., 2020), transformer-based models have become a staple of Natural Language Processing as fine-tuning or transferring knowledge from these models often outperforms learning a model on the task directly. While our taggers are based on BERT models (Devlin et al., 2018), we otherwise use the generative power of GPT2 (Radford et al., 2019) to provide unlabeled data for the semi-supervised training. GPT2 has been finetuned and used to generate unlabeled data for classification in a high resource context (He et al., 2021).

3 Methods

This section provides details on the tri-training process for sentence tagging and how we levy language modeling as an unlabeled data provider.

3.1 Tri-training

Algorithm 1 Tri-training ((Zhou and Li, 2005), (Ruder and Plank, 2018))

for $i \in \{1..3\}$ **do**
  $m_i \leftarrow train\_model(sampling(L), m_i)$
while Any m_i still learns **do**
  for $i \in \{1..3\}$ **do**
    $L_i \leftarrow \emptyset$
    $j, k \leftarrow \{1..3\} - |i|$
    for $x \in U$ **do**
      if $m_j(x) = m_k(x)$ **then**
        $L_i \leftarrow L_i \cup \{(x, m_j(x))\}$
  for $i \in \{1..3\}$ **do**
    $m_i \leftarrow train\_model(L_i \cup L, m_i)$

Tri-training is an inductive semi-supervised learning (Van Engelen and Hoos, 2020) method using an ensemble of three models. The models are trained in a supervised learning manner on a set of labeled and pseudo-labeled data. As we try to solve

[1]https://github.com/HugoBoulanger/Tritraining-Gen

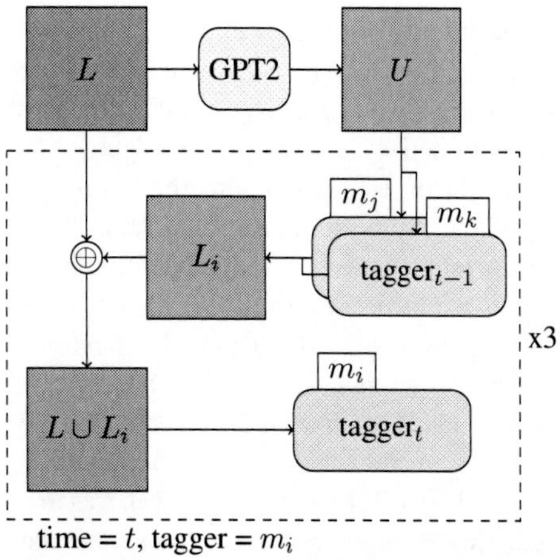

Figure 1: Tri-training with unlabeled data U generation. In rectangles are the data sets, and in rounded rectangles are the different models. The procedure is shown at episode t for model m_i. The initialization is not represented and is done by sampling with replacement from L.

a NER task, the models we use for the ensemble are taggers. Further description of the taggers can be found in the experiments section. We describe the Algorithm 1 in the following paragraphs, and we show our additions in Figure 1.

Tri-training. Tri-training is an episodic training method that stops when each model of the ensemble has stopped improving. The most crucial feature of tri-training is the construction of the training set of the models. This is shown from line 4 to line 9 in Algorithm 1 and in the second line of Figure 1. For each model m_i, a pseudo-labeled set L_i is constructed. L_i is composed of the unlabeled sentences $x \in U$ for which the predictions of the models m_j and m_k $i \notin \{j, k\}$ are equal. These predictions are added to L_i alongside x as their pseudo-labels. A threshold can also be used to remove uncertain annotations. However, it was concluded that it was not necessary for simple tri-training (Ruder and Plank, 2018). The models are then trained on both the natural and synthetic data $L \cup L_i$. L is the labeled training data. In our case, it represents any subset of the training corpus made for the low resource setting as explained in section 4.2. The operations described above are repeated until all models have stopped learning.

Initialization. The central part of Algorithm 1 described above assumes that models are sufficiently trained and different to create varied pseudo-labels. To achieve these prerequisites, we pre-train the models. The models m_i are pre-trained on different random subsets of the labeled data L. These subsets are made by sampling with replacement from the training set. This operation is also referred to as *bootstrap sampling* in (Zhou and Li, 2005). Sampling the pre-training data is done to introduce variety in the train sets of the three models without incurring performance losses.

Inference. For inference, we obtain an ensemble of 3 different models that can be used together with a voting system. We keep the labels with the highest summed score across the three models.

As a semi-supervised learning algorithm, tri-training requires a substantial amount of unlabeled examples. The specificity of our study is the use of a generator to create the unlabeled examples.

3.2 Generation

Applying semi-supervised learning methods is more complicated when there is no unlabeled data. We used the text of the labeled data as the context for the generation model. We use the generation model in two different ways: (i) follow-up sentence generation and (ii) sentence completion, as shown in Figure 2.

The first generation method we use is follow-up sentence generation. Large language models like GPT-2 (Radford et al., 2019) are trained on texts containing multiple sentences. This kind of model should be able to generate the follow-up sentence from the context. Using these models out-of-the-box should work without any finetuning. We apply follow-up sentence generation to generate new examples. With this method, we aim to generate new sentences that are within the same domain but have different structures.

The second method we use is sentence completion. We remove the end of the sentence and complete it using the language model for this method. We aim to generate alternative contexts to the part of the sentence we keep with this method. While this method might bring more variations by taking out random portions of the sentences, it is easier to use this way.

3.3 Evaluation

We aim at evaluating whether the data generated with large language models is of sufficient quality to serve as unlabeled data in a tri-training scenario. To that end, we evaluate the performances of the

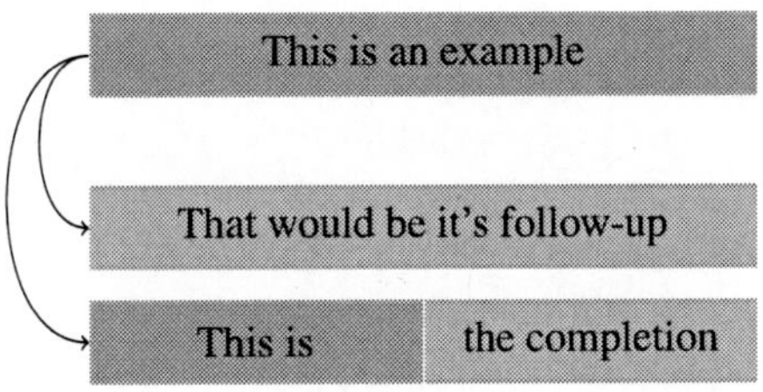

Figure 2: Generation methods examples. In blue is the initial example and in red is the generated text. The first generated example is from sentence follow-up, and the second is from sentence completion.

tri-trained models against the performances of a single model trained on the same amount of labeled natural data.

We do not reduce the size of our testing sets as we aim to compare our method to existing results. Our evaluation is comparative between our tri-training method and no augmentation method. We want to see whether there are increases in performance in a low-resource setting. Comparisons are made between a tagger trained on one subset against the ensemble of taggers obtained via our tri-training and generation method on the same subset. The sampling of subsets is seeded as explained in Section 4.2. We average results over those seeds to reduce the impact of selection biases.

4 Experiments

In this section, we describe the technical details of the experiments and explain the variants tested.

4.1 Datasets

The task we are working on is the Named Entity Recognition (NER) task. The goal of this task is to find mentions associated with certain concepts in sequences of text. In practice, this is done by assigning labels representing the concepts and the position within the mention to each of the tokens of the text. The corpora we are using are CoNLL 2003 English (Sang and De Meulder, 2003) and I2B2 (Uzuner et al., 2011). CoNLL is a corpus of Reuters news annotated with four different concepts: person, location, organization, and miscellaneous. The difficulties of this corpus reside in the various types of information portrayed within. From geopolitical news to tables of sports results, the input format varies greatly. I2B2 is a corpus of medical records annotated with three different concepts: problem, treatment, and test. These corpora are classic corpora for the NER task and cover

	I2B2	CoNLL
Train line count	11482	14986
Test line count	27625	3683
BERT base	84.0	90.0
BERT large	85.0	**92.0**
BioBERT	**86.6**	

Table 1: Reference models used as topline for our work and viability check against current state of the art. F_1 of BERT + classifier models on I2B2 and CoNLL using different pre-trained models. Metrics computed by seqeval (Ramshaw and Marcus, 1995) (Nakayama, 2018). Best model based on development set F1, trained on 50 epochs, with batch size of 32.

diverse specialty domains. These complete datasets contain enough data to be considered an ideal case for their respective tasks. We have tested our tagger architecture (see 4.3) on the full-sized data in order to verify its quality and select the best pre-trained BERT model available. This topline can be seen in Table 1. Our experiment focuses on low resources; the maximum size of the training data is less than 10% of the full set. We do not expect to reach topline results with our method at this quantity of data. However, we have to look at how much of the gap between topline and baseline is bridged by our method.

4.2 Low resource setting

The purpose of our method is to be used in a low-resource setting. We simulate such a setting by sampling a small number of labeled examples from the training set to create a new training set. We also consider that the quantity of data is small enough that all of the data is labeled. For our experiment, we reduce the training set to a subset S_{1000} of size 1000 by sampling without replacement using ten different seeds. This is where the sampling bias is induced. S_{1000} contains less than 10% of each of our sets. The seeding is done to reduce the variability of results due to sampling biases. Most of the results will be averaged over the ten seeds. We cut each subset S_{1000} in a series of subsets: $S_{50} \subset S_{100} \subset S_{250} \subset S_{500} \subset S_{1000}$. This is useful to evaluate the impact of the addition of new examples. For each seed, we obtain five subsets of labeled data.

4.3 Tagger

This section presents the architecture shared by all the taggers we train. It is a simple BERT +

		S_{50}	S_{100}	S_{250}	S_{500}	S_{1000}
I2B2	baseline	36.23±5.80	49.22±3.23	64.34±1.43	71.39±0.75	77.38±0.64
	Δunique	+3.93±1.89	+2.56±2.37	+1.89±1.25	+1.93±0.70	+1.28±0.84
	Δensemble	+4.32±1.82	+3.08±2.38	+2.45±1.23	+2.49±0.73	+1.80±0.84
CoNLL	baseline	59.87±3.32	69.20±3.92	80.65±1.99	84.74±0.89	87.70±0.38
	Δunique	+2.33±2.01	+0.08±3.64	+1.06±1.11	+0.54±0.83	+0.27±0.37
	Δensemble	+2.98±1.98	+0.84±3.68	+1.77±1.17	+1.14±0.71	+0.71±0.40

Table 2: F_1 score on baseline averaged across seeds. Average of the deltas between the performances of each individual tri-trained tagger and their respective baselines at Δunique lines. Average of the deltas between the performances of tri-trained ensembles and their respective baselines at Δensemble lines. Corpora used are I2B2 and CoNLL.

classifier architecture. The classifier is a two-layer feed-forward network with a hidden size of 768 and ReLU (rectified linear unit) activation. Dropout with $p = 0.1$ is applied between BERT and the classifier during training. The model is trained with the Adam optimizer with an initial learning rate of 10^{-5}. We train all taggers for tri-training and baseline for 1000 epochs with early stopping when the development set F_1 score stops increasing for 20 epochs (40 epochs for a subset of size 50). The sentence batch size is 16.

While we refer to our tagger architecture as BERT + classifier, we have tried different pre-trained BERT models[2][3][4] as shown in Table 1 and have settled on two different models. For CoNLL, the best results were obtained with BERT large cased (Devlin et al., 2018), and for I2B2, with BioBERT base cased (Lee et al., 2020).

4.4 Generation

We generate the unlabeled set U with GPT-2 (Radford et al., 2019). We use HuggingFace's implementation[5]. The text from the labeled train set is used as the context to generate entailed examples. With each labeled example, we generate five follow-up sentences. We also use the language model for sentence completion. In this case, we cut the original text and complete it using the model. Each labeled example is cut to 75%, 50%, and 25% of its length. In each of these cases, we generate five completed sentences. This amounts to a total of 20 synthetic examples per natural example. It is, in practice, slightly less than that because we filter out sequences made exclusively of different types of whitespace, newlines, and other such noise. Generated examples can be seen in Figure 3

4.5 Tri-training

The main focus of this article is the use of tri-training without natural unlabeled data. We use the unlabeled data generated, as explained previously, as the unlabeled data of tri-training. Tri-training requires one development set and one validation set: the first for the training of each model m_i, the second to validate the stagnation of the models across episodes. We chose to split the corpora's initial development set in half to fulfill each of those purposes. As this is a first experiment, we exclude sentences without tags from the pseudo-labeled set. This is done to avoid a possible problem at very low resources where the pre-trained models are not trained enough and produce sentences with empty tag sequences where they should not. However, our results show that these precautions might not be necessary. The result of the tri-training procedure is an ensemble of three models. Inference using this ensemble is done with a simple voting system. Voting is done by summing the scores output of each tag across all models and picking the highest.

4.6 Results

In this section, we present the results obtained across the different subsets.

Baseline. Baseline are the results of models trained in a supervised manner only on the natural training data. For each subset S_n, it is an average of 10 scores. The results in Table 2 show consistent performance increases between each subset sizes. Seqeval (Ramshaw and Marcus, 1995) (Nakayama, 2018) is used to compute the results. I2B2 $F1$ range from 36.2 (size 50) to 77.4 (size 1000), and

[2] `https://huggingface.co/bert-base-uncased`

[3] `https://huggingface.co/bert-large-cased`

[4] `https://huggingface.co/dmis-lab/biobert-base-cased-v1.1`

[5] `https://huggingface.co/gpt2`

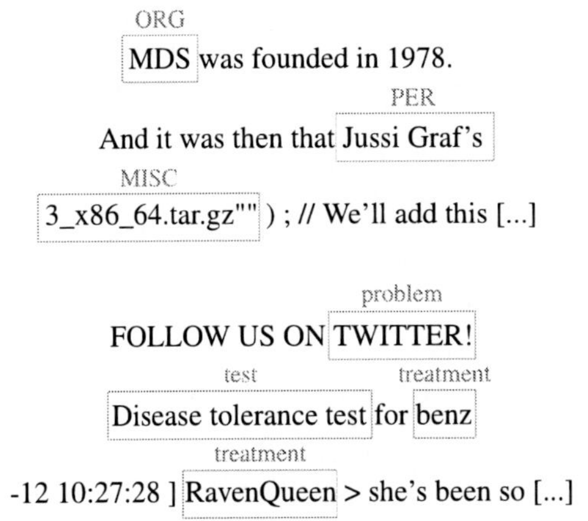

Figure 3: Examples of generation. The three first examples are from CoNLL and the three last from I2B2. Each series is formed of an example of completion and two examples of sentence follow-up. The examples were cherry-picked to show both positive and negative aspects of generation, be of short length, and be labeled by the models. On CoNLL's completion example, only a full stop was added. On I2B2's completion example, the context was "FOLLOW" and was too short and generic to bring the sentence to the medical domain. The second examples for both corpora are okay. The third examples for both corpora happen when short formulaic sentences are used as context. For CoNLL, it is the common -DOCSTART- and for I2B2, it was a date.

CoNLL $F1$ range from 59.9 (size 50) to 87.7 (size 1000). As discussed in Section 3.3, smaller sizes show a higher standard deviation with 5.8 for I2B2 and 3.3 for CoNLL at size 50.

Δunique. Tri-training produces three trained models supposed to be used as an ensemble of models. With constraints such as memory consumption or inference time, one might want to use a single model for inference. For such cases, we have reported the results of single models. The Δunique results show the deltas between each of the three individual models m_i and the baseline. For each subset S_n, it is an average of 30 deltas.

Δensemble. The purpose of tri-training is to obtain an ensemble of three models. We report the results of the ensembles by computing the deltas between the performances of the ensembles and their respective baselines. These results can be found within Table 2 at the Δensemble line and in Figure 4.

Our method obtains higher results on average on all subsets and on both corpora. Generally, on

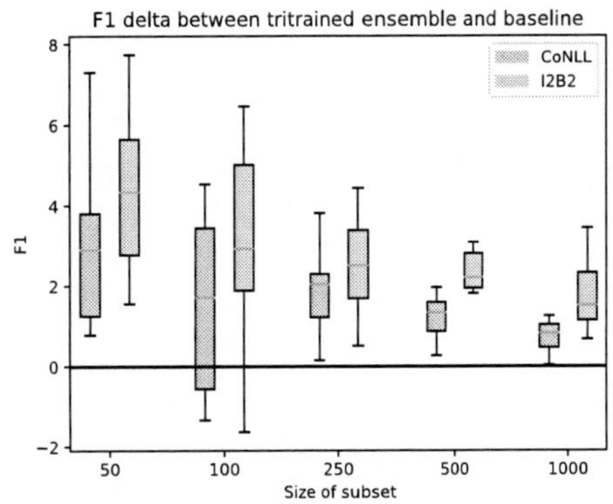

Figure 4: Boxplot of CoNLL and I2B2 deltas between tri-trained ensemble and baseline (Δensemble). For each subset size, the left boxplot is CoNLL, the right boxplot is I2B2.

I2B2, tri-training allows for a Δensemble to range from +4.32 (S_{50}) to +1.80 (S_{1000}). On CoNLL, it otherwise ranges from +2.98 (S_{50}) to +0.71 (S_{1000}). The Δunique shows, as expected, lower gains than Δensemble, ranging from +3.93 (S_{50}) to +1.28 (S_{1000}) for I2B2 and +2.33 (S_{50}) to +0.27 (S_{1000}) for CoNLL.

Out of the 50 individual runs for each corpus, one is negative for I2B2, and five are negative for CoNLL. Impacts of the negative results are seen on the average results of CoNLL at subset size 100. Three seeds yield negative gains at this size, with one having extreme (-8.6 points) negative gains. Removing this extreme result in the average calculation brings the Δensemble score closer to expected values (+1.89). Performances of individual models on CoNLL are within the standard deviation of negative results. This is not the case for I2B2. These results show that using the ensemble is a more stable solution. Overall, the method is most consistent with subsets of size 250 plus, as the average performance of tri-trained ensembles is above the standard deviation of the baseline.

5 Discussion

While our low-resource setting allows us to compare the impact of the training method in an otherwise similar context, it does not fully represent the nature of the problem. Building the development and test set is also a low resource problem. Reducing the test set to simulate low-resource will only make any comparison meaningless. Simulating the development set in the low resource context is an improvement that could be made.

It is also to note that while the application domain is low resource, it is necessary to have a sizeable open-domain language model in the target language. Trying this method in languages other than English must be tested. Multilingual models might be the solution to the generalization of this method. As it stands, availability of large language model is the hardest limitation of this method.

6 Conclusion

Leveraging pre-trained models to improve performances on specific tasks is a common approach. With recent improvements to language modeling, recent models are often used directly to solve tasks. Direct usage is the method we use to build our taggers. However, we propose a new use for these sizeable models. They can serve as unlabeled data generators for semi-supervised learning. In particular, we have shown that we can use this method to gain significant improvements to the performances of taggers on NER and Clinical Concept Extraction in a low resource context. We gain between 3 and 4 points of F_1 score on subsets of data of size 50. Gains are overall positive on the sizes of the subsets we have tested. The higher the gains, the lower the data size is. We have shown that large language models are suitable tools to generate unlabeled examples for semi-supervised learning for NER.

Acknowledgements

This work was granted access to the HPC resources of IDRIS under the allocation 2021-AD011013018 made by GENCI. This work was granted access to the HPC resources of Saclay-IA through the Lab-IA machine. This work has been supported by the project PSPC AIDA: 2019-PSPC-09 funded by BPI-France.

References

Avrim Blum and Tom Mitchell. 1998. Combining labeled and unlabeled data with co-training. In *Proceedings of the eleventh annual conference on Computational learning theory*, pages 92–100.

Tom Brown, Benjamin Mann, Nick Ryder, Melanie Subbiah, Jared D Kaplan, Prafulla Dhariwal, Arvind Neelakantan, Pranav Shyam, Girish Sastry, Amanda Askell, et al. 2020. Language models are few-shot learners. *Advances in neural information processing systems*, 33:1877–1901.

Y Chen, C Zhou, T Li, H Wu, X Zhao, K Ye, and J Liao. 2019. Named entity recognition from chinese adverse drug event reports with lexical feature based bilstm-crf and tri-training. *Journal of Biomedical Informatics*, 96:103252–103252.

Jacob Devlin, Ming-Wei Chang, Kenton Lee, and Kristina Toutanova. 2018. Bert: Pre-training of deep bidirectional transformers for language understanding. *arXiv preprint arXiv:1810.04805*.

Bosheng Ding, Linlin Liu, Lidong Bing, Canasai Kruengkrai, Thien Hai Nguyen, Shafiq Joty, Luo Si, and Chunyan Miao. 2020. Daga: Data augmentation with a generation approach for low-resource tagging tasks. *arXiv preprint arXiv:2011.01549*.

Thomas Dopierre, Christophe Gravier, and Wilfried Logerais. 2021. Protaugment: Intent detection meta-learning through unsupervised diverse paraphrasing. In *Proceedings of the 59th Annual Meeting of the Association for Computational Linguistics and the 11th International Joint Conference on Natural Language Processing (Volume 1: Long Papers)*, pages 2454–2466.

Xuanli He, Islam Nassar, Jamie Kiros, Gholamreza Haffari, and Mohammad Norouzi. 2021. Generate, annotate, and learn: Generative models advance self-training and knowledge distillation. *arXiv preprint arXiv:2106.06168*.

Jinhyuk Lee, Wonjin Yoon, Sungdong Kim, Donghyeon Kim, Sunkyu Kim, Chan Ho So, and Jaewoo Kang. 2020. Biobert: a pre-trained biomedical language representation model for biomedical text mining. *Bioinformatics*, 36(4):1234–1240.

David McClosky, Eugene Charniak, and Mark Johnson. 2006. Effective self-training for parsing. In *Proceedings of the main conference on human language technology conference of the North American Chapter of the Association of Computational Linguistics*, pages 152–159. Citeseer.

Hiroki Nakayama. 2018. seqeval: A python framework for sequence labeling evaluation. Software available from https://github.com/chakki-works/seqeval.

Antoine Neuraz, Leonardo Campillos Llanos, Anita Burgun, and Sophie Rosset. 2018. Natural language understanding for task oriented dialog in the biomedical domain in a low resources context. *arXiv preprint arXiv:1811.09417*.

Alec Radford, Karthik Narasimhan, Tim Salimans, and Ilya Sutskever. 2018. Improving language understanding by generative pre-training.

Alec Radford, Jeffrey Wu, Rewon Child, David Luan, Dario Amodei, and Ilya Sutskever. 2019. Language models are unsupervised multitask learners. *OpenAI Blog*, 1(8):9.

Colin Raffel, Noam Shazeer, Adam Roberts, Katherine Lee, Sharan Narang, Michael Matena, Yanqi Zhou, Wei Li, and Peter J Liu. 2020. Exploring the limits of transfer learning with a unified text-to-text transformer. *Journal of Machine Learning Research*, 21:1–67.

Lance Ramshaw and Mitch Marcus. 1995. Text chunking using transformation-based learning. In *Third Workshop on Very Large Corpora*.

Sebastian Ruder. 2019. *Neural Transfer Learning for Natural Language Processing*. Ph.D. thesis, National University of Ireland, Galway.

Sebastian Ruder and Barbara Plank. 2018. Strong baselines for neural semi-supervised learning under domain shift. In *Proceedings of the 56th Annual Meeting of the Association for Computational Linguistics (Volume 1: Long Papers)*, pages 1044–1054.

Erik Tjong Kim Sang and Fien De Meulder. 2003. Introduction to the conll-2003 shared task: Language-independent named entity recognition. In *Proceedings of the Seventh Conference on Natural Language Learning at HLT-NAACL 2003*, pages 142–147.

Rico Sennrich, Barry Haddow, and Alexandra Birch. 2016. Improving neural machine translation models with monolingual data. In *Proceedings of the 54th Annual Meeting of the Association for Computational Linguistics (Volume 1: Long Papers)*, pages 86–96.

Özlem Uzuner, Brett R South, Shuying Shen, and Scott L DuVall. 2011. 2010 i2b2/va challenge on concepts, assertions, and relations in clinical text. *Journal of the American Medical Informatics Association: JAMIA*, 18(5):552.

Jesper E Van Engelen and Holger H Hoos. 2020. A survey on semi-supervised learning. *Machine Learning*, 109(2):373–440.

Ashish Vaswani, Noam Shazeer, Niki Parmar, Jakob Uszkoreit, Llion Jones, Aidan N Gomez, Łukasz Kaiser, and Illia Polosukhin. 2017. Attention is all you need. In *Advances in neural information processing systems*, pages 5998–6008.

Wei Wang, Vincent W Zheng, Han Yu, and Chunyan Miao. 2019. A survey of zero-shot learning: Settings, methods, and applications. *ACM Transactions on Intelligent Systems and Technology (TIST)*, 10(2):1–37.

Jason Wei and Kai Zou. 2019. EDA: Easy data augmentation techniques for boosting performance on text classification tasks. In *Proceedings of the 2019 Conference on Empirical Methods in Natural Language Processing and the 9th International Joint Conference on Natural Language Processing (EMNLP-IJCNLP)*, pages 6382–6388, Hong Kong, China. Association for Computational Linguistics.

David Yarowsky. 1995. Unsupervised word sense disambiguation rivaling supervised methods. In *33rd annual meeting of the association for computational linguistics*, pages 189–196.

Zhi-Hua Zhou and Ming Li. 2005. Tri-training: Exploiting unlabeled data using three classifiers. *IEEE Transactions on knowledge and Data Engineering*, 17(11):1529–1541.

ANTS: A Framework for Retrieval of Text Segments in Unstructured Documents

Brian Chivers, Mason P. Jiang, Wonhee Lee, Amy Ng, Natalya I. Rapstine, Alex Storer

Stanford University

{bchivers,mpjiang,wolee,awn,nrapstin,astorer}@stanford.edu

Abstract

Text segmentation and extraction from unstructured documents can provide business researchers with a wealth of new information on firms and their behaviors. However, the most valuable text is often difficult to extract consistently due to substantial variations in how content can appear from document to document. Thus, the most successful way to extract this content has been through costly crowdsourcing and training of manual workers. We propose the Assisted Neural Text Segmentation (ANTS) framework to identify pertinent text in unstructured documents from a small set of labeled examples. ANTS leverages deep learning and transfer learning architectures to empower researchers to identify relevant text with minimal manual coding. Using a real world sample of accounting documents, we identify targeted sections 96% of the time using only 5 training examples.

1 Introduction

Datasets of text documents hold enormous amounts of raw information, particularly for social scientists and business researchers. An individual document contains not only declarative statements and facts, but also style, theme and sentiment information that can be used to evaluate diverse research questions.

Researchers have spent decades developing frameworks and techniques to distill text into features that are easily integrated into existing research practices. One common practice is to use vetted word lists to compute a score for a particular topic or theme. For example, Loughran and Mcdonald (2011) use a vetted word list to identify the degree of uncertain language used in financial documents, and count the number of occurrences as a proxy for the amount of prospective discussion. Dictionary approaches such as LIWC (Tausczik and Pennebaker, 2009) match words to predefined psycholinguistic categories, allowing researchers to identify broad themes including "anxiety" and "religion".

More computationally sophisticated methods such as word embeddings (Mikolov et al., 2013) and topic modeling algorithms (Blei et al., 2003) provide the capability to measure prevalence of topics within documents, as well as the relationships between words and how they may shift over time. The development of transformer models such as BERT (Bi-directional Encoder Representations from Transformers) (Devlin et al., 2019) have opened a new frontier of text processing, with models trained to categorize, summarize or answer specific questions from input text.

Despite all these advancements, valuable pieces of information remain difficult to extract or categorize in large unstructured documents. Word lists and dictionaries can fail to capture the immense variety of language that can be used to talk about a single topic. Topic modeling algorithms may not capture a specific concept in one overarching topic. Thus, to ensure maximum quality, many researchers resort to manual methods to effectively characterize the text data from their documents. One approach is to begin by identifying only the segments of interest, so that only relevant text can be utilized by subject matter experts or computational methods. To manually select these relevant subsets, researchers frequently work with undergraduates or other research assistants, or they post tasks to pools of remote workers using platforms like Amazon's Mechanical Turk (MTurk). In either method, using humans to extract specific pieces of text from large documents is costly and time consuming.

We propose a general deep learning framework to provide Assisted Neural Text Segmentation (ANTS) as a way to facilitate identification of text segments of interest for researchers. The primary goal of this general framework aims to reduce the amount of time subject matter experts must spend

Proceedings of the Third Workshop on Deep Learning for Low-Resource Natural Language Processing, pages 38 - 47
July 14, 2022

manually coding documents or identifying and training effective research assistants. The ANTS framework has four steps:

1. Label a small handful of documents indicating the relevant section of text
2. Fine-tune a pre-trained deep transformer model (e.g., BERT) on the labeled dataset
3. Classify new text with the fine-tuned model
4. Infer the section of interest from the model's classification scores combined with domain knowledge from the research question

In this paper, we present a specific problem of extracting Human Capital Disclosure (HCD) sections from Form 10-K filings created by corporations for regulatory Securities and Exchange Commission (SEC) filings. We also illustrate a few strategies to elevate the performance of our model without annotating additional training data. Through similar means, we hope to provide a less costly and time consuming pathway for researchers to identify relevant segments of text from unstructured documents.

2 Related Work

With modern advancements in deep learning technology and the increased need for processing large text datasets, researchers have been optimizing the task of automated text segmentation. Common applications of this natural language processing (NLP) task include information retrieval (Oh et al., 2007; Nguyen et al., 2021), topic segmentation (Arnold et al., 2019; Aumiller et al., 2021), and document summarization (Chuang and Yang, 2000). These tasks can take either linear or hierarchical approaches, with the latter taking into account structural representation of topics within documents (Glavaš and Swapna, 2020).

Generally, the development of neural models from scratch for text segmentation tasks requires large training datasets (Koshorek et al., 2018) and high computational costs. In response, researchers have turned to pre-trained deep transformer models such as BERT, which offers high performance on NLP tasks and the possibility of fine-tuning its base model towards specific domains. Various transformer-based model architectures and linear, hierarchical, and multilevel models have been explored and evaluated for their performance on text segmentation.

For domain-independent models, Lukasik et al. (2020) introduced three new BERT architectures to segment documents and discourses by predicting on break points instead of classifying every piece of text. These novel architectures showed that a simple cross-segment BERT model using only local context (sequences of tokens before and after a potential break point) can perform as competitively as more complex hierarchical BERT models. Yoong et al. (2021) also developed three BERT models—BERT-NSP, BERT-SEP and BERT-SEGMENT—to perform a text tiling task (dividing a document or dialogue into semantically coherent text segments) and demonstrated that BERT-SEP, which considers the relatedness of adjacent sentences as well as information from the whole document, outperformed graph-based or bi-directional LSTM (Long Short-Term Memory) models. Lo et al. (2021) developed a two-level transformer framework incorporating language-specific or domain-specific pre-trained BERT transformers as sentence encoders, which outperformed state-of-the-art text segmentation models on a semantic coherence measure.

To develop domain-specific models, often with limited labeled training data, researchers have tested how transformer-based language models pre-trained on large amounts of general-domain data can be leveraged and adapted for a specific domain. To extract content elements from regulatory filings and property lease agreements, Zhang et al. (2020) segmented documents into paragraphs and trained BERT at the paragraph level, which achieved reasonable accuracy. They also found that training with fewer than 100 documents was sufficient to achieve an F1 score similar to that of the same model trained with the entire set of documents. Araci (2019) introduced FinBERT, a fine-tuned BERT model for the financial domain, by conducting additional pre-training and fine-tuning of BERT using text from financial news articles. FinBERT outperformed other pre-trained models with as few as 250 training examples in a sentiment analysis task involving financial phrases.

We go beyond the works mentioned that only provided information retrieval, topic segmentation, or document summarization to extract any targeted section that a social science researcher needs through a quick and manual-labor saving framework. Building on the above related works, we focus on refining a generic transformer model

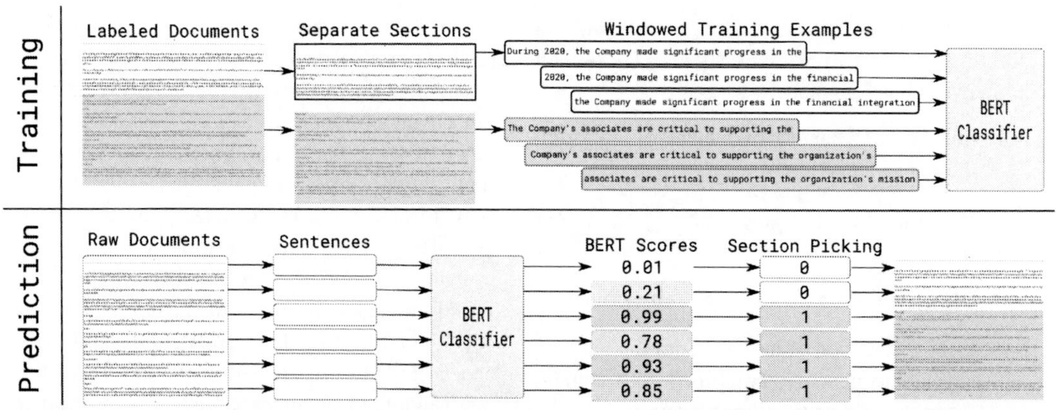

Figure 1: An illustration of the Assisted Neural Text Segmentation (ANTS) framework. In the Training stage (top pane), we fine-tune a pre-trained BERT model for text classification on hand-labeled documents that are separated into pertinent (green) and non-pertinent (white) sections. We augment our collection of training examples by creating sliding windows of tokens from the labeled sections. In the Prediction stage (bottom pane), we use our fine-tuned model on unseen documents to compute classification scores on individual sentences. We utilize these scores with a threshold method to identify a single, continuous section of relevant text for each document.

on a single domain-specific task to extract a targeted section of text in a low-resource setting. We use this test case to illustrate a framework that a social science researcher can use in place of training and recruiting manual labor.

3 Data

The Securities and Exchange Commission (SEC) requires that publicly traded companies file financial disclosures at regular intervals. The Form 10-K is an annual report that contains information about a company's business operations, financial results, and management. In November 2020, the SEC began to require its registrants to include a disclosure of their human capital resources in their Form 10-K. This resulting section is of interest to accounting researchers who want to characterize how firms discuss their human capital and whether specific diversity metrics are divulged (Choi et al., 2022).

We use MTurk to train workers to identify the described Human Capital Disclosures (HCD) section in 393 Form 10-K documents filed by S&P 500 firms from November 2020 through March 2021. The HCD section is a single, continuous segment of text located within each Form 10-K. It appears under various titles (e.g., "Human Capital", "Human Resources", "Talent", "Employee Engagement"), which span a range of sub-section topics (e.g., hiring, benefits and compensation, diversity, culture) of different lengths and combinations. We employ human labor for this extraction task due to this lack of uniformity in the section names, content, and location of the HCD section among Form 10-K documents. We use this manually collected data as a test case for our ANTS framework. In later sections, we will describe how documents are randomly sampled to obtain training and test sets to evaluate our framework.

4 Methods

In this section, we describe the ANTS framework (outlined in Figure 1) in more detail and how it is used in the scope of our specific test case. Our framework expands upon the general structure and methodologies of machine learning systems. We employ a few strategies within the framework to maximize the performance of our fine-tuned model on our task without adding more labeled documents. In training, we explore a windowing method to expand the size of our input data. In prediction, we use an approach combining the prediction scores of individual sentences and blocks of sentences to optimize our ability to locate the targeted single, continuous HCD section. Our implementation of the methods described below can be found at darc.stanford.edu/ants.

4.1 Label Training Data

To begin, documents are manually annotated to be used as inputs for training (green boxes in Training panel of Figure 1). We discuss our training inputs as documents to match how this framework might be used by researchers who are more familiar with handling and labeling whole documents. For our specific problem, MTurk workers manually identified a single HCD section within Form 10-K documents.

After manual labeling, we separate the text within our documents into positive and negative sections. In this case, the positive section is the HCD section and the negative section is the rest of the document. Since a given HCD section may be relatively scarce in content (~1000 tokens on average from the collected sample), we increase the amount of training examples in our dataset by windowing over each section. In this approach, illustrated in the Training panel of Figure 1, given a specific window size N, we take the first N tokens of the positive section (in green), and label that window as 1. This is the first training example for our model. Next, we move one token over, and take another window of N tokens. This is repeated until there are no more tokens in the section. We perform the same windowing for the negative section (in white), except with a label of 0. In our test case, we use a window size of 34 tokens to coincide with the median number of tokens per sentence in our sample of documents. The window size hyperparameter can be varied depending on the use case, where smaller windows might contribute too little context for the model to learn on, while larger windows might provide too few examples.

4.2 Fine-tune BERT

To fine-tune BERT, we use the implementation of BERT for binary classification from Wolf et al. (2020) We train only the final classification layer with a batch size of 32 and a learning rate of $1e^{-5}$ for 4 epochs on a 3:1 (negative:positive) balanced training set, selecting the best model based on the validation set performance. All other layer weights in the model are frozen. The training dataset was split 9:1 for training and validation. After the training/validation split, we balance the training set with a 3:1 ratio of negative to positive examples. This balancing is accomplished by under-sampling negative examples to achieve the desired ratio.

We use GPU resources on Google Colab for the initial exploration and development of our training framework, and a high performance computing cluster for final training. We run the final training using a single GPU on the Stanford High Performance Computing Sherlock cluster.

To better represent the range of performance of the fine-tuned models from our training framework in this paper, we take a random sample of input documents from the available set of labeled documents and fine-tune a BERT model using that sample instead of the full set of labeled documents. We denote a model trained on a random sample of input documents by Model$_i$, for $i = 1, \ldots, M$, where M is set to 20 in our examples. For Model$_i$, we randomly sample a number of training documents, and use the remaining documents as the test set for that model. In the prediction phase, we pick the epoch with the least validation loss during training for every Model$_i$.

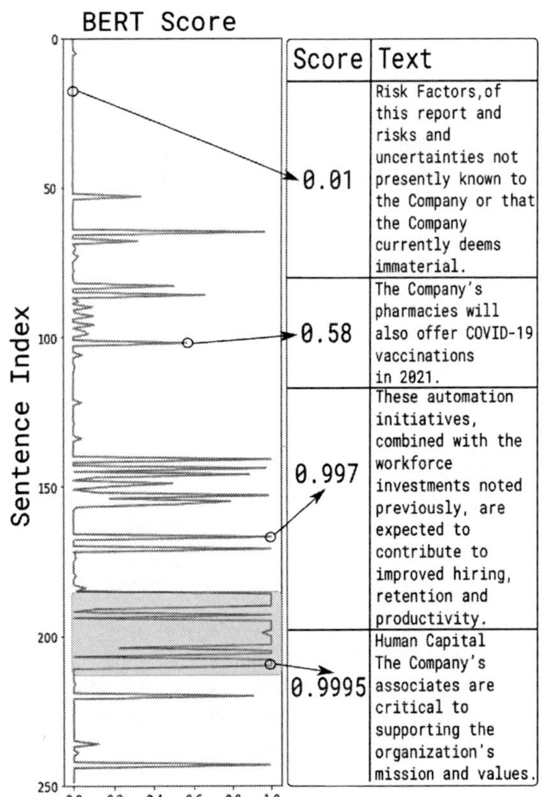

Figure 2: Example of single sentence (1-block) probabilistic scores (red line) generated during the prediction phase for a single document accompanied by sample sentence text. High scores (such as 0.9995) indicate a strong correlation with the language of the positive training examples and low scores (such as 0.01) indicate the opposite. The targeted Human Capital Disclosure (HCD) section is highlighted in green.

4.3 Classify New Text

Now that we have a fine-tuned BERT model to identify the language we are looking for, we use that model to classify text in unseen documents. For each document, we tokenize the text into sentences (Prediction panel of Figure 1) using the Python NLTK package (Bird et al., 2009) in preparation for prediction on the sentence-level. We choose to predict on sentences as they represent the most natural breaking points within a document. As an output, the model provides a probabilistic classification score for each sentence.

In our test case, we generate prediction scores for both single sentences (1-block) and for larger blocks of five sentences (5-block). In the 5-block instance, we create blocks of 5 sentences with a step size of 1 sentence, similar to the windowing strategy in training. Our rationale for generating scores for 5-blocks is to take advantage of the additional context provided by neighboring sentences to help classify the central sentence. This way, shorter sentences with less contextual information, but that are still part of the target section, are more likely to be classified properly in the method we use to identify HCD sections from the model output. This strategy is another demonstration of maximizing the available information from a scarce amount of data.

4.4 Identify Targeted Section

After running prediction and obtaining scores for each sentence in a document, we need to make a decision on which sentences are associated with our section of interest. In some use cases, where a straightforward categorization of individual sentences is sufficient, a simple threshold can be chosen to make this decision. This threshold can be tuned based on the desired outcome metrics. In our test case, where we need to find a single, continuous section of text, a more complex approach is necessary.

The choice of a section identification method is complicated by the distribution of sentence scores generated by the model. Figure 2 illustrates the score distribution (in red) as a function of sentence index for an example document. The targeted HCD section is highlighted in green. Generally, higher scores indicate a strong correlation with the language of the positive training examples and lower scores indicate the opposite. There are a few situations to consider.

First, there are sentences that are part of the targeted section and should become true positive predictions. However, the distribution of scores within the highlighted green area shows that there are individual sentences with lower scores that could end up as false negative predictions. These may simply be shorter sentences with less contextual information or they could actually contain irrelevant text, but happen to be in the targeted section. In our task of capturing the HCD section as presented in each Form 10-K document, we want to capture these sentences.

Furthermore, there are sentences with relatively high scores (such as the 0.997 example sentence and many of the other peaks outside of the highlighted green area) that contain relevant content based on the provided training examples, but are not contained within the targeted section. This is not unexpected in our case as companies are required to discuss their human capital resources in Item 1 of their Form 10-K, but this does not forbid them from discussing related content outside of Item 1. This situation can lead to many false positive predictions in our case, that could actually be relevant data in a different use case.

Finally, there are sentences with scores in the middle (such as the 0.58 example sentence). These could appear within or outside of the targeted section and the chosen method must accommodate these sentences.

In consideration of these factors, we use the combined information provided by the 1-block and 5-block scores to determine the predicted single, continuous HCD section for each test document. To start, we calculate a threshold for which to evaluate the output scores by compiling the 1-block scores produced by the Model$_i$ given a particular set of parameters and taking the median value of scores that are less than or equal to 0.5. For each document, we then find the longest continuous section of 1-block scores that fall under that threshold. After that, we seek the longest continuous section of 5-block scores that fall under the threshold and has an overlap with the longest 1-block section. The sentence endpoints of this 5-block section determine the predicted HCD section for each document. We believe this approach provides the best balance in our attempt to capture as much of the true HCD section as possible.

5 Results

Our results are reported using the aforementioned sample of 393 Form 10-K documents from S&P 500 companies. We use three evaluation metrics: precision, recall, and Jaccard index. Precision represents how well our section identification algorithm captures positive sentences, penalizing the situation where sentences outside of the true HCD section are determined to be part of that section. In practice, however, extraneous sentences at the outside edges of the HCD section may be acceptable if most of the section itself is correctly labeled. For this, we rely on the recall score, which represents how much of the targeted section is captured. Finally, to capture both the precision and recall metrics together, we use the Jaccard index, which penalizes both false positives and false negatives.

We calculate the three metrics described above for each predicted HCD section from a document varying the number of training documents for each Model_i. To characterize the performance of Model_i, we take the mean score from all predicted documents. Documents without a predicted HCD section receive a score of zero for each metric. The plots in Figure 3 show these mean scores.

5.1 Training on Sentences versus Windows

To illustrate the effectiveness of the windowing method described earlier in the labeling phase of training, we test the ANTS framework by constructing training examples using windowing and no windowing (sentence-only) training datasets. For the no windowing model, we tokenize the separated positive and negative sections into sentences, each of which then constitutes a single training example for the BERT model. The training datasets for Model_i are created from the same set of documents and the evaluation metrics are derived from predictions on the remaining documents not used in training. For sentence-level and window-level approaches, the training and test sets used in training and evaluating Model_i are the same. All other hyperparameters are held constant.

Figures 3a (sentence training) and 3b (window training) show the three chosen evaluation metrics as a function of the number of training documents ranging from 1 to 19 documents with a step size of 2 and using just the 1-block scores to predict the HCD section. In other words, we choose the longest continuous section of 1-block scores that fall under the threshold described earlier. For this particular comparison, we omit the usage of 5-block scores to focus on the difference achieved just with windowing. Each dot in the displayed score distribution represents the performance of Model_i for each number of training documents and the dashed lines represent the trend of the mean score value of all 20 Model_i's.

A few notable differences can be seen between Figures 3a and 3b. First, we see a sharp contrast in the distribution of scores across Model_i's at any given document size. In the no windowing case, a model's Jaccard index for a given Model_i can range anywhere from zero to around 0.7. Strikingly, this wide spread can be observed anywhere from a number of training documents of 7 documents all the way to 19 documents. Although the overall mean performance (dashed line) displays an upward trend, this spread illustrates that if the "wrong" N documents are chosen for sentence-only training, then poor results may be observed even with large N. The score distributions in the windowed case are much narrower, mitigating the impact of selecting any particular documents for training.

Additionally, though less dramatic than the spread, there is an overall improvement in performance across the three metrics in the windowed models versus the sentence-only ones. In particular, the performance of the models trained with windows saturates after only a training input size of about 5 documents or so. The same cannot be said, and is also difficult to observe, in the models trained with sentences. This is likely caused by the substantial increase in effective training data resulting from the windowing method, which leads to a lower requirement on the number of documents needed for training.

Based on the observations above, using the windowing method during training in the ANTS framework is an effective way of improving the predictability and overall performance of the resulting fine-tuned model. At the same time, it reduces the number of manually labeled training documents required.

5.2 Varied Number of Training Documents

We train our model on various training input sizes, measured by the number of documents used. As mentioned earlier, we choose document as the input size unit to match how this framework might be used by social science (particularly business)

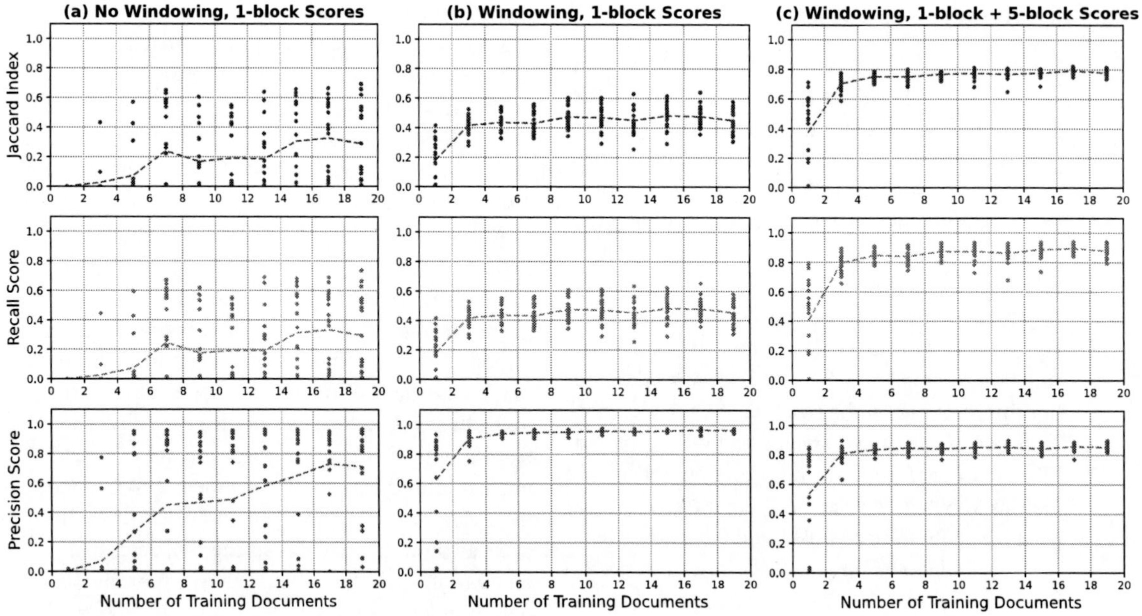

Figure 3: The x-axis represents the number of training documents and each dot in the graph represents a mean score for all test documents for Model_i trained on a random subsample of the input labeled documents. The mean Jaccard (blue), recall (red), and precision (green) scores of predicted Human Capital Disclosure (HCD) sections are calculated across a set of test documents. Test set for Model_i consists of the remaining documents not used for training of Model_i. The dashed lines show the trend of the mean score value for all Model_i through Model_M, where $M = 20$ at each training input size. (a) Results for training on sentences only and using just 1-block scores to predict the HCD section. (b) Results for training on windows and using just 1-block scores to predict the HCD section. (c) Results for training on windows and using both 5-block and 1-block scores to predict the HCD section.

researchers who are more familiar with handling collections of documents. We use Figure 3c to discuss our findings. Figure 3c shows the same metrics described for Figures 3a and 3b, but using windowing during training and the aid of 5-block scores in finding the right section. The effectiveness of employing 5-block scores is described in the next section.

Based on the score distributions shown, there is a noticeable increase in performance as a function of the number of training documents used for fewer than 5 documents, but then a clear saturation after that point. This same behavior was noted for the results in Figure 3b, but is more evident here. Furthermore, the spread in the scores across Model_i's also reduces markedly as a function of the number of training documents, also steadying at around 5 documents. This indicates that after a certain number of training documents, the predictability of the model performance is quite stable, which provides some leeway as to which training documents are chosen.

Of particular interest from a practical perspective is that the point of saturation for both performance and spread is reached at only around 5 documents. There is merely a 3.4% difference in mean Jaccard index between training on 5 documents versus 19 documents. This somewhat unexpected result illustrates that for a defined section identification task like this one, not very much training data is necessary in the ANTS framework for a fine-tuned BERT model to achieve adequate classification performance. Moreover, at 5 training documents, the model already captures part of the targeted section in 96% of the unseen documents.

5.3 Using 5-block Scores in Section Identification

As discussed in Methods, we use a combination of 1-block and 5-block scores to optimize the prediction of the HCD section for each document. The differences in Figures 3b and 3c emphasize the validity of this approach. To start, there is a clear gap in performance as reflected by the mean Jaccard index after the point of saturation (5 documents) is reached. In the case of using only 1-block scores, the Jaccard index ranges from 0.43 to 0.48. However, in the case of using both 1-block and 5-block data, the Jaccard index ranges from 0.75 to 0.79. Looking closer at the precision and recall scores, it is clear that this dramatic difference in Jaccard index can be attributed to the sizable improvement in recall shown in Figure 3c. In fact, the precision scores are higher in the case of using only 1-block scores in Figure 3b. This means that the chosen section identification algorithm captures more of the targeted section during prediction, but at the expense of falsely including sentences just outside the edges of the section. For our test case, this is acceptable and for other use cases, this can be tuned.

As a result of calculating 5-block scores for this section identification method, the overall time spent during the prediction phase is longer. However, the performance gains for our use case are significant and additional annotated data is not required. The results here further illustrate the possibility and effectiveness of stretching out scarce text data in this framework.

5.4 Utility of "False Positives"

The section identification scheme that we choose de-emphasizes other sentences that have high classification scores, but lay outside of the actual HCD section. For instance, the sentence with score 0.997 outside of the highlighted green area in Figure 2. However, these resulting "false positive" sentences could be relevant content to a researcher even though they do not fall in the targeted section. We perform a text similarity analysis to determine whether these sentences are indeed relevant. To do this, we divide the sentences of each document into 3 categories:

1. **Actual Positive** sentences identified by workers to be part of the HCD section,
2. **False Positive** sentences determined by the 1-block model to be positive, but did not fall into the HCD section, and
3. **Negative** sentences determined by the 1-block model not to be positive and did not fall into the HCD section.

We remove English stop words from the text and then compute a TFIDF matrix for each of the three categories using the Python Scikit-learn package (Pedregosa et al., 2011). We then calculate the cosine similarity between the matrices. Notably, we find that the similarity between Actual Positive and False Positive text is very high (0.88) relative to the same measure between Actual Positive and Negative (0.38) text. For False Positive and Negative text, the similarity is 0.42. This supports the idea that the model potentially captures text relevant to the HCD section that is ignored in the scope of this paper, but may still be of value in a different context.

6 Conclusions

In this paper, we propose a practical framework to extract continuous segments of text from unstructured documents, with a particular focus on text-intensive research in business and social science. The ANTS framework utilizes a pre-trained BERT model to identify targeted sections 96% of the time using only 5 training examples. This general framework can enable subject matter experts to accelerate their research by reducing the time commitment needed to extract large amounts of relevant text given a very small number of training examples. Our proof of concept using Human Capital Disclosure sections of SEC filings demonstrates that manually coding only a few documents provides enough training data for a model to effectively identify the relevant section of the remaining documents. Furthermore, the success of this framework opens a number of other valuable research questions from the same documents. For instance, what distinguishes the official HCD text from thematically similar data (as flagged by ANTS) in the remainder of the document? Or, how did companies report human capital information prior to the SEC's disclosure requirement?

The ANTS framework provides the opportunity for researchers to use additional domain knowledge to integrate the sentence-level scores from a trained model. In this report we use a section picking algorithm that is constrained to identify only a single contiguous section to mirror the SEC filing structure. An ANTS framework that could, for instance, identify boilerplate language from corporate charters, could be tuned based on the known length, location and number of boilerplate sections. The wealth of trained models also provides the opportunity to extract or flag relevant text from semi-structured documents (e.g., HTML), spoken text transcriptions or social media posts.

While our proof of concept only returns flagged sections as an output, it suggests an application as a successor to "word list" based research methods. Work such as Loughran and Mcdonald (2011) describes counting words and phrases as a proxy for an underlying theme, such as uncertainty. Using ANTS, researchers can identify sections of interest and prepare document scores from aggregating model results. Taking human capital disclosures and diversity as an example, ANTS could be trained with language on workforce diversity from SEC filings, and then used to generate a diversity score by counting the number of sentences discussing diversity. This work could circumvent the technical and arduous task of building word lists, and provide context aware metrics that can flag a diversifying workforce without false positives from a diversifying supply chain.

Taken together, the ANTS framework demonstrates a rich set of avenues that can be used to accelerate, augment and amplify the work of academic researchers in the social sciences. As deep learning tools are released on free and reduced cost platforms (e.g., Colab, OpenAI, HuggingFace), researchers will build effective datasets from larger, more diverse and more subtle text sources. We hope that ANTS can be leveraged to facilitate this growth in text data and democratize deep learning advances in new and unexpected ways.

7 Acknowledgment

Some of the computing for this project was performed on the Sherlock cluster. We would like to thank Stanford University and the Stanford Research Computing Center for providing computational resources and support that contributed to these research results.

References

Dogu Araci. FinBERT: Financial Sentiment Analysis with Pre-trained Language Models. *ArXiv*, abs/1908.10063, 8 2019. URL https://arxiv.org/abs/1908.10063.

Sebastian Arnold, Rudolf Schneider, Philippe Cudré-Mauroux, Felix A Gers, and Alexander Löser. SECTOR: A Neural Model for Coherent Topic Segmentation and Classification. *Transactions of the Association for Computational Linguistics*, 7:169–184, 2019. doi: 10.1162/tacl/a/00261. URL https://aclanthology.org/Q19-1011.

Dennis Aumiller, Satya Almasian, S Lackner, and Michael Gertz. Structural text segmentation of legal documents. *Proceedings of the Eighteenth International Conference on Artificial Intelligence and Law*, 2021. URL https://doi.org/10.1145/3462757.3466085.

Steven Bird, Edward Loper, and Ewan Klein. *Natural Language Processing with Python*. O'Reilly Media Inc., 2009.

David M. Blei, Andrew Y. Ng, Michael I. Jordan, and John Lafferty. Latent dirichlet allocation. *Journal of Machine Learning Research*, 3, 2003. URL https://dl.acm.org/doi/10.5555/944919.944937.

Jung Ho Choi, Joseph Pacelli, Kristina M. Rennekamp, and Sorabh Tomar. Do Jobseekers Value Diversity Information? Evidence from a Field Experiment. *SSRN Electronic Journal*, 2022. ISSN 1556-5068. doi: 10.2139/ssrn.4025383.

Wesley T Chuang and Jihoon Yang. Extracting sentence segments for text summarization: a machine learning approach. *Proceedings of the 23rd annual international ACM SIGIR conference on Research and development in information retrieval*, pages 152–159, 2000. URL https://doi.org/10.1145/345508.345566.

Jacob Devlin, Ming-Wei Chang, Kenton Lee, and Kristina Toutanova. BERT: Pre-training of Deep Bidirectional Transformers for Language Understanding. *ArXiv*, abs/1810.04805, 2019. URL https://arxiv.org/abs/1810.04805.

Goran Glavaš and Somasundaran Swapna. Two-level transformer and auxiliary coherence modeling for improved text segmentation. *Proceedings of the AAAI Conference on Artificial Intelligence*, 2020. URL https://ojs.aaai.org/index.php/AAAI/article/view/6284.

Omri Koshorek, Adir Cohen, Noam Mor, Michael Rotman, and Jonathan Berant. Text Segmentation as a Supervised Learning Task. *NAACL HLT 2018 - 2018 Conference of the North American Chapter of the Association for Computational Linguistics: Human Language Technologies - Proceedings of the Conference*, 2:469–473, 3 2018. doi: 10.18653/v1/n18-2075. URL https://arxiv.org/abs/1803.09337v1.

Kelvin Lo, Yuan Jin, Weicong Tan, Ming Liu, Lan Du, and Wray Buntine. Transformer over Pre-trained Transformer for Neural Text Segmentation with Enhanced Topic Coherence. *ArXiv*, abs/2110.07160, 2021. URL https://arxiv.org/abs/2110.07160.

Tim Loughran and Bill Mcdonald. When Is a Liability Not a Liability? Textual Analysis, Dictionaries, and 10-Ks. *Journal of Finance*, 66(1):35–65, 2 2011. ISSN 00221082. doi: 10.1111/J.1540-6261.2010.01625.X.

Michal Lukasik, Boris Dadachev, Gonçalo Simões, and Kishore Papineni. Text Segmentation by Cross Segment Attention, 2020. URL https://arxiv.org/abs/2004.14535.

Tomas Mikolov, Kai Chen, Greg Corrado, and Jeffrey Dean. Efficient Estimation of Word Representations in Vector Space. *1st International Conference on Learning Representations, ICLR 2013 - Workshop Track Proceedings*, 1 2013. doi: 10.48550/arxiv.1301.3781. URL https://arxiv.org/abs/1301.3781v3.

Minh Tien Nguyen, Dung Tien Le, and Linh Le. Transformers-based information extraction with limited data for domain-specific business documents. *Engineering Applications of Artificial Intelligence*, 97:104100, 1 2021. ISSN 0952-1976. doi: 10.1016/J.ENGAPPAI.2020.104100. URL https://www.sciencedirect.com/science/article/pii/S0952197620303481.

Hyo Jung Oh, Sung Hyon Myaeng, and Myung Gil Jang. Semantic passage segmentation based on sentence topics for question answering. *Information Sciences*, 177(18):3696–3717, 9 2007. ISSN 0020-0255. doi: 10.1016/J.INS.2007.02.038. URL https://doi.org/10.1016/j.ins.2007.02.038.

F. Pedregosa, G. Varoquaux, A. Gramfort, V. Michel, B. Thirion, O. Grisel, M. Blondel, P. Prettenhofer, R. Weiss, V. Dubourg, J. Vanderplas, A. Passos, D. Cournapeau, M. Brucher, M. Perrot, and E. Duchesnay. Scikit-learn: Machine Learning in Python. *Journal of Machine Learning Research*, 12:2825–2830, 2011.

Yla R. Tausczik and James W. Pennebaker. The Psychological Meaning of Words: LIWC and Computerized Text Analysis Methods. *Journal of Language and Social Psychology*, 29(1):24–54, 12 2009. ISSN 0261927X. doi: 10.1177/0261927X09351676. URL https://journals.sagepub.com/doi/abs/10.1177/0261927x09351676.

Thomas Wolf, Lysandre Debut, Victor Sanh, Julien Chaumond, Clement Delangue, Anthony Moi, Pierric Cistac, Tim Rault, Remi Louf, Morgan Funtowicz, Joe Davison, Sam Shleifer, Patrick von Platen, Clara Ma, Yacine Jernite, Julien Plu, Canwen Xu, Teven Le Scao, Sylvain Gugger, Mariama Drame, Quentin Lhoest, and Alexander Rush. Transformers: State-of-the-Art Natural Language Processing. In *Proceedings of the 2020 Conference on Empirical Methods in Natural Language Processing: System Demonstrations*, pages 38–45, Online, 10 2020. Association for Computational Linguistics. doi: 10.18653/v1/2020.emnlp-demos.6. URL https://aclanthology.org/2020.emnlp-demos.6.

Siang Yun Yoong, Yao Chung Fan, and Fang Yie Leu. On Text Tiling for Documents: A Neural-Network Approach. *Lecture Notes in Networks and Systems*, 159 LNNS:265–274, 2021. ISSN 23673389. doi: 10.1007/978-3-030-61108-8/26. URL https://link.springer.com/chapter/10.1007/978-3-030-61108-8_26.

Ruixue Zhang, Wei Yang, Luyun Lin, Zhengkai Tu, Yuqing Xie, Zihang Fu, Yuhao Xie, Luchen Tan, Kun Xiong, and Jimmy Lin. Rapid Adaptation of BERT for Information Extraction on Domain-Specific Business Documents. *ArXiv*, abs/2002.01861, 2 2020. ISSN 2331-8422. URL https://arxiv.org/abs/2002.01861v1.

Cross-TOP: Zero-Shot Cross-Schema Task-Oriented Parsing

Melanie Rubino
Amazon Alexa AI
New York, USA
rubinome@amazon.com

Nicolas Guenon des Mesnards
Amazon Alexa AI
New York, USA
mesnarn@amazon.com

Uday Shah
Amazon Alexa AI
New York, USA
shahuda@amazon.com

Nanjiang Jiang
Department of Linguistics
The Ohio State University
jiang.1879@osu.edu

Weiqi Sun
Amazon Alexa AI
New York, USA
weiqisun@amazon.com

Konstantine Arkoudas
Amazon Alexa AI
New York, USA
arkoudk@amazon.com

Abstract

Deep learning methods have enabled task-oriented semantic parsing of increasingly complex utterances. However, a single model is still typically trained and deployed for each task separately, requiring labeled training data for each, which makes it challenging to support new tasks, even within a single business vertical (e.g., food-ordering or travel booking). In this paper we describe Cross-TOP (Cross-Schema Task-Oriented Parsing), a zero-shot method for complex semantic parsing in a given vertical. By leveraging the fact that user requests from the same vertical share lexical and semantic similarities, a single cross-schema parser is trained to service an arbitrary number of tasks, seen or unseen, within a vertical. We show that Cross-TOP can achieve high accuracy on a previously unseen task without requiring any additional training data, thereby providing a scalable way to bootstrap semantic parsers for new tasks. As part of this work we release the FoodOrdering dataset, a task-oriented parsing dataset in the food-ordering vertical, with utterances and annotations derived from five schemas, each from a different restaurant menu.

1 Introduction

Propelled by deep learning, task-oriented parsing has made significant strides, moving away from flat intents and slots towards more complex tree-based semantics that can represent compositional meaning structures (Gupta et al., 2018; Aghajanyan et al., 2020; Rongali et al., 2020; Mansimov and Zhang, 2021). However, most semantic parsing systems remain task-specific: they can only produce representations with the set of intents and slots seen during training. To support multiple tasks, this approach requires collecting data, training, and maintaining a model for each task separately. This is costly when multiple tasks need to be supported, as is usually the case for digital voice assistants such as Alexa and Google Assistant, which may need to support hundreds or thousands of different tasks in a given business vertical (e.g., restaurants in the food-ordering vertical, hotels in the travel vertical, and so on).

In this paper we present Cross-TOP, a method for building a single semantic parsing model that can support an arbitrary number of tasks in a given vertical. User requests pertaining to the same vertical have lexical and semantic similarities; their main differences lie in their unique schemas. In the food-ordering domain, for example, a customer may request a main dish with various options and possibly a drink and a side. However, depending on the specific restaurant menu, the output semantic representations can differ greatly; see Figure 1.

Cross-TOP makes use of a powerful pre-trained transformer-based encoder-decoder language model, with schema-specific context added to the input along with the utterance. In this way, the model learns to generate parses for a new, unseen task, by attending to the schema in the input rather than by needing to see it during training. We show that this approach is quite effective and provides a quick solution to the practical problem of bootstrapping semantic parsers for new tasks within a vertical, using a single model in production.

The parser is trained on a number of initial tasks, where each task has some training data available. Moreover, we assume that every task has a unique

Proceedings of the Third Workshop on Deep Learning for Low-Resource Natural Language Processing, pages 48 - 60
July 14, 2022 ©2022 Association for Computational Linguistics

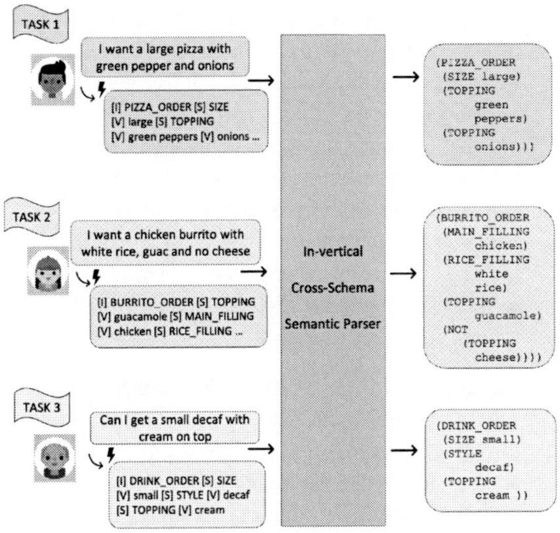

Figure 1: The Cross-TOP parser processes utterances from multiple tasks with different schemas. The lightning bolts represent fuzzy matching, which is used to append schema elements to the input (cf. Section 2).

schema. That schema consists of all possible intents and slots for the task at hand; both intents and slots can be arbitrarily nested (compositional). For every slot S, the schema also includes natural-language phrases for the various values of S. All schemas for the five tasks in our dataset can be found in Appendix B. Cross-TOP uses constrained decoding to ensure that it generates well-formed parses that can be resolved to executable representations that can be directly used by the back end.

Most zero-shot cross-schema semantic parsing work has been in the context of the Text-to-SQL task (Zhong et al., 2020; Lin et al., 2020; Wang et al., 2020; Rubin and Berant, 2021; Yu et al., 2020; Gan et al., 2021). Cross-schema task-oriented parsing introduces its own challenges. In SQL, the schemas are database schemas, and the parser is trained on some initial databases and then evaluated on another database. There is a lot of invariant structure across different tasks in the output space (since output sequences are always SQL queries), as well as common patterns in how SQL structures tend to align with natural language. However, for the schemas defined in task-oriented parsing for the food-ordering domain, the only invariant structures are the parentheses and some lexical overlap among the intents and slots. Therefore, cross-schema parsing in general is more challenging for task-oriented parsing. However, restricting the scope to a given vertical imposes more common structure that can prove helpful.

To evaluate our methodology, we focus on tasks in the food-ordering domain, where each task contains examples from a restaurant with the schema generated from its menu. Our main contributions are as follows:

- We present a new technique for zero-shot intra-vertical cross-schema semantic parsing that jointly encodes utterance tokens and schema elements.
- We release a new task-oriented parsing dataset for food ordering to evaluate similar efforts. The FoodOrdering dataset includes examples from five restaurants, totaling close to 30,000 synthetically-generated training examples and 963 human-generated test utterances with labels.
- We show that our method achieves up to 73% exact match accuracy on a previously unseen ordering task, proving the method's viability for effortlessly handling a new task.

2 Model

Our method trains a single schema-aware model to serve multiple tasks and bootstrap new ones from the same business vertical in a zero-shot setting. It leverages the transfer learning capabilities of a transformer-based pretrained encoder-decoder language model.

Terminology Each *task* is defined by a unique *schema* consisting of *intents*, *slots* belonging to those intents, and *catalogs* enumerating the possible *slot values* for each slot. For example, in the pizza-ordering task the `TOPPING` slot belongs to the `PIZZAORDER` intent, and values for this slot could be `mushrooms`, `pepperoni`, and so on. In our predefined catalogs, multiple slot values could refer to the same *slot value entity*, for example `peppers` and `green peppers` can both be mapped to `TOPPING_PEPPERS`—or perhaps `TOPPING_35`—in the back end. Cross-TOP predicts parse trees that contain slot values, which are then entity-resolved into those unique back-end identifiers through this many-to-1 mapping.

A task schema can optionally define *invocation keywords* for each intent, to identify how these are expressed in natural language, for example $\{$*drink*, *drinks*$\}$ for a `DRINK_ORDER` intent. This is used for augmenting model input with *fuzzy-matched* schema elements later on. Fuzzy string-matching algorithms compute lexical similarity between strings. If some schema elements have a significant overlap with certain utterance tokens, then there is a "match" and that schema element will be appended to the input utterance before encoding.

Model Inputs As just mentioned, to achieve zero-shot cross-schema parsing, we append fuzzy-matched schema elements to input utterances. Given an utterance u, assume our fuzzy-matching process (described later) determined that the intents i_1 and i_2 are present in the request, with slot/slot-values $s_{1,1}/v_{1,1}$ for i_1, as well as $s_{2,1}/v_{2,1}$ and $s_{2,2}/v_{2,2}$ for i_2[1]. The input to Cross-TOP is then serialized into the following format:

u [I] i_1 [S] $s_{1,1}$ [V] $v_{1,1}$ [I] i_2 [S] $s_{2,1}$ [V] $v_{2,1}$ [S] $s_{2,2}$ [V] $v_{2,2}$

where markers [I], [S], [V] indicate that the following tokens are intents, slots and slot values, respectively. An example is given in Figure 2.

Input

```
I want a large-size pizza with peppers
[I] PIZZAORDER : pizza
[S] SIZE [V] large [S] TOPPING [V] peppers
```

Target

```
( PIZZAORDER ( SIZE large )( TOPPING peppers ))
```

Figure 2: Cross-TOP is trained to attend to input utterances augmented with fuzzy-matched schema elements.

Our format is inspired from BRIDGE (Lin et al., 2020), but instead of table/column/column-value in a database schema, task-oriented parsing schemas uses intent/slot/slot-value. While the longer input sequences increase the computation required for inference, the latency impact is mitigated by the parallelizability of the transformer architecture.

Model Outputs The model is trained to generate a linearized parse tree similar to the target shown in Figure 2, which is reminiscent of the TOP *decoupled* notation (Aghajanyan et al., 2020). TOP decoupled is itself derived from the TOP notation (Gupta et al., 2018) by removing tokens that are not direct children of slot nodes. Unlike TOP decoupled, leaf nodes in our output semantics are not tokens copied from the source utterance, but instead must be valid *slot values* belonging to the task's catalogs. As exemplified in Figure 2, the fuzzy-matched slot value for the utterance segment `large-size` is the catalog entry `large`. It can happen that utterance token and catalog value are identical, as is the case for `peppers` here. By predicting slot values instead of unresolved utterance tokens, Cross-TOP jointly learns to perform semantic parsing and entity resolution, thus eliminating the need to train and maintain a separate entity resolution system for every new task.

Fuzzy-Matching Details The viability of our schema-aware encoding depends on our ability to extract the proper schema elements. We leverage the fuzzy-matching method from the BRIDGE codebase[2] and compute lexical similarity scores between an input utterance and every slot value.[3] If multiple slot values representing the same entity match the utterance, we pick the one with the higher similarity score. Slots are added to the input if at least one of their slot values was added.[4] Intents are added to the input if at least one of their slots is added.[5]

In addition, if any of the predefined intent invocation keywords (cf. **Terminology**) fuzzy-match the utterance, then that intent is added along with the fuzzy-matched keyword, for example adding `[I] PIZZAORDER : pizza` instead of simply `[I] PIZZAORDER`. Given that intent names can be arbitrary and carry little semantic content, this design helps the pretrained language model by bridging the gap between natural language and back-end executable representations.

Constrained Decoding The target parses contain only schema elements and parentheses. Cross-TOP leverages constrained decoding at inference time to generate valid catalog values and parses according to the schema. For example, the string `(DRINK_ORDER (SIZE coke))` is not valid, as the slot value `coke` is not a catalog entry for the slot `SIZE`. In this work we also implement a

[1]There can be more than one slot value v identified for the same slot s, in which case the input will be of the form: u [I] i_1 [S] $s_{1,1}$ [V] $v_{1,1,1}$ [V] $v_{1,1,2}$ ...

[2]https://github.com/salesforce/TabularSemanticParsing

[3]This works in a vertical with small catalogs, such as restaurant menus. To make it scale to much larger catalogs, one could use sub-linear fuzzy string-matching algorithms and offline parallel processing.

[4]Slots that are parents of other slots are also provided with catalog entries to allow fuzzy matching. For example, a `NOT` slot for negation will use {*with no, without, hold the* ...}.

[5]A slot shared across two intents will trigger both their inclusion, but experiments indicate that the neural parser can learn to discard such false detection.

parentheses-balancing constraint, as well as a set of valid next-token constraints, where each vocabulary subword has a corresponding entry in a dictionary mapping it to a list of valid subwords that may follow it. The content of such a dictionary is task-specific but is built programmatically from the task schema. The detailed constraints are provided in Appendix D. Section 5 quantifies the benefits of constrained decoding in the zero-shot setting.

3 The FoodOrdering Dataset

We release a dataset for cross-schema zero-shot task-oriented parsing: the FoodOrdering dataset,[6] comprising five food-ordering tasks for five fictitious restaurants: PIZZA, SUB, BURRITO, BURGER and COFFEE.

Dataset Construction To gauge zero-shot capabilities, only three out of five tasks come with training data. For SUB and BURRITO, the training portion of the data was synthetically generated by sampling around 50 human-designed templates for which slot values are themselves sampled from predefined catalogs. The catalogs and templates are released along with the dataset, but a couple of examples are given in Table 4. We generated up to 10,000 unique pairs of natural language and target parses. For PIZZA we randomly sampled 10,000 utterances out of the 2.5M provided by Arkoudas et al. (2021). All five tasks have evaluation data generated by humans and collected through Mechanical Turk; see Appendix A for details. MTurk workers generated natural language orders, which were then annotated internally. More examples can be found in Appendix C.

Dataset Statistics All tasks follow a common structure of intents and slots, but each task has a different number of intents, slots and slot values. In Table 1, the #SltValEntities column does not count the total number of slot values, but rather the total number of slot value entities, which are resolved slot values (cf. **Terminology**). BURRITO has 7 distinct intents while COFFEE is a single-intent task. The design differences between the task schemas reflect a real-world setting: each restaurant comes with its own preexisting back end that dictates the design and contents of the corresponding schema. On average there are 1.7 intents and 6.2 slots per utterance, and an average depth[7] of 3.4. Detailed numbers are provided in Table 5 of Appendix C.

Task Schemas Each task has a unique schema, but all schemas are governed by similar rules: only slot nodes can be children of intent nodes, and there is no limit on the number of intents per utterance nor slots per intent. Slot nodes can be parents either of slot values or of other slots. NOT is an example of a generic (task-agnostic) slot that allows us to negate any slot that admits negation, such as TOPPING. Refer to Appendix B for the details of the five schemas.

4 Experimental Setup

Our experimental setup reflects the practical scenario of having to scale a technology to service multiple applications under constrained production resources. We consider a single model to serve all tasks, so we train with synthetic data for only three of the tasks (PIZZA, BURRITO and SUB), and test zero-shot generalization on two unseen tasks (BURGER and COFFEE).

Training Details In this work we use BART-Large (Lewis et al., 2020), a transformer-based pretrained encoder-decoder language model. We fine-tune the publicly available 24-layer BART-Large checkpoint[8] totaling 406M parameters, using the `transformers` codebase. We expand the target vocabulary by adding special tokens for input markers `[I]`, `[S]` and `[V]`. The training dataset was created by concatenating synthetic data from the three training tasks. Models are trained for 50 epochs with early stopping patience of 4, using cross-entropy sequence loss and the `AdamW` optimizer. We use the human-generated data of the three training tasks as our development set for early stopping and hyperparameter tuning. Hyperparameter tuning is described in Appendix E. Our best model uses a batch size of 16, learning rate `1e-05` and linear learning rate scheduler with warm-up ratio of 0.1. The hyperparameter `no_repeat_ngram_size` was disabled by setting it to 0.

Evaluation Details We use Unordered Exact match accuracy (Unordered EM) to measure per-

[6] https://github.com/amazon-research/food-ordering-semantic-parsing-dataset

[7] Queries are by design multi-intent, hence implicitly rooted in a parent ORDER node, which is factored in the computation of depth.

[8] https://huggingface.co/facebook/bart-large

Dataset	#Train/Synthetic	#Eval	#Int	#Slt	#SltValEntities	Example utterance
PIZZA	10,000	348	2	10	166	*"Can i get one large pie with no cheese and a coke."*
BURRITO	9,982	191	7	11	34	*"One carnitas quesadilla with white rice and black beans."*
SUB	10,000	161	3	8	62	*"Get me a cold cut combo with mayo and extra pickles."*
BURGER	0*	161	3	9	44	*"A vegan burger with onions and a side of sweet potato fries."*
COFFEE	0*	104	1	9	43	*"One regular latte cinnamon iced with one extra espresso shot."*

Table 1: FoodOrdering dataset statistics: sizes of training and evaluation sets, as well as numbers of intents, slots, and resolved slot value entities defined in each task's schema. *BURGER and COFFEE have no training data, as they are used to evaluate zero-shot learning.

formance. It checks for an exact match between the golden and predicted trees, where sibling order does not matter. The golden parse trees are executable representations (ready for consumption by an appropriate back end) that contain resolved entity names instead of slot values identified by utterance segments. These entities are fully determined by the many-to-1 mapping mentioned in Section 2. Validation performance is computed on the aggregated validation sets for the three training tasks. Test performance is reported for tasks individually. We used a beam size of 6 for validation and testing.

Pre-Processing and Post-Processing When appending the schema elements to the input utterance we do not include the slot/slot-value pair `NUMBER, 1` from the fuzzy matching process if it's the only quantity matched.[9] This choice was made after observing that the slot values `a/an` can easily trigger false positives in fuzzy matching. For example, in the utterance *an order of two sprites*, the numeric quantity to extract is *two*, but the token *an* would trigger an extra unnecessary match. At inference time, if no `NUMBER` was generated for an intent, we add back `(NUMBER 1)` as a default to the predicted parse tree. Before computing unordered EM scores, all slot values are resolved into the appropriate entity names using the many-to-1 mapping mentioned earlier.

5 Results and Analysis

In the zero-shot setting, Cross-TOP achieves 73% unordered EM on BURGER and 55% on COFFEE (Table 2). The rest of this section presents an analysis of our results.

Schema-aware encoding enables zero-shot transfer learning. The main strength of Cross-TOP is training and maintaining a single model that can serve multiple tasks within the same business vertical, and bootstrapping new tasks without retraining. The zero-shot results in Table 2 support the claim that joint learning over utterance tokens and matched schema elements achieves this objective. For completeness, we show that the zero-shot ability does not simply come from the conjunction of constrained decoding and BART's extensive pretraining: we perform an ablation exercise where the input to BART-Large contains no schema information at all, but constrained decoding is enabled. As can be seen in the second row of Table 2, accuracy drops precipitously, by 46 and 23 absolute points for BURGER and COFFEE, respectively. A manual analysis of the predictions shows that in the overwhelming majority of cases, this model only generates intents and slots that it has seen before in training and thus fails to correctly parse utterances that have unseen intents/slots. On a subset of 108 BURGER utterances with at least one intent unseen in training, the schema-oblivious approach only gets 4% unordered EM, compared to 64% for Cross-TOP.

Schema-aware decoding ensures proper executable parses. Schema-aware constrained decoding ensures that Cross-TOP generates fully executable parse trees. Without this component, performance drops by 20 absolute points, as shown in the third row of Table 2. By looking at 15 predicted ut-

[9]Note that we do keep those slot/slot-value pairs for quantities larger than 1.

terances where the output predictions change by removing constrained decoding, we found that 93.3% of BURGER utterances and 60% of COFFEE utterances contained at least one invalid slot/slot-value combination. While using constrained decoding on these utterances is guaranteed to rule out invalid combinations, this does not ensure that the result will be correct. However, on inspection we found that constrained decoding transforms 60% of BURGER and 33.3% of COFFEE mismatched utterances to be completely correct. Table 6 in Appendix D illustrates how constrained decoding can help with specific examples.

Cross-TOP improves as more training tasks are added. While our main result shows that training with only few tasks allows zero-shot transfer to new tasks with no retraining, a realistic production scenario would be to periodically retrain the model by incorporating new training data. To quantify the benefits of adding more tasks, we compare training Cross-TOP using one, two or three tasks. The results for training on one task are an average over three models, one trained on PIZZA only, one on BURRITO and one on SUB. Likewise, results for training on two tasks are an average of three models, one trained on PIZZA+BURRITO, one on BURRITO+SUB and the other on PIZZA+SUB. As shown in Table 2, going from 1 to 2 tasks doubles performance for BURGER, and using 3 tasks almost triples the performance for both test tasks, confirming that the model learns general patterns that govern all schemas in the food-ordering vertical.

Dependency on fuzzy matching Cross-TOP relies on the quality of the fuzzy-matching process that determines which schema elements are encoded along with the utterance tokens. It can be challenging to recover from a fuzzy matching failure that ends up omitting a slot value from the input. In BURGER, such failures account for only 1% of all test utterances. In COFFEE that phenomenon is more prominent, with 7% of test utterances presenting at least one missing element from the fuzzy-matched schema. These limitations can be addressed by making the fuzzy-matching algorithm more robust and/or by adding unrecognized slot values as extra entries in the slot's catalog. The latter option is appealing, as it involves no model retraining, but does not suffice, as there is no obvious way to automate it. We upper-bound the impact of any candidate fix by providing an oracle schema for all utterances, and observe in the last row of Table 2 that it brings an absolute improvement of 2 absolute point in BURGER and 5 absolute points in COFFEE.

	Burger	Coffee
Cross-TOP	73.3 ± 3.6	54.8 ± 5.7
w/o schema-augmented input	26.5 ± 1.5	31.7 ± 1.0
w/o constrained decoding	53.0 ± 4.2	33.3 ± 7.2
training only on 1 task	25.4 ± 1.6	19.9 ± 3.3
training only on 2 tasks	52.4 ± 2.7	34.0 ± 3.5
w/ oracle schema	75.6 ± 4.3	59.4 ± 7.1

Table 2: Cross-TOP zero-shot unordered EM accuracy, averaged over 3 seeds, along with various ablations. The $\pm$ signs indicate the standard error across seeds.

6 Related Work

Slot Filling Traditionally, task-oriented parsing for flat intents and slots has been framed as a combination of intent classification and slot labeling (Sarikaya et al., 2016), possibly with an additional domain classification component. Several authors have addressed zero-shot solutions in this field. QASF (Du et al., 2021) is a QA-driven approach that extracts slot-filler spans from utterances using a question-answering model. Both Bapna et al. (2017) and Siddique et al. (2021) tag words with slots using slot descriptions and context-aware representations of the utterance. These solutions don't apply to structured (compositional) semantic representations, or to multiple intents in a single utterance, both of which are handled by Cross-TOP.

Task-Oriented Parsing In the more general area of task-oriented parsing, where hierarchical representations are featured, the authors are not aware of other zero-shot cross-schema work. There is some work in the few-shot setting (Chen et al., 2020), where data from multiple domains is used during an additional stage of fine-tuning combined with meta-learning.

Text-to-SQL Some of the most relevant related zero-shot work is in text-to-SQL semantic parsing. In this area, a challenging dataset, SPIDER (Yu et al., 2018), is the most common dataset used to test zero-shot solutions. The GAZP (Zhong et al., 2020) method generates synthetic training data for the new schema environment and requires a retraining of the neural parser, not making it as convenient of a zero-shot method. RAT-SQL (Wang et al., 2020) moves away from needing to retrain the parser, and focuses on jointly encoding the schema and utterance tokens. BRIDGE (Lin et al., 2020) is the main inspiration for our work, as it encodes the utterance and schema together, and augments the input with anchor texts, which are database values from tables, designed to better bridge utterance tokens to database tables, columns and values. Another notable contribution intended to bridge the gap between natural language and machine-executable representations is the work of Gan et al. (2021), which leverages an intermediate representation to go from text to SQL.

7 Conclusion

We presented Cross-TOP, a zero-shot method for cross-schema task-oriented parsing that eliminates the need to retrain and maintain a new model for every new task in a business vertical. We released a new dataset illustrative of five real-world applications in the food-ordering vertical. We showed that Cross-TOP reaches up to 73% EM accuracy in zero-shot transfer, making it a viable technique for quickly bootstrapping a parser for a new task.

Future work could further enrich the joint encoding of utterances and task schemas, while an additional thread of work could study how to best leverage limited annotated data that may be available for a new task.

Acknowledgments

We would like to thank Beiye Liu, Emre Barut, Ryan Gabbard, and anonymous reviewers for providing valuable feedback on this work.

References

Armen Aghajanyan, Jean Maillard, Akshat Shrivastava, Keith Diedrick, Michael Haeger, Haoran Li, Yashar Mehdad, Veselin Stoyanov, Anuj Kumar, Mike Lewis, and Sonal Gupta. 2020. Conversational semantic parsing. In *Proceedings of the 2020 Conference on Empirical Methods in Natural Language Processing (EMNLP)*, pages 5026–5035, Online. Association for Computational Linguistics.

Konstantine Arkoudas, Nicolas Guenon des Mesnards, Melanie Rubino, Sandesh Swamy, Saarthak Khanna, and Weiqi Sun. 2021. Pizza: a task-oriented semantic parsing dataset.

Ankur Bapna, Gokhan Tur, Dilek Hakkani-Tur, and Larry Heck. 2017. Towards zero-shot frame semantic parsing for domain scaling.

Xilun Chen, Asish Ghoshal, Yashar Mehdad, Luke Zettlemoyer, and Sonal Gupta. 2020. Low-resource domain adaptation for compositional task-oriented semantic parsing. In *Proceedings of the 2020 Conference on Empirical Methods in Natural Language Processing (EMNLP)*, pages 5090–5100, Online. Association for Computational Linguistics.

Xinya Du, Luheng He, Qi Li, Dian Yu, Panupong Pasupat, and Yuan Zhang. 2021. QA-driven zero-shot slot filling with weak supervision pretraining. In *Proceedings of the 59th Annual Meeting of the Association for Computational Linguistics and the 11th International Joint Conference on Natural Language Processing (Volume 2: Short Papers)*, pages 654–664, Online. Association for Computational Linguistics.

Yujian Gan, Xinyun Chen, Jinxia Xie, Matthew Purver, John R Woodward, John Drake, and Qiaofu Zhang. 2021. Natural sql: Making sql easier to infer from natural language specifications. In *Findings of the Association for Computational Linguistics: EMNLP 2021*, pages 2030–2042.

Sonal Gupta, Rushin Shah, Mrinal Mohit, Anuj Kumar, and Mike Lewis. 2018. Semantic parsing for task oriented dialog using hierarchical representations. In *Proceedings of the 2018 Conference on Empirical Methods in Natural Language Processing*, pages 2787–2792, Brussels, Belgium. Association for Computational Linguistics.

Mike Lewis, Yinhan Liu, Naman Goyal, Marjan Ghazvininejad, Abdelrahman Mohamed, Omer Levy, Veselin Stoyanov, and Luke Zettlemoyer. 2020. BART: Denoising sequence-to-sequence pre-training for natural language generation, translation, and comprehension. In *Proceedings of the 58th Annual Meeting of the Association for Computational Linguistics*, pages 7871–7880, Online. Association for Computational Linguistics.

Xi Victoria Lin, Richard Socher, and Caiming Xiong. 2020. Bridging textual and tabular data for cross-domain text-to-SQL semantic parsing. In *Findings of the Association for Computational Linguistics: EMNLP 2020*, pages 4870–4888, Online. Association for Computational Linguistics.

Elman Mansimov and Yi Zhang. 2021. Semantic parsing in task-oriented dialog with recursive insertion-based encoder. *arXiv preprint arXiv:2109.04500*.

Subendhu Rongali, Luca Soldaini, Emilio Monti, and Wael Hamza. 2020. Don't parse, generate! a sequence to sequence architecture for task-oriented semantic parsing. In *Proceedings of The Web Conference 2020*, pages 2962–2968.

Ohad Rubin and Jonathan Berant. 2021. SmBoP: Semi-autoregressive bottom-up semantic parsing. In *Proceedings of the 5th Workshop on Structured Prediction for NLP (SPNLP 2021)*, pages 12–21, Online. Association for Computational Linguistics.

R. Sarikaya, P. A. Crook, A. Marin, M. Jeong, J.P. Robichaud, A. Celikyilmaz, Y.B. Kim, A. Rochette, O. Z. Khan, X. Liu, D. Boies, T. Anastasakos, Z. Feizollahi, N. Ramesh, H. Suzuki, R. Holenstein, E. Krawczyk, and V. Radostev. 2016. An overview of end-to-end language understanding and dialog management for personal digital assistants. In *2016 IEEE Spoken Language Technology Workshop (SLT)*, pages 391–397.

AB Siddique, Fuad Jamour, and Vagelis Hristidis. 2021. Linguistically-enriched and context-awarezero-shot slot filling. In *Proceedings of the Web Conference 2021*, pages 3279–3290.

Bailin Wang, Richard Shin, Xiaodong Liu, Oleksandr Polozov, and Matthew Richardson. 2020. RAT-SQL: Relation-aware schema encoding and linking for text-to-SQL parsers. In *Proceedings of the 58th Annual Meeting of the Association for Computational Linguistics*, pages 7567–7578, Online. Association for Computational Linguistics.

Tao Yu, Chien-Sheng Wu, Xi Victoria Lin, Bailin Wang, Yi Chern Tan, Xinyi Yang, Dragomir R. Radev, Richard Socher, and Caiming Xiong. 2020. Grappa: Grammar-augmented pre-training for table semantic parsing. *CoRR*, abs/2009.13845.

Tao Yu, Rui Zhang, Kai Yang, Michihiro Yasunaga, Dongxu Wang, Zifan Li, James Ma, Irene Li, Qingning Yao, Shanelle Roman, Zilin Zhang, and Dragomir Radev. 2018. Spider: A large-scale human-labeled dataset for complex and cross-domain semantic parsing and text-to-SQL task. In *Proceedings of the 2018 Conference on Empirical Methods in Natural Language Processing*, pages 3911–3921, Brussels, Belgium. Association for Computational Linguistics.

Victor Zhong, Mike Lewis, Sida I. Wang, and Luke Zettlemoyer. 2020. Grounded adaptation for zero-shot executable semantic parsing. In *Proceedings of the 2020 Conference on Empirical Methods in Natural Language Processing (EMNLP)*, pages 6869–6882, Online. Association for Computational Linguistics.

Appendix

A Mechanical Turk Instructions

The instructions given to the workers were templated as shown in Figure 3. The tasks can be described as natural language text generation with a constrained menu. The number of responses was limited to 3 submissions per worker in order to balance diversity of responses and responsiveness ratios. The respondent's location had to be either US or CA, and the *master* worker qualification was required.[10] The tasks were designed, timed and priced to ensure that the compensation of respondents lies above the US and CA minimum hourly wages. The dataset went through an internal review process to ensure it abides by the company's required standards. Overall we collected answers form about 60 distinct workers for BURGER, SUB and COFFEE and about 90 for BURRITO, for a total of 183 unique individuals. The menus used for each collection are given in Figure 4.

B Task Schemas

Detailed schemas for each task, describing intent names, slot names, and slot properties, are given as supplementary material, along with the full catalog values for each slot.[11] For illustration purposes, Figure 5 shows the schema for BURRITO. Note that not all schemas need to share identical slots for similar intents. For example the BURGER schema has a `SIZE` slot for the `DRINK_ORDER` and `SIDE_ORDER` intents, while the BURRITO task does not. This is a design choice meant to reflect a real-life setting where the back end for one restaurant might support such property while another might not. This is a challenging—though realistic—obstacle our model needs to overcome.

C Dataset Construction Details

Part of the dataset comes from the publicly available PIZZA dataset (Arkoudas et al., 2021). We are following the conditions of use as defined by the license[12] and will release our dataset under the same license. The collection of new data was done through Mechanical Turk. Respondents were constrained to submit a single utterance for an order containing potentially more than one suborder. Hence, some utterances contained periods and question marks, indicating a sharp separation between two requests. To better reflect the fact that these users would likely have broken their request into multiple ones in an vocal interaction, we split those utterances into pieces. Other punctuation marks like commas, and non-ASCII characters, were simply removed, but utterances were not split around them. Numerical values were spelled out (e.g., *2 large cokes* $\rightarrow$ *two large cokes*). Finally, utterance text was lower-cased. Annotation was carried out internally by two annotators located in the US. Utterances displaying too much ambiguity for human annotators were removed. In Table 3 we provide examples of the collected utterances, and their linearized semantics. As can be seen in the table, utterances have varying degrees of complexity, which results in linearized trees of varying depths and widths. Synthetic data was generated by sampling human-designed templates, illustrated in Table 4. For SUB we used 32 templates and for BURRITO we used 46. Some statistics on the degree of compositionality of human and synthetic orders are given in Table 5.

D Constrained Decoding Details

In what follows we list the actual constraints implemented in this work in the form of allowed transitions. Any element on the left of the arrow can be followed by elements on the right:

$$\begin{cases} \texttt{BOS} & \rightarrow \{\text{"(}X\text{"}, X = \text{valid intent}\} \\ \text{"("} & \rightarrow \{X, X = \text{valid intent or slot}\} \\ \text{")"} & \rightarrow \{\text{")" or "(" or } \texttt{EOS}\} \\ \text{intent} & \rightarrow \{\text{"(}X\text{"}, X = \text{a valid slot}\} \\ \text{slot} & \rightarrow \{X, X = \text{compatible value}\} \\ \texttt{(COMPLEX} & \rightarrow \texttt{(QUANTITY} \end{cases}$$

One could think of imposing more grammar-based constraints, for example, allowing only valid intent-slot combinations, or only allowing negatable slots after `(NOT`, since some of these—like `SIZE`—cannot be negated. Examples of how constrained decoding helped can be found in Table 6.

E Computational Details

Hyperparameter tuning was performed on learning rates [`5e-04`, `1e-05`, `5e-05`, `1e-06`] and batch sizes `[16, 24, 48, 64]` across three seeds.

[10] workers with high ratings according to MTurk API.

[11] https://github.com/amazon-research/food-ordering-semantic-parsing-dataset

[12] https://github.com/amazon-research/pizza-semantic-parsing-dataset/blob/main/LICENSE

Dataset	Natural Language	Semantic representation after entity resolution
PIZZA	five medium pizzas with tomatoes and ham	(PIZZAORDER (NUMBER 5) (SIZE medium) (TOPPING ham) (TOPPING tomatoes))
PIZZA	i'll have one pie along with pesto and ham but avoid olives	(PIZZAORDER (NOT (TOPPING olives)) (NUMBER 1) (TOPPING ham) (TOPPING pesto))
PIZZA	i wanted to have two dr peppers three pepsis and a sprite	(DRINKORDER (DRINKTYPE dr_pepper) (NUMBER 2)) (DRINKORDER (DRINKTYPE pepsi) (NUMBER 3)) (DRINKORDER (DRINKTYPE sprite) (NUMBER 1))
BURRITO	burrito with steak cheese guacamole sour cream and fresh tomato salsa	(BURRITO_ORDER (NUMBER 1) (MAIN_FILLING steak) (TOPPING cheese) (TOPPING guacamole) (TOPPING sour_cream) (SALSA_TOPPING fresh_tomato_salsa))
BURRITO	i'd also like a bottled water please	(DRINK_ORDER (NUMBER 1) (DRINK_TYPE bottled_water))
BURRITO	i'd like a lemonade with a side of chips	(DRINK_ORDER (NUMBER 1) (DRINK_TYPE tractor_lemonade) (SIDE_ORDER (NUMBER 1) (SIDE_TYPE chips))
SUB	steak and cheese sandwich with lettuce cucumbers and olives	(SANDWICH_ORDER (NUMBER 1) (BASE_SANDWICH steak_and_cheese) (TOPPING lettuce) (TOPPING cucumbers) (TOPPING black_olives))
SUB	i will order a chicken and bacon ranch sandwich and on that please put american cheese chipotle southwest sauce lettuce tomatoes pickles with a side of doritos and two chocolate chip cookies	(SANDWICH_ORDER (NUMBER 1) (BASE_SANDWICH chicken_and_bacon_ranch) (TOPPING american_cheese) (TOPPING chipotle_southwest) (TOPPING lettuce) (TOPPING tomatoes) (TOPPING pickles)) (SIDE_ORDER (NUMBER 1) (SIDE_TYPE doritos_nacho_cheese)) (SIDE_ORDER (NUMBER 2) (SIDE_TYPE chocolate_chip))
BURGER	hi can i have the double cheeseburger with ketchup and onions and french fries on the side	(MAIN_DISH_ORDER (NUMBER 1) (MAIN_DISH_TYPE double_cheese_burger) (TOPPING ketchup) (TOPPING onion)) (SIDE_ORDER (NUMBER 1) (SIDE_TYPE french_fries))
BURGER	veggie burger with lettuce and bacon large curly fry and a small iced tea	(MAIN_DISH_ORDER (NUMBER 1) (MAIN_DISH_TYPE vegan_burger) (TOPPING lettuce) (TOPPING bacon)) (SIDE_ORDER (NUMBER 1) (SIZE large) (SIDE_TYPE curly_fries)) (DRINK_ORDER (NUMBER 1) (SIZE small) (DRINK_TYPE iced_tea))
COFFEE	i'd like a large hot chocolate with whipped cream	(DRINK_ORDER (NUMBER 1) (SIZE large) (DRINK_TYPE hot_chocolate) (TOPPING whipped_cream))
COFFEE	one regular latte light roast with an extra espresso shot and honey added and one large cappuccino with caramel syrup in that one	(DRINK_ORDER (NUMBER 1) (SIZE regular) (DRINK_TYPE latte) (ROAST_TYPE light_roast) (TOPPING honey) (TOPPING (ESPRESSO_SHOT 1))) (DRINK_ORDER (NUMBER 1) (SIZE large) (DRINK_TYPE cappuccino) (TOPPING caramel_syrup))

Table 3: Example utterances obtained from Mechanical Turk collection and their corresponding machine-executable representation.

Dataset	Template	Example catalog values
SUB	{prelude} {number} {side_type}	{prelude} = *i want to order* {side_type} = *sunchips*
SUB	{prelude} {number} {base_sandwich} with {topping1} and {topping2}	{base_sandwich} = *chicken teriyaki* {topping1} = *bacon*
BURRITO	{prelude} {number} {main_filling} {entity_name} with {salsa_topping}	{main_filling} = *barbacoa* {entity_name} = *burrito*
BURRITO	{prelude} {number} side of {side_type1} and {side_type2} and {number} {drink_type}	{side_type1} = *chips* {side_type2} = *guac*

Table 4: Example templates and catalog values used for sampling synthetic data.

We use the human-generated data of the three training tasks as our development set for early stopping and hyperparameter tuning. Including this and general experimentation, we estimate our total

	#Intent per utterance	#Slots per utterance	Avg utterance depth
Synthetic Data			
PIZZA	1.77	5.77	3.44
BURRITO	1.57	6.50	3.48
SUB	1.79	6.24	3.37
Human-generated Data			
PIZZA	1.25	6.13	3.62
BURRITO	1.39	5.78	3.12
SUB	1.69	5.99	3.07
BURGER	1.97	7.17	3.04
COFFEE	1.05	5.34	3.2

Table 5: Statistics on the degree of compositionality in each task, for synthetic and human-generated data.

Dataset	Natural Language Utterance	Prediction w/o constraints	Prediction w/ constraints
BURGER	i'll have a hamburger topped with bacon and ketchup along with a large coke and large order of french fries	(MAIN_DISH_ORDER (MAIN_DISH_TYPE hamburger) (TOPPING bacon) (TOPPING ketchup)) (DRINK_ORDER (SIZE large) (DRINK_TYPE coke)) (SIDE_ORDER (NUMBER large) (SIDE_TYPE french fries))	(MAIN_DISH_ORDER (MAIN_DISH_TYPE hamburger) (TOPPING bacon) (TOPPING ketchup)) (DRINK_ORDER (SIZE large) (DRINK_TYPE coke)) (SIDE_ORDER (NUMBER a) (SIZE large) (SIDE_TYPE french fries))
COFFEE	i'd like an iced cappuccino with caramel syrup and whipped cream	(DRINK_ORDER (STYLE iced cappuccino) (TOPPING caramel syrup) (TOPPING whipped cream))	(DRINK_ORDER (STYLE iced) (DRINK_TYPE cappuccino) (TOPPING caramel syrup) (TOPPING whipped cream))

Table 6: Example utterances where constrained decoding helps fix invalid slot/slot value combinations.

computation cost to be about 2 weeks GPU hours.

MTurk prompt

Suppose you want to place your usual order at your favorite *type of restaurant* (like *examples of such venues*) for you, your partner, your family or your group of friends. Your task is to enter your order exactly as you would say it, verbatim, when you place the order at that restaurant.

IMPORTANT: This restaurant has a limited menu provided below. Only order items available on the menu, but do so with the same words you usually use when ordering these items:

**** Picture of restaurant Menu ****

Write as you would speak. Make sure that:

- you write your order exactly as you would say it
- your usual order may include many items and if so, include them all when you enter your order below
- if you complete multiple HITs, vary the type of orders you place. The orders should be usual orders you, your friends or family place, but with varying number or types of items, toppings, sides or drinks.

Enter your order below, using the limited menu above, exactly as you would say it at the restaurant :

**** Type order here ****

Figure 3: Template prompt given to Mechanical Turk workers, common across all 4 tasks. The only significant attribute varying across tasks was the menu to order from.

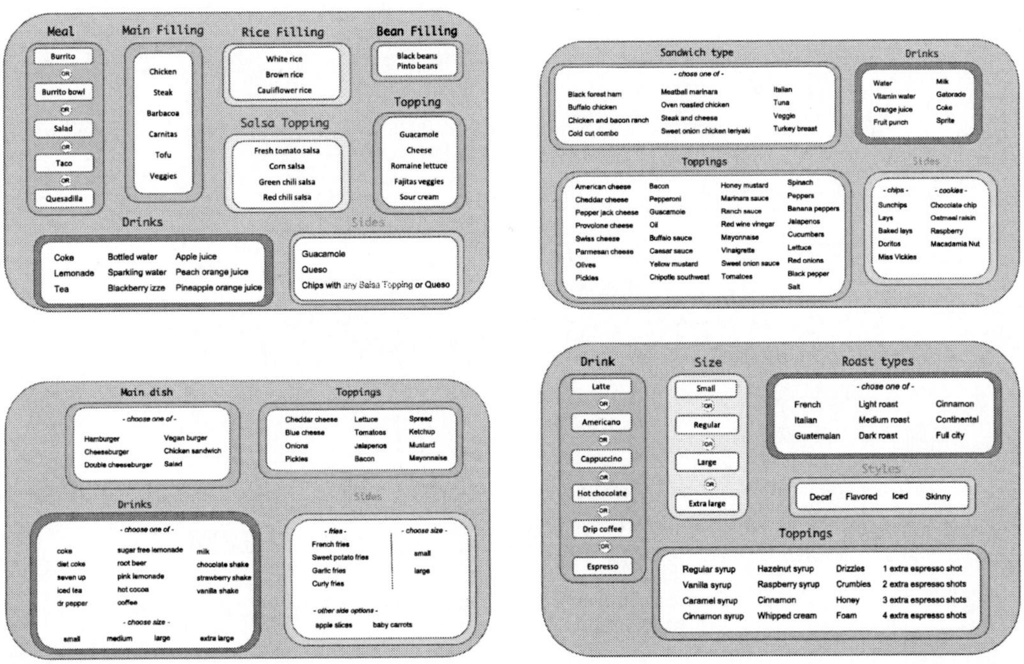

Figure 4: Menus shown to Mechanical Turk workers for each task: BURRITO (top-left), SUB (top-right), BURGER (bottom-left) and COFFEE (bottom-right).

```
{
  "name": "BURRITO",
  "intents": [
    {"name": "BURRITO_ORDER",
     "invocation_keywords": ["burrito", "burritos"],
      "slots": [
      {"name": "NUMBER"}, {"name": "MAIN_FILLING", "quantifiable": true},
      {"name": "RICE_FILLING", "negatable": true, "quantifiable": true},
      {"name": "BEAN_FILLING", "negatable": true, "quantifiable": true},
      {"name": "SALSA_TOPPING", "negatable": true, "quantifiable": true},
      {"name": "TOPPING", "negatable": true, "quantifiable": true}
      ]
    },
    {"name": "BURRITO_BOWL_ORDER",
      "invocation_keywords": ["burrito bowl", "burrito bowls", "bowl", "bowls"],
      "slots": [
      {"name": "NUMBER"}, {"name": "MAIN_FILLING", "quantifiable": true},
      {"name": "RICE_FILLING", "negatable": true, "quantifiable": true},
      {"name": "BEAN_FILLING", "negatable": true, "quantifiable": true},
      {"name": "SALSA_TOPPING", "negatable": true, "quantifiable": true},
      {"name": "TOPPING", "negatable": true, "quantifiable": true}
      ]
    },
    {"name": "SALAD_ORDER",
     "invocation_keywords": ["salad", "salads"],
      "slots": [
      {"name": "NUMBER"}, {"name": "MAIN_FILLING", "quantifiable": true},
      {"name": "RICE_FILLING", "negatable": true, "quantifiable": true},
      {"name": "BEAN_FILLING", "negatable": true, "quantifiable": true},
      {"name": "SALSA_TOPPING", "negatable": true, "quantifiable": true},
      {"name": "TOPPING", "negatable": true, "quantifiable": true}
      ]
    },
    {"name": "TACO_ORDER",
     "invocation_keywords": ["taco", "tacos"],
      "slots": [
      {"name": "NUMBER"}, {"name": "MAIN_FILLING", "quantifiable": true},
      {"name": "RICE_FILLING", "negatable": true, "quantifiable": true},
      {"name": "BEAN_FILLING", "negatable": true, "quantifiable": true},
      {"name": "SALSA_TOPPING", "negatable": true, "quantifiable": true},
      {"name": "TOPPING", "negatable": true, "quantifiable": true}
      ]
    },
    {"name": "QUESADILLA_ORDER",
     "invocation_keywords": ["quesadilla", "quesadillas"],
      "slots": [
      {"name": "NUMBER"}, {"name": "MAIN_FILLING", "quantifiable": true},
      {"name": "RICE_FILLING", "negatable": true, "quantifiable": true},
      {"name": "BEAN_FILLING", "negatable": true, "quantifiable": true},
      {"name": "SALSA_TOPPING", "negatable": true, "quantifiable": true},
      {"name": "TOPPING", "negatable": true, "quantifiable": true}
      ]
    },
    {"name": "SIDE_ORDER",
    "invocation_keywords": ["side of chip", "sides of chips"],
      "slots": [
        {"name": "NUMBER"},
        {"name": "SIDE_TYPE"},
        {"name": "SALSA_TOPPING", "negatable": true, "quantifiable": true}
      ]
    },
    {"name": "DRINK_ORDER",
     "invocation_keywords": ["drink", "drinks"],
      "slots": [
        {"name": "NUMBER"},
        {"name": "DRINK_TYPE"}
      ]
    }
  ]
}
```

Figure 5: Task schema for the BURRITO restaurant.

Help from the Neighbors: Estonian Dialect Normalization Using a Finnish Dialect Generator

Mika Hämäläinen[1], Khalid Alnajjar[1] and Tuuli Tuisk[2]
[1]École Normale Supérieure and CNRS, Paris, France
[2]University of Tartu, Estonia
firstname.lastname@{cnrs.fr[1],ut.ee[2]}

Abstract

While standard Estonian is not a low-resourced language, the different dialects of the language are under-resourced from the point of view of NLP, given that there are no vast hand normalized resources available for training a machine learning model to normalize dialectal Estonian to standard Estonian. In this paper, we crawl a small corpus of parallel dialectal Estonian - standard Estonian sentences. In addition, we take a savvy approach of generating more synthetic training data for the normalization task by using an existing dialect generator model built for Finnish to "dialectalize" standard Estonian sentences from the Universal Dependencies tree banks. Our BERT based normalization model achieves a word error rate that is 26.49 points lower when using both the synthetic data and Estonian data in comparison to training the model with only the available Estonian data. Our results suggest that synthetic data generated by a model trained on a more resourced related language can indeed boost the results for a less resourced language.

1 Introduction

Estonian itself can hardly be characterized as low-resourced due to a variety of NLP tools (Orasmaa et al., 2016; Kaalep et al., 2018; Laur et al., 2020) and corpora (Kaalep et al., 2010; Altrov and Pajupuu, 2012; Muischnek et al., 2016) available for the language. What still remains a difficult and severely under-resourced task to tackle is non-standard dialectal language. Estonian has a rich morphology which means that an individual word can have several different inflectional forms. In terms of dialects, this means that all of the different inflectional forms of a given word can be slightly different in different dialects of the language. This poses a challenge for NLP methods that are mostly trained on standard Estonian.

While the written standard is something people follow when they write official text such as published books or newspapers, people tend to communicate using dialect in more informal settings such as when sending messages or emails with friends and family or when engaging in discussion on online forums. This type of an every day language use is beyond the reach of current NLP methods for Estonian.

For other languages such as Finnish (Partanen et al., 2019), Swedish (Hämäläinen et al., 2020a) and German (Scherrer et al., 2019), dialect normalization has been seen as good way of dealing with the issue of non-standard language. If a model can normalize dialectal text to a standard norm, then all normative language NLP models can be applied on that data. Normalization has been shown to improve results in a variety of tasks such as parsing (van der Goot et al., 2020) and neologism retrieval (Säily et al., 2021).

Unfortunately, Estonian does not have vast dialectal resources available with aligned normalizations with dialectal sentences. For this reason, we establish a new methodology for producing synthetic dialectal Estonian - standard Estonian sentence pairs using a Finnish dialect generation model. The data and the models presented in this paper have been released openly on Zenodo[1].

Estonian dialects are traditionally divided into northern and southern groups, that differ on phonological, morphological as well as on lexical levels. According to the general Estonian dialect classification (Pajusalu et al., 2018), there are three main dialect groups. (1) The North Estonian dialect group consists of the Eastern, Insular, Central, and Western dialects. (2) The Northeastern Coastal dialect group consists of the Northeastern and the Coastal dialects. (3) The South Estonian group consists of the Mulgi, Tartu, and Võru dialects. In recent decades, the question of Seto has been debated. The distinction between Seto and Võru has been justified for instance on a syntactic level

[1]https://zenodo.org/record/6558469

Proceedings of the Third Workshop on Deep Learning for Low-Resource Natural Language Processing, pages 61 - 66
July 14, 2022 ©2022 Association for Computational Linguistics

(Lindström et al., 2014). The dominant contact languages for Estonian dialects are Swedish, Russian, Latvian, and Votic. Finnish, Ingrian and Livonian have influenced somewhat less (Lindström et al., 2019).

2 Related work

There have been several different approaches to text normalization in the past (Bollmann, 2019). In this section, we will give a quick overview of the common approaches.

Dialectal text normalization has been tackled by using normalization rules and heuristics (Bollmann et al., 2011; Khan and Karim, 2012; Sidarenka et al., 2013). Later on, algorithmic approaches have been used for the task (Saloot et al., 2014; Rehan et al., 2018; Poolsukkho and Kongkachandra, 2018).

Very frequently, normalization is modeled as a character-level machine translation task. There are several research papers that use a statistical machine translation approach with a character level n-gram language model of varying lengths (Schlippe et al., 2010; De Clercq et al., 2013; Schlippe et al., 2013; Scherrer and Erjavec, 2013).

More recently, neural machine translation has been used on a character level for the normalization task (Bollmann and Søgaard, 2016; Ruzsics et al., 2019; Hämäläinen et al., 2019). The approaches consist typically of a bi-directional LSTM model and an attention mechanism. This approach has also been used with word2vec to extract and train an OCR post-correction model in an unsupervised way (Hämäläinen and Hengchen, 2019).

With the emergence of general purpose language models, many recent papers present work on using such models for text normalization. BERT (Muller et al., 2019; Plank et al., 2020), BART (Bucur et al., 2021) and RoBERTa (Kubal and Nagvenkar, 2021), for instance, have all been use lately to solve the task.

3 Dialect data

Since there is no dialectal corpus with standard normalizations available for Estonian, we have to crawl one relying on the accessible resources. The Institute of Estonian Language has released some dialectal dictionaries online[2]. Some of these contain example sentences in one of the dialects and their normalization in standard Estonian. In particular, we found that the dialectal dictionaries for Mulgi[3], Kihnu[4] and Hiiu[5] dialects had such aligned dialectal-standard Estonian sentence pairs.

We proceeded to crawl the aforementioned dictionaries. The dictionaries do not have an index of lemmas or any other means of browsing them apart from search queries. For this reason, we use the full text query the online dictionaries have to find occurrences of a given word in anywhere within the dictionary entries. We do this query for the 10,000 most frequent words[6] recorded in the Eesti kirjakeele sagedussõnastik (Kaalep and Muischnek, 2002) which is based on a relatively large 1 million word corpus. This crawling approach leads to the same texts being crawled multiple times, and for this reason, we remove all duplicates.

Some of the dialectal example sentences have additional annotation such as stress marked on top of the vowels. We clean the data of any additional marking and punctuations so that we are left with characters that are part of the Estonian alphabets. Furthermore, we ensure that the dialectal sentence and its normalization have an equal number of words. This step is needed because sometimes the example sentences were not normalized or were not fully normalized. This way we can clear all wrongly aligned sentences from the data. This resulted in 14510 aligned dialectal-normative Estonian sentences.

In Table 1, we can see examples of the data. As we can see, sometimes the dictionary authors had adapted a very strict normalization strategy; on top of just normalizing the sentence to follow the standard Estonian morphology and orthography, they had occasionally normalized dialectal words to completely different words that are part of the standard language. This is different from the vast dialect corpus available for Finnish (Kotimaisten kielten keskus, 2014), where the normalization does not replace any existing words with different ones. This fact alone makes this Estonian corpus more difficult to normalize automatically.

We split the corpus randomly to 70% training, 15% validation and 15% testing. This split is used for all the models we train that include Estonian data in their training. All models are evaluated with this test split.

[2]https://portaal.eki.ee/sonaraamatud.html

[3]https://eki.ee/dict/mulgisuur

[4]http://www.eki.ee/dict/kihnu

[5]http://www.eki.ee/dict/hiiu

[6]https://www.cl.ut.ee/ressursid/sagedused/table1.txt

Dialectal	Normalized	Translation
na joove kõrdamisi ütest laasist	nad joovad kordamööda ühest klaasist	they take turns drinking from one glass
Siis oli tiädmätä jäen ning oksõndan	Siis oli teadvuse kaotanud ja oksendanud	Then he had lost consciousness and vomited
ärä tettä alatude inemistege tegemist	ära tee alatute inimestega tegemist	don't deal with naughty people

Table 1: Examples of the corpus

4 Dialect normalization

We train BERT-based (Devlin et al., 2018) models to do Estonian normalization using Transformers Python library (Wolf et al., 2020). We model the task as a sequence to sequence task, where the model is trained to predict a normalized version of a sentence given a dialectal sentence. The model consists of a BERT based encoder and decoder models similarly to the architecture proposed in Rothe et al. (2020).

We build our models on EstBERT[7] (Tanvir et al., 2021) which is a BERT model trained solely on Estonian data using the Estonian National Corpus. We train three models: one with Estonian only data, one only with synthetic data and one with both types of data. We train the models for 3 epochs.

4.1 Generating synthetic Finnish data

Because Finnish and Estonian are closely related languages, we want to experiment whether synthetically produced dialectal Finnish data can improve the Estonian normalization models. Standard Estonian is closer to dialectal Finnish than standard Finnish, so it makes sense that a Finnish dialect like data could improve the results. It is important to note at this stage that this is not a Finnish to Estonian translation task. Finnish and Estonian are two very different languages and a model that can translate between the two languages has hardly anything to do with dialect normalization.

We use the Finnish dialect generation models presented by Hämäläinen et al. (2020b) to convert standard Estonian sentences into a pseudo Estonian dialect. The dialect generation models are available through Murre Python library[8]. The dialect generator supports over 20 Finnish dialects, and we need to indicate which dialect we want to generate when we use the model. Ideally, we would like to pick the dialect closest to the Estonian dialectal data, because Finland is a relatively large country and dialects further away from Estonia are already linguistically rather distant.

[7] tartuNLP/EstBERT

[8] https://github.com/mikahama/murre

In order to find out which Finnish dialect produces the most Estonian dialect like output, we generate a dialectal version for each standard Estonian sentence in our corpus in each Finnish dialect. We compare the WER (word error rate) of each dialectal output to the correct dialectal Estonian sentence in the corpus that corresponds to the normalized sentence that was used to produce the dialectal sentences.

The results of the experiment, as seen in Table 2, indicate that Etelä-Karjala dialect gives an output closest to the Estonian dialectal data. For this reason, we pick this dialect to adapt sentences from the Estonian Universal Dependencies (UD) treebanks to a pseudo Estonian dialect. The treebanks have some noise, so we filter out all sentences that contain alphabets that are not part of Estonian such as *å*, *ø* or *ω* because they are an indication of non-Estonian sentences or non-Estonian words appearing in a sentence. We want the correct Estonian data to be of a very high quality, so we ensure that only sentences that have correct Estonian alphabets are retained. We also clear the sentences from non-alphabets such as numbers, punctuations and emojis.

Estonian has slightly different vowels than Finnish. The same speech sound [y] is written *y* in Finnish and *ü* in Estonian. For this reason, we replace *ü* with *y* before we pass it to the dialect generation model, and then we replace *y*s back to *ü*s in the output. Estonian also has one more vowel Finnish does not have, *õ*. In practice, both Estonian *ö* and *õ* are mapped to a single vowel *ö* in the Finnish phonetic system. We deal with this by excluding all Estonian UD sentences that have both *ö* and *õ*, so that the input can have either *ö* or *õ*. In case the input has *õ*, it is first replaced with *ö* and after the dialectal form has been generated, all *ö*s are replaced back to *õ*s.

After the dialect adaptation, we do a simple post-processing where we match the voice of plosives of each word in the dialectal output and the standard Estonian input. This means that if the Estonian word contained voiced plosives *d*, *b* or *g* without their unvoiced variants and if the dialectal output

Finnish dialect	WER
Etelä-Häme	0.84
Etelä-Karjala	0.80
Etelä-Pohjanmaa	0.83
Etelä-Satakunta	0.82
Etelä-Savo	0.83
Eteläinen Keski-Suomi	0.83
Inkerinsuomalaismurteet	0.81
Kaakkois-Häme	0.82
Kainuu	0.84
Keski-Karjala	0.82
Keski-Pohjanmaa	0.83
Länsi-Satakunta	0.81
Länsi-Uusimaa	0.81
Länsipohja	0.81
Läntinen Keski-Suomi	0.82
Peräpohjola	0.81
Pohjoinen Keski-Suomi	0.85
Pohjoinen Varsinais-Suomi	0.81
Pohjois-Häme	0.82
Pohjois-Karjala	0.84
Pohjois-Pohjanmaa	0.84
Pohjois-Satakunta	0.82
Pohjois-Savo	0.85

Table 2: The WER between the Finnish dialect generator output and the Estonian dialect sentence. The lower the WER, the closer the output is to Estonian dialect.

had the corresponding unvoiced variant *t, p* or *k*, we replace the unvoiced consonant with the voiced variant. For example, *lambad* (sheep) is dialectalized to *lampaat*, which we convert to *lambaad*. This is important because Finnish dialects often unvoice voiced consonants, whereas the Estonian ones use voiced plosives frequently.

The generated data consists of over 336000 synthetically generated samples where the source side is in pseudo Estonian dialect produced by the Finnish dialect generator for Etelä-Karjala dialect and the target is clean standard Estonian from the UD tree banks. We split this data into 85% for training and 15% for validation.

5 Results and evaluation

In this section, we present the results of our models using WERs. Word Error Rate[9] is a commonly used metric to assess the quality of normalization models as it shows how far away the normalization predicted by a computational model is from the ground truth in terms of substitutions, insertions and deletions. We also calculate a token level accuracy which shows how many times a token was correctly normalized in the exact position it appeared in the sentence.

[9] We use the implementation from https://github.com/nsmartinez/WERpp

	WER	Accuracy
No normalization	74.09	0.257
Estonian only	77.74	0.240
Synthetic data only	73.84	0.256
Synthetic data and Estonian data	**55.25**	**0.471**

Table 3: The results of the BERT model with different datasets

The results can be seen in Table 3. The first row of the table shows how far away the dialectal sentence is from the standard Estonian one without applying a normalization. The WER and the accuracy were the best for the model that was trained on both the synthetic data and the Estonian data. These results are far from perfect, as even the best model makes mistakes around half of the time. However, the results look promising in the sense that the data augmentation improved the results drastically. It is interesting to see that neither the synthetic data nor the Estonian data alone seem to take the model too far, but when combined the results are way better. This is probably due to the fact that the Estonian data is rather small and training a model solely based on it is difficult, and that the synthetic data, while it helps the model to learn a mapping from something that looks like Estonian to standard Estonian, is does not represent the true difference between real Estonian dialects and the standard language. It is to be said, that with the amount of data we have at hand, it is unlikely that the model can ever learn to normalize Estonian the same way the dictionary authors had normalized the dialectal sentences, because then the model would need to also learn a mapping between dialectal words and more standard language.

6 Conclusions

We have shown that despite Estonian not having enough data on its own to train a dialect normalization model, using a Finnish dialect generator model with some orthographic conversion rules to produce synthetic data can boost the results. Although the results were promising, the best WER is still relatively high. This is partially due to the normalization strategy used in the original data. Nevertheless we believe that experimenting more with synthetic data in the future can help us push the WER lower.

7 Acknowledgments

This work was supported in part by the French government under management of Agence Nationale de la Recherche as part of the "Investissements d'avenir" program, reference ANR19-P3IA-0001 (PRAIRIE 3IA Institute). The work was also supported by the CNRS funded International Research Network Cyclades (Corpora and Computational Linguistics for Digital Humanities).

References

Rene Altrov and Hille Pajupuu. 2012. Estonian emotional speech corpus: theoretical base and implementation. In *4th international workshop on corpora for research on emotion sentiment & social signals (ES3)*, pages 50–53. Citeseer.

Marcel Bollmann. 2019. A large-scale comparison of historical text normalization systems. In *Proceedings of the 2019 Conference of the North American Chapter of the Association for Computational Linguistics: Human Language Technologies, Volume 1 (Long and Short Papers)*, pages 3885–3898.

Marcel Bollmann, Florian Petran, and Stefanie Dipper. 2011. Rule-based normalization of historical texts. In *Proceedings of the Workshop on Language Technologies for Digital Humanities and Cultural Heritage*, pages 34–42.

Marcel Bollmann and Anders Søgaard. 2016. Improving historical spelling normalization with bi-directional LSTMs and multi-task learning. In *Proceedings of COLING 2016, the 26th International Conference on Computational Linguistics: Technical Papers*, pages 131–139, Osaka, Japan. The COLING 2016 Organizing Committee.

Ana-Maria Bucur, Adrian Cosma, and Liviu P. Dinu. 2021. Sequence-to-sequence lexical normalization with multilingual transformers. In *Proceedings of the Seventh Workshop on Noisy User-generated Text (W-NUT 2021)*, pages 473–482, Online. Association for Computational Linguistics.

Orphée De Clercq, Bart Desmet, Sarah Schulz, Els Lefever, and Véronique Hoste. 2013. Normalization of dutch user-generated content. In *9th International conference on Recent Advances in Natural Language Processing (RANLP 2013)*, pages 179–188. Incoma.

Jacob Devlin, Ming-Wei Chang, Kenton Lee, and Kristina Toutanova. 2018. Bert: Pre-training of deep bidirectional transformers for language understanding. *arXiv preprint arXiv:1810.04805*.

Mika Hämäläinen and Simon Hengchen. 2019. From the paft to the fiiture: a fully automatic nmt and word embeddings method for ocr post-correction. In *Proceedings of the International Conference on Recent Advances in Natural Language Processing (RANLP 2019)*, pages 431–436.

Mika Hämäläinen, Niko Partanen, and Khalid Alnajjar. 2020a. Normalization of different swedish dialects spoken in finland. In *GeoHumanities'20: Proceedings of the 4th ACM SIGSPATIAL Workshop on Geospatial Humanities*, page 24–27, United States. ACM.

Mika Hämäläinen, Niko Partanen, Khalid Alnajjar, Jack Rueter, and Thierry Poibeau. 2020b. Automatic dialect adaptation in finnish and its effect on perceived creativity. In *Proceedings of the 11th International Conference on Computational Creativity (ICCC'20)*. Association for Computational Creativity.

Mika Hämäläinen, Tanja Säily, Jack Rueter, Jörg Tiedemann, and Eetu Mäkelä. 2019. Revisiting nmt for normalization of early english letters. In *Proceedings of the 3rd Joint SIGHUM Workshop on Computational Linguistics for Cultural Heritage, Social Sciences, Humanities and Literature*. The Association for Computational Linguistics.

Heiki-Jaan Kaalep, Sjur Nørstebø Moshagen, and Trond Trosterud. 2018. Estonian morphology in the giella infrastructure. In *Baltic HLT*, pages 47–54.

Heiki-Jaan Kaalep and Kadri Muischnek. 2002. *Eesti kirjakeele sagedussõnastik*. Tartu Ülikool.

Heiki-Jaan Kaalep, Kadri Muischnek, Kristel Uiboaed, and Kaarel Veskis. 2010. The estonian reference corpus: Its composition and morphology-aware user interface. In *Baltic HLT*, pages 143–146.

Osama A Khan and Asim Karim. 2012. A rule-based model for normalization of sms text. In *2012 IEEE 24th International Conference on Tools with Artificial Intelligence*, volume 1, pages 634–641. IEEE.

Kotimaisten kielten keskus. 2014. Suomen kielen näytteitä, ladattava versio. Kielipankki.

Divesh Kubal and Apurva Nagvenkar. 2021. Multilingual sequence labeling approach to solve lexical normalization. In *Proceedings of the Seventh Workshop on Noisy User-generated Text (W-NUT 2021)*, pages 457–464, Online. Association for Computational Linguistics.

Sven Laur, Siim Orasmaa, Dage Särg, and Paul Tammo. 2020. Estnltk 1.6: Remastered estonian nlp pipeline. In *Proceedings of The 12th Language Resources and Evaluation Conference*, pages 7152–7160.

Liina Lindström, Maarja-Liisa Pilvik, Mirjam Ruutma, and Kristel Uiboaed. 2019. On the use of perfect and pluperfect in estonian dialects: Frequency and language contacts. *Uralica Helsingiensia*, 1(14):155–193.

Liina Lindström, Kristel Uiboaed, and Virve-Anneli Vihman. 2014. Varieerumine tarvis-/vaja-konstruktsioonides keelekontaktide valguses. *Keel ja Kirjandus*, pages 8–9.

Kadri Muischnek, Kaili Müürisep, and Tiina Puolakainen. 2016. Estonian dependency treebank: from constraint grammar tagset to universal dependencies. In *Proceedings of the Tenth International Conference on Language Resources and Evaluation (LREC'16)*, pages 1558–1565.

Benjamin Muller, Benoit Sagot, and Djamé Seddah. 2019. Enhancing BERT for lexical normalization. In *Proceedings of the 5th Workshop on Noisy User-generated Text (W-NUT 2019)*, pages 297–306, Hong Kong, China. Association for Computational Linguistics.

Siim Orasmaa, Timo Petmanson, Alexander Tkachenko, Sven Laur, and Heiki-Jaan Kaalep. 2016. EstNLTK - NLP toolkit for Estonian. In *Proceedings of the Tenth International Conference on Language Resources and Evaluation (LREC'16)*, pages 2460–2466, Portorož, Slovenia. European Language Resources Association (ELRA).

Karl Pajusalu, Tiit Hennoste, Ellen Niit, Peeter Päll, and Jüri Viikberg. 2018. *Eesti murded ja kohanimed [Estonian dialects and place names]. 3rd edition.* Tallinn: Eesti Keele Sihtasutus.

Niko Partanen, Mika Hämäläinen, and Khalid Alnajjar. 2019. Dialect text normalization to normative standard Finnish. In *Proceedings of the 5th Workshop on Noisy User-generated Text (W-NUT 2019)*, pages 141–146, Hong Kong, China. Association for Computational Linguistics.

Barbara Plank, Kristian Nørgaard Jensen, and Rob van der Goot. 2020. DaN+: Danish nested named entities and lexical normalization. In *Proceedings of the 28th International Conference on Computational Linguistics*, pages 6649–6662, Barcelona, Spain (Online). International Committee on Computational Linguistics.

Sanphet Poolsukkho and Rachada Kongkachandra. 2018. Text normalization on thai twitter messages using ipa similarity algorithm. In *2018 International Joint Symposium on Artificial Intelligence and Natural Language Processing (iSAI-NLP)*, pages 1–5. IEEE.

Palak Rehan, Mukesh Kumar, and Sarbjeet Singh. 2018. A modular approach for social media text normalization. In *Information and Decision Sciences*, pages 187–195. Springer.

Sascha Rothe, Shashi Narayan, and Aliaksei Severyn. 2020. Leveraging pre-trained checkpoints for sequence generation tasks. *Transactions of the Association for Computational Linguistics*, 8:264–280.

Tatyana Ruzsics, Massimo Lusetti, Anne Göhring, Tanja Samardžić, and Elisabeth Stark. 2019. Neural text normalization with adapted decoding and pos features. *Natural Language Engineering*, 25(5):585–605.

Tanja Säily, Eetu Mäkelä, and Mika Hämäläinen. 2021. From plenipotentiary to puddingless: Users and uses of new words in early english letters. In *Multilingual Facilitation*, pages 153–169. University of Helsinki.

Mohammad Arshi Saloot, Norisma Idris, and Rohana Mahmud. 2014. An architecture for malay tweet normalization. *Information Processing & Management*, 50(5):621–633.

Yves Scherrer and Tomaž Erjavec. 2013. Modernizing historical slovene words with character-based smt. In *BSNLP 2013-4th Biennial Workshop on Balto-Slavic Natural Language Processing*.

Yves Scherrer, Tanja Samardžić, and Elvira Glaser. 2019. Digitising swiss german: how to process and study a polycentric spoken language. *Language Resources and Evaluation*, 53(4):735–769.

Tim Schlippe, Chenfei Zhu, Jan Gebhardt, and Tanja Schultz. 2010. Text normalization based on statistical machine translation and internet user support. In *Eleventh annual conference of the international speech communication association*.

Tim Schlippe, Chenfei Zhu, Daniel Lemcke, and Tanja Schultz. 2013. Statistical machine translation based text normalization with crowdsourcing. In *2013 IEEE International Conference on Acoustics, Speech and Signal Processing*, pages 8406–8410. IEEE.

Uladzimir Sidarenka, Tatjana Scheffler, and Manfred Stede. 2013. Rule-based normalization of german twitter messages. In *Proc. of the GSCL Workshop Verarbeitung und Annotation von Sprachdaten aus Genres internetbasierter Kommunikation*.

Hasan Tanvir, Claudia Kittask, Sandra Eiche, and Kairit Sirts. 2021. EstBERT: A pretrained language-specific BERT for Estonian. In *Proceedings of the 23rd Nordic Conference on Computational Linguistics (NoDaLiDa)*, pages 11–19, Reykjavik, Iceland (Online). Linköping University Electronic Press, Sweden.

Rob van der Goot, Alan Ramponi, Tommaso Caselli, Michele Cafagna, and Lorenzo De Mattei. 2020. Norm it! lexical normalization for Italian and its downstream effects for dependency parsing. In *Proceedings of the 12th Language Resources and Evaluation Conference*, pages 6272–6278, Marseille, France. European Language Resources Association.

Thomas Wolf, Lysandre Debut, Victor Sanh, Julien Chaumond, Clement Delangue, Anthony Moi, Pierric Cistac, Tim Rault, Remi Louf, Morgan Funtowicz, Joe Davison, Sam Shleifer, Patrick von Platen, Clara Ma, Yacine Jernite, Julien Plu, Canwen Xu, Teven Le Scao, Sylvain Gugger, Mariama Drame, Quentin Lhoest, and Alexander Rush. 2020. Transformers: State-of-the-art natural language processing. In *Proceedings of the 2020 Conference on Empirical Methods in Natural Language Processing: System Demonstrations*, pages 38–45, Online. Association for Computational Linguistics.

Exploring Diversity in Back Translation for Low-Resource Machine Translation

Laurie Burchell and **Alexandra Birch** and **Kenneth Heafield**
Institute for Language, Cognition, and Computation
School of Informatics, University of Edinburgh
10 Crichton Street, Edinburgh, EH8 9AB, UK
{laurie.burchell,a.birch,kenneth.heafield}@ed.ac.uk

Abstract

Back translation is one of the most widely used methods for improving the performance of neural machine translation systems. Recent research has sought to enhance the effectiveness of this method by increasing the 'diversity' of the generated translations. We argue that the definitions and metrics used to quantify 'diversity' in previous work have been insufficient. This work puts forward a more nuanced framework for understanding diversity in training data, splitting it into lexical diversity and syntactic diversity. We present novel metrics for measuring these different aspects of diversity and carry out empirical analysis into the effect of these types of diversity on final neural machine translation model performance for low-resource English↔Turkish and mid-resource English↔Icelandic. Our findings show that generating back translation using nucleus sampling results in higher final model performance, and that this method of generation has high levels of both lexical and syntactic diversity. We also find evidence that lexical diversity is more important than syntactic for back translation performance.

1 Introduction

The data augmentation technique of back translation (BT) is used in nearly every current neural machine translation (NMT) system to reach optimal performance (Edunov et al., 2020; Barrault et al., 2020; Akhbardeh et al., 2021, *inter alia*). It involves creating a pseudo-parallel dataset by translating target-side monolingual data into the source language using a secondary NMT system (Sennrich et al., 2016). In this way, it enables the incorporation of monolingual data into the NMT system. Whilst adding data in this way helps nearly all language pairs, it is particularly important for low-resource NMT where parallel data is scarce by definition.

Because of its ubiquity, there has been extensive research into how to improve BT (Burlot and Yvon, 2018; Hoang et al., 2018; Fadaee and Monz, 2018; Caswell et al., 2019), especially in ways which increase the 'diversity' of the back-translated dataset (Edunov et al., 2018; Soto et al., 2020). Previous work (Gimpel et al., 2013; Ott et al., 2018; Vanmassenhove et al., 2019) has found that machine translations lack the diversity of human productions. This is because most translation systems use some form of maximum a-posteriori (MAP) estimation, meaning that they will always favour the most probable output. Edunov et al. (2018) and Soto et al. (2020) argue that this makes standard BT data worse training data since it lacks 'richness' or diversity.

Despite the focus on increasing diversity in BT, what 'diversity' actually means in the context of NMT training data is ill-defined. In fact, Tevet and Berant (2021) point out that there is no standard metric for measuring diversity. Most previous work uses the BLEU score between candidate sentences or another n-gram based metric to estimate similarity (Zhu et al., 2018; Hu et al., 2019; He et al., 2018; Shen et al., 2019; Shu et al., 2019; Holtzman et al., 2020; Thompson and Post, 2020). However, such metrics mostly measure changes in the vocabulary or spelling. Because of this, they are likely to be less sensitive to other kinds of variety such as changes in structure.

We argue that quantifying 'diversity' using n-gram based metrics alone is insufficient. Instead, we split diversity into two aspects: variety in the word choice and spelling, and variety in structure. We call these aspects *lexical diversity* and *syntactic diversity* respectively. Here, we follow recent work in natural language generation and particularly paraphrasing (e.g. Iyyer et al., 2018; Krishna et al., 2020; Goyal and Durrett, 2020; Huang and Chang, 2021; Hosking and Lapata, 2021) which explicitly models the meaning and form of the input separately. Of course, there are likely more kinds of diversity than this, but this distinction provides

Proceedings of the Third Workshop on Deep Learning for Low-Resource Natural Language Processing, pages 67 - 79
July 14, 2022

a common-sense framework to extend our understanding of the concept. To our knowledge, no other previous work in data augmentation has attempted to isolate and automatically measure syntactic and lexical diversity.

Building from our definition, we introduce novel metrics aimed at measuring lexical and syntactic diversity separately. We then carry out an empirical study into what effect training data with these two kinds of diversity has on final NMT performance in the context of low-resource machine translation. We do this by creating BT datasets using different generation methods and measuring their diversity. We then evaluate what impact different aspects of diversity have on final model performance. We find that a high level of diversity is beneficial for final NMT performance, though lexical diversity seems more important than syntactic diversity. Importantly though there are limits to both; the data should not be so 'diverse' that it affects the adequacy of the parallel data.

We summarise our contributions as follows:

- We put forward a more nuanced definition of 'diversity' in NMT training data, splitting it into *lexical diversity* and *syntactic diversity*. We present two novel metrics for measuring these different aspects of diversity.
- We carry out empirical analysis into the effect of these types of diversity on final NMT model performance for low-resource English↔Turkish and mid-resource English↔Icelandic.
- We find that nucleus sampling is the highest-performing method of generating BT, and it combines both lexical and syntactic diversity.
- We make our code publicly available.[1]

2 Methods

We explain each method we use for creating diverse BT datasets in Section 2.1, then discuss our metrics for diversity in Section 2.2.

2.1 Generating diverse back translation

We use four methods to generate diverse BT datasets: beam search, pure sampling, nucleus sampling, and syntax-group fine-tuning. The first three were chosen because they are in common use and so more relevant for future work. The last, syntax-group fine-tuning, aims to increase syntactic diversity specifically and so allows us to separate its effect on final NMT performance from lexical diversity. For each method, we create a diverse BT dataset by generating three candidate translations for each input sentence. This allows us to measure diversity whilst keeping the 'meaning' of the sentence as similar as possible. In this way, we measure inter-sentence diversity as a proxy for the diversity of the dataset as a whole. We discuss our datasets in detail in Section 3.1.

Beam search Beam search is the most common search algorithm used to decode in NMT systems. Whilst it is generally successful in finding a high-probability output, the translations it produces tend to lack diversity since it will always default to the most likely alternative in the case of ambiguity (Ott et al., 2018). We use beam search to generate three datasets for each language pair, using a beam size of five and no length penalty:

- *base*: three million input sentences used to generate one output per input (BT dataset length: three million)
- *beam*: three million input sentences used to generate three outputs per input (BT dataset length: nine million)
- *base-big*: nine million input sentences used to generate one output per output (BT dataset length: nine million)

Pure sampling An alternative to beam search is sampling from the model distribution. At each decoding step, we sample from the learned distribution without restriction to generate output. This method means we are likely to generate a much wider range of tokens than restricting our choice to those which are most likely (as in beam search). However, it also means that the generated text is less likely to be adequate (have the same meaning as the input) as the output space does not necessary restrict itself to choices which best reflect the meaning of the input. In other words, the output may be diverse, but it may not be the kind of diversity that we want for NMT training data.

We create one dataset per language pair (*sampling*) by generating three candidate translations for each of the three million monolingual input sentences. This results in nine-million line

[1] github.com/laurieburchell/exploring-diversity-bt

BT dataset. We set our beam size to five when generating.

Nucleus sampling Nucleus or top-p sampling is another sampling-based method, introduced by Holtzman et al. (2020). Unlike pure sampling, which samples from the entire distribution, top-p sampling only samples from the highest probability tokens whose cumulative probability mass exceeds the pre-chosen threshold p. The intuition is that when only a small number of tokens are likely, we want to limit our sampling space to those. However, when there are many likely hypotheses, we want to widen the number of tokens we might sample from. We chose this method in the hope it represents a middle ground between high-probability but repetitive beam search generations, and more diverse but potentially low-adequacy pure sampling generation. We create one dataset per language pair (*nucleus*) by generating three hypothesis translations for each of the three million monolingual input sentences. Each dataset is therefore nine million lines long. We set the beam size to five and p to 0.95.

Syntax-group fine-tuning For our analysis in this paper, we want to generate diverse BT in a way which focuses on syntactic diversity over lexical diversity, so that we can separate out its effect on final NMT performance. We therefore take a fine-tuning approach for our final generation method. To do this, we generate the dependency parse of each sentence in the English side of the parallel data for each language pair using the Stanford neural network dependency parser (Chen and Manning, 2014). We then label each pair of parallel sentences in the training data according to the first split in the corresponding syntactic parse tree. We then create three fine-tuning training datasets out of the three biggest syntactic groups.[2] Finally, we take NMT models trained on parallel data alone and restart training on each syntactic-group dataset, resulting in three NMT systems which are fine-tuned to produce a particular syntactic structure. We are only able to create models this way which translate into English, as good syntactic parsers are not available for the other languages in our study.

To verify this method works as expected, we translated the test set for each language pair with the model trained on parallel data only. We then

[2]For English–Turkish, we combine the third and fourth largest syntactic groups to create the third fine-tuning dataset, as the third-largest syntactic group alone was not large enough for successful fine-tuning.

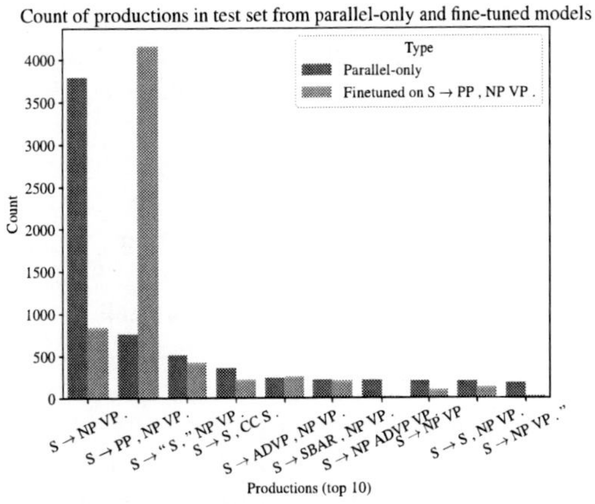

Figure 1: The count of the top-ten syntactic groups produced by the parallel-only Turkish→English NMT model compared to the number of those productions produced by a Turkish→English NMT model fine-tuned on the second-most common syntactic group (`S -> PP NP VP .`). The fine-tuned model produces more examples of the required syntactic group. Input data is the combined WMT test sets.

translated the same test set with each fine-tuned model and checked it was producing more of the required syntactic group. We did indeed find that fine-tuning resulted in more candidate sentences from the required group. Figure 1 gives an example of the different pattern of productions between the parallel-only model and a model fine-tuned on a particular syntactic group (`S -> PP NP VP .`)

2.2 Diversity metrics

We use three primary metrics to measure lexical and syntactic diversity: i-BLEU, i-chrF, and tree kernel difference. As mentioned in Section 2.1, we generate three output sentences for each input to our BT systems and measure inter-sentence diversity as a proxy for the diversity produced by the system. Due to compute time, we calculate all inter-sentence metrics over a sample of 30,000 sentence groups rather than the whole BT dataset.

i-BLEU Following previous work, we calculate the BLEU score between all sentence pairs generated from the same input (Papineni et al., 2002), take the mean and then subtract it from one to give inter-sentence or i-BLEU (Zhu et al., 2018). We believe that lexical diversity as we define it is the main driver of this metric, since BLEU scores are calculated based on n-gram overlap and so the biggest changes to the score will result from changes to the words used (though changes in ordering of words and their morphology will also have an effect). The higher the i-BLEU score, the higher the diversity of output.

i-chrF Building from i-BLEU, we introduce i-chrF, which is generated in the same way as i-BLEU but using chrF (Popović, 2015). Since chrF is also based on n-gram overlap, we believe it will also mostly measure lexical diversity. However, i-chrF is based on character rather than word overlap, and so should be less affected by morphological changes to the form of words than i-BLEU. We calculate both chrF and BLEU scores using the sacreBLEU toolkit (Post, 2018).

Tree kernel difference We propose a novel metric which focuses on syntactic diversity: mean tree kernel difference. To calculate it, we first generate the dependency parse of each candidate sentence using the Stanford neural network dependency parser (Chen and Manning, 2014). We replace all terminals with a dummy token to minimise the effect of lexical differences, then we calculate the tree kernel for each pair of parses using code from Conklin et al. (2021), which is in turn based on Moschitti (2006). Finally, we calculate the mean across all pairs to give the mean tree kernel difference for each set of generated sentences.

We are only able to calculate the tree kernel metric for the English datasets due to the lack of reliable parsers in Turkish and Icelandic, though this method could extend to any language with a reasonable parser available. The higher the score, the higher the diversity of the output.

Summary statistics We calculate mean word length, mean sentence length, and vocabulary size over the entire generated dataset as summary statistics. We use the definition of 'word' as understood by the bash `wc` command to calculate all metrics, since we are only interested in a rough measure to check for degenerate results.

3 Experiments

Having discussed the methods by which we generate diverse BT datasets and the metrics with which we measure the diversity in these datasets, we now outline our experimental set up for testing the effect of training data diversity on final NMT model performance.

3.1 Data and preprocessing

We carry out our experiments on two language pairs: low-resource Turkish–English and mid-resource Icelandic–English. These languages are sufficiently low-resource that augmenting the training data will likely be beneficial, but well-resourced enough that we can still train a reasonable back-translation model on the available parallel data alone.

Data provenance The Turkish–English parallel data is from the WMT 2018 news translation task (Bojar et al., 2018). The training data is from the SETIMES dataset, a parallel dataset of news articles in Balkan languages (Tiedemann, 2012). We use the development set from WMT 2016 and the test sets from WMT 2016–18.

The Icelandic–English parallel data is from the WMT 2021 news translation task (Akhbardeh et al., 2021). There are four sources of training data: ParIce (Barkarson and Steingrímsson, 2019), filtered as described in Jónsson et al. (2020); Paracrawl (Bañón et al., 2020); WikiMatrix (Schwenk et al., 2021); and WikiTitles[3]. We use the development and test sets provided for WMT 2021.

The English monolingual data is made up of news crawl data from 2016 to 2020, version 16 of news-commentary crawl,[4] and crawled news discussions from 2012 to 2019.[5] The Turkish monolingual data is news crawl data from 2016 to 2020.[6] The Icelandic monolingual data is made up of news crawl data from 2020, and part one of the Icelandic Gigaword dataset (Steingrímsson et al., 2018).

Data cleaning Our cleaning scripts are adapted from those provided by the Bergamot project.[7] The full data preparation procedure is provided in the repo accompanying this paper. After cleaning, the Turkish–English parallel dataset contains 202 thousand lines and the Icelandic–English parallel dataset contains 3.97 million lines. The English, Icelandic, and Turkish cleaned monolingual datasets contain 487 million, 39.9 million, and 26.1 million lines respectively. We select 9 million lines of each monolingual dataset for BT at random since all the monolingual datasets are the same domain as the test sets.

[3] `data.statmt.org/wikititles/v3`

[4] `data.statmt.org/news-commentary/v16`

[5] `data.statmt.org/news-discussions/en`

[6] `data.statmt.org/news-crawl`

[7] `github.com/browsermt/students/tree/master/train-student`

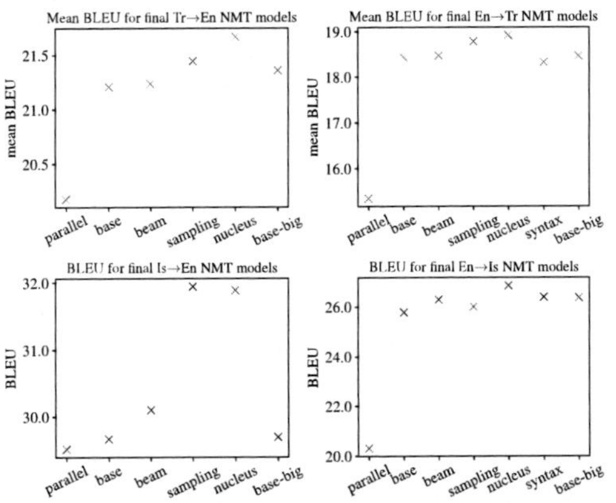

Figure 2: Mean BLEU score on WMT test sets for English↔Turkish and English↔Icelandic models trained on different BT datasets. For English↔Turkish, we give the mean score on WMT 16, WMT 17, and WMT 18 test sets. For English↔Icelandic, we give the score on the WMT 21 test set.

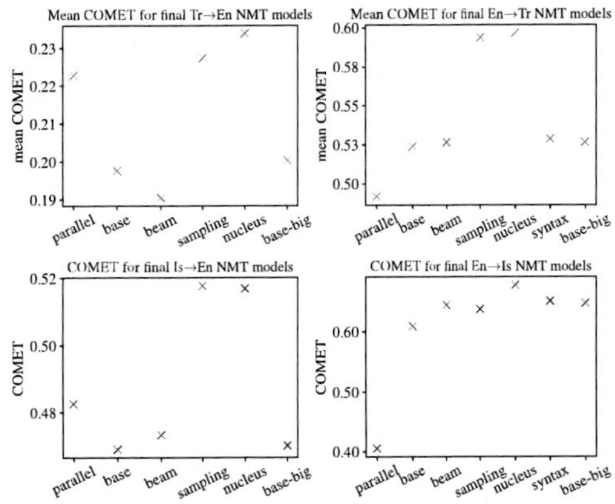

Figure 3: Mean COMET score on WMT test sets for English↔Turkish and English↔Icelandic models trained on different BT datasets. For English↔Turkish, we give the mean score on WMT 16, WMT 17, and WMT 18 test sets. For English↔Icelandic, we give the score on the WMT 21 test set.

Text pre-processing We learn a joint BPE model with SentencePiece using the concatenated training data for each language pair (Kudo and Richardson, 2018). We set vocabulary size to 16,000 and character coverage to 1.0. All other settings are default. We apply this model to the training, development, and test data. We remove the BPE segmentation before calculating any metrics.

3.2 Model training

Model architecture and infrastructure All NMT models in this paper are transformer models (Vaswani et al., 2017). We give full details about hyper-parameters and infrastructure in Appendix A.2.

Parallel-only models for back translation For each language pair and in both directions, we train an NMT model on the cleaned parallel data alone using the relevant hyper-parameter settings in Table 5. We measure the performance of these models by calculating the BLEU score (Papineni et al., 2002) using the sacreBLEU toolkit (Post, 2018)[8] and by evaluating the translations with COMET using the `wmt20-comet-da` model (Rei et al., 2020).

Generating back translation For each language pair and in each direction, we use the trained parallel-only models to generate back translation datasets as described in Section 2.1. We translate the same three million sentences of monolingual data each time for consistency, translating an additional six million lines of monolingual data for the *base-big* dataset.

Training final models We train final models for each language direction on the concatenation of the parallel data and each back-translation dataset (back-translation on the source side, original monolingual data as target). We measure the final performance of these models using BLEU and COMET as before.

4 Results and Analysis

4.1 Final model performance

Figures 2 and 3 show the mean BLEU and COMET scores achieved by the final models trained on the concatenation of the parallel data and the different BT datasets. In most cases, adding any BT data to the training data results in some improvement over the parallel-only baseline for both scores. However, augmenting the training data with BT produced with nucleus sampling nearly always results in the strongest performance, with mean gains of 2.88 BLEU or 0.078 COMET. This compares to mean gains of 2.24 BLEU or 0.026 COMET when using the baseline BT dataset of three million lines translated with beam search. Pure sampling tends to perform similarly but not quite as well as nucleus sampling. Based on this result, we suggest that

[8] `BLEU|nrefs:1|case:mixed|eff:no|tok:13a|smooth:exp|version:2.0.0`

Dataset	*base-big*	*beam*	*sampling*	*nucleus*
Sent. len.	12.23	12.21	13.11	12.74
Word. len.	8.19	8.17	8.37	8.28
Vocab	1.6M	1.0M	5.6M	3.4M
i-BLEU	-	38.11	86.69	83.27
i-chrF	-	17.91	58.84	53.95

Table 1: Diversity metrics for the Turkish BT datasets (original language: English) used to train the Tr→En models. Inter-sentence metrics are calculated on a sample of 30k triplets. 'M' = million.

Dataset	*base-big*	*beam*	*sampling*	*nucleus*
Sent. len.	15.65	14.79	14.92	14.73
Word len.	6.54	6.91	7.33	7.15
Vocab.	1.3M	0.82M	11M	5.6M
i-BLEU	-	30.89	86.41	79.67
i-chrF	-	16.09	66.06	57.83

Table 2: Diversity metrics for the Icelandic BT datasets (original language: English) used to train the Is→En models. Inter-sentence metrics are calculated on a sample of 30k triplets. 'M' = million.

Dataset	*base+*	*beam*	*sampl.*	*nucleus*	*syntax*
Sent. len.	16.98	17.03	17.85	17.54	17.28
Word len.	6.05	6.04	6.25	6.11	6.06
Vocab	0.89M	0.54M	4.9M	2.5M	0.64M
i-BLEU	-	30.74	83.52	78.92	42.26
i-chrF	-	16.28	57.16	51.82	23.32
Kernel	-	72.20	97.33	95.91	83.43

Table 3: Diversity metrics for the English BT datasets (original language: Turkish) used to train the En→Tr models. Inter-sentence metrics are calculated on a sample of 30k triplets. 'M' = million.

Dataset	*base+*	*beam*	*sampl.*	*nucleus*	*syntax*
Sent. len.	20.45	22.75	21.34	21.13	18.29
Word len.	5.83	5.83	6.33	6.08	5.89
Vocab.	0.66M	0.41M	12M	5.6M	0.49M
i-BLEU	-	22.75	92.31	88.86	77.17
i-chrF	-	11.95	72.20	67.16	56.90
Kernel	-	65.72	99.35	98.74	99.40

Table 4: Diversity metrics for the English BT datasets (original language: Icelandic) used to train the En→Is models. Inter-sentence metrics are calculated on a sample of 30k triplets. 'M' = million.

future work generate BT with nucleus sampling rather than pure sampling.

4.2 Diversity metrics

We give the diversity metrics for each language pair and each generated dataset in Tables 1 to 4.[9] Sentence and word lengths are comparable across the same language for all generation methods, suggesting that each method is generating tokens from roughly the right language distribution. However, the vocabulary size is much larger for *nucleus* compared to *base* or *beam*, and *sampling* is around twice that of *nucleus*. Examining the data, we find many neologisms (that is, 'words' which do not appear in the training data) for *nucleus* and more still for *sampling*. We note that the *syntax-groups* dataset has a much smaller vocabulary again; this is what we would hope if the generation method is producing syntactic rather than lexical diversity as required. We give representative examples of generated triples in Appendix A.1, along with some explanation of how the phenomena they demonstrate fit into the general trend of the dataset.

Effect on performance With respect to the inter-sentence diversity metrics (i-BLEU, i-chrF, and tree kernel scores), we see that the *sampling* dataset has the highest diversity scores, followed by *nucleus*, then *syntax*, then *beam*. Taken together with the performance scores and the summary statistics, this suggests that NMT data benefits from a high level of diversity, but not so high that the two halves of the parallel data no longer have the same meaning (as shown by the very high vocabulary size for *sampling*).

Metric correlation There is a high correlation between i-BLEU, i-chrF, and tree kernel score for the *beam*, *sampling*, and *nucleus* datasets. This is not entirely unexpected: it is likely to be difficult if not impossible to disentangle lexical and syntactic diversity, since changing sentence structure would also affect the word choice and vice versa.

This correlation is much weaker for the *syntax-groups* dataset: whilst the tree-kernel scores are comparable to the *sampling* and *nucleus* datasets, there is a much smaller increase in the other (lexical) diversity scores. This suggests that this generation method encourages relatively more syntactic variation than lexical compared to the other diverse generation method, as was its original aim (see paragraph on syntax-group fine-tuning in section 2.1). The fact that the final model trained on this BT dataset has lower performance compared to other forms of diversity suggests that lexical diversity is more important than syntactic diversity when undertaking data augmentation. We leave it

[9] We omit *base* for reasons of space and because its different length to the other datasets makes comparison difficult (3 million lines compared to 9 million for the others).

to future work to investigate this hypothesis further.

4.3 Data augmentation versus more monolingual data

The right-most cross in each quadrant of Figures 2 and 3 gives the performance of *base-big*, the dataset where we simply add six million more lines of new data rather than carrying out data augmentation. Interestingly, pure and nucleus sampling both often outperform *base-big*. This may be because the model over-fits to too much back-translated data, whereas having multiple sufficiently-diverse pseudo-source sentences for each target sentence has a regularising effect on the model.

To further support this hypothesis, Figure 4 gives training perplexity for the first 50,000 steps of training for the final Icelandic→English models, which are representative of the results for the other language pairs. We see that the *base-big* dataset has the lowest training perplexity at each step, suggesting this data is easier to model. Conversely, the model has highest training perplexity on the *sampling* and *nucleus* datasets, suggesting generating the data this way has a regularising effect.

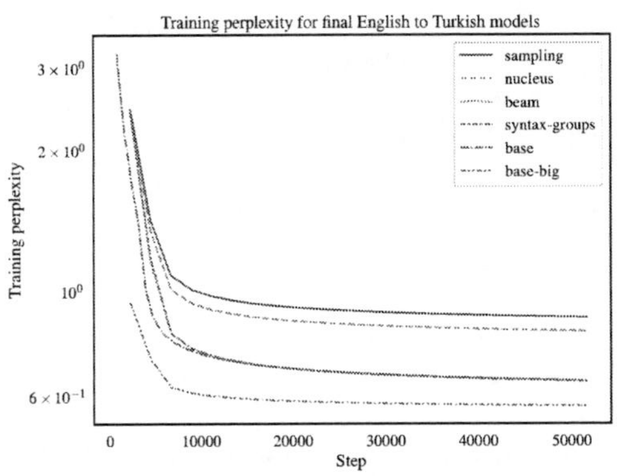

Figure 4: Mean training perplexity for the first 50 thousand steps of training for final English→Turkish models. The model has highest training perplexity on the *sampling* then *nucleus* datasets. The lowest training perplexity is on the *beam* and *base-big* datasets.

4.4 Translationese effect

Several studies have found that back-translated text is easier to translate than forward-translated text, and so inflates intrinsic metrics like BLEU (Edunov et al., 2020; Graham et al., 2020; Roberts et al., 2020). To use a concrete example, the WMT test sets for English to Turkish are made up of half native English translated into Turkish, and half native Turkish translated into English. We want models that perform well when translating *from* native text (in this example: the native English side), as this is the usual direction of translation. However, half the test set is made up of translations on the source side. The translationese effect means that the model will usually get higher scores on this half of the test set, potentially inflating the score. Consequently, the intrinsic metrics could suggest choosing a model that does not actually perform well on the desired task (translating *from* native text).

We investigate this effect in our own work by examining the mean BLEU scores for each model on each half of the test sets, giving the results in Figure 5. Each bar indicates the mean percentage change in BLEU scores over the parallel-only baseline model for the models trained on the different BT datasets, so a larger bar means a better performing model. The left-hand bars in each quadrant show the performance of each model on the back-translated half of the test set (*to native*) and the right-hand bars give the performance of each model on the forward-translated half of the test set (*from native*).

We see a significant translationese effect for all models, as the percentage change in scores over the baseline are much higher when the models translate already translated text (the left-hand side bars are higher than the right-hand ones). However, it appears that the *nucleus* dataset is less affected by the translationese effect than the other datasets, since it shows less of a decline in performance when translating native text. This may be due to a similar regularising effect as discussed previously, as it is more difficult for the model to overfit to BT data when it is generated with nucleus sampling. A direction for future research is how to obtain the benefits of using monolingual data (as BT does) without exacerbating the translationese effect.

5 Related work

Improving back translation The original paper introducing BT by Sennrich et al. (2016) found that using a higher-quality NMT system for BT led to higher BLEU scores in the final trained system. This finding was corroborated by Burlot and Yvon (2018), and following work has investigated further ways to improve NMT. These include iterative BT (Hoang et al., 2018), targeting difficult words (Fadaee and Monz, 2018), and tagged BT (Caswell et al., 2019). Section 3.2.1 of Haddow et al. (2021)

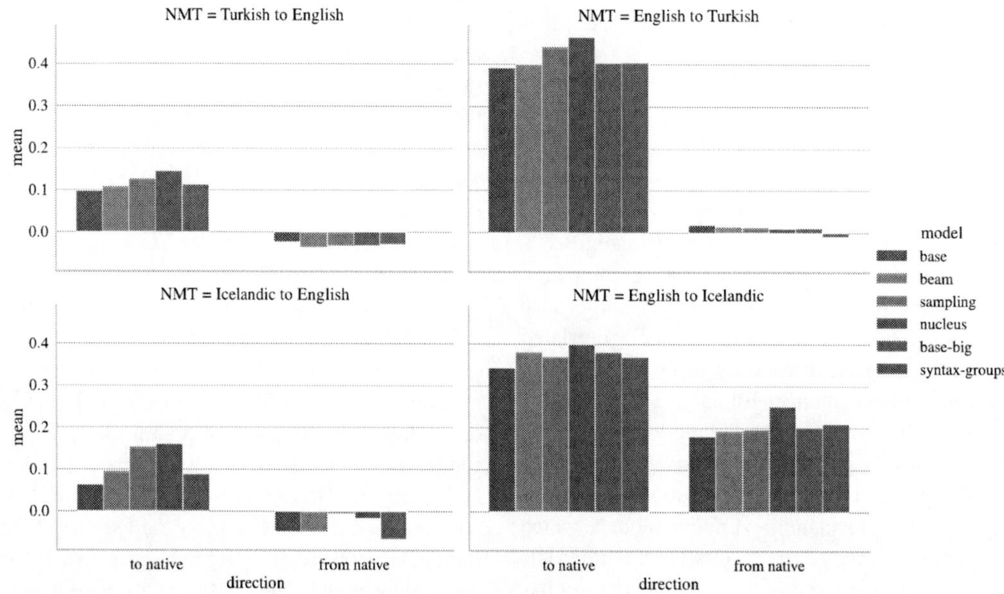

Figure 5: The mean percentage change in BLEU score for each model on the test set(s) over the parallel-only models, separated by language direction. The left-hand side (*to native*) has translated text on the source side and native text on the target side of the test set (back translation). The right-hand side (*from native*) has native text on the source side and translated text on the target side of the test set.

presents a comprehensive survey of BT and its variants as applied to low-resource NMT.

Diversity in machine translation Most of the work on the lack of diversity in machine-translated text are in the context of automatic evaluation (Edunov et al., 2020; Graham et al., 2020; Roberts et al., 2020). As for diversity in BT specifically, Edunov et al. (2018) argue that MAP prediction, as is typically used to generate BT through beam search, leads to overly-regular synthetic source sentences which do not cover the true data distribution. They propose instead generating BT with sampling or noised beam outputs, and find model performance increases for all but the lowest resource scenarios. Alternatively, Soto et al. (2020) generate diverse BT by training multiple machine-translation systems with varying architectures.

Generating diversity Increasing diversity in BT is part of the broader field of diverse generation, by which we mean methods to vary the surface form of a production whilst keeping the meaning as similar as possible. Aside from generating diverse translations (Gimpel et al., 2013; He et al., 2018; Shen et al., 2019; Nguyen et al., 2020; Li et al., 2021), it is also used in question answering systems (Sultan et al., 2020), visually-grounded generation (Vijayakumar et al., 2018), conversation models (Li et al., 2016), and particularly paraphrasing (Mallinson et al., 2017; Wieting and Gimpel, 2018; Hu et al., 2019; Thompson and Post, 2020; Goyal and Durrett, 2020; Krishna et al., 2020). Some recent work such as Iyyer et al. (2018), Huang and Chang (2021), and Hosking and Lapata (2021) explicitly model the meaning and the form of the input separately. In this way, they aim to vary the syntax of the output whilst preserving the semantics so as to generate more diverse paraphrases. Unfortunately, these methods are difficult to apply to a low-resource scenario as they require external resources (e.g. accurate syntactic parsers, large-scale paraphrase data) which are not available for most of the world's languages.

6 Conclusion

In this paper, we introduced a two-part framework for understanding diversity in NMT data, splitting it into *lexical diversity* and *syntactic diversity*. Our empirical analysis suggests that whilst high amounts of both types of diversity are important in training data, lexical diversity may be more beneficial than syntactic. In addition, achieving high diversity in BT should not be at the expense of adequacy. We find that generating BT with nucleus sampling results in the highest final NMT model performance for our systems. Future work could investigate further the affect of high lexical diversity on BT independent of syntactic diversity.

Acknowledgements

This work was supported in part by the UKRI Centre for Doctoral Training in Natural Language Processing, funded by the UKRI (grant EP/S022481/1) and the University of Edinburgh, School of Informatics and School of Philosophy, Psychology & Language Sciences. It was also supported by funding from the European Union's Horizon 2020 research and innovation programme under grant agreement No 825299 (GoURMET) and funding from the UK Engineering and Physical Sciences Research Council (EPSRC) fellowship grant EP/S001271/1 (MTStretch).

The experiments in this paper were performed using resources provided by the Cambridge Service for Data Driven Discovery (CSD3) operated by the University of Cambridge Research Computing Service (www.csd3.cam.ac.uk), provided by Dell EMC and Intel using Tier-2 funding from the Engineering and Physical Sciences Research Council (capital grant EP/P020259/1), and DiRAC funding from the Science and Technology Facilities Council (www.dirac.ac.uk).

Finally, the authors would like to thank our anonymous reviewers for their time and helpful comments, and we give special thanks to Henry Conklin and Bailin Wang for their help with tree kernels and many useful discussions.

References

Farhad Akhbardeh, Arkady Arkhangorodsky, Magdalena Biesialska, Ondřej Bojar, Rajen Chatterjee, Vishrav Chaudhary, Marta R. Costa-jussa, Cristina España-Bonet, Angela Fan, Christian Federmann, Markus Freitag, Yvette Graham, Roman Grundkiewicz, Barry Haddow, Leonie Harter, Kenneth Heafield, Christopher Homan, Matthias Huck, Kwabena Amponsah-Kaakyire, Jungo Kasai, Daniel Khashabi, Kevin Knight, Tom Kocmi, Philipp Koehn, Nicholas Lourie, Christof Monz, Makoto Morishita, Masaaki Nagata, Ajay Nagesh, Toshiaki Nakazawa, Matteo Negri, Santanu Pal, Allahsera Auguste Tapo, Marco Turchi, Valentin Vydrin, and Marcos Zampieri. 2021. Findings of the 2021 conference on machine translation (WMT21). In *Proceedings of the Sixth Conference on Machine Translation*, pages 1–88, Online. Association for Computational Linguistics.

Marta Bañón, Pinzhen Chen, Barry Haddow, Kenneth Heafield, Hieu Hoang, Miquel Esplà-Gomis, Mikel L. Forcada, Amir Kamran, Faheem Kirefu, Philipp Koehn, Sergio Ortiz Rojas, Leopoldo Pla Sempere, Gema Ramírez-Sánchez, Elsa Sarrías, Marek Strelec, Brian Thompson, William Waites, Dion Wiggins, and Jaume Zaragoza. 2020. ParaCrawl: Web-scale acquisition of parallel corpora. In *Proceedings of the 58th Annual Meeting of the Association for Computational Linguistics*, pages 4555–4567, Online. Association for Computational Linguistics.

Starkaður Barkarson and Steinþór Steingrímsson. 2019. Compiling and filtering ParIce: An English-Icelandic parallel corpus. In *Proceedings of the 22nd Nordic Conference on Computational Linguistics*, pages 140–145, Turku, Finland. Linköping University Electronic Press.

Loïc Barrault, Magdalena Biesialska, Ondřej Bojar, Marta R. Costa-jussà, Christian Federmann, Yvette Graham, Roman Grundkiewicz, Barry Haddow, Matthias Huck, Eric Joanis, Tom Kocmi, Philipp Koehn, Chi-kiu Lo, Nikola Ljubešić, Christof Monz, Makoto Morishita, Masaaki Nagata, Toshiaki Nakazawa, Santanu Pal, Matt Post, and Marcos Zampieri. 2020. Findings of the 2020 conference on machine translation (WMT20). In *Proceedings of the Fifth Conference on Machine Translation*, pages 1–55, Online. Association for Computational Linguistics.

Lukas Biewald. 2020. Experiment tracking with weights and biases. Software available from wandb.com.

Ondřej Bojar, Christian Federmann, Mark Fishel, Yvette Graham, Barry Haddow, Philipp Koehn, and Christof Monz. 2018. Findings of the 2018 conference on machine translation (WMT18). In *Proceedings of the Third Conference on Machine Translation: Shared Task Papers*, pages 272–303, Belgium, Brussels. Association for Computational Linguistics.

Franck Burlot and François Yvon. 2018. Using monolingual data in neural machine translation: a systematic study. In *Proceedings of the Third Conference on Machine Translation: Research Papers*, pages 144–155, Brussels, Belgium. Association for Computational Linguistics.

Isaac Caswell, Ciprian Chelba, and David Grangier. 2019. Tagged back-translation. In *Proceedings of the Fourth Conference on Machine Translation (Volume 1: Research Papers)*, pages 53–63, Florence, Italy. Association for Computational Linguistics.

Danqi Chen and Christopher Manning. 2014. A fast and accurate dependency parser using neural networks. In *Proceedings of the 2014 Conference on Empirical Methods in Natural Language Processing (EMNLP)*, pages 740–750, Doha, Qatar. Association for Computational Linguistics.

Henry Conklin, Bailin Wang, Kenny Smith, and Ivan Titov. 2021. Meta-learning to compositionally generalize. In *Proceedings of the 59th Annual Meeting of the Association for Computational Linguistics and the 11th International Joint Conference on Natural Language Processing (Volume 1: Long Papers)*, pages 3322–3335, Online. Association for Computational Linguistics.

Sergey Edunov, Myle Ott, Michael Auli, and David Grangier. 2018. Understanding back-translation at scale. In *Proceedings of the 2018 Conference on Empirical Methods in Natural Language Processing*, pages 489–500, Brussels, Belgium. Association for Computational Linguistics.

Sergey Edunov, Myle Ott, Marc'Aurelio Ranzato, and Michael Auli. 2020. On the evaluation of machine translation systems trained with back-translation. In *Proceedings of the 58th Annual Meeting of the Association for Computational Linguistics*, pages 2836–2846, Online. Association for Computational Linguistics.

Marzieh Fadaee and Christof Monz. 2018. Back-translation sampling by targeting difficult words in neural machine translation. In *Proceedings of the 2018 Conference on Empirical Methods in Natural Language Processing*, pages 436–446, Brussels, Belgium. Association for Computational Linguistics.

Kevin Gimpel, Dhruv Batra, Chris Dyer, and Gregory Shakhnarovich. 2013. A systematic exploration of diversity in machine translation. In *Proceedings of the 2013 Conference on Empirical Methods in Natural Language Processing*, pages 1100–1111, Seattle, Washington, USA. Association for Computational Linguistics.

Tanya Goyal and Greg Durrett. 2020. Neural syntactic preordering for controlled paraphrase generation. In *Proceedings of the 58th Annual Meeting of the Association for Computational Linguistics*, pages 238–252, Online. Association for Computational Linguistics.

Yvette Graham, Christian Federmann, Maria Eskevich, and Barry Haddow. 2020. Assessing human-parity in machine translation on the segment level. In *Findings of the Association for Computational Linguistics: EMNLP 2020*, pages 4199–4207, Online. Association for Computational Linguistics.

Barry Haddow, Rachel Bawden, Antonio Valerio Miceli Barone, Jindrich Helcl, and Alexandra Birch. 2021. Survey of low-resource machine translation. *CoRR*, abs/2109.00486.

Xuanli He, Gholamreza Haffari, and Mohammad Norouzi. 2018. Sequence to sequence mixture model for diverse machine translation. In *Proceedings of the 22nd Conference on Computational Natural Language Learning*, pages 583–592, Brussels, Belgium. Association for Computational Linguistics.

Vu Cong Duy Hoang, Philipp Koehn, Gholamreza Haffari, and Trevor Cohn. 2018. Iterative back-translation for neural machine translation. In *Proceedings of the 2nd Workshop on Neural Machine Translation and Generation*, pages 18–24, Melbourne, Australia. Association for Computational Linguistics.

Ari Holtzman, Jan Buys, Li Du, Maxwell Forbes, and Yejin Choi. 2020. The curious case of neural text degeneration. In *International Conference on Learning Representations*.

Tom Hosking and Mirella Lapata. 2021. Factorising meaning and form for intent-preserving paraphrasing. In *Proceedings of the 59th Annual Meeting of the Association for Computational Linguistics and the 11th International Joint Conference on Natural Language Processing (Volume 1: Long Papers)*, pages 1405–1418, Online. Association for Computational Linguistics.

J Edward Hu, Rachel Rudinger, Matt Post, and Benjamin Van Durme. 2019. Parabank: Monolingual bitext generation and sentential paraphrasing via lexically-constrained neural machine translation. In *Proceedings of the AAAI Conference on Artificial Intelligence*, volume 33, pages 6521–6528.

Kuan-Hao Huang and Kai-Wei Chang. 2021. Generating syntactically controlled paraphrases without using annotated parallel pairs. In *Proceedings of the 16th Conference of the European Chapter of the Association for Computational Linguistics: Main Volume*, pages 1022–1033, Online. Association for Computational Linguistics.

Mohit Iyyer, John Wieting, Kevin Gimpel, and Luke Zettlemoyer. 2018. Adversarial example generation with syntactically controlled paraphrase networks. In *Proceedings of the 2018 Conference of the North American Chapter of the Association for Computational Linguistics: Human Language Technologies, Volume 1 (Long Papers)*, pages 1875–1885, New Orleans, Louisiana. Association for Computational Linguistics.

Haukur Páll Jónsson, Haukur Barri Símonarson, Vésteinn Snæbjarnarson, Steinþór Steingrímsson, and Hrafn Loftsson. 2020. Experimenting with different machine translation models in medium-resource settings. In *International Conference on Text, Speech, and Dialogue*, pages 95–103. Springer.

Kalpesh Krishna, John Wieting, and Mohit Iyyer. 2020. Reformulating unsupervised style transfer as paraphrase generation. In *Proceedings of the 2020 Conference on Empirical Methods in Natural Language Processing (EMNLP)*, pages 737–762, Online. Association for Computational Linguistics.

Taku Kudo and John Richardson. 2018. SentencePiece: A simple and language independent subword tokenizer and detokenizer for neural text processing. In *Proceedings of the 2018 Conference on Empirical Methods in Natural Language Processing: System Demonstrations*, pages 66–71, Brussels, Belgium. Association for Computational Linguistics.

Jicheng Li, Pengzhi Gao, Xuanfu Wu, Yang Feng, Zhongjun He, Hua Wu, and Haifeng Wang. 2021. Mixup decoding for diverse machine translation. In *Findings of the Association for Computational Linguistics: EMNLP 2021*, pages 312–320, Punta Cana, Dominican Republic. Association for Computational Linguistics.

Jiwei Li, Michel Galley, Chris Brockett, Jianfeng Gao, and Bill Dolan. 2016. A diversity-promoting objective function for neural conversation models. In *Proceedings of the 2016 Conference of the North American Chapter of the Association for Computational Linguistics: Human Language Technologies*, pages 110–119, San Diego, California. Association for Computational Linguistics.

Jonathan Mallinson, Rico Sennrich, and Mirella Lapata. 2017. Paraphrasing revisited with neural machine translation. In *Proceedings of the 15th Conference of the European Chapter of the Association for Computational Linguistics: Volume 1, Long Papers*, pages 881–893, Valencia, Spain. Association for Computational Linguistics.

Alessandro Moschitti. 2006. Making tree kernels practical for natural language learning. In *11th Conference of the European Chapter of the Association for Computational Linguistics*, pages 113–120, Trento, Italy. Association for Computational Linguistics.

Xuan-Phi Nguyen, Shafiq Joty, Kui Wu, and Ai Ti Aw. 2020. Data diversification: A simple strategy for neural machine translation. *Advances in Neural Information Processing Systems*, 33:10018–10029.

Myle Ott, Michael Auli, David Grangier, and Marc'Aurelio Ranzato. 2018. Analyzing uncertainty in neural machine translation. In *Proceedings of the 35th International Conference on Machine Learning*, volume 80 of *Proceedings of Machine Learning Research*, pages 3956–3965. PMLR.

Myle Ott, Sergey Edunov, Alexei Baevski, Angela Fan, Sam Gross, Nathan Ng, David Grangier, and Michael Auli. 2019. fairseq: A fast, extensible toolkit for sequence modeling. In *Proceedings of the 2019 Conference of the North American Chapter of the Association for Computational Linguistics (Demonstrations)*, pages 48–53, Minneapolis, Minnesota. Association for Computational Linguistics.

Kishore Papineni, Salim Roukos, Todd Ward, and Wei-Jing Zhu. 2002. Bleu: a method for automatic evaluation of machine translation. In *Proceedings of the 40th Annual Meeting of the Association for Computational Linguistics*, pages 311–318, Philadelphia, Pennsylvania, USA. Association for Computational Linguistics.

Maja Popović. 2015. chrF: character n-gram F-score for automatic MT evaluation. In *Proceedings of the Tenth Workshop on Statistical Machine Translation*, pages 392–395, Lisbon, Portugal. Association for Computational Linguistics.

Matt Post. 2018. A call for clarity in reporting BLEU scores. In *Proceedings of the Third Conference on Machine Translation: Research Papers*, pages 186–191, Brussels, Belgium. Association for Computational Linguistics.

Ricardo Rei, Craig Stewart, Ana C Farinha, and Alon Lavie. 2020. COMET: A neural framework for MT evaluation. In *Proceedings of the 2020 Conference on Empirical Methods in Natural Language Processing (EMNLP)*, pages 2685–2702, Online. Association for Computational Linguistics.

Nicholas Roberts, Davis Liang, Graham Neubig, and Zachary C. Lipton. 2020. Decoding and diversity in machine translation. In *Advances in Neural Information Processing Systems*, volume 33. Curran Associates, Inc.

Holger Schwenk, Vishrav Chaudhary, Shuo Sun, Hongyu Gong, and Francisco Guzmán. 2021. WikiMatrix: Mining 135M parallel sentences in 1620 language pairs from Wikipedia. In *Proceedings of the 16th Conference of the European Chapter of the Association for Computational Linguistics: Main Volume*, pages 1351–1361, Online. Association for Computational Linguistics.

Rico Sennrich, Barry Haddow, and Alexandra Birch. 2016. Improving neural machine translation models with monolingual data. In *Proceedings of the 54th Annual Meeting of the Association for Computational Linguistics (Volume 1: Long Papers)*, pages 86–96, Berlin, Germany. Association for Computational Linguistics.

Tianxiao Shen, Myle Ott, Michael Auli, and Marc'Aurelio Ranzato. 2019. Mixture models for diverse machine translation: Tricks of the trade. In *Proceedings of the 36th International Conference on Machine Learning*, volume 97 of *Proceedings of Machine Learning Research*, pages 5719–5728. PMLR.

Raphael Shu, Hideki Nakayama, and Kyunghyun Cho. 2019. Generating diverse translations with sentence codes. In *Proceedings of the 57th Annual Meeting of the Association for Computational Linguistics*, pages 1823–1827, Florence, Italy. Association for Computational Linguistics.

Xabier Soto, Dimitar Shterionov, Alberto Poncelas, and Andy Way. 2020. Selecting backtranslated data from multiple sources for improved neural machine translation. In *Proceedings of the 58th Annual Meeting of the Association for Computational Linguistics*, pages 3898–3908, Online. Association for Computational Linguistics.

Steinþór Steingrímsson, Sigrún Helgadóttir, Eiríkur Rögnvaldsson, Starkaður Barkarson, and Jón Guðnason. 2018. Risamálheild: A very large Icelandic text corpus. In *Proceedings of the Eleventh International Conference on Language Resources and Evaluation (LREC 2018)*, Miyazaki, Japan. European Language Resources Association (ELRA).

Md Arafat Sultan, Shubham Chandel, Ramón Fernandez Astudillo, and Vittorio Castelli. 2020. On the importance of diversity in question generation for QA. In *Proceedings of the 58th Annual Meeting of the Association for Computational Linguistics*, pages 5651–5656, Online. Association for Computational Linguistics.

Guy Tevet and Jonathan Berant. 2021. Evaluating the evaluation of diversity in natural language generation. In *Proceedings of the 16th Conference of the European Chapter of the Association for Computational Linguistics: Main Volume*, pages 326–346, Online. Association for Computational Linguistics.

Brian Thompson and Matt Post. 2020. Paraphrase generation as zero-shot multilingual translation: Disentangling semantic similarity from lexical and syntactic diversity. In *Proceedings of the Fifth Conference on Machine Translation*, pages 561–570, Online. Association for Computational Linguistics.

Jörg Tiedemann. 2012. Parallel data, tools and interfaces in OPUS. In *Proceedings of the Eighth International Conference on Language Resources and Evaluation (LREC'12)*, pages 2214–2218, Istanbul, Turkey. European Language Resources Association (ELRA).

Eva Vanmassenhove, Dimitar Shterionov, and Andy Way. 2019. Lost in translation: Loss and decay of linguistic richness in machine translation. In *Proceedings of Machine Translation Summit XVII: Research Track*, pages 222–232, Dublin, Ireland. European Association for Machine Translation.

Ashish Vaswani, Noam Shazeer, Niki Parmar, Jakob Uszkoreit, Llion Jones, Aidan N Gomez, Ł ukasz Kaiser, and Illia Polosukhin. 2017. Attention is all you need. In *Advances in Neural Information Processing Systems*, volume 30. Curran Associates, Inc.

Ashwin Vijayakumar, Michael Cogswell, Ramprasaath Selvaraju, Qing Sun, Stefan Lee, David Crandall, and Dhruv Batra. 2018. Diverse beam search for improved description of complex scenes. *Proceedings of the AAAI Conference on Artificial Intelligence*, 32(1).

John Wieting and Kevin Gimpel. 2018. ParaNMT-50M: Pushing the limits of paraphrastic sentence embeddings with millions of machine translations. In *Proceedings of the 56th Annual Meeting of the Association for Computational Linguistics (Volume 1: Long Papers)*, pages 451–462, Melbourne, Australia. Association for Computational Linguistics.

Yaoming Zhu, Sidi Lu, Lei Zheng, Jiaxian Guo, Weinan Zhang, Jun Wang, and Yong Yu. 2018. Texygen: A benchmarking platform for text generation models. In *The 41st International ACM SIGIR Conference on Research and Development in Information Retrieval*, SIGIR '18, page 1097–1100, New York, NY, USA. Association for Computing Machinery.

A Appendix

A.1 Representative examples from back-translated datasets (translated from Icelandic)

Original *Þjóðverjar hafa tekið forræðið og stefnt er að stofnun stórríkis.*

Beam

- The Germans have taken custody and are aimed at the establishment of a large state.
- The Germans have taken custody and are aimed at the creation of a large state.
- The Germans have taken custody and are aimed at establishing a large state.

Comment: Only one or two words differ between sentences (underlined).

Sampling

- The Germz governmentregluru has committed suicide, intending to organise a major state.
- The Germano had ensured that British commanders in France would be aides of theærd rapidly.
- And the need to defend and establish theseUCtions are all organized intomissions from Iraqéttihe.

Comment: Sentences show large variation in structure and vocabulary, but they contain many non-dictionary words (underlined) and adequacy is low.

Nucleus

- Germany has taken custody and aimed to establish a large country.
- The German government initiated a group operation, to establish capital city.
- The Germany has managed to make an example of their full widowed demands.

Comment: There is a moderate amount of variation between sentences in terms of syntax and vocabulary, but no non-dictionary words. Some phrases lack adequacy (underlined).

Syntax-groups

- The Germans have taken custody and are aimed at the establishment of a large state.
- The Icelandic Institute of Natural History
- As a result, the Germans have taken control of the country and are aimed at establishing a large state.

Comment: The second and third sentences contain hallucinations, presumably in order to generate according to the syntactic templates (underlined).

A.2 Model architecture and infrastructure

All NMT models in this paper are transformer models (Vaswani et al., 2017). We conducted a hyper-parameter search for each language pair, training English↔Turkish and English↔Icelandic NMT models and using the BLEU score as the optimisation metric. We give the settings which differ to *transformer-base* in Table 5. We use the same hyper-parameter settings for all models trained for the same language pair.

We use the Fairseq toolkit to train all our NMT models (Ott et al., 2019). We train on four NVIDIA A100-SXM-80GB GPUs and use CUDA 11.1 plus a Python 3.8 Conda environment provided in the Github repo. We generate on one GPU, since to our knowledge the Fairseq toolkit does not support multi-GPU decoding. We use Weights and Biases for experiment tracking (Biewald, 2020).

	tr–en	is–en
Dropout	0.6	0.3
Activation dropout	0.1	0
Attention dropout	0.1	
Learning rate	0.001	
L.R. scheduler	Inv. square root	
Optimiser	Adam	
Optimiser parameters	0.9, 0.98	
Label smoothing	0.1	
Shared embeddings	all	
Batch size	64	
Update frequency	16	
Patience	15	

Table 5: Hyper-parameter settings for NMT transformer models trained for each language pair. All other settings are the default for *transformer-base*.

Punctuation Restoration in Spanish Customer Support Transcripts using Transfer Learning

Xiliang Zhu, Shayna Gardiner, David Rossouw
Tere Roldán, Simon Corston-Oliver
Dialpad Canada Inc.
{xzhu, sgardiner, davidr}@dialpad.com
{tere.roldan, scorston-oliver}@dialpad.com

Abstract

Automatic Speech Recognition (ASR) systems typically produce unpunctuated transcripts that have poor readability. In addition, building a punctuation restoration system is challenging for low-resource languages, especially for domain-specific applications. In this paper, we propose a Spanish punctuation restoration system designed for a real-time customer support transcription service. To address the data sparsity of Spanish transcripts in the customer support domain, we introduce two transfer-learning-based strategies: 1) domain adaptation using out-of-domain Spanish text data; 2) cross-lingual transfer learning leveraging in-domain English transcript data. Our experiment results show that these strategies improve the accuracy of the Spanish punctuation restoration system.

1 Introduction

Automatic Speech Recognition (ASR) systems play an increasingly important role in our daily lives, with a wide range of applications in different domains such as voice assistant, customer support and healthcare. However, ASR systems usually generate an unpunctuated word stream as the output. Unpunctuated speech transcripts are difficult to read and reduce overall comprehension (Jones et al., 2003) . Punctuation restoration is thus an important post-processing task on the output of ASR systems to improve general transcript readability and facilitate human comprehension.

Punctuation restoration for transcripts of Spanish-speaking customer support telephone dialogue is a non-trivial task. First, real-world human conversation transcripts have unique characteristics compared to common written text, e.g., filler words and false starts are common in spoken dialogue. Moreover, further challenges arise when addressing noisy ASR transcripts in a specific domain, as the lexical data distribution can be quite different compared to public Spanish datasets. Examples of Spanish sentences from different sources are shown below:

- **Written text in Wikipedia**: *El español o castellano es una lengua romance procedente del latín hablado, perteneciente a la familia de lenguas indoeuropeas.* (Spanish or Castilian is a Romance language derived from spoken Latin, belonging to the Indo-European language family.)
- **Written text in customer support**: *Mire, quería ver si me podían ayudar.* (Look, I wanted to see if you guys could help me)
- **Noisy ASR transcript in customer support**: *Mire, este, es que, que- quería ver si me podían ayudar.* (Look, well, so I, I wanted to see if you could help me)

Recent advances in transformer-based pre-trained models have been proven successful in many NLP tasks across different languages. For Spanish, available pre-trained resources include multilingual models such as multilingual BERT (mBERT) (Devlin et al., 2019) and XLM-RoBERTa (XLM-R) (Conneau et al., 2020), as well as monolingual models such as BETO (Cañete et al., 2020). However, large pre-trained models are trained on various written text sources such as Wikipedia and CommonCrawl (Wenzek et al., 2019), which are very distant from what we are trying to address in noisy ASR transcripts in the customer support domain. While Spanish is not usually considered a low-resource language in many NLP tasks, it is much more challenging to acquire sufficient training data in Spanish for our domain-specific task, since most of the publicly-available Spanish datasets do not come from natural human conversations, and have little coverage in the customer support domain.

In addressing the challenge of in-domain data sparsity we make the following contributions:

Proceedings of the Third Workshop on Deep Learning for Low-Resource Natural Language Processing, pages 80 - 89
July 14, 2022 ©2022 Association for Computational Linguistics

1. We propose a punctuation restoration system dedicated for Spanish based on pre-trained models, and examine the feasibility of various pre-trained models for this task.

2. We adopt a domain adaptation approach utilizing out-of-domain Spanish text data.

3. We implement a data modification strategy and match in-domain English transcripts with Spanish punctuation usage, and propose a cross-lingual transfer approach using English transcripts.

4. We demonstrate that our proposed transfer learning approaches (domain adaptation and cross-lingual transfer) can sufficiently improve the overall performance of Spanish punctuation restoration in our customer support domain, without any model-level modifications.

2 Background

Punctuation restoration is the task of inserting appropriate punctuation marks in the appropriate position on the unpunctuated text input. A variety of approaches have been used for punctuation restoration, most of which are built and evaluated on one language: English. The use of classic machine learning models such as n-gram language model (Gravano et al., 2009) and conditional random fields (Lu and Ng, 2010) are common in early studies. More recently, deep neural networks such as Long Short-Term Memory (LSTM) (Hochreiter and Schmidhuber, 1997) and transformers (Vaswani et al., 2017) have been adopted in (Tilk and Alumäe, 2015) and (Courtland et al., 2020).

Punctuation conventions differ between Spanish and English. Namely, in addition to the equivalents of English and Spanish periods, commas, terminating question marks and terminating exclamation marks, we must also account for the inverted question marks (¿) and inverted exclamation marks (¡) used to introduce these respective clauses in Spanish. There has been limited work done in Spanish punctuation restoration and in most cases Spanish is covered as part of the multilingual training. (Li and Lin, 2020) proposed a multilingual LSTM including the support for Spanish. (González-Docasal et al., 2021) uses a transformer-based model with both lexical and acoustic inputs for Spanish and Basque.

Transfer learning has been widely studied and applied in NLP applications for low-resource languages (Alyafeai et al., 2020). Domain adaptation and cross-lingual learning both fall under the category of transductive transfer learning, where source and target share the same task but labeled data is only available in source (Ruder et al., 2019). Data selection is among the data-centric methods used in domain adaptation, which aims to select the best matching data for a new domain (Ramponi and Plank, 2020). (Fu et al., 2021) uses data selection to improve English punctuation restoration with out-of-domain datasets. Recent advances in multilingual language models such as mBERT and XLM-R have shown great potential in cross-lingual zero-shot learning, wherein a multilingual model can be trained on the target task in a high-resource language, and afterwards applied to the unseen target languages by zero-shot learning (Hedderich et al., 2021). (Wu and Dredze, 2019) and (Pires et al., 2019) demonstrate the effectiveness of mBERT as a zero-shot cross-lingual transfer model in various NLP tasks, such as classification and natural language inference.

3 Methods

3.1 System Description

Pre-trained transformer-based models have been widely adopted for various NLP tasks since the introduction of BERT (Devlin et al., 2019). Publicly available pre-trained models for Spanish include the multilingual models mBERT and XLM-R and the BERT-like monolingual model BETO. In this work, we evaluate all three pre-trained models in our experiments and compare their performance in both proposed domain adaptation and cross-lingual transfer approaches.

Using pre-trained models as a starting point, we formulate the Spanish punctuation restoration problem as a sequence labeling task, where the model predicts one punctuation class for each input word token. Instead of covering all possible Spanish punctuation marks, we only include nine target punctuation classes that are commonly used and important in terms of improving transcript readability:

- OPEN_QUESTION: **¿** should be added at the start of this word token.
- CLOSE_QUESTION: **?** should be added at the end of this word token.

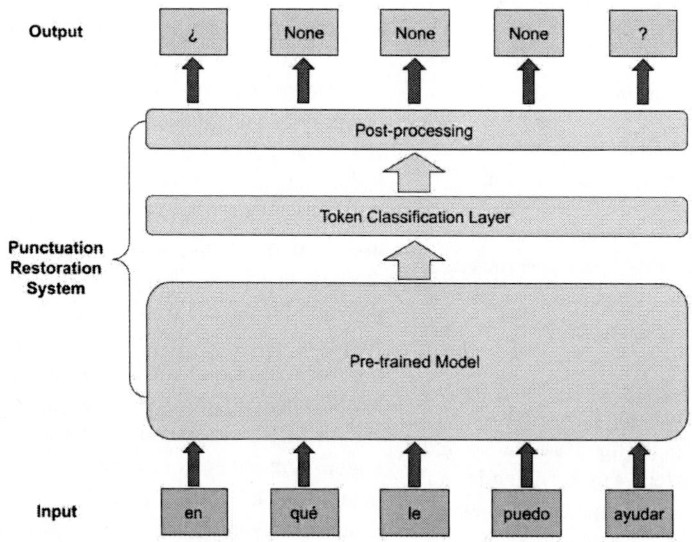

Figure 1: Our punctuation restoration system, showing the process of predicting "*en qué le puedo ayudar*" as "*¿En qué le puedo ayudar?*" (How can I help you?).

- FULL_QUESTION: **¿** and **?** should be added at the start and end of this word token respectively.
- OPEN_EXCLAMATION: **¡** should be added at the start of this word token.
- CLOSE_EXCLAMATION: **!** should be added at the end of this word token.
- FULL_EXCLAMATION: **¡** and **!** should be added at the start and end of this word token respectively.
- COMMA: **,** should be added at the end of this word token.[1]
- PERIOD: **.** should be added at the end of this word token.
- NONE: no punctuation should be associated with this word token.

The input to the Spanish punctuation restoration system is a transcribed utterance emitted by the ASR system. The ASR system outputs an utterance if an endpoint (long pause or speaker change) is detected in the audio. The length of a given utterance can vary, each utterance can contain multiple sentences, meaning that there can be multiple terminating punctuation marks – period, question mark and exclamation mark – in a single utterance.

The punctuation restoration model structure is illustrated in Figure 1. We add a token classification layer on top of the pre-trained models. Raw model prediction results are also post-processed by a set of simple heuristics to mitigate the error caused by unmatched predictions for paired punctuation marks. For instance, a predicted OPEN_QUESTION class will be changed to NONE if there is no matched CLOSE_QUESTION prediction in the same utterance. [2]

3.2 Datasets

It is essential to acquire in-domain manual transcripts that come from real customer support scenarios to build a punctuation restoration model that fits the customer support domain. However, only around 5,000 in-domain transcribed Spanish utterances from call recordings could be obtained at this early product development stage. Addition-

[1]The insertion of commas as decimal separators is not included here.

[2]This post-processing step may not always produce the correct result, but the overall prediction accuracy was improved by adding this post-processing in our experiments.

Spanish out-of-domain (LDC) examples
Ah, qué bueno, yo conozco mucho cubano pero más que todo en Filadelfia. (Ah, how good, I know many Cubans but especially in Philadelphia.)
Bueno, mira, eh, ¿sus papás, cuántos años llevan casados? (Well, look, uhm, your parents, how long have they been married?)
Spanish out-of-domain (OpenSubtitle) examples
Sé que lo que estoy pidiéndote es difícil. (I know that what I'm asking you is hard.)
Sí, da un poco de tristeza. (Yes, it makes you a little bit sad.)
Spanish in-domain examples
Buenas tardes, ¿cómo le puedo ayudar? (Good afternoon, how can I help you?)
Pues no me funciona y lo he intentado varias veces. (So, it doesn't work and I've tried several times)
English in-domain examples
I don't find this app very helpful, I'm calling to cancel my subscription.
Hi, this is Tom, how can I help you today?

Table 1: Examples of Spanish and English utterances.

ally, there are around 200,000 in-domain manually transcribed English utterances from our call center product.

We supplemented this in-domain Spanish data with the Linguistic Data Consortium (LDC) Fisher Spanish Speech and Fisher Spanish Transcripts corpora (Graff et al., 2010). These corpora consist of audio files and transcripts for approximately 163 hours of telephone conversations from native Spanish speakers. These recordings are a good match to the acoustic properties of our telephone conversations, but the transcripts, which are mostly social calls with predefined topics, do not match the domain of customer support conversations.

The Spanish portion of the OpenSubtitle corpus (Lison and Tiedemann, 2016) also contains a variety of human-to-human conversation, albeit from movies rather than from spontaneous conversational speech. Spanish OpenSubtitle offers 179 million sentences from 192,000 subtitle files, and can provide our models with good exposure to exclamation marks, which are not included in the LDC dataset. However, the movie topics are generally distant from our business-specific, customer support domain.

Some examples from both in-domain and out-of-domain data sources are illustrated in Table 1. External out-of-domain datasets usually have various Spanish punctuation marks outside our supported range as described in 3.1. After reviewing the datasets from a linguistic perspective, we first apply a set of conversion rules to those unsupported punctuation marks without affecting the readability and semantic meanings: we delete quotation marks, replace colons and semicolons with commas, and replace ellipses with periods.

3.3 Domain Adaptation

Many machine learning applications have the assumption that training and testing datasets follow the same underlying distribution. But for our target task in the customer support domain, we mostly have to rely on external data such as LDC and Spanish OpenSubtitle during the training process, due to the lack of in-domain Spanish data. This will therefore cause a mismatch between our training and testing data in terms of its distribution, and consequently, performance will drop in our target task. Therefore, to mitigate this distribution mismatch, we apply domain adaptation on external Spanish datasets from two directions: data selection and data augmentation.

3.3.1 Data Selection

As described in 3.2, Spanish OpenSubtitle has a total of over 179 million sentences, which is much larger than our other data sources. However, the vast majority of the data in the Spanish OpenSubtile corpus are fundamentally distinct from our target customer support domain, and randomly sampling from out-of-domain datasets could hurt the model performance. Thus, following the procedure in (Fu et al., 2021), we first train a 4-gram language model using our Spanish in-domain data, and then sample the 100,000 utterances from the OpenSubtitle corpus with lowest perplexity (i.e. the highest language model similarity to the in-domain data).

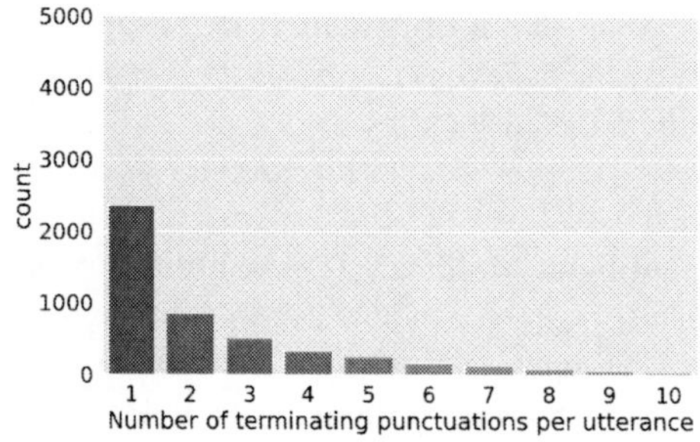

(a) in-domain

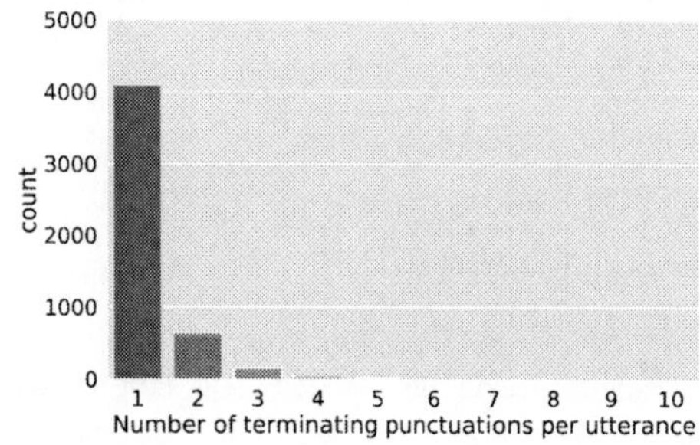

(b) LDC-before augmentation

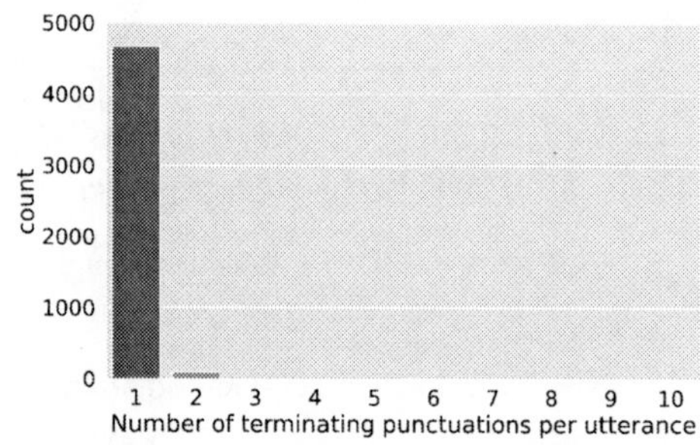

(c) OpenSubtitle-before augmentation

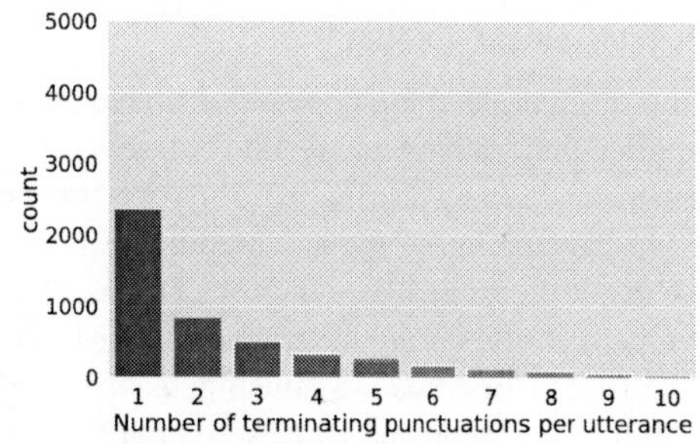

(d) LDC-after augmentation

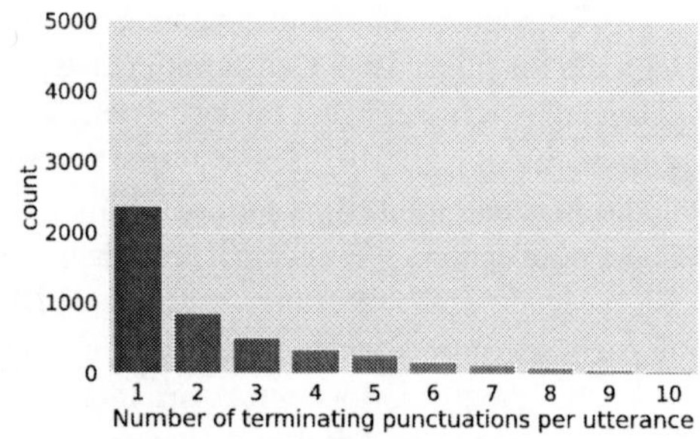

(e) OpenSubtitle-after augmentation

Figure 2: Comparison of number of terminating punctuations per utterance distribution in in-domain, LDC and OpenSubtitle datasets, before and after data augmentation.

Since the telephone conversation transcripts in the LDC corpora are closer to our target domain and there are only 130,000 utterances in this dataset, we do not perform further data selection on the LDC data for training purposes.

3.3.2 Data Augmentation

Most of the data in LDC and OpenSubtitle datasets is segmented into single sentences. However, as described in 3.1, the input to our punctuation restoration system will be composed of larger blocks of utterances rather than single sentences. To illustrate this difference, we investigate how many terminating punctuation marks occur in each input from external datasets and in-domain data, respectively.

As shown in Figure 2(a)(b)(c), our in-domain data has a much wider distribution in terms of the number of terminating punctuation marks in a single utterance. However, the majority of samples in both LDC and OpenSubtitle consist of only one sentence each. It is necessary to augment the out-of-domain datasets to cover the wider spread of distribution exhibited in our in-domain data, based on the fact that this will affect how many terminating punctuation marks the model tends to predict per input utterance. We therefore apply data augmentation by concatenating sentences in these corpora, in proportion to the spread seen in our in-domain dataset, so that the overall terminating punctuation distribution in out-of-domain datasets matches our in-domain data. As Figure 2(d)(e) shows, the

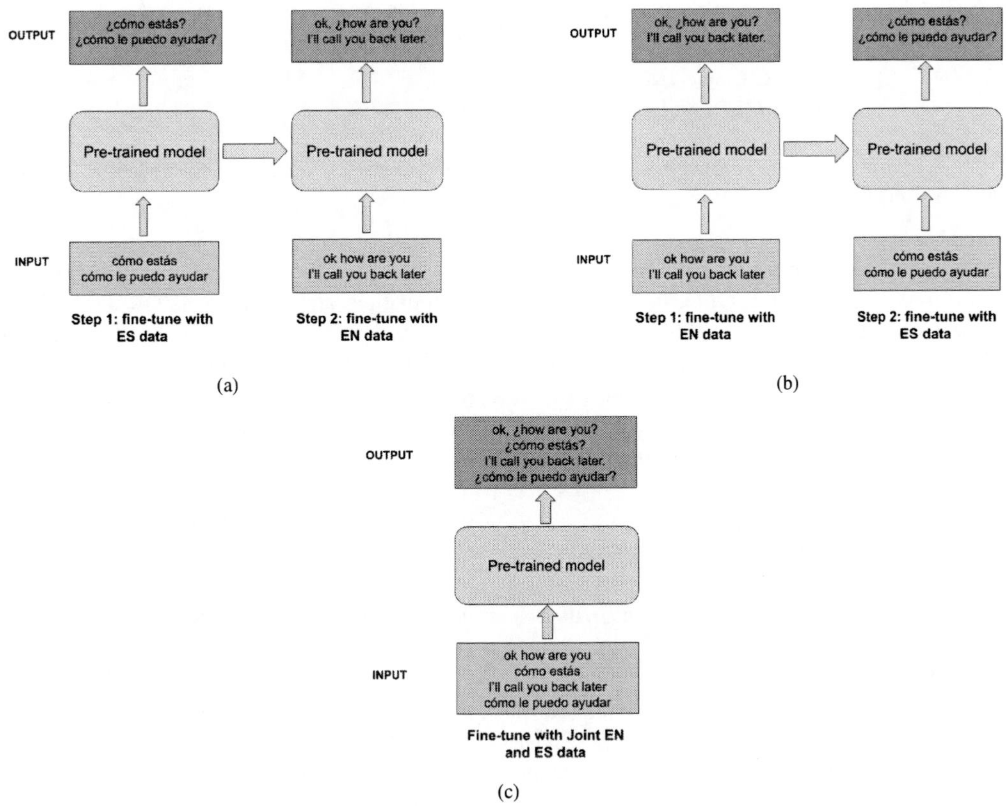

Figure 3: Diagram of three proposed fine-tuning strategies. (a) **ES->EN**, (b) **EN->ES**, (c) **Joint EN, ES**

augmented results for the LDC and OpenSubtitle corpora more closely match the distribution of our in-domain Spanish data.

3.4 Cross-lingual Transfer

Multilingual language models such as mBERT and XLM-R advanced zero-shot cross-lingual transfer learning for low-resource languages (Hedderich et al., 2021). Instead of using cross-lingual transfer as zero-shot, we utilize our English in-domain data (described in 3.2) to fine-tune multilingual pre-trained models in addition to our available Spanish datasets to improve our Spanish punctuation restoration system. However, punctuation conventions differ between languages; to better leverage cross-lingual transfer learning, we first convert the punctuation usage in the source language to appropriately match the punctuation conventions in the target language.

Since this study involves matching English punctuation to Spanish, the task is not insurmountable: most of the punctuation marks and their usages are the same across these two languages. Periods are used to terminate a declarative sentence in both languages, and the usage of commas to separate words or phrases is very similar. Therefore, no modifications are required for these two punctuation marks.

One more significant challenge for this task is the fact that question marks and exclamation marks do work somewhat differently in Spanish writing than in English. Namely, in addition to the terminating role played in both languages by standard question marks (to denote the end of an interrogative sentence) and standard exclamation marks (to denote the end of an exclamatory sentence), Spanish writing conventions also require the addition of an inverted question mark or an inverted exclamation mark, which occur at the beginning of the clause that contains the question or exclamation. For example:

- **English**: *Hi, how are you today?*
- **Spanish**: *Hola, ¿cómo estás hoy?*

For each question mark and exclamation mark in our English training data, we add an open question

Training Data	BETO	mBERT	XLM-R
LDC	51.3%	50.2%	51.8%
LDC + Selected OpenSubtitle	52.1%	51.5%	53.2%
Augmented (LDC + Selected OpenSubtitle)	**53.7%**	**52.1%**	**54.7%**

Table 2: F1 score performance comparison using the LDC and OpenSubtitle datasets, before and after our domain adaptation approaches.

mark or exclamation mark, respectively, at the start of the word chunk that the terminating question or exclamation mark is in.

For example, consider the following English utterance:

"OK, how can I help you?"

For cross-lingual transfer training, it will be modified to:

"OK, ¿how can I help you?"

By doing this conversion, the model will learn to predict punctuation as it should occur in Spanish contexts during the fine-tuning phase, even though what it actually sees are English utterances with Spanish punctuation.

To determine the best way to transfer the in-domain distribution from English (**EN**) to Spanish (**ES**) in the punctuation restoration task, we investigate three fine-tuning strategies for cross-lingual transfer learning:

1. Fine-tune the pre-trained models in two steps, Spanish first then English. Noted as **"ES->EN"**.

2. Fine-tune the pre-trained models in two steps, English first then Spanish. Noted as **"EN->ES"**.

3. Fine-tune the pre-trained models in one step, with joint English and Spanish data. Noted as **"Joint EN, ES"**

Diagrams of three fine-tuning strategies are illustrated in Figure 3. Note that our objective is to build a model for Spanish, but it is still worth experimenting with **"ES->EN"** setting to establish the impact of more in-domain data albeit in a different language.

4 Evaluation

4.1 Evaluation Setup

We evaluate our proposed transfer learning approaches using the datasets described in 3.2. Using the model architecture shown in Figure 1, we fine-tune pre-trained models using various data combinations and fine-tuning strategies to demonstrate the effectiveness of our proposed approaches. Pre-trained models including both monolingual (BETO) and multilingual (MBERT and XLM-R) are explored and evaluated.

The Spanish punctuation restoration system is intended to operate in real-time so that customer-support agents can review prior information communicated by a customer and to provide the input to product features such as automatically retrieving information to assist the agent. As shown in (Fu et al., 2021), reducing the number of layers from deep pre-trained models does not significantly impact accuracy for the punctuation restoration task. To reduce the computation time during inference, we take only the first six layers from the pre-trained models as our starting point.

To evaluate the model accuracy in our target customer support domain, we split our in-domain Spanish manual transcripts into three parts: the training set (60%), the validation set (10%) and the test set (30%). The Spanish in-domain training set is over-sampled to make the size comparable to the other datasets. The performance of every model is evaluated on the in-domain test set after being fine-tuned on various combinations of training sources and processes.

4.2 Performance with Domain Adaptation

We evaluate the F1 score performance before and after the domain adaptation approaches proposed in 3.3. Pre-trained models are fine-tuned using the combinations of LDC and selected OpenSubtitle datasets only, and then evaluated on our in-domain test set. The results are shown in Table 2. Both data selection and data augmentation improve the overall F1 score performance for all three pre-trained models, which demonstrates the effectiveness of our domain adaptation approaches for the Spanish punctuation restoration task. Among three different models, XLM-R shows the best performance under this setup, and outperforms the monolingual BETO model after domain adaptation.

Training data and strategy	BETO	mBERT	XLM-R
ES only (no cross-lingual transfer)	62.8%	61.5%	62.9%
ES->EN	N/A	59.1%	60.7%
EN->ES	N/A	62.0%	63.5%
Joint EN,ES	N/A	62.4%	**64.4%**

Table 3: F1 score performance comparison with and without cross-lingual transfer. ***ES***: the combination of Spanish datasets including (1) Augmented (LDC + Selected OpenSubtitle) as described in Table 2; (2) Spanish in-domain transcripts. ***EN***: English in-domain transcripts.

Gold \ Prediction	CLOSE_QUESTION	PERIOD
CLOSE_QUESTION	223	106
PERIOD	37	2177

Table 4: Confusion matrix of CLOSE_QUESTION and PERIOD on test set, using best performing XLM-R in 4.3

4.3 Performance with Cross-lingual transfer

To understand the effect of cross-lingual transfer, we use all the available data sources described in 3.2. We separate the Spanish datasets (LDC, selected OpenSubtitle and Spanish in-domain transcripts) from the English one (English in-domain transcripts), and fine-tune the pre-trained models using three different strategies described in 3.4 (“**ES->EN**”, “**EN->ES**” and “**Joint EN, ES**”) as shown in Figure 3.

Table 3 shows our results on cross-lingual transfer learning: multilingual models (mBERT and XLM-R) both show performance gain with “**Joint EN, ES**” and “**EN->ES**” training. However, “**ES->EN**” training actually results in lower accuracy than models trained without cross-lingual transfer. As for the comparison with the monolingual model (BETO) which is not feasible for the direct cross-lingual transfer, XLM-R produces similar results as BETO without cross-lingual transfer, but XLM-R outperforms BETO by 1.5% F1 score after joint training with both Spanish and English datasets. mBERT becomes comparable to BETO after cross-lingual transfer as well.

5 Future Work

When analysing the prediction errors, we found that many CLOSE_QUESTION classes are predicted as PERIOD by the model, as shown in Table 4. This is a common behavior across all three pre-trained models, and is possibly due to the linguistic properties of Spanish. Because Spanish clauses do not require an overt subject noun phrase, and because Spanish has considerable variability in constituent order, it is often the case that there is no structural indication of whether an utterance should be interpreted as a declarative or as a question. Instead, intonation is used to make this distinction. For example, "*hablan español*" ("they speak Spanish" or "do they speak Spanish") becomes a question with rising intonation. Future work in this area might focus on incorporating such acoustic information into punctuation restoration tasks.

6 Conclusion

For this study, we trained and tested a Spanish punctuation restoration system for the customer support domain based on pre-trained transformer models. To address in-domain data sparsity in Spanish, transfer learning approaches were applied in two directions: domain adaptation and cross-lingual transfer. We explored and fine-tuned three different pre-trained models with our transfer learning approaches for this task; our results demonstrate that the domain adaptation method improves the accuracy of all three pre-trained models. Cross-lingual transfer with joint training of English and Spanish datasets improves the performance of both multilingual pre-trained models. XLM-R substantially outperforms the monolingual BETO after cross-lingual transfer and achieves the best F1 score in our Spanish punctuation restoration task.

References

Zaid Alyafeai, Maged Saeed AlShaibani, and Irfan Ahmad. 2020. A survey on transfer learning in natural language processing. *CoRR*, abs/2007.04239.

José Cañete, Gabriel Chaperon, Rodrigo Fuentes, Jou-

Hui Ho, Hojin Kang, and Jorge Pérez. 2020. Spanish pre-trained bert model and evaluation data. In *PML4DC at ICLR 2020*.

Alexis Conneau, Kartikay Khandelwal, Naman Goyal, Vishrav Chaudhary, Guillaume Wenzek, Francisco Guzmán, Edouard Grave, Myle Ott, Luke Zettlemoyer, and Veselin Stoyanov. 2020. Unsupervised cross-lingual representation learning at scale. In *Proceedings of the 58th Annual Meeting of the Association for Computational Linguistics*, pages 8440–8451, Online. Association for Computational Linguistics.

Maury Courtland, Adam Faulkner, and Gayle McElvain. 2020. Efficient automatic punctuation restoration using bidirectional transformers with robust inference. In *Proceedings of the 17th International Conference on Spoken Language Translation*, pages 272–279, Online. Association for Computational Linguistics.

Jacob Devlin, Ming-Wei Chang, Kenton Lee, and Kristina Toutanova. 2019. BERT: Pre-training of deep bidirectional transformers for language understanding. In *Proceedings of the 2019 Conference of the North American Chapter of the Association for Computational Linguistics: Human Language Technologies, Volume 1 (Long and Short Papers)*, pages 4171–4186, Minneapolis, Minnesota. Association for Computational Linguistics.

Xue-Yong Fu, Cheng Chen, Md Tahmid Rahman Laskar, Shashi Bhushan, and Simon Corston-Oliver. 2021. Improving punctuation restoration for speech transcripts via external data. In *Proceedings of the Seventh Workshop on Noisy User-generated Text (W-NUT 2021)*, pages 168–174, Online. Association for Computational Linguistics.

Ander González-Docasal, Aitor García-Pablos, Haritz Arzelus, and Aitor Álvarez. 2021. Autopunct: A bert-based automatic punctuation and capitalisation system for spanish and basque. *Procesamiento del Lenguaje Natural*, 67(0):59–68.

David Graff, Shudong Huang, Ingrid Cartagena, Kevin Walker, and Christopher Cieri. 2010. Fisher spanish - transcripts ldc2010t04.

Agustin Gravano, Martin Jansche, and Michiel Bacchiani. 2009. Restoring punctuation and capitalization in transcribed speech. In *2009 IEEE International Conference on Acoustics, Speech and Signal Processing*, pages 4741–4744.

Michael A. Hedderich, Lukas Lange, Heike Adel, Jannik Strötgen, and Dietrich Klakow. 2021. A survey on recent approaches for natural language processing in low-resource scenarios. In *Proceedings of the 2021 Conference of the North American Chapter of the Association for Computational Linguistics: Human Language Technologies*, pages 2545–2568, Online. Association for Computational Linguistics.

Sepp Hochreiter and Jürgen Schmidhuber. 1997. Long short-term memory. *Neural Computation*, 9(8):1735–1780.

Douglas Jones, Florian Wolf, Edward Gibson, Elliott Williams, Evelina Fedorenko, Douglas Reynolds, and Marc Zissman. 2003. Measuring the readability of automatic speech-to-text transcripts.

Xinxing Li and Edward Lin. 2020. A 43 Language Multilingual Punctuation Prediction Neural Network Model. In *Proc. Interspeech 2020*, pages 1067–1071.

Pierre Lison and Jörg Tiedemann. 2016. OpenSubtitles2016: Extracting large parallel corpora from movie and TV subtitles. In *Proceedings of the Tenth International Conference on Language Resources and Evaluation (LREC'16)*, pages 923–929, Portorož, Slovenia. European Language Resources Association (ELRA).

Wei Lu and Hwee Tou Ng. 2010. Better punctuation prediction with dynamic conditional random fields. In *Proceedings of the 2010 Conference on Empirical Methods in Natural Language Processing*, pages 177–186, Cambridge, MA. Association for Computational Linguistics.

Telmo Pires, Eva Schlinger, and Dan Garrette. 2019. How multilingual is multilingual BERT? In *Proceedings of the 57th Annual Meeting of the Association for Computational Linguistics*, pages 4996–5001, Florence, Italy. Association for Computational Linguistics.

Alan Ramponi and Barbara Plank. 2020. Neural unsupervised domain adaptation in NLP—A survey. In *Proceedings of the 28th International Conference on Computational Linguistics*, pages 6838–6855, Barcelona, Spain (Online). International Committee on Computational Linguistics.

Sebastian Ruder, Anders Søgaard, and Ivan Vulić. 2019. Unsupervised cross-lingual representation learning. In *Proceedings of ACL 2019, Tutorial Abstracts*, pages 31–38.

Ottokar Tilk and Tanel Alumäe. 2015. LSTM for punctuation restoration in speech transcripts. In *Proc. Interspeech 2015*, pages 683–687.

Ashish Vaswani, Noam Shazeer, Niki Parmar, Jakob Uszkoreit, Llion Jones, Aidan N Gomez, Ł ukasz Kaiser, and Illia Polosukhin. 2017. Attention is all you need. In *Advances in Neural Information Processing Systems*, volume 30. Curran Associates, Inc.

Guillaume Wenzek, Marie-Anne Lachaux, Alexis Conneau, Vishrav Chaudhary, Francisco Guzmán, Armand Joulin, and Edouard Grave. 2019. CCNet: Extracting high quality monolingual datasets from web crawl data. *CoRR*.

Shijie Wu and Mark Dredze. 2019. Beto, bentz, becas: The surprising cross-lingual effectiveness of BERT. In *Proceedings of the 2019 Conference on Empirical*

Methods in Natural Language Processing and the 9th International Joint Conference on Natural Language Processing (EMNLP-IJCNLP), pages 833–844, Hong Kong, China. Association for Computational Linguistics.

Pre-training Data Quality and Quantity for a Low-Resource Language: New Corpus and BERT Models for Maltese

Kurt Micallef[1] kurt.micallef@um.edu.mt
Albert Gatt[2,3] a.gatt@uu.nl
Marc Tanti[3] marc.tanti@um.edu.mt
Lonneke van der Plas[4,3] lonneke.vanderplas@idiap.ch
Claudia Borg[1] claudia.borg@um.edu.mt

[1]Department of Artificial Intelligence, University of Malta
[2]Information and Computing Sciences, Utrecht University
[3]Institute of Linguistics and Language Technology, University of Malta
[4]Idiap Research Institute

Abstract

Multilingual language models such as mBERT have seen impressive cross-lingual transfer to a variety of languages, but many languages remain excluded from these models. In this paper, we analyse the effect of pre-training with monolingual data for a low-resource language that is not included in mBERT – Maltese – with a range of pre-training set ups. We conduct evaluations with the newly pre-trained models on three morphosyntactic tasks – dependency parsing, part-of-speech tagging, and named-entity recognition – and one semantic classification task – sentiment analysis. We also present a newly created corpus for Maltese, and determine the effect that the pre-training data size and domain have on the downstream performance. Our results show that using a mixture of pre-training domains is often superior to using Wikipedia text only. We also find that a fraction of this corpus is enough to make significant leaps in performance over Wikipedia-trained models. We pre-train and compare two models on the new corpus: a monolingual BERT model trained from scratch (BERTu), and a further pre-trained multilingual BERT (mBERTu). The models achieve state-of-the-art performance on these tasks, despite the new corpus being considerably smaller than typically used corpora for high-resourced languages. On average, BERTu outperforms or performs competitively with mBERTu, and the largest gains are observed for higher-level tasks.

1 Introduction

Language Models have become a core component in many Natural Language Processing (NLP) tasks. These models are typically pre-trained on unlabelled texts, and then further fine-tuned using labelled data relevant to the target task. Transformer-based (Vaswani et al., 2017) contextual models such as BERT (Devlin et al., 2019) have gained success since the fine-tuning step is relatively inexpensive, while attaining state-of-the-art results in various syntactic and semantic tasks.

While the bulk of work with the BERT family of models focuses on English, there have been some monolingual models developed for other languages as well (Martin et al., 2020; Polignano et al., 2019; Antoun et al., 2020; de Vries et al., 2019; Virtanen et al., 2019; Agerri et al., 2020; inter alia). These monolingual models have been trained on large volumes of data, typically amounting to billions of tokens. In contrast, it is challenging to find publicly available corpora of this size for low-resource languages. The evaluation benchmarks for downstream tasks on these languages are also limited, and tend to be dominated by low-level structural tagging tasks.

To counteract the lack of large volumes of monolingual corpora for low-resource languages, a number of multilingual models have been released, such as mBERT (Devlin et al., 2019) and XLM-R (Conneau et al., 2020). These multilingual models were pre-trained on more than one language at a time by combining corpora from different languages, usually sourced from Wikipedia. Several works have demonstrated the efficacy of these multilingual models, especially for languages without a language-specific model (Kondratyuk and Straka, 2019; Wu and Dredze, 2019). Benchmark results have improved for many languages by leveraging cross-linguistic features learnt by these multilingual models (Conneau et al., 2020).

However, the gains with multilingual models may vary depending on the language being considered. The "curse of multilinguality" limits the language-specific features that these models can learn, since the limited model capacity has to be

Proceedings of the Third Workshop on Deep Learning for Low-Resource Natural Language Processing, pages 90 - 101
July 14, 2022 ©2022 Association for Computational Linguistics

shared between multiple languages (Conneau et al., 2020). Models such as mBERT use WordPiece tokenisation (Johnson et al., 2017), which splits words into various sub-tokens, thereby reducing the number of unknown tokens. However, the vocabulary representations for multilingual models tend to be sub-optimal for specific languages, because words tend to be split into a higher number of sub-tokens (Rust et al., 2021). Moreover, these models may still be biased in favour of over-representing sub-tokens common to a certain subset of languages over others. Due to the data imbalance across languages, lower-resourced languages tend to be disadvantaged, as there is relatively less pre-training data available compared to the other languages considered in the multilingual model (Wu and Dredze, 2020).

Apart from the tension between languages in a multilingual model, other factors are at play as well. Most prominently, many languages are never seen by these multilingual models (Muller et al., 2021), since these are typically trained on the largest-available corpora (e.g. mBERT was pre-trained on the 104 languages with the greatest Wikipedia presence). Such criteria exclude many of the world's languages, including Maltese, the focus of this paper. This issue is exacerbated even further when the language uses a script which is either different to its closely related languages (Muller et al., 2021), or which is never seen during pre-training, thereby encoding most of the input with out-of-vocabulary tokens (Pfeiffer et al., 2021). In fact, Muller et al. (2021) show that the language transfer capability of a multilingual model to an unseen language is dependent on the degree to which the target language is related to languages already included in the multilingual model.

In this work we focus on the Maltese language, an official EU language spoken primarily in Malta and in some small communities around the world (Brincat, 2011). It is the only Semitic language written exclusively with a Latin script, containing a few additional characters with diacritic marks (ċ, ġ, ħ, ż). The language also has strong influences from Romance languages such as Italian, as well as English. The Semitic influence is largely exhibited in the grammatical structure through complex morphological characteristics, whilst the non-Semitic aspect is predominantly observed in its vocabulary, with extensive lexical borrowing from Italian and English.

In the context of NLP, Maltese is a low-resource language (Rosner and Borg, 2022) and is not part of the languages covered by either mBERT or XLM-R. Muller et al. (2021) find that mBERT underperforms non-contextual baselines on Maltese, but benefits when pre-trained further on raw Maltese data. Similarly, Chau et al. (2020) further pre-train mBERT but impute the 99 unused tokens present in the model with language specific tokens, yielding better results. This confirms previous findings by Wang et al. (2020), who also extend mBERT's vocabulary to accommodate unseen languages, but do so by extending the vocabulary and model dimensionality, hence increasing its footprint.

Motivated by the limitations of existing multilingual models and the deficiency of publicly available corpora for Maltese, we set out to pre-train a new monolingual language model for Maltese and compare it to the alternative strategy of further pre-training an existing multilingual model. We study, in particular, the impact that the pre-training data size and domain has on the performance in downstream tasks. The main contributions of this work are as follows:

1. We develop a new corpus of Maltese text.
2. Using this new data, language models for Maltese are pre-trained.
3. We compare the newly pre-trained models and find that both models improve the state-of-the-art on three structural tagging tasks – dependency parsing, part-of-speech tagging, and named-entity recognition – and one semantic classification task – sentiment analysis.
4. We demonstrate that in a low-resource setting, pre-training using text from varied domains is often superior to solely using Wikipedia, and that matching the domain to target task is beneficial when this is available.
5. We also provide an analysis on the effects of the pre-training size, shedding new light on how much pre-training data is needed to attain significant improvements in performance.

We make this new corpus, the newly pre-trained language models, and the code publicly available[1].

[1]The corpus and the language models are available at the Hugging Face Hub at `https://huggingface.co/datasets/MLRS/korpus_malti`, `https://huggingface.co/MLRS/BERTu`, and `https://huggingface.co/MLRS/mBERTu`. The code is available at `https://github.com/MLRS/BERTu`.

2 Corpus

In this work, we build a new unlabelled text corpus, which we call the **Korpus Malti v4.0 (KM)**. This builds on and extends an existing corpus, Korpus Malti v3.0[2], which is approximately half the size.

Rather than scraping the web randomly for Maltese text, we collect text data from specific sources, including both online and offline. Although this does incur additional effort in data collection, and results in a smaller dataset compared to large-scale web-scraping initiatives, it has the benefit of resulting in a less noisy dataset, while offering greater control over sources. For comparison, the Maltese portion of the OSCAR data (Ortiz Suárez et al., 2019), which is sourced entirely from the web, contains texts which, to a native speaker, suggest that they are automatically generated through the use of a low-quality machine translation system, a common pitfall of web-scraping for low-resource languages (Kreutzer et al., 2022). We also expect to find a small proportion of code-switched texts, as this is a pre-dominant phenomenon for Maltese in domains such as social media or transcribed speech. In addition, the data is separated into different domains, and the source for each document is available as part of the metadata. This allows data users to select data subsets which are more appropriate for their particular use-case, such as domain-adaptive pre-training (Lee et al., 2019; Gururangan et al., 2020; inter alia), whilst enabling tracing back to the original source, or omission in case unforeseen ethical or privacy issues come to light. In short, the goal was to build a good quality training dataset, while avoiding at least some of the pitfalls identified with opportunistic, web-scale data initiatives (Bender et al., 2021; Rogers, 2021).

Data is collected from a variety of sources, including online news sources, legal texts, transcripts of speeches and debates, blogs, Wikipedia, etc. Before texts are included in the corpus, we filter non-Maltese sentences using language identification using LiD (Lui and Baldwin, 2014), and perform de-duplication using Onion (Pomikálek, 2011).

The resulting data, split into 19 different domains, is summarised by Table 1.

To the best of our knowledge, there is no corpus of this size available for Maltese. We also note that this data is a significant increase over Wikipedia data, which is what is usually available and used in low-resource scenarios. The Wikipedia data makes up less than 1% of the entire corpus in terms of both tokens and sentences.

Despite this substantial increase in data, we emphasise that a corpus of under 500M tokens is still substantially smaller than is typically used for higher-resourced languages. For example, Devlin et al. (2019) pre-train BERT using a combined corpus of 3.3B words for English (approximately 16GB). Larger models have since exceeded these pre-training sizes by a wide margin – for example, RoBERTa is pre-trained on 161GB of text (Liu et al., 2019). Monolingual models for languages other than English, typically use smaller corpora than English models, but their size is still significantly larger than ours – for example AraBERT was pre-trained on a corpus of 24GB (Antoun et al., 2020) and BERTje was pre-trained on a corpus of 12GB (de Vries et al., 2019).

3 Language Models

Using this new corpus, two new language models are pre-trained for Maltese: a monolingual model (**BERTu**) and a multilingual model (**mBERTu**). In both cases, pre-training is performed using the Masked Language Modelling Objective (MLM) only, since the Next Sentence Prediction (NSP) objective was found to be detrimental to downstream performance (Joshi et al., 2020; Liu et al., 2019). Other than that, pre-training largely follows the pre-training setup of BERT (Devlin et al., 2019). This allows for a better comparison with already available models. The pre-training data from all domains is combined, shuffled, and split into 85% and 15% for training and validation sets respectively.

BERTu We pre-train a monolingual BERT model from scratch on the new unlabelled data, using the $\text{BERT}_{\text{BASE}}$ architecture with 12 transformer layers, a hidden size of 768, and 12 attention heads. The vocabulary is initialised with 52K tokens. Pre-training is done across 1M steps, with a sequence length of 128 for the first 90% of the steps and a sequence length of 512 for the remaining 10% steps. A batch size of 512 is used, which amounts to approximately 30 epochs in total, and a warmup of 1% of the total number of steps. We use mixed-precision training to ease memory requirements. Training was performed on 8 A100 GPUs for the first 90% steps and 16 A100 GPUs for the remaining 10% steps, taking approximately 53 hours.

[2]See: `https://mlrs.research.um.edu.mt`

data subset	documents	sentences	tokens	size
belles_lettres	195	299 762	4 454 906	21.82MB
blogs	25 436	807 628	14 562 039	74.45MB
comics	62	2 413	44 768	233.22KB
court	2 663	694 227	11 881 638	61.91MB
eu_docs	2 974	5 099 564	135 811 945	773.25MB
government_gazette	2 974	1 881 034	39 771 556	203.61MB
gov_docs	272	120 209	1 900 842	10.79MB
law_eu	71	4 433 235	98 582 031	541.13MB
law_mt	2 596	401 118	7 631 651	38.84MB
legal	3	4 784	83 581	490.67MB
nonfiction	2 177	208 763	3 902 436	20.01MB
parliament	6 198	3 935 906	82 294 520	433.09MB
press_eu	5 483	413 317	9 774 919	55.73MB
press_mt	46 782	713 886	17 679 904	93.15MB
speeches	62	2 067	51 259	286.63MB
theses	19	11 545	310 243	1.63MB
umlib_oar	11 688	963 606	21 235 949	106.11MB
web_general	2	685 873	14 741 525	75.22MB
wiki	3 469	79 134	1 885 661	9.73MB
all	131 429	20 758 071	466 601 373	2.52GB

Table 1: Korpus Malti v4.0 corpus distribution. *belles_lettres* is largely composed of literary works; the *government_gazzette* consists of text from the official newsletter of the Maltese government; *umlib_oar* is a miscellaneous collection of previously published non-fiction texts, available in the public domain via the University of Malta Library Open Access Repository.

mBERTu Similar to Chau et al. (2020) and Muller et al. (2021) we also pre-train mBERT further on Maltese. Since the embedding weights are not randomly initialised, as is the case for the monolingual model, we follow Rust et al. (2021) and pre-train for 250K steps. A sequence length of 512 is used throughout, keeping the rest of the hyper-parameters the same as the monolingual pre-training. To better fit the Maltese language, the mBERT vocabulary is augmented with Maltese tokens following the procedure from Chau et al. (2020), by replacing the unused tokens reserved in the original vocabulary. Specifically, we train a tokeniser with a vocabulary size of 5 000 tokens on the data and choose the set of 99 tokens which reduce the number of `[UNK]` tokens the most in the target data. Training was performed on 32 A100 GPUs, and took around 46 hours to complete.

4 Evaluation

An evaluation for the language models described in Section 3 is presented here. **mBERT** without any additional pre-training is used as one of the baselines. In addition, we pre-train two language models on the Maltese Wikipedia data as additional baselines. This allows us to analyse the limitations that could be faced when following the common practice of using Wikipedia data, for the specific case of low-resource languages with a comparatively small Wikipedia footprint.

Following the same setup of the main models, a monolingual model (**BERTu Wiki**) and a multilingual model (**mBERTu Wiki**) are pre-trained. The same hyper-parameters described in Section 3 are used, but the batch size and number of steps are decreased to prevent overfitting due to the smaller data size. To this end, the batch size is set to 64 and the total number of steps set to 30 500 and 7 600 steps for the monolingual and multilingual models, respectively. This was deemed appropriate since it would amount to the same number of epochs as the models pre-trained on the entire corpus.

4.1 Tasks

The language models are fine-tuned on the following downstream tasks. A summary of the datasets and fine-tuning architectures used is given below.

Dependency Parsing (DP) The Maltese Universal Dependencies Treebank (MUDT) (Čéplö, 2018) is used for this task using the provided training, validation, and testing splits. The data is composed of 2 074 human-annotated sentences from 4 different high-level domains. Similar to Chau et al. (2020), Muller et al. (2021), and Chau and Smith (2021), we use a Biaffine graph-based prediction layer (Dozat and Manning, 2017) and use the Labelled Attachment Score (LAS) as the main evaluation metric, but also report the Unlabelled Attachment Score (UAS).

Part-of-Speech Tagging (POS) The MLRS POS data (Gatt and Čéplö, 2013), is used for this task. This data is composed of 6 167 human-annotated sentences – 426 of which overlap with the MUDT data (Čéplö, 2018) – and are stratified into 8 domains. We combine the data from the different domains, shuffle it, and split the data into 80%, 10%, and 10% for training, validation, and testing sets, respectively. The annotations are language-specific tags (using the XPOS scheme) and we follow the tag mapping in MUDT (Čéplö, 2018) to also produce tags in the Universal Part of Speech tagset (UPOS). To evaluate tagging with these two tagsets, we use a linear layer, and use accuracy as the evaluation metric.

Named-Entity Recognition (NER) The Maltese annotations for the WikiAnn data (Pan et al., 2017) are used for this task, using the data splits from Rahimi et al. (2019). The data is made up of 300 sentences derived from Wikipedia. Following Chau and Smith (2021), a Conditional Random Field layer is used for this task, and we use F1 as the evaluation metric.

Sentiment Analysis (SA) We use the Maltese sentiment analysis dataset by Martínez-García et al. (2021), which is a collection of 815 sentences, using the provided training, validation, and testing splits. The texts in this data originate from comments on news articles and social media posts, and are a combination of two datasets from Cortis and Davis (2019) and Dingli and Sant (2016). A linear prediction layer is used, and we use the macro-averaged F1 score as the evaluation metric.

We largely use the hyper-parameters from Chau and Smith (2021), but optimise the learning rate, batch size, and dropout on the validation set of each task. Table 2 shows the chosen hyper-parameters. Fine-tuning is performed for at most 200 epochs, with an early stopping of 20 epochs on the validation set.

Name	DP	POS	NER	SA
Learning Rate	5e-4	5e-4	5e-4	1e-4
Batch Size	128	128	64	32
Dropout	0.3	0.3	0.2	0.5

Table 2: Fine-tuning hyper-parameters

4.2 Results

The results on all tasks are summarised in Table 3. Consistent with the results reported by Muller et al. (2021) and Chau and Smith (2021), BERTu Wiki generally underperforms mBERT, and mBERTu Wiki performs better than mBERT. Whilst they show this for Dependency Parsing, Part-of-Speech tagging, and Named Entity Recognition, we demonstrate that this also holds for Sentiment Analysis.

Our baseline results diverge slightly from previous results on the Named-Entity Recognition task, where BERTu Wiki performs slightly better than mBERT. We suspect that this is due to a slightly different pre-training setup than that used by Muller et al. (2021) and Chau and Smith (2021)[3], but we analyse this further in Section 5.1. However, these results remain consistent with regards to BERTu Wiki not performing as well as mBERTu Wiki.

Both language models pre-trained with the KM data perform significantly better than all the other baselines, on all tasks except for Named-Entity Recognition, where the trend is similar, but does not reach statistical significance. This underlines the value of this new corpus. When compared to the Wikipedia language models, the most noticeable improvements can be seen between the BERTu models, across all tasks. A more detailed analysis on this is presented in Section 5.2, but intuitively this finding makes sense since mBERTu models are exposed to significantly more data, making them less specific to Maltese.

The gap in performance between the BERTu and mBERTu models is much less for the KM pre-trained models than it is for the Wikipedia pre-trained models. In fact, on average, the BERTu KM model performs better than the mBERTu KM model on all tasks except Part-of-Speech tagging.

[3]Muller et al. (2021) pre-train for at most 10 epochs whilst Chau and Smith (2021) pre-train for at most 20 epochs (choosing the best performing model on based on the validation set). Both use a smaller-sized BERT architecture with 6 layers and pre-train with a maximum sequence length of 128.

Data	Model	UAS	LAS
Wiki	BERTu	80.95 ± 0.25	74.16 ± 0.20
	mBERTu	88.74 ± 0.11	82.59 ± 0.19
N/A	mBERT	84.83 ± 0.31	77.22 ± 0.34
KM	BERTu	**92.31 ± 0.15**	**88.14 ± 0.21**
	mBERTu	*92.10 ± 0.14	*87.87 ± 0.18

(a) Dependency Parsing

Data	Model	span F1
Wiki	BERTu	67.96 ± 2.20
	mBERTu	*85.01 ± 2.92
N/A	mBERT	65.41 ± 2.06
KM	BERTu	**86.77 ± 3.55**
	mBERTu	*86.60 ± 2.49

(b) Named Entity Recognition

Data	Model	UPOS	XPOS
Wiki	BERTu	97.27 ± 0.11	97.01 ± 0.07
	mBERTu	97.95 ± 0.13	97.83 ± 0.08
N/A	mBERT	97.26 ± 0.15	97.20 ± 0.14
KM	BERTu	98.58 ± 0.02	*98.54 ± 0.03
	mBERTu	**98.66 ± 0.03**	**98.58 ± 0.04**

(c) Part-of-Speech tagging

Data	Model	macro-F1
Wiki	BERTu	53.95 ± 2.70
	mBERTu	56.05 ± 3.24
N/A	mBERT	55.99 ± 3.63
KM	BERTu	**78.96 ± 1.95**
	mBERTu	*76.79 ± 1.79

(d) Sentiment Analysis

Table 3: Experimental results, grouped by the underlying language model and additional pre-training data used. All figures shown are the mean and standard deviations over 5 runs with different random seeds. The best performing models for each metric are **bolded**. Values marked with * are not found to be significantly worse than the best model (using a 1-tailed t-test with a p-value = 0.05 with Bonferroni correction).

For Part-of-Speech tagging we also note that the baseline results are already quite high, probably due to the relatively larger labelled data, which may partially mask the effects of the KM models.

Overall, Sentiment Analysis is the task where the most gains are made with respect to the baselines. The KM-trained models are over 20 F1 points higher than the best performing baseline. This finding provides evidence that, unlike syntactic tasks, where structural information could potentially be shared across related clusters of languages, semantic tasks such as Sentiment Analysis will benefit much more from language-specific embeddings.

5 Analysis

In this section we build on the results presented in Section 4.2, and analyse the effect that the pre-training data has on performance on the downstream tasks.

5.1 Data Domain

In this subsection we take advantage of the fact that the data is stratified by domains. Here, we analyse the impact of pre-training using data from different domains, compared to a single domain, namely Wikipedia, which is commonly used in multilingual models and low-resource settings. For this purpose, we consider the BERTu Wiki and mBERTu Wiki baselines from Section 4 as single-domain models. We compare them to language models pre-trained with the same amount of data but from different domains, which are referred to as “Mixed” in this discussion.

We determine the size using the number of sentences, since this would directly effect the number of epochs and allows us to keep an identical pre-training setup as the Wikipedia-trained models. Since the Maltese Wikipedia data is composed of 79 134 sentences, the Mixed language models are also pre-trained with the same amount of sentences, split into training and validation sets as the Wikipedia models. A comparison of the downstream task performance for these language models is plotted in Figure 1.

At this small scale of data, both Wiki and Mixed mBERTu models consistently perform better than the mBERT models, owing to the multilingual representation power of these models. The Mixed models perform better than their Wikipedia counterparts on Part-of-Speech tagging and Sentiment Analysis. On Dependency Parsing, there is a slight improvement on the mBERTu model but a slight degradation on the BERTu model.

For Named-Entity Recognition, the Wikipedia models perform better than the Mixed ones. Since the dataset for this task originates from Wikipedia as well, this indicates that matching the pre-training data domain to the target domain boosts performance, supporting the findings by Gururangan et al. (2020). In fact, mBERTu Wiki surpasses mBERT, and proves to be a competitive baseline, as shown in Table 3b. On the other hand, mBERTu Mixed

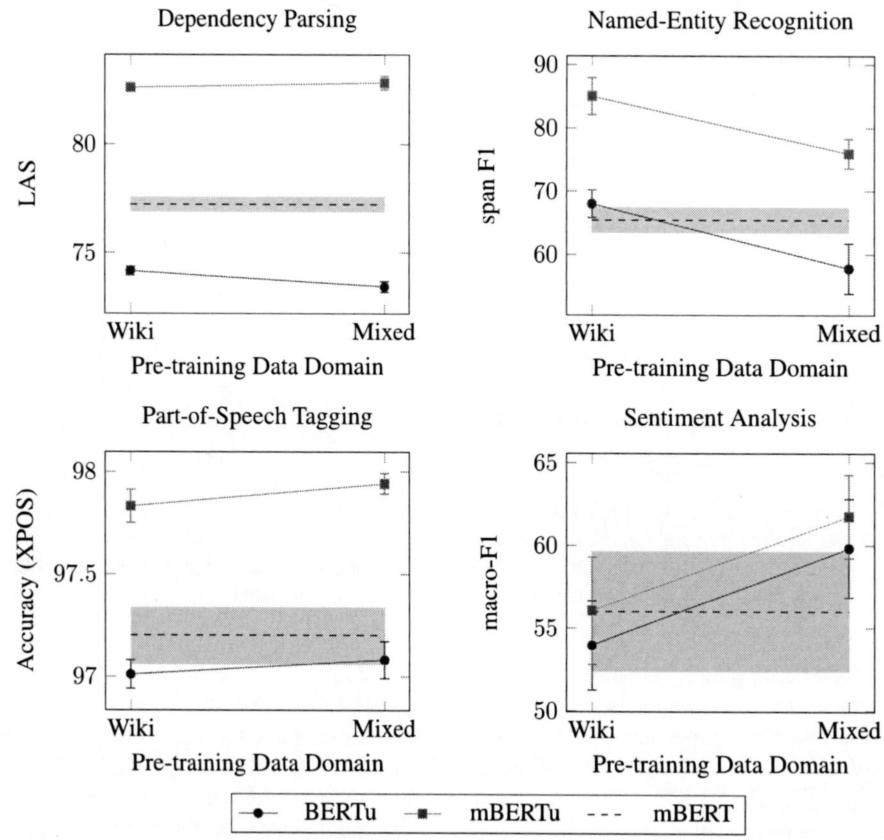

Figure 1: Downstream task performance with different pre-training data domains. All values are the mean over 5 runs with different random seeds. The standard deviation is represented by the corresponding error bars and shaded area.

performs worse than mBERT.

The opposite is true for Sentiment Analysis, as BERTu Mixed turns out to be a more competitive baseline than mBERT. The improvement is so pronounced for this task that the BERTu Mixed model not only performs better than the BERTu Wiki counterpart, but also better than mBERTu Wiki. Even though this dataset contains texts exhibiting stylistic features expected in social media text, a mixture of domains is helpful, probably since Wikipedia texts tend to be quite structured and neutral in terms of the writing style and tone. The results on sentiment analysis suggest that pre-training on a diversity of domains contribute to more effective learning of features relevant to discourse semantic tasks, compared to tasks involving morpho-syntactic tagging. We leave further investigation of this, on a broader range of semantically-oriented tasks, for future work.

Overall, these results emphasise the importance of having pre-training data from sources close to the target data, even for low-resource settings.

5.2 Data Size

From Table 3, it is clear that the KM corpus translates to better performance on downstream tasks, regardless of whether a monolingual or a multilingual model is used. To better understand the relationship between the data size and performance, we pre-train several language models with varying data sizes.

We do this by fixing the desired data proportion and scaling the pre-training data to satisfy this proportion, keeping the original training and validation split. In tandem, the original 1M and 250K steps and batch size used in Section 3 are scaled down with the data size to pre-train for the same number of epochs as the models with the entire data. Language models at 10% intervals are pre-trained, with 100% being the original models from

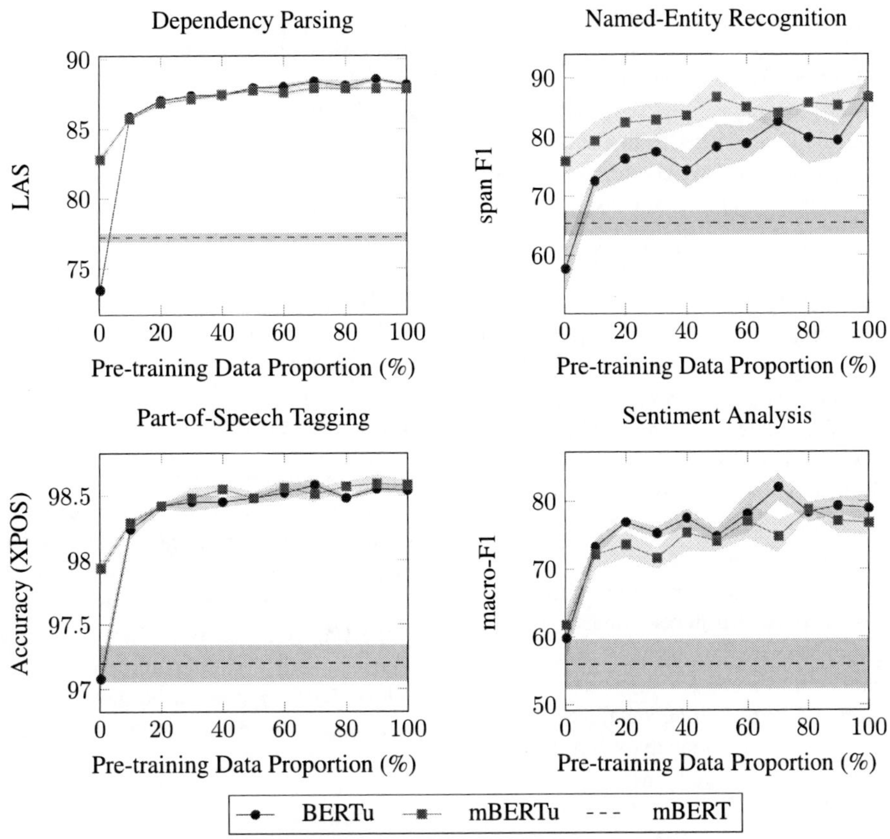

Figure 2: Downstream task performance as the pre-training data size grows. All values are the mean over 5 runs with different random seeds. The standard deviation being represented by the corresponding shaded area.

Section 3. In this analysis, we also include the BERTu Mixed and mBERTu Mixed models from Section 5.1, which use 0.38% of the data, estimated as a proportion of sentences.

After pre-training, each language model is fine-tuned on each of the downstream tasks in the same setup considered in Section 4. These results are visualised in Figure 2.

As expected, the performance generally improves with more pre-training data. Surprisingly, the performance gap between the monolingual and multilingual models is drastically reduced with just 10% of the data. With this little data all configurations outperform mBERT. For Named-Entity Recognition this is also the case but it takes around 70% of the data for BERTu and mBERTu to start achieving very close performance.

It is also noticeable that the gradual increase is not monotonic, although it is more stable for Dependency Parsing and Part-of-Speech tagging. Suprisingly, BERTu with 70% of the data performs better than with 100% of the data on Sentiment Analysis. Similarly, mBERTu with 50% of the data performs better than with 100% of the data on Named-Entity Recognition. One possible explanation may be due to the relationship between the number of steps and batch size chosen, but further investigation is warranted.

On Sentiment Analysis, BERTu is consistently better than mBERTu with 10% or more of the data, and is at times significantly better. This finding gives some evidence that monolingual representations seem better suited for fine-tuning on semantic tasks in a specific language.

6 Conclusion

In this work we analyse the impact of pre-training data on downstream task performance in a low-resource setting, specifically focusing on Maltese. We present a newly developed corpus of around 500M tokens, which allows us to study how the pre-training data size and domain translates in downstream performance differences. Using BERT as our architecture, we compare a monolingual language model, pre-trained from scratch, to a further pre-trained multilingual model, in a number of pre-training configurations. We conduct an evaluation on a both syntactic and semantic tasks.

In line with previous findings on domain pre-training (Gururangan et al., 2020; inter alia), we find that matching the pre-training domain to the target task domain, results in improvements. Moreover, we demonstrate that pre-training language models with varied domains is often beneficial over pre-training solely with Wikipedia. These adjustments were in certain cases enough to surpass mBERT, underlining the importance of having pre-training data more suited to the target task, even at a small scale.

Whilst we show that further pre-training data does improve downstream performance, the gains are linear with exponential increases in data. In fact, substantial improvements are observed with a small proportion of the pre-training data, over language models trained with Wikipedia-sized data. This echoes the findings made by Martin et al. (2020) with a small pre-training subset, although our reduced data setup is considerably smaller.

Using the whole corpus, we also pre-train two new language models: BERTu, a monolingual BERT model, trained from scratch, and mBERTu, which is the result of further pre-training mBERT. These models demonstrate state-of-the-art results in Dependency Parsing, Part-of-Speech Tagging, Named-Entity Recognition, and Sentiment Analysis. Moreover, we show that in general, BERTu performs better than mBERTu, as well as other baselines. Through this, we also demonstrate that language-specific pre-training is most beneficial for higher-level tasks.

Despite these considerable improvements, the pre-training setups used in this work are as close as possible to the baselines, to allow for a more controlled comparison. Hence, in the future, we plan to experiment with more language-specific tuning to push the state-of-the-art even further.

Even though this new corpus will undoubtedly improve the state of resources available for Maltese, the language is by no means a highly-resourced one. The corpus we use is significantly smaller than typically used corpora for higher-resourced languages. We also remark that the quantity of labelled data is still scarce, and at times non-existent for certain tasks. Although we include a semantically-oriented task in our evaluation, future work should investigate the efficacy of these models in more complex Natural Language Understanding scenarios.

We make this corpus and the models publicly available to foster further work and improvements for various NLP applications for Maltese. We also hope that this work inspires work in other low-resource languages, since we show that the amount of data needed to achieve considerable improvements, does not need to be overly ambitious.

Acknowledgements

This work is partially funded by the Malta Digital Innovation Authority (MDIA) under the Malta AI Strategy Framework 2019. We also acknowledge LT-Bridge Project (GA 952194) and DFKI for access to the Virtual Laboratory. We are also grateful to the University of Malta Libraries for granting access to their digital open repository and to the many Maltese authors who gave permission for their work to be included in the Korpus Malti v4.0.

References

Rodrigo Agerri, Iñaki San Vicente, Jon Ander Campos, Ander Barrena, Xabier Saralegi, Aitor Soroa, and Eneko Agirre. 2020. Give your text representation models some love: the case for Basque. In *Proceedings of the 12th Language Resources and Evaluation Conference*, pages 4781–4788, Marseille, France. European Language Resources Association.

Wissam Antoun, Fady Baly, and Hazem Hajj. 2020. AraBERT: Transformer-based model for Arabic language understanding. In *Proceedings of the 4th Workshop on Open-Source Arabic Corpora and Processing Tools, with a Shared Task on Offensive Language Detection*, pages 9–15, Marseille, France. European Language Resource Association.

Emily M Bender, Timnit Gebru, Angelina McMillan-Major, and Shmargaret Shmitchell. 2021. On the Dangers of Stochastic Parrots: Can Language Models Be Too Big? In *Proceedings of the fourth ACM Conference on Fairness, Accountability, and Transparency (FAccT'21)*, Online. Association for Computing Machinery.

Joseph Brincat. 2011. *Maltese and other languages: A linguistic history of Malta*. Midsea Books, Malta.

Slavomír Čéplö. 2018. *Constituent order in Maltese: A quantitative analysis*. Ph.D. thesis, Charles University, Prague.

Ethan C. Chau, Lucy H. Lin, and Noah A. Smith. 2020. Parsing with multilingual BERT, a small corpus, and a small treebank. In *Findings of the Association for Computational Linguistics: EMNLP 2020*, pages 1324–1334, Online. Association for Computational Linguistics.

Ethan C. Chau and Noah A. Smith. 2021. Specializing multilingual language models: An empirical study. In *Proceedings of the 1st Workshop on Multilingual Representation Learning*, pages 51–61, Punta Cana, Dominican Republic. Association for Computational Linguistics.

Alexis Conneau, Kartikay Khandelwal, Naman Goyal, Vishrav Chaudhary, Guillaume Wenzek, Francisco Guzmán, Edouard Grave, Myle Ott, Luke Zettlemoyer, and Veselin Stoyanov. 2020. Unsupervised cross-lingual representation learning at scale. In *Proceedings of the 58th Annual Meeting of the Association for Computational Linguistics*, pages 8440–8451, Online. Association for Computational Linguistics.

Keith Cortis and Brian Davis. 2019. A social opinion gold standard for the Malta government budget 2018. In *Proceedings of the 5th Workshop on Noisy User-generated Text (W-NUT 2019)*, pages 364–369, Hong Kong, China. Association for Computational Linguistics.

Wietse de Vries, Andreas van Cranenburgh, Arianna Bisazza, Tommaso Caselli, Gertjan van Noord, and Malvina Nissim. 2019. BERTje: A dutch BERT model.

Jacob Devlin, Ming-Wei Chang, Kenton Lee, and Kristina Toutanova. 2019. BERT: Pre-training of deep bidirectional transformers for language understanding. In *Proceedings of the 2019 Conference of the North American Chapter of the Association for Computational Linguistics: Human Language Technologies, Volume 1 (Long and Short Papers)*, pages 4171–4186, Minneapolis, Minnesota. Association for Computational Linguistics.

Alexei Dingli and Nicole Sant. 2016. Sentiment analysis on Maltese using machine learning. In *The Tenth International Conference on Advances in Semantic Processing (SEMAPRO 2016)*, pages 21–25.

Timothy Dozat and Christopher D. Manning. 2017. Deep biaffine attention for neural dependency parsing. In *5th International Conference on Learning Representations, ICLR 2017, Toulon, France, April 24-26, 2017, Conference Track Proceedings*. OpenReview.net.

Albert Gatt and Slavomír Čéplö. 2013. Digital Corpora and Other Electronic Resources for Maltese. In *Proceedings of the International Conference on Corpus Linguistics*, pages 96–97. UCREL, Lancaster, UK.

Suchin Gururangan, Ana Marasović, Swabha Swayamdipta, Kyle Lo, Iz Beltagy, Doug Downey, and Noah A. Smith. 2020. Don't stop pretraining: Adapt language models to domains and tasks. In *Proceedings of the 58th Annual Meeting of the Association for Computational Linguistics*, pages 8342–8360, Online. Association for Computational Linguistics.

Melvin Johnson, Mike Schuster, Quoc V. Le, Maxim Krikun, Yonghui Wu, Zhifeng Chen, Nikhil Thorat, Fernanda Viégas, Martin Wattenberg, Greg Corrado, Macduff Hughes, and Jeffrey Dean. 2017. Google's multilingual neural machine translation system: Enabling zero-shot translation. *Transactions of the Association for Computational Linguistics*, 5:339–351.

Mandar Joshi, Danqi Chen, Yinhan Liu, Daniel S. Weld, Luke Zettlemoyer, and Omer Levy. 2020. SpanBERT: Improving pre-training by representing and predicting spans. *Transactions of the Association for Computational Linguistics*, 8:64–77.

Dan Kondratyuk and Milan Straka. 2019. 75 languages, 1 model: Parsing Universal Dependencies universally. In *Proceedings of the 2019 Conference on Empirical Methods in Natural Language Processing and the 9th International Joint Conference on Natural Language Processing (EMNLP-IJCNLP)*, pages 2779–2795, Hong Kong, China. Association for Computational Linguistics.

Julia Kreutzer, Isaac Caswell, Lisa Wang, Ahsan Wahab, Daan van Esch, Nasanbayar Ulzii-Orshikh, Allahsera Tapo, Nishant Subramani, Artem Sokolov, Claytone Sikasote, Monang Setyawan, Supheakmungkol Sarin, Sokhar Samb, Benoît Sagot, Clara Rivera, Annette Rios, Isabel Papadimitriou, Salomey Osei, Pedro Ortiz Suarez, Iroro Orife, Kelechi Ogueji, Andre Niyongabo Rubungo, Toan Q. Nguyen, Mathias Müller, André Müller, Shamsuddeen Hassan Muhammad, Nanda Muhammad, Ayanda Mnyakeni, Jamshidbek Mirzakhalov, Tapiwanashe Matangira, Colin Leong, Nze Lawson, Sneha Kudugunta, Yacine Jernite, Mathias Jenny, Orhan Firat, Bonaventure F. P. Dossou, Sakhile Dlamini, Nisansa de Silva, Sakine Çabuk Ballı, Stella Biderman, Alessia Battisti, Ahmed Baruwa, Ankur Bapna, Pallavi Baljekar, Israel Abebe Azime, Ayodele Awokoya, Duygu Ataman, Orevaoghene Ahia, Oghenefego Ahia, Sweta Agrawal, and Mofetoluwa Adeyemi. 2022. Quality at a glance: An audit of web-crawled multilingual datasets. *Transactions of the Association for Computational Linguistics*, 10:50–72.

Jinhyuk Lee, Wonjin Yoon, Sungdong Kim, Donghyeon Kim, Sunkyu Kim, Chan Ho So, and Jaewoo Kang. 2019. BioBERT: a pre-trained biomedical language representation model for biomedical text mining. *Bioinformatics*, 36(4):1234–1240.

Yinhan Liu, Myle Ott, Naman Goyal, Jingfei Du, Mandar Joshi, Danqi Chen, Omer Levy, Mike Lewis, Luke Zettlemoyer, and Veselin Stoyanov. 2019. RoBERTa: A robustly optimized BERT pretraining approach. *CoRR*, abs/1907.11692.

Marco Lui and Timothy Baldwin. 2014. Accurate language identification of Twitter messages. In *Proceedings of the 5th Workshop on Language Analysis for Social Media (LASM)*, pages 17–25, Gothenburg, Sweden. Association for Computational Linguistics.

Louis Martin, Benjamin Muller, Pedro Javier Ortiz Suárez, Yoann Dupont, Laurent Romary, Éric de la Clergerie, Djamé Seddah, and Benoît Sagot. 2020. CamemBERT: a tasty French language model. In *Proceedings of the 58th Annual Meeting of the Association for Computational Linguistics*, pages 7203–7219, Online. Association for Computational Linguistics.

Antonio Martínez-García, Toni Badia, and Jeremy Barnes. 2021. Evaluating morphological typology in zero-shot cross-lingual transfer. In *Proceedings of the 59th Annual Meeting of the Association for Computational Linguistics and the 11th International Joint Conference on Natural Language Processing (Volume 1: Long Papers)*, pages 3136–3153, Online. Association for Computational Linguistics.

Benjamin Muller, Antonios Anastasopoulos, Benoît Sagot, and Djamé Seddah. 2021. When being unseen from mBERT is just the beginning: Handling new languages with multilingual language models. In *Proceedings of the 2021 Conference of the North American Chapter of the Association for Computational Linguistics: Human Language Technologies*, pages 448–462, Online. Association for Computational Linguistics.

Pedro Javier Ortiz Suárez, Benoît Sagot, and Laurent Romary. 2019. Asynchronous pipelines for processing huge corpora on medium to low resource infrastructures. Proceedings of the Workshop on Challenges in the Management of Large Corpora (CMLC-7) 2019. Cardiff, 22nd July 2019, pages 9–16, Mannheim. Leibniz-Institut für Deutsche Sprache.

Xiaoman Pan, Boliang Zhang, Jonathan May, Joel Nothman, Kevin Knight, and Heng Ji. 2017. Cross-lingual name tagging and linking for 282 languages. In *Proceedings of the 55th Annual Meeting of the Association for Computational Linguistics (Volume 1: Long Papers)*, pages 1946–1958, Vancouver, Canada. Association for Computational Linguistics.

Jonas Pfeiffer, Ivan Vulić, Iryna Gurevych, and Sebastian Ruder. 2021. UNKs everywhere: Adapting multilingual language models to new scripts. In *Proceedings of the 2021 Conference on Empirical Methods in Natural Language Processing*, pages 10186–10203, Online and Punta Cana, Dominican Republic. Association for Computational Linguistics.

Marco Polignano, Pierpaolo Basile, Marco De Gemmis, Giovanni Semeraro, and Valerio Basile. 2019. AlBERTo: Italian bert language understanding model for NLP challenging tasks based on tweets. In *6th Italian Conference on Computational Linguistics, CLiC-it 2019*, volume 2481, pages 1–6. CEUR.

Jan Pomikálek. 2011. *Removing boilerplate and duplicate content from web corpora*. Ph.D. thesis, Masaryk university, Faculty of informatics, Brno, Czech Republic.

Afshin Rahimi, Yuan Li, and Trevor Cohn. 2019. Massively multilingual transfer for NER. In *Proceedings of the 57th Annual Meeting of the Association for Computational Linguistics*, pages 151–164, Florence, Italy. Association for Computational Linguistics.

Anna Rogers. 2021. Changing the world by changing the data. In *Proceedings of the 59th Annual Meeting of the Association for Computational Linguistics and the 11th International Joint Conference on Natural Language Processing (Volume 1: Long Papers)*, pages 2182–2194, Online. Association for Computational Linguistics.

Mike Rosner and Claudia Borg. 2022. *Report on the Maltese Language*. Language Technology Support of Europe's Languages in 2020/2021. Maria Giagkou, Stelios Piperidis, Georg Rehm, Jane Dunne (Series Editors). Available online at `https://european-language-equality.eu/deliverables/`.

Phillip Rust, Jonas Pfeiffer, Ivan Vulić, Sebastian Ruder, and Iryna Gurevych. 2021. How good is your tokenizer? on the monolingual performance of multilingual language models. In *Proceedings of the 59th Annual Meeting of the Association for Computational Linguistics and the 11th International Joint Conference on Natural Language Processing (Volume 1: Long Papers)*, pages 3118–3135, Online. Association for Computational Linguistics.

Ashish Vaswani, Noam Shazeer, Niki Parmar, Llion Uszkoreit, Jakob an Jones, Aidan N Gomez, Ł ukasz Kaiser, and Illia Polosukhin. 2017. Attention is all you need. In *Advances in Neural Information Processing Systems*, volume 30. Curran Associates, Inc.

Antti Virtanen, Jenna Kanerva, Rami Ilo, Jouni Luoma, Juhani Luotolahti, Tapio Salakoski, Filip Ginter, and Sampo Pyysalo. 2019. Multilingual is not enough: Bert for finnish.

Zihan Wang, Karthikeyan K, Stephen Mayhew, and Dan Roth. 2020. Extending multilingual BERT to low-resource languages. In *Findings of the Association for Computational Linguistics: EMNLP 2020*, pages 2649–2656, Online. Association for Computational Linguistics.

Shijie Wu and Mark Dredze. 2019. Beto, bentz, becas: The surprising cross-lingual effectiveness of BERT. In *Proceedings of the 2019 Conference on Empirical Methods in Natural Language Processing and the 9th International Joint Conference on Natural Language Processing (EMNLP-IJCNLP)*, pages 833–844, Hong Kong, China. Association for Computational Linguistics.

Shijie Wu and Mark Dredze. 2020. Are all languages created equal in multilingual BERT? In *Proceedings of the 5th Workshop on Representation Learning for NLP*, pages 120–130, Online. Association for Computational Linguistics.

Building an Event Extractor with Only a Few Examples

Pengfei Yu[1]*, **Zixuan Zhang**[1]*, **Clare Voss**[3], **Jonathan May**[2], **Heng Ji**[1]
[1]University of Illinois Urbana-Champaign [2]University of South California
[3]U.S. Army Combat Capabilities Development Command Army Research Laboratory
{pengfei4,zixuan11,hengji}@illinois.edu
jonmay@isi.edu, clare.r.voss.civ@army.mil

Abstract

Supervised event extraction models require a substantial amount of training data to perform well. However, event annotation requires a lot of human effort and costs much time, which limits the application of existing supervised approaches to new event types. In order to reduce manual labor and shorten the time to build an event extraction system for an arbitrary event ontology, we present a new framework to train such systems much more efficiently without large annotations. Our event trigger labeling model uses a weak supervision approach, which only requires a set of keywords, a small number of examples and an unlabeled corpus, on which our approach automatically collects weakly supervised annotations. Our argument role labeling component performs zero-shot learning, which only requires the names of the argument roles of new event types. The source codes of our event trigger detection[1] and event argument extraction[2] models are publicly available for research purposes. We also release a dockerized system connecting the two models into an unified event extraction pipeline[3].

1 Introduction

Supervised event extraction models require sufficient training data to achieve a good performance. However, event annotation is a challenging task costing a lot of time and manual effort due to the sparsity of event mentions in natural language and the potentially large number of emergent event types that human annotators need to keep in mind during annotation. Therefore, annotation becomes a bottleneck that slows down the development of supervised event extraction systems whenever a new scenario of interest emerges with new event types in need of new data.

In order to meet the needs of fast development of event extraction systems for emergent new event types, we present a novel framework that can train event extraction systems with very few resources. Our proposed framework includes a weakly supervised approach to train a event trigger labeling model and a zero-shot model for argument role labeling. Our proposed weakly supervised event trigger labeling model only requires a few keywords and a small number of example event mentions. In our experiments on the ACE 2005 English dataset,[4] we use 4.9 keywords and 7.3 example mentions per event type on average, which are all extracted from the ACE annotation guidelines. We also propose a zero-shot argument role labeling model that only requires the argument role names of new event types to perform the task. Since such information is typically included in the target ontology and annotation guidelines, we believe this required input costs much less than human annotations. Our framework can be applied to any new event types. Our trigger labeling component outperforms existing few-shot and zero-shot methods (Huang et al., 2018; Li et al., 2021; Feng et al., 2020) on ACE 2005 English dataset.

2 Approach

Our framework includes two components: a trigger labeling model trained from a few keywords and example mentions per each new event type and an unlabeled corpus; and a zero-shot argument role labeling model which only needs the corresponding argument role names for extraction.

2.1 Event Trigger Labeling

As shown in Figure 1, our framework requires a list of keywords $\{k_1, \dots, k_M\}$ for each target

*These authors contributed equally to this work.

[1]https://github.com/Perfec-Yu/efficient-event-extraction

[2]https://github.com/zhangzx-uiuc/zero-shot-event-arguments

[3]https://hub.docker.com/repository/docker/zixuan11/event-extractor

[4]https://catalog.ldc.upenn.edu/LDC2006T06

Proceedings of the Third Workshop on Deep Learning for Low-Resource Natural Language Processing, pages 102 - 109
July 14, 2022 ©2022 Association for Computational Linguistics

event type and a set of event mentions as input. Our goal is to annotate an unlabeled corpus $\mathcal{C} = \{s_1, s_2, \ldots, s_N\}$, which is a collection of sentences s_i, and train a model on the weakly supervised annotations. The corpus for weak supervision is disjoint from the evaluation corpus.

Keyword Representation For each keyword k_i, we first find all its occurrences (including morphological inflection) in the corpus and summarize the semantics of each keyword into distributed representations by aggregating the hidden representation of each keyword occurrence using a large-scale language model $\mathcal{M}$ inspired by Meng et al. (2020). $\mathcal{M}$ functions as a sentence encoder to transform tokens in a sentence into hidden representations. A keyword occurrence consists of a sentence $s_j \in \mathcal{C}$ and a token offset (b_{ij}, e_{ij}) indicating the starting and ending offsets of k_i. We average the token hidden representations from the language model $\mathcal{M}$ within the token span as the representation for the j-th occurrence, and use the mean vector of all occurrences as the keyword representation $\boldsymbol{k}_i$. This process is shown in the top right corner of Figure 1.

Keyword Clustering and Annotation Since some keywords have similar meanings, we propose an additional clustering step to group similar keywords together to find mentions of novel trigger words not in the keyword list. We show an example in Figure 1 for the `Attack` event. We apply spherical KMeans (Lloyd, 1982) to acquire a set of cluster centers for an event type$\{\boldsymbol{c}_1, \boldsymbol{c}_2, \ldots, \boldsymbol{c}_m\}$. Letting $\boldsymbol{t}$ denote the representation of a token in an unlabeled sentence according to $\mathcal{M}$, we compute the score $S(t)$ of the token being an event trigger as the cosine similarity with the closest cluster representation for all the event type's clusters: $S(t) = \max_i \text{cos\_sim}(\boldsymbol{c}_i, \boldsymbol{t})$. We accept a token as an event trigger of this type if the score $S(t)$ exceeds a threshold value. We select the threshold for which this annotation procedure achieves the best trigger labeling F1 score on example sentences.

Training with Example-based Denoising At each minibatch training step, let B_w be a sampled batch from the weakly supervised data. We further sample a batch B_e from the example mentions (from the human annotation guidelines). We compute the information consistency between B_w and B_e as $d = \mathbb{I}(\nabla_\theta \mathcal{L}_{B_e}^\top \nabla_\theta \mathcal{L}_{B_w} > 0)$ where $\mathbb{I}$ is the indicator function, $\mathcal{L}$ is the loss with respect to either the example batch or the weakly supervised batch, and θ is the set of model parameters. If $d = 0$, the training gradient has deviated far from the example gradient, in which case we discard the training data for loss computation. The overall loss is $\mathcal{L}_B = d\lambda\mathcal{L}_{B_w} + (1 - d\lambda)\mathcal{L}_{B_e}$, where λ is a hyperparameter that interpolates joint training on example data and weakly supervised data.

2.2 Event Argument Role Labeling

Our zero-shot event argument extraction model only requires the event argument role names (usually single words or phrases) for each event type (e.g., the event argument role names *Giver, Beneficiary, Recipient* and *Place* for event type *Transaction: Transfer-Money*). Note that our model does not require any detailed information such as natural language descriptions, example annotations or external resources (Zhang et al., 2021). Our model is trained on existing event argument roles with annotations, and is using zero-shot learning to generalize well to any new argument roles.

Zero-shot Training and Classification Inspired from many typical zero-shot learning tasks such as zero-shot image classification (Xian et al., 2018; Liu et al., 2018b), we take a similar approach to build a shared embedding space for both role label semantics and the contextual text features between triggers and arguments. Given an input sentence, we first perform named entity recognition (NER) with Spacy[5] to extract all entity mentions in a sentence. After that, given the event role names $\{r_1, r_2, \cdots, r_R\}$ for a certain event type, we first obtain the semantic embeddings $\{\boldsymbol{r}_1, \boldsymbol{r}_2, \cdots, \boldsymbol{r}_R\}$ using the pretrained language model BERT (Devlin et al., 2019). We also use BERT to get the representation vectors for all extracted event triggers $\boldsymbol{t}_i$ and entity mentions $\boldsymbol{e}_i$ within the sentence, and concatenate the vectors as $[\boldsymbol{t}_i, \boldsymbol{e}_i]$ to represent a trigger-entity pair. The intuition here is to learn two separate neural network projection functions to map each role label and trigger-entity pair into a single shared embedding space, where each trigger-entity pair stays near its correct roles and far from all other event argument roles. During training, we minimize the cosine distance between each $[\boldsymbol{t}_i, \boldsymbol{e}_i]$ and its role label $\boldsymbol{r}_i$, while maximizing the distance between $[\boldsymbol{t}_i, \boldsymbol{e}_i]$ and all other role labels. Specifically, if we use $\mathcal{R}$ to represent the set of all argument role embeddings and use $\boldsymbol{x}_i = [\boldsymbol{t}_i, \boldsymbol{e}_i]$

[5] `https://spacy.io/api/entityrecognizer`

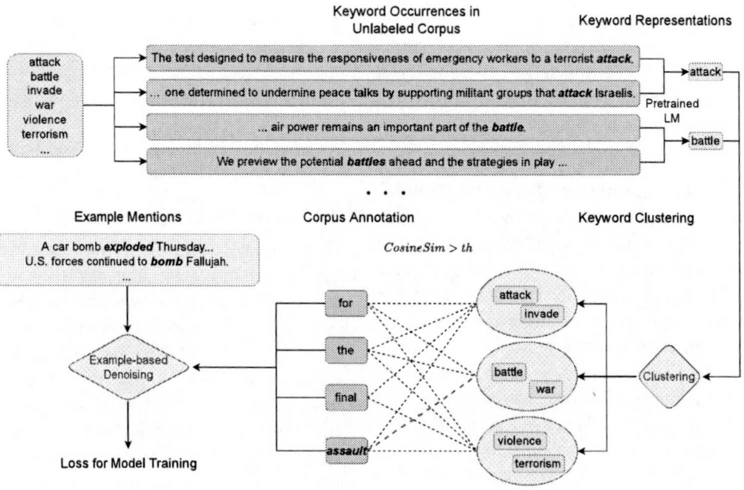

Figure 1: The weakly supervised event trigger labeling framework

to represent trigger-entity pairs, the training objective is to minimize the hinge loss $\mathcal{L}_i = \sum_{j \neq i, \boldsymbol{r}_j \in \mathcal{R}} \max\left(m - C(\boldsymbol{x}_i, \boldsymbol{r}_i) + C(\boldsymbol{x}_i, \boldsymbol{r}_j)\right)$, where $C(\boldsymbol{x}, \boldsymbol{r})$ denotes the cosine similarity. In this way, the trigger-entity pair representations tend to be centered around their argument role labels. During testing, we directly classify each trigger-entity pair as its nearest role label.

3 Evaluation

3.1 Dataset

We evaluate our models with the English portion of the ACE 2005 dataset. It contains 33 event types with 22 event argument role types. We use the training split as the weak supervision corpus, while in zero-shot event argument role labeling, we follow previous work (Huang et al., 2018; Zhang et al., 2021) and use the 10 most frequent event types as training types and other event types along with their role types for testing.

Dataset	Split	#Sents	#Ents	#Events
ACE05-E	Train	17,172	29,006	4,202
	Dev	923	2,451	450
	Test	832	3,017	403

Table 1: Dataset statistics.

3.2 Results

Event Detection. We evaluate event detection performance on two tasks. The first is the traditional trigger labeling. The model detects trigger spans from sentences and predicts an event type for each span. The second task is sentence level event detection (Feng et al., 2020), where the model predicts whether a sentence contains a mention of each event type. We evaluate both of the tasks with the F1 score. To further evaluate the impact of weak supervision, we compare with the **Example** baseline, which uses the same architecture but is trained only with example mentions in the human annotation guidelines. We also show ablation results for the keyword clustering step and example-based denoising step. As an efficient approach for event detection, we also compare with other zero-shot and few-shot methods for each task, as specified next below. We provide more implementation details in the Appendix.

We show the performance of our framework on trigger labeling in Table 2. We compare with the reported performance using two zero-shot methods: **ZSL** (Huang et al., 2018) and **TapKey** (Li et al., 2021). Our framework has the best performance among all the methods. We also show some inconsistent weakly supervised annotations ($d = 0$ in the denoising step in Section 2.1) from the denoising component in Table 3 to demonstrate the effectiveness of the denoising component. To further understand the effect of weak supervision, we compare the weakly supervised results with supervised models trained on varying percentages of training data

Full ACE Ontology (33 Types)	P	R	F
TapKey (Li et al., 2021)	-	-	52.1
Example	57.2	63.0	59.8
Ours	65.6	60.8	**63.1**
w/o denoising	62.2	61.1	61.6
w/o clustering	61.3	59.7	60.4
ACE Subset (23 Types)	P	R	F
ZSL (Huang et al., 2018)	75.5	36.3	49.1
Ours	66.3	60.5	**63.3**

Table 2: Trigger labeling performance (in %). Huang et al. (2018) evaluated on a 23-event-type subset of the complete ACE event ontology. We compute our model's performance on these types for comparison. The slots with "-" are unreported results.

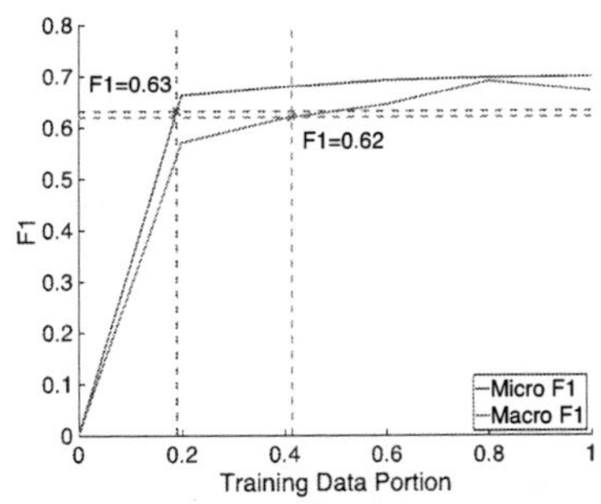

Figure 2: Supervised performance with respect to training data portion. Dotted lines indicate the performance of the weakly supervised methods.

in Figure 2. For sentence-level detection, we compare with the best few-shot (9-shot) results (Feng et al., 2020) in Table 4. Our weakly supervised approach has improved the performance.

Error	Inconsistent Weak Supervision
False Positive	... a minute fraction of the sum of **money**[`Transfer-Money`] ...
False Negative	... concerns our ability to *travel*[`Transport`].

Table 3: Inconsistent weakly supervised annotations from the denoising step.

Method	P	R	F
9-shot (Feng et al., 2020)	54.5	57.0	61.8
Example	66.4	68.0	66.9
Ours	66.2	74.2	**69.9**

Table 4: Sentence level event detection result (%).

Event Argument Extraction. In our experiments of event argument extraction, we use the top 10 frequent event types in ACE dataset for training and the other 23 types for testing. We report the precision, recall, and F1 scores on the test split of ACE dataset as shown in Table 5.

Models / Role Types	Prec	Rec	F1
Our Model	39.6	49.7	**41.5**
(Huang et al., 2018)	-	-	14.7
`Start-Position:Entity`	48.5	76.2	59.3
`Justice:Defendant`	55.0	44.0	48.9
`Justice:Agent`	45.5	45.5	45.5

Table 5: Event argument role labeling performance on ACE dataset. We report both overall scores and also top-3 scores on specific event argument roles.

4 Related Work

Supervised Event Detection Event detection under supervised settings has been widely studied (Ji and Grishman, 2008; Chen et al., 2015; Feng et al., 2016; Liu et al., 2017, 2018a, 2019a; Lu et al., 2019; Ding et al., 2019; Yan et al., 2019; Tong et al., 2020; Du and Cardie, 2020; Li et al., 2021). Other methods on joint information extraction (Li et al., 2013; Wadden et al., 2019; Lin et al., 2020) also include event detection as a subtask. However, supervised methods heavily rely on human annotations to perform well.

Weakly Supervised Event Extraction Some previous weakly supervised event extraction methods aim at augmenting data for existing event types. Ferguson et al. (2018) propose a semi-supervised method which requires a strong supervised event extractor for data collection. Chen et al. (2017) propose a distant supervision based framework using Freebase Compound Value Types (CVTs). Wang et al. (2019) follow Chen et al. (2015) and introduce a novel adversarial training method to denoise the noisy training data for event extraction.

Zero-shot Event Argument Extraction In zero-shot learning (Zhang and Saligrama, 2015; Romera-Paredes and Torr, 2015; Zhang et al., 2017), the model is required to make predictions on types that are not observed during training. Such a problem setting has also been widely explored in Computer Vision, especially for zero-shot image classification (Gu et al., 2021; Hanouti and Borgne, 2022). In terms of zero-shot event extraction, Huang et al. (2018) propose a semantic similarity based learning method, and more recently, Zhang et al. (2021) further use resources from external corpus as weakly-supervised example annotations.

5 Conclusions

In this work we present an efficient event extraction framework that can be trained with only a few keywords and example event mentions per new event type. We use weak supervision for trigger labeling and apply a zero-shot framework for argument role labeling. Our framework can collect training data and build models for emergent new event types in a significantly shortened time without needing to acquire large-scale human annotations.

Acknowledgement

This research is based upon work supported in part by U.S. DARPA LORELEI Program No. HR0011- 15-C-0115, U.S. DARPA AIDA Program No. FA8750-18-2-0014 and KAIROS Program No. FA8750-19-2-1004. The views and conclusions contained herein are those of the authors and should not be interpreted as necessarily representing the official policies, either expressed or implied, of DARPA, or the U.S. Government. The U.S. Government is authorized to reproduce and distribute reprints for governmental purposes notwithstanding any copyright annotation therein.

References

Yubo Chen, Shulin Liu, Xiang Zhang, Kang Liu, and Jun Zhao. 2017. Automatically labeled data generation for large scale event extraction. In *Proceedings of the 55th Annual Meeting of the Association for Computational Linguistics (Volume 1: Long Papers)*, pages 409–419, Vancouver, Canada. Association for Computational Linguistics.

Yubo Chen, Liheng Xu, Kang Liu, Daojian Zeng, and Jun Zhao. 2015. Event extraction via dynamic multi-pooling convolutional neural networks. In *Proceedings of the 53rd Annual Meeting of the Association for Computational Linguistics and the 7th International Joint Conference on Natural Language Processing (Volume 1: Long Papers)*, pages 167–176, Beijing, China. Association for Computational Linguistics.

Jacob Devlin, Ming-Wei Chang, Kenton Lee, and Kristina Toutanova. 2019. BERT: Pre-training of deep bidirectional transformers for language understanding. In *Proceedings of the 2019 Conference of the North American Chapter of the Association for Computational Linguistics: Human Language Technologies, Volume 1 (Long and Short Papers)*, pages 4171–4186, Minneapolis, Minnesota. Association for Computational Linguistics.

Ning Ding, Ziran Li, Zhiyuan Liu, Haitao Zheng, and Zibo Lin. 2019. Event detection with trigger-aware lattice neural network. In *Proceedings of the 2019 Conference on Empirical Methods in Natural Language Processing and the 9th International Joint Conference on Natural Language Processing (EMNLP-IJCNLP)*, pages 347–356, Hong Kong, China. Association for Computational Linguistics.

Xinya Du and Claire Cardie. 2020. Event extraction by answering (almost) natural questions. In *Proceedings of the 2020 Conference on Empirical Methods in Natural Language Processing (EMNLP)*, pages 671–683, Online. Association for Computational Linguistics.

Rui Feng, Jie Yuan, and Chao Zhang. 2020. Probing and fine-tuning reading comprehension models for few-shot event extraction. *arXiv preprint arXiv:2010.11325*.

Xiaocheng Feng, Lifu Huang, Duyu Tang, Heng Ji, Bing Qin, and Ting Liu. 2016. A language-independent neural network for event detection. In *Proceedings of the 54th Annual Meeting of the Association for Computational Linguistics (Volume 2: Short Papers)*, pages 66–71, Berlin, Germany. Association for Computational Linguistics.

James Ferguson, Colin Lockard, Daniel Weld, and Hannaneh Hajishirzi. 2018. Semi-supervised event extraction with paraphrase clusters. In *Proceedings of the 2018 Conference of the North American Chapter of the Association for Computational Linguistics: Human Language Technologies, Volume 2 (Short Papers)*, pages 359–364, New Orleans, Louisiana. Association for Computational Linguistics.

Xiuye Gu, Tsung-Yi Lin, Weicheng Kuo, and Yin Cui. 2021. Zero-shot detection via vision and language knowledge distillation. *arXiv preprint arXiv:2104.13921*.

Celina Hanouti and Hervé Le Borgne. 2022. Learning semantic ambiguities for zero-shot learning. *arXiv preprint arXiv:2201.01823*.

Lifu Huang, Heng Ji, Kyunghyun Cho, Ido Dagan, Sebastian Riedel, and Clare Voss. 2018. Zero-shot transfer learning for event extraction. In *Proceedings of the 56th Annual Meeting of the Association for Computational Linguistics (Volume 1: Long Papers)*, pages 2160–2170, Melbourne, Australia. Association for Computational Linguistics.

Heng Ji and Ralph Grishman. 2008. Refining event extraction through cross-document inference. In *Proceedings of ACL-08: HLT*, pages 254–262, Columbus, Ohio. Association for Computational Linguistics.

Qi Li, Heng Ji, and Liang Huang. 2013. Joint event extraction via structured prediction with global features. In *Proceedings of the 51st Annual Meeting of the Association for Computational Linguistics (Volume 1: Long Papers)*, pages 73–82, Sofia, Bulgaria. Association for Computational Linguistics.

Sha Li, Heng Ji, and Jiawei Han. 2021. Document-level event argument extraction by conditional generation. In *Proceedings of the 2021 Conference of the North American Chapter of the Association for Computational Linguistics: Human Language Technologies, Volume 1 (Long and Short Papers)*. Association for Computational Linguistics.

Ying Lin, Heng Ji, Fei Huang, and Lingfei Wu. 2020. A joint neural model for information extraction with global features. In *Proceedings of the 58th Annual Meeting of the Association for Computational Linguistics*, pages 7999–8009, Online. Association for Computational Linguistics.

Jian Liu, Yubo Chen, Kang Liu, and Jun Zhao. 2019a. Neural cross-lingual event detection with minimal parallel resources. In *Proceedings of the 2019 Conference on Empirical Methods in Natural Language Processing and the 9th International Joint Conference on Natural Language Processing (EMNLP-IJCNLP)*, pages 738–748, Hong Kong, China. Association for Computational Linguistics.

Shaobo Liu, Rui Cheng, Xiaoming Yu, and Xueqi Cheng. 2018a. Exploiting contextual information via dynamic memory network for event detection. In *Proceedings of the 2018 Conference on Empirical Methods in Natural Language Processing*, pages 1030–1035, Brussels, Belgium. Association for Computational Linguistics.

Shichen Liu, Mingsheng Long, Jianmin Wang, and Michael I Jordan. 2018b. Generalized zero-shot learning with deep calibration network. In *Advances in Neural Information Processing Systems*, pages 2005–2015.

Shulin Liu, Yubo Chen, Kang Liu, and Jun Zhao. 2017. Exploiting argument information to improve event detection via supervised attention mechanisms. In *Proceedings of the 55th Annual Meeting of the Association for Computational Linguistics (Volume 1: Long Papers)*, pages 1789–1798, Vancouver, Canada. Association for Computational Linguistics.

Yinhan Liu, Myle Ott, Naman Goyal, Jingfei Du, Mandar Joshi, Danqi Chen, Omer Levy, Mike Lewis, Luke Zettlemoyer, and Veselin Stoyanov. 2019b. Roberta: A robustly optimized BERT pretraining approach. *CoRR*, abs/1907.11692.

Stuart P. Lloyd. 1982. Least squares quantization in PCM. *IEEE Trans. Inf. Theory*, 28(2):129–136.

Ilya Loshchilov and Frank Hutter. 2019. Decoupled weight decay regularization. In *7th International Conference on Learning Representations, ICLR 2019, New Orleans, LA, USA, May 6-9, 2019*. OpenReview.net.

Yaojie Lu, Hongyu Lin, Xianpei Han, and Le Sun. 2019. Distilling discrimination and generalization knowledge for event detection via delta-representation learning. In *Proceedings of the 57th Annual Meeting of the Association for Computational Linguistics*, pages 4366–4376, Florence, Italy. Association for Computational Linguistics.

Yu Meng, Yunyi Zhang, Jiaxin Huang, Chenyan Xiong, Heng Ji, Chao Zhang, and Jiawei Han. 2020. Text classification using label names only: A language model self-training approach. In *Proceedings of the 2020 Conference on Empirical Methods in Natural Language Processing (EMNLP)*, pages 9006–9017, Online. Association for Computational Linguistics.

Bernardino Romera-Paredes and Philip Torr. 2015. An embarrassingly simple approach to zero-shot learning. In *International conference on machine learning*, pages 2152–2161. PMLR.

Meihan Tong, Bin Xu, Shuai Wang, Yixin Cao, Lei Hou, Juanzi Li, and Jun Xie. 2020. Improving event detection via open-domain trigger knowledge. In *Proceedings of the 58th Annual Meeting of the Association for Computational Linguistics*, pages 5887–5897, Online. Association for Computational Linguistics.

David Wadden, Ulme Wennberg, Yi Luan, and Hannaneh Hajishirzi. 2019. Entity, relation, and event extraction with contextualized span representations. In *Proceedings of the 2019 Conference on Empirical Methods in Natural Language Processing and the 9th International Joint Conference on Natural Language Processing (EMNLP-IJCNLP)*, pages 5784–5789, Hong Kong, China. Association for Computational Linguistics.

Xiaozhi Wang, Xu Han, Zhiyuan Liu, Maosong Sun, and Peng Li. 2019. Adversarial training for weakly supervised event detection. In *Proceedings of the 2019 Conference of the North American Chapter of the Association for Computational Linguistics: Human Language Technologies, Volume 1 (Long and Short Papers)*, pages 998–1008, Minneapolis, Minnesota. Association for Computational Linguistics.

Adina Williams, Nikita Nangia, and Samuel Bowman. 2018. A broad-coverage challenge corpus for sentence understanding through inference. In *Proceedings of the 2018 Conference of the North American Chapter of the Association for Computational Linguistics: Human Language Technologies, Volume 1 (Long Papers)*, pages 1112–1122, New Orleans, Louisiana. Association for Computational Linguistics.

Yongqin Xian, Tobias Lorenz, Bernt Schiele, and Zeynep Akata. 2018. Feature generating networks for zero-shot learning. In *Proceedings of the IEEE conference on computer vision and pattern recognition*, pages 5542–5551.

Haoran Yan, Xiaolong Jin, Xiangbin Meng, Jiafeng Guo, and Xueqi Cheng. 2019. Event detection with multi-order graph convolution and aggregated attention. In *Proceedings of the 2019 Conference on Empirical Methods in Natural Language Processing and the*

9th International Joint Conference on Natural Language Processing (EMNLP-IJCNLP)*, pages 5766–5770, Hong Kong, China. Association for Computational Linguistics.

Hongming Zhang, Haoyu Wang, and Dan Roth. 2021. Zero-shot Label-aware Event Trigger and Argument Classification. In *Findings of the Association for Computational Linguistics: ACL-IJCNLP 2021*, pages 1331–1340, Online. Association for Computational Linguistics.

Li Zhang, Tao Xiang, and Shaogang Gong. 2017. Learning a deep embedding model for zero-shot learning. In *Proceedings of the IEEE conference on computer vision and pattern recognition*, pages 2021–2030.

Ziming Zhang and Venkatesh Saligrama. 2015. Zero-shot learning via semantic similarity embedding. In *Proceedings of the IEEE international conference on computer vision*, pages 4166–4174.

A Implementation Details

A.1 Spherical KMeans for Keyword Clustering

Compared with traditional KMeans (Lloyd, 1982), there are two modifications in spherical KMeans. Firstly, the cluster assignment at each iteration step is decided according to the cosine similarities to the cluster centers instead of the Euclidean distance. Besides, after computing the cluster centers as the mean vectors of those keyword representations that are assigned to the corresponding clusters, we add an additional normalizing step to make all cluster centers have unit norm. We use the implementation in `https://github.com/jasonlaska/spherecluster` for experiments.

A.2 Implementation Details for Trigger Labeling

We adopt a sequence labeling model for trigger labeling. Since we observe very few consecutive trigger spans, we use a simplified 'IO' tagging method instead of 'BIO' tagging. Specifically, we assign each token in a sentence a label 'I-<Event_type>' if it is in a trigger span of the corresponding event type. For the model architecture, we use Roberta-Large (Liu et al., 2019b) to encode each token in the sentences into a hidden representation. Then we adopt an additional linear layer to classify each token into one of the tags. We use training batch size of 8 sentences. We truncate sentences to contain at most 96 tokens. For optimization, we use AdamW (Loshchilov and Hutter, 2019) optimizer with initial learning rate 10^{-5}. We also use a linear warmup with 1200 warmup steps. We run experiments with 4 random seeds and report the average score.

A.3 Implementation Details for Sentence-level Event Detection

We use a Roberta-Large model finetuned on MultiNLI (Williams et al., 2018) dataset for textual entailment. The input to the model consists of a candidate sentence and an event-type-specific entailment sentence, such as *Agent attacked Target* for `Attack` event. The complete list of used entailment sentences can be found in the supplementary materials. The model outputs scores for the three labels: s_e for *entailment*, s_n *neutral* and s_c *contradiction*. We compute the probability of mentioning an event as $P(Mention) = \frac{e^{s_e}}{e^{s_e}+e^{s_n+s_c}}$. We use cross entropy loss to train the model. For evaluation, consider the candidate sentence mentioning an event if the probability of entailment is greater than 0.5. We use the same training hyper-parameters as trigger labeling. We run experiments with 4 random seeds and report the average score.

A.4 Implementation Details for Weak Supervision

For the weak annotation, The threshold is chosen from 0.4 to 1.0 with 0.05 incremental steps. We choose the threshold as 0.65 to have the best F1 score on the example mentions. Since we use the ACE 2005 English training corpus for weak supervision, we also compute the F1 score of the weakly supervised annotation directly. The F1 score is 0.46.

For the example-based denoising, we choose the weight parameter $\lambda = 0.7$ for trigger labeling and $\lambda = 0.5$ for sentence-level event detection.

B Keywords and Example Mentions

We show keywords for each event type in Table 6. We include example mentions in the supplementary materials. We have a total of 173 sentences and 241 event mentions in the example data.

Event Type	Keywords
Business:Declare-Bankruptcy	bankruptcy, broke, broken, bankrupt
Business:End-Org	failure, shut, collapse, fold
Business:Merge-Org	merger, merge
Business:Start-Org	initiate, establish, established, launch
Conflict:Attack	conflict, shoot, war, fighting, violence, attack, surge, battle, terrorism, invasion, coalition, warfare, explode, invade, pound, combat, fought
Conflict:Demonstrate	rally, protest, demonstration, demonstrate, riot
Contact:Meet	talk, meet, meeting, seminar, summit, dialogue
Contact:Phone-Write	call, phone, letter, email, video, cable, telephone, correspondence, mail, dial
Justice:Acquit	acquittal
Justice:Appeal	appeal
Justice:Arrest-Jail	jail, arrest, imprison
Justice:Charge-Indict	charge, accuse, indictment, accusation
Justice:Convict	convict
Justice:Execute	execute, execution
Justice:Extradite	deport, expel, extradite
Justice:Fine	penalty, fine, fee, penalize
Justice:Pardon	mercy, forgive, pardon
Justice:Release-Parole	parole, release, free
Justice:Sentence	sentence
Justice:Sue	sue, lawsuit
Justice:Trial-Hearing	trial, hearing, testify
Life:Be-Born	birth, born
Life:Die	die, death, suicide, murder, kill, slaughter, survive, killing, stabbed, fatal
Life:Divorce	divorce, split
Life:Injure	hurt, harm, hit, wound, injure, injured, wounded
Life:Marry	wedding, marry, wed
Movement:Transport	head, move, retreat, leave, visit, trip, travel, shift, tour, remove, return, arrive, carry, moving, ship, journey, transport, cruise, transition, deploy
Personnel:Elect	elect, election, vote, voting, poll, electoral, voter
Personnel:End-Position	resign, former, previous, fire, late, retire, dismiss, formerly, defunct
Personnel:Nominate	name, nominate
Personnel:Start-Position	appoint, employ, hire
Transaction:Transfer-Money	pay, spend, compensate, borrow, transfer, donate, lend
Transaction:Transfer-Ownership	buy, buying, acquire, purchase, acquisition, takeover, obtain

Table 6: Keywords used for each event type. Although we performed lemmatization for matching, there are some situations that lemmatization cannot handle perfectly. Therefore we also include various tenses for some verbs.

Task Transfer and Domain Adaptation for Zero-Shot Question Answering

Xiang Pan* New York University xp2030@nyu.edu

Alex Sheng* New York University alexsheng4@gmail.com

David Shimshoni* New York University ds5396@nyu.edu

Aditya Singhal* New York University adis@nyu.edu

Sara Rosenthal IBM Research AI sjrosenthal@us.ibm.com

Avirup Sil IBM Research AI avi@us.ibm.com

Abstract

Pretrained language models have shown success in various areas of natural language processing, including reading comprehension tasks. However, when applying machine learning methods to new domains, labeled data may not always be available. To address this, we use supervised pretraining on source-domain data to reduce sample complexity on domain-specific downstream tasks. We evaluate zero-shot performance on domain-specific reading comprehension tasks by combining task transfer with domain adaptation to fine-tune a pretrained model with no labelled data from the target task. Our approach outperforms Domain-Adaptive Pretraining on downstream domain-specific reading comprehension tasks in 3 out of 4 domains.

1 Introduction

Pretrained language models (Liu et al., 2019; Wolf et al., 2020) require substantial quantities of labeled data to learn downstream tasks. For domains that are novel or where labeled data is in short supply, supervised learning methods may not be suitable (Zhang et al., 2020; Madasu and Rao, 2020; Rietzler et al., 2020). Collecting sufficient quantities of labeled data for each new application can be resource intensive, especially when aiming for both a specific task type and a specific data domain. By traditional transfer learning methods, it is prohibitively difficult to fine-tune a pretrained model on a domain-specific downstream task for which there is no existing training data. In light of this, we would like to use more readily available labeled in-domain data from unrelated tasks to domain-adapt our fine-tuned model.

In this paper, we consider a problem setting where we have a domain-specific target task (QA) for which we do not have any in-domain training data (SQuAD). However, we assume that we have generic training data for the target task type, and in-domain training data for another task. To address this problem setting, we present Task and Domain Adaptive Pretraining (T+DAPT), a technique that combines domain adaptation and task adaptation to improve performance in downstream target tasks. We evaluate the effectiveness of T+DAPT in zero-shot domain-specific machine reading comprehension (MRC) (Hazen et al., 2019; Reddy et al., 2020; Wiese et al., 2017) by pretraining on in-domain NER data and fine-tuning for generic domain-agnostic MRC on SQuADv1 (Rajpurkar et al., 2018), combining knowledge from the two different tasks to achieve zero-shot learning on the target task. We test the language model's performance on domain-specific reading comprehension data taken from 4 domains: News, Movies, Biomedical, and COVID-19. In our experiments, RoBERTa-Base models trained using our approach perform favorably on domain-specific reading comprehension tasks compared to baseline RoBERTa-Base models trained on SQuAD as well as Domain Adaptive Pretraining (DAPT). Our code is publicly available for reference. [1]

We summarize our contributions as follows:

- We propose Task and Domain Adaptive Pretraining (T+DAPT) combining domain adaptation and task adaptation to achieve zero-shot learning on domain-specific downstream tasks.
- We experimentally validate the performance of T+DAPT, showing our approach performs favorably compared to both a previous approach (DAPT) and a baseline RoBERTa fine-tuning approach.
- We analyze the adaptation performance on different domains, as well as the behavior of

*Equal Contribution

[1] https://github.com/adityaarunsinghal/Domain-Adaptation

Proceedings of the Third Workshop on Deep Learning for Low-Resource Natural Language Processing, pages 110 - 116
July 14, 2022 ©2022 Association for Computational Linguistics

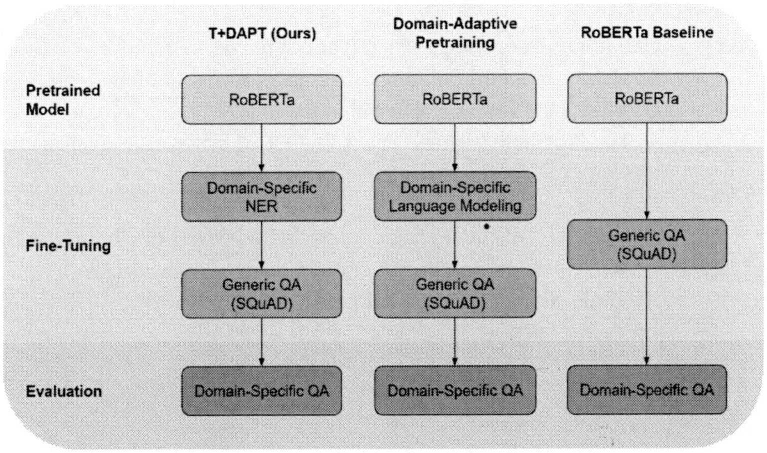

Figure 1: sequential transfer learning procedures of T+DAPT, DAPT, and a RoBERTa baseline for zero-shot question answering.

DAPT and T+DAPT under various experimental conditions.

2 Related Work

It has been shown that pretrained language models can be domain-adapted with further pretraining (Pruksachatkun et al., 2020) on unlabeled in-domain data to significantly improve the language model's performance on downstream supervised tasks in-domain. This was originally demonstrated by BioBERT (Lee et al., 2019). Gururangan et al. (2020) further explores this method of domain adaptation via unsupervised pretraining, referred to as Domain-Adaptive Pretraining (DAPT), and demonstrates its effectiveness across several domains and data availability settings. This procedure has been shown to improve performance on specific domain reading comprehension tasks, in particular in the biomedical domain (Gu et al., 2021). In this paper, as a baseline for comparison, we evaluate the performance of DAPT-enhanced language models in their respective domains, both in isolation with SQuAD1.1 fine-tuning and in conjunction with our approach that incorporates the respective domain's NER task. DAPT models for two of our domains, News and Biomedical, are initialized from pretrained weights as provided by the authors of Gururangan et al. (2020). We train our own DAPT baselines on the Movies and COVID-19 domains. Xu et al. (2020) explore methods to reduce catastrophic forgetting during language model fine-tuning. They apply topic modeling on the MS MARCO dataset (Bajaj et al., 2018) to generate 6 narrow domain-specific data sets, from which we use BioQA and MoviesQA as domain-specific reading comprehension benchmarks.

3 Experiments

We aim to achieve zero-shot learning for an unseen domain-specific MRC task by fine-tuning on both a domain transfer task and a generic MRC task. The model is initialized by pretrained RoBERTa weights (Liu et al., 2019), then fine-tuned using our approach with a domain-specific supervised task to augment domain knowledge, and finally trained on SQuAD to learn generic MRC capabilities to achieve zero-shot MRC in the target domain on an unseen domain-specific MRC task without explicitly training on the final task. This method is illustrated in Figure 1.

3.1 Datasets

We explore the performance of this approach in the Movies, News, Biomedical, and COVID-19 domains. Specifically, our target domain-specific MRC tasks are MoviesQA (Xu et al., 2020), NewsQA (Trischler et al., 2017), BioQA (Xu et al., 2020), and CovidQA (Möller et al., 2020), respectively. We choose to use named entity recognition (NER) as our supervised domain adaptation task for all four target domains, as labeled NER data is widely available across various domains. Furthermore, NER and MRC share functional similarities, as both rely on identifying key tokens in a text as entities or answers. The domain-specific NER tasks are performed using supervised training data

Dataset	Dev Set	Sample
MoviesQA	755	Q: After its re-opening, which types of movies did the Tower Theatre show? A: second and third run movies, along with classic films
NewsQA	934	Q: Who is the struggle between in Rwanda? A: The struggle pits ethnic Tutsis, supported by Rwanda, against ethnic Hutu, backed by Congo.
BioQA	4,790	Q: What is hemophilia? A: a bleeding disorder characterized by low levels of clotting factor proteins.
CovidQA	2,019	Q: What is the molecular structure of bovine coronavirus? A: single-stranded, linear, and nonsegmented RNA

Table 1: Overview of the domain-specific MRC datasets used in our experiments. The number of question-answer pairs in the train set and development set for each domain is shown, along with a sample question-answer pair from each domain. The datasets share the same format as SQuAD.

from the MIT Movie Corpus (Liu et al., 2013), CoNLL 2003 News NER (Tjong Kim Sang and De Meulder, 2003), NCBI-Disease (Doğan et al., 2014) and COVID-NER [2]. The domain-specific language modeling tasks for DAPT are performed using unsupervised text from IMDB (Maas et al., 2011), the RealNews Corpus (Zellers et al., 2020), the Semantic Scholar Open Research Corpus (Lo et al., 2020) and the Covid-19 Corpus [3].

3.2 Methods

We compare our approach (T+DAPT) to a previous approach (DAPT) as well as a baseline model. For the baseline, the pretrained RoBERTa-Base model is fine-tuned on SQuAD and evaluated on domain-specific MRC without any domain adaptation. In the DAPT approach, RoBERTa-Base is first initialized with fine-tuned DAPT weights (NewsRoBERTa and BioRoBERTa) provided by Gururangan et al. (2020) or implemented ourselves using the methodology described in Gururangan et al. (2020) and different Movies and COVID-19 datasets (Maas et al., 2011; Danescu-Niculescu-Mizil and Lee, 2011; Pang et al., 2019). These models are initialized by DAPT weights—which have been fine-tuned beforehand on unsupervised text corpora for domain adaptation—from the HuggingFace model hub (Wolf et al., 2020), fine-tuned on SQuAD, and evaluated on domain-specific MRC.

3.3 Results

We compare the effectiveness of our approach, which uses NER instead of language modeling (as in DAPT) for the domain adaptation method in a sequential training regime. Our experiments cover every combination of domain (Movies, News, Biomedical, or COVID) and domain adaptation method (T+DAPT which uses named entity recognition vs. DAPT which uses language modeling vs. baseline with no domain adaptation at all).

Our results are presented in Table 2. We use F1 score to evaluate the QA performance of each model in its target domain. In our experiments, DAPT performs competitively with baseline models and outperforms in one domain (CovidQA). Our T+DAPT approach (RoBERTA + Domain NER + SQuAD) outperforms the baseline in three out of four domains (Movies, Biomedical, COVID) and outperforms DAPT in three out of four domains (Movies, News, Biomedical). We also test a combination of DAPT and T+DAPT by retraining DAPT models on domain NER then SQuAD, and find that this combined approach underperforms compared to either T+DAPT alone or DAPT alone in all four domains. We further discuss the possible reasons for these results in Section 4.

4 Analysis

Specific domains learn from adaptation: Our approach shows promising performance gains when used for zero-shot domain-specific question answering, particularly in the biomedical, movies, and COVID domains, where the MRC datasets were designed with the evaluation of domain-specific features in mind. Performance gains are less apparent in the News domain, where the NewsQA dataset was designed primarily to evaluate causal reasoning and inference abilities—which correlate strongly with SQuAD and base-

[2] https://github.com/tsantosh7/COVID-19-Named-Entity-Recognition

[3] https://github.com/davidcampos/covid19-corpus

RoBERTa Retraining Procedure	MoviesQA	NewsQA	BioQA	CovidQA
SQuAD1.1	67.1	**57.0**	58.0	42.0
DAPT + SQuAD1.1	60.7	54.4	57.8	**47.2**
T+DAPT (ours)	**68.0**	56.0	**58.9**	42.7
DAPT + *T+DAPT*	66.4	54.2	55.1	43.1

Table 2: F1 score of pretrained RoBERTa-Base models on dev sets of MRC datasets for given domains with the stated retraining regimens

line RoBERTa pretraining—rather than domain-specific features and adaptation. The lack of performance gains from either T+DAPT or DAPT in the News domain could also possibly be attributed to the nature of the domain: Gururangan et al. (2020) found that the News domain had the highest vocabulary overlap of any domain (54.1%) with the RoBERTa pretraining corpus, so the baseline for this domain could have had an advantage in the News domain that would be lost due to catastrophic forgetting while little relevant knowledge is gained from domain adaptation. We perform follow-up experiments with varying amounts of epochs and training data in SQuAD fine-tuning to analyze the tradeoff between more thorough MRC fine-tuning and better preservation of source domain knowledge from DAPT and auxiliary domain adaptation tasks. The results from these runs are in the Appendix (Table 4).

When does DAPT succeed or fail: In zero-shot QA, DAPT performs competitively with the baseline in all domains and outperforms in the COVID domain. This builds upon the results of Gururangan et al. (2020), which reports superior performance on tasks like relation classification, sentiment analysis, and topic modeling, but does not address reading comprehension tasks, which DAPT may not have originally been optimized for. Unsupervised language modeling may not provide readily transferable features for reading comprehension, as opposed to NER which identifies key tokens and classifies those tokens into specific entities. These entities are also often answer tokens in reading comprehension, lending to transferable representations between NER and reading comprehension. Another possible factor is that RoBERTa was pretrained on the English Wikipedia corpus, the same source that the SQuAD questions were drawn from. Because of this, it is possible that pretrained RoBERTa already has relevant representations that would provide an intrinsic advantage for SQuAD-style reading comprehension which would be lost due to catastrophic forgetting after retraining on another large language modeling corpus in DAPT.

In the COVID domain, we use the article dataset from Wang et al. (2020). These articles also make the basis for the CovidNER and CovidQA (Möller et al., 2020) datasets, which may explain the large performance improvement from DAPT in this domain. These results suggest that the performance of DAPT is sensitive to the similarity of its language modeling corpus to the target task dataset.[1]

5 Conclusion

We evaluate the performance of our T+DAPT approach with domain-specific NER, achieving positive results in a zero-shot reading comprehension setting in four different domain-specific QA datasets. These results indicate that our T+DAPT approach robustly improves performance of pretraining language models in zero-shot domain QA across several domains, showing that T+DAPT is a promising approach to domain adaptation in low-resource settings for pretrained language models, particularly when directly training on target task data is difficult.

In future work, we intend to explore various methods to improve the performance of T+DAPT by remedying catastrophic forgetting and maximizing knowledge transfer. For this we hope to emulate the regularization used by Xu et al. (2020) and implement multi-task learning and continual learning methods like AdapterNet (Hazan et al., 2018). In order to improve the transferability of learned features, we will explore different auxiliary tasks such as NLI and sentiment analysis in addition to few-shot learning approaches.

6 Ethical Considerations

Question answering systems are useful tools in complement to human experts, but the "word-of-

[1] Additional experiments in the COVID domain with different auxiliary tasks are presented in the Appendix A.1

BioQA Samples
Q: what sugar is found in rna DAPT: ribose, whereas the sugar in DNA is deoxyribose T+DAPT: ribose
Q: normal blood pressure range definition DAPT: 120 mm Hg1 T+DAPT: a blood pressure of 120 mm Hg1 when the heart beats (systolic) and a blood pressure of 80 mm Hg when the heart relaxes (diastolic)
MoviesQA Samples
Q: what is cyborgs real name DAPT: Victor Stone/Cyborg is a hero from DC comics most famous for being a member of the Teen Titans T+DAPT: Victor Stone
Q: who plays klaus baudelaire in the show DAPT: Liam Aiken played the role of Klaus Baudelaire in the 2004 movie A Series of Unfortunate Events. T+DAPT: Liam Aiken

Table 3: Samples from BioQA and MoviesQA where T+DAPT achieves exact match with the label answer, and DAPT produces a different answer. Answers from each approach are shown side-by-side for comparison.

machine effect" (Longoni and Cian, 2020) demonstrates the effects of a potentially dangerous overtrust in the results of such systems. While the methods proposed in this paper would allow more thorough usage of existing resources, they also bestow confidence and capabilities to models which may not have much domain expertise. T+DAPT models aim to mimic extensively domain-trained models, which are themselves approximations of real experts or source documents. Use of domain adaptation methods for low-data settings could propagate misinformation from a lack of source data. For example, while making an information-retrieval system for biomedical and COVID information could become quicker and less resource-intensive using our approach, people should not rely on such a system for medical advice without extensive counsel from a qualified medical professional.

References

Payal Bajaj, Daniel Campos, Nick Craswell, Li Deng, Jianfeng Gao, Xiaodong Liu, Rangan Majumder, Andrew McNamara, Bhaskar Mitra, Tri Nguyen, Mir Rosenberg, Xia Song, Alina Stoica, Saurabh Tiwary, and Tong Wang. 2018. Ms marco: A human generated machine reading comprehension dataset. *arXiv:1611.09268 [cs]*.

Cristian Danescu-Niculescu-Mizil and Lillian Lee. 2011. Chameleons in imagined conversations: A new approach to understanding coordination of linguistic style in dialogs.

Rezarta Islamaj Doğan, Robert Leaman, and Zhiyong Lu. 2014. Ncbi disease corpus: A resource for disease name recognition and concept normalization. *Journal of Biomedical Informatics*, 47:1–10.

Yu Gu, Robert Tinn, Hao Cheng, Michael Lucas, Naoto Usuyama, Xiaodong Liu, Tristan Naumann, Jianfeng Gao, and Hoifung Poon. 2021. Domain-specific language model pretraining for biomedical natural language processing.

Suchin Gururangan, Ana Marasović, Swabha Swayamdipta, Kyle Lo, Iz Beltagy, Doug Downey, and Noah Smith. 2020. Don't stop pretraining: Adapt language models to domains and tasks.

Alon Hazan, Yoel Shoshan, Daniel Khapun, Roy Aladjem, and Vadim Ratner. 2018. Adapternet - learning input transformation for domain adaptation.

Timothy J. Hazen, Shehzaad Dhuliawala, and Daniel Boies. 2019. Towards domain adaptation from limited data for question answering using deep neural networks. *arXiv:1911.02655 [cs]*.

Jinhyuk Lee, Wonjin Yoon, Sungdong Kim, Donghyeon Kim, Sunkyu Kim, Chan Ho So, and Jaewoo Kang. 2019. Biobert: a pre-trained biomedical language representation model for biomedical text mining. *Bioinformatics*.

Jingjing Liu, Panupong Pasupat, Yining Wang, Scott Cyphers, and Jim Glass. 2013. Query understanding enhanced by hierarchical parsing structures.

Yinhan Liu, Myle Ott, Naman Goyal, Jingfei Du, Mandar Joshi, Danqi Chen, Omer Levy, Mike Lewis, Luke Zettlemoyer, and Veselin Stoyanov. 2019. Roberta: A robustly optimized bert pretraining approach.

Kyle Lo, Lucy Lu Wang, Mark Neumann, Rodney Kinney, and Dan S. Weld. 2020. S2orc: The semantic scholar open research corpus.

Chiara Longoni and Luca Cian. 2020. Artificial intelligence in utilitarian vs. hedonic contexts: The "word-of-machine" effect. *Journal of Marketing*.

Andrew Maas, Raymond Daly, Peter Pham, Dan Huang, Andrew Ng, and Christopher Potts. 2011. Learning word vectors for sentiment analysis.

Avinash Madasu and Vijjini Anvesh Rao. 2020. Sequential domain adaptation through elastic weight consolidation for sentiment analysis. *arXiv:2007.01189 [cs]*.

Timo Möller, Anthony Reina, Raghavan Jayakumar, and Malte Pietsch. 2020. COVID-QA: A question answering dataset for COVID-19. In *Proceedings of the 1st Workshop on NLP for COVID-19 at ACL 2020*, Online. Association for Computational Linguistics.

Timo Möller, Anthony Reina, Raghavan Jayakumar, and Malte Pietsch. 2020. Covid-qa: A question answering dataset for covid-19.

Bo Pang, Lillian Lee, and Shivakumar Vaithyanathan. 2019. Thumbs up? sentiment classification using machine learning techniques.

Yada Pruksachatkun, Jason Phang, Haokun Liu, Phu Mon Htut, Xiaoyi Zhang, Richard Yuanzhe Pang, Clara Vania, Katharina Kann, and Samuel R. Bowman. 2020. Intermediate-task transfer learning with pretrained models for natural language understanding: When and why does it work?

Pranav Rajpurkar, Jian Zhang, Konstantin Lopyrev, and Percy Liang. 2018. Squad: 100,000+ questions for machine comprehension of text.

Revanth Gangi Reddy, Bhavani Iyer, Md Arafat Sultan, Rong Zhang, Avi Sil, Vittorio Castelli, Radu Florian, and Salim Roukos. 2020. End-to-end qa on covid-19: Domain adaptation with synthetic training.

Alexander Rietzler, Sebastian Stabinger, Paul Opitz, and Stefan Engl. 2020. Adapt or get left behind: Domain adaptation through BERT language model finetuning for aspect-target sentiment classification. In *Proceedings of the 12th Language Resources and Evaluation Conference*, pages 4933–4941, Marseille, France. European Language Resources Association.

Erik F. Tjong Kim Sang and Fien De Meulder. 2003. Introduction to the conll-2003 shared task. *Proceedings of the seventh conference on Natural language learning at HLT-NAACL 2003*.

Adam Trischler, Tong Wang, Xingdi Yuan, Justin Harris, Alessandro Sordoni, Philip Bachman, and Kaheer Suleman. 2017. Newsqa: A machine comprehension dataset.

Lucy Lu Wang, Kyle Lo, Yoganand Chandrasekhar, Russell Reas, Jiangjiang Yang, Doug Burdick, Darrin Eide, Kathryn Funk, Yannis Katsis, Rodney Michael Kinney, et al. 2020. Cord-19: The covid-19 open research dataset. In *Proceedings of the 1st Workshop on NLP for COVID-19 at ACL 2020*.

Jerry Wei, Chengyu Huang, Soroush Vosoughi, and Jason Wei. 2020. What are people asking about covid-19? a question classification dataset. In *Proceedings of the 1st Workshop on NLP for COVID-19 at ACL 2020*.

Georg Wiese, Dirk Weissenborn, and Mariana Neves. 2017. Neural domain adaptation for biomedical question answering.

Thomas Wolf, Lysandre Debut, Victor Sanh, Julien Chaumond, Clement Delangue, Anthony Moi, Pierric Cistac, Tim Rault, Rémi Louf, Morgan Funtowicz, Joe Davison, Sam Shleifer, Patrick von Platen, Clara Ma, Yacine Jernite, Julien Plu, Canwen Xu, Teven Le Scao, Sylvain Gugger, Mariama Drame, Quentin Lhoest, and Alexander M. Rush. 2020. Huggingface's transformers: State-of-the-art natural language processing.

Y. Xu, X. Zhong, A. J. J. Yepes, and J. H. Lau. 2020. Forget me not: Reducing catastrophic forgetting for domain adaptation in reading comprehension. *arXiv:1911.00202 [cs]*.

Rowan Zellers, Ari Holtzman, Hannah Rashkin, Yonatan Bisk, Ali Farhadi, Franziska Roesner, Yejin Choi, and Paul Allen. 2020. Defending against neural fake news.

Rong Zhang, Revanth Gangi Reddy, Md Arafat Sultan, Vittorio Castelli, Anthony Ferritto, Radu Florian, Efsun Sarioglu Kayi, Salim Roukos, Avirup Sil, and Todd Ward. 2020. Multi-stage pre-training for low-resource domain adaptation. *arXiv:2010.05904 [cs]*.

A Appendix

RoBERTa Adaptation Procedure	CovidQA
CovidQA (upper bound)	52.1416
SQuAD only	42.0485
DAPT	47.2190
CovidNER	42.6584
CovidQCLS	42.6300
DAPT+Covid-NER	43.0710
DAPT+Covid-QCLS	**45.8314**
DAPT+CovidNER+CovidQCLS	43.0854

Table 4: Zero-shot F1 performance of RoBERTa-Base models on dev sets of QA data for COVID domain with SQuAD1.1 following different intermediate pretraining regimens. The CovidQA upper bound score is attained by training directly on the CovidQA train set.

Model	NewsQA
RoBERTa-Base	
1 Epoch, 1000 Samples	19.9953
2 Epochs, 1000 Samples	35.2666
2 Epochs, 5000 Samples	47.0090
2 Epochs, All Samples	**56.9803**
2 Epochs, All Samples (Head)	05.5891
NewsRoBERTa (DAPT)	
1 Epoch, 1000 Samples	17.9025
2 Epochs, 1000 Samples	28.4453
2 Epochs, 5000 Samples	44.1206

Table 5: Zero-shot F1 performance of RoBERTa-Base models on NewsQA following different amounts of SQuAD fine-tuning. For comparison the score of our News model from the main paper with 2 epochs and all samples is included as an upper bound, alongside a head tuning baseline where all weights are frozen except the classifier layer.

A.1 Experiment Details and Additional Experiments

Freezing Layer - We tried to freeze the bottom layer after NER training and only train the QA layer on SQuAD, the performance is worse than fine-tuning the whole RoBERTa and QA layer. NER and QA may not rely on the exact same features for the final task which may be the reason that freezing causes a performance decrease.

Different Training Epoch and Training Examples - When selecting the best performance model, we use a validation set in target domain to evaluate the performance. From Table 5, we show our trials with different amounts of SQuAD training in the News Domain and how it affected performance in NewsQA.

Different Training Order - We tried to use different training order, for example, we train on SQuAD1.1 task first and then on NER, the F1 score is 42.15 in CovidQA, which has some improvement, but QA as the last task performs better.

Another Auxiliary Task - In the Covid domain, we also do experiments on a more QA-relevant task, question classification (QCLS) (Wei et al., 2020). We show the result in Table 4. The experiments show that QCLS task have more improvements than NER task. In addition, we test the model trained on CovidQA as the performance upper bound.

Let the Model Decide its Curriculum for Multitask Learning

Neeraj Varshney, Swaroop Mishra, Chitta Baral
Arizona State University
{nvarshn2, srmishr1, cbaral}@asu.edu

Abstract

Curriculum learning strategies in prior multi-task learning approaches arrange datasets in a difficulty hierarchy either based on human perception or by exhaustively searching the optimal arrangement. However, human perception of difficulty may not always correlate well with machine interpretation leading to poor performance and exhaustive search is computationally expensive. Addressing these concerns, we propose two classes of techniques to arrange training instances into a learning curriculum based on difficulty scores computed via model-based approaches. The two classes i.e Dataset-level and Instance-level differ in granularity of arrangement. Through comprehensive experiments with 12 datasets, we show that instance-level and dataset-level techniques result in strong representations as they lead to an average performance improvement of 4.17% and 3.15% over their respective baselines. Furthermore, we find that most of this improvement comes from correctly answering the difficult instances, implying a greater efficacy of our techniques on difficult tasks.

1 Introduction

In recent times, Multi-Task Learning (MTL) (Caruana, 1997) i.e. developing one *Generalist* model capable of handling multiple tasks has received significant attention from the NLP community (Aghajanyan et al., 2021; Lu et al., 2020; Sanh et al., 2019; Clark et al., 2019; Mishra et al., 2022). Developing a single model in MTL has several advantages over multiple *Specialist* models as it (i) can leverage knowledge gained while learning other tasks and perform better in limited-data scenarios (Crammer and Mansour, 2012; Ruder et al., 2017), (ii) prevents overfitting to a single task, thus providing a regularization effect and increasing robustness (Clark et al., 2019; Evgeniou and Pontil, 2004), and (iii) provides storage and efficiency benefits because only one model needs to be maintained for all the tasks (Bingel and Søgaard, 2017).

Prior work has shown that presenting training instances ordered by difficulty level benefits not only humans but also machines (Elman, 1993; Xu et al., 2020). Arranging instances in a difficulty hierarchy i.e Curriculum Learning (easy to hard) and Anti-Curriculum Learning (hard to easy) has been studied in MTL setup (McCann et al., 2018; Pentina et al., 2015). These techniques arrange datasets either based on human perception of difficulty or by exhaustively searching the optimal arrangement. However, both these approaches have several limitations. Firstly, human perception of difficulty may not always correlate well with machine interpretation, for instance, a dataset that is easy for humans could be difficult for machines to learn or vice-versa. Secondly, exhaustive search is computationally expensive and becomes intractable as the number and size of datasets increase.

In this work, we propose two classes of techniques that enable models to form their own learning curriculum in a difficulty hierarchy. The two classes i.e Dataset-level and Instance-level differ in the granularity of arrangement. In dataset-level techniques, we arrange **datasets** based on the average difficulty score of their instances and train the model sequentially such that all the instances of a dataset are learned together. In instance-level techniques, we relax the dataset boundaries and order **instances** solely based on their difficulty scores. We leverage two model-based approaches to compute the difficulty scores (Section 2).

We experiment with 12 datasets covering various NLP tasks and show that instance and dataset-level techniques result in stronger representations with an average performance gain of 4.17% and 3.15% over their respective baselines. Furthermore, we analyze model predictions and find that difficult instances contribute most to this improvement implying greater effectiveness of our techniques on difficult tasks. We note that our techniques are generic and can be employed in any MTL setup.

Proceedings of the Third Workshop on Deep Learning for Low-Resource Natural Language Processing, pages 117 - 125
July 14, 2022 ©2022 Association for Computational Linguistics

In summary, our contributions are as follows:

1. **Incorporating Machine Interpretation of Difficulty in MTL**: We introduce a novel framework for MTL that goes beyond human intuition of sample difficulty and provides model the flexibility to form its own curriculum at two granularities: instance-level and dataset-level.
2. **Performance Improvement**: We experiment with 12 NLP datasets and show that instance and dataset-level techniques lead to a considerable performance improvement of 4.17% and 3.15%. We note that our curriculum arrangement techniques can be used in conjunction with other multi-task learning methods such as dynamic sampling (Gottumukkala et al., 2020) and pre-finetuning (Aghajanyan et al., 2021) to further improve their performance.
3. **Efficacy on Difficult Instances**: Our experiments in low-data regime reveal that the proposed techniques are most effective on difficult instances. This makes them more applicable for real-world tasks as they are often more difficult than abstract toy tasks and provide limited training instances.

2 Difficulty Score Computation

In this section, we describe two model-based difficulty computation methods based on recent works.

2.1 Cross Review Method

Xu et al. (2020) proposed a method that requires splitting the training dataset D into N equal meta-datasets (M_1 to M_N) and training a separate model on each meta-dataset with identical architecture. Then, each training instance is inferred using the models trained on other meta-datasets and the average prediction confidence is subtracted from 1 to get the difficulty score. Mathematically, score of instance i ($\in M_k$) is calculated as,

$$s_i = 1 - \frac{\sum_{j \in (1,...,N), j \neq k} c_{ji}}{N-1}$$

where c_{ji} is prediction confidence on instance i given by the model trained on M_j.

2.2 Average Confidence Across Epochs

In this method, the difficulty score is computed by simply averaging the prediction confidences across epochs of a single model and subtracting it from 1.

$$s_i = 1 - \frac{\sum_{j=1}^{E} c_{ji}}{E}$$

where the model is trained till E epochs and c_{ji} is prediction confidence of the correct answer given by the model at j^{th} checkpoint. This method is based on recent works that analyze the behavior of model during training i.e "training dynamics" (Swayamdipta et al., 2020) and during evaluation (Varshney et al., 2022a).

Algorithm 1: General Training Structure

```
Input:
D: the training dataset,
{S_1, ..., S_K}: splits created from D
frac: fraction of previous split
Initialization: Model M
for i ← 1 to K do
    train_data = S_i
    for j ← 1 to i − 1 do
        sampled_S_j = Sampler(S_j, frac)
        train_data += sampled_S_j
    end
    Train M with train_data
end
Train M with D
```

3 Proposed Techniques

Addressing the limitations of current approaches highlighted in Section 1, we propose two classes of techniques to arrange training instances that allow models to form the learning curriculum based on their own difficulty interpretation. The technique classes i.e Dataset-Level and Instance-Level leverage difficulty scores computed using methods described in section 2 and follow the general training structure shown in Algorithm 1. The training dataset D is divided into K splits ($S_1, ..., S_K$) based on the difficulty score, and model M is trained sequentially on these ordered splits. Furthermore, while training the model on split S_i, a fraction ($frac$) of instances from previous splits ($S_j(j < i)$) is also included in training to avoid catastrophic forgetting (Carpenter and Grossberg, 1988) i.e forgetting the previous splits while learning a new split. Note that D is a collection of multiple datasets in the MTL setup. The final step requires training on the entire dataset D as the evaluation sets often contain instances of all tasks and difficulty levels. Dataset-level and Instance level techniques vary in the way splits ($S_1, ..., S_K$) are created as described below:

Dataset-level techniques: In this technique class, each **dataset** represents a split and is arranged

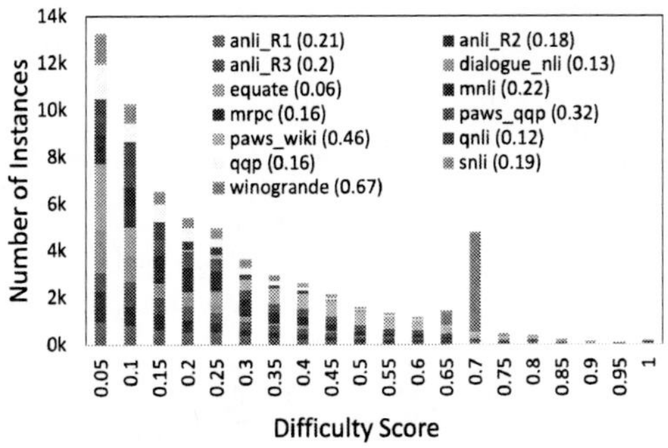

Figure 1: Distribution of instances based on difficulty score computed using Average Confidence method. Difficulty score of datasets are shown in the legends.

based on the average difficulty score of its instances i.e score of a dataset D_k is calculated as:

$$d_k = \frac{\sum_{i \in D_k} s_i}{|D_k|}$$

where, s_i is the difficulty score of instance $i \in D_k$.

Instance-level techniques: Here, we relax the dataset boundaries and arrange **instances** solely based on their difficulty scores. We study two approaches of dividing instances into splits $(S_1, ..., S_K)$: **Uniform and Distribution-based splitting**. In the former, we create K uniform splits from D, while in the latter, we divide based on the distribution of scores such that instances with similar scores are grouped in the same split[1]. The latter approach can result in unequal split sizes as we show in Figure 1 that the number of instances varies greatly across difficulty scores.

4 Experiments

Datasets: We experiment with 12 datasets covering various sentence pair tasks, namely, Natural Language Inference (SNLI (Bowman et al., 2015), MultiNLI (Williams et al., 2018), Adversarial NLI (Nie et al., 2020)), Paraphrase Identification (QQP (Iyer et al., 2017), MRPC (Dolan and Brockett, 2005), PAWS (Zhang et al., 2019)), Commonsense Reasoning (Winogrande (Sakaguchi et al., 2020)), Question Answering NLI (QNLI (Wang et al., 2018)), Dialogue NLI (DNLI (Welleck et al., 2019)), and Numerical Reasoning (Stress Test of Equate (Ravichander et al., 2019)). For evaluation on robustness and generalization parameters, we use HANS (McCoy et al., 2019) and Stress Test (Naik et al., 2018) datasets.

[1]Refer to Appendix for details

Setup: We experiment in a low-resource regime limiting the number of training instances of each dataset to 5000. This enables evaluating our techniques in a fair and comprehensive manner as transformer models achieve very high accuracy when given large datasets. Furthermore, inspired by decaNLP (McCann et al., 2018), we reformulate all the tasks in our MTL setup as span identification Question Answering tasks[1]. This allows creating a single model to solve the tasks that originally have different output spaces.

Implementation Details: We use three values of $frac$: 0, 0.2, and 0.4 (refer Algorithm 1), $N = 5$ (in Cross Review method), and $E = 5$ (in Average Confidence method). For distribution-based splitting, we experiment by dividing D into 3 and 5 splits[1]. These hyper-parameters are selected based on development dataset performance.

Baseline Methods: In MTL, *heterogeneous* batching where all the datasets are combined and a batch is randomly sampled has been shown to be much more effective than *homogeneous* and *partitioned* batching strategies (Gottumukkala et al., 2020). Therefore, we use it as the baseline for instance-level techniques. For dataset-level techniques, we generate multiple dataset orders and take the average performance as the baseline. We average these baseline scores across 3 different runs.

5 Results and Analysis

Table 1 shows the efficacy of our proposed curriculum learning techniques.

Performance Improvement: *Instance and Dataset-level techniques achieve an average improvement of 4.17% and 3.15% over their respective baseline methods.* This improvement in consistent across all the datasets and also outperforms single-task performance in most cases. Furthermore, we find that *models leveraging Average Confidence method (2.2) outperform their counterparts using the Cross Review method (2.1)*[1] *rendering Average Confidence approach as more effective both in terms of performance and computation as Cross Review requires training multiple models (one for each meta-dataset).*

Uniform Vs Distribution based splitting: *In instance-level experiments, distribution-based splitting shows slight improvement over uniform split-*

Datasets	Single-Task		Instance-Level								Dataset-Level			
			Heterogeneous(B)		Uniform		Distribution (D)		D with $frac$=0.4		Random Order(B)		Proposed Order	
	EM	F1	EM	F1	EM	F1	EM	F1	EM	F1	EM	F1	EM	F1
SNLI	77.26	77.42	74.55	74.62	77.79	**77.79**	77.64	77.7	77.65	77.65	77.7	77.75	78.94	**79.05**
MNLI Mismatched	65.98	66.12	62.07	62.14	66.14	66.3	66.71	**66.78**	66.6	66.66	66.29	66.4	69.15	**69.28**
MNLI Matched	65.33	65.45	61.23	61.36	65.85	65.96	66.91	**67.01**	66.82	66.85	65.96	66.09	69.18	**69.33**
Winogrande	50	50	47.34	50	50.24	**50.27**	50	50.12	49.82	49.85	47.99	49.85	48.37	**50.3**
QNLI	74.21	74.23	66.78	66.81	70.42	70.44	71.81	**71.81**	71.38	71.38	70.35	70.39	73.75	**73.79**
EQUATE	98.99	98.99	98.99	98.99	99.14	99.21	99.57	**99.57**	99.28	99.28	99.57	99.57	99.57	**99.57**
QQP	80.04	80.06	75.34	75.35	78.89	78.9	79.23	**79.25**	79.11	79.12	79.23	79.26	80.27	**80.29**
MRPC	80.98	80.98	74.42	74.45	74.05	74.05	75.95	**75.98**	75.4	75.4	75.73	75.77	79.08	**79.08**
PAWS Wiki	52.45	52.49	55.92	56.01	53.15	53.16	54.39	54.47	70.59	**70.62**	56.44	56.51	80.33	**80.34**
PAWS QQP	68.25	68.41	73.03	73.03	69	69	71.83	71.83	78.84	**78.84**	73.08	73.12	83.46	**83.46**
ANLI R1	42.2	42.57	38.1	38.28	42.1	42.13	45.7	**45.7**	43.2	43.33	42.9	**43.04**	42.3	42.58
ANLI R2	38.1	38.78	35	35	39.8	**39.9**	38.9	39.05	37.2	37.25	38.4	**38.5**	36.8	36.97
ANLI R3	39.25	39.38	36.17	36.24	38.5	**38.62**	38.17	38.24	36.5	36.56	37.92	**38.03**	37.25	37.4
DNLI	84.68	84.83	80.36	80.48	83.51	**83.57**	83.15	83.2	82.09	82.12	82.52	82.59	82.67	**82.73**
HANS	-	-	49.06	49.07	48.95	49.01	48.3	48.38	49.39	**49.45**	48.22	**48.27**	48	48.09
Stress Test	-	-	55.28	55.44	56.2	56.31	58.66	**58.77**	57.7	57.75	56.74	56.84	59.94	**60.15**

Table 1: Results on performing curriculum learning using the proposed techniques with difficulty scores computed via Average Confidence approach. Note that $frac$ is 0 unless otherwise mentioned. B means baseline and D with $frac$=0.4 column represents Distribution based splitting with value of $frac$ as 0.4.

ting. We attribute this to the superior inductive bias resulting from the collation of instances with similar difficulty scores to the same split.

Effect of adding instances from previous splits: *For dataset-level techniques, we find that it does not provide any improvement.* This is because all the instances of a dataset are grouped in a single split therefore, adding instances from other splits doesn't contribute much to the inductive bias. Furthermore, *in the case of instance-level, it leads to a performance improvement* because previous splits contain instances of the same dataset hence, providing the inductive bias.

Difficulty Scores Analysis: Figure 1 shows the distribution of training instances of all datasets with difficulty scores computed using Average confidence (2.2) method. This distribution reveals that instances across datasets and within every dataset vary greatly in difficulty as they are widely spread across the difficulty scores. Comparing the average difficulty score of all datasets (shown in legends of Figure 1) shows that *Equate and QNLI are easy-to-learn while PAWS and Winogrande are relatively difficult-to-learn.* Furthermore, *around 32% of the training instances get assigned a difficulty score of* ≤ 0.1 *hinting at either the presence of dataset artifacts or the inherent easiness of these instances.* A similar observation is made with Cross Review method with the percentage being 37%.

Test Set Analysis: We also compute difficulty scores of test instances and plot the performance improvement achieved by our approach over the baseline method for every difficulty score bucket

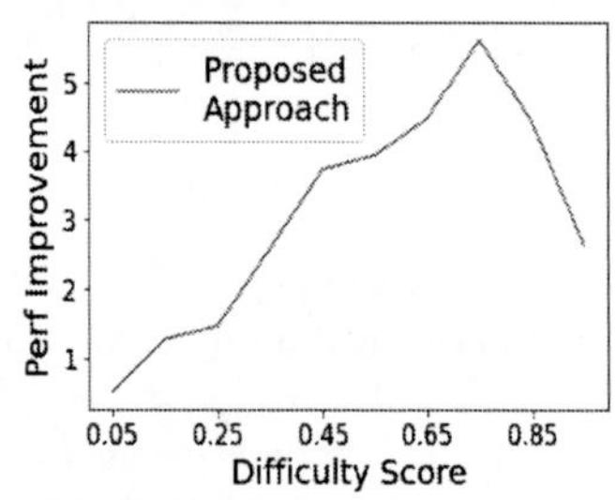

Figure 2: Performance improvement vs Difficulty score for dataset level techniques.

in Figure 2. We find that *the proposed technique is effective especially on instances with high difficulty scores*. This implies a greater efficacy of our techniques on tasks that contain difficult instances.

6 Conclusion

In this paper, we proposed two classes of techniques for MTL that allow models to form the learning curriculum based on their own interpretation of difficulty. Comprehensive experiments with 12 datasets showed that our techniques lead to a performance improvement of 4.17% and 3.15%. Furthermore, we found that difficult instances contribute most to this improvement, implying a greater efficacy of our techniques on difficult tasks. We hope that our techniques and findings will foster development of stronger multi-task learning models as our curriculum arrangement techniques can be used in conjunction with other multi-task learning methods such as dynamic sampling (Gottumukkala et al., 2020) and pre-finetuning (Aghajanyan et al., 2021) to further improve their performance.

Acknowledgements

We thank the anonymous reviewers for their insightful feedback. This research was supported by DARPA SAIL-ON program.

References

Armen Aghajanyan, Anchit Gupta, Akshat Shrivastava, Xilun Chen, Luke Zettlemoyer, and Sonal Gupta. 2021. Muppet: Massive multi-task representations with pre-finetuning. In *Proceedings of the 2021 Conference on Empirical Methods in Natural Language Processing*, pages 5799–5811, Online and Punta Cana, Dominican Republic. Association for Computational Linguistics.

Joachim Bingel and Anders Søgaard. 2017. Identifying beneficial task relations for multi-task learning in deep neural networks. In *Proceedings of the 15th Conference of the European Chapter of the Association for Computational Linguistics: Volume 2, Short Papers*, pages 164–169, Valencia, Spain. Association for Computational Linguistics.

Samuel R. Bowman, Gabor Angeli, Christopher Potts, and Christopher D. Manning. 2015. A large annotated corpus for learning natural language inference. In *Proceedings of the 2015 Conference on Empirical Methods in Natural Language Processing*, pages 632–642, Lisbon, Portugal. Association for Computational Linguistics.

Gail A. Carpenter and Stephen Grossberg. 1988. The art of adaptive pattern recognition by a self-organizing neural network. *Computer*, 21(3):77–88.

Rich Caruana. 1997. Multitask learning. *Machine learning*, 28(1):41–75.

Kevin Clark, Minh-Thang Luong, Urvashi Khandelwal, Christopher D. Manning, and Quoc V. Le. 2019. BAM! born-again multi-task networks for natural language understanding. In *Proceedings of the 57th Annual Meeting of the Association for Computational Linguistics*, pages 5931–5937, Florence, Italy. Association for Computational Linguistics.

Koby Crammer and Yishay Mansour. 2012. Learning multiple tasks using shared hypotheses. *Advances in Neural Information Processing Systems*, 25:1475–1483.

William B Dolan and Chris Brockett. 2005. Automatically constructing a corpus of sentential paraphrases. In *Proceedings of the Third International Workshop on Paraphrasing (IWP2005)*.

Jeffrey L Elman. 1993. Learning and development in neural networks: The importance of starting small. *Cognition*, 48(1):71–99.

Theodoros Evgeniou and Massimiliano Pontil. 2004. Regularized multi–task learning. In *Proceedings of the tenth ACM SIGKDD international conference on Knowledge discovery and data mining*, pages 109–117.

Ananth Gottumukkala, Dheeru Dua, Sameer Singh, and Matt Gardner. 2020. Dynamic sampling strategies for multi-task reading comprehension. In *Proceedings of the 58th Annual Meeting of the Association for Computational Linguistics*, pages 920–924.

Shankar Iyer, Nikhil Dandekar, and Kornél Csernai. 2017. First quora dataset release: Question pairs. *data. quora. com*.

Sébastien Jean, Orhan Firat, and Melvin Johnson. 2019. Adaptive scheduling for multi-task learning. *arXiv preprint arXiv:1909.06434*.

Eliyahu Kiperwasser and Miguel Ballesteros. 2018. Scheduled multi-task learning: From syntax to translation. *Transactions of the Association for Computational Linguistics*, 6:225–240.

Jiasen Lu, Vedanuj Goswami, Marcus Rohrbach, Devi Parikh, and Stefan Lee. 2020. 12-in-1: Multi-task vision and language representation learning. In *The IEEE/CVF Conference on Computer Vision and Pattern Recognition (CVPR)*.

Bryan McCann, Nitish Shirish Keskar, Caiming Xiong, and Richard Socher. 2018. The natural language decathlon: Multitask learning as question answering. *arXiv preprint arXiv:1806.08730*.

Tom McCoy, Ellie Pavlick, and Tal Linzen. 2019. Right for the wrong reasons: Diagnosing syntactic heuristics in natural language inference. In *Proceedings of the 57th Annual Meeting of the Association for Computational Linguistics*, pages 3428–3448, Florence, Italy. Association for Computational Linguistics.

Swaroop Mishra, Arindam Mitra, Neeraj Varshney, Bhavdeep Sachdeva, Peter Clark, Chitta Baral, and Ashwin Kalyan. 2022. NumGLUE: A suite of fundamental yet challenging mathematical reasoning tasks. In *Proceedings of the 60th Annual Meeting of the Association for Computational Linguistics (Volume 1: Long Papers)*, pages 3505–3523, Dublin, Ireland. Association for Computational Linguistics.

Aakanksha Naik, Abhilasha Ravichander, Norman Sadeh, Carolyn Rose, and Graham Neubig. 2018. Stress test evaluation for natural language inference. In *Proceedings of the 27th International Conference on Computational Linguistics*, pages 2340–2353, Santa Fe, New Mexico, USA. Association for Computational Linguistics.

Yixin Nie, Adina Williams, Emily Dinan, Mohit Bansal, Jason Weston, and Douwe Kiela. 2020. Adversarial NLI: A new benchmark for natural language understanding. In *Proceedings of the 58th Annual Meeting of the Association for Computational Linguistics*, pages 4885–4901, Online. Association for Computational Linguistics.

Anastasia Pentina, Viktoriia Sharmanska, and Christoph H Lampert. 2015. Curriculum learning of multiple tasks. In *Proceedings of the IEEE Conference on Computer Vision and Pattern Recognition*, pages 5492–5500.

Abhilasha Ravichander, Aakanksha Naik, Carolyn Rose, and Eduard Hovy. 2019. EQUATE: A benchmark evaluation framework for quantitative reasoning in natural language inference. In *Proceedings of the 23rd Conference on Computational Natural Language Learning (CoNLL)*, pages 349–361, Hong Kong, China. Association for Computational Linguistics.

Sebastian Ruder, Joachim Bingel, Isabelle Augenstein, and Anders Søgaard. 2017. Sluice networks: Learning what to share between loosely related tasks. *ArXiv*, abs/1705.08142.

Keisuke Sakaguchi, Ronan Le Bras, Chandra Bhagavatula, and Yejin Choi. 2020. Winogrande: An adversarial winograd schema challenge at scale. In *Proceedings of the AAAI Conference on Artificial Intelligence*, volume 34, pages 8732–8740.

Victor Sanh, Thomas Wolf, and Sebastian Ruder. 2019. A hierarchical multi-task approach for learning embeddings from semantic tasks. In *Proceedings of the AAAI Conference on Artificial Intelligence*, volume 33, pages 6949–6956.

Swabha Swayamdipta, Roy Schwartz, Nicholas Lourie, Yizhong Wang, Hannaneh Hajishirzi, Noah A. Smith, and Yejin Choi. 2020. Dataset cartography: Mapping and diagnosing datasets with training dynamics. In *Proceedings of the 2020 Conference on Empirical Methods in Natural Language Processing (EMNLP)*, pages 9275–9293, Online. Association for Computational Linguistics.

Neeraj Varshney, Swaroop Mishra, and Chitta Baral. 2022a. ILDAE: Instance-level difficulty analysis of evaluation data. In *Proceedings of the 60th Annual Meeting of the Association for Computational Linguistics (Volume 1: Long Papers)*, pages 3412–3425, Dublin, Ireland. Association for Computational Linguistics.

Neeraj Varshney, Swaroop Mishra, and Chitta Baral. 2022b. Towards improving selective prediction ability of NLP systems. In *Proceedings of the 7th Workshop on Representation Learning for NLP*, pages 221–226, Dublin, Ireland. Association for Computational Linguistics.

Alex Wang, Amanpreet Singh, Julian Michael, Felix Hill, Omer Levy, and Samuel Bowman. 2018. GLUE: A multi-task benchmark and analysis platform for natural language understanding. In *Proceedings of the 2018 EMNLP Workshop BlackboxNLP: Analyzing and Interpreting Neural Networks for NLP*, pages 353–355, Brussels, Belgium. Association for Computational Linguistics.

Sean Welleck, Jason Weston, Arthur Szlam, and Kyunghyun Cho. 2019. Dialogue natural language inference. In *Proceedings of the 57th Annual Meeting of the Association for Computational Linguistics*, pages 3731–3741, Florence, Italy. Association for Computational Linguistics.

Adina Williams, Nikita Nangia, and Samuel Bowman. 2018. A broad-coverage challenge corpus for sentence understanding through inference. In *Proceedings of the 2018 Conference of the North American Chapter of the Association for Computational Linguistics: Human Language Technologies, Volume 1 (Long Papers)*, pages 1112–1122, New Orleans, Louisiana. Association for Computational Linguistics.

Benfeng Xu, Licheng Zhang, Zhendong Mao, Quan Wang, Hongtao Xie, and Yongdong Zhang. 2020. Curriculum learning for natural language understanding. In *Proceedings of the 58th Annual Meeting of the Association for Computational Linguistics*, pages 6095–6104.

Poorya Zaremoodi and Gholamreza Haffari. 2019. Adaptively scheduled multitask learning: The case of low-resource neural machine translation. In *Proceedings of the 3rd Workshop on Neural Generation and Translation*, pages 177–186, Hong Kong. Association for Computational Linguistics.

Yuan Zhang, Jason Baldridge, and Luheng He. 2019. PAWS: Paraphrase adversaries from word scrambling. In *Proceedings of the 2019 Conference of the North American Chapter of the Association for Computational Linguistics: Human Language Technologies, Volume 1 (Long and Short Papers)*, pages 1298–1308, Minneapolis, Minnesota. Association for Computational Linguistics.

Appendix

A Statistics of Evaluation Datasets

In this work, we experiment with 12 datasets spanning over several NLU tasks. Table 4 shows the statistics of the evaluation sets.

B Implementation Details

We use the huggingface implementation of BERT-Base model, batch size 16, learning rate $5e-5$ for our experiments. We use three values of $frac$: 0, 0.2, and 0.4 (refer Algorithm 1), $N = 5$ (in Cross Review method), and $E = 5$ (in Average Confidence method). For distribution based splitting, we experiment by dividing D into 3 and 5 splits. The results reported in the paper are for 3 splits. These hyper-parameters are selected based on performance on the dev dataset. We adjust the per gpu training batch size and gradient accumulation accordingly to fit in our 4 Nvidia V100 16GB GPUs.

Context – Question	Datasets
C: Kyle doesn't wear leg warmers to bed, while Logan almost always does. he is more likely to live in a colder climate. **false**, or true ? **Q:** Kyle is more likely to live in a colder climate.	Winogrande
C: In order for an elevator to be legal to carry passengers in some jurisdictions it must have a solid inner door. **false**, or true ? **Q:** What is another name for a freight elevator? Does the context sentence contain answer to this question ?	QNLI
C: What makes a great problem solver? false, or **true**? **Q:** How can I be a fast problem solver? Are the two sentences semantically equivalent?	QQP, MRPC, PAWS
C: i sell miscellaneous stuff in local fairs . **contradiction**, or neutral, or entailment ? **Q:** i used to work a 9 5 job as a telemarketer . Consistency of the dialogues ?	DNLI
C: 205 total Tajima' s are currently owned by the dealership. contradiction, or neutral, **entailment** ? **Q:** less than 305 total Tajima' s are currently owned by the dealership.	Equate
C: Two collies are barking as they play on the edge of the ocean contradiction, or neutral, or **entailment** ? **Q:** Two dogs are playing together.	SNLI, MNLI, ANLI

Table 2: Illustrative examples (Context (C) - Question (Q) pairs) of different types of training datasets considered in this work. We transform all these datasets to Question-Answering format in order to use a single model for all these tasks. Answers are highlighted in **bold**.

Datasets	Instance-Level Uniform Splitting + Prev		Dataset-Level Proposed Order with $frac$=0.4		AC on Proposed Order	
	EM	F1	EM	F1	EM	F1
SNLI	76.19	76.2	77.09	77.11	77	77.02
MNLI Mismatched	64.54	64.55	65.83	65.85	65.36	65.41
MNLI Matched	63.63	63.64	66.06	66.08	64.72	64.77
Winogrande	50.48	50.48	50.6	50.94	48.43	49.79
QNLI	68.16	68.17	71.24	71.25	72.23	72.26
EQUATE	99.71	99.71	99.43	99.43	99.57	99.57
QQP	77.61	77.61	79.32	79.32	79.68	79.71
MRPC	72.15	72.15	76.07	76.07	77.55	77.55
PAWS Wiki	52.11	52.13	69.48	69.48	52.92	52.95
PAWS QQP	68.7	68.7	69.75	69.75	66.62	66.69
ANLI R1	41.9	41.93	43.8	43.88	44.7	44.8
ANLI R2	37.8	37.85	36.8	36.83	37.4	37.5
ANLI R3	37.58	37.62	36.5	36.53	36.83	36.83
DNLI	82.55	82.58	83.64	83.66	81.83	81.93
HANS	49.76	49.77	48.24	48.28	50.25	50.26
Stress Test	56.07	56.09	57.55	57.57	58.79	58.87
Average	62.43	62.45	64.46	64.5	63.37	63.49

Table 3: Results of instance-level and dataset-level techniques.

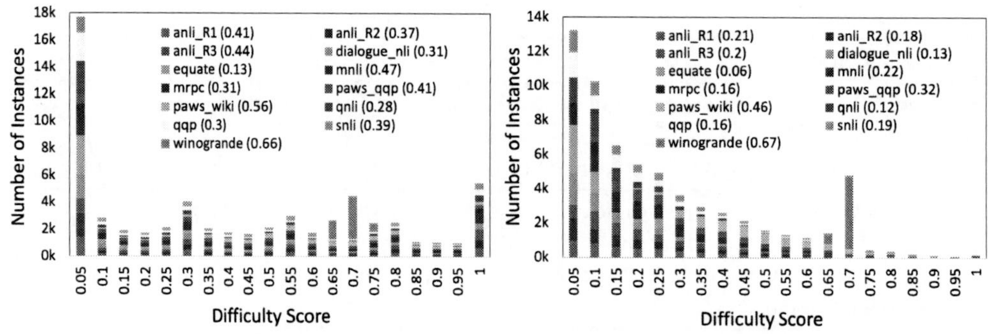

(a) Cross Review approach

(b) Average Confidence approach

Figure 3: Distribution of instances based on difficulty scores computed using (a) Cross Review approach and (b) Average Confidence approach.

Dataset	Size	Dataset	Size
SNLI	9824	MNLI	19645
Winogrande	1654	QNLI	5650
PAWS qqp	671	PAWS wiki	7987
MRPC	1630	ANLI R1	1000
ANLI R2	1000	ANLI R3	1000
DNLI	16408	HANS	30000
Equate	696	QQP	40371
Stress Test	136464		

Table 4: Statistics of the evaluation datasets.

We keep the maximum sequence length of 512 for our experiments to ensure that the model uses the full context.

C Dataset Examples

Table 2 shows examples of different types of datasets used in this work. We transform all these datasets to Question-Answering format in order to use a single model for all these tasks.

D Difficulty Scores

Figure 3 shows the distribution of difficulty scores computed using Cross Review and Average Confidence approach.

E Results

Table 3 shows the results of instance-level and dataset-level techniques.

F Analysis

In table 5, we compare the performance of random order and the proposed order (developed using our curriculum strategy) across all difficulty scores for instance level techniques.

Difficulty Score	Instances	Random Order	Proposed Order
0.1	63736	94.86	93.77
0.2	18703	87.8	85.55
0.3	28035	81.85	79.85
0.4	17238	74.5	72.81
0.5	21502	65.03	65.84
0.6	17338	57.69	57.94
0.7	21255	46.75	48.92
0.8	18058	38.36	44.05
0.9	22327	26.8	33.07
1	46008	9.17	14.05

Table 5: Comparing performance of random order and the proposed order (developed using our curriculum strategy) across all difficulty scores for instance level techniques.

G Scheduling in Multi-task Learning

Scheduling in multi-task learning has attracted a lot of attention, especially for the machine translation task (Zaremoodi and Haffari, 2019; Kiperwasser and Ballesteros, 2018; Jean et al., 2019). Such approaches can be adapted for our tasks and can further improve the multi-task performance. We leave these explorations for future work.

H Limitations of Computing Difficulty Scores using Model-based Techniques

In addition to arranging the training instances into a learning curriculum, computing difficulty scores using model-based techniques has shown its benefits in several other areas, such as improving selective prediction ability (Varshney et al., 2022b), understanding training dynamics (Swayamdipta et al., 2020), and efficient evaluations (Varshney et al., 2022a). However, these techniques present a few challenges:

1. **Computation:** They involve calculating the difficulty scores of training instances which requires additional computation. However, this computation is only required during training and not required during inference. Hence, it does not add any computational overhead at inference time when deployed in an application.
2. **Noisy Instances:** Training instances that are wrongly annotated/noisy will most certainly get assigned a very high difficulty score and hence will be learned at the end during training. This is unlikely to hamper learning when the number of noisy instances is small. However, it may negatively impact the model's learning when the training dataset has a non-trivial number of noisy instances. We plan to investigate this in our future work.

AfriTeVa: Extending "Small Data" Pretraining Approaches to Sequence-to-Sequence Models

Odunayo Ogundepo, Akintunde Oladipo, Mofetoluwa Adeyemi, Kelechi Ogueji and **Jimmy Lin**

David R. Cheriton School of Computer Science, University of Waterloo

{oogundep,aooladip,moadeyem,kelechi.ogueji,jimmylin}@uwaterloo.ca

Abstract

Pretrained language models represent the state of the art in NLP, but the successful construction of such models often requires large amounts of data and computational resources. Thus, the paucity of data for low-resource languages impedes the development of robust NLP capabilities for these languages. There has been some recent success in pretraining encoder-only models solely on a combination of low-resource African languages, exemplified by AfriBERTa. In this work, we extend the approach of "small data" pretraining to encoder–decoder models. We introduce AfriTeVa, a family of sequence-to-sequence models derived from T5 that are pretrained on 10 African languages from scratch. With a pretraining corpus of only around 1GB, we show that it is possible to achieve competitive downstream effectiveness for machine translation and text classification, compared to larger models trained on much more data. All the code and model checkpoints described in this work are publicly available at https://github.com/castorini/afriteva.

1 Introduction

Transfer learning has driven many recent advances in natural language processing, and leveraging pretrained models for downstream tasks has produced state-of-the-art results on many tasks. These results can be attributed to general-purpose knowledge that is gained when a model is pretrained on a data-rich task (Raffel et al., 2020). This paradigm also extends to multilingual settings, where a model is pretrained on text in multiple languages and then fine-tuned for downstream tasks in those languages. Some of these models, for example, mBERT and XML-R (Conneau et al., 2020), have been trained on large combination of languages comprised of high-resource and low-resource languages, amounting to many gigabytes of data.

Due to the effectiveness of transfer learning on downstream tasks, T5 (Raffel et al., 2020) introduced a unified framework where all NLP tasks can be framed as a text-to-text problem, enabling us to train a single model for multiple tasks. This framework is simple and effective by enabling knowledge transfer from high-resource to low-resource tasks (Nagoudi et al., 2022). Unlike BERT-based models, which are encoder-only models, T5 and its multilingual variants such as mT5 (Xue et al., 2021b) and byT5 (Xue et al., 2021a) are encoder–decoder models that are more suited for natural language tasks involving generation. Both mT5 and byT5 were trained on 100+ languages, of which only 13 were low-resource African languages, making up less than 6% of the total training data. Despite the existence of 2000+ African languages (Eberhard et al., 2019), only a few of them are featured in pretraining, and thus it is unclear how effective these models generalize to those languages.

The paucity of data for many African languages has been a stumbling block for developing robust NLP capabilities. However, some works have shown that it is possible to train language models with smaller amounts of data, albeit on encoder-only models. For example, Micheli et al. (2020) obtained good results on the French Question Answering Dataset (FQuAD) by pretraining on as little as 100MB of text. Directly related to our present study, AfriBERTa (Ogueji et al., 2021) pretrained a RoBERTa-based model from scratch on 10 African languages with only around 1GB of data, outperforming mBERT and XLM-R on tasks in several languages. Given this context, we pose the following research question:

Research Question: Can "small data" pretraining for low-resource African languages exemplified by AfriBERTa be extended from encoder-only models to encoder–decoder models?

Proceedings of the Third Workshop on Deep Learning for Low-Resource Natural Language Processing, pages 126 - 135
July 14, 2022 ©2022 Association for Computational Linguistics

To answer this research question, we pretrained encoder–decoder models in low-resource settings using relatively little data and evaluated our models against other models that have been pretrained on much more data. We introduce AfriTeVa, a family of pretrained transformer-based sequence-to-sequence models derived from T5, pretrained on 10 low-resource African languages. AfriTeVa gets its name from the fact that "V" is the Roman numeral for "5", which reflects its membership in the T5 family. We pretrained from random initialization with only around 1GB of data (using the same corpus as AfriBERTa) and evaluated our models on text classification and machine translation. To the best of our knowledge, this is the first encoder–decoder model pretrained solely on low-resource African languages.

With respect to our research question, our results are suggestive but not conclusive. AfriTeVa demonstrates better results than mT5, but falls short of other models pretrained with richer resources. However, existing experiments conflate several factors that we have not successfully untangled. Nevertheless, our preliminary study sets the ground for future work.

2 Related Work

2.1 NLP for African Languages

Interest in low-resource African languages has increased in recent years. However, the question of how NLP capabilities can be scaled to many of these languages has yet to be answered fully (Nekoto et al., 2020). Adebara and Abdul-Mageed (2022) highlighted the challenges of using and extending current NLP technologies to communities with different fabrics and languages. A common characteristic of African languages is the absence of large monolingual data for pretraining, which directly impacts the ability to build high-quality language models for these languages.

Some of the more recent work in benchmarking and advancing the state of machine translation for African languages include the following: Adelani et al. (2022) investigated how to best leverage existing pretrained models for machine translation in 16 languages. They also released a corpus comprising machine translation data in all 16 languages. Emezue and Dossou (2021) released MMTAfrica, which is a many-to-many multilingual translation system for 6 African languages. Duh et al. (2020) provided a benchmark state-of-the-art neural machine translation system on two African languages, Somali and Swahili, while Martinus and Abbott (2019) leveraged current neural machine translation techniques to train translation models for 5 African languages.

Some researchers have been interested in methods to adapt already pretrained models to unseen languages, thus enabling the ability to pretrain in high-resource settings and extend to low-resource languages. Liu et al. (2021) introduced a continual pretraining framework to adapt the mBART model for machine translation to unseen languages, while Baziotis et al. (2020) incorporated an LM as a prior by adding a regularization term for low-resource machine translation.

2.2 Multilingual Pretrained Models

XLM-R (Conneau et al., 2020), mBERT, and mT5 (Xue et al., 2021b) have extended masked language modelling to multilingual settings by jointly pretraining large transformer models on up to 100+ languages. This work demonstrates the effectiveness of multilingual models on downstream tasks, even for low-resource languages. This has been attributed to shared vocabulary items, generalizable representations the model learns (Artetxe et al., 2020), and model architectures (K et al., 2020).

Still, these models contain only a handful of African languages. Ogueji et al. (2021) explored the viability of pretraining multilingual models *from scratch* using only limited amounts of data on a number of African languages—this is the "small data" pretraining approach we referred to in the introduction. They demonstrated the competitiveness of this "small data" approach and released comparatively smaller models that match and in some cases exceed the effectiveness of larger models pretrained on much more data. As a follow-up, Oladipo et al. (2022) explored the effect of vocabulary size and other factors affecting transfer in AfriBERTa-based models. Our work builds on this thread: We wondered if the approach taken by AfriBERTa can be extended to encoder–decoder models.

3 Experimental Setup

Following the T5 architecture (Raffel et al., 2020), we consider 3 model sizes for AfriTeVa: small (64M parameters), base (229M parameters), and large (745M parameters). Each model is similar in configuration to their T5 counterparts.

	Small	Base	Large
# of Layers	6	12	24
# of Attention Heads	8	12	16
# of Parameters	64M	229M	745M
Batch Size	256	128	64
Optimizer		Adafactor	
ϵ		1e-6	
Weight Decay		1e-3	
Learning rate		3e-4	
Warmup steps		40000	
Vocabulary size		70000	

Table 1: **Model Configurations:** model configurations and training hyperparameters.

3.1 Pretraining

To adapt the T5 architecture (Raffel et al., 2020; Xue et al., 2021b) to African languages, we pretrained AfriTeVa on the AfriBERTa corpus (Ogueji et al., 2021), a multilingual corpus comprising 10 low-resource African languages: Afaan Oromoo, Amharic, Gahuza, Hausa, Igbo, Nigerian Pidgin, Somali, Swahili, Tigrinya, and Yorùbá. Table 2 presents characteristics of text in each language in more detail. As we can see, the languages vary in terms of morphology and typology. Amharic, Somali, and Tigrinya have subject–object–verb (SOV) word order while the other languages have subject–verb–object (SVO) word order. The languages also belong to different written scripts, another aspect of diversity.

In addition to AfriTeVa pretrained with only African languages, we also pretrained another model jointly with English and the 10 languages listed above. We sampled 1,500,000 English sentences from the Common Crawl[1] to match the language with the most sentences, which is Swahili. Our models were pretrained with a vocabulary size of 70,000 tokens learned using a SentencePiece unigram subword tokenizer (Kudo and Richardson, 2018). The model that includes English in pretraining used a different tokenizer with the same vocabulary size.

We pretrained AfriTeVa using the masked language modelling "span-corruption" training objective in T5, where consecutive spans of dropped-out tokens are replaced by a single sentinel token that does not correspond to any wordpiece in the tokenizer. We pretrained our models for 500,000 steps with effective batch sizes shown in Table 1. Model perplexity during training was evaluated on varying amounts of sentences sampled from the different languages, consisting of roughly 440,000 sentences for the models without English, and 540,000 sentences for the model with English.

All pretraining and fine-tuning experiments were conducted using the Huggingface transformers library (Wolf et al., 2020) on a TPU VM of type v3-8 provisioned on Google Cloud using the JAX/FLAX framework. All models were pretrained using a learning rate of 3e-4 and a maximum sequence length of 512 tokens using the Adafactor optimizer (Shazeer and Stern, 2018).

3.2 Fine-Tuning

Given the lack of benchmark datasets that would be appropriate for sequence-to-sequence models for low-resource African languages, we focused on two downstream tasks: machine translation and text classification.

Text Classification: We performed text classification on news title topic classification datasets for Hausa and Yorùbá (Hedderich et al., 2020). The authors established strong baselines using multilingual pretrained language models and multilingual pretrained language models + English adaptive fine-tuning. We cast the text classification task into a text-to-text format where the decoder generates two tokens; the class token and an end-of-sequence token. More precisely, the text classification task is framed as:

input: sentence [eos]
output: label [eos]

We do not use a task prefix for these experiments. In cases where the class labels are in a language not seen during pretraining or do not exist as a single token in the vocabulary, we replace them with randomly chosen tokens from the vocabulary and fine-tune. During inference, we map the tokens back to the initial labels.

To fine-tune our models, we used PyTorch Lightning with a batch-size of 16, a constant learning rate of 0.0003, and the Adam optimizer. We report F_1 scores averaged over 3 runs with different random seeds.

Machine Translation: We fine-tuned and evaluated all models on machine translation datasets in the news domain, focusing on 7 African languages. We used publicly available parallel data for the following languages: Hausa (6k sentences),[2]

[1] https://data.statmt.org/cc-100/

[2] https://www.statmt.org/wmt21/translation-task.html

Language	Lang code	Family	Word Order	Script	# Sent.	# Tok.	Size (GB)
Afaan Oromoo	orm	Afro–Asiatic	SVO	Latin	410,840	6,870,959	0.051
Amharic	amh	Afro–Asiatic	SOV	Ge'ez	525,024	1,303,086	0.213
Gahuza	gah	Niger–Congo	SVO	Latin	131,952	3,669,538	0.026
Hausa	hau	Afro–Asiatic	SVO	Latin	1,282,996	27,889,299	0.150
Igbo	igb	Niger–Congo	SVO	Latin	337,081	6,853,500	0.042
Nigerian Pidgin	pcm	English–Creole	SVO	Latin	161,842	8,709,498	0.048
Somali	som	Afro–Asiatic	SOV	Latin	995,043	27,332,348	0.170
Swahili	swa	Niger–Congo	SVO	Latin	1,442,911	30,053,834	0.185
Tigrinya	tig	Afro–Asiatic	SOV	Ge'ez	12,075	280,397	0.027
Yorùbá	yor	Niger–Congo	SVO	Latin	149,147	4,385,797	0.027
Total (African languages only)					5,448,911	108,800,600	0.939
English	eng	Indo–European	SVO	Latin	1,500,000	35,053,400	0.264
Total (Including English)					6,948,911	143,854,000	1.203

Table 2: **Dataset Information:** Characteristics and the size of data in each language, including number of sentences and tokens, and uncompressed size on disk. The table also shows the written scripts and family that each language belongs to, along with its language code.

Igbo (10k sentences) (Ezeani et al., 2020), Yorùbá (10k sentences) (Adelani et al., 2021), Swahili (30k sentences),[3] Luganda (7k sentences), Luo (7k sentences) and Pcm (8k sentences) (Adelani et al., 2022). The datasets contain train, dev, and test folds for the individual languages. All machine translation corpora are publicly available.[4]

To fine-tune our models for machine translation, we trained for 10 epochs using a beam size of 10 and a constant learning rate of 0.0003. As is standard, BLEU score (Papineni et al., 2002) was the evaluation metric.

3.3 Models Comparisons

Here we compare AfriTeVa with existing multilingual language models that were pretrained on low-resource African languages. Table 3 shows a high-level breakdown of model features.

mT5 (Xue et al., 2021b) is a multilingual variant of T5 (Raffel et al., 2020) that was pretrained on 107 languages, but includes only 13 African languages, making up less than 6% of the training corpus.

byT5 (Xue et al., 2021a) is a transformer pretrained on byte sequences using the same corpora as mT5; its model size is similar to mT5 and T5.

AfriMT5 and **AfriByT5** (Adelani et al., 2022) are multilingual sequence-to-sequence models that were adapted from mT5 and byT5, respectively. These models were further pretrained on 18 African languages plus English and French, starting from existing mT5 and byT5 checkpoints.

[3]https://opus.nlpl.eu/GlobalVoices.php

[4]https://github.com/masakhane-io/lafand-mt

XLM-R (Conneau et al., 2020) is an encoder-only model based on RoBERTa (Zhuang et al., 2021). It was pretrained on a corpus consisting of 100 languages, of which only 8 were African languages.

AfriBERTa (Ogueji et al., 2021) is also an encoder-only model based on RoBERTa, pretrained from scratch with "small data", as already discussed.

M2M-100 (Fan et al., 2021) is a multilingual encoder–decoder model that was pretrained for many-to-many multilingual translation using parallel data in 100 languages. M2M-100 can translate directly between any pair of the 100 languages covered in training, including 18 African languages.

mBART50 (Tang et al., 2020) is a multilingual encoder–decoder model trained for machine translation in 50 languages. The model was fine-tuned on many translation directions at the same time, and covers 3 African languages in pretraining.

4 Results and Discussion

4.1 Machine Translation

We present our machine translation results in Table 4 and Table 5. We compared the results of different sequence-to-sequence models fine-tuned for two directions, to and from English, for each language in our dataset. Evaluation was performed on both the model variants pretrained only with the AfriBERTa corpus as well as the variant that includes English in the pretraining corpus. For comparison, machine Translation results for mT5, byT5, AfriMT5, AfriByT5, mBART50, and M2M-100 were copied from Adelani et al. (2022).

Model	# Params	Model Family	African Languages Covered
XLM-R (Conneau et al., 2020)	270M	Encoder-only	Afaan Oromoo, Afrikaans, Amharic, Hausa, Malagasy, Somali, Swahili, Xhosa
AfriBERTa (Ogueji et al., 2021)	112M	Encoder-only	Afaan Oromoo, Amharic, Gahuza, Hausa, Igbo, Nigerian Pidgin, Somali, Swahili, Tigrinya, Yorùbá
mT5 (Xue et al., 2021b)	582M	Encoder–Decoder	Afrikaans, Amharic, Chichewa, Hausa, Igbo, Malagasy, Somali, Shona, Sotho, Swahili, Xhosa, Yorùbá, Zulu
byT5 (Xue et al., 2021a)	582M	Encoder–Decoder	Afrikaans, Amharic, Chichewa, Hausa, Igbo, Malagasy, Somali, Shona, Sotho, Swahili, Xhosa, Yorùbá, Zulu
AfriMT5, AfriByT5 (Adelani et al., 2022)	582M	Encoder–Decoder	Afrikaans, Amharic, Arabic, Chichewa, Hausa, Igbo, Malagasy, Oromo, Nigerian Pidgin, Rwanda-Rundi, Sesotho, Shona, Somali, Swahili, Xhosa, Yorùbá, Zulu
mBART50 (Tang et al., 2020)	610M	Encoder–Decoder	Afrikaans, Swahili, Xhosa
M2M-100 (Fan et al., 2021)	418M	Encoder–Decoder	Afrikaans, Amharic, Fulah Ganda, Hausa, Igbo, Lingala, Luganda, Northern Sotho, Swahili, Swati, Wolof Somali, Swahili, Swati, Wolof, Xhosa, Yorùbá, Zulu
AfriTeVa (ours)	229M	Encoder–Decoder	Afaan Oromoo, Amharic, Gahuza, Hausa, Igbo, Nigerian Pidgin, Somali, Swahili, Tigrinya, Yorùbá

Table 3: **Model Comparisons:** a high-level comparison of our model with similar large multilingual pretrained language models featuring low-resource African languages.

Focusing on variants of AfriTeVa, we find improved BLEU scores on all languages as we scale up our models. In both translation directions for most languages, we obtain our best BLEU scores using AfriTeVa base + En. Only when translating English into Nigerian Pidgin do we see a drop in BLEU score for AfriTeVa base + En. In Table 5, scores improved by an average of 3 points as we go from small to large when translating from English to the various African languages. When translating to English, we observed average improvements of 4 points. With AfriTeVa large, scores improved by an extra BLEU point over AfriTeVa base.

What do these empirical results say with respect to our research question? The most pertinent comparison is between mT5 and AfriTeVa base + En: the former is pretrained on 100+ languages while the latter is only pretrained on the much smaller AfriBERTa corpus. The fact that AfriTeVa base + En outperforms mT5 (with a smaller model, no less) suggests the viability of the "small data" pretraining approach, so in this respect, these experimental results affirm our hypothesis.

The situation, however, is a bit more complex. AfriMT5, which starts with the mT5 backbone and performs further pretraining, outperforms AfriTeVa base + En. The AfriMT5 pretraining corpus comprises 12GB data in 20 languages, including English and French. This suggests that massive multilanguage pretraining remains useful as model initialization, which in turn would suggest that "small data" pretraining still cannot compete. However, this is not a fair comparison for at least two reasons: (1) AfriMT5 is a larger model, and (2) the pretraining corpus of AfriMT5 is much larger than the 1GB AfriBERTa corpus. Thus, a fair comparison would be pretraining with the AfriMT5 corpus from scratch with the same model size as mT5. We leave this for future work.

The effectiveness of byT5 and AfriByT5 further complicates our analysis. We see that byT5 alone achieves excellent BLEU scores. AfriByT5, which benefits from additional pretraining starting from a byT5 backbone, is only marginally better. In particular, byT5 appears to generate high-quality output for Luganda and Luo, two languages that it had never encountered before during pretraining. These results suggest that tokenization is consequential in ways we do not yet fully understand. Once again, this is interesting future work.

We provide evaluation results for M2M-100 and mBART50 only as a reference, since we do not feel that they represent fair comparisons. All models discussed above derive from the T5 family, and thus it is easier to isolate the source of the translation quality differences. For comparisons to M2M-100 and mBART50, it is difficult to perform attribution analysis to understand the underlying factors contributing to effectiveness. Furthermore, both of these models are specialized for machine translation, whereas the T5-based models can be adapted to multiple downstream tasks.

Model	# params	hau	ibo	pcm	swa	yor	lug	luo	avg
				translation *into* English					
mT5 (Xue et al., 2021b)	582M	5.9	18.0	42.2	29.0	7.9	11.5	6.7	17.3
		✓	✓	x	✓	✓	✗	✗	
ByT5 (Xue et al., 2021a)	582M	14.0	**20.8**	**43.4**	28.8	9.6	19.3	**11.9**	21.1
		✓	✓	✗	✓	✓	✗	✗	
AfriMT5 (Adelani et al., 2022)	582M	10.7	19.1	44.7	30.7	**11.5**	14.8	9.4	20.1
AfriByT5 (Adelani et al., 2022)	582M	**14.7**	20.5	43.4	**29.0**	10.4	**20.6**	12.4	**21.6**
		✓	✓	✓	✓	✓	✗	✗	
AfriTeVa Small	64M	4.7	7.9	32.3	15.5	3.7	5.1	4.2	10.4
AfriTeVa Base	229M	9.0	13.4	35.9	19.9	7.2	9.4	6.8	14.5
AfriTeVa Large	745M	11.4	15.2	36.8	21.3	8.2	10.5	7.7	15.9
AfriTeVa Base + En	229M	12.5	20.4	37.1	26.2	9.5	11.7	10.2	18.2
		✓	✓	✓	✓	✓	✗	✗	
M2M-100 (Fan et al., 2021)	418M	17.2	18.5	44.7	29.9	13.5	18.5	19.4	23.1
		✓	✓	✗	✓	✓	✓	✓	
mBART50 (Tang et al., 2020)	610M	12.3	16.4	44.4	29.2	9.8	14.1	10.2	19.5
		✗	✗	✗	✗	✗	✗	✗	

Table 4: **Machine Translation Results (lang–en) :** BLEU scores when translating from each African language to English. All models were fine-tuned on each language using data in the news domain. Checkmarks indicate that the model was pretrained on that language. AfriMT5 and AfriByT5 were further pretrained using the mT5 base and byT5 base checkpoints, respectively (Adelani et al., 2022). The highest reported BLEU scores are shown in bold for T5 models; overall best BLEU scores are underlined.

Model	# params	hau	ibo	pcm	swa	yor	lug	luo	avg
				translation *from* English					
mT5 (Xue et al., 2021b)	582M	2.4	14.1	33.5	23.2	2.2	3.5	3.2	11.7
		✓	✓	✗	✓	✓	✗	✗	
ByT5 (Xue et al., 2021a)	582M	8.8	18.6	32.4	26.6	6.2	11.3	8.8	16.1
		✓	✓	✗	✓	✓	✗	✗	
AfriMT5 (Adelani et al., 2022)	582M	4.5	15.4	**34.5**	26.7	4.7	5.9	4.5	13.7
AfriByT5 (Adelani et al., 2022)	582M	9.8	**19.3**	32.5	**27.5**	**7.1**	**12.2**	**9.0**	**16.8**
		✓	✓	✗	✓	✓	✗	✗	
AfriTeVa Small	64M	4.3	8.1	30.3	16.1	2.9	2.6	4.1	9.8
AfriTeVa Base	229M	7.2	13.2	31.7	20.3	4.9	5.3	6.6	12.7
AfriTeVa Large	745M	8.9	15.7	31.5	20.6	6.0	6.2	6.8	13.7
AfriTeVa Base + En	229M	**10.1**	17.3	28.7	24.3	6.8	8.7	8.6	14.9
		✓	✓	✓	✓	✓	✗	✗	
M2M-100 (Fan et al., 2021)	418M	14.4	20.3	33.2	27.0	9.6	13.0	10.8	18.3
		✓	✓	✗	✓	✓	✓	✓	
mBART50 (Tang et al., 2020)	610M	11.8	14.8	33.9	22.1	7.5	9.7	9.6	15.6
		✗	✗	✗	✗	✗	✗	✗	

Table 5: **Machine Translation Results (en–lang) :** BLEU scores when translating from English to each African language. All models were fine-tuned on each language using data in the news domain. Checkmarks indicate that the model was pretrained on that language. AfriMT5 and AfriByT5 were pretrained further using the mT5 base and byT5 base checkpoints, respectively (Adelani et al., 2022). The highest reported BLEU scores are shown in bold for T5 models; overall best BLEU scores are underlined.

Language	mBERT	XLM-R base	AfriBERTa large	mT5 base	AfriTeVa small	AfriTeVa base	AfriTeVa large
	(172M)	(270M)	(126M)	(582M)	(64M)	(229M)	(745M)
hau	83.03	85.62	**90.86**	86.80	88.75	88.25	89.80
yor	71.61	71.07	**83.22**	75.46	80.15	80.51	82.26

Table 6: **Text Classification Results:** F_1 scores averaged over 3 random seeds. mBERT, XLM-R, and AfriBERTa results were obtained from Ogueji et al. (2021)

4.2 Text Classification

Text classification F_1 results are presented in Table 6, based on the experimental settings described in Section 3.2. Note that while it is possible to adapt sequence-to-sequence models for classification tasks, as we have done, intuitively, encoder-only models are more suitable for text classification tasks. AfriTeVa small outperforms mBERT and XLM-R on both languages despite having significantly fewer parameters. However, AfriTeVa base is still outperformed by AfriBERTa large by an average of 3 F_1 points on Yorùbá and 2 F_1 points on Hausa. Our models also perform better than mT5 on both languages. As with machine translation, we see improvements as we scale our model from 64M parameters to 745M parameters. However, the gains are modest here.

What do these text classification results say with respect to our research question? Once again, the pertinent comparison is between mT5 and AfriTeVa, since we are primarily concerned with the viability of "small data" pretraining. Here, our results are consistent with the machine translation experiments: it does appear that we can pretrain full encoder–decoder models from scratch using relatively small amounts of data.

4.3 Limitations

Encoder–decoder models are best suited for natural language generation tasks such as summarization, question answering, machine translation, etc. Cross-lingual datasets are often used as benchmarks to evaluate multilingual pretrained models. Despite our efforts to evaluate on as many tasks as possible, many existing datasets feature few to no African languages. For example, popular cross-lingual datasets such as WikiLingua (Ladhak et al., 2020), XQuAD (Artetxe et al., 2020), and Tydi QA (Clark et al., 2020) only contain Swahili.

Existing machine translation systems in many low-resource languages require much larger parallel corpora to improve translation quality. Examples include languages such as Yorùbá, Igbo, and Luganda. To improve such systems, there is a need for high-quality data in multiple domains. While there are existing efforts to curate parallel datasets such as JW300 (Agić and Vulić, 2019), Yorùbá (Adelani et al., 2021), Igbo (Ezeani et al., 2020), Fon (Emezue and Dossou, 2020), parallel corpora for bi-directional translation in Amharic, Tigrigna, Afan-Oromo, Wolaytta, and Ge'ez (Teferra Abate et al., 2018), there is a need for continued research to creating high-quality datasets to further drive advances in low-resource machine translation (Fan et al., 2021).

5 Conclusions

In this work, we present AfriTeVa, a family of multilingual T5 models that were pretrained from scratch on 10 low-resource African languages with only around 1GB of data (with an additional variant model that includes English data in pretraining). Answering our research question, we have verified that it is possible to pretrain encoder–decoder models on relatively small amounts of data, but there remain conflating factors we have yet to fully understand. Although we do not reach the state of the art, our models achieve competitive results on text classification and machine translation benchmarks. We also highlight some of the limitations of evaluating sequence-to-sequence models for African languages. Finally, we release code and pretrained models to drive further work in multilingual models for African languages.

Acknowledgments

This research was supported in part by the Natural Sciences and Engineering Research Council (NSERC) of Canada and an AI for Social Good grant from the Waterloo AI Institute. Computational resources were provided by Compute Ontario and Compute Canada. We also thank the Google TRC program for providing us free cloud TPU access.

References

Ife Adebara and Muhammad Abdul-Mageed. 2022. Towards afrocentric NLP for African languages: Where we are and where we can go. In *Proceedings of the 60th Annual Meeting of the Association for Computational Linguistics (Volume 1: Long Papers)*, pages 3814–3841, Dublin, Ireland. Association for Computational Linguistics.

David Adelani, Dana Ruiter, Jesujoba Alabi, Damilola Adebonojo, Adesina Ayeni, Mofe Adeyemi, Ayodele Esther Awokoya, and Cristina España-Bonet. 2021. The effect of domain and diacritics in Yoruba–English neural machine translation. In *Proceedings of Machine Translation Summit XVIII: Research Track*, pages 61–75, Virtual. Association for Machine Translation in the Americas.

David Ifeoluwa Adelani, Jesujoba Oluwadara Alabi, Angela Fan, Julia Kreutzer, Xiaoyu Shen, Machel Reid, Dana Ruiter, Dietrich Klakow, Peter Nabende, Ernie Chang, Tajuddeen Gwadabe, Freshia Sackey, Bonaventure F. P. Dossou, Chris Chinenye Emezue, Colin Leong, Michael Beukman, Shamsuddeen Hassan Muhammad, Guyo Dub Jarso, Oreen Yousuf, Andre Niyongabo Rubungo, Gilles Hacheme, Eric Peter Wairagala, Muhammad Umair Nasir, Benjamin Ayoade Ajibade, Tunde Oluwaseyi Ajayi, Yvonne Wambui Gitau, Jade Abbott, Mohamed Ahmed, Millicent Ochieng, Anuoluwapo Aremu, Perez Ogayo, Jonathan Mukiibi, Fatoumata Ouoba Kabore, Godson Koffi Kalipe, Derguene Mbaye, Allahsera Auguste Tapo, Victoire Memdjokam Koagne, Edwin Munkoh-Buabeng, Valencia Wagner, Idris Abdulmumin, Ayodele Awokoya, Happy Buzaaba, Blessing Sibanda, Andiswa Bukula, and Sam Manthalu. 2022. A few thousand translations go a long way! Leveraging pre-trained models for African news translation. In *Proceedings of the 2022 Annual Conference of the North American Chapter of the Association for Computational Linguistics*.

Željko Agić and Ivan Vulić. 2019. JW300: A wide-coverage parallel corpus for low-resource languages. In *Proceedings of the 57th Annual Meeting of the Association for Computational Linguistics*, pages 3204–3210, Florence, Italy. Association for Computational Linguistics.

Mikel Artetxe, Sebastian Ruder, and Dani Yogatama. 2020. On the cross-lingual transferability of monolingual representations. In *Proceedings of the 58th Annual Meeting of the Association for Computational Linguistics*, pages 4623–4637, Online. Association for Computational Linguistics.

Christos Baziotis, Barry Haddow, and Alexandra Birch. 2020. Language model prior for low-resource neural machine translation. In *Proceedings of the 2020 Conference on Empirical Methods in Natural Language Processing (EMNLP)*, pages 7622–7634, Online. Association for Computational Linguistics.

Jonathan H. Clark, Eunsol Choi, Michael Collins, Dan Garrette, Tom Kwiatkowski, Vitaly Nikolaev, and Jennimaria Palomaki. 2020. TyDi QA: A benchmark for information-seeking question answering in typologically diverse languages. *Transactions of the Association for Computational Linguistics*, 8:454–470.

Alexis Conneau, Kartikay Khandelwal, Naman Goyal, Vishrav Chaudhary, Guillaume Wenzek, Francisco Guzmán, Edouard Grave, Myle Ott, Luke Zettlemoyer, and Veselin Stoyanov. 2020. Unsupervised cross-lingual representation learning at scale. In *Proceedings of the 58th Annual Meeting of the Association for Computational Linguistics*, pages 8440–8451, Online. Association for Computational Linguistics.

Kevin Duh, Paul McNamee, Matt Post, and Brian Thompson. 2020. Benchmarking neural and statistical machine translation on low-resource African languages. In *Proceedings of the 12th Language Resources and Evaluation Conference*, pages 2667–2675, Marseille, France. European Language Resources Association.

David M. Eberhard, Gary F. Simons, and Charles D. Fennig. 2019. *Ethnologue: Languages of the World*. SIL International, Dallas.

Chris Chinenye Emezue and Bonaventure F. P. Dossou. 2021. MMTAfrica: Multilingual machine translation for African languages. In *Proceedings of the Sixth Conference on Machine Translation*, pages 398–411, Online. Association for Computational Linguistics.

Chris Chinenye Emezue and Femi Pancrace Bonaventure Dossou. 2020. FFR v1.1: Fon-French neural machine translation. In *Proceedings of the The Fourth Widening Natural Language Processing Workshop*, pages 83–87, Seattle, USA. Association for Computational Linguistics.

Ignatius Ezeani, Paul Rayson, Ikechukwu E. Onyenwe, Chinedu Uchechukwu, and Mark Hepple. 2020. Igbo-English machine translation: An evaluation benchmark. *arXiv:2004.00648*.

Angela Fan, Shruti Bhosale, Holger Schwenk, Zhiyi Ma, Ahmed El-Kishky, Siddharth Goyal, Mandeep Baines, Onur Celebi, Guillaume Wenzek, Vishrav Chaudhary, Naman Goyal, Tom Birch, Vitaliy Liptchinsky, Sergey Edunov, Michael Auli, and Armand Joulin. 2021. Beyond English-Centric Multilingual Machine Translation. *Journal of Machine Learning Research*, 22(107):1–48.

Michael A. Hedderich, David Adelani, Dawei Zhu, Jesujoba Alabi, Udia Markus, and Dietrich Klakow. 2020. Transfer learning and distant supervision for multilingual transformer models: A study on African languages. In *Proceedings of the 2020 Conference on Empirical Methods in Natural Language Processing (EMNLP)*, pages 2580–2591, Online. Association for Computational Linguistics.

Karthikeyan K, Zihan Wang, Stephen Mayhew, and Dan Roth. 2020. Cross-lingual ability of multilingual BERT: An empirical study. In *International Conference on Learning Representations*.

Taku Kudo and John Richardson. 2018. SentencePiece: A simple and language independent subword tokenizer and detokenizer for neural text processing. In *Proceedings of the 2018 Conference on Empirical Methods in Natural Language Processing: System Demonstrations*, pages 66–71, Brussels, Belgium. Association for Computational Linguistics.

Faisal Ladhak, Esin Durmus, Claire Cardie, and Kathleen McKeown. 2020. WikiLingua: A new benchmark dataset for cross-lingual abstractive summarization. In *Findings of the Association for Computational Linguistics: EMNLP 2020*, pages 4034–4048, Online. Association for Computational Linguistics.

Zihan Liu, Genta Indra Winata, and Pascale Fung. 2021. Continual mixed-language pre-training for extremely low-resource neural machine translation. In *Findings of the Association for Computational Linguistics: ACL-IJCNLP 2021*, pages 2706–2718, Online. Association for Computational Linguistics.

Laura Martinus and Jade Z. Abbott. 2019. A focus on neural machine translation for African languages. *arXiv:1906.05685*.

Vincent Micheli, Martin d'Hoffschmidt, and François Fleuret. 2020. On the importance of pre-training data volume for compact language models. In *Proceedings of the 2020 Conference on Empirical Methods in Natural Language Processing (EMNLP)*, pages 7853–7858, Online. Association for Computational Linguistics.

El Moatez Billah Nagoudi, AbdelRahim Elmadany, and Muhammad Abdul-Mageed. 2022. AraT5: Text-to-text transformers for Arabic language generation. In *Proceedings of the 60th Annual Meeting of the Association for Computational Linguistics (Volume 1: Long Papers)*, pages 628–647, Dublin, Ireland. Association for Computational Linguistics.

Wilhelmina Nekoto, Vukosi Marivate, Tshinondiwa Matsila, Timi Fasubaa, Taiwo Fagbohungbe, Solomon Oluwole Akinola, Shamsuddeen Muhammad, Salomon Kabongo Kabenamualu, Salomey Osei, Freshia Sackey, Rubungo Andre Niyongabo, Ricky Macharm, Perez Ogayo, Orevaoghene Ahia, Musie Meressa Berhe, Mofetoluwa Adeyemi, Masabata Mokgesi-Selinga, Lawrence Okegbemi, Laura Martinus, Kolawole Tajudeen, Kevin Degila, Kelechi Ogueji, Kathleen Siminyu, Julia Kreutzer, Jason Webster, Jamiil Toure Ali, Jade Abbott, Iroro Orife, Ignatius Ezeani, Idris Abdulkadir Dangana, Herman Kamper, Hady Elsahar, Goodness Duru, Ghollah Kioko, Murhabazi Espoir, Elan van Biljon, Daniel Whitenack, Christopher Onyefuluchi, Chris Chinenye Emezue, Bonaventure F. P. Dossou, Blessing Sibanda, Blessing Bassey, Ayodele Olabiyi, Arshath Ramkilowan, Alp Öktem, Adewale Akinfaderin, and Abdallah Bashir. 2020. Participatory research for low-resourced machine translation: A case study in African languages. In *Findings of the Association for Computational Linguistics: EMNLP 2020*, pages 2144–2160, Online. Association for Computational Linguistics.

Kelechi Ogueji, Yuxin Zhu, and Jimmy Lin. 2021. Small data? No problem! Exploring the viability of pretrained multilingual language models for low-resourced languages. In *Proceedings of the 1st Workshop on Multilingual Representation Learning*, pages 116–126, Punta Cana, Dominican Republic. Association for Computational Linguistics.

Akintunde Oladipo, Odunayo Ogundepo, Kelechi Ogueji, and Jimmy Lin. 2022. An exploration of vocabulary size and transfer effects in multilingual language models for African languages. In *Proceedings of the 3rd Workshop on African Natural Language Processing*.

Kishore Papineni, Salim Roukos, Todd Ward, and Wei-Jing Zhu. 2002. BLEU: A method for automatic evaluation of machine translation. In *Proceedings of the 40th Annual Meeting on Association for Computational Linguistics*, ACL '02, page 311–318, USA. Association for Computational Linguistics.

Colin Raffel, Noam Shazeer, Adam Roberts, Katherine Lee, Sharan Narang, Michael Matena, Yanqi Zhou, Wei Li, and Peter J. Liu. 2020. Exploring the limits of transfer learning with a unified text-to-text transformer. *Journal of Machine Learning Research*, 21(140):1–67.

Noam Shazeer and Mitchell Stern. 2018. Adafactor: Adaptive learning rates with sublinear memory cost. In *Proceedings of the 35th International Conference on Machine Learning*, pages 4596–4604.

Yuqing Tang, Chau Tran, Xian Li, Peng-Jen Chen, Naman Goyal, Vishrav Chaudhary, Jiatao Gu, and Angela Fan. 2020. Multilingual translation with extensible multilingual pretraining and finetuning. *arXiv:2008.00401*.

Solomon Teferra Abate, Michael Melese, Martha Yifiru Tachbelie, Million Meshesha, Solomon Atinafu, Wondwossen Mulugeta, Yaregal Assabie, Hafte Abera, Binyam Ephrem, Tewodros Abebe, Wondimagegnhue Tsegaye, Amanuel Lemma, Tsegaye Andargie, and Seifedin Shifaw. 2018. Parallel corpora for bi-directional statistical machine translation for seven Ethiopian language pairs. In *Proceedings of the First Workshop on Linguistic Resources for Natural Language Processing*, pages 83–90, Santa Fe, New Mexico, USA. Association for Computational Linguistics.

Thomas Wolf, Lysandre Debut, Victor Sanh, Julien Chaumond, Clement Delangue, Anthony Moi, Pierric Cistac, Tim Rault, Rémi Louf, Morgan Funtowicz, Joe Davison, Sam Shleifer, Patrick von Platen, Clara Ma, Yacine Jernite, Julien Plu, Canwen Xu, Teven Le Scao, Sylvain Gugger, Mariama Drame, Quentin Lhoest, and Alexander M. Rush. 2020. Transformers: State-of-the-art natural language processing. In *Proceedings of the 2020 Conference on Empirical*

Methods in Natural Language Processing: System Demonstrations, pages 38–45, Online. Association for Computational Linguistics.

Linting Xue, Aditya Barua, Noah Constant, Rami Al-Rfou, Sharan Narang, Mihir Kale, Adam Roberts, and Colin Raffel. 2021a. ByT5: Towards a token-free future with pre-trained byte-to-byte models. *arXiv:2105.13626*.

Linting Xue, Noah Constant, Adam Roberts, Mihir Kale, Rami Al-Rfou, Aditya Siddhant, Aditya Barua, and Colin Raffel. 2021b. mT5: A massively multilingual pre-trained text-to-text transformer. In *Proceedings of the 2021 Conference of the North American Chapter of the Association for Computational Linguistics: Human Language Technologies*, pages 483–498, Online. Association for Computational Linguistics.

Liu Zhuang, Lin Wayne, Shi Ya, and Zhao Jun. 2021. A robustly optimized BERT pre-training approach with post-training. In *Proceedings of the 20th Chinese National Conference on Computational Linguistics*, pages 1218–1227, Huhhot, China. Chinese Information Processing Society of China.

Few-shot Learning for Sumerian Named Entity Recognition

Guanghai Wang Yudong Liu and **James Hearne**
Computer Science Department
Western Washington University
Bellingham, Washington 98225
{wangg5,liuy2,hearne}@wwu.edu

Abstract

This paper presents our study in exploring the task of named entity recognition (NER) in a low resource setting, focusing on few-shot learning on the Sumerian NER task. The Sumerian language is deemed as an extremely low-resource language due to that (1) it is a long dead language, (2) highly skilled language experts are extremely scarce. NER on Sumerian text is important in that it helps identify the actors and entities active in a given period of time from the collections of tens of thousands of texts in building socio-economic networks of the archives of interest. As a text classification task, NER tends to become challenging when the amount of annotated data is limited or the model is required to handle new classes. The Sumerian NER is no exception. In this work, we propose to use two few-shot learning systems, ProtoBERT and NNShot, to the Sumerian NER task. Our experiments show that the ProtoBERT NER generally outperforms both the NNShot NER and the fully supervised BERT NER in low resource settings on the predictions of rare classes. In particular, F1-score of ProtoBERT on unseen entity types on our test set has achieved 89.6% that is significantly better than the F1-score of 84.3% of the BERT NER.

1 Introduction

Named Entity Recognition (NER), as a fundamental task in Natural Language Processing, aims to locate and classify named entities such as people, organizations, and locations, etc. The Ur III period (ca. 2112-2004 BC), spanning about 100 years, has a particularly rich source of texts, comprising at least 100,000 documents. These are primarily financial records and potentially support investigations of economic activity in Ancient Mesopotamian society. To give but one example, Liu (2021) aims to do a prosopographical study of individuals delivering animals to the Puzriš-Dagan organization during the Ur III period and identifies the individuals, their family relations and royal status of the historical actors delivering animals, as well as the variety of animals involved. NER applied to this domain can efficiently help Assyriologists recover and analyze the social-economical activities and thus provide a better understanding of the social organization and dynamics of ancient Mesopotamian history.

There is a broad effort in the community of Assyriologists, in collaboration of Computer Scientists, to build reproducible socio-economic networks from the Ur III archives (Journal et al., 2021). This effort shows that the application of NER to these texts is of great use in the quantitative study of Assyriology.

In this work, we conduct experiments to apply models that are based on prototypical networks (Snell et al., 2017) and nearest neighbour classification to the Sumerian NER task. Specifically, we adapt two few-shot learning systems, ProtoBERT (Ding et al., 2021) and NNShot (Yang and Katiyar, 2020), to the Sumerian NER task and have achieved good performance in prediction of rare classes. In summary, our contributions are as follows: (1) We construct two few-shot learning systems, ProtoBERT and NNShot, and apply them on the Sumerian NER task. To the best of our knowledge, this is the first work exploring Sumerian NER task using the few-shot learning approach. (2) We demonstrate that the ProtoBERT approach considerably and consistently outperforms the fully supervised BERT-based model and has shown to be well-suited for prediction of rare class with few labelled examples.

2 Previous Work

Previous studies on Sumerian NER are few, partially due to the lack of language resources and meaningful collaborations between researchers in Computer Science and Assyriology. The few studies include Luo et al. (2015) and Liu et al. (2016). Luo et al. (2015) uses the DL-CoTrain algorithm

Proceedings of the Third Workshop on Deep Learning for Low-Resource Natural Language Processing, pages 136 - 145
July 14, 2022 ©2022 Association for Computational Linguistics

for personal name identification to minimize the use of the annotated data. The system achieves a high recall (92.5%) and a low precision (56.0%). Liu et al. (2016) chooses to fully utilize the annotated data by applying a wide range of supervised algorithms, including Decision Tree, Gradient Boosting, Logistic Regression, Naive Bayes, SVM and Random Forest, to predict personal names. The supervised approach shows an opposite behavior with a low recall (around 65%) and a high precision (around 86%). A more recent work (Bansal et al., 2021) investigates the Sumerian Machine Translation task in low-resource settings. They also built a variety of algorithms, including HMM, Rules+CRF, Bi-LSTM+CRF, FLAIR and RoBERTa, on the POS and NER tasks on the Sumerian dataset. For the NER task, RoBERTa achieves the best F1-score (95.3%) on a set of 12 entity types and the simple CRF model with well-defined rules significantly outperforms the rest of the models and is the second best with F1-score of 91.3%. We adapt their labelled Sumerian dataset in this work. As they only reported the overall F-scores of those NER systems on the 12 entity types without describing how the dataset is split, their result is not directly comparable with ours. More details about the dataset will be given in Section 3.

One of the key problems for low-resource NER is the lack of annotated data. As one of the common strategies, cross-lingual NER attempts to address this challenge by transferring knowledge from one or more high-resource source languages with abundant annotated data to a low-resource target language with few or no labels. The knowledge transfer is either through annotation projection from the source language to the target language (Bharadwaj et al., 2016; Xie et al., 2018; Feng et al., 2018; Rahimi et al., 2019) or through using a shared encoder in a multi-task architecture (Lin et al., 2018; Kruengkrai et al., 2020). Along the research line of enabling parameter reuse across a variety of tasks, Pfeiffer et al. (2020) proposes MAD-X, an adapter-based framework which includes language adapters, task adapters and invertible adapters, in a multilingual context. MAD-X outperforms the state of the art in cross-lingual transfer on NER across diverse languages. However, the highest F1-score is achieved on Arabic which is 59.41%. For other low-resource languages, such as Icelandic, Quechua and so on, the F1-scores are mostly around 30-50%. Cross-lingual methods have achieved notable success, but in certain circumstances, such as insufficient pre-training corpora or when the target language is far from the source language, their performance suffers. Sumerian language, as a long dead language, suffers both which makes the cross-lingual methods not readily apply.

Few-shot classification (Vinyals et al., 2016; Bao et al., 2019) can effectively recognize new classes from very few labelled examples and thus has recently drawn a lot of attention. Snell et al. (2017) proposed Prototypical Networks based on the idea that there exists an embedding space in which images of the same class cluster around a single prototype representation for each class. In other words, two images of the same class should be close to each other, and two images of the different class will be far away. Adapting this idea from image classification, Fritzler et al. (2019); Hou et al. (2020); Ding et al. (2021) address the few-shot NER problem and have achieved considerable success. Yang and Katiyar (2020) proposed token-level nearest neighbor classification based methods for the few-shot NER problem to address some potential issues of prototypical NER in learning class prototypes, such as learning a noisy prototype of the 'O' class.

Usually the overall F1-scores are high if BERT is chosen as backbone encoder in deep learning NER systems (Devlin et al., 2019). However, Tänzer et al. (2022) demonstrates that BERT fails to predict minority classes when the number of examples is limited. They observe that BERT needs at least 25 examples of a minority label to start learning on the CoNNL-03 dataset (Sang and De Meulder, 2003). If the examples are fewer than 25, the F1-score will be 0. When the examples exceed 100, the performance improves rapidly. They also observe similar phenomena on other datasets. For example, learning on the JNLPBA dataset (Collier and Kim, 2004) requires at least 50 examples. They also construct a prototypical few-shot learning model to overcome BERT's limitation. The results show the few-shot learning model consistently surpasses the performance of BERT on minority classes. For instance, it is outperforming BERT by 40 F1 points on LOC class when the dataset has 15 sentences containing that class. All this has shown that few-shot learning is well suited for the setting when the number of labelled examples is very constrained, which further justifies our choice of exploring this approach in the Sumerian NER task. And our experimental results have also echoed their findings.

The paper is organized as follows. In Section 3 we give a more detailed description of the Sumerian NER task and the dataset. In Section 4 we describe our models. Section 5 contains the description of our experimental setup and the report and analysis of the results. We conclude our work with some discussion of the future work in Section 6.

3 Dataset and task description

The dataset we used in this work is originally from the CDLI database (Cuneiform Digital Library Initiative `http://cdli.ucla.edu/`). CDLI is a project that curates an electronic documentation of ancient cuneiform texts, comprised of cuneiform texts, images, transliterations and sundry information concerning the Ur III period and its immediate aftermath. It is a joint project of the University of California, Los Angeles, the University of Oxford, and the Max Planck Institute for the History of Science, Berlin.

Although the texts we are investigating were originally written in cuneiform script, CDLI provides them in transliterated form, using the English alphabet. Fig. 1 shows a tablet from CDLI repository, (id P407107). An image of the original tablet with its cuneiform inscription is on the left; the transliteration is in the middle and the modern English translation appears on the right.

As aforementioned, we adapt the labelled Sumerian dataset and the tagset directly from Bansal et al. (2021). The dataset has 22,728 sentences, 61,478 tokens, and 12 entity types (not including the O type that indicates a word is not a named entity of interest). All these entity types, their meaning and counts in the dataset are shown in Table 1. The tablet in Fig. 1 demonstrates an example with multiple named entity types in it. According to a domain expert, *den-lil2-la2* in line 2 on the obverse is labelled as the named entity tag 'DN' (Divine Name), *ki-maszki* in line 3 labelled as 'GN' (Geographical Name), *a-mur-dsuen* and *ur-ku3-nun-na* in line 2 and 3 on the reverse are labelled as 'PN' (Personal Name), and *ses-da-gu7* in line 4 labelled as 'MN' (Month Name). The task of a few-shot Sumerian NER tagger is to identify these named entity types from the transliterations of tablets based on a few labelled examples.

The counts in Table 1 show that the dataset is quite unbalanced. Some entity types have many more labelled examples than others. For example, entity types 'EN', 'MN', 'ON' and 'TN' only have tens of labelled examples. The least entity type is 'AN' which only has 1 example. On the contrary, 'PN' has a dominant number of examples in the dataset, over half of that of the non-named entity type 'O'. We decide to discard 'AN', 'ON' and 'EN' entity types from our training and test process. For tag 'AN' and 'ON', the number of their labelled examples is too low to enable an effective episodic-based few-shot learning process. Even though 'EN' tag has the same number of examples as the 'TN' tag, because of the data splitting and relabelling issues described in Sec. 5.1 and Sec. 5.3, we choose to drop it from our tag set as well. However, we still report the experimental results both without and with the 'EN' tag in Table 6 and Table 7, respectively. More details about data splitting and relabeling can be found in Section 5.1.

Tag	Meaning	Count
DN	Divine Name	900
FN	Field Name	1,463
GN	Geographical Name	1,351
PN	Personal Name	17,729
RN	Royal Name	150
SN	Settlement Name	521
WN	Watercourse Name	304
EN	Ethnos Name	60
MN	Month Name	79
ON	Object Name	18
TN	Temple Name	60
O	Others	38,822
AN	Agricultural Name	1

Table 1: Twelve NER tags and O-tag, their meanings and counts in the dataset

4 Methods

In the following, we will describe three models applied to the low-resource Sumerian NER task. They are BERT+LC, ProtoBERT and NNShot. As Transformer-based pre-trained language models (Devlin et al., 2019) have shown significant impact on the NER task, a pre-trained language model (PLM) on Sumerian will also be used in our NER models. In our experiment, we adapt a PLM on Sumerian explored in Bansal et al. (2021). The PLM is pre-trained using RoBERTa (Liu et al., 2019) on their Sumerian monolingual dataset.

Cuneiform Tablet	Transliteration	English Translation
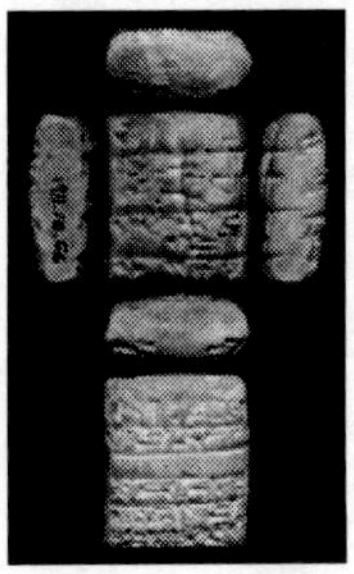	&P407107 = HSS 68, 209	
	@tablet	
	@obverse	
	1. 4(u) la2 1(disz@t) udu	39 sheep
	2. kasz-de2-a {d}en-lil2-la2	for banquet of Enlil
	3. u4 ki-masz{ki} ba-hul	when Kimash was destroyed
	4. u4 2(u) 4(disz)-kam	on the 24th day
	@reverse	
	1. zi-ga	were withdrawn
	2. bala a-mur-{d}suen	which were bala-tax of Amur-Suen
	3. ki ur-ku3-nun-na	from Ur-kununa
	blank space	
	4. iti ses-da-gu7	Month: eating sheshda
	5. mu us2-sa ur-bi2-lum{ki} ba-hul	Year after: Urbilum was destroyed

Figure 1: Tablet no. P407107 inscribed with the original Sumerian cuneiform script, the digitized transliteration, and human-translated English text line by line.

4.1 BERT+LC

Although a supervised setting is not the main goal of this work, it is nevertheless interesting to explore the standard setup of using the BERT model with a linear classifier built on top of its encoding representations, and compare it with the few-shot learning models. The model is trained to minimize the cross-entropy loss on the given training data. More details on the hyper-parameters and data setup can be found in Sec. 4.4 and Sec. 5.1, respectively.

4.2 ProtoBERT

ProtoBERT (Ding et al., 2021) is a few-shot learning model that combines the few-shot capabilities of prototypical networks (Snell et al., 2017) with the BERT's pre-trained knowledge. The model aims to build an embedding space through the training process so all the inputs can be clustered around its own "prototype" that represents the centroid of the class each input is associated with. Classifying a new input can then be done by finding its closest centroid and being assigned with the corresponding entity type. The training process is organized into a series of "episodes". Each episode consists of a support set and a query set that are randomly sampled from the training set. As a support set contains a limited number of "training" examples and a query set "test" examples, each episode essentially mimics the test-time scenario in a few-shot learning setting. In an N-way K-shot learning setup, each support set has N classes and K samples per class and the query set has N classes as well.

In our implementation, we follow the algorithm in (Ding et al., 2021) and run 500 episodes for training. In this model, for each class c, its prototype p_c is calculated by averaging the embeddings of examples that belong to class c in the support set S:

$$p_c = \frac{1}{|S_c|} \sum_{x \in S_c} f(x) \tag{1}$$

where S_c denotes the set of all elements in S that belong to class c and function f denotes the BERT architecture augmented with a linear classifier. The model parameter of f is updated after each episode in the training process by minimizing the cross-entropy loss between the probability calculated through softmax and the one-hot ground-truth label of x.

After computing all prototypes in a support set S, we compute the distance from each input x in the query set Q to each prototype. As used in Ding et al. (2021), we also use the squared Euclidean distance as the metric function $d(f(x), p) = \|f(x) - p\|_2^2$. Once we get the distances between x and all the prototypes, a softmax function is used to compute the prediction distribution of x over all prototypes. The entity type of the nearest prototype is the prediction of x.

4.3 NNShot

NNShot (Yang and Katiyar, 2020) is a few-shot learning method based on token-level nearest neighbor classification. Unlike ProtoBERT where the training classes are clustered based on the token representations, NNShot does the inference on a query example directly based on the nearest neighbor metric. That is, NNShot simply computes the distance score between example x in the query set and all examples in the support set. It then assigns x the label of the example in the support set that is closest to x. In this work, we use the same distance metric as we use in ProtoBERT.

4.4 Hyper-parameters

We experimentally set a fixed collection of hyper-parameters across all the datasets. The Adam optimizer (Kingma and Ba, 2015) is used in the training stage. The learning rate is $1e^{-3}$. For BERT+LC, we set the batch size as 16. For few-shot learning systems, we use 2-way $5 \sim 10$ shot setting as suggested in Ding et al. (2021) for building a support set. This strategy allows each class in a support set to have a variable number of examples between 5 to 10, which effectively alleviates the sampling constraint between the two classes. All the models are implemented using the Hugging Face library[1].

5 Experiments

5.1 Data and tag processing

In the following, we describe how we split the tag set and generate our training, dev and test datasets accordingly for each model.

5.1.1 Tagset and dataset splitting

We largely follow the work of (Ding et al., 2021) for our tag set and data set splitting. We first divide the 12 entity types into three mutually disjoint subsets so the entity types in the test set are "new" classes or "unseen" in the training set, and vice versa. In practice, new entity types may appear in an existing or new data set or a new domain where no insufficient number of annotated examples has become available. To be aligned with a realistic setting, we reserve the entity types that have fewer examples for the test set, and those that have more examples for the training set. Based on the characteristics of our dataset, and common practice, for each specific entity type, we placed 5 to 10 examples. However, it turns out that the numbers of examples of entity types 'AN' and 'ON' are too low (1 and 18, respectively) for our few-shot learning models to get stable results. Thus we drop these two entity types from our tag set and filter out those sentences that have 'AN' or 'ON' entity type when we construct training, dev and test sets.

With this setup, we generate the train, dev and test sets where each set only contains instances of its own pre-assigned entity types. As the average sentence length in our dataset is quite small which is around three, all the entity types except for 'EN' do not co-occur with other entity types in a same sentence. However, almost all of the sentences containing 'EN' also contain other entity types, including 'PN', 'GN', etc. Relabelling (Yang and Katiyar, 2020) as a common strategy in few-shot learning systems to get mutually disjoint subsets is when a sentence has more than one entity type, any entity type that does not belong to the pre-assigned set is relabelled as 'O' type. We follow this process for the 'EN' tag and conduct the experiment. As the number of 'EN' tokens is only 60 out of 61,478 in the entire dataset, and 'EN' is the only tag that involves relabelling, we also experimentally exclude 'EN' and conduct the experiment. Experiments show a significant improvement in system performance (24 point increase in F-1) without 'EN' and relabelling. In the setup without relabelling, we drop 'EN' along with 'AN' and 'ON' from the 12 entity types which leaves us 9 types among which the top-4 are 'DN', 'FN', 'GN' and 'PN' and are assigned to the training set, 'MN' and 'TN' to the test set, and 'RN', 'SN' and 'WN' to the dev set. Type 'O' is present across all the three subsets. In total, 73 sentences are removed from the dataset owing to this process, accounting for around 0.3% of the total number of the sentences in the dataset. We first report the experimental results of all the models in the setting of not including 'EN' in Sec. 5.2. The results with 'EN' are presented and discussed in Sec 5.3 where the influence of relabelling is discussed in detail.

5.1.2 Data and tags for BERT+LC

The remaining data is split into training and test sets based on their pre-assigned entity types. Since BERT+LC is fully supervised, it cannot handle unseen classes in the test phase. For that reason, a few examples of 'MN' and 'TN' need to be reinserted into the training set. Because our dataset is very small compared to other widely studied languages and BERT+LC requires more data than the few-shot learning setting, we omit the dev set at this step. That means BERT+LC's training set contains all 9 entity types. However, we only include 8 examples of 'MN' and 'TN' in this training set to make it comparable with the few-shot learning models that only use $5 \sim 10$ examples in each

[1]https://huggingface.co

Model	Dev	Test
BERT+LC	——	0.843
NNShot	0.714	0.857
ProtoBERT	**0.823**	**0.896**

Table 2: F1-scores for all models on test set and few-shot models on dev set.

Model	Entity	P	R	F1
BERT+LC	MN	**1.0**	0.914	**0.955**
	TN	**1.0**	0.378	0.549
NNShot	MN	0.869	0.883	0.876
	TN	0.735	0.926	**0.820**
ProtoBERT	MN	0.949	**0.933**	0.941
	TN	0.703	**0.963**	0.813

Table 3: Precision (P), Recall (R) and F1-score of individual entity types on test set.

Model	Entity	P	R	F1
NNShot	SN	0.595	0.581	0.588
	WN	**0.789**	0.818	0.803
	RN	0.636	0.840	0.724
ProtoBERT	SN	**0.714**	**0.789**	**0.750**
	WN	0.765	**0.912**	**0.832**
	RN	**0.857**	**0.960**	**0.906**

Table 4: Precision (P), Recall (R) and F1-score of individual entity types on dev set.

support set for each entity type.

5.1.3 Data and tags for few-shot learning systems

Section 5.1.2 describes the augmentation of the training set for the BERT+LC model but the test set remains the same across the 3 models. To construct the training and dev sets for the few-shot learning models, we select sentences containing 'DN', 'FN', 'GN' and 'PN' for the training set and sentences having 'RN', 'SN' and 'WN' for the dev set.

Fig. 2 summarizes our process of splitting the set of entity tags and data for the three models. Without including 'EN' and relabelling, the training sets for the BERT+LC model and the two few-shot learning systems have 22,530 sentences and 21,642 sentences, respectively. The dev set has 498 sentences, and test set 107 sentences.

5.2 Results

Table 2 summarizes the overall results of the three models on the test dataset, and the results of the two few-shot learning models on the dev set, when not including 'EN'. As shown in Fig. 2 and described in Sec. 5.1, the training dataset that used by BERT+LC model is the combination of training set used by ProtoBERT and NNShot, dev set, 8 instances of entity type 'MN' and 8 instances of entity type 'TN' but the test data remains the same across the three models. In our few-shot systems, we use a 2-way $5 \sim 10$ shot setting. All the F1-scores we report are micro averaged F1-score.

As shown, both ProtoBERT and NNShot perform better than BERT+LC on the test set. NNShot outperforms BERT+LC by 1.4% F1-score and ProtoBERT outperforms BERT+LC by 5.3% F1-score. The gap between NNShot and ProtoBERT becomes more evident on the dev set with ProtoBERT outperforming NNShot by over 10% F1-score. This suggests that ProtoBERT can outperform NNShot by a larger margin when they run on a larger dataset.

We further analyze the performance of the three models on the individual entity types on the dev and test sets. The results are summarized in Table 3 and Table 4, respectively. Table 3 shows that predictions on 'MN' are overwhelmingly better than that on 'TN'. We believe this is mainly because 'MN' as month name is a much easier entity type to identify than 'TN' (a temple name). Among the three models, BERT+LC system produces the best F1-score on 'MN' that is 1.4% higher than that of ProtoBERT. However, BERT+LC produces the worst performance on 'TN' with an F1-score of 54.9%, around 27% lower than that of NNShot and ProtoBERT. This is mainly due to its low recall on 'TN' even though its precision is 100%. A further post-processing step often takes place when conducting NER using Sumerian data: we allow a domain expert to go over the automatically identified name list (or a sample of the list) for further verification. We believe a system that has a higher recall is more useful in practice than a system that has a 100% precision but low recall. That said, we think ProtoBERT has its own advantages in practice than the other two systems in low-shot settings. This is consistently suggested by Table 3 and Table 4 with the high recall scores of ProtoBERT in all the individual entity types across dev and test set. Table 4 shows that ProtoBERT dominantly outperforms NNShot on all the individual entity types on dev set in F1-score and recall. The only place where ProtoBERT falls behind NNShot is on 'WN' by 2.4% in precision.

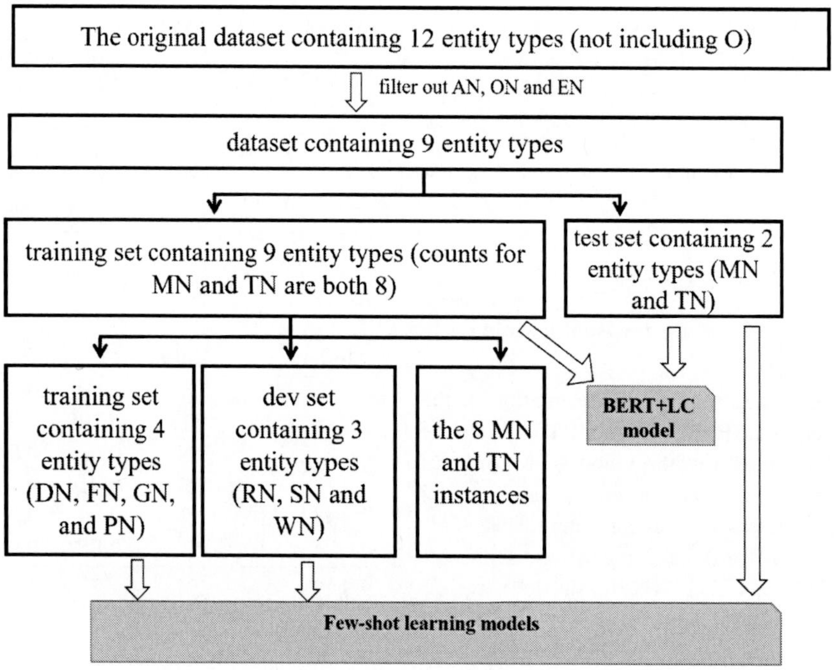

Figure 2: The process of tag and data splitting for three models

Model	Dev	Test
BERT+LC	—	**0.822**
NNShot	0.714	0.821
ProtoBERT	**0.823**	0.659

Table 5: F1-score of few-shot learning models on test set with EN.

5.3 Discussion on the influence of relabeling

NER is a sequence labeling problem and it is very common that a sentence contains several different entity types. For few-shot learning systems, we keep entity types in training, dev and test sets mutually disjoint because we want to test the systems on unseen entity types. A common strategy for avoiding the same entity types from occurring in different subsets is relabeling. Tokens in the training set whose labels belong to the test set are relabelled to 'O' type. Same operation is performed on test set and dev set to keep these subsets mutually disjoint. Fortunately, in our Sumerian dataset, the sentences are normally short and the majority of them only contain one of the twelve types. For most of the entity types, we can easily select sentences that only contain one entity type and no need to relabel any tokens in those sentences. However, 'EN' is an exception. Almost every sentence that has 'EN' entity type has the existence of multiple other entity types, which means all those entity types should be relabelled to 'O' when we include 'EN' in our target tag set. As 'EN' was initially assigned as an entity type for the test set, we did our first experiment with 'EN' included in the test set and ran all the three models on this set. Table 5 shows that the performance of ProtoBERT drops dramatically. F1-score drops to 65.6% (with 'EN') from 89.6% (without 'EN'). In this setting, the result of BERT+LC is produced by adding 8 randomly sampled 'EN' examples to the model's training set, and the rest of 'EN' examples goes to the test set.

Table 6 shows the confusion matrix calculated on the test set both without and with the 'EN' type to see how the results of ProtoBERT are allocated. The first column of the table with entity types is the gold labels in test set. The first row shows what label each gold label was predicted to be by the system. As shown in the table, with 'EN' included in the test set, 54 'O' are labeled to 'TN' and 52 'O' are labeled to 'EN'. That means with the inclusion of 'EN' many more false positive for 'TN' and 'EN' are produced. We believe this is mainly caused by the fact that almost all the sentences that have 'EN' also have many other entity types and these entity types are relabelled to 'O'. In ProtoBERT, when

Test set without EN				
	O	MN	TN	
O (118)	108	3	7	
MN (60)	0	56	4	
TN (27)	1	0	26	
Test set with EN				
	O	MN	TN	EN
O (225)	157	2	**54**	**52**
MN (60)	1	58	1	0
TN (27)	2	0	25	0
EN (50)	**12**	0	0	38

Table 6: Prediction of ProtoBERT on test set without and with EN.

Test set without EN				
	O	MN	TN	
O (118)	109	7	2	
MN (60)	0	53	7	
TN (27)	1	1	25	
Test set with EN				
	O	MN	TN	EN
O (225)	251	1	6	7
MN (60)	6	50	0	4
TN (27)	7	0	20	0
EN (50)	12	0	0	38

Table 7: Prediction of NNShot on test set without and with EN.

we calculate prototypes for each class, we average all the tokens in support set with the same entity type. After we relabel some tokens to 'O', the prototype of 'O' becomes noisy. That's why the model often gets confused between 'O' type and other types such as 'EN' or 'TN', which leads to poor performance of a model. Again, 'MN' as an easy entity type shows to be stable and is not affected by this relabelling as much.

Table 7 shows that the influence of relabeling for NNShot is not as obvious as that for ProtoBERT. The main reason is that the model is based on token-level nearest neighbor classification. When we query a token, it goes to find its closest example and uses its type which can counteract to a certain extent the effect of 'O' type relabeling issue.

Previous work of few-shot learning systems on English also shows the performance is not as good as expected (Fritzler et al., 2019; Huang et al., 2020; Ding et al., 2021). As the prototypes in their work are also learnt from a similar relabelling process, it could be one of the reasons that affects the system performance. Yang and Katiyar (2020) proposes STRUCTSHOT for few-shot NER to better model the label dependencies in a sentence. Although the label dependency issue in Sumerian NER is not as outstanding, it still exists. We are planning to leave it as future work to further investigate effective ways to deal with the relabelling issues caused by the 'O' type.

6 Conclusions and Future Work

We have applied three models, BERT+LC, NNShot and ProtoBERT, to explore the Sumerian NER in low resource settings, and have presented our preliminary results. This is the first work of exploring few-shot NER on the Sumerian language dataset. Our experiments show that ProtoBERT as a few-shot learning model has consistently outperformed the fully supervised model BERT+LC model in few-shot settings and has generally achieved better performance than NNShot. Though as a token-level nearest neighbour classification method, NNShot is less sensitive to the noisy 'O' type that is introduced by the relabeling step, it may not be as stable as ProtoBERT owing to the nearest neighbor mechanism in the training stage. We show that BERT-LC fails to do a good job in learning more examples in few-shot settings. While we investigate the efficacy of prototypical networks-based ProtoBERT and nearest neighbour metric-based NNShot learning models in the few-shot Sumerian NER task, it will be particularly interesting to 1) extend our work to a larger test set; 2) explore new methods such as STRUCTSHOT (Yang and Katiyar, 2020) to solve the noisy 'O' type issue introduced by relabelling; 3) experiment on using more sophisticated cross-lingual approaches including adapter-based models on Sumerian NER.

Acknowledgements

We thank Dr. ChangYu Liu, Professor at Nanjing Normal University, for his assistance with the tablet example in this paper.

References

Rachit Bansal, Himanshu Choudhary, Ravneet Punia, Niko Schenk, Jacob L Dahl, and Émilie Pagé-Perron. 2021. How low is too low? a computational perspective on extremely low-resource languages. arXiv:2105.14515.

Yujia Bao, Menghua Wu, Shiyu Chang, and Regina Barzilay. 2019. Few-shot text classification with distributional signatures. *arXiv preprint arXiv:1908.06039.*

Akash Bharadwaj, David R Mortensen, Chris Dyer, and Jaime G Carbonell. 2016. Phonologically aware neural model for named entity recognition in low resource transfer settings. In *Proceedings of the 2016 Conference on Empirical Methods in Natural Language Processing*, pages 1462–1472.

Nigel Collier and Jin-Dong Kim. 2004. Introduction to the bio-entity recognition task at JNLPBA. In *Proceedings of the International Joint Workshop on Natural Language Processing in Biomedicine and its Applications (NLPBA/BioNLP)*, pages 73–78, Geneva, Switzerland. COLING.

Jacob Devlin, Ming-Wei Chang, Kenton Lee, and Kristina Toutanova. 2019. BERT: Pre-training of deep bidirectional transformers for language understanding. In *Proceedings of the 2019 Conference of the North American Chapter of the Association for Computational Linguistics: Human Language Technologies, Volume 1 (Long and Short Papers)*, pages 4171–4186, Minneapolis, Minnesota. Association for Computational Linguistics.

Ning Ding, Guangwei Xu, Yulin Chen, Xiaobin Wang, Xu Han, Pengjun Xie, Hai-Tao Zheng, and Zhiyuan Liu. 2021. Few-nerd: A few-shot named entity recognition dataset. arXiv:2105.07464.

Xiaocheng Feng, Xiachong Feng, Bing Qin, Zhangyin Feng, and Ting Liu. 2018. Improving low resource named entity recognition using cross-lingual knowledge transfer. In *IJCAI*, volume 1, pages 4071–4077.

Alexander Fritzler, Varvara Logacheva, and Maksim Kretov. 2019. Few-shot classification in named entity recognition task. In *Proceedings of the 34th ACM/SIGAPP Symposium on Applied Computing*, SAC '19, page 993–1000, New York, NY, USA. Association for Computing Machinery.

Yutai Hou, Wanxiang Che, Yongkui Lai, Zhihan Zhou, Yijia Liu, Han Liu, and Ting Liu. 2020. Few-shot slot tagging with collapsed dependency transfer and label-enhanced task-adaptive projection network. *arXiv preprint arXiv:2006.05702.*

Jiaxin Huang, Chunyuan Li, Krishan Subudhi, Damien Jose, Shobana Balakrishnan, Weizhu Chen, Baolin Peng, Jianfeng Gao, and Jiawei Han. 2020. Few-shot named entity recognition: A comprehensive study. arXiv:2012.14978.

IDEAH Journal, Anya Kulikov, Adam Anderson, and Niek Veldhuis. 2021. Sumerian networks: Classifying text groups in the drehem archives. *IDEAH*. Https://ideah.pubpub.org/pub/q22859lx.

Diederik P. Kingma and Jimmy Ba. 2015. Adam: A method for stochastic optimization. arXiv:1412.6980.

Canasai Kruengkrai, Thien Hai Nguyen, Sharifah Mahani Aljunied, and Lidong Bing. 2020. Improving low-resource named entity recognition using joint sentence and token labeling. In *Proceedings of the 58th Annual Meeting of the Association for Computational Linguistics*, pages 5898–5905, Online. Association for Computational Linguistics.

Ying Lin, Shengqi Yang, Veselin Stoyanov, and Heng Ji. 2018. A multi-lingual multi-task architecture for low-resource sequence labeling. In *Proceedings of the 56th Annual Meeting of the Association for Computational Linguistics (Volume 1: Long Papers)*, pages 799–809.

Changyu Liu. 2021. Prosopography of individuals delivering animals to puzriš-dagan in ur iii mesopotamia. *Akkadica*, 142:113–142.

Yinhan Liu, Myle Ott, Naman Goyal, Jingfei Du, Mandar Joshi, Danqi Chen, Omer Levy, Mike Lewis, Luke Zettlemoyer, and Veselin Stoyanov. 2019. Roberta: A robustly optimized bert pretraining approach. arXiv:1907.11692.

Yudong Liu, James Hearne, and Bryan Conrad. 2016. Recognizing proper names in ur iii texts through supervised learning. In *Proceedings of the Twenty-Ninth International Florida Artificial Intelligence Research Society Conference*, page 535–540, Florida, USA.

Liang Luo, Yudong Liu, James Hearne, and Clinton Burkhart. 2015. Unsupervised sumerian personal name recognition. In *Proceedings of the Twenty-Eighth International Florida Artificial Intelligence Research Society Conference*, page 193–198, Florida, USA.

Jonas Pfeiffer, Ivan Vulić, Iryna Gurevych, and Sebastian Ruder. 2020. MAD-X: An Adapter-Based Framework for Multi-Task Cross-Lingual Transfer. In *Proceedings of the 2020 Conference on Empirical Methods in Natural Language Processing (EMNLP)*, pages 7654–7673, Online. Association for Computational Linguistics.

Afshin Rahimi, Yuan Li, and Trevor Cohn. 2019. Massively multilingual transfer for ner. *arXiv preprint arXiv:1902.00193.*

Erik F. Tjong Kim Sang and Fien De Meulder. 2003. Introduction to the conll-2003 shared task: Language-independent named entity recognition.

Jake Snell, Kevin Swersky, and Richard S. Zemel. 2017. Prototypical networks for few-shot learning. arXiv:1703.05175.

Michael Tänzer, Sebastian Ruder, and Marek Rei. 2022. Memorisation versus generalisation in pre-trained language modelsl perspective on extremely low-resource languages. arXiv:2105.00828.

Oriol Vinyals, Charles Blundell, Timothy Lillicrap, Daan Wierstra, et al. 2016. Matching networks for one shot learning. *Advances in neural information processing systems*, 29.

Jiateng Xie, Zhilin Yang, Graham Neubig, Noah A Smith, and Jaime Carbonell. 2018. Neural cross-lingual named entity recognition with minimal resources. *arXiv preprint arXiv:1808.09861*.

Yi Yang and Arzoo Katiyar. 2020. Simple and effective few-shot named entity recognition with structured nearest neighbor learning. arXiv:2010.02405.

Deep Learning-Based Morphological Segmentation for Indigenous Languages: A Study Case on Innu-Aimun

Ngoc Tan Le
Université du Québec à Montréal
le.ngoc_tan@uqam.ca

Antoine Cadotte
Université du Québec à Montréal
cadotte.antoine@courrier.uqam.ca

Mathieu Boivin
Université de Montréal
mathieu.boivin.2@umontreal.ca

Fatiha Sadat
Université du Québec à Montréal
sadat.fatiha@uqam.ca

Abstract

Recent advances in the field of deep learning have led to a growing interest in the development of NLP approaches for low-resource and endangered languages. Nevertheless, relatively little research, related to NLP, has been conducted on indigenous languages. These languages are considered to be filled with complexities and challenges that make their study incredibly difficult in the NLP and AI fields. This paper focuses on the morphological segmentation of indigenous languages, an extremely challenging task because of polysynthesis, dialectal variations with rich morpho-phonemics, misspellings and resource-limited scenario issues. The proposed approach, towards a morphological segmentation of Innu-Aimun, an extremely low-resource indigenous language of Canada, is based on deep learning. Experiments and evaluations have shown promising results, compared to state-of-the-art rule-based and unsupervised approaches.

1 Introduction

Over the past decade, we have observed a successful growth in the deep learning-based approaches in several Natural Language Processing (NLP) applications. This has helped to create NLP tools and applications in resource-rich languages. On the other hand, for low-resource languages, few applications of NLP have been studied for multiple reasons (Mager et al., 2018b).

In particular, for indigenous languages, NLP applications have to deal with linguistics challenges such as polysynthesis, diversity of grammatical features of morphology, dialect variation with rich morpho-phonemics, misspellings due to noisy or scarce training data and low resource scenario challenges (Littell et al., 2018; Joanis et al., 2020). Moreover, morphological segmentation for indigenous polysynthetic languages is especially challenging because these languages have often multiple individual morphemes by word and several meanings per morpheme.

The current research focuses on the morphological segmentation task for indigenous languages, with a case study on Innu-Aimun, also called Montagnais[1]. Innu-Aimun is an Algonquian polysynthetic language spoken by over 10,000 Innu in Labrador and Quebec in Eastern Canada[2]. We choose this indigenous language for this specific NLP task because it has not yet been investigated thus far.

The main focus consists of how to develop indigenous language technology and linguistic resources, with the aim of helping the indigenous communities in the revitalization and preservation of their languages. Thus, we propose in the current study, a deep learning-based morphological segmentation for Innu-Aimun. Our contribution to the current research is twofold. Firstly, it proposes a deep learning-based word segmenter for indigenous languages. Secondly, it empirically compares the proposed approach, in a case study of Innu-Aimun, with multiple baselines such as Finite-State Transducer, Morfessor, and Adaptor Grammar-based approaches.

Overall, this study aims to serve as a benchmark for developing NLP tools and applications, which will help revitalize and preserve indigenous languages, while taking into account indigenous cultural realities and knowledge.

The paper is structured as follows: Section 2 highlights morphological analyzers for indigenous languages, with a description of Innu-Aimun. Our proposed approach is described in Section 3. Section 4 presents the experimental results, compared to other state-of-the-art approaches. Section 5 discusses our evaluations, while providing an error analysis. Finally, Section 6 presents the conclusion as well as potential future work.

[1] https://www.thecanadianencyclopedia.ca/en/article/innu-montagnais-naskapi

[2] https://en.wikipedia.org/wiki/Innu-Aimun

Proceedings of the Third Workshop on Deep Learning for Low-Resource Natural Language Processing, pages 146 - 151
July 14, 2022 ©2022 Association for Computational Linguistics

2 Related work

2.1 Morphological segmentation in Indigenous languages

Many indigenous languages in Canada, in the Americas and around the world have in common that they are polysynthetic. Most also share a context of extremely low or scarce resource. While morphological segmentation is highly useful—if not unavoidable—for indigenous NLP applications, data and knowledge scarcity make its development very challenging.

When there exists no language-specific tool, NLP tasks often make use of unsupervised approaches for segmentation. Byte-pair encoding (BPE) segmentation, introduced by Sennrich et al. (2016), is a common one for Neural Machine Translation. The technique has been used by (Joanis et al., 2020; Le and Sadat, 2020), for instance, to produce an Inuktitut-English NMT baseline using the Nunavut Hansard corpus.

In cases where there is a lack of annotated data, rule-based approaches, such as those based on Finite-State Transducers (FST), have been used the most. Farley (2012) proposed an FST-based morphological analyser for Inuktitut (one of Canada's most resourced and documented indigenous languages). Harrigan et al. (2017) developed an FST morphological model for Plains Cree. Arppe et al. (2017) applied the same approach partially adapted to East Cree. Mager et al. (2018a) proposed a probabilistic approach to an FST model for Wixarika (huichol).

Other proposed approaches are hybrid, adding knowledge or rules to unsupervised methods. Eskander et al. (2019) proposed an approach based on Adaptor Grammars (Johnson et al., 2006), and applied it to four Uto-Aztecan polysynthetic languages. Pan et al. (2020) combined BPE segmentation and rule-based segmentation for Uyghur, a morphologically rich language.

For deep learning-based approach, Kann et al. (2018) used the neural network-based seq2seq models for Mexican polysynthetic languages. Micher (2019) applied a recurrent neural network-based approach to deal with the word segmentation for Inuktitut.

2.2 Innu-Aimun language

Innu-Aimun is the language of the Innu, an indigenous people formerly known as the Montagnais (Mollen, 2006). This language is found in the Quebec and Labrador provinces of Canada, in a dozen communities (Baraby et al., 2017). It is a polysynthetic indigenous language, a member of the Algonquian family and is related to Cree and Naskapi with which it forms a dialectic continuum (Drapeau, 2014). Statistics Canada estimated the number of speakers at 11,360 in 2016 [3].

Although Innu-Aimun is fundamentally an oral language, its orthography was standardized in 1989 (Mollen, 2006). A first dictionnary based on the standard orthography, for Innu-French, was published in 1991 (Drapeau, 1991). There exists today a more complete, trilingual and pan-dialectal dictionnary that is being continuously updated and is available online[4]. Other online resources include a verb conjugation web application (Baraby and Junker, 2011), based on work of Baraby (1998).

The aforementioned online tools have been part of an effort by Junker et al. (2016) to develop a series of Web tools for Innu-Aimun language maintenance. This project, primarily, aimed at bilingual speakers, which also includes several primary language resources (*e.g.* lexicons, grammars, conversational guides, etc.), educational online games and a catalog of audio and written Innu-Aimun works[5].

Other than online tools, very few language technologies have been developed for Innu-Aimun, to our knowledge. A search-engine with flexible orthography has been developed by Junker and Stewart (2008) and integrated with an online dictionnary (Junker et al., 2016), in conjunction with an equivalent tool for East Cree. Other research projects have targeted the construction of Innu-Aimun corpora Cadotte et al. (2022). Drapeau and Lambert-Brétière (2013) proposed an annotated, multimodal corpus with translations. An NRC Canada indigenous languages technology project (Kuhn et al., 2020) aimed to transcribe oral recordings of several indigenous languages in Canada, including Innu-Aimun.

3 Our proposed approach

3.1 Model overview

In this paper, we focus on the surface segmentation (Ruokolainen et al., 2016; Kann et al., 2018; Liu et al., 2021), where a term is segmented in a substrings sequence.

[3]Statistics Canada: The Aboriginal languages of First Nations people, Métis and Inuit

[4]`https://dictionary.Innu-Aimun.ca/`

[5]Tshakapesh Institute - Catalogue

Given an Innu-Aimun word, the segmentation process consists of breaking down the word into separate morphemes, for example, *uminushima* → *u-minush-im-a* (in English: *her/his cats*). Our model is made following these steps: (1) apply the Transformer-based encoder-decoder architecture, with a multihead self attention mechanism (Vaswani et al., 2017); (2) deal with surface segmentation, while considering the monotonic aspect of morphotactics (that is, the constraints on the ordering of morphemes) (Figure 1). We train the positional embeddings using the position of each element in a sequence.

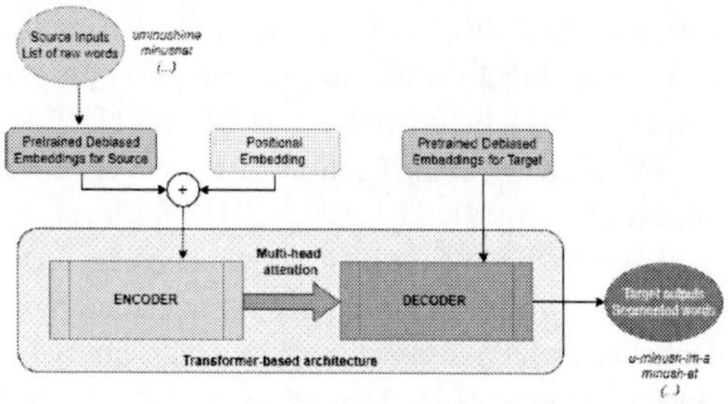

Figure 1: Architecture of our framework: Deep Learning-based Morphological segmentation for indigenous language, with pretrained debiased word-based embedding for source-target, and positional embedding.

3.2 Deep Learning-based morphotactics modeling

We model a deep learning-based morphological segmenter using the Transformer-based encoder-decoder architecture.

In the encoder, the input sequence is encoded at character level. Then the embedding layer is incorporated with pre-trained embeddings at multiple levels such as character, affix (prefixes and suffixes), along with multiheaded attention over the input sequence, that helps finding morpheme boundaries related to the whole word.

To ensure the monotonic aspect of morphotactics, the positional embeddings are used to encode the order of each element of a sequence in both the encoder and the decoder.

The decoder uses the same concept of multihead attention over itself and also the encoder. The attention mechanism allows to align input sequences to the correct corresponding output sequences that are segmented in individual morphemes (Figure 1).

4 Experiments and Evaluations

4.1 Data Preparation

A small corpus was manually collected from multiple resources such as the Website of Aimun-Mashinaikan-French-English dictionary Innu[6] as well as open source grammar books and the online Innu lessons platform[7] that are available at the Tshakapesh Institute (Drapeau, 2014; Mollen, 2006).

The collected experimental corpus contains 500 word bases (roots) and 500 affixes (prefixes, suffixes). A training set, crawled from the Aimun-Mashinaikan dictionary Innu, consists of 30,118 terms, used as raw word lists, non segmented, with length between 2 and 46 characters. A small golden testing set, containing 250 unique terms, was manually segmented with the help of an Innu language teacher from the Uashat Mak Mani-utenam community[8].

4.2 Training settings

We configured several baselines: (1) based on a simple weighted Finite-State Transducer (FST) to maximise the morpheme frequency (Richardson and Tyers, 2021), (2) based on Morfessor version 2.0 (Virpioja et al., 2013) to learn the morpheme boundaries using minimum description length optimization, and (3) based on the Adaptor Grammar approach. We used the MorphAGram toolkit (Eskander et al., 2020), with two settings: standard setting (AdaGra-Std) and scholar seeded setting (AdaGra-SS). We adopted the best learning settings: the best standard *PrefixStemSuffix+SuffixMorph* grammar and the best scholar-seeded grammar, as explained in (Eskander et al., 2019), for Innu-Aimun.

We configured a deep-learning based model (T-DeepLo) with an encoder-decoder Transformer model (Vaswani et al., 2017), based entirely on the multihead self-attention mechanism. For the hyperparameters, we used 4-layer both in the encoder and in the decoder. The batch size was set at 32. The initial learning rate was set to 0.0001. The hidden dimension was set at 256, and dropout with a rate of 0.2. The model is trained with 8 multihead attention in the encoder and in the decoder, using Adam optimizer (Kingma and Ba, 2014).

[6] https://dictionary.Innu-Aimun.ca/Words

[7] https://lessons.innu.atlas-ling.ca/

[8] https://www.itum.qc.ca/

4.3 Results

	Precision	Recall	F1
FST	52.71	42.96	46.11
Morfessor	43.33	38.01	40.49
AdaGra-Std	53.78	43.18	47.91
AdaGra-SS	70.45	61.36	65.60
T-DeepLo	81.27	77.15	79.16

Table 1: Evaluation on the test set using the different settings.

The performances of all the models were evaluated using the conventional automatic metrics in the field of NLP, such as Precision, Recall and F1-score.

For the unsupervised methods, we noticed that the scholar-seeded learning (AdaGra-SS) model outperformed all the other baselines, with 70.45%, 61.36%, 65.60% in terms of Precision, Recall and F1 score, respectively (Table 1). We observed both precision and recall were significantly improved while injecting a list of affixes (prefixes and suffixes) during the training. However, the Morfessor model showed the worst results, with only 40.49% in terms of F1.

The Transformer-based DeepLo model obtained the best performance across all metrics, with gains of +10.82%, +15.79%, +13.56% in terms of Precision, Recall and F1 score, respectively, compared to the AdaGra-SS model (Table 1). The T-DeepLo model showed the ability to learn and to extract more complex features, relying on the multihead self attention mechanism.

We performed an error analysis in order to shed some light on how the models were able to learn and recognize the morpheme boundary of a sequence. Table 2 shows sample prediction outputs from all the models on the test set.

5 Error analysis

Due to the complex linguistic peculiarities of Innu-Aimun and its dialectal variations, a word can be pronounced in several ways. Thus, its transcription poses more challenges in the segmentation task. Besides, a word in Innu-Aimun is always composed of a central core (root), including a verb.

With the help of an Innu language teacher, we made observations and reviewed the data and predictions to determine if the segmentation results were correct and discover the errors. Basically, our models tend to over-segment more complex morphemes due to the linguistic irregularities and the morphotactic phenomena, to detect common lexical suffixes such as *ap*, *tsh* or grammatical ending suffixes such as *at*, *eu*, *t*, *n*, *it*, *mi* or *uk*. In particular, we observed an over-segmentation in the FST and Morfessor models. These models tend to segment a term into several sub-morphemes (Table 2). The same phenomena are found in other models of AdaGra-Std and AdaGra-SS. Furthermore, the T-DeepLo model was able to better detect morpheme boundaries.

All models failed when dealing with out-of-vocabulary words. For example, here, the term *mitshuap* (meaning: *house*), which was not seen in the training, was segmented into multiple morphemes (Table 2).

Another challenge is related to the over-segmentation of all the models, down to character level, due to the length of prefixes and suffixes between one and multiple characters. For example, some models divided a term up to a character level (Table 2): (FST) **u a** pa tamu; mi **t** shu **a p**; (Morfessor) **u** apa tamu; (AdaGra-Std) minu sha **t**; (AdaGra-SS) **u** apa tamu.

6 Conclusion and Perspectives

We presented a deep learning-based method for morphological segmentation for Innu-Aimun, an indigenous language of Canada, which can be considered as a first research study on the subject, so far.

Our evaluations showed promising results. Thus, the proposed deep learning-based method, incorporating pre-trained embeddings at multiple levels, helped finding morpheme boundaries related to the whole word. This study makes an important contribution by focusing on morpheme segmentation in the low-resource indigenous language. Furthermore, through this research, we noted the importance of close collaboration and consultation with the Innu indigenous community, to ensure that language technologies are developed with respect and in accordance with the community's revitalisation objectives.

Acknowledgements

The authors are grateful to the community of Uashat Mak Mani-Utenam, Samuel Marticotte for his role in initiating this project, Mrs. Denise Jourdain for sharing her knowledge and experience,

Reference	FST	Morfessor	AdaGra-Std	AdaGra-SS	T-DeepLo
akushi ńua	**akushińua**	akushi **ń ua**	akushi ńua	akushi ńua	akushi ńua
minush at	minush at	**minu sh** at	**minu sha t**	minush at	minush at
mi tshuap	mi **t shu a p**	mi **tsh uap**	mi **tshu ap**	mi **tsh uap**	**mitshuap**
pashu e u	**pa shu eu**	**pashueu**	**pa sh** ueu	pash **u eu**	pashu **eu**
tshika papata n	**tshi ka pa pa ta n**	**tshi ka papa tan**	tshika **papatan**	tshika **papatan**	tshika **pa patan**
u minush im a	u minush **ima**	u **minu sh ima**	u minush **ima**	u minush im a	u minush im a
uapat am u	**u a pa tamu**	**u apa tamu**	**uapa tamu**	**u apa tamu**	**u apa tamu**

Table 2: Illustrations of morpheme segmentation predictions on the test set using the different settings such as Finite-State Transducer, Morfessor, Standard setting (AdaGra-Std), Scholar seeded setting (AdaGra-SS), and Deep learning-based (T-DeepLo). Strings in bold are incorrectly segmented.

Prof. Yvette Mollen and Prof. Jimena Terraza from Kiuna College, for their precious advices and feedbacks. The authors also thank the anonymous reviewers for their valuable comments.

References

Antti Arppe, Marie-Odile Junker, and Delasie Torkornoo. 2017. Converting a comprehensive lexical database into a computational model: The case of East Cree verb inflection. In *Proceedings of the 2nd Workshop on the Use of Computational Methods in the Study of Endangered Languages*, pages 52–56, Honolulu. Association for Computational Linguistics.

Anne-Marie Baraby. 1998. Guide pratique des principales conjugaisons en Montagnais. *Sept-Iles: Institut culturel et éducatif montagnais*.

Anne-Marie Baraby and Marie-Odile Junker. 2011. Conjugaisons des verbes innus.

Anne-Marie Baraby, Marie-Odile Junker, and Yvette Mollen. 2017. A 45-year old language documentation program first aimed at speakers: the case of the Innu.

Antoine Cadotte, Tan Ngoc Le, Boivin Boivin, and Fatiha Sadat. 2022. Challenges and perspectives for innu-aimun within indigenous language technologies. In *Proceedings of the Fifth Workshop on the Use of Computational Methods in the Study of Endangered Languages*, pages 99–108, Dublin, Ireland. Association for Computational Linguistics.

Lynn Drapeau. 1991. *Dictionnaire montagnais-français*. Presses de l'Université du Québec.

Lynn Drapeau. 2014. *Grammaire de la langue innue*. Presses de l'Université du Québec.

Lynn Drapeau and Renée Lambert-Brétière. 2013. The innu language documentation project. In *Proceedings of the 17th Foundation for Endangered Languages Conference*.

Ramy Eskander, Francesca Callejas, Elizabeth Nichols, Judith L Klavans, and Smaranda Muresan. 2020. Morphagram, evaluation and framework for unsupervised morphological segmentation. In *Proceedings of The 12th Language Resources and Evaluation Conference*, pages 7112–7122.

Ramy Eskander, Judith L Klavans, and Smaranda Muresan. 2019. Unsupervised morphological segmentation for low-resource polysynthetic languages. In *Proceedings of the 16th Workshop on Computational Research in Phonetics, Phonology, and Morphology*, pages 189–195.

Benoit Farley. 2012. The uqailaut project. *URL http://www.inuktitutcomputing.ca*.

Atticus G. Harrigan, Katherine Schmirler, Antti Arppe, Lene Antonsen, Trond Trosterud, and Arok Wolvengrey. 2017. Learning from the computational modelling of Plains Cree verbs. *Morphology*, 27(4):565–598.

Eric Joanis, Rebecca Knowles, Roland Kuhn, Samuel Larkin, Patrick Littell, Chi-kiu Lo, Darlene Stewart, and Jeffrey Micher. 2020. The Nunavut Hansard Inuktitut–English parallel corpus 3.0 with preliminary machine translation results. In *Proceedings of the 12th Language Resources and Evaluation Conference*, pages 2562–2572, Marseille, France. European Language Resources Association.

Mark Johnson, Thomas Griffiths, and Sharon Goldwater. 2006. Adaptor grammars: A framework for specifying compositional nonparametric bayesian models. In *Advances in Neural Information Processing Systems*, volume 19. MIT Press.

Marie-Odile Junker, Yvette Mollen, Hélène St-Onge, and Delasie Torkornoo. 2016. Integrated web tools for Innu language maintenance. In *Papers of the 44th Algonquian Conference*, pages 192–210.

Marie-Odile Junker and Terry Stewart. 2008. Building search engines for Algonquian languages. *Algonquian Papers-Archive*, 39.

Katharina Kann, Manuel Mager, Ivan Meza-Ruiz, and Hinrich Schütze. 2018. Fortification of neural morphological segmentation models for polysynthetic minimal-resource languages. *arXiv preprint arXiv:1804.06024*.

Diederik P Kingma and Jimmy Ba. 2014. Adam: A method for stochastic optimization. *arXiv preprint arXiv:1412.6980*.

Roland Kuhn, Fineen Davis, Alain Désilets, Eric Joanis, Anna Kazantseva, Rebecca Knowles, Patrick Littell, Delaney Lothian, Aidan Pine, Caroline Running Wolf, Eddie Santos, Darlene Stewart, Gilles Boulianne, Vishwa Gupta, Brian Maracle Owennatékha, Akwiratékha' Martin, Christopher Cox, Marie-Odile Junker, Olivia Sammons, Delasie Torkornoo, Nathan Thanyehténhas Brinklow, Sara Child, Benoît Farley, David Huggins-Daines, Daisy Rosenblum, and Heather Souter. 2020. The Indigenous Languages Technology project at NRC Canada: An empowerment-oriented approach to developing language software. In *Proceedings of the 28th International Conference on Computational Linguistics*, pages 5866–5878, Barcelona, Spain (Online). International Committee on Computational Linguistics.

Tan Ngoc Le and Fatiha Sadat. 2020. Low-resource NMT: an empirical study on the effect of rich morphological word segmentation on Inuktitut. In *Proceedings of the 14th Conference of the Association for Machine Translation in the Americas (Volume 1: Research Track)*, pages 165–172, Virtual. Association for Machine Translation in the Americas (AMTA 2020).

Patrick Littell, Anna Kazantseva, Roland Kuhn, Aidan Pine, Antti Arppe, Christopher Cox, and Marie-Odile Junker. 2018. Indigenous language technologies in canada: Assessment, challenges, and successes. In *Proceedings of the 27th International Conference on Computational Linguistics*, pages 2620–2632.

Zoey Liu, Robert Jimerson, and Emily Prud'hommeaux. 2021. Morphological segmentation for seneca. In *Proceedings of the First Workshop on Natural Language Processing for Indigenous Languages of the Americas*, pages 90–101.

Manuel Mager, Diónico Carrillo, and Ivan Meza. 2018a. Probabilistic Finite-State morphological segmenter for Wixarika (huichol) language. *Journal of Intelligent & Fuzzy Systems*, 34(5):3081–3087. Publisher: IOS Press.

Manuel Mager, Ximena Gutierrez-Vasques, Gerardo Sierra, and Ivan Meza-Ruiz. 2018b. Challenges of language technologies for the indigenous languages of the Americas. In *Proceedings of the 27th International Conference on Computational Linguistics*, pages 55–69, Santa Fe, New Mexico, USA. Association for Computational Linguistics.

Jeffrey Micher. 2019. Bootstrapping a neural morphological generator from morphological analyzer output for inuktitut. In *Proceedings of the Workshop on Computational Methods for Endangered Languages*, volume 2, page 7.

Yvette Mollen. 2006. Transmettre un héritage: la langue innue. *Cap-aux-Diamants: la revue d'histoire du Québec*, (85):21–25. Publisher: Les Éditions Cap-aux-Diamants inc.

Yirong Pan, Xiao Li, Yating Yang, and Rui Dong. 2020. Morphological word segmentation on agglutinative languages for neural machine translation.

Ivy Richardson and Francis M Tyers. 2021. A morphological analyser for k'iche'. *Procesamiento del Lenguaje Natural*, 66:99–109.

Teemu Ruokolainen, Oskar Kohonen, Kairit Sirts, Stig-Arne Grönroos, Mikko Kurimo, and Sami Virpioja. 2016. A comparative study of minimally supervised morphological segmentation. *Computational Linguistics*, 42(1):91–120.

Rico Sennrich, Barry Haddow, and Alexandra Birch. 2016. Neural machine translation of rare words with subword units. In *Proceedings of the 54th Annual Meeting of the Association for Computational Linguistics (Volume 1: Long Papers)*, pages 1715–1725, Berlin, Germany. Association for Computational Linguistics.

Ashish Vaswani, Noam Shazeer, Niki Parmar, Jakob Uszkoreit, Llion Jones, Aidan N Gomez, Łukasz Kaiser, and Illia Polosukhin. 2017. Attention is all you need. In *Advances in neural information processing systems*, pages 5998–6008.

Sami Virpioja, Peter Smit, Stig-Arne Grönroos, Mikko Kurimo, et al. 2013. Morfessor 2.0: Python implementation and extensions for morfessor baseline.

Clean or Annotate: How to Spend a Limited Data Collection Budget

Derek Chen
ASAPP, New York, NY
dchen@asapp.com

Zhou Yu
Columbia University, NY
zy2461@columbia.edu

Samuel R. Bowman
New York University, NY
bowman@nyu.edu

Abstract

Crowdsourcing platforms are often used to collect datasets for training machine learning models, despite higher levels of inaccurate labeling compared to expert labeling. There are two common strategies to manage the impact of such noise: The first involves aggregating redundant annotations, but comes at the expense of labeling substantially fewer examples. Secondly, prior works have also considered using the entire annotation budget to label as many examples as possible and subsequently apply denoising algorithms to implicitly clean the dataset. We find a middle ground and propose an approach which reserves a fraction of annotations to *explicitly* clean up highly probable error samples to optimize the annotation process. In particular, we allocate a large portion of the labeling budget to form an initial dataset used to train a model. This model is then used to identify specific examples that appear most likely to be incorrect, which we spend the remaining budget to relabel. Experiments across three model variations and four natural language processing tasks show our approach outperforms or matches both label aggregation and advanced denoising methods designed to handle noisy labels when allocated the same finite annotation budget.

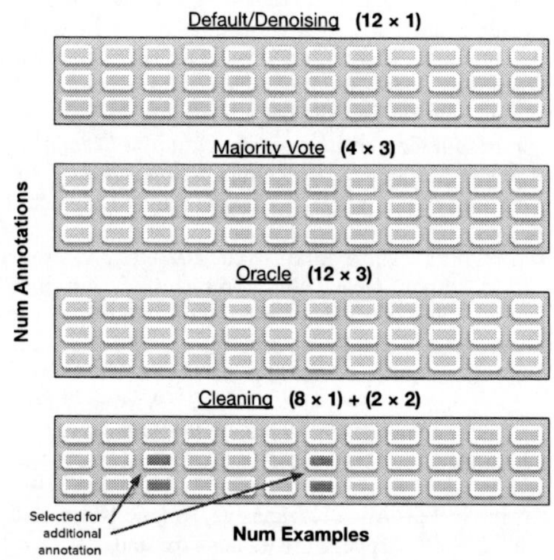

Figure 1: Data cleaning reserves a small portion of the annotation budget for targeted relabeling of examples that are identified as especially likely to be noisy. In contrast, the default and denoising methods spend the entire budget upfront, yielding lower quality data.

1 Introduction

Modern machine learning often depends on heavy data annotation efforts. To keep costs in check while maintaining speed and scalability, many people turn to non-specialist crowd-workers through platforms like Mechanical Turk. Although crowdsourcing reduces costs to a reasonable level, it also tends to produce substantially higher error rates compared with expert labeling. The classic approach for improving reliability in classification tasks is to perform redundant annotations which are later aggregated using a majority vote to form a single gold label (Snow et al., 2008; Sap et al., 2019a; Potts et al., 2021; Sap et al., 2019b). This solution is easy to understand and implement, but comes at the expense of severely reducing the number of labeled examples available for training.

As an alternative, researchers have made great strides in designing automatic label cleaning methods, noise-insensitive training schemes and other mechanisms to work with noisy data (Sukhbaatar et al., 2015; Han et al., 2018; Tanaka et al., 2018). For example, some methods learn a noise transition matrix for reweighting the label (Dawid and Skene, 1979; Goldberger and Ben-Reuven, 2017), while others modify the loss (Ghosh et al., 2017; Patrini et al., 2017). Another set of options generate cleaned examples from mislabeled ones through semi-supervised pseudo-labeling (Jiang et al., 2018; Li et al., 2020). However, empirically getting many of these techniques to work well in practice is often a struggle due to the difficulty of training extra model components.

Proceedings of the Third Workshop on Deep Learning for Low-Resource Natural Language Processing, pages 152 - 168
July 14, 2022 ©2022 Association for Computational Linguistics

We avoid the complexity of repairing or reweighting the labels of existing annotations by instead obtaining wholly new annotations from crowdworkers for a selected subset of samples. In doing so, our proposed methods require no extra model parameters to train, yet still retains the benefits of high label quality. Concretely, we start by allocating a large portion of the labeling budget to obtain an initial training dataset. The examples in this dataset are annotated in a single pass, and we would expect some percentage of them to be incorrectly labeled. However, enough of the labels should be correct to train a reasonable base model. Next, we take advantage of the recently trained model to identify incorrectly labeled examples, and then spend the remaining budget to relabel those examples. Finally, we train a new model using the original data combined with the cleaned data.

The key ingredient of our method is a function for selecting which examples to re-annotate. We consider multiple approaches for identifying candidates for relabeling, none of which have been applied before to denoising data within NLP settings. In all cases, relabeling the target examples relies on neither training any extra model components nor on tuning sensitive hyper-parameters. By using the existing annotation pipeline, the implementation becomes relatively trivial.

To test the generalizability of our method, we compare against multiple baselines on four tasks spanning multiple natural language formats. This departs from previous studies on human labeling in NLP, which focus exclusively on text classification (Wang et al., 2019; Jindal et al., 2019; Tayal et al., 2020). The control baseline and denoising baselines perform a single annotation per example. The majority vote baseline triples the annotations per example, but consequently is trained on only one third the number of examples to meet the annotation budget. We lastly include an oracle baseline that lifts the restriction on a fixed budget and instead uses all available annotations. We test across three model types, ranging from small ones taking minutes to train up to large transformer models which require a week to reach convergence. We find that under the same fixed annotation budget, cleaning methods match or surpass all baselines.

In summary, our contributions include:

1. We examine an alternative direction to learning with noisy labels that appear when data is collected under low-resource settings.
2. We build four versions of our approach that vary in how they target examples to relabel.
3. We compare against a number of baselines, many of which have never been implemented before in the natural language setting.

Overall, our *Large Loss* method, which selects examples for relabeling by the size of their training loss, performs the best out of all variations we consider despite requiring no extra parameters to train.

2 Related Work

The standard method for learning in the presence of unreliable annotation is to perform redundant annotation, where each example is annotated multiple times and a simple majority vote determines the final label (Snow et al., 2004; Russakovsky et al., 2015; Bowman et al., 2015). While effective, this can be costly since it severely reduces the amount of data collected. To tackle this problem, researchers have developed several alternative methods for dealing with noisy data that can be broken down into three categories.

Denoising Techniques Noisy training examples can be thought of as the result of perturbing the true, underlying labels by some source of noise. One group of methods assume the source of noise is from confusing one label *class* for another, and is resolved by reverting the errors through a noise transition matrix (Sukhbaatar et al., 2015; Goldberger and Ben-Reuven, 2017). Other methods work under the assumption that labeling errors occur due to *annotator* biases (Raykar et al., 2009; Rodrigues and Pereira, 2018), such as non-expert labelers (Welinder et al., 2010; Guan et al., 2018) or spammers (Hovy et al., 2013; Khetan et al., 2018). Finally, some methods model the noise of each individual *example*, either through expectation-maximization (Dawid and Skene, 1979; Whitehill et al., 2009; Mnih and Hinton, 2012), or neural networks (Felt et al., 2016; Jindal et al., 2019).

Another set of methods modify the loss function to make the model more robust to noise (Patrini et al., 2017). For example, some methods add a regularization term (Tanno et al., 2019), while others bound the amount of loss contributed by individual training examples (Ghosh et al., 2017; Zhang and Sabuncu, 2018). The learning procedure can also be modified such that the importance of training examples is dynamically reweighted to prevent overfitting to noise (Jiang et al., 2018).

Pseudo-labeling represents a final set of methods that either devise new labels for noisy data (Reed et al., 2015; Tanaka et al., 2018) or generate wholly new training examples (Arazo et al., 2019; Li et al., 2020). Other approaches from this family use two distinct networks to produce examples for each other to learn from (Han et al., 2018; Yu et al., 2019).

Budget Constrained Data Collection Our work also falls under research studying how to maximize the benefit of labeled data given a fixed annotation budget. Khetan and Oh (2016) apply model-based EM to model annotator noise, allowing singly-labeled data to outperform multiply-labeled data when annotation quality goes above a certain threshold. Bai et al. (2021) show that similar trade-offs exist when performing domain adaptation on a constrained budget. Zhang et al. (2021) observe that difficult examples benefit from additional annotations, so optimal spending actually varies the amount of labels given to each example. Our approach actively targets examples for relabeling based on its likelihood of noise, whereas they randomly select examples for multi-labeling without considering its characteristics.

Human in the Loop Finally, our work is also related to data labeling with humans. Annotators can be assisted through iterative labeling where models suggest labels for each training example (Settles, 2011; Schulz et al., 2019), or through active learning where models suggest which examples to label (Settles and Craven, 2008; Ash et al., 2020). In both cases, forward facing decisions are made on incoming batches of *unlabeled* data. In contrast, our methods look back to previously collected data to select examples for *relabeling*. These activities are orthogonal to each other and can both be included when training a model. (See Appendix C)

Lastly, re-active learning from (Sheng et al., 2008; Lin et al., 2016) proposes to relabel examples based on their predicted impact by retraining a classifier from scratch for every iteration of annotation. Accordingly, their method is impractical when adapted to the large Transformer models studied in this paper[1]. Instead, we identify examples to relabel through much less computationally expensive means, making the process tractable for real-life deployment.

[1]Training a large language model (such as RoBERTa-Large) until convergence can easily take a day or longer. Doing so each time for 12k annotations would take 30+ years.

3 Methods Under Study

We study how to maximize model performance given a static data annotation budget. Concretely, we are given some model M for a target task, along with a budget as measured by B number of annotations, where each annotation allows us to apply a possibly noisy labeling function $f_r(x)$, where r is the number of redundant annotations applied to a single example. Annotating some set of unlabeled instances produces noisy examples $(X, f_r(X)) = (X, \tilde{Y})$. Our goal is to achieve the best score possible for some primary evaluation metric S on a given task by cleaning the noisy labels $\tilde{Y} \xrightarrow{clean} Y$. Afterwards, we train a model with the cleaned data and then test it on a separate test set. For all our experiments, we set $B = 12,000$ as the total annotation budget.

As a default setting, we start with a *Control* baseline which uses the entire budget to annotate 12k examples, once each ($n = 12,000; r = 1$). To simulate a single annotation, we randomly sample a label from the set of labels offered for each example by the dataset. To obtain more accurate labels, people often perform multiple annotations on each example and use *Majority Vote* to aggregate the annotations. Accordingly, as a second baseline we annotate 4k examples three times each ($n = 4,000; r = 3$), matching the same total budget as before. In the event of a tie, we randomly select one of the candidate labels. Finally, we also include an *Oracle* baseline which uses the gold label for 12k examples ($n = 12,000; r = 3|5$). The gold label is either given by the dataset or generated by majority vote, where the label might result from aggregating five annotations rather than just three annotations.

3.1 Noise Correction Baselines

We consider four advanced baselines, all of which perform a single annotation per example ($n = 12,000, r = 1$) as seen in Figure 1. (1) (Goldberger and Ben-Reuven, 2017) propose applying a noise *Adaptation* layer which models the error probability of label classes. This layer is initialized as an identity matrix, which biases the layer to act as if there is no confusion in the labels. This noise transition matrix is then learned as a non-linear layer on top of the baseline model M to denoise predictions. The layer is discarded during final inference since gold labels are used during test time and are assumed to no longer be noisy.

(2) The *Crowdlayer* also operates by modeling the error probability, but assumes the noise arises due to annotator error, so a noise transition matrix is created for each worker (Rodrigues and Pereira, 2018). Once again, this matrix is learned with gradient descent and removed for final inference. (3) The *Forward* correction method from (Patrini et al., 2017) adopts a loss correction approach which modifies the training objective. Given $-\log p(\hat{y} = \tilde{y}|x)$ as the original loss, Forward modifies this to become $-log \sum_{j=1}^{c} T_{ji} p(\hat{y} = y|x)$ where c is the number of classes being predicted, and both i and j are used to index the number of classes. Matrix T is represented as a neural network that is learned jointly during pre-training. (4) Lastly, the *Bootstrap* method proposed by (Reed et al., 2015) generates pseudo-labels by gradually interpolating the predicted label $\hat{y}$ with the given noisy label $\tilde{y}$. We apply their recommended *hard* bootstrap variant which uses the one-hot prediction for interpolation since this was shown to work better in their experiments.

3.2 Cleaning through Targeted Relabeling

Rather than maximizing the number of examples annotated given our budget, we propose reserving a portion of the budget for reannotating the labels most likely to be incorrect. Specifically, we start by annotating a large number of examples one time each using the majority of the budget ($n_a = 10,000; r = 1$). We then pretrain a model M_1 using this noisy data, and observe either the model's training dynamics or output predictions to target examples for relabeling. Next, we use the remaining budget to annotate those examples two more times ($n_b = 1,000; r = 2$), allowing us to obtain a majority vote on those examples. The final training set is formed by combining the 1k multiply-annotated examples with the remaining 9k singly-annotated examples. We wrap up by initializing a new model M_2 with the weights from M_1 and fine-tune it with the clean data until convergence. We experiment with four approaches for discovering the most probable noisy labels:

Area Under the Margin AUM identifies problematic labels by tracking the margin between the likelihood assigned to the target label class and the likelihood of the next highest class as training progresses (Pleiss et al., 2020). Intuitively, if the gap between these two likelihoods is large, then the model is confident of its argmax prediction, presumably because the training label is correct. On the other hand, if the gap between them is small, or even negative, then the model is uncertain of its prediction, presumably because the label is noisy. AUM averages the margins over all training epochs and targets the examples with the smallest margins for relabeling.

Cartography Dataset Cartography is a technique for mapping the training dynamics of a dataset to diagnose its issues (Swayamdipta et al., 2020). The intuition is largely the same as AUM, such that Cartography also chooses consistently low-confidence (ie. low probability) examples for relabeling. We take the suggestion from Section 5 of their paper to detect mislabeled examples by tracking the mean model probability of the true label across epochs. Note that unlike AUM, Cartography tracks the final model outputs after the softmax, rather than the logits before the softmax. These can lead to different rankings since Cartography does not take the other probabilities in the distribution into account.

Large Loss (Arpit et al., 2017) found that correctly labeled examples are easier for a model to learn, and thus incur a small loss during training, whereas incorrectly labeled examples produce a large loss. Inspired by this observation and other similar works (Jiang et al., 2018), the Large Loss method selects examples for cleaning by ranking the top n_b examples where the model achieves the largest loss during the optimal stopping point. The ideal stopping point is the moment after the model has learned to fit the clean data, but before it has started to memorize the noisy data (Zhang et al., 2017). We approximate this stopping point by performing early stopping during training when the progression of the development set fails to improve for three epochs in a row. We then use the earlier checkpoint for identifying errors.

Prototype We lastly consider identifying noisy labels as those which are farthest away compared to the other training data (Lee et al., 2018). More specifically, we use a pretrained model to map all training examples into the same embedding space. Then, we select the vectors for each label class to form clusters where the centroid of each cluster is the "prototype" (Snell et al., 2017). Finally, we define outliers as those far away from the centroid for their given class, as measured by Euclidean distance, which are then selected for cleaning.

4 Experiments

4.1 Datasets and Tasks

To test our proposal, we select datasets that span across four natural language processing tasks. We choose these datasets because they provide multiple labels per example, allowing us to simulate single- and multiple-annotation scenarios.

Offense The Social Bias Frames dataset collects instances of biases and implied stereotypes found in text (Sap et al., 2020). We extract just the label of whether a statement is offensive for binary classification.

NLI We adopt the MultiNLI dataset for natural language inference (Williams et al., 2018). The three possible label classes for each sentence pair are *entailment*, *contradiction*, and *neutral*.

Sentiment Our third task uses the first round of the DynaSent corpus for four-way sentiment analysis (Potts et al., 2021). The possible labels are *positive*, *negative*, *neutral*, and *mixed*.

QA Our final task is question answering with examples coming from the NewsQA dataset (Trischler et al., 2017). The input includes a premise taken from a news article, along with a query related to the topic. The target label consists of two indexes representing the start and end locations within the article that extract a span of text answering the query. Unlike the other tasks, the format for QA is span selection rather than classification. Due to this distinction, certain denoising methods that assume a fixed set of candidate labels are omitted from comparison.

4.2 Training Configuration

In our experiments, we fine-tune parameters during initial training with only six runs, which is composed of three learning rates and two levels of dropout at 0.1 and 0.05. Occasionally, when varying dropout had no effect, we consider doubling the batch size instead from 16 to 32. We found an appropriate range of learning rates by initially conducting some sanity checks on a sub-sample of development data for each task and model combination. Learning rates were chosen from the set of [1e-6, 3e-6, 1e-5, 3e-5, 1e-4]. When a technique contained method-specific variables, we defaulted to the suggestions offered in their respective papers. We do not expect any of the methods to be particularly sensitive to specific hyperparameters.

4.3 Model Variations

We select three models for comparison that represent strong options at their respective model sizes. We repeat the process of example identification and simulated re-annotation separately for each model. We use all models as a pre-trained encoders to embed the text inputs of the different tasks we study.

DeBERTa-XLarge is our large model, which contains 750 million parameters and currently is the state-of-the-art on many natural language understanding tasks (He et al., 2021). DistilRoBERTa represents a distilled version of RoBERTa-base (Liu et al., 2019). It contains 82 million parameters, compared to the 125 million parameters found in RoBERTa. Learning follows the distillation process set by DistillBERT where a student model is trained to match the soft target probabilities produced by the larger teacher model (Sanh et al., 2019). Fine-tuning DistilRoBERTa is approximately 60-70 times faster compared to fine-tuning DeBERTa-XLarge on the same task.

For the final model, we avoid using Transformers altogether and instead use the FastText bag-of-words encoder (Joulin et al., 2017). The FastText embeddings are left unchanged during training, so the only learned parameters are in the 2-layer MLP we use for producing the model's final output. The same output prediction setup is used for all models, with a 300-dimensional hidden state. Training the FastText models run roughly 100-120 faster compared to working with DeBERTa-XLarge.

5 Major Results

Table 1 displays results across all models types and tasks, with each row representing a different technique. All rows except the Oracle were trained using the same label budget of 12,000 annotations.[2] In some cases, a method may surpass the Oracle since we conducted limited hyperparameter tuning, but as expected, the Oracle model outperforms all other methods overall. Notably, the Control setting always beats the Majority setting. In fact, Majority is consistently the lowest-performing method on all models and tasks, showing that improved label quality is never quite enough to overcome the reduction in annotation quantity. Adaptation is the best among denoising methods, achieving the

[2]Our annotation amount is much less than total available data for a task so our results are not directly comparable to prior work. For example, DynaSent train set includes 94,459 examples and Social Bias Frames contains 43,448 examples.

Methods	FastT	DRoB	DeXL	Avg
Oracle	*78.0*	*81.8*	*86.2*	*82.0*
Control	77.0	81.4	86.0	81.5
Majority	76.2	80.4	84.5	80.4
Adaptation	**77.8**	81.5	**86.1**	**81.8**
Crowdlayer	77.1	81.4	85.4	81.3
Bootstrap	77.1	81.2	85.1	81.2
Forward	77.5	81.2	84.9	81.2
Large Loss	77.7	**81.6**	85.4	81.6
AUM	77.5	81.5	85.3	81.4
Cartography	77.3	81.2	85.0	81.2
Prototype	77.7	81.4	85.5	81.5

(a) Offensive Language Detection from SBF

Methods	FastT	DRoB	DeXL	Avg
Oracle	*40.7*	*49.7*	*88.3*	*59.6*
Control	40.1	48.5	87.4	58.7
Majority	38.5	46.2	86.1	56.9
Adaptation	40.6	**49.4**	87.8	**59.2**
Crowdlayer	40.2	48.7	87.4	58.7
Bootstrap	**40.8**	49.3	87.4	59.1
Forward	40.6	48.6	87.3	58.8
Large Loss	40.5	48.9	87.8	59.1
AUM	40.3	49.0	87.1	58.8
Cartography	40.1	48.1	87.0	58.4
Prototype	40.4	48.6	**88.0**	59.0

(b) Natural Language Inference from MNLI

Methods	FastT	DRoB	DeXL	Avg
Oracle	*55.5*	*57.3*	*73.2*	*62.0*
Control	54.0	57.2	72.7	61.3
Majority	52.4	55.8	71.2	59.8
Adaptation	53.8	56.8	72.6	61.1
Crowdlayer	53.9	57.2	72.7	61.2
Bootstrap	54.1	**57.4**	72.7	61.4
Forward	53.5	57.3	73.0	61.4
Large Loss	**55.6**	**57.4**	**73.1**	**62.0**
AUM	55.4	56.5	72.6	61.5
Cartography	55.0	56.6	72.0	61.2
Prototype	55.1	57.1	**73.1**	61.7

(c) Sentiment Analysis from DynaSent

Methods	FastT	DRoB	DeXL	Avg
Oracle	—	*7.94*	*52.3*	*30.1*
Control	—	6.90	50.3	28.6
Majority	—	5.89	47.9	26.9
Adaptation	—	—	—	—
Crowdlayer	—	—	—	—
Bootstrap	—	6.72	50.5	28.6
Forward	—	—	—	—
Large Loss	—	**6.95**	**51.5**	**29.2**
AUM	—	6.69	**51.5**	29.1
Cartography	—	6.24	51.0	28.6
Prototype	—	—	—	—

(d) Question Answering from NewsQA

Table 1: Aggregated results for all method and model combinations, averaged over three seeds. Model names are abbreviated for space: FastT is FastText, DRoB is DistilRoBERTa, and DeXL is DeBERTa-XLarge. Avg is the average across models for that method. FastText doesn't produce context-dependent representations, and so is not usable on the QA task.

strongest results in two out of four settings. Large Loss is the best among cleaning methods, with the highest scores in the remaining two tasks. Prototypical is also a strong runner-up. Large Loss is the best overall method due to its consistency since it never drops below second on all tasks.

Variance among the three seeds is fairly consistent for all models and methods within the same task. Specifically, the standard deviation for offense detection and NLI are both around 0.5, with sentiment analysis and QA around 1.5 and 4.5, respectively. We do not see any strong trends across tasks, nor any outliers for a specific method.

Breakdown by Task Table 1a contains the results for offense language detection, where we see that Large Loss and Adaptation are the only methods to overtake the Control. These two are also the best overall performers on natural language inference as seen in Table 1b. The cleaning methods really shine on sentiment analysis and question answering where even the worst cleaning method often tops the best denoising method. We hypothesize this happens because the denoising methods work best in simple classification tasks, which we further explore in the next section. A handful of results are not reported in Table 1d since they refer to methods that are designed exclusively for classification tasks, and cannot be directly transferred to span selection.

Breakdown by Model The larger models perform better than the smaller models in terms of downstream accuracy, but somewhat surprisingly, there does not seem to be any clear patterns in relation to the method. In other words, if a particular method performs well (poorly) with one model size, it tends to also do well (poorly) when

	Large	AUM	Cart	Proto
Large Loss	1.000	0.541	0.000	0.316
AUM	---	1.000	0.001	0.212
Cartography	---	---	1.000	0.025
Prototype	---	---	---	1.000

Table 2: Jaccard similarity for all pairs of targeted relabeling methods on the sentiment analysis task. Large, Cart and Proto are short for Large Loss, Cartography and Prototype, respectively. Results for other tasks available in Appendix A.

Methods	Offense	NLI	Sentiment	QA
Default	81.6	48.9	57.4	6.95
Random	80.9	48.0	55.8	6.41
Cross	81.7	48.4	57.3	6.56

Table 3: Ablation results that vary the method of identifying errors for relabeling. Default uses the same model for error selection and training.

applied to the other model sizes too. One possible exception to this is the Prototype method showing strong performance with DeBERTA-XLarge. This is possibly because a stronger model produces more valuable hidden state representations for determining outliers. Since method performance is largely independent of the model size, we use DistillRoBERTa as the encoder for simplicity in the upcoming analyses.

Ablation How can we be sure that the cleaning methods are actually exhibiting a small, but consistent gain over the baselines rather than just natural variation? Perhaps the scores are close simply because all the methods use the same amount of training data. If the cleaning methods are indeed adding value, then they should perform much better than random selection. To measure this, we replace the pre-trained DistilRoBERTa model with a uniform sampler to identify examples for cleaning.

Active learning has been shown to exhibit significant decrease when transferring across model types (Lowell et al., 2019). In contrast, we argue that our method is not active learning since it is not directly dependent on the specific abilities of the target model. To test this claim, we also conduct an additional ablation whereby we replace one model type for another. Namely, we use the DeBERTa-XLarge model to select examples for cleaning, then train on the DistilRoBERTa model.

The results in Table 3 show that randomly selecting data points to relabel indeed lowers the final performance by a noticeable amount. By comparison, cross training models leads to a negligible drop in performance. We believe this occurs because targeted relabeling produces clean data, and clean data is useful regardless of the situation.

6 Discussion and Analysis

To better understand how the proposed clean methods operate, we conduct additional analysis with the sentiment analysis task.

Methods	Precision	GoEmotions	Synthetic
Oracle	—	*55.8*	*57.9*
Control	—	54.8	56.6
Majority	—	53.0	55.2
Adaptation	—	54.8	56.5
Crowdlayer	—	54.9	56.4
Bootstrap	—	55.0	**57.0**
Forward	—	53.9	56.2
Large Loss	56.8	**55.2**	56.5
AUM	60.4	54.6	56.1
Cartography	19.0	54.3	56.4
Prototype	46.6	55.1	56.7

Table 4: This table contains results for the three different post-hoc analyses. Left column is precision of the model in identifying mislabeled examples. Right columns are results training on extended datasets. All scores are average of three seeds on DistillRoBERTa.

How well do clean methods select items? We compare the four proposed methods by first looking at the amount of overlap in the examples selected for relabeling. To calculate this, we gather all examples chosen for relabeling by their likelihood of annotation error. For a given pair of methods, we then find the size of their intersection and divide by the size of their union, which yields the Jaccard similarity. As shown in Table 2, AUM and Large Loss have high overlap meaning that they select similar examples for cleaning. We additionally calculate the precision of each method by counting the number of times a label targeted for relabeling did not match the oracle label, and therefore legitimately requires cleaning. Based on Table 4, we once again see reasonable performance for the Large Loss cleaning method.

Qualitative examples for sentiment analysis are displayed in Table 5, which were chosen as the most likely examples of label errors according to their respective methods. Large Loss consistently discovers 'neutral' labels that were mis-labeled as

Method	Input Text	Label
Large Loss	That's usually how it go goes.	MIXED
	I always order "to-go"	MIXED
	It's $15 bucks for a beer since I used a drink ticket	MIXED
	We usually frequent the settlers ridge location.	MIXED
	I went on June 4th around 10:30.	MIXED
AUM	So fine, no problem.	POSITIVE
	A sirloin hotdog wrapped in bacon.	NEUTRAL
	For many years, I have gone to the Pet Smart down the street.	NEUTRAL
	I was always so happy here when it was managed by Johnny.	NEUTRAL
	I ordered the pad Thai noodles, chicken chow mien and egg rolls.	POSITIVE
Cartography	The food and customer service was fantastic when you first opened	POSITIVE
	The servers were pleasant.	POSITIVE
	Our waiter was overly friendly and informational.	MIXED
	Family owned and operated these folks are killing it	POSITIVE
	I really thought the young folks behind the counter were outgoing and seemed to enjoy their jobs	POSITIVE
Prototype	This should be a fun family place!	NEGATIVE
	Hotel was awesome.	NEGATIVE
	Great service for many years on our cars, but always at an additional price.	NEUTRAL
	Salad was great but a bit small.	NEUTRAL
	We had to specify the order *multiple* times, but eventually when the food came it was actually pretty good.	NEUTRAL

Table 5: Sentiment Analysis examples each method identified as being most likely to be label errors.

'mixed', while Prototype also does a good job uncovering label errors, finding 'positive' examples mislabeled as 'negative'. Overall, we see that the best performing cleaning methods do seem to pick up on meaningful patterns.

How many examples should be cleaned? All cleaning experiments so far have been run with n_a = 10,000 examples with n_b = 1,000 samples chosen for relabeling. This is equivalent to using up $\lambda = \frac{5}{6}$ of the labeling budget upfront, with the remaining annotations saved for later. This λ ratio was chosen as a reasonable default, but can also be tuned to be higher or lower. Figure 2 shows the results of varying the λ parameter from a range of $\frac{1}{6}$ to $\frac{11}{12}$. Based on the results, choosing $\lambda = \frac{2}{3}$ would have actually been the best option. This translates to n_a = 8,000 examples with n_b = 2,000 of those examples selected for re-labeling. As a sanity check, we also try dropping the n_b cleaned examples when retraining, keeping only the noisy data. As seen in Figure 2, the performance decreases as expected.

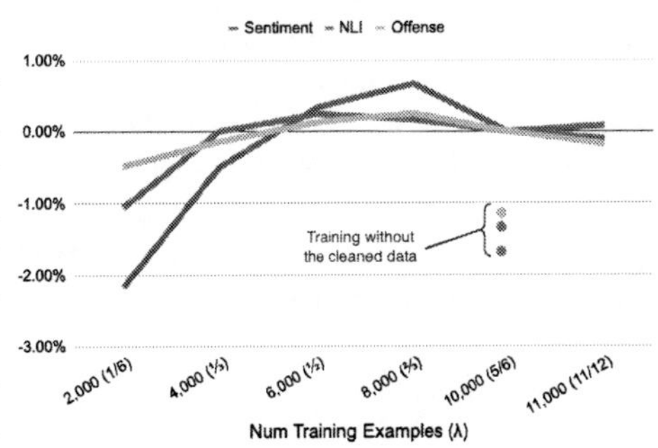

Figure 2: Varying the number of training examples changes the amount of budget remaining for cleaning. 10,000 examples is set as the default and the percent change is measured in comparison to this point.

What if we increase the number of classes? Based on the trends in the task breakdown of section 5, denoising methods seem to perform worse than explicit relabeling methods as the task gets harder. Most denoising methods may even become intractable for complex settings, such as those which require span selection. To test this hypothesis, we extend our setup to the GoEmotions dataset, where the goal of the task is to predict the emotion associated with a given utterance (Demszky et al., 2020). Whereas previous tasks dealt with 2-4 classes, the GoEmotions dataset requires a model to select from 27 granular emotions and a neutral option, for a total of 28 classes. Intuitively, we would expect the denoising methods to struggle since the pairwise interactions among classes has grown exponentially larger. The results in Table 4 reveal that Large Loss again outperforms all other methods in prediction accuracy. Notably, Adaptation in particular continues to exhibit lower than average scores compared to other methods. This supports our claim that relabeling methods are more robust as the number of classes grows.

What happens if noise is synthetically created? Many of the advanced denoising methods were originally tested on synthetically generated noise, whereas the noise in our datasets originates from noisy annotations, caused by the inherent ambiguity of natural language text (Pavlick and Kwiatkowski, 2019; Chen et al., 2020). Perhaps this partially explains how our proposed relabeling methods are able to outperform prior work. To study this further, we create a perturbed dataset starting from the gold DynaSent examples. Specifically, we randomly sample replacement labels according to a fabricated noise transition matrix, rather than sampling from the label distribution provided by annotators. (More details in Appendix D.) With noise coming from an explicit transition matrix, it might be easier for all models to pick up on this pattern.

The middle column of Table 4 shows that all eight cleaning methods perform on par with each other. When comparing the variance on this dataset with synthetic noise against the original DynaSent dataset with natural noise, the standard deviation drops from 0.34 down to 0.28, highlighting the uniformity in performance among the eight methods. The denoising methods work as intended on synthetic noise, but such assumptions may not hold on real data with more nuanced errors.

7 Conclusion

Noisy data is a common problem when annotating data under low resource settings. Performing redundant annotation on the same examples to mitigate noise leads to having even less data to work with, so we propose data cleaning instead through targeted relabeling. We apply our methods on multiple model sizes and NLP tasks of varying difficulty, which show that saving a portion of a labeling budget for re-annotation matches or outperforms other baselines despite requiring no extra parameters to train or hyper-parameters to tune. Intuitively, our best method can be summarized as double-checking the examples that the model gets wrong to see if it is actually an incorrect label causing problems.

Thus, to make the most out of the scarce labeled data available, we believe a best practice should include targeting examples for cleaning rather than spending the entire annotation budget upfront. Future work includes exploring more sophisticated techniques for identifying examples to relabel and understanding how such cleaning models perform on additional NLP tasks such as machine translation or dialogue state tracking, which have distinct output formats.

Acknowledgements

The authors would like to sincerely thank the reviewers for their attention to detail when reading through the paper. Their insightful questions and advice have noticeably improved the final manuscript. We would also like to thank ASAPP for sponsoring the costs of this project. Finally, we would like to acknowledge the helpful feedback from discussions with members of the Columbia Dialogue Lab.

References

Eric Arazo, Diego Ortego, Paul Albert, Noel E. O'Connor, and Kevin McGuinness. 2019. Unsupervised label noise modeling and loss correction. In *Proceedings of the 36th International Conference on Machine Learning, ICML 2019, 9-15 June 2019, Long Beach, California, USA*, volume 97 of *Proceedings of Machine Learning Research*, pages 312–321. PMLR.

Devansh Arpit, Stanislaw Jastrzebski, Nicolas Ballas, David Krueger, Emmanuel Bengio, Maxinder S. Kanwal, Tegan Maharaj, Asja Fischer, Aaron C. Courville, Yoshua Bengio, and Simon Lacoste-Julien. 2017. A closer look at memorization in deep networks. In *Proceedings of the 34th International Conference on Machine Learning, ICML 2017, Sydney, NSW, Australia, 6-11 August 2017*, volume 70 of *Proceedings of Machine Learning Research*, pages 233–242. PMLR.

Jordan T. Ash, Chicheng Zhang, Akshay Krishnamurthy, John Langford, and Alekh Agarwal. 2020. Deep batch active learning by diverse, uncertain gradient lower bounds. In *8th International Conference on Learning Representations, ICLR 2020, Addis Ababa, Ethiopia, April 26-30, 2020*. OpenReview.net.

Fan Bai, Alan Ritter, and Wei Xu. 2021. Pre-train or annotate? domain adaptation with a constrained budget. *ArXiv*, abs/2109.04711.

Yoshua Bengio, Jérôme Louradour, Ronan Collobert, and Jason Weston. 2009. Curriculum learning. In *Proceedings of the 26th Annual International Conference on Machine Learning, ICML 2009, Montreal, Quebec, Canada, June 14-18, 2009*, volume 382 of *ACM International Conference Proceeding Series*, pages 41–48. ACM.

Samuel R. Bowman, Gabor Angeli, Christopher Potts, and Christopher D. Manning. 2015. A large annotated corpus for learning natural language inference. In *Proceedings of the 2015 Conference on Empirical Methods in Natural Language Processing, EMNLP 2015, Lisbon, Portugal, September 17-21, 2015*, pages 632–642. The Association for Computational Linguistics.

Tongfei Chen, Zhengping Jiang, Adam Poliak, Keisuke Sakaguchi, and Benjamin Van Durme. 2020. Uncertain natural language inference. In *Proceedings of the 58th Annual Meeting of the Association for Computational Linguistics, ACL 2020, Online, July 5-10, 2020*, pages 8772–8779. Association for Computational Linguistics.

Alexander Philip Dawid and Allan M Skene. 1979. Maximum likelihood estimation of observer error-rates using the EM algorithm. *Journal of the Royal Statistical Society: Series C (Applied Statistics)*, 28(1):20–28.

Dorottya Demszky, Dana Movshovitz-Attias, Jeongwoo Ko, Alan Cowen, Gaurav Nemade, and Sujith Ravi. 2020. GoEmotions: A Dataset of Fine-Grained Emotions. In *Proceedings of the 58th Annual Meeting of the Association for Computational Linguistics, ACL 2020, Online, July 5-10, 2020*, pages 4040–4054. Association for Computational Linguistics.

Paul Felt, Eric K. Ringger, and Kevin D. Seppi. 2016. Semantic annotation aggregation with conditional crowdsourcing models and word embeddings. In *COLING 2016, 26th International Conference on Computational Linguistics, Proceedings of the Conference: Technical Papers, December 11-16, 2016, Osaka, Japan*, pages 1787–1796. ACL.

Aritra Ghosh, Himanshu Kumar, and P. S. Sastry. 2017. Robust loss functions under label noise for deep neural networks. In *Proceedings of the Thirty-First AAAI Conference on Artificial Intelligence, February 4-9, 2017, San Francisco, California, USA*, pages 1919–1925. AAAI Press.

Jacob Goldberger and Ehud Ben-Reuven. 2017. Training deep neural-networks using a noise adaptation layer. In *5th International Conference on Learning Representations, ICLR 2017, Toulon, France, April 24-26, 2017, Conference Track Proceedings*. OpenReview.net.

Melody Y. Guan, Varun Gulshan, Andrew M. Dai, and Geoffrey E. Hinton. 2018. Who said what: Modeling individual labelers improves classification. In *Proceedings of the Thirty-Second AAAI Conference on Artificial Intelligence, (AAAI-18), the 30th innovative Applications of Artificial Intelligence (IAAI-18), and the 8th AAAI Symposium on Educational Advances in Artificial Intelligence (EAAI-18), New Orleans, Louisiana, USA, February 2-7, 2018*, pages 3109–3118. AAAI Press.

Bo Han, Quanming Yao, Xingrui Yu, Gang Niu, Miao Xu, Weihua Hu, Ivor W. Tsang, and Masashi Sugiyama. 2018. Co-teaching: Robust training of deep neural networks with extremely noisy labels. In *Advances in Neural Information Processing Systems 31: Annual Conference on Neural Information Processing Systems 2018, NeurIPS 2018, December 3-8, 2018, Montréal, Canada*, pages 8536–8546.

Steve Hanneke. 2014. Theory of disagreement-based active learning. *Found. Trends Mach. Learn.*, 7(2-3):131–309.

Pengcheng He, Xiaodong Liu, Jianfeng Gao, and Weizhu Chen. 2021. DeBERTa: Decoding-enhanced BERT with disentangled attention. In *9th International Conference on Learning Representations, ICLR 2021, Virtual Event, Austria, May 3-7, 2021*. OpenReview.net.

Dirk Hovy, Taylor Berg-Kirkpatrick, Ashish Vaswani, and Eduard H. Hovy. 2013. Learning whom to trust with MACE. In *Human Language Technologies:*

Conference of the North American Chapter of the Association of Computational Linguistics, Proceedings, June 9-14, 2013, Westin Peachtree Plaza Hotel, Atlanta, Georgia, USA, pages 1120–1130. The Association for Computational Linguistics.

Lu Jiang, Deyu Meng, Shoou-I Yu, Zhen-Zhong Lan, Shiguang Shan, and Alexander G. Hauptmann. 2014. Self-paced learning with diversity. In *Advances in Neural Information Processing Systems 27: Annual Conference on Neural Information Processing Systems 2014, December 8-13 2014, Montreal, Quebec, Canada*, pages 2078–2086.

Lu Jiang, Deyu Meng, Qian Zhao, Shiguang Shan, and Alexander G. Hauptmann. 2015. Self-paced curriculum learning. In *Proceedings of the Twenty-Ninth AAAI Conference on Artificial Intelligence, January 25-30, 2015, Austin, Texas, USA*, pages 2694–2700. AAAI Press.

Lu Jiang, Zhengyuan Zhou, Thomas Leung, Li-Jia Li, and Li Fei-Fei. 2018. MentorNet: Learning data-driven curriculum for very deep neural networks on corrupted labels. In *Proceedings of the 35th International Conference on Machine Learning, ICML 2018, Stockholmsmässan, Stockholm, Sweden, July 10-15, 2018*, volume 80 of *Proceedings of Machine Learning Research*, pages 2309–2318. PMLR.

Ishan Jindal, Daniel Pressel, Brian Lester, and Matthew S. Nokleby. 2019. An effective label noise model for DNN text classification. In *Proceedings of the 2019 Conference of the North American Chapter of the Association for Computational Linguistics: Human Language Technologies, NAACL-HLT 2019, Minneapolis, MN, USA, June 2-7, 2019, Volume 1 (Long and Short Papers)*, pages 3246–3256. Association for Computational Linguistics.

Armand Joulin, Edouard Grave, Piotr Bojanowski, and Tomás Mikolov. 2017. Bag of tricks for efficient text classification. In *Proceedings of the 15th Conference of the European Chapter of the Association for Computational Linguistics, EACL 2017, Valencia, Spain, April 3-7, 2017, Volume 2: Short Papers*, pages 427–431. Association for Computational Linguistics.

Ashish Khetan, Zachary C. Lipton, and Animashree Anandkumar. 2018. Learning from noisy singly-labeled data. In *6th International Conference on Learning Representations, ICLR 2018, Vancouver, BC, Canada, April 30 - May 3, 2018, Conference Track Proceedings*. OpenReview.net.

Ashish Khetan and Sewoong Oh. 2016. Achieving budget-optimality with adaptive schemes in crowdsourcing. In *Advances in Neural Information Processing Systems 29: Annual Conference on Neural Information Processing Systems 2016, December 5-10, 2016, Barcelona, Spain*, pages 4844–4852.

M. Pawan Kumar, Benjamin Packer, and Daphne Koller. 2010. Self-paced learning for latent variable models. In *Advances in Neural Information Processing Systems 23: 24th Annual Conference on Neural Information Processing Systems 2010. Proceedings of a meeting held 6-9 December 2010, Vancouver, British Columbia, Canada*, pages 1189–1197. Curran Associates, Inc.

Kuang-Huei Lee, Xiaodong He, Lei Zhang, and Linjun Yang. 2018. Cleannet: Transfer learning for scalable image classifier training with label noise. In *2018 IEEE Conference on Computer Vision and Pattern Recognition, CVPR 2018, Salt Lake City, UT, USA, June 18-22, 2018*, pages 5447–5456. Computer Vision Foundation / IEEE Computer Society.

Junnan Li, Richard Socher, and Steven C. H. Hoi. 2020. Dividemix: Learning with noisy labels as semi-supervised learning. In *8th International Conference on Learning Representations, ICLR 2020, Addis Ababa, Ethiopia, April 26-30, 2020*. OpenReview.net.

Christopher H. Lin, Mausam, and Daniel S. Weld. 2016. Re-active learning: Active learning with relabeling. In *Proceedings of the Thirtieth AAAI Conference on Artificial Intelligence, February 12-17, 2016, Phoenix, Arizona, USA*, pages 1845–1852. AAAI Press.

Yinhan Liu, Myle Ott, Naman Goyal, Jingfei Du, Mandar Joshi, Danqi Chen, Omer Levy, Mike Lewis, Luke Zettlemoyer, and Veselin Stoyanov. 2019. RoBERTa: A robustly optimized BERT pretraining approach. *ArXiv*, abs/1907.11692.

David Lowell, Zachary C. Lipton, and Byron C. Wallace. 2019. Practical obstacles to deploying active learning. In *Proceedings of the 2019 Conference on Empirical Methods in Natural Language Processing and the 9th International Joint Conference on Natural Language Processing, EMNLP-IJCNLP 2019, Hong Kong, China, November 3-7, 2019*, pages 21–30. Association for Computational Linguistics.

Volodymyr Mnih and Geoffrey E. Hinton. 2012. Learning to label aerial images from noisy data. In *Proceedings of the 29th International Conference on Machine Learning, ICML 2012, Edinburgh, Scotland, UK, June 26 - July 1, 2012*. icml.cc / Omnipress.

Giorgio Patrini, Alessandro Rozza, Aditya Krishna Menon, Richard Nock, and Lizhen Qu. 2017. Making deep neural networks robust to label noise: A loss correction approach. In *2017 IEEE Conference on Computer Vision and Pattern Recognition, CVPR 2017, Honolulu, HI, USA, July 21-26, 2017*, pages 2233–2241. IEEE Computer Society.

Ellie Pavlick and Tom Kwiatkowski. 2019. Inherent disagreements in human textual inferences. *Trans. Assoc. Comput. Linguistics*, 7:677–694.

Geoff Pleiss, Tianyi Zhang, Ethan R. Elenberg, and Kilian Q. Weinberger. 2020. Identifying mislabeled data using the area under the margin ranking. In *Advances in Neural Information Processing Systems 33: Annual Conference on Neural Information Processing Systems 2020, NeurIPS 2020, December 6-12, 2020, virtual*.

Christopher Potts, Zhengxuan Wu, Atticus Geiger, and Douwe Kiela. 2021. Dynasent: A dynamic benchmark for sentiment analysis. In *Proceedings of the 59th Annual Meeting of the Association for Computational Linguistics and the 11th International Joint Conference on Natural Language Processing, ACL/IJCNLP 2021, (Volume 1: Long Papers), Virtual Event, August 1-6, 2021*, pages 2388–2404. Association for Computational Linguistics.

Vikas C. Raykar, Shipeng Yu, Linda H. Zhao, Anna K. Jerebko, Charles Florin, Gerardo Hermosillo Valadez, Luca Bogoni, and Linda Moy. 2009. Supervised learning from multiple experts: whom to trust when everyone lies a bit. In *Proceedings of the 26th Annual International Conference on Machine Learning, ICML 2009, Montreal, Quebec, Canada, June 14-18, 2009*, volume 382 of *ACM International Conference Proceeding Series*, pages 889–896. ACM.

Scott E. Reed, Honglak Lee, Dragomir Anguelov, Christian Szegedy, Dumitru Erhan, and Andrew Rabinovich. 2015. Training deep neural networks on noisy labels with bootstrapping. In *3rd International Conference on Learning Representations, ICLR 2015, San Diego, CA, USA, May 7-9, 2015, Workshop Track Proceedings*.

Filipe Rodrigues and Francisco C. Pereira. 2018. Deep learning from crowds. In *Proceedings of the Thirty-Second AAAI Conference on Artificial Intelligence, (AAAI-18), the 30th innovative Applications of Artificial Intelligence (IAAI-18), and the 8th AAAI Symposium on Educational Advances in Artificial Intelligence (EAAI-18), New Orleans, Louisiana, USA, February 2-7, 2018*, pages 1611–1618. AAAI Press.

Olga Russakovsky, Jia Deng, Hao Su, Jonathan Krause, Sanjeev Satheesh, Sean Ma, Zhiheng Huang, Andrej Karpathy, Aditya Khosla, Michael S. Bernstein, Alexander C. Berg, and Li Fei-Fei. 2015. Imagenet large scale visual recognition challenge. *Int. Journal of Computer Vision*, 115(3):211–252.

Victor Sanh, Lysandre Debut, Julien Chaumond, and Thomas Wolf. 2019. DistilBERT, a distilled version of BERT: smaller, faster, cheaper and lighter. *ArXiv*, abs/1910.01108.

Maarten Sap, Ronan Le Bras, Emily Allaway, Chandra Bhagavatula, Nicholas Lourie, Hannah Rashkin, Brendan Roof, Noah A. Smith, and Yejin Choi. 2019a. ATOMIC: an atlas of machine commonsense for if-then reasoning. In *The Thirty-Third AAAI Conference on Artificial Intelligence, AAAI 2019, The Thirty-First Innovative Applications of Artificial Intelligence Conference, IAAI 2019, The Ninth AAAI Symposium on Educational Advances in Artificial Intelligence, EAAI 2019, Honolulu, Hawaii, USA, January 27 - February 1, 2019*, pages 3027–3035. AAAI Press.

Maarten Sap, Saadia Gabriel, Lianhui Qin, Dan Jurafsky, Noah A. Smith, and Yejin Choi. 2020. Social bias frames: Reasoning about social and power implications of language. In *Proceedings of the 58th Annual Meeting of the Association for Computational Linguistics, ACL 2020, Online, July 5-10, 2020*, pages 5477–5490. Association for Computational Linguistics.

Maarten Sap, Hannah Rashkin, Derek Chen, Ronan Le Bras, and Yejin Choi. 2019b. Social iqa: Commonsense reasoning about social interactions. In *Proceedings of the 2019 Conference on Empirical Methods in Natural Language Processing and the 9th International Joint Conference on Natural Language Processing, EMNLP-IJCNLP 2019, Hong Kong, China, November 3-7, 2019*, pages 4462–4472. Association for Computational Linguistics.

Claudia Schulz, Christian M. Meyer, Jan Kiesewetter, Michael Sailer, Elisabeth Bauer, Martin R. Fischer, Frank Fischer, and Iryna Gurevych. 2019. Analysis of automatic annotation suggestions for hard discourse-level tasks in expert domains. In *Proceedings of the 57th Annual Meeting of the Association for Computational Linguistics*, pages 2761–2772, Florence, Italy. Association for Computational Linguistics.

Ozan Sener and Silvio Savarese. 2018. Active learning for convolutional neural networks: A core-set approach. In *6th International Conference on Learning Representations, ICLR 2018, Vancouver, BC, Canada, April 30 - May 3, 2018, Conference Track Proceedings*. OpenReview.net.

Burr Settles. 2011. Closing the loop: Fast, interactive semi-supervised annotation with queries on features and instances. In *Proceedings of the 2011 Conference on Empirical Methods in Natural Language Processing*, pages 1467–1478, Edinburgh, Scotland, UK. Association for Computational Linguistics.

Burr Settles and Mark Craven. 2008. An analysis of active learning strategies for sequence labeling tasks. In *Proceedings of the 2008 Conference on Empirical Methods in Natural Language Processing*, pages 1070–1079, Honolulu, Hawaii. Association for Computational Linguistics.

Victor S. Sheng, Foster J. Provost, and Panagiotis G. Ipeirotis. 2008. Get another label? improving data quality and data mining using multiple, noisy labelers. In *Proceedings of the 14th ACM SIGKDD International Conference on Knowledge Discovery and Data Mining, Las Vegas, Nevada, USA, August 24-27, 2008*, pages 614–622. ACM.

Jake Snell, Kevin Swersky, and Richard S. Zemel. 2017. Prototypical networks for few-shot learning.

In *Advances in Neural Information Processing Systems 30: Annual Conference on Neural Information Processing Systems 2017, December 4-9, 2017, Long Beach, CA, USA*, pages 4077–4087.

Rion Snow, Daniel Jurafsky, and Andrew Y. Ng. 2004. Learning syntactic patterns for automatic hypernym discovery. In *Advances in Neural Information Processing Systems 17 [Neural Information Processing Systems, NIPS 2004, December 13-18, 2004, Vancouver, British Columbia, Canada]*, pages 1297–1304.

Rion Snow, Brendan O'Connor, Daniel Jurafsky, and Andrew Y. Ng. 2008. Cheap and fast - but is it good? evaluating non-expert annotations for natural language tasks. In *2008 Conference on Empirical Methods in Natural Language Processing, EMNLP 2008, Proceedings of the Conference, 25-27 October 2008, Honolulu, Hawaii, USA, A meeting of SIGDAT, a Special Interest Group of the ACL*, pages 254–263. ACL.

Sainbayar Sukhbaatar, Joan Bruna, Manohar Paluri, Lubomir Bourdev, and Rob Fergus. 2015. Training convolutional neural networks with noisy labels. In *3rd International Conference on Learning Representations, ICLR 2015, San Diego, CA, USA, May 7-9, 2015, Workshop Track Proceedings*.

Swabha Swayamdipta, Roy Schwartz, Nicholas Lourie, Yizhong Wang, Hannaneh Hajishirzi, Noah A. Smith, and Yejin Choi. 2020. Dataset cartography: Mapping and diagnosing datasets with training dynamics. In *Proceedings of the 2020 Conference on Empirical Methods in Natural Language Processing, EMNLP 2020, Online, November 16-20, 2020*, pages 9275–9293. Association for Computational Linguistics.

Daiki Tanaka, Daiki Ikami, Toshihiko Yamasaki, and Kiyoharu Aizawa. 2018. Joint optimization framework for learning with noisy labels. In *2018 IEEE Conference on Computer Vision and Pattern Recognition, CVPR 2018, Salt Lake City, UT, USA, June 18-22, 2018*, pages 5552–5560. Computer Vision Foundation / IEEE Computer Society.

Ryutaro Tanno, Ardavan Saeedi, Swami Sankaranarayanan, Daniel C. Alexander, and Nathan Silberman. 2019. Learning from noisy labels by regularized estimation of annotator confusion. In *IEEE Conference on Computer Vision and Pattern Recognition, CVPR 2019, Long Beach, CA, USA, June 16-20, 2019*, pages 11244–11253. Computer Vision Foundation / IEEE.

Kshitij Tayal, Rahul Ghosh, and Vipin Kumar. 2020. Model-agnostic methods for text classification with inherent noise. In *Proceedings of the 28th International Conference on Computational Linguistics, COLING 2020 - Industry Track, Online, December 12, 2020*, pages 202–213. International Committee on Computational Linguistics.

Simon Tong and Daphne Koller. 2001. Support vector machine active learning with applications to text classification. *J. Mach. Learn. Res.*, 2:45–66.

Adam Trischler, Tong Wang, Xingdi Yuan, Justin Harris, Alessandro Sordoni, Philip Bachman, and Kaheer Suleman. 2017. NewsQA: A machine comprehension dataset. In *Proceedings of the 2nd Workshop on Representation Learning for NLP, Rep4NLP at ACL 2017, Vancouver, Canada, August 3, 2017*, pages 191–200. Association for Computational Linguistics.

Hao Wang, Bing Liu, Chaozhuo Li, Yan Yang, and Tianrui Li. 2019. Learning with noisy labels for sentence-level sentiment classification. In *Proceedings of the 2019 Conference on Empirical Methods in Natural Language Processing and the 9th International Joint Conference on Natural Language Processing, EMNLP-IJCNLP 2019, Hong Kong, China, November 3-7, 2019*, pages 6285–6291. Association for Computational Linguistics.

Peter Welinder, Steve Branson, Serge J. Belongie, and Pietro Perona. 2010. The multidimensional wisdom of crowds. In *Advances in Neural Information Processing Systems 23: 24th Annual Conference on Neural Information Processing Systems 2010. Proceedings of a meeting held 6-9 December 2010, Vancouver, British Columbia, Canada*, pages 2424–2432. Curran Associates, Inc.

Jacob Whitehill, Paul Ruvolo, Tingfan Wu, Jacob Bergsma, and Javier R. Movellan. 2009. Whose vote should count more: Optimal integration of labels from labelers of unknown expertise. In *Advances in Neural Information Processing Systems 22: 23rd Annual Conference on Neural Information Processing Systems 2009. Proceedings of a meeting held 7-10 December 2009, Vancouver, British Columbia, Canada*, pages 2035–2043. Curran Associates, Inc.

Adina Williams, Nikita Nangia, and Samuel R. Bowman. 2018. A broad-coverage challenge corpus for sentence understanding through inference. In *Proceedings of the 2018 Conference of the North American Chapter of the Association for Computational Linguistics: Human Language Technologies, NAACL-HLT 2018, New Orleans, Louisiana, USA, June 1-6, 2018, Volume 1 (Long Papers)*, pages 1112–1122. Association for Computational Linguistics.

Xingrui Yu, Bo Han, Jiangchao Yao, Gang Niu, Ivor W. Tsang, and Masashi Sugiyama. 2019. How does disagreement help generalization against label corruption? In *Proceedings of the 36th International Conference on Machine Learning, ICML 2019, 9-15 June 2019, Long Beach, California, USA*, volume 97 of *Proceedings of Machine Learning Research*, pages 7164–7173. PMLR.

Chiyuan Zhang, Samy Bengio, Moritz Hardt, Benjamin Recht, and Oriol Vinyals. 2017. Understanding deep learning requires rethinking generalization.

In *5th International Conference on Learning Representations, ICLR 2017, Toulon, France, April 24-26, 2017, Conference Track Proceedings*. OpenReview.net.

Shujian Zhang, Chengyue Gong, and Eunsol Choi. 2021. Learning with different amounts of annotation: From zero to many labels. In *Proceedings of the 2021 Conference on Empirical Methods in Natural Language Processing, EMNLP 2021, Virtual Event / Punta Cana, Dominican Republic, 7-11 November, 2021*, pages 7620–7632. Association for Computational Linguistics.

Zhilu Zhang and Mert R. Sabuncu. 2018. Generalized cross entropy loss for training deep neural networks with noisy labels. In *Advances in Neural Information Processing Systems 31: Annual Conference on Neural Information Processing Systems 2018, NeurIPS 2018, December 3-8, 2018, Montréal, Canada*, pages 8792–8802.

A Additional Quantitative Results

Looking at Figure 3, the similarity scores for offensive language detection and natural language inference largely match up with the scores found in sentiment analysis. In particular, Large Loss and AUM exhibit higher overlap with each other. Additionally, Prototype shows a medium overlap and Cartography shows no overlap at all with the other methods. We reach a similar conclusion that the Large Loss method is a reasonable technique.

B Additional Qualitative Examples

More examples can be found in Table 6 on the next page. We see that Large Loss is once again quite accurate in picking up labeling errors. Prototype for NLI does a great job at finding examples labeled as 'entailment' which should be something else. The hypotheses for all the selected examples contain negative sentiment, which may be located far away from the entailment examples in the embedding space. Cartography exhibits a pattern of always choosing examples labeled as 'contradiction'.

C Comparison to Learning Schemes

On the surface, targeting examples for relabeling contains may seem similar to active learning or curriculum learning. Although there are certainly some parallels between these techniques, these are fundamentally different learning paradigms.

Active learning methods typically choose new examples to label based on the uncertainty of the model (Tong and Koller, 2001; Hanneke, 2014) or on the diversity they can add to the existing distribution (Sener and Savarese, 2018; Ash et al., 2020). Although sample noise can also be measured through model uncertainty, denoising and active learning do not have the same goal. More specifically, the noise of a training example is related to how its label is somehow incorrect. Perhaps the start of a span was not properly selected or an example that should not be tagged was accidentally included. More simply, an example is mislabeled as class A, when in fact it belongs to class B. This situation is not possible with active learning because the examples in active learning do not have labels yet! The entire point of active learning is to choose which examples should be labeled next (Settles and Craven, 2008; Settles, 2011). Thus, when we try to identify examples for cleaning, we are *re*-labeling rather than labeling for the first time.

Curriculum learning also selects examples for training based on model uncertainty (Bengio et al., 2009) and diversity maximization (Jiang et al., 2014). It could be interpreted that easier examples are those that contain less noise, which would connect to our proposed process. However, traditional curriculum learning chooses these examples upfront rather than based on modeling dynamics (Jiang et al., 2015). Extensions have been made under the umbrella of self-paced curriculum learning whereby examples are chosen for a curriculum based on how they react to a model's behavior (Kumar et al., 2010). This is indeed similar to how we can choose to relabel examples based on the model loss. This aspect of relabeling though is the key distinction – we *act* on these examples in an attempt to denoise the dataset. On the other hand, self-paced learning simply feeds those same examples back into the model without any modification.

D Data Preprocessing

D.1 Synthetic Data Generation

The synthetic dataset is created by applying an explicit noise transition matrix with 20% noise. Since the original dataset contains four classes, we start with an empty 4x4 matrix. The labels should not be confused most of the time so we assign a likelihood of 0.8 across the diagonal of the matrix. Next, we randomly select another class for each row to receive 0.1 likelihood of confusion. This leaves 0.1 for each row to be divided between the two remaining classes, which receive 0.05 each. For each example in the oracle dataset, we use the original label to select a single row from the constructed noise transition matrix. Lastly, we are able to sample a new label according to the weights provided by this 4-D vector. In contrast, the original sampling procedure obtained its weights according to the normalized label distribution provided by the annotations.

D.2 GoEmotions Preprocessing

To prepare the GoEmotions dataset, we filter the raw data to include only examples that have at least three annotators and a clear majority vote (used for determining the gold label). We then cross-reference this against the proposed data splits offered by the authors which have high inter-annotator agreement. From this joint pool of examples, we sample 12k training examples to match the setting of all our other experiments. This results in

	Large	AUM	Cart	Proto
Large Loss	1.000	0.637	0.000	0.190
Area Margin	---	1.000	0.000	0.125
Cartography	---	---	1.000	0.166
Prototype	---	---	---	1.000

(a) Jaccard similarity on Social Bias Frames

	Large	AUM	Cart	Proto
Large Loss	1.000	0.545	0.000	0.191
Area Margin	---	1.000	0.000	0.202
Cartography	---	---	1.000	0.152
Prototype	---	---	---	1.000

(b) Jaccard similarity on MNLI dataset

Figure 3: Jaccard similarity overlap for all pairs of targeted relabeling methods on the offensive language detection task and the natural language inference task.

12000/2954/2946 examples for train, development and test splits respectively.

E Limitations

Our proposed methods are limited to studying noise which comes from human annotators acting in good faith. Other sources of label noise include errors which occur due to spammers, distant supervision (as commonly seen in Named Entity Recognition), and/or pseudo-labels from bootstrapping. Within interactive settings, such as for dialogue systems, models may also encounter noisy user inputs such as out-of-domain requests or ambiguous queries. Our methods would not work well in those regimes either.

Method	Premise	Hypothesis	Label
Large Loss	Why shouldn't he be?	He doesn't actually want to be that way.	ENTAILMENT
	How do they feel about your being a Theater major?	They don't know you're a theater major, do they?	ENTAILMENT
	Defication of humankind as supreme.	Humankind is not supreme.	ENTAILMENT
	These are artists who are either emerging as leaders in their fields or who have already become well known.	These artists are becoming well known in their fields.	CONTRADICTION
	As he stepped across the threshold, Tommy brought the picture down with terrific force on his head.	Tommy stepped across a threshold and put a picture down on his head.	CONTRADICTION
AUM	And if, as ultimately happened, no settlement resulted, we could shrug our shoulders, say, 'Hey, we tried.'	Even if an agreement could not be reach we could say we tried.	ENTAILMENT
	Companies that were foreign had to accept Indian financial participation and management.	Foreign companies had to take Italian money	CONTRADICTION
	... he's been tireless about pursuing both celebrity and the cause of popular history ever since.	He never wanted any attention and kept to himself all the time.	CONTRADICTION
	Two more weeks with my cute TV satellite dish have increased my appreciation of it.	My appreciation of my satellite dish has increased.	ENTAILMENT
	Each working group met several times to develop recommendations for ... legal services delivery system	Each working met more than once to discuss changes to the legal services delivery system.	ENTAILMENT
Cartography	A detailed English explanation of the plot is always provided, and wireless recorded commentary units ...	You'll have to figure the plot out on your own.	CONTRADICTION
	I just loved Cinderella . I also saw my sisters as the wicked stepsisters sometimes, and I was Cinderella ...	I really disliked Cinderella and could never relate to her.	CONTRADICTION
	The judge gave vent to a faint murmur of disapprobation and the prisoner in the dock leant forward angrily.	The prisoner in the dock remained still and and expressionless	CONTRADICTION
	Jon was about to require a lot from her.	Jon needed nothing to do with her.	CONTRADICTION
	I know you'll enjoy being a part of the Herron School of Art and Gallery.	You will detest the Herron School of Art and Gallery and have nothing to do with it	CONTRADICTION
Prototype	Why shouldn't he be?	He doesn't actually want to be that way.	ENTAILMENT
	I like this area a whole lot and it's, it's growing so much and I just want to be near my family ...	I really despise living in this location and would prefer to be farther away from my relatives.	ENTAILMENT
	The air is warm.	The arid air permeates the surrounding land.	ENTAILMENT
	Inside the Oval: White House Tapes From FDR to Clinton	No tapes were recorded in the white house	ENTAILMENT
	He became even more concerned as its route changed moving into another sector's airspace.	He wasn't worried at all for the plane	ENTAILMENT

Table 6: Natural language inference examples that each method identified as being most likely to be label errors. Sentences were truncated in some cases for brevity.

Unsupervised Knowledge Graph Generation Using Semantic Similarity Matching

Lixian Liu[a], Amin Omidvar[a], Zongyang Ma[a], Ameeta Agrawal[b], Aijun An[a]
[a]Department of Electrical Engineering and Computer Science, York University, Canada
[b]Department of Computer Science, Portland State University, USA
lixian@my.yorku.ca, omidvar@yorku.ca, mzyone@gmail.com
ameeta@cs.pdx.edu, aan@eecs.yorku.ca

Abstract

Knowledge Graphs (KGs) are directed labeled graphs representing entities and the relationships between them. Most prior work focuses on supervised or semi-supervised approaches which require large amounts of annotated data. While unsupervised approaches do not need labeled training data, most existing methods either generate too many redundant relations or require manual mapping of the extracted relations to a known schema. To address these limitations, we propose an unsupervised method for KG generation that requires neither labeled data nor manual mapping to the predefined relation schema. Instead, our method leverages sentence-level semantic similarity for automatically generating relations between pairs of entities. Our proposed method outperforms two baseline systems when evaluated over four datasets.

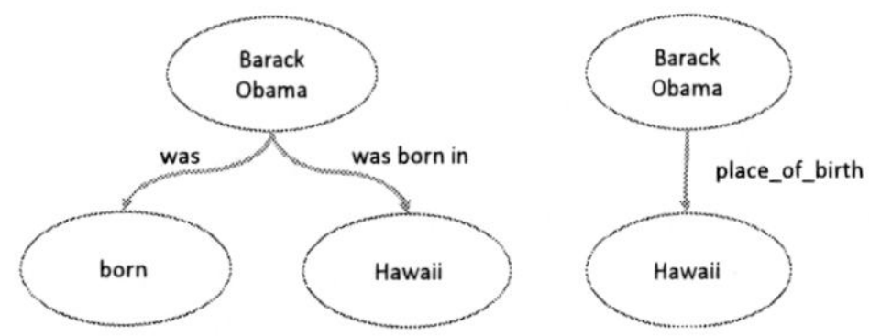

Figure 1: A KG generated using Stanford OpenIE (left) and our method (right) for the input sentence "*Barack Obama was born in Hawaii*".

1 Introduction

A knowledge graph (KG) is a directed labeled graph in which nodes represent entities and edges are labeled by well-defined relationships between entities. Formally, given a set E of entities and a set R of relations, a knowledge graph is a set T of triples, where $T \subseteq E \times R \times E$. A triple $t \in T$ can be expressed as (e_h, r, e_t), where $e_h \in E$, $r \in R$, $e_t \in E$, and e_h and e_t are referred to as the head entity and the tail entity, respectively. As a structured representation of world knowledge, knowledge graphs have been used in a number of applications such as Web search (Singhal, 2012; Wang et al., 2019a), question answering (Huang et al., 2019) and recommender systems (Wang et al., 2019b).

Knowledge graphs can be constructed automatically from text. Most of the automatic KG generation methods are supervised or semi-supervised, where a large set of labeled data is required to train a KG generation model (e.g., PCNN (Zeng et al., 2015), OLLIE (Schmitz et al., 2012), ReVerb (Fader et al., 2011)). However, creating labeled data is labor-intensive and the generated graph is limited to the specific domain of the training corpus. In addition, supervised methods can only extract a predefined set of relations occurring in the training data and the model needs to be re-trained to work with other new relation schemas.

Unsupervised KG models (e.g., Stanford OpenIE (Angeli et al., 2015)), on the other hand, do not need labeled training corpus. They often use syntactic parsing and a set of rules to extract relationships between two entities in a sentence. Although not normally confined to a predefined set of relations, too many unuseful or inaccurate relations can be generated. In Figure 1, the left graph presents an example KG using triples generated with Stanford OpenIE (Angeli et al., 2015), while the right graph presents the KG generated using our proposed method, both using the same single input sentence. In addition, in case only relations in a predefined set need to be generated, the unsupervised methods do not normally provide a mechanism to map the extracted relation to a known one in the set of relations

In a project to build knowledge graphs from news articles where no labeled data are given, we propose an unsupervised knowledge graph generation method using semantic similarity (KGSS) that does not need a labeled set of training data nor a complicated set of syntactic rules for KG

Proceedings of the Third Workshop on Deep Learning for Low-Resource Natural Language Processing, pages 169 - 179
July 14, 2022 ©2022 Association for Computational Linguistics

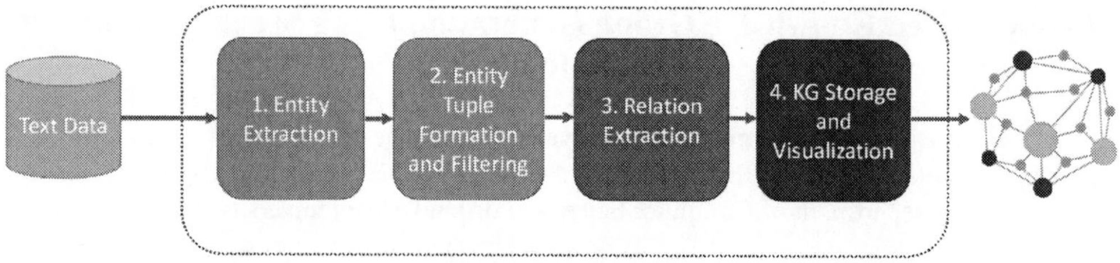

Figure 2: An overview of KGSS, our proposed unsupervised KG generation system.

generation. The method can work with any set of relations that a user prefers, and uses semantic similarity matching to automatically identify the relation between two entities. A salient feature of our method is the use of a pretrained language model (Reimers and Gurevych, 2019) to compute and measure the similarity between the sentence embedding and the embedding of candidate triples formed by the two entities and a candidate relation. The best matching candidate relation is identified as the relation between the two entities.

Since most supervised models underperform in low-resource settings where no or very limited labeled data are provided, our proposed unsupervised approach can extract useful relations from unlabeled data and can also be used to create a labeled data set for distant supervised learning, which can potentially lead to better results. In this paper, we focus on describing and evaluating the unsupervised method.

The contributions of this paper are as follows:

- We propose a novel unsupervised KG generation system that requires no labeled data.
- Our method is flexible and can work with any set of relations. The results of the empirical evaluation (automatic as well as human) demonstrate that our system significantly outperforms two state-of-the-art unsupervised methods for KG generation.
- To facilitate research in KG construction or information extraction from news articles, we develop a new dataset called NewsKG21[1] that was created from recent news articles.

[1]The NewsKG21 dataset and the code for our KG generation and visualization are available under the open source license at `https://github.com/lixianliu12/KGSS`

2 Related Work

Research on KG construction falls under supervised, semi-supervised, or unsupervised categories. For the supervised methods, we name two of them. Bastos et al. (2021) propose the RECON model to extract relations from a sentence and align them to the KG, using a graph neural network for obtaining the sentence representations. Then a neural classifier is adopted to predict the relation of each entity pair in the sentence. Another supervised learning method for KG construction is SpERT (Eberts and Ulges, 2020), which is a span-based deep learning model with the attention mechanism, targeting to extract entities and relations jointly. Semi-supervised approaches such as ReVerb (Fader et al., 2011), OLLIE (Schmitz et al., 2012), and Stanford OpenIE (Angeli et al., 2015), to name a few, leverage linguistic features (e.g., dependency trees and POS tags) with many human-defined patterns and existing knowledge bases (e.g., Wikidata (Vrandečić and Krötzsch, 2014), DBpedia (Auer et al., 2007)) to extract triples. These systems have a supervision component. For example, Stanford OpenIE uses distant supervision to create a noisy corpus of sentences annotated with relation mentions and train a logistic regression classifier to decide which action to perform on an edge on the parse tree when extracting relations. However, these systems miss many potential triples in a sentence since they use verbs as a signal to identify triples, whereas many relational triples may not be connected with a verb. They also tend to generate redundant triples and require manual mapping of the extracted relations to a fixed relation schema.

The earliest unsupervised approaches (i.e., heuristics approaches) (Suchanek et al., 2007; Auer et al., 2007; Bollacker et al., 2008) were applied to Wikipedia data, building the pioneering Knowledge Graphs (e.g., YAGO, DBpedia, Freebase). However, these approaches leverage additional

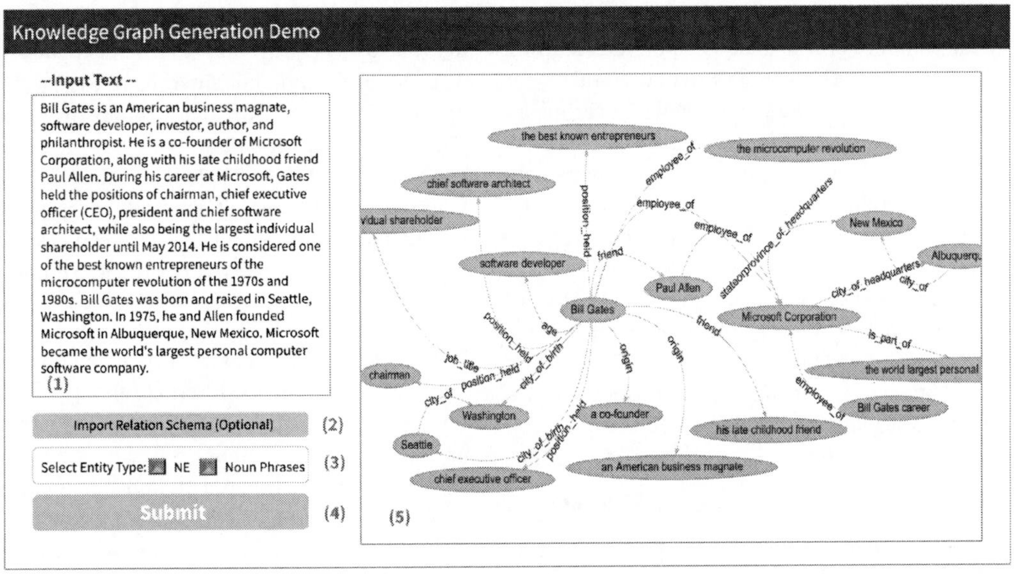

Figure 3: A demo of our system. (1) An input box for users to enter text. (2) A button for users to select their preferred relation schema; if nothing is imported, a default relation schema is used. (3) Users can select the type of entities to be extracted; if nothing is selected, both Named Entity and Noun will be extracted. (4) A submit button. (5) An interactive KG will be generated and visualized where the users can drag the nodes around to modify the presentation of the graph as desired.

knowledge to construct the graph, for example, the Wikipedia hierarchical categories in (Suchanek et al., 2007). Another drawback of these approaches is that they are slow and costly to build the KG. The resultant KGs are also restricted to a specific domain of corpus. MAMA (Wang et al., 2020), an unsupervised KG construction model, uses the attention weight matrices of a pre-trained language model (e.g., BERT (Devlin et al., 2018)) to extract the candidate triples. For mapping the extracted relations to a fixed schema, they follow the method of Stanford OpenIE (Angeli et al., 2015) requiring some manual annotations. Goswami et al. (2020) propose the RE-Flex framework for unsupervised relation extraction, where given a set of relations, each of them is rewritten as a cloze template (e.g., the cloze template of DraftBy is *X was created by Y*, where X and Y denote subject and object respectively.). Then the cloze template is semantically matched with the context (e.g., "Bill Gates founded Microsoft") to determine if the context has the relation or not. Another simliar work is proposed in (Tran et al., 2020) where the importance of the feature ENTITY TYPE for relation extraction is emphasized in their model called EType+. However, the feed-forward neural network classifier which is incorporated in their EType+ model makes their method not entirely unsupervised.

3 Proposed Model: KGSS

Given a document, our system generates a knowledge graph from the document. Figure 2 illustrates an overview of our system, KGSS, which consists of four modules: *entity extraction, entity tuple formation and filtering, relation extraction, and KG storage and visualization*, and Figure 3 illustrates the user interface of our system and visualizes a KG generated given an input paragraph based on a relation schema in TACRED* with 6 additional relations: *loc:province_of, loc:country_of, loc:city_of, org:is_part_of, per:position_held* and *per:friend*. Since our proposed system is unsupervised, it can flexibly work with any user-specified relation schema.

3.1 Entity Extraction

The first step in our system is co-reference resolution, which identifies and replaces different expressions of the same real-world entity with the same expression. We use an end-to-end neural coreference resolution model (Lee et al., 2017) from AllenNLP (Gardner et al., 2018) for this task.

In the second step, our system extracts all entities. We allow the user to specify in the user interface whether they would like to extract only named entities or also include other noun phrases. A named entity (NE) refers to a real-world object associated with a name, for example - a person, an organization, or a location (e.g., Barack Obama, Apple Inc., New York City). We use a transition-based algorithm (Lample et al., 2016) from the spaCy[2] library to detect all the NEs in a given sentence. There are 18 categories of NEs, such as PER (for person), ORG (for organization), and LOC (for location) in the spaCy *en_core_web_lg* pipeline for the NER task. We keep the NEs in all categories. In addition, if noun phrases are to be included, we extract all noun phrases (also called noun chunks) as candidate entities.

3.2 Entity Tuple Formation and Filtering

After extracting entities, we form a set of entity tuples for each sentence as follows. For each sentence s in the input document, let $E = (e_1, e_2, ..., e_k)$ be the list of identified entities in s, where e_i occurs before e_j in s when $i < j$. The set T of entity tuples for s contains all pairs $\langle e_i, e_j \rangle$ such that e_i occurs before e_j in s, that is, $T = \{\langle e_i, e_j \rangle | i < j\}$. We refer to this tuple formation rule as TF1. Thus, for a sentence containing k extracted entities, there are $\frac{k(k-1)}{2}$ entity tuples in its T. As an example, consider the sentence "*Barack Obama was born in Honolulu and graduated from Columbia University.*". The list of extracted entities is *Barack Obama, Honolulu, Columbia University*, and the set of entity tuples is ⟨Barack Obama, Honolulu⟩, ⟨Barack Obama, Columbia University⟩, and ⟨Honolulu, Columbia University⟩.

However, not all entity tuples lead to generation of good relations between the two entities. Thus, we use some heuristic rules to filter out unpromising tuples. Recall that NEs have categories. We use NE_{PER} to denote an NE in the person category, NE_{ORG} an organization NE, and NE_{LOC} a location NE. In addition, we denote all noun phrases as NE_{NOUN}. Not all the combinations of entities will yield meaningful relations between them. For instance, a location subject is most likely to not have a relation with its non-location object (Wang, 2020). Thus, we leverage the NE types and apply the following rules to keep quality candidate tuples and filter out some invalid ones: Rule TF2: keep all the tuples whose head entity is a NE_{PER}, a NE_{ORG} or a NE_{LOC}, and Rule TF3: if the first entity is a NE_{LOC}, keep the tuple if the second entity is also a NE_{LOC}; otherwise remove the tuple.

Thus, after applying filtering rules, the final set of entity tuples from the previous example is ⟨Barack Obama, Honolulu⟩ and ⟨Barack Obama, Columbia University⟩. Tuple ⟨Honolulu, Columbia University⟩ is filtered out due to Rule TF2, which is beneficial because a relation between Honolulu and Columbia University is not visibly helpful.

3.3 Relation Extraction

We denote the final set of entity tuples for a sentence after applying the filtering rules as F. Each tuple in F is in the format of *head-tail*, denoted as $\langle e_h, e_t \rangle$. Our algorithm for finding the relation between e_h and e_t is based on semantic matching.

Given a tuple $\langle e_h, e_t \rangle$, its sentence s and a set of pre-defined relations $R = (r_1, r_2, \dots, r_n)$, we collect all the tokens between e_h and e_t in s (including e_h and e_t) and name this sequence of tokens as P_{sub}. For each relation r_i in R, we also construct a sequence of tokens as "$e_h r_i e_t$" and name it R_i. Using a state-of-the-art embedding model, Sentence-BERT (SBERT)[3] (Reimers and Gurevych, 2019), we compute the semantic similarity between P_{sub} and R_i by obtaining the embeddings of P_{sub} and R_i and computing their cosine similarity. We do this for all the r_i's in R and select the relation r_i whose R_i has the highest similarity score with P_{sub}. If this highest similarity score is higher than a threshold[4], then r_i is selected as the relation between e_h and e_t. This generates a triple (e_h, r_i, e_t) for the knowledge graph. This process is repeated for all the entity tuples for sentence s and for all sentences in the input document. A triple is removed if it has been generated from a previous sentence.

Figure 4 shows an example sentence, its two entities ⟨Barack Obama, Columbia University⟩, the P_{sub} formed by the two entities, the R_i's and the generated triple for the entity tuple. Note that even though the P_{sub} span is considerably long, SBERT helps generate the correct relation in this case because of contextual knowledge encoded within such pretrained language models, thus validating the effectiveness of using semantic similarity in

[2]https://spacy.io/

[3]We use *distilbert-base-nli-stsb-mean-tokens* as the pretrained model.

[4]We set this threshold to 0.8 in our experiments based on the following experiment in the NYT dataset: beginning at 0 and increasing by 0.2 on each test until the threshold reaches 1, and we found that setting the threshold at 0.8 yielded the best F-score results. We use this threshold for all the other datasets.

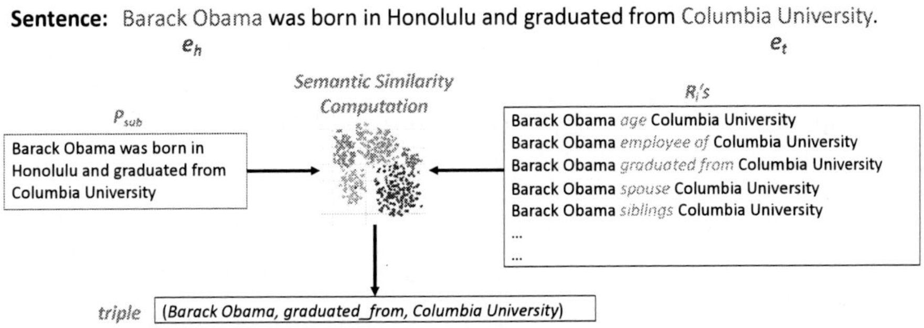

Figure 4: An example for Relation Extraction phase. At the top is the sentence with e_h and e_t denoting head and tail entities, respectively. P_{sub} is the part of sentence between e_h and e_t. R_i's are the sequences formed by the two entities and a relation. The final extracted triple for the two entities is also shown.

Dataset	# Sentence	# Relations	Example Sentences	Triple
TACRED	15509	42	*Both Konin and Alessi think so.*	(Alessi, no_relation, Konin)
TACRED*	3325	41	*Miettinen hired for WPS champ Sky Blue.*	(Miettinen, per:employee_of, Sky Blue)
NYT	5000	24	*At the time, she lived in Hollis, Queens.*	(Hollis, neighborhood_of, Queens); (Queens, contains, Hollis)
WEBNLG	703	246	*Bionico is a dessert containing sour cream from Mexico.*	(Bionico, country, Mexico); (Bionico, ingredient, cream)
NewsKG21	685	91	*Kevin Feige is married to Caitlin, a cardiothoracic nurse.*	(Kevin Feige, spouse, Caitlin); (Caitlin, job_title, cardiothoracic nurse)

Table 1: Dataset statistics. TACRED* is a subset of TACRED without instances containing triples with "no_relation".

KG relation extraction.

3.4 Optional Pattern-Based Rules

To further improve relation extraction in the news domain, we apply the following pattern-based rules based on our observation of their occurrence frequency in news articles: (1) Relation Extraction Rule 1 (RE1): if an entity tuple contains a noun phrase and a named entity of type Person (NE_{PER}) and the noun phrase is immediately before a NE_{PER} in the sentence (such as in "U.S. President Biden"), we assign "job title" as the relation; (2) Relation Extraction Rule 2 (RE2): if the two entities in a tuple appear as NE_{LOC}, NE_{LOC} in the sentence (such as in "Seattle, Washington"), the "is part of" relation is generated; and Relation Extraction Rule 3 (RE3): relation "job title" is generated in the tuple with the pattern $NE_{PER}, noun\ phrase$ (such as in "Caitlin, a cardiothoracic nurse").

We would like to emphasize that these rules are optional and even without these heuristics, our method outperforms the other unsupervised approaches, as demonstrated in Table 4 in section 5.3. Please also note that these rules may not be 100% accurate, but none of the existing KG generation methods is 100% accurate. These optional heuristics can better extract relations when two entities are next to each other in a sentence, where SBERT may not have enough information to correctly identify the relation between the two entities. We will show that these rules lead to a better overall result on news domains. Our goal here is to demonstrate that optional domain specific rules can be used to further improve the quality of the generated triples. If our purpose is to generate more labeled data for distant supervision, the use of these rules can reduce the overall noise ratio.

4 Evaluation Datasets

We evaluate our KG system by comparing the generated triples to manually annotated triples from three benchmark information extraction datasets and a new dataset on the news domain, all for English language.

4.1 Benchmark Datasets

The three benchmark datasets are: (i) **TACRED** (Zhang et al., 2017), (ii) **NYT** (Riedel et al., 2010), and (iii) **WEBNLG** (Gardent et al., 2017). Only their test datasets are used in our evaluation because our method does not need training. Each of the datasets contains a set of independent sentences and one or more ground truth triples for each sentence. TACRED has 41 relations originally from the TAC KBP yearly challenges [5] with a newly created relation called "no_relation"[6]. This dataset was manually constructed from an underlying corpus from TAC KBP where each sentence is labeled with a single ground truth triple and a standard evaluation tool is provided. NYT and WEBNLG datasets have 24 and 246 predefined relations, respectively. In both datasets, a sentence may have more than one ground truth triple. The statistics of the three benchmark datasets and our manually-created dataset are given in Table 1.

4.2 New Dataset: NewsKG21

Our goal in this research is to create a KG from news articles in order to build question-answering tools for editors of a news agency. The benchmark datasets we can obtain are not completely in the news domain. To evaluate our method on the news domain, we created a new dataset named `NewsKG21`. Another reason for us to develop a new KG generation dataset is that many public benchmark KG datasets are of poor quality since they were created mostly via crowdsourcing (e.g., in the TACRED dataset, the ground truth label for "AIG SELLS ALICO TO METLIFE" is ('ALICO', 'parents', 'AIG'), which is wrong). The evaluation results based on such datasets may be misleading. As a result, we carefully created a new dataset with as little noise as possible.

Four volunteers assisted in the creation of this dataset. One is an author of this paper, and the others are senior undergraduate Computer Science students. We selected 685 sentences from news articles published in 2021 in CNN, CBC, USNEWS, The Star, and Wikipedia News. From the 685 sentences, 1247 unique triples were manually generated. We divided the dataset into two parts: a test data set containing 271 sentences and 705 ground truth triples and a training set with 414 sentences and 542 ground truth triples. To prevent bias and advantages for a certain system, no system was engaged in the dataset creation process. Only the testing set is used to assess all unsupervised models.

5 Experiments and Discussion

5.1 Baselines and Metrics

We compare our system with two other state-of-the-art unsupervised systems[7], **Stanford OpenIE** (Angeli et al., 2015) and **MAMA** (with the BERT_{LARGE} option) (Wang et al., 2020).

Entity tuple extraction: To compare the extracted entities with those in the ground truth data, we use *Token Set Ratio*[8], to calculate the similarity between two entities. Given an extracted entity E and the ground truth entity G, *Token Set Ratio* is defined as $\frac{2M}{T}$ where T is the total number of tokens in both E and G (that is, $|E| + |G|$ where $|X|$ is the number of tokens in entity X), M is the number of matched tokens between E and G, and tokens are separated by spaces in the entity (that is, tokens are basically the words in the entity). For example, if E is "Trudeau" and G is "Justin Trudeau", the token set ratio is 2/3.

This entity matching method is used for all the evaluated methods. Empirically, the threshold of string similarity is set to 0.9 for all the systems. The need for partial matching over exact matching is motivated by the observation that some gold standard annotations in the benchmark datasets are incompletely-matched entities. For example, "Apollo 12" appears as an entity in the original text, but it appears as "Apollo" in the gold standard triple in a benchmark dataset.

Triple generation: For a fair comparison, we also map the extracted relations from all the methods (including Stanford OpenIE and MAMA) to each of the dataset's relations using the same method, i.e., using SBERT embeddings for computing the cosine similarity between extracted relations and predefined relations in the schema, and selecting the one with the highest similarity score. We chose this relation mapping approach for Stanford OpenIE and MAMA instead of their original

[5] https://tac.nist.gov/

[6] The results of the evaluation including the "no_relation" instances can be found in Appendix A.

[7] Although Stanford OpenIE was trained in a semi-supervised way, we use their pre-trained version and do not fine-tune it on our training dataset. Thus, we consider our use of their method as unsupervised.

[8] https://pypi.org/project/fuzzywuzzy/

Dataset	System	P %	R %	F1 %
TACRED*	Stanford OpenIE	18.4	3.0	5.2
	MAMA	12.6	2.3	3.8
	(Ours) KGSS	**43.5**	**27.6**	**33.8**
NYT	Stanford OpenIE	2.7	1.5	1.9
	MAMA	1.7	7.2	2.8
	(Ours) KGSS	**25.7**	**29.2**	**27.3**
WEBNLG	Stanford OpenIE	2.5	6.5	3.6
	MAMA	5.1	6.0	5.5
	(Ours) KGSS	**8.4**	**9.1**	**8.7**
NewsKG21	Stanford OpenIE	7.1	11.3	8.7
	MAMA	2.1	6.1	3.2
	(Ours) KGSS	**24.6**	**20.4**	**22.3**

Table 2: The results of KG triple extraction.

System	P %	R %	F1 %
Stanford OpenIE	19.2	30.9	23.7
MAMA	11.4	32.8	16.9
KGSS	**45.1**	**48.7**	**46.8**

Table 3: Results of entity tuple extraction (e_h, e_t) on NewsKG21

System	P %	R %	F1 %
Stanford OpenIE	7.1	11.3	8.7
MAMA	2.1	6.1	3.2
KGSS (without rules)	10.5	12.1	11.2
KGSS with RE 1	**13.1**	**15.7**	**14.3**
KGSS with RE 1 & 2	**16.1**	**19.3**	**17.5**
KGSS with RE 1, 2 & 3	**16.5**	**20.1**	**18.1**
KGSS with 3 REs & tail type	**24.6**	**20.4**	**22.3**

Table 4: Results of triple extraction (e_h, r, e_t) on NewsKG21 dataset, without relation extraction rules (top) and with relation extraction rules (bottom). Adding rules improves the performance.

manual relation mapping techniques, which are irreproducible in our experiments.

For the TACRED* dataset, we calculate precision, recall, and F-score with the provided standard evaluation script. As the TACRED* dataset also contains pronouns and nouns as entities in the ground truth triples, we also extract these in addition to the named entities and omit the coreference resolution in our system for this dataset in order to have a fair comparison because both baselines can detect pronouns and nouns as entities. In our system, the user can choose types of entities that can be identified. For the NYT and WEBNLG datasets, we calculate the standard F1 score as $F1 = (2 * p * r)/(p + r)$, with $p = \frac{c}{m}$ and $r = \frac{c}{g}$, where c denotes the number of correctly extracted triples, m is the total number of extracted triples, and g is the number of triples in the annotated dataset.

5.2 Results and Discussion

Table 2 presents the results of KG triple generation over the four datasets. We note that our method KGSS consistently outperforms both unsupervised baselines across all the datasets by considerable margins on all the three metrics. One possible explanation for the improvement gains achieved by KGSS as compared to the unsupervised baselines is that the baseline methods tend to extract triples using verbs as signals which causes them to miss many triples, whereas our method generates the triples using semantic similarity from sentence embeddings. The baseline models also generate redundant triples which lowers their precision.

It is worth noting that among the four datasets, WEBNLG is the most challenging one for KGSS, with much lower performance than that on other datasets. This is most likely because of the large number of relation types in its schema (more than 200 as compared to other datasets having less than 100 relations). We conjecture that some relations may be too semantically similar for SBERT to distinguish from each other.

In terms of qualitative analysis, looking at the visual KG shown in Figure 3 generated for an excerpt from a Wikipedia article, we notice that all mentions of 'Bill Gates' and 'Gates' get correctly resolved to a single entity, i.e., 'Bill Gates', (and similarly, 'Microsoft Corporation' and 'Microsoft' get resolved to 'Microsoft Corporation') which helps prevent generating redundant triples. Another strength of the system can be seen in the form of triples such as ⟨Bill Gates, friend, Paul Allen⟩, ⟨Albuquerque, city of, New Mexico⟩ and ⟨Seattle, city of, Washington⟩. Also, all the various positions held by Gates are captured well, thus highlighting the role of such systems as helpful tools for summarizing long pieces of unstructured text into a concise visual representation.

5.3 Ablation Experiments

In Table 3, we evaluate the three systems on the NewsKG21 dataset one the task of entity tuple extraction, which means that we only compare the performance of systems generating pairs of head and tail entities to the ground truth in the dataset. We see that our method is better than Stanford OpenIE and MAMA which is most likely attributed to our entity tuple filtering rules (TF1, 2, and 3) that can remove some noisy entity pairs while preserving a large number of meaningful tuples.

We also evaluate the three relation extraction rules described in Section 3.4. The results in Table 4 show that each rule helps to enhance the performance of our system as all the three measures increase as we apply more rules. The F-score is increased by around 7% after applying the three rules all together. One significant point to notice is that our system outperforms the other two unsupervised methods even when no heuristic rules are used.

By analyzing the generated triples, we realized that some incorrect triples can be avoided if we consider the entity types of a relation in relation extraction. For example, the spouse relation can only connect two entities of the person type. Thus, we add the type of the tail entity in each relation in our relation schema. Note the head entity type is already in the schema, similar to the schema in the TACRED dataset. With such information in the relation schema, we are able to eliminate some candidate relations given an entity tuple. For example, if the entity tuple is "Trump, New York", any relations whose head and tail entity types do not match Person and Location (such as the *spouse* relation) are not considered as candidates.

The last row of Table 4 demonstrates that by using the tail entity type for each relation in the schema, we can raise the F-score of our system by 4% points. This is another advantage of our system, which uses an entity-type aware method for eliminating unpromising triple extraction results, which the Stanford OpenIE and MAMA systems do not have. In addition, we run an ablation test on the NewsKG21 dataset using the tuple filtering criteria specified in section 3.2. As seen in Table 5, each rule contributes to the improvement of overall performance of our system.

One interesting finding is that, of the three systems, MAMA gets the lowest score on the NewsKG21 dataset since it extracts entity tuples based on information contained in a pre-trained language model BERT. As such, MAMA will approach its KG generation limit if the input articles are not from the language model's underlying corpus, such as our NewsKG21 dataset which is produced from the recent news stories.

Filtering Rule	P %	R %	F1 %
No Rule	12.9	25.4	17.1
TF 1	18.5	24.3	20.9
TF 1 & 2	19.1	23.4	21.1
TF 1, 2 & 3	20.9	23.4	**22.1**

Table 5: KGSS's performance on triple extraction with various tuple filtering methods on NewsKG21.

System	P %	R %	F1 %
Stanford OpenIE	33.5 ± 9.0	34.6 ± 15.9	34.0
MAMA	2.7 ± 2.6	10.3 ± 6.9	4.3
KGSS	34.1 ± 10.0	37.8 ± 12.7	**35.9**

Table 6: Results of human evaluation on the performance of triple extraction on NewsKG21.

5.4 Human Evaluation

In addition to automatic evaluation, we conduct human evaluation of our proposed system's triple extraction performance by comparing it to two baseline models: Stanford OpenIE and MAMA. Five human evaluators participated in our study, none of whom was told beforehand which systems they were assessing; more specifically, the names of each model were hidden. We chose 30 sentences at random from the NEWSKG21 dataset, and each participant graded the quality of triples generated by each system on each sentence based on the following criteria: (i) how accurate the extracted triples are in regard to the original text; and (ii) how thoroughly the extracted triples cover the true relations in the original sentence. Each evaluator was asked to assign a score from 0 to 1 to each generated triple on precision and to the set of triples generated from a sentence on recall, with 0 indicating entirely incorrect, 1 indicating completely accurate, and a value in between indicating partially correct.

The results in Table 6 show that Stanford OpenIE performs much better on human evaluation than on automatic evaluation. This is because only evaluating the system based on automatically match with the ground truth in the dataset may not accurately reflect the performance of a system. However, the results in Table 6 confirm that our system outperforms the two baseline models.

Although unsupervised approaches may allow more interpretable and flexible methods, they are not without limitations. The effectiveness of our unsupervised algorithm is partly dependent on the accuracy of the existing NER tools that we incorporate into our pipeline. Similarly, the semantic matching phase's performance may be less effective when the relation schema contains similar relation names. In addition, if training data are available, supervised methods can achieve much better results as shown in Table 9 in Appendix C. Nevertheless, our unsupervised method can work when no training data are available and can potentially be used to create labeled data (although noisy) for distant supervised learning to bootstrap knowledge graph generation.

6 Conclusions

We presented a novel unsupervised method for knowledge graph generation without the need for labeled data or manual mapping of extracted relations to a predefined relation schema (as in two previous unsupervised methods). A salient feature of the method is that it uses semantic similarity matching to find relations between entities. In addition, our system can work with any set of relations that the user prefers, flexibility that other methods, especially the supervised ones, do not have. We also created a new data set from news articles that will be shared with the community.

Our evaluation results demonstrate the effectiveness of our system which significantly outperforms two state-of-the-art unsupervised models over four different datasets. We also develop an open source interactive KG generation and visualization tool. As future work, we will evaluate effectiveness of using our method for bootstrapping knowledge graph generation with distant supervision.

Acknowledgements

We would like to thank our volunteer annotators Iris Chang, Rhitabrat Pokharel, and Andrew Jeon for their help in creating our NewsKG21 dataset. We are thankful to the anonymous reviewers for their helpful suggestions.

References

Gabor Angeli, Melvin Jose Johnson Premkumar, and Christopher D Manning. 2015. Leveraging linguistic structure for open domain information extraction. In *Proceedings of the 53rd Annual Meeting of the Association for Computational Linguistics and the 7th International Joint Conference on Natural Language Processing (Volume 1: Long Papers)*, pages 344–354.

Sören Auer, Christian Bizer, Georgi Kobilarov, Jens Lehmann, Richard Cyganiak, and Zachary Ives. 2007. Dbpedia: A nucleus for a web of open data. In *The semantic web*, pages 722–735. Springer.

Anson Bastos, Abhishek Nadgeri, Kuldeep Singh, Isaiah Onando Mulang', Saeedeh Shekarpour, Johannes Hoffart, and Manohar Kaul. 2021. RECON: relation extraction using knowledge graph context in a graph neural network. In *WWW '21: The Web Conference 2021, Virtual Event / Ljubljana, Slovenia, April 19-23, 2021*, pages 1673–1685. ACM / IW3C2.

Kurt Bollacker, Colin Evans, Praveen Paritosh, Tim Sturge, and Jamie Taylor. 2008. Freebase: a collaboratively created graph database for structuring human knowledge. In *Proceedings of the 2008 ACM SIGMOD international conference on Management of data*, pages 1247–1250.

Jacob Devlin, Ming-Wei Chang, Kenton Lee, and Kristinax Toutanova. 2018. Bert: Pre-training of deep bidirectional transformers for language understanding. *arXiv preprint arXiv:1810.04805*.

Markus Eberts and Adrian Ulges. 2020. Span-based joint entity and relation extraction with transformer pre-training. In *ECAI 2020 - 24th European Conference on Artificial Intelligence, 29 August-8 September 2020, Santiago de Compostela, Spain, August 29 - September 8, 2020 - Including 10th Conference on Prestigious Applications of Artificial Intelligence (PAIS 2020)*, volume 325 of *Frontiers in Artificial Intelligence and Applications*, pages 2006–2013. IOS Press.

Anthony Fader, Stephen Soderland, and Oren Etzioni. 2011. Identifying relations for open information extraction. In *Proceedings of the 2011 conference on empirical methods in natural language processing*, pages 1535–1545.

Claire Gardent, Anastasia Shimorina, Shashi Narayan, and Laura Perez-Beltrachini. 2017. Creating training corpora for nlg micro-planning. In *55th annual meeting of the Association for Computational Linguistics (ACL)*.

Matt Gardner, Joel Grus, Mark Neumann, Oyvind Tafjord, Pradeep Dasigi, Nelson Liu, Matthew Peters, Michael Schmitz, and Luke Zettlemoyer. 2018. Allennlp: A deep semantic natural language processing platform. *arXiv preprint arXiv:1803.07640*.

Ankur Goswami, Akshata Bhat, Hadar Ohana, and Theodoros Rekatsinas. 2020. Unsupervised relation extraction from language models using constrained cloze completion. *CoRR*, abs/2010.06804.

Wenti Huang, Yiyu Mao, Zhan Yang, Lei Zhu, and Jun Long. 2020. Relation classification via knowledge graph enhanced transformer encoder. *Knowledge-Based Systems*, 206:106321.

Xiao Huang, Jingyuan Zhang, Dingcheng Li, and Ping Li. 2019. Knowledge graph embedding based question answering. In *Proceedings of the Twelfth ACM International Conference on Web Search and Data Mining*, pages 105–113.

Guillaume Lample, Miguel Ballesteros, Sandeep Subramanian, Kazuya Kawakami, and Chris Dyer. 2016. Neural architectures for named entity recognition. In *Proceedings of the 2016 Conference of the North American Chapter of the Association for Computational Linguistics: Human Language Technologies*, pages 260–270, San Diego, California. Association for Computational Linguistics.

Kenton Lee, Luheng He, Mike Lewis, and Luke Zettlemoyer. 2017. End-to-end neural coreference resolution. In *Proceedings of the 2017 Conference on Empirical Methods in Natural Language Processing*, pages 188–197, Copenhagen, Denmark. Association for Computational Linguistics.

Jie Liu, Shaowei Chen, Bingquan Wang, Jiaxin Zhang, Na Li, and Tong Xu. 2021. Attention as relation: learning supervised multi-head self-attention for relation extraction. In *Proceedings of the Twenty-Ninth International Conference on International Joint Conferences on Artificial Intelligence*, pages 3787–3793.

Peng Qi, Yuhao Zhang, Yuhui Zhang, Jason Bolton, and Christopher D Manning. 2020. Stanza: A python natural language processing toolkit for many human languages. *arXiv preprint arXiv:2003.07082*.

Nils Reimers and Iryna Gurevych. 2019. Sentence-bert: Sentence embeddings using siamese bert-networks. *arXiv preprint arXiv:1908.10084*.

Sebastian Riedel, Limin Yao, and Andrew McCallum. 2010. Modeling relations and their mentions without labeled text. In *Joint European Conference on Machine Learning and Knowledge Discovery in Databases*, pages 148–163. Springer.

Michael Schmitz, Stephen Soderland, Robert Bart, Oren Etzioni, et al. 2012. Open language learning for information extraction. In *Proceedings of the 2012 joint conference on empirical methods in natural language processing and computational natural language learning*, pages 523–534.

Amit Singhal. 2012. Introducing the Knowledge Graph: things, not strings. `https://blog.google/products/search/introducing-knowledge-graph-things-not/`. [Online; accessed 01-July-2021].

Fabian M Suchanek, Gjergji Kasneci, and Gerhard Weikum. 2007. Yago: a core of semantic knowledge. In *Proceedings of the 16th international conference on World Wide Web*, pages 697–706.

Thy Thy Tran, Phong Le, and Sophia Ananiadou. 2020. Revisiting unsupervised relation extraction. In *Proceedings of the 58th Annual Meeting of the Association for Computational Linguistics*, pages 7498–7505, Online. Association for Computational Linguistics.

Denny Vrandečić and Markus Krötzsch. 2014. Wikidata: a free collaborative knowledgebase. *Communications of the ACM*, 57(10):78–85.

Chenguang Wang, Xiao Liu, and Dawn Song. 2020. Language models are open knowledge graphs. *arXiv preprint arXiv:2010.11967*.

Peilu Wang, Hao Jiang, Jingfang Xu, and Qi Zhang. 2019a. Knowledge graph construction and applications for web search and beyond. *Data Intelligence*, 1(4):333–349.

Xiang Wang, Xiangnan He, Yixin Cao, Meng Liu, and Tat-Seng Chua. 2019b. Kgat: Knowledge graph attention network for recommendation. In *Proceedings of the 25th ACM SIGKDD International Conference on Knowledge Discovery & Data Mining*, pages 950–958.

Zina Wang. 2020. Unsupervised and supervised learning of complexrelation instances extraction in natural language. Master's thesis, Delft University of Technology.

Daojian Zeng, Kang Liu, Yubo Chen, and Jun Zhao. 2015. Distant supervision for relation extraction via piecewise convolutional neural networks. In *Proceedings of the 2015 conference on empirical methods in natural language processing*, pages 1753–1762.

Yuhao Zhang, Victor Zhong, Danqi Chen, Gabor Angeli, and Christopher D Manning. 2017. Position-aware attention and supervised data improve slot filling. In *Proceedings of the 2017 Conference on Empirical Methods in Natural Language Processing*, pages 35–45.

A Experiments on TACRED dataset including *no_relation* relationship

Table 7 compares our system's performance to Stanford OpenIE and MAMA on the TACRED dataset, which includes the relation: no_relation. In this experiment, if the relation confidence rate returned from SBERT is less than 0.8, our system will return no_relation. Although the total performance of all three systems decreases, our system still outperforms the other two cutting-edge models.

System	P %	R %	F1 %
Stanford OpenIE	6.6	3.0	4.1
MAMA	2.4	2.2	2.3
(Ours) KGSS	**14.3**	**27.6**	**18.8**

Table 7: The performance of triple extraction on TACRED including relationship "no_relation".

B Comparing performance of different algorithms on entity extraction

For entity extraction, we compare the performance of the named entity recognition (NER) systems

Dataset	Library	P %	R %	F1 %	Runtime (sec)
TACRED*	spaCy	29.3	86.4	43.7	145
	Stanza	29.2	88.6	43.9	1355
NYT	spaCy	57.5	99.6	72.9	51
	Stanza	56.8	99.9	72.4	454
WEBNLG	spaCy	86.7	86.5	86.6	6
	Stanza	91.5	91.6	91.5	47

Table 8: Performance of spaCy and Stanza for entity extraction

from two libraries, namely spaCy[9] and Stanza[10] (Qi et al., 2020) on the three benchmark datasets. A detected NE is considered to be correct if it partially matches the entities in the ground truth dataset via fuzzy string matching. The precision, recall, and F1 scores for both the tools are presented in Table 2, where we observe that while spaCy and Stanza are comparable in terms of their F1 scores, Stanza is about 8 times more computationally expensive. Thus, we select spaCy for NER and tokenization in all our experiments.

C Performance of the supervised KG models

Table 9 shows the performance of the state of the art supervised KG models: TransEN (Huang et al., 2020) on the TACRED dataset, and AaR (Liu et al., 2021) on the NYT and WEBNLG datasets. All the models are trained on the training data of each dataset and evaluated on the test data of the corresponding dataset. The results are taken from the references.

System	Dataset	P %	R %	F1 %
TransEN	TACRED	68.3	66.2	67.3
AaR	NYT	88.1	78.5	83.0
AaR	WEBNLG	89.5	86.0	87.7

Table 9: The performance of the state of the art supervised KG models on the TACRED, NYT, and WEBNLG datasets.

[9]https://spacy.io/

[10]https://stanfordnlp.github.io/stanza/

FarFetched: Entity-centric Reasoning and Claim Validation for the Greek Language based on Textually Represented Environments

Dimitris Papadopoulos
Technical University of Crete
Chania, Greece
dpapadopoulos6@isc.tuc.gr

Katerina Metropoulou
National Technical University of Athens
Athens, Greece
kmetropoulou@mail.ntua.gr

Nikolaos Matsatsinis
Technical University of Crete
Chania, Greece
nmatsatsinis@isc.tuc.gr

Nikolaos Papadakis
Hellenic Army Academy
Vari, Greece
npapadakis@sse.gr

Abstract

Our collective attention span is shortened by the flood of online information. With *FarFetched*, we address the need for automated claim validation based on the aggregated evidence derived from multiple online news sources. We introduce an entity-centric reasoning framework in which latent connections between events, actions, or statements are revealed via entity mentions and represented in a graph database. Using entity linking and semantic similarity, we offer a way for collecting and combining information from diverse sources in order to generate evidence relevant to the user's claim. Then, we leverage textual entailment recognition to quantitatively determine whether this assertion is credible, based on the created evidence. Our approach tries to fill the gap in automated claim validation for less-resourced languages and is showcased on the Greek language, complemented by the training of relevant semantic textual similarity (STS) and natural language inference (NLI) models that are evaluated on translated versions of common benchmarks.

1 Introduction

Motivation: The wider diffusion of the Web since the dawn of Web 2.0 has enabled instantaneous access to an expanding universe of information. The entire nature of news consumption has shifted dramatically, as individuals increasingly rely on the Internet as their major source of information. While people access, filter and blend several websites into intricate patterns of media consumption, this wealth of information contained in billions of online articles inevitably creates a poverty of attention and a need to efficiently allocate this attention among the many sources that may absorb it. Verifying whether a given claim coheres with the knowledge hidden in the vast amount of published information is a fundamental problem in NLP, taking into account that the arrival of new information may weaken or retract the initially supported inference. The problem is more apparent in less-resourced languages that lack the necessary linguistic resources for building meaningful NLP applications.

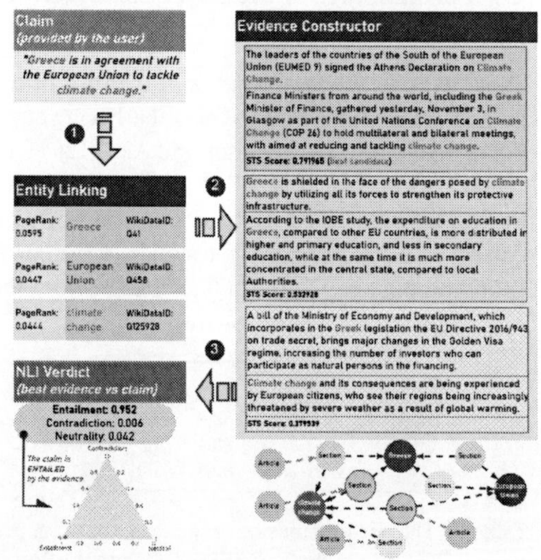

Figure 1: Claim validation example (translated from Greek) based on aggregated evidence using *FarFetched*.

Approach and Contribution: *FarFetched* is a modular framework that enables people to verify any kind of textual claim based on the incorporated evidence from textual news sources. It combines a series of processes to periodically crawl for news articles and annotate their context with named entities. Given a user claim, *FarFetched* derives a relevant subset of the stored content based on its

Proceedings of the Third Workshop on Deep Learning for Low-Resource Natural Language Processing, pages 180 - 191
July 14, 2022 ©2022 Association for Computational Linguistics

semantic similarity with the provided claim, thus being able to reason about its validity in an NLI setting (Figure 1). While the proposed framework focuses on the less-resourced Greek language, its modular architecture allows the integration of pre-trained models for any language. Moreover, it is capable of topic-agnostic, evidence-aware assessment of arbitrary textual claims in a fully automated manner, without relying on feature engineering, curated sources and manual intervention.

The main contributions of this work are summarized as follows: a) to formalize, develop and evaluate a claim validation and reasoning approach based on the aggregated knowledge derived from the continuous monitoring of news sources, and b) to train, evaluate and share SotA models for the STS and NLI downstream tasks for the Greek language that support the core functionalities of our framework.[1]

2 Related Work

Our work comprises functionalities comparable to those of fact checking frameworks, targeting the assignment of a truth value to a claim made in a particular context (Vlachos and Riedel, 2014). For most related approaches (Zhang et al., 2021; Majithia et al., 2019; Zhou et al., 2019; Ciampaglia et al., 2015; Goasdoué et al., 2013) the evidence to support or refute a claim is derived from a trustworthy source (e.g. Wikipedia, crowdsourced tagging or expert annotators). Interesting deviations are DeClarE (Popat et al., 2018) that searches for web articles related to a claim considering their in-between relevance using an attention mechanism, and ClaimEval (Samadi et al., 2016), based on first-order logic to contextualise prior knowledge from a set of the highest page-ranked websites.

FarFetched can be distinguished from the aforementioned works by four major points: a) evidence collection is disentangled from manual annotation but relies on a constantly updating feed of news articles instead; b) claim validation based on the accumulated evidence relies on the effective combination of entity linking and attention-based models; c) our approach provides interpretable reasoning based on the aggregated evidence of multiple sources without assessing their truthfulness as opposed to most fact checking frameworks; and d) the outcome of the process is dynamic as the continuous integration of new information may lead to a shift in the verdict of the validated claim.

Recent advances in the field of *event-centric* NLP have introduced event representation methods based on narrative event chains (Vossen et al., 2015), knowledge graphs (Tang et al., 2019; Vossen et al., 2016), QA pairs (Michael et al., 2018) or event network embeddings (Zeng et al., 2021) to capture connections among events in a global context. Our method relies on an *entity-centric* approach instead, where the identified entities are used as connectors between events, actions, facts, statements or opinions, thus revealing latent connections between the articles containing them. A few similar approaches have been proposed for combining world knowledge with event extraction methods to represent coherent events, but rely either on causal reasoning to generate plausible predictions (Radinsky et al., 2012) or on QA models that require the accompanying news source to be provided along with the user's question (Jin et al., 2021).

The latest advances regarding the technological concepts that comprise our methodology are provided below:

Entity linking (EL) resolves the lexical ambiguity of entity mentions and determines their meanings in context. Typical EL approaches aim at identifying named entities in mention spans and linking them to entries of a KG (e.g. Wikidata, DBpedia) thus resolving their ambiguity. Recent methods combine the aforementioned tasks using local compatibility and topic similarity features (Delpeuch, 2019), pagerank-based wikification (Brank et al., 2017a) —used also in *FarFetched*— or neural end-to-end models that jointly detect and disambiguate mentions with the help of context-aware mention embeddings (Kolitsas et al., 2018).

The recent interest for encapsulating diverse semantic sentence features into fixed-size vectors has resulted in SotA systems for Semantic Textual Similarity (STS) based on supervised cross-sentence attention (Raffel et al., 2020), Deep Averaging Networks (DAN) (Cer et al., 2018) or siamese and triplet BERT-Networks (Reimers and Gurevych, 2019) to acquire meaningful sentence embeddings that can be compared using cosine similarity. The latter approach is leveraged in our case to train an STS model for the Greek language using transfer learning.

Finally, the task of Natural Language Inference

[1]Code and benchmark datasets: `https://github.com/lighteternal/FarFetched_NLP`

(NLI) -also known as Recognizing Textual Entailment (RTE)- associates an input pair of premise and hypothesis phrases into one of three classes: contradiction, entailment and neutral. Ferreira and Vlachos, 2016 modeled fact checking as a form of RTE to predict whether a premise, typically part of a trusted source, is for, against, or observing a given claim. SotA NLI models typically rely on Transformer variants with global attention mechanisms (Beltagy et al., 2020), siamese network architectures (Reimers and Gurevych, 2019) (also used in *FarFetched* to train a Greek NLI model), autoregressive language models for capturing long-term dependencies (Yang et al., 2019) and denoising autoencoders (Lewis et al., 2020).

3 Methodology

3.1 Problem Definition

Given a user claim in free text, we tackle the problem of deciding whether this statement is plausible based on the currently accumulated knowledge from news sources. We also acknowledge the problem of constructing relevant evidence from multiple sources by analysing the information contained in online articles and the need for efficiently extracting only contextually and semantically relevant excerpts to verify or refute the user's claim. While our work does not primarily focus on better sentence embeddings and natural language inference techniques, we also target the lack of such models for the Greek language.

3.2 Our approach

FarFetched combines a series of *offline* (i.e. performed periodically) operations to accumulate data from various news sources and annotate their context with named entities. It also encompasses a number of *online* operations (i.e. upon user input) to assess the validity of a claim in free text. First, it identifies the entities included in the provided claim and leverages these as a starting point to derive a relevant subset of the stored textual information as candidate evidence. Each candidate is then compared with the claim in terms of textual similarity, in order to finally conclude on the most relevant evidence (premise) to reason about the validity of the claim (hypothesis) in an NLI setting. The distinct modules that comprise the framework are visualised in Figure 2. The process that *FarFetched* follows to evaluate a claim is summarized in Algorithm 1, while each module is described in greater detail in the following subsections.

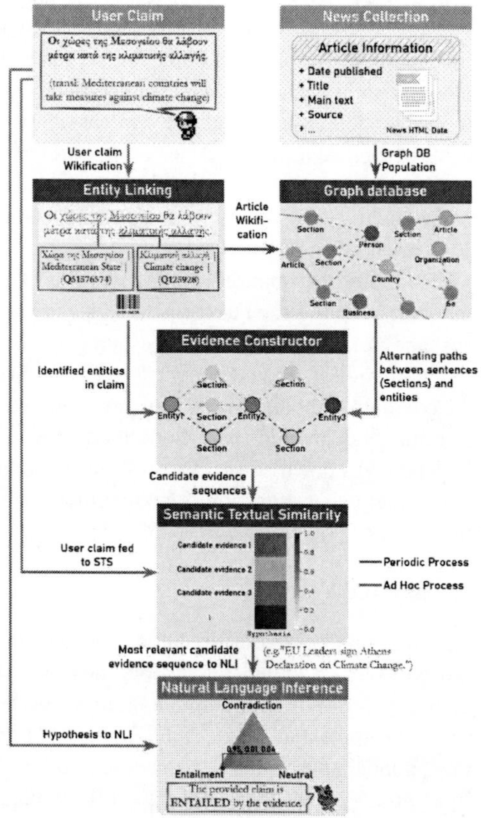

Figure 2: The *FarFetched* modular framework.

3.2.1 News Collection

A multilingual, open-source crawler and extractor for heterogeneous website structures is leveraged to incorporate information from various news sources (Hamborg et al., 2017). It is capable of extracting the major properties of news articles (i.e., title, lead paragraph, main content, publication date, author, etc.), featuring full website extraction and requiring only the root URL of a news website to crawl it completely.

3.2.2 Graph Database Population

The crawled articles are forwarded to a graph database (Webber, 2012) that initially stores only two types of nodes: `Article`, which represents a news article with its aforementioned properties and `Section` that represents a sentence of each article's main text (i.e. concatenated title and article body). Each `Article` node is linked to one or more `Section` nodes via the `HAS_SECTION` relationship.

Algorithm 1 Claim Evaluation

Input: A claim c provided by the user in natural language.
Output: Most relevant evidence seq^* (sequence of article excerpts) based on the input claim c along with its STS_score^* and $NLI\_score < c, e, n >$.

Entity Linking: Find the set of entities $(e_1, ..., e_n) \in E$, where $e \exists c$ and $|E| = n$
$S \leftarrow \varnothing$
Graph database search: Find all shortest paths p between the alternating entities e and sentences s: $p \leftarrow (e_1, s_a, e_2, ..., e_{n-1}, s_k, e_n) \in P$
if $P = \varnothing$ **then**
    $s \in P \iff s$ has at least 1 entity mention
end if
for $p_i \in P$ **do**
    $seq_i \leftarrow (s_a, ..., s_k)$
    $S \leftarrow S \cup seq_i$ (sequence seq_i added to candidate evidence set)
end for
$STS\_Scores \leftarrow \varnothing$
for $seq_i \in S$ **do**
    Semantic Textual Similarity: Compare $seq_i \in S$ to c (each candidate evidence sequence to the claim) and calculate STS_score_i
    $STS\_Scores \leftarrow STS\_Scores \cup STS\_score_i$
end for
Find the candidate seq^* with the highest similarity to the claim: $STS\_score^* \leftarrow max(STS\_Scores)$
$seq^* \leftarrow argmax(STS\_score^*)$
Natural Language Inference: Compare seq^* to c (the best candidate evidence to the claim) and calculate the scores for contradiction, entailment and neutrality $NLI\_score < c, e, n >$

3.2.3 Entity Linking

Given that our approach relies on largely unstructured textual documents that lack explicit semantic information, Entity Linking (EL) constitutes a central role in revealing latent connections between seemingly uncorrelated article sections. To this end, *FarFetched* employs a type of semantic enrichment and entity disambiguation technique known as wikification (Brank et al., 2017b), which involves using Wikipedia concepts as a source of semantic annotation. It applies pagerank-based wikification on input text to identify phrases that refer to entities of the target knowledge base (Wikipedia) and return their corresponding WikiData Entity ID. The latter is used as a unique identifier for storing the entities as `Entity` nodes to the graph database and for linking them with the crawled article `Section` nodes, resulting to a more tightly connected graph, where article sections are connected to WikiData entities via the `HAS_ENTITY` relationship. The virtual graph of Figure 3 represents the structure (labels and relationships) of the graph database. It should be noted that an entity node might have an additional label (e.g. `Person`, `City`, `Business`) except for the generic `Entity` one, based on the WikiData class taxonomy.

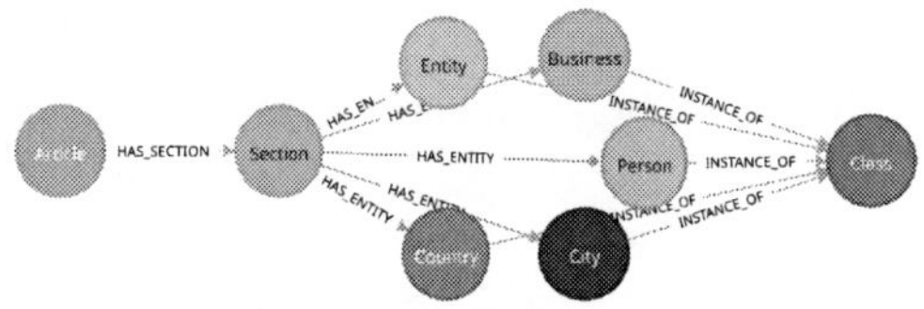

Figure 3: Final structure of the graph database.

3.2.4 Evidence Constructor

In a typical NLI setting, a premise represents our knowledge or evidence regarding an event and is used to infer whether a relevant hypothesis follows from it or not. In our case, article sections focusing on the same entities as the user's claim could potentially lead to the construction of useful evidence towards the validation of this claim. We can therefore leverage the entity-annotated article sections of our graph database to collect relevant evidence by aggregating information from multiple sources. To this end, we developed an evidence construction process that comprises the following steps:

1. The claim provided by the user passes through the Entity Linking phase and one or more entities (WikiData concepts) are identified.

2. The graph database is queried for all possible shortest paths that contain article sections between the identified entities. Given the implemented graph structure and n Entity nodes, this translates to a minimum path length of $2(n-1)$ alternating Entity-Section nodes as shown in Figure 4. Since the existence of such path is not guaranteed, in cases that no path is found the algorithm will select an article section if it contains at least one mentioned entity.

3. The article sections contained in these paths are concatenated to form a set of candidate evidence sequences. Their relevance with the claim at hand is assessed during the Semantic Textual Similarity phase.

3.2.5 Semantic Textual Similarity

We train and apply a sentence embeddings method to extract and compare the vector representations

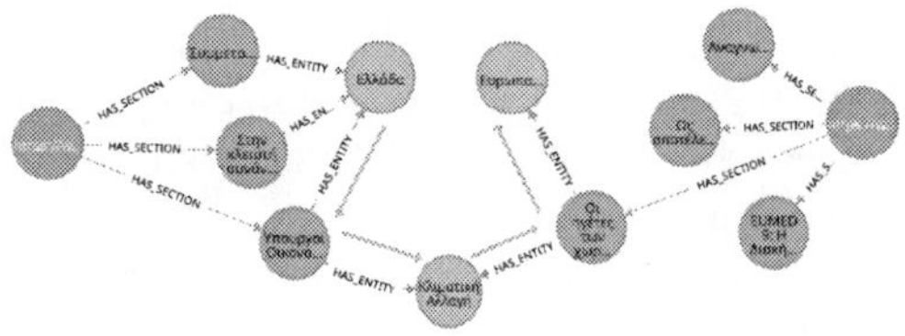

Figure 4: Shortest path example: The 3 entities (in brown) are connected with 2 article sections (in blue).

of the user's claim with each candidate evidence sequence, in order to select the most semantically relevant candidate for the final NLI phase. Despite the abundance of multilingual language models (e.g. m-BERT, XLM) that cover most common languages, pretrained multilingual sentence embeddings models do not generally perform well in downstream tasks for less-resourced languages like Greek (Koutsikakis et al., 2020). Furthermore, given that the vector spaces between languages are not aligned, sentences with the same content in different languages could be mapped to different locations in the common vector space. To overcome this obstacle, we trained a Greek sentence embeddings model on parallel EN-EL (English-Greek) sentence pairs following a multilingual knowledge distillation approach (Reimers and Gurevych, 2020a). Our Greek student model (XLM-RoBERTa) was trained on parallel pairs to produce vectors for the EN-EL sentences that are close to the teacher's pretrained English model ones (DistilRoBERTa). Using the trained model, we are able to compare the produced vector representations between the claim and each concatenated candidate evidence sequence with regard to STS in terms of cosine similarity and forward the best candidate to the last phase of the claim validation process, namely Natural Language Inference.

3.2.6 Natural Language Inference

The last step of our process leverages NLI to determine whether the user claim (hypothesis) is entailed by, contradicted, or neutral to the most relevant evidence (premise) of the previous phase. To tackle the aforementioned multilinguality issues of pretrained language models on less-resourced languages, we finetuned a Greek *sentence-transformers* Cross-Encoder (Reimers and Gurevych, 2019) (*XLM-RoBERTa-base*) model for the NLI task. The model was trained on the Greek and English version of the combined SNLI (Bowman et al., 2015) and MultiNLI (Williams et al., 2018) corpora (AllNLI). We used the English-to-Greek machine translation model by Papadopoulos et al., 2021 to create the Greek version of the AllNLI dataset. The trained model takes the premise-hypothesis pair as input and predicts one of the following labels for each case: "contradiction": c, "entailment": e or "neutral": n. The logits for each class are then converted to probabilities using the softmax function. These labels along with their probability scores can be used to assess whether the claim is verified by the accumulated knowledge of the candidate evidence.

4 Experiments

4.1 Setup

The technical details for each building block of *FarFetched* are provided below:

News Collection and Storage: The *news-please* (Hamborg et al., 2017) Python library was used to ingest an initial corpus of news articles to support our experiments. The root URLs of two popular Greek news sites served as the starting point in order to recursively crawl news from a diverse topic spectrum, spanning from 2018 until 2021. We collected 13,236 articles, containing 31,358 sections in total. A *Neo4j* graph DBMS was used to store the crawled articles and sections as nodes and create their in-between relationships.

Entity Linking: A Python script producing POST requests to the *JSI Wikifier* web API (Brank et al., 2017a) was implemented to annotate the article sections and enrich the graph database with WikiData entities. A total of 2,516 WikiData entities of different types (e.g. sovereign states, cities, humans, organizations, academic institutions etc.) were identified in the crawled articles. A *pageRankSqThreshold* of 0.80 was set for pruning the annotations on the basis of their pagerank score.

Evidence Constructor: We implemented Algorithm 1 as a Python script that executes a parametrizable Cypher query to construct candidate evidence sequences; the identified entities in the claim are used as parameters and the concatenated article sections that link these entities together are returned. For our experiments, the maximum number of relationships between the alternating Sections and Entities was set to $2(n-1)$ (shortest path), while the script returns candidate evidence sequences in descending order based on path length. These parameters can be modified if longer candidate evidence sequences are required.

Semantic Similarity: We finetuned a bilingual (Greek-English) *XLM-RoBERTa-base* model (~270M parameters with 12-layers, 768-hidden-state, 3072 feed-forward hidden-state, 8-heads) using 340MB of parallel (EN-EL) sentences from various sources (e.g. OPUS, Wikimatrix, Tatoeba) leveraging the *sentence-transformers* library (Reimers and Gurevych, 2020b). The model was trained for 4 epochs with a batch size of 16 on a machine with a single NVIDIA GeForce RTX3080 (10GB of VRAM) for a total of 28 GPU-hours (single run).

Natural Language Inference: We finetuned a Cross-Encoder *XLM-RoBERTa-base* model of the same architecture on the created Greek-English AllNLI dataset (100MB) using *sentence-transformers*. The model was trained on the same hardware setting for a single epoch, using a train batch size of 6 for 22 GPU-hours (single run).

4.2 Main results

In this section we perform a quantitative and qualitative demonstration of *FarFetched*'s overall performance and also provide individual results for our STS and NLI models based on benchmark datasets.

4.2.1 End-to-end performance

Given the particularity of *FarFetched* in evidence collection (data originating from constantly updating web content), a quantitative evaluation of its performance is quite challenging. To combat the lack of relevant benchmarks for the Greek language, we leveraged the FEVER dataset by Thorne et al. 2018, which models the assessment of truthfulness of written claims as a joint information retrieval and natural language inference task using evidence from Wikipedia. Each row of the dataset comprises a claim in free text, a list of evidence information including a URL to the Wikipedia page of the corresponding evidence and an annotated label (SUPPORTS, REFUTES, NOT ENOUGH INFO). We manually translated a subset of 150 claims from the FEVER validation set from English to Greek and populated the graph database with the content of the corresponding Wikipedia URLs, which was automatically translated into Greek (due to its size), using the NMT model by Papadopoulos et al., 2021. We report *FarFetched*'s performance in terms of accuracy, precision, recall and F1-score on Table 1.

The results indicate a balanced precision and recall for the REFUTES and SUPPORTS classes,

Label	Precision	Recall	F1-score
NOT ENOUGH INFO	.36	.80	.49
REFUTES	.91	.72	.80
SUPPORTS	.84	.70	.76
Weighted Average	**.82**	**.73**	**.75**
Label accuracy (overall)		.73	

Table 1: *FarFetched* claim validation performance on Greek FEVER subset.

while precision is relatively lower for the NOT ENOUGH INFO case. This can be partially attributed to the challenges of applying wikification on the automatically translated evidence content, leading to some claims not being linked to their corresponding evidence. Although the above results are not directly comparable to those of similar systems tested on the original English FEVER dataset, they show a significant gain over the baseline model of Thorne et al. 2018 (label accuracy of 0.49). Based on a large comparative study conducted by Bekoulis et al. 2021, *FarFetched* scores in the upper 30th percentile in terms of accuracy (scores ranging from 0.45 to 0.84); however, to the best of our knowledge none of these systems covers the Greek language.

We also provide a set of qualitative examples based on real data that aim at showcasing the capabilities of our system while also acknowledging the dynamicity of the evidence collection process. These scenarios are translated into English to facilitate readability. They include two parts each and are shown in Tables 2, 3 and 4. The original examples (in Greek) are available in the Appendix.

In *Scenario 1*, two contradicting user claims (1a, 1b) with the same entity mentions are provided by the user (Table 2). Since they refer to the same entities, the Evidence Constructor returns the same candidate evidence sequences for both claims in order to evaluate their validity. The most relevant one (STS score in bold) is selected for the NLI phase, where the verdict is that the evidence entails the first claim (1a) and contradicts the second (1b).

In *Scenario 2*, we investigate the sensitivity of our approach in exploiting new information to evaluate a claim (Table 3). The claim initially triggers the Evidence Constructor which returns multiple candidate evidence sequences, in descending STS order (yellow rows). During the NLI evaluation phase, the verdict is entailment, but with a low probability of 0.571 (2a). The same hypothesis is evaluated in Scenario 2b, after the addition of new information appended to the evidence list (blue

User Claim (Scenario 1)	NLI score
Denmark and Austria believe that the European Union should increase aid to refugees. **(1a)**	c: 0.014 **e: 0.958** n: 0.028
Denmark disagrees with Austria on the management of immigration issues in the European Union. **(1b)**	**c: 0.951** e: 0.002 n: 0.047
Candidate Evidence Sequences (↓ similarity)	
Austria and Denmark also want to increase EU support for countries hosting refugees near crisis hotspots so that they do not travel to Europe. • **STS Score: 0.8505**	
Checked by police at the Airport Police Departments ... the foreigners presented forged travel documents ... in order to leave the country for other EU countries like France, Germany, Italy, Austria, the Netherlands, Denmark, Spain and Norway. • STS Score: 0.2283	

Table 2: Demonstration of FarFetched on *Scenario 1*.

row). The new evidence is clearly more relevant to the claim at hand, which is successfully identified by *FarFetched*'s STS component that selects it as the best candidate, providing a more confident entailment score of 0.891 (2b). This shift in NLI verdict is visualized in Figure 5. Since *FarFetched* relies on the constantly updating evidence, monitoring such shifts could be useful for identifying trend changes, especially for cases that benefit from long-term planning (business, market, politics etc.)

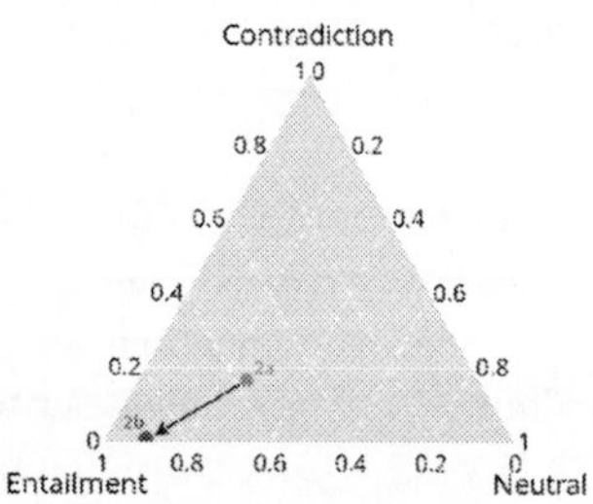

Figure 5: Shift in NLI verdict from Scenario 2a to Scenario 2b of Table 3.

Scenario 3 is similar to 2, as one claim is evaluated on an initial set of candidate evidence sequences (3a) followed by a new relevant article section with contradicting evidence collected by the Evidence Collector in 3b (Table 4). However, in this case the new evidence is an excerpt from a person's interview. While our approach correctly identifies the relevance of this new evidence to the claim thus affecting the NLI verdict, it does not distinguish between opinions and factual evidence. This is discussed in more detail in Section 5.

User Claim (Scenario 2)	NLI score initial (2a)	NLI score updated (2b)
The United States plans to impose sanctions on Iran.	c: 0.170 **e: 0.571** n: 0.259	c: 0.012 **e: 0.891** n: 0.097
Candidate Evidence Sequences (↓ similarity)		
Iran faces dilemma over whether to comply of Washington or will lead to collapse. The sanctions that came back in force today, will force the government of the Islamic Republic to accept the US claims regarding the Iranian nuclear program and Iranian activities in the Middle East East because, otherwise, the regime will be in danger to collapse, claimed Israel Kats, the Israeli minister responsible for Information Services. • **STS Score: 0.6665**		
Why Greece was exempted from US sanctions on Iran. New US sanctions on oil exports from Iran have been in force since November 5. • STS Score: 0.6324		
"We are always in favor of diplomacy and talks ... But the Conversations need honesty ... The US is pushing again sanctions on Iran and withdraw from the nuclear deal "(of 2015) and then they want to have conversations with us", Rohani said in a speech that was broadcast live on television. • STS Score: 0.5151		
NEW: Following the collapse of the last talks between the US and Iran, the announcement of additional sanctions is expected in the coming days. • **STS Score: 0.7195**		

Table 3: Demonstration of FarFetched on *Scenario 2*.

User Claim (Scenario 3)	NLI score initial (3a)	NLI score updated (3b)
Apple is trying to compete with Netflix in the production of television content.	c: 0.004 **e: 0.967** n: 0.029	**c: 0.982** e: 0.008 n: 0.010
Candidate Evidence Sequences (↓ similarity)		
Apple is expected to spend about $ 2 billion this year creating original content that it hopes will compete with Netflix, Hulu and Amazon, already established in the television audience. • **STS Score: 0.7107**		
NEW: "We're not trying to compete with Netflix on TV," an Apple spokesman said in an interview. • **STS Score: 0.7134**		

Table 4: Demonstration of FarFetched on *Scenario 3*.

4.2.2 STS performance

The performance of our semantic similarity model was evaluated on the test subset of the STS2017 benchmark dataset (Cer et al., 2017). Given that the original dataset does not provide sentence pairs in Greek, we manually created a cross-lingual version for the English-Greek pair. The performance is measured using Pearson (r) and Spearman (ρ) correlation between the predicted and gold similarity scores (Table 5). We also provide results regarding translation matching accuracy, evaluating the source and target language embeddings in terms of cosine similarity. Our model achieves a slightly better performance in both evaluations compared to the current state-of-the-art multilingual model by Reimers and Gurevych, 2019.

Model	STS2017		Translation Matching	
	r	ρ	**Acc. (en2el)**	**Acc. (el2en)**
STS-XLM-RoBERTa-base (Ours)	**83.30**	**84.32**	**98.05**	**97.80**
Paraphrase-multilingual-mpnet-base-v2 (UKP-TUDA)	82.71	82.70	97.50	97.35

Table 5: STS model comparison on EN-EL version of STS2017 and in terms of translation matching accuracy.

4.2.3 NLI performance

We benchmark our trained NLI model on the Greek subset of the XNLI dataset (Conneau et al., 2018) that contains 5,010 premise-hypothesis pairs (Table 6). Despite not having used the XNLI dataset during the training phase, we achieve a 1% gain over the multilingual XLM-R (Conneau et al., 2020) and are on par with the monolingual Greek-BERT by Koutsikakis et al., 2020. Since our model was trained on a mixture of Greek and English sentence pairs, it is more suitable for corpora that also contain English terms (e.g. technology, science topics) without suffering from the under-representability of the Greek language occurring in multilingual models.

Model	F1-score
NLI-XLM-RoBERTa-base (Ours)	**78.3**
Greek-BERT (AUEB)	78.6 ± 0.62
XLM-RoBERTa-base (Facebook)	77.3 ± 0.41
M-BERT (Google AI Language)	73.5 ± 0.49

Table 6: NLI model comparison in terms of F1-score on the Greek subset of XNLI-test dataset.

5 Limitations

We acknowledge that *FarFetched* is possible to encounter errors in 3 main areas; these limitations are briefly addressed below.

Entity Linking: Highly ambiguous entities and name variations pose challenges to any entity linking method. Since we claim that our approach is entity-centric, a wrong entity annotation may lead to irrelevant candidate evidence sequences and increase the probability of "neutral" NLI verdicts. Moreover, the tunable sensitivity of the integrated wikification module implies a trade-off between a precision-oriented and a recall-oriented strategy, the latter resulting in more annotated articles, but also being prone to false-positive annotations.

Evidence Construction: This initial version of our approach relies solely on the STS comparison between the evidence and the claim, based on a shortest path approach as discussed in Section 3.2.4. In cases that involve a larger number of entities in the user claim, calculating the shortest path between the alternating Entity-Section nodes can be computationally cumbersome. Moreover, there is no guarantee that the shortest path is able to capture the most relevant candidate evidence sequences; to this end, outputting the top n best candidates is considered, providing a user with an overview of the extracted news excerpts together with their NLI outcome. Finally, neither a temporal evaluation of the evidence with regard to the claim nor a distinction between opinions and facts is considered; all candidates are treated as equal.

Natural Language Inference: Recognizing the entailment between a pair of sentences partially depends on the tense and aspect of the predications. Tense plays an important role in determining the temporal location of the predication (i.e. past, present or future), while the aspectual auxiliaries signify an event's internal constituency (e.g. whether an action is completed or in progress). While the work of Kober et al., 2019 indicates that language models substantially encode morphosyntactic information regarding tense and aspect, they are unable to reason based only on these properties. To this end, claims with a high presence of such semantic properties should be avoided.

6 Conclusions

In this work, we presented a novel approach for claim validation and reasoning based on the accumulated knowledge from the continuous ingestion and processing of news articles. *FarFetched* is able to evaluate the validity of any arbitrary textual claim by automatically retrieving and aggregating evidence from multiple sources, relying on the pillars of entity linking, semantic textual similarity and natural language inference.

We showcased the effectiveness of our method on the FEVER benchmark as well as on diverse scenarios and acknowledged its limitations. As byproducts of our work, we trained and open-sourced an NLI and an STS model for the less-resourced Greek language, achieving state-of-the-art performance on the XNLI and STS2017 benchmarks respectively. While our framework fills the gap in automated claim validation for Greek, its modular architecture allows it to be repurposed for any language for which the corresponding models exist.

For future work, we intend to address the limitations of our method mentioned in Section 5, focusing primarily on an optimal entity linking setting, as well as on a more robust strategy for constructing relevant candidate evidence sequences.

Acknowledgments

The research work of Dimitris Papadopoulos was supported by the Hellenic Foundation for Research and Innovation (HFRI) under the HFRI PhD Fellowship grant (Fellowship Number: 50, 2nd call).

References

Giannis Bekoulis, Christina Papagiannopoulou, and Nikos Deligiannis. 2021. A review on fact extraction and verification. *ACM Comput. Surv.*, 55(1).

Iz Beltagy, Matthew E. Peters, and Arman Cohan. 2020. Longformer: The long-document transformer. *CoRR*, abs/2004.05150.

Samuel R. Bowman, Gabor Angeli, Christopher Potts, and Christopher D. Manning. 2015. A large annotated corpus for learning natural language inference. In *Proceedings of the 2015 Conference on Empirical Methods in Natural Language Processing*, pages 632–642, Lisbon, Portugal. Association for Computational Linguistics.

Janez Brank, Gregor Leban, and Marko Grobelnik. 2017a. Annotating documents with relevant wikipedia concepts. *Proceedings of SiKDD.*

Janez Brank, Gregor Leban, and Marko Grobelnik. 2017b. Annotating documents with relevant wikipedia concepts. In *Proceedings of the Slovenian Conference on Data Mining and Data Warehouses (SiKDD 2017)*, pages 218–223.

Daniel Cer, Mona Diab, Eneko Agirre, Iñigo Lopez-Gazpio, and Lucia Specia. 2017. SemEval-2017 task 1: Semantic textual similarity multilingual and crosslingual focused evaluation. In *Proceedings of the 11th International Workshop on Semantic Evaluation (SemEval-2017)*, pages 1–14, Vancouver, Canada. Association for Computational Linguistics.

Daniel Cer, Yinfei Yang, Sheng-yi Kong, Nan Hua, Nicole Limtiaco, Rhomni St. John, Noah Constant, Mario Guajardo-Cespedes, Steve Yuan, Chris Tar, Brian Strope, and Ray Kurzweil. 2018. Universal sentence encoder for English. In *Proceedings of the 2018 Conference on Empirical Methods in Natural Language Processing: System Demonstrations*, pages 169–174, Brussels, Belgium. Association for Computational Linguistics.

Giovanni Luca Ciampaglia, Prashant Shiralkar, Luis M Rocha, Johan Bollen, Filippo Menczer, and Alessandro Flammini. 2015. Computational fact checking from knowledge networks. *PloS one*, 10(6):e0128193.

Alexis Conneau, Kartikay Khandelwal, Naman Goyal, Vishrav Chaudhary, Guillaume Wenzek, Francisco Guzmán, Edouard Grave, Myle Ott, Luke Zettlemoyer, and Veselin Stoyanov. 2020. Unsupervised cross-lingual representation learning at scale. In *Proceedings of the 58th Annual Meeting of the Association for Computational Linguistics*, pages 8440–8451, Online. Association for Computational Linguistics.

Alexis Conneau, Ruty Rinott, Guillaume Lample, Adina Williams, Samuel Bowman, Holger Schwenk, and Veselin Stoyanov. 2018. XNLI: Evaluating cross-lingual sentence representations. In *Proceedings of the 2018 Conference on Empirical Methods in Natural Language Processing*, pages 2475–2485, Brussels, Belgium. Association for Computational Linguistics.

Antonin Delpeuch. 2019. Opentapioca: Lightweight entity linking for wikidata. *arXiv preprint arXiv:1904.09131.*

William Ferreira and Andreas Vlachos. 2016. Emergent: a novel data-set for stance classification. In *Proceedings of the 2016 Conference of the North American Chapter of the Association for Computational Linguistics: Human Language Technologies*, pages 1163–1168, San Diego, California. Association for Computational Linguistics.

François Goasdoué, Konstantinos Karanasos, Yannis Katsis, Julien Leblay, Ioana Manolescu, and Stamatis Zampetakis. 2013. Fact checking and analyzing the web. In *Proceedings of the 2013 ACM SIGMOD International Conference on Management of Data*, SIGMOD '13, page 997–1000, New York, NY, USA. Association for Computing Machinery.

Felix Hamborg, Norman Meuschke, Corinna Breitinger, and Bela Gipp. 2017. news-please: A generic news crawler and extractor. In *Proceedings of the 15th International Symposium of Information Science*, pages 218–223.

Woojeong Jin, Rahul Khanna, Suji Kim, Dong-Ho Lee, Fred Morstatter, Aram Galstyan, and Xiang Ren. 2021. ForecastQA: A question answering challenge for event forecasting with temporal text data. In *Proceedings of the 59th Annual Meeting of the Association for Computational Linguistics and the 11th International Joint Conference on Natural Language Processing (Volume 1: Long Papers)*, pages 4636–4650, Online. Association for Computational Linguistics.

Thomas Kober, Sander Bijl de Vroe, and Mark Steedman. 2019. Temporal and aspectual entailment. In *Proceedings of the 13th International Conference on Computational Semantics - Long Papers*, pages 103–119, Gothenburg, Sweden. Association for Computational Linguistics.

Nikolaos Kolitsas, Octavian-Eugen Ganea, and Thomas Hofmann. 2018. End-to-end neural entity linking. In *Proceedings of the 22nd Conference on Computational Natural Language Learning*, pages 519–529, Brussels, Belgium. Association for Computational Linguistics.

John Koutsikakis, Ilias Chalkidis, Prodromos Malakasiotis, and Ion Androutsopoulos. 2020. Greek-bert: The greeks visiting sesame street. In *11th Hellenic Conference on Artificial Intelligence*, SETN 2020, page 110–117, New York, NY, USA. Association for Computing Machinery.

Mike Lewis, Yinhan Liu, Naman Goyal, Marjan Ghazvininejad, Abdelrahman Mohamed, Omer Levy, Veselin Stoyanov, and Luke Zettlemoyer. 2020. BART: Denoising sequence-to-sequence pre-training for natural language generation, translation, and comprehension. In *Proceedings of the 58th Annual Meeting of the Association for Computational Linguistics*, pages 7871–7880, Online. Association for Computational Linguistics.

Sarthak Majithia, Fatma Arslan, Sumeet Lubal, Damian Jimenez, Priyank Arora, Josue Caraballo, and Chengkai Li. 2019. ClaimPortal: Integrated monitoring, searching, checking, and analytics of factual claims on Twitter. In *Proceedings of the 57th Annual Meeting of the Association for Computational Linguistics: System Demonstrations*, pages 153–158, Florence, Italy. Association for Computational Linguistics.

Julian Michael, Gabriel Stanovsky, Luheng He, Ido Dagan, and Luke Zettlemoyer. 2018. Crowdsourcing question-answer meaning representations. In *Proceedings of the 2018 Conference of the North American Chapter of the Association for Computational Linguistics: Human Language Technologies, Volume 2 (Short Papers)*, pages 560–568, New Orleans, Louisiana. Association for Computational Linguistics.

Dimitris Papadopoulos, Nikolaos Papadakis, and Nikolaos Matsatsinis. 2021. PENELOPIE: Enabling open information extraction for the Greek language through machine translation. In *Proceedings of the 16th Conference of the European Chapter of the Association for Computational Linguistics: Student Research Workshop*, pages 23–29, Online. Association for Computational Linguistics.

Kashyap Popat, Subhabrata Mukherjee, Andrew Yates, and Gerhard Weikum. 2018. DeClarE: Debunking fake news and false claims using evidence-aware deep learning. In *Proceedings of the 2018 Conference on Empirical Methods in Natural Language Processing*, pages 22–32, Brussels, Belgium. Association for Computational Linguistics.

Kira Radinsky, Sagie Davidovich, and Shaul Markovitch. 2012. Learning to predict from textual data. *Journal of Artificial Intelligence Research*, 45:641–684.

Colin Raffel, Noam Shazeer, Adam Roberts, Katherine Lee, Sharan Narang, Michael Matena, Yanqi Zhou, Wei Li, and Peter J. Liu. 2020. Exploring the limits of transfer learning with a unified text-to-text transformer. *Journal of Machine Learning Research*, 21(140):1–67.

Nils Reimers and Iryna Gurevych. 2019. Sentence-BERT: Sentence embeddings using Siamese BERT-networks. In *Proceedings of the 2019 Conference on Empirical Methods in Natural Language Processing and the 9th International Joint Conference on Natural Language Processing (EMNLP-IJCNLP)*, pages 3982–3992, Hong Kong, China. Association for Computational Linguistics.

Nils Reimers and Iryna Gurevych. 2020a. Making monolingual sentence embeddings multilingual using knowledge distillation. In *Proceedings of the 2020 Conference on Empirical Methods in Natural Language Processing (EMNLP)*, pages 4512–4525, Online. Association for Computational Linguistics.

Nils Reimers and Iryna Gurevych. 2020b. Making monolingual sentence embeddings multilingual using knowledge distillation. In *Proceedings of the 2020 Conference on Empirical Methods in Natural Language Processing*. Association for Computational Linguistics.

Mehdi Samadi, Partha Talukdar, Manuela Veloso, and Manuel Blum. 2016. Claimeval: Integrated and flexible framework for claim evaluation using credibility of sources. *Proceedings of the AAAI Conference on Artificial Intelligence*, 30(1).

Jizhi Tang, Yansong Feng, and Dongyan Zhao. 2019. Learning to update knowledge graphs by reading news. In *Proceedings of the 2019 Conference on Empirical Methods in Natural Language Processing and the 9th International Joint Conference on Natural Language Processing (EMNLP-IJCNLP)*, pages 2632–2641, Hong Kong, China. Association for Computational Linguistics.

James Thorne, Andreas Vlachos, Christos Christodoulopoulos, and Arpit Mittal. 2018. FEVER: a large-scale dataset for fact extraction and VERification. In *Proceedings of the 2018 Conference of the North American Chapter of the Association for Computational Linguistics: Human Language Technologies, Volume 1 (Long Papers)*, pages 809–819, New Orleans, Louisiana. Association for Computational Linguistics.

Andreas Vlachos and Sebastian Riedel. 2014. Fact checking: Task definition and dataset construction.

In *Proceedings of the ACL 2014 Workshop on Language Technologies and Computational Social Science*, pages 18–22, Baltimore, MD, USA. Association for Computational Linguistics.

Piek Vossen, Rodrigo Agerri, Itziar Aldabe, Agata Cybulska, Marieke van Erp, Antske Fokkens, Egoitz Laparra, Anne-Lyse Minard, Alessio Palmero Aprosio, German Rigau, et al. 2016. Newsreader: Using knowledge resources in a cross-lingual reading machine to generate more knowledge from massive streams of news. *Knowledge-Based Systems*, 110:60–85.

Piek Vossen, Tommaso Caselli, and Yiota Kontzopoulou. 2015. Storylines for structuring massive streams of news. In *Proceedings of the First Workshop on Computing News Storylines*, pages 40–49, Beijing, China. Association for Computational Linguistics.

Jim Webber. 2012. A programmatic introduction to neo4j. In *Proceedings of the 3rd Annual Conference on Systems, Programming, and Applications: Software for Humanity*, SPLASH '12, page 217–218, New York, NY, USA. Association for Computing Machinery.

Adina Williams, Nikita Nangia, and Samuel Bowman. 2018. A broad-coverage challenge corpus for sentence understanding through inference. In *Proceedings of the 2018 Conference of the North American Chapter of the Association for Computational Linguistics: Human Language Technologies, Volume 1 (Long Papers)*, pages 1112–1122, New Orleans, Louisiana. Association for Computational Linguistics.

Zhilin Yang, Zihang Dai, Yiming Yang, Jaime Carbonell, Russ R Salakhutdinov, and Quoc V Le. 2019. Xlnet: Generalized autoregressive pretraining for language understanding. In *Advances in Neural Information Processing Systems*, volume 32. Curran Associates, Inc.

Qi Zeng, Manling Li, Tuan Lai, Heng Ji, Mohit Bansal, and Hanghang Tong. 2021. GENE: Global event network embedding. In *Proceedings of the Fifteenth Workshop on Graph-Based Methods for Natural Language Processing (TextGraphs-15)*, pages 42–53, Mexico City, Mexico. Association for Computational Linguistics.

Zijian Zhang, Koustav Rudra, and Avishek Anand. 2021. *FaxPlainAC: A Fact-Checking Tool Based on EXPLAINable Models with HumAn Correction in the Loop*, page 4823–4827. Association for Computing Machinery, New York, NY, USA.

Jie Zhou, Xu Han, Cheng Yang, Zhiyuan Liu, Lifeng Wang, Changcheng Li, and Maosong Sun. 2019. GEAR: Graph-based evidence aggregating and reasoning for fact verification. In *Proceedings of the 57th Annual Meeting of the Association for Computational Linguistics*, pages 892–901, Florence, Italy. Association for Computational Linguistics.

A Appendix: Original examples (in Greek) of Tables 2, 3 and 4.

User Claim (Scenario 1)	**NLI score**
Η Δανία και η Αυστρία πιστεύουν ότι η Ευρωπαϊκή Ένωση πρέπει να αυξήσει τη βοήθεια προς τους πρόσφυγες. **(1a)**	c: 0.014 **e: 0.958** n: 0.028
Η Δανία διαφωνεί με την Αυστρία σχετικά με τη διαχείριση των μεταναστευτικών θεμάτων στην Ευρωπαϊκή Ένωση. **(1b)**	**c: 0.951** e: 0.002 n: 0.047
Candidate Evidence Sequences (↓ similarity)	
Η Αυστρία και η Δανία θέλουν να ενισχυθεί επίσης η υποστήριξη της ΕΕ προς κράτη που υποδέχονται πρόσφυγες κοντά σε εστίες κρίσεις, ώστε οι πρόσφυγες αυτοί να μην ταξιδεύουν προς την Ευρώπη. • **STS Score: 0.8505**	
Σε έλεγχο από αστυνομικούς των Αστυνομικών Τμημάτων Αερολιμένων ... οι αλλοδαποί επέδειξαν πλαστά ταξιδιωτικά έγγραφα προκειμένου να αναχωρήσουν από τη χώρα για άλλες χώρες της ΕΕ όπως η Γαλλία, Γερμανία, Ιταλία, Αυστρία, Ολλανδία, Δανία, Ισπανία και Νορβηγία. • STS Score: 0.2283	

Table 7: Demonstration of FarFetched on *Scenario 1* in Greek language.

User Claim (Scenario 2)	**NLI score** initial (2a)	**NLI score** updated (2b)
Οι Ηνωμένες Πολιτείες σχεδιάζουν να επιβάλλουν κυρώσεις στο Ιράν.	c: 0.170 **e: 0.571** n: 0.259	c: 0.012 **e: 0.891** n: 0.097
Candidate Evidence Sequences (↓ similarity)		
Το Ιράν μπροστά στο δίλημμα αν θα συμμορφωθεί προς τις υποδείξεις της Ουάσινγκτον ή θα οδηγηθεί σε κατάρρευση Οι κυρώσεις που επανήλθαν σε ισχύ σήμερα, θα αναγκάσουν την κυβέρνηση της Ισλαμικής Δημοκρατίας να δεχθεί τις αξιώσεις των ΗΠΑ όσον αφορά το ιρανικό πυρηνικό πρόγραμμα και τις ιρανικές δραστηριότητες στην περιοχή της Μέσης Ανατολής διότι, σε διαφορετική περίπτωση, το καθεστώς θα κινδυνεύσει να καταρρεύσει, υποστήριξε ο Ισραέλ Κατς, ο ισραηλινός υπουργός αρμόδιος για τις Υπηρεσίες Πληροφοριών. • **STS Score: 0.6665**		
Γιατί εξαιρέθηκε η Ελλάδα από τις αμερικανικές κυρώσεις στο Ιράν. Από τις 5 Νοεμβρίου βρίσκονται σε ισχύ οι νέες κυρώσεις των ΗΠΑ για εξαγωγές πετρελαίου από το Ιράν. • STS Score: 0.6324		
«Είμαστε πάντα υπέρ της διπλωματίας και των συνομιλιών ... Όμως οι συνομιλίες χρειάζονται εντιμότητα ... Οι ΗΠΑ επιβάλλουν εκ νέου κυρώσεις στο Ιράν και αποσύρονται από την πυρηνική συμφωνία (του 2015) και μετά θέλουν να κάνουν συνομιλίες μαζί μας», δήλωσε ο Ροχανί σε ομιλία του που μεταδόθηκε ζωντανά από την τηλεόραση. • STS Score: 0.5151		
Μετά το ναυάγιο των τελευταίων συνομιλιών μεταξύ ΗΠΑ και Ιράν αναμένεται η ανακοίνωση επιπλέον κυρώσεων τις επόμενες ημέρες. • **STS Score: 0.7195**		

Table 8: Demonstration of FarFetched on *Scenario 2* in Greek language.

User Claim (Scenario 3)	**NLI score** initial (3a)	**NLI score** updated (3b)
Η Apple προσπαθεί να ανταγωνιστεί την Netflix στην παραγωγή τηλεοπτικού περιεχομένου.	c: 0.004 **e: 0.967** n: 0.029	**c: 0.982** e: 0.008 n: 0.010
Candidate Evidence Sequences (↓ similarity)		
Η Apple αναμένεται να δαπανήσει φέτος περίπου 2 δισεκατομμύρια δολάρια με σκοπό τη δημιουργία πρωτότυπου περιεχομένου που ελπίζει ότι θα ανταγωνιστεί τις ήδη εδραιωμένες στο τηλεοπτικό κοινό υπηρεσίες των Netflix, Hulu και Amazon. • **STS Score: 0.7107**		
«Δεν προσπαθούμε να ανταγωνιστούμε το Netflix στην τηλεόραση», δήλωσε εκπρόσωπος της Apple σε συνέντευξή του. • **STS Score: 0.7134**		

Table 9: Demonstration of FarFetched on *Scenario 3* in Greek language.

Alternative non-BERT model choices for the textual classification in low-resource languages and environments

Syed Mustavi Maheen, Moshiur Rahman Faisal, Rafakat Rahman, Md. Shahriar Karim
Department of Electrical and Computer Engineering
North South University, Dhaka, Bangladesh
{mustavi.maheen, moshiur.faisal, rafakat.rahman}@northsouth.edu
shahriar.karim@northsouth.edu

Abstract

Natural Language Processing (NLP) tasks in non-dominant and low-resource languages have not experienced significant progress. Although pre-trained BERT models are available, GPU-dependency, large memory requirement, and data scarcity often limit their applicability. As a solution, this paper proposes a fusion chain architecture comprised of one or more layers of CNN, LSTM, and BiLSTM and identifies precise configuration and chain length. The study shows that a simpler, CPU-trainable non-BERT fusion CNN + BiLSTM + CNN is sufficient to surpass the textual classification performance of the BERT-related models in resource-limited languages and environments. The fusion architecture competitively approaches the state-of-the-art accuracy in several Bengali NLP tasks and a six-class emotion detection task for a newly developed Bengali dataset. Interestingly, the performance of the identified fusion model, for instance, CNN + BiLSTM + CNN, also holds for other low-resource languages and environments. Efficacy study shows that the CNN + BiLSTM + CNN model outperforms BERT implementation for Vietnamese languages and performs almost equally in English NLP tasks experiencing artificial data scarcity. For the GLUE benchmark and other datasets such as Emotion, IMDB, and Intent classification, the CNN + BiLSTM + CNN model often surpasses or competes with BERT-base, TinyBERT, DistilBERT, and mBERT. Besides, a position-sensitive self-attention layer role further improves the fusion models' performance in the Bengali emotion classification. The models are also compressible to as low as $\approx 5\times$ smaller through pruning and retraining, making them more viable for resource-constrained environments. Together, this study may help NLP practitioners and serve as a blueprint for NLP model choices in textual classification for low-resource languages and environments.

1 Introduction

Many developed nations are now considering deep learning approaches for tackling textual toxicity in social media. But countries lacking substantial socio-economic capacity and technological infrastructures are lagging. The current trend of NLP research evolves mainly around a few dominant languages, leaving NLP research for many low-resource languages unattended or less explored (Joshi et al., 2020). The NLP tasks in low-resource languages generally suffer from exceptionally scarce resources, ranging from lack of annotated data to insufficient computational facilities. In contrast, most NLP breakthroughs that achieve high accuracy are computationally intensive, making it more challenging for societies suffering from inadequate technological infrastructures. For instance, while the bidirectional transformer BERT has about 340 millions parameters (Devlin et al., 2018), a more advanced model GPT-3 (Brown et al., 2020), has about 170 billions parameters, requiring extensive GPU/TPU support and memory storage that may be unaffordable for low-resource societies. As a result, low-resource languages and environments are frequently left out with little attention from the NLP community (Joshi et al., 2020).

Further complicating matters, the serverless free deployment of deep learning models, as commonly done using Amazon Web Services (AWS) and Google Cloud Platform (GCP), is restrictive for larger model size (Han et al., 2015a,b). Also, latency increases with increasing memory requirement and model size, suggesting memory-intensive device GPU/TPU for faster inference and response. These additional financial costs limit access to BERT models for NLP community works in resource-constrained environments (Strubell et al., 2019). One intriguing question thus arises: could computationally less-expensive non-BERT models reduce GP/TPU dependency and associated fi-

Proceedings of the Third Workshop on Deep Learning for Low-Resource Natural Language Processing, pages 192 - 202
July 14, 2022

nancial cost without affecting the classification accuracy for textual classification in a low-resource context?

The multilingual-BERT (mBERT) (Devlin et al., 2018; Pires et al., 2019) and its reduced versions (Abdaoui et al., 2020), other compressed BERT modifications, such as TinyBERT (Jiao et al., 2019), MobileBERT (Sun et al., 2020), are a few viable models proposed for many languages and contexts, including the low-resource ones. Nevertheless, these models require additional fine-tuning and training for target-specific NLP tasks, requiring GPU/TPU support even in a resource-constrained context. Also, size of these models may not be optimal for deployment in low-end devices. So, textual classification in many non-dominant languages remains rudimentary, leaving the communities unequipped against the increasing toxicity and abusive comments on social platforms. Besides, many textual classification tasks do not require a rigorous use of linguistic semantics. So, models that are structured well against the semantics, for instance, the BERT models, may not always be the most optimal choice in NLP tasks less dependent on language semantics. Thus, a viable trade-off between the deployability, scarce resources, and DNN models' accuracy in NLP tasks for low-resource languages and environments needs unraveling.

As a solution, this study integrates local and global dependencies in sentences by bringing alternative DNN models into a hybrid model structure, namely the fusion chain models. Subsequently, a rigorous architecture search identifies deployable DNN models for low-resource languages, with an improved understanding on a few intriguing questions such as:

- How effective are the homogeneous (of similar layers) and heterogeneous (of different layers) form of fusion of one or more DNN layers in textual classification tasks?
- What chain length is optimal to maintain accuracy and reduce the difference between training and validation loss?
- How helpful the self-attention is for fusion models, and what is its optimal position?

We identify that classification accuracy is sensitive to fusion chain length, beyond which classification accuracy deteriorates considerably. Subsequent exploration of the identified fusion models reveals a position-sensitive performance of the self-attention layer for the newly annotated six-class Bengali emotion dataset.

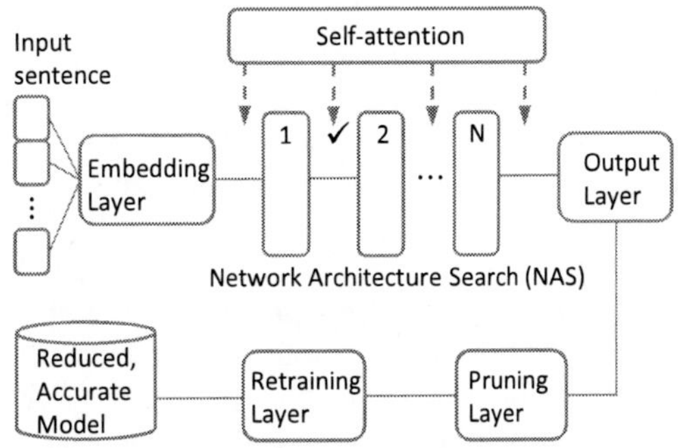

Figure 1: The word embedding layer acts as the input for the fusion of DNN layers during the NAS process. In the NAS, CNN, LSTM or BiLSTM layer are all considered as the initial layer, however the subsequent layers depended on the type of initial layer chosen finally resulting the three alternative chain-structures. The output from the DNN fusion requires pruning and retraining to generate the deployable models.

2 Related Works

Previous works attempted alternative deep learning models in NLP tasks for low-resource languages and environments. For instance, using a teacher-student framework, the BERT distillation with simpler models such as CBoW + FFN and BiLSTM as the student models for the limited availability of labeled data (Wasserblat et al., 2020). While such models are more deployable in low-end devices, the training still relies on a memory-hungry and costly setup requiring GPU/TPU as well as large unlabelled data for student model training. Alternative approaches consider freezing the BERT-layer outcomes by assessing their roles in the classification process (Grießhaber et al., 2020), requiring GPU/TPU support to train. Also, the sequence of frozen layers may vary across alternative datasets, and hence, the accuracy for a particular set of frozen layers becomes context-dependent. Instead, we investigate if a simple, CPU-trainable CNN and RNN fusion layer stack can achieve textual classification accuracy in NLP tasks where syntactical knowledge is less influential than the keywords or sentiment-based phrases. To find out such alternative non-BERT models, we propose fusion-chain architecture comprising one or more CNN and RNN layers and perform a rigorous network architecture search (NAS). Interestingly, the NAS process identifies a few optimal candidate models capable of achieving accuracy comparable to the baseline models, as elaborated further in the subsequent sections.

The emergence of more advanced deep neural networks capable of learning the word orders and information dependency in sentences replaces the classical machine learning models (Mikolov et al., 2013) in many NLP tasks. Precisely, the neural network models of the form of RNN (LSTM, BiLSTM) or CNN independently, or in combination with a pre-trained word embedding facility such as word2vec (Mikolov et al., 2013), fasttext (Joulin et al., 2016), have become the standard alternatives. For instance, Dynamic CNN architecture (DCNN) performs semantic modeling to identify words' short and long-range relations in sentences (Kalchbrenner et al., 2014). Whereas the CNN-based models are good at local and position-invariant feature extraction, the LSTM/BiLSTM models explicitly treat sentences as a sequence of words and capture sentence-level (for instance, syntactical (Zhu et al., 2015)) dependencies. Also, a few alternative attempts integrate local and global textual dependencies using CNN and RNN architectures (known as hybrid models) to improve accuracy of textual classification reviewed thoroughly in (Minaee et al., 2021).

Intriguingly, the hybrid models also appear promising for target-specific sequential analysis, as evident from quantifying the function of specific DNA sequences (Quang and Xie, 2016). Named Entity Recognition (NER) tasks also employ a hybrid approach by merging BiLSTM and CNN models (Chiu and Nichols, 2016). One of the initial works leveraging the advantages of both CNN and RNN architectures for textual classification is the Convolutional-LSTM (C-LSTM). Precisely, in C-LSTM, n-gram features extracted by a CNN layer are fed to the LSTM layer for learning the intra-sentence sequential dependence of words (Zhou et al., 2015). Authors in (Zhang et al., 2016) also tried a hybrid model with LSTM outputs fed to a CNN layer in document modeling. Alternative models include an attention mechanism with either CNN or RNN architecture to optimize textual classification performance further. For instance, Attention-Based Bidirectional Long Short-Term Memory Networks (Att-BLSTM) capture the position variant semantic information from the sentences (Basiri et al., 2021). Another study implements an attention-based Convolutional Neural Network (ABCNN) to model a pair of sentences (Yin et al., 2016). However, most of the studied hybrid models are single and two-layer models and did not explore the relevance of a larger stacking depth in textual classification tasks. The optimal fusion length and the order of the layers are still debatable and context-dependent. Besides, these CPU-implementable models facilitate the exploration and deployment of DNN models in low-resourced environments devoid of adequate advanced computing devices and facilities.

Algorithm 1 Fusion chain generation in NAS

```
Require: Input and Embedding Layer
Require: N = Max. fusion chain length
Require: RNN = LSTM | BiLSTM
Require: Initial Fusion Layer = CNN | RNN
Ensure: i = RandomNumber (1 to N − 1)
  Fusion Model = Initial Fusion Layer
  for
     x ← 0 to i do
     if x is even then
        Layer ← RNN
     else if x is odd then
        Layer ← CNN
     end if
     Append Layer to Fusion model
     Append GlobalMaxPooling, Output Layer
     Return: Fusion model
     if Fusion chain length > N then
        BREAK
     end if
  end for
```

3 Models and Methods

3.1 Proposed fusion chain models

Alternative DNN versions possess different strengths in NLP tasks. For instance, CNN (LeCun et al., 1998) models are good at position invariant text classification tasks, whereas the RNN (Elman, 1990) models are more pertinent for sequential processing of the input texts. However, the basic RNN structure frequently suffers from vanishing gradient problems, and the improved RNN variants are—Long Short Term Memory (LSTM) (Hochreiter and Schmidhuber, 1997) and Gated Recurrent Unit (GRU) (Cho et al., 2014). Many NLP tasks such as sentiment analysis, emotion detection, have striking similarity, as the attributes are largely keywords dependent. Because of the sequential structures of

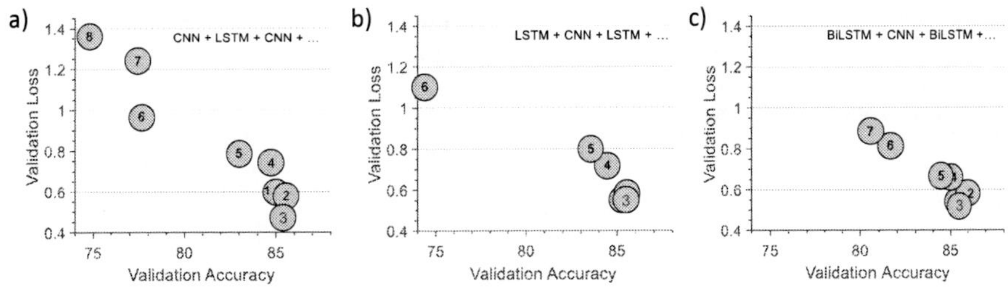

Figure 2: a, b, c) Optimal chain length for the three alternative fusion chain models studied extensively as part of the NAS.

LSTM and GRU, and their ability to remember previous text sequences, they perform well where context-dependencies are crucial (Yin et al., 2017). Another variant of LSTM, the Bidirectional LSTM (BiLSTM), comprises two LSTMs taking input sequence in forward and reverse directions, exhibits improved performance over single-LSTM in many applications (Huang et al., 2015). While each deep learning variant has its strength, a legitimate question thus arises—if a fusion model, formed with the DNN variants in a fusion chain, enhance performance of textual classification. An immediate next interesting question thus becomes the optimal chain length of the proposed fusion model.

3.2 Optimal length of the fusion chain

Textual classification accuracy depends on the context length of a word in a sentence. Fusing multiple DNN layers can increase the context length, but the optimal stacking depth for the DNN layers remains elusive and requires unravelling. The proposed fusion architecture follows a generic structure— it starts with an input layer, followed by an embedding layer that generates an embedding matrix for the given input sentence. A DNN layer is introduced immediately next to the embedding layer. Subsequently, additional DNN layers are added to form a fusion chain model of DNN layers, as schematically shown in Fig. 1. We performed random search for an the optimal fusion chain length, using several performance objectives, including the higher classification accuracy. The network architecture search (NAS) for an optimal chain length randomly generates even and odd numbers to decide if the next stacking to be done by an LSTM/BiLSTM (for even) or CNN (for odd) layer. The current fusion process does not consider similar DNN layers to be stacked together. The maximum length of fusion chain considered in the NAS is eight, beyond which the classification accuracy becomes considerably low (data not shown). The NAS process for optimal fusion chain length is summarized in algorithm 1.

3.3 Generalized random search

We implemented a generalized random search for a set of hyper-parameters in Keras (Chollet et al., 2018) and used it in all the experiments conducted for the analysis of fusion chain models. Interestingly, the random search process needs manual tuning of only one parameter, namely the maximum word length of a sentence that affects the shape of attention and LSTM layers. With this little tuning, the search process as developed in this study remains applicable for other similar textual classification tasks. Each layer in the random search is accompanied by an activation layer, a batch normalization layer, and a dropout layer to minimize the overfitting error. The CNN and RNN layers here also include kernel, bias, and activity regularizers (see the supplemental data for details).

3.4 Metrics used for comparison

The initial architecture search uses classification accuracy on the test dataset and the loss difference (LD = validation loss - training loss) as the performance metrics. The classification accuracy is defined as (TP + TN)/(TP + TN + FP + FN) with TP, TN, FP, FN are true positive, true negative, false positive, and false negative, respectively. The random search also considers early stopping to control the overfitting error [1]. For a comparison between the baseline models and the CNN + BiLSTM + CNN fusion model, we also considered other metrics, such as the number of parameters (# params), number of floating point operations (# FLOPs). Generally, experiments conducted in this study consider a 80% (training) and 20% (testing)

[1]Data and codes are available here in this link

Table 1: Performance of alternative fusion models for the new 6-class emotion Bengali dataset.

Model structure	Accuracy (T)	LD
Classical Machine Learning Models		
1. SVM	41.93	NA
2. KNN	72.79	NA
3. Random Forest	81.43	NA
Fusion models		
4. CNN + CNN + CNN	85.62	0.491
5. LSTM + LSTM	85.43	0.541
6. CNN + LSTM + CNN	86.61	0.283
7. LSTM + CNN + LSTM	85.74	0.483
8. BiLSTM + BiLSTM	86.54	0.126
9. BiLSTM + CNN + CNN	85.25	0.143
10. CNN + BiLSTM + CNN	84.54	-0.058
11. BiLSTM + LSTM	85.14	0.206
12. BiLSTM + LSTM + BiLSTM	85.49	0.057
13. BiLSTM + CNN + BiLSTM	85.86	-0.005
Fusion models + attention		
14. CNN + attn. + BiLSTM + CNN	86.83	
15. CNN + attn. + LSTM + CNN	86.91	
BERT models		
16. mBERT	86.62	0.457
17. Bangla BERT	86.17	0.177

split, and use fasttext (Joulin et al., 2016) as word embedding method.

3.5 Datasets

The study considers datasets across different languages and contexts for the efficacy demonstration of CNN + BiLSTM + CNN fusion. We developed a new Bengali corpus for 6-class emotion classification, as well as used other previously developed Bengali datasets for different NLP tasks– i) Six-class emotion Bengali dataset (Das et al., 2021), ii) Hate Speech Bengali dataset (Romim et al., 2021), and iii) DeepHateExplainer Bengali dataset (Karim et al., 2020). As examples of non-Bengali languages that relate the low-resource contexts, we consider the **Vietnamese** (Ho et al., 2019) and **Indonesian** (Saputri et al., 2018) datasets. The low-resource contexts in English considers an artificial data scarcity for the Stanford Sentiment Treebank 2 (**SST-2**), (Socher et al., 2013), emotion classification dataset (**Emotion**) (Saravia et al., 2018), and the Internet Movie Database (**IMDB**) review dataset (Maas et al., 2011). Finally, the efficacy study of the CNN + BiLSTM + CNN fusion model also considers evaluating the model on the on the General Language Understanding Evaluation the **GLUE benchmark** (Wang et al., 2018); however, we used randomly chosen 250 samples only from each classes to mimic artificial data scarcity.

3.6 Baseline models

We compare CNN + BiLSTM + CNN and other fusion models as identified against the models previously introduced for resource-constrained environments. A few such models are BERT-base (uncased) (Devlin et al., 2018), mBERT (Abdaoui et al., 2020), DistilBERT (Sanh et al., 2019), and TinyBERT (Jiao et al., 2019). The chosen models are all BERT related, and a few of which, for instance, DistilBERT, and TinyBERT, come with reduced size and additional fine-tuning for the resource-constrained environments and low-end devices. Besides the GLU benchmark, the mBERT is also used for the textual classification in Bengali.

4 Results and Discussion

Optimal fusion chain length of fusion models: The NAS process identifies (see Fig. 2a, b, c) that stacking unlimited DNN layers do not improve performance of the fusion models. Instead, the accuracy and LD of the textual classification deteriorate after the chain length attains an optimal value. Interestingly, chain-structure of length three or fewer layers yield the optimal performance (shown in Fig. 2a, b, c) irrespective of the fact whether fusion models start with any of the CNN, LSTM, BiLSTM layers. The NAS considers three fusion chains:

- CNN + LSTM + CNN + LSTM + . . . + CNN
- LSTM + CNN + LSTM + CNN + . . . + LSTM
- BiLSTM + CNN + BiLSTM + . . . + BiLSTM

A comparison between the competing models for our newly developed corpus of emotion classification reveals that accuracy deteriorates as the chain length goes beyond three. As it appeared, the accuracy gradually reduces to lower values as the length increases beyond three (shown in Fig. 2a, b, c). Among the models with a chain length of three or less, a model with a chain length of three is the smallest in LD values among the three allowed chains. A fusion chain that starts with a CNN layer attains the lowest validation loss and is explored further in subsequent analysis by replacing the LSTM layer with a BiLSTM layer.

GLUE benchmark with artificial data scarcity: The GLUE benchmark datasets have different sentence classification tasks. The performance evaluation of CNN + BiLSTM + CNN for all the categories has been done by assuming an artificial data scarcity. Precisely, the artificial scarcity considers only 250 samples from each class. As reported, the proposed CNN + BiLSTM + CNN model frequently outperforms baseline

Table 2: Efficacy study of CNN + BiLSTM + CNN fusion model considers GLUE benchmark datasets. Here, M and B stand for Millions and Billions, respectively. Only 250 samples were collected randomly to mimic a low-resource setup artificially for each class, among which 80% and 20% were for training and testing purposes. Here, accuracy colored in red is the highest, whereas the bold black is the next highest accuracy attained. The baseline models are all pre-trained versions available in `https://huggingface.co/models`

Model	# Params	# FLOPs	CoLA	WNLI	QQP	QNLI	RTE
BERT-base	109M	22.04B	63	46	61	70	75
mBERT	110M	22.04B	64	49	66	**73**	71
DistilBERT	52.2M	22.04B	65	47	65	74	76
TinyBERT	14.5M	0.119B	48	39	49	53	57
CNN + BiLSTM + CNN	0.4M	1.50M	**64**	65	71	**73**	81
CNN + LSTM + CNN	0.37M	1.43M	60	**64**	69	74	81
CNN + BiLSTM	0.38M	1.47M	62	62	**70**	71	**79**

Table 3: Comparison between CNN + BiLSTM + CNN model and BERT with frozen layers as in (Grießhaber et al., 2020) for 1000 randomly selected samples from SST-2 dataset (Socher et al., 2013).

Methods	Model structure	SST-2
	no frozen layer	0.78 ± 0.059
BERT	layer 1,2,3 frozen	0.80 ± 0.045
	layer 9,10,11 frozen	0.84 ± 0.013
Fusion	CNN + BiLSTM + CNN	0.80

models and approximates the rest for all different classification tasks available in GLUE benchmark (shown in Table 2). For instance, the comparison considers both the SST-2 (Socher et al., 2013) and CoLA (Warstadt et al., 2019) datasets for the single sentence classification task, and the CNN + BiLSTM + CNN model achieves the second-highest accuracy (64% for CoLA) marked as bold black with Distilled BERT accuracy at the top with 65% accuracy. Interestingly, in 4 sentence inference task (dataset RTE (Bentivogli et al., 2009)), the CNN + BiLSTM + CNN model achieves 81% accuracy exceeding all the other baseline models in the presence of artificial scarcity. In another inference task dataset, QNLI (Rajpurkar et al., 2016), the fusion model CNN + LSTM + CNN attains the maximum accuracy (74%) with CNN + BiLSTM + CNN and mBERT following it with an accuracy of 73%. The GLUE benchmark also includes three-sentence similarity tasks, and the CNN + BiLSTM+ CNN performed equally well for datasets such as QQP (Chen et al., 2018) with the highest and immediate next best performances with 71% and 70%, respectively. These experiments on different NLP tasks of the GLUE benchmark demonstrate the ability of CNN + BiLSTM + CNN models to perform better in data scarcity and low-end computational facilities.

Fusion and BERT models have comparable accuracy for a newly developed Bengali corpus: A few fusion chain models perform closely with BERT models for Bengali 6-class emotion corpus we developed (see supplemental information). Precisely, the Bangla BERT and mBERT models achieve 86.17% and 86.62%, whereas the CNN + LSTM + CNN fusion model reports an accuracy 86.61% (Table 1, row 6). The accuracy further improves for the same dataset with a self-attention layer added immediately after the initial CNN layer with an accuracy of 86.83% and 86.91% respectively (Table 1, row 14, 15). We primarily emphasized on minimizing overfitting error by lowering the difference between the validation loss and training. As observed, fusion models containig BiLSTM layers demonstrate a tendency of lowering the LD (Table 1, row: 8, 9, 10, 12, 13), and in fact, obtains the lowest LD = 0.057 among alternative fusion models. Interestingly, the fusion models performed very closely with the mBERT model, and in fact, outperformed mBERT in lowering the generalization error. For instance, reported mBERT LD = 0.457 (Table 1, row 16), whereas the CNN + LSTM + CNN model has a low LD = 0.28. The fusion models also perform well across other Bengali text classification datasets. For instance, CNN + BiLSTM + CNN model outperforms mBERT and BanglaBERT implementation for the reported dataset in (Das et al., 2021). In another dataset of Bengali hate speech detection (Romim et al., 2021), the fusion model with self-attention CNN + attn. + BiLSTM + CNN outperforms all the previous DNN and ML implementations, as evident from Table 4. However, for the dataset in (Karim et al., 2020), the fusion models fail to match the BERT-variants' performance (see Table 4) and surpass only the other DNN models. However, these datasets generally contain few thousands of samples for each classes, and do not necessarily represent data scarcity. Fur-

Table 4: Performance comparison between fusion models and alternative DNN and BERT models for various NLP-tasks in Bengali language. Here, A ≡ self-attention layer.

Group	Model structure	Accuracy (%)	Ref.
Six-class emotion Bengali dataset (Das et al., 2021)			
DNN	CNN + A + LSTM + CNN	**64.26**	Ours
	CNN + A + BiLSTM + CNN	**65.24**	
	CNN + A + GRU + CNN	**64.73**	
	CNN + BiLSTM	55.68	(2021)
	BiLSTM	58.08	(2021)
BERT	mBERT	64.63	(2021)
	Bangla-BERT	62.24	
	XLM-R	69.61	
Hate Speech Bengali dataset (Romim et al., 2021)			
ML	SVM	87.80	(2021)
DNN	fasttext + LSTM	84.30	(2021)
	fasttext + BiLSTM	86.55	
	word2vec + LSTM	83.85	
	CNN + A + BiLSTM + CNN	**88.65**	Ours
DeepHateExplainer (Karim et al., 2020)			
DNN	LSTM	75	(2020)
	BiLSTM	78	
	CNN + A + BiLSTM + CNN	**83.56**	Ours
BERT	Bangla-BERT	86	(2020)
	mBERT-cased	85	
	XML-Roberta	87	

ther exploration of the fusion models for other low-resources languages and contexts reveal the resilience of the identified models. For instance, the IMDB dataset (Maas et al., 2011) and the Emotion dataset (Saravia et al., 2018) were randomly reduced to mimick low-resource contexts. Subsequently, mBERT performance for the reduced datasets (5%, 10% for IMDB and 0.01%, 0.02% for Emotion) was compared against the fusion models' performance.

As appeared in Table 4, fusion models outperformed in all instances; in fact, it performed significantly better for the smaller dataset size considered. Ability of fusion models also remain equally competitive in other English NLP tasks, as demonstrated from classification accuracy comparison (see Table 6) between the fusion models and other BERT, DNN based implementation as in (Larson et al., 2019). Specifically, the fusion models attain a comparable accuracy of 93.62%, 93.28% as opposed to BERT-base's 94.4% reported in (Larson et al., 2019). Interestingly, the proposed method also perform competitively with the other low-resource fine-tuning, for instance, the freezing of BERT-layer approach as in (Grießhaber et al., 2020). Precisely, the CNN + BiLSTM + CNN model achieves higher accuracy than the BERT-base model reported, and almost equally perform to other tuned BERT-models of frozen layers, for a randomly selected 1000 samples from the SST-2 dataset (see Table 3).

Table 5: Training cost comparison between the baseline and fusion models using the average time per epoch for all the GLUE benchmark datasets studied.

Model	Average Time per Epoch (second)				
	CoLA	WNLI	QQP	QNLI	RTE
BERT-base	1286	1321	895	1421	783
mBERT	2540	1721	1296	2671	1026
DistilBERT	783	982	662	941	386
TinyBERT	19.6	24.4	19.8	24.4	18.8
CNN + BiLSTM + CNN	1.92	3.36	3.33	3.36	2.21
CNN + LSTM + CNN	1.25	3.26	2.25	3.18	1.11
CNN + BiLSTM	1.23	4.21	3	4.16	2.58

Table 6: Performance comparison between fusion models and alternative DNN and transformers models across different languages and datasets. Here, A ≡ attn.

Method	Model structure	Accuracy (%)	Ref.
Artificial scarcity: (5%, 10%) of **IMDB** dataset (Maas et al., 2011)			
Fusion	CNN + A + BiLSTM + CNN	(**84.79**, **85.10**)	Ours
BERT	mBERT	(81.40, 84.79)	-
Scarcity: (0.01%, 0.02%) **Emotion** dataset (Saravia et al., 2018)			
Fusion	CNN + A + LSTM + CNN	(**84.65**, **89.87**)	Ours
BERT	mBERT	(79.5, 89.57)	-
100% of **Intent Classification** dataset (Larson et al., 2019)			
BERT	BERT-base	94.3	(2019)
Others	CNN	89.8	
	MLP	90.1	
Fusion	CNN + BiLSTM + CNN	**93.62**	Ours
	CNN + LSTM + CNN	**93.28**	
100% of the **Vietnamese** dataset (Ho et al., 2019)			
Fusion	CNN + LSTM + CNN	54.76	Ours
	CNN + BiLSTM + CNN	54.54	
BERT	BERT-base	53.18	
100% of the **Indonesian** dataset (Saputri et al., 2018)			
Fusion	CNN + LSTM + CNN	54.76	Ours
	CNN + BiLSTM + CNN	54.54	
BERT	BERT-base	53.18	

Position-sensitive self-attention role of fusion models in new Bengali corpus: An attention layer may aid in capturing the necessary information for a sequence to sequence model. We also investigated how adding a self-attention layer to the fusion model affects the accuracy of the the newly developed 6-class Bengali emotion corpus. However, an immediate question arises—what the optimal position of the attention layer be within a fusion chain. To answer this, we execute four different experiments, utilizing a self-attention layer in four alternative places: between the embedding and the first CNN layer, between the first CNN layer and the first LSTM layer, between the first LSTM layer and the second CNN layer, and between the second CNN layer and the final output

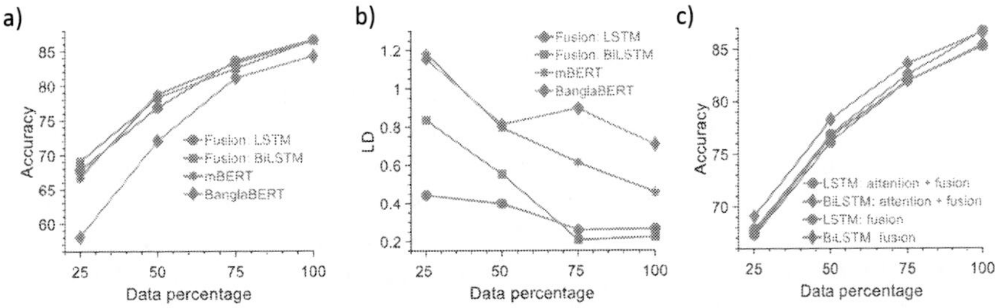

Figure 3: Performance comparison between the fusion (CNN + attn. + LSTM/BiLSTM + CNN) and mBERT model on 25%, 50%, 75% and 100% of a new 6-class Bengali emotion dataset. The dataset was split randomly to produce an artificial scarcity. In Fig. 3a-b, the green (square), red (circle), blue (asterisks), and yellow (diamond) lines represent CNN + attn. + LSTM + CNN (Fusion: LSTM), CNN + attn. + BiLSTM + CNN (Fusion: BiLSTM), mBERT and BanglaBERT models' performance, respectively. a) Accuracy comparison of all the four models for varying data size. b) The loss difference (LD) progression for different data sizes– the smaller the loss, the better the performance is. c) An inclusion of a self-attention layer improves fusion models' performance (blue lines).

Table 7: Deployable form for a few DNN-based fusion models before and after the pruning and retraining for the six-class Bengali emotion dataset developed in this study.

Serial	Fusion architecture	Retrained Accuracy	Accuracy		Size (zip, MB)	
			Before pruning	After Pruning	Before Pruning	After Pruning
1	LSTM + LSTM	86.19	85.43	85.18	33.45	6.32
2	**CNN + LSTM + CNN**	**86.36**	86.61	85.54	34.81	6.60
3	LSTM + CNN + LSTM	85.28	85.74	84.24	34.27	6.45

layer. As observed, the model provides an accuracy of 85.79% and a loss difference of 0.205 if the attention layer is placed between the embedding and the first DNN layer. Interestingly, the accuracy increased to 86.68%, and the loss difference reduced to 0.164 if the attention layer posits between the first CNN and first LSTM layer. It was the highest accuracy produced and the lowest loss difference of 0.164 among the alternative self-attention position tried. An attention layer between the LSTM and the second CNN layers generates shape mismatch and stops the model from training. Final experiment that places attention between the second CNN and output layer produces an accuracy of 85.79% with a 0.285 loss difference. These experiments show that for the 6-class Bengali emotion classification, a position-sensitive attention layer makes a difference in classification accuracy and reduces overfitting error. The accuracy improvement because of the self-attention layer still holds if an artificial scarcity for the new corpus is produced by considering 25%, 50%, 75% of the complete dataset, as shown in Fig. 3c. However, further analysis with other datasets and languages would clarify whether self-attention layer roles, as observed here in Fig. 3, are context-dependent or generic, and are beyond the scope of this study.

Fusion models robustly perform in data scarcity: One intriguing query on the fusion model would be to assess its ability to perform in data scarcity. An experiment designed to compare how the proposed fusion models and mBERT perform in data scarcity randomly segregates the Bengali 6-class emotion dataset into 25%, 50%, 75%, and 100% categories. The artificial data scarcity is analogous to the low-resource contexts, mimicking the lack of sufficient annotated data common for many low-resource languages. The comparison considers CNN + attn. + LSTM + CNN and CNN + attn. + BiLSTM + CNN and compare with mBERT. The fusion models perform better for the 25% case and match or surpass the mBERT performance in other scarce data cases (shown in Fig. 3a). Besides, the fusion models decrease LD in all the artificially produced scarce cases studied. A close comparison (Fig. 3b) shows that the LD of mBERT (blue line) remains way above the LDs reported by the fusion models. For the 25% case, the LD value is doubled for mBERT, indicating an advantage of fusion models in low-resource contexts.

Fusion models are computationally less expensive: Along with other factors, the computational cost of an NLP model also depends on its size and the FLOPs count. A comparison of these metrics between the baseline models and the fusion models exhibits that fusion models are more advantageous for a small number of annotated samples (shown in Table 2). For instance, the fusion model CNN

+ BiLSTM/LSTM + CNN roughly does 100 times fewer FLOPs. Also, for most GLUE datasets, the fusion model outperforms the TinyBERT in the presence of data scarcity. Some of the BERT models demonstrate equal accuracy for some GLUE benchmark datasets. However, these models are computationally extensive because of their high #Params and #FLOPs. Although costs related to FLOPs are decreasing, it requires hardware upgradation from GPU to TPU. Whereas the GPU itself is a computationally extensive device in low-resource environments, let alone the use of TPU. So, the low #FLOPs requirement in CNN + BiLSTM + CNN provides an edge over the memory-hungry BERT models in low-resource contexts. Besides, the possibility of a low computational cost of the CNN + BiLSTM + CNN model can also be predicted by comparing the average time per epoch calculation, an ensemble representation of all the individual times per epoch for alternative GLUE benchmark data considered. The average time per epoch over GLUE benchmark data is about 3 seconds for the CNN + BiLSTM + CNN model. In contrast, the same becomes as high as 1000 seconds or more for the different baseline models implemented in the experiment.

Besides, pruning and retraining reduce the fusion models further and increase their deployability in low-end devices and web platforms. Precisely, the CNN + LSTM + CNN model achieves almost a $5\times$ reduction in size from 34.81MB to a model size of 6.60MB, as in Table 7. The TinyBERT model may be as small as about 16MB, but it is pre-trained in the English language requiring further tuning in other languages for better accuracy. For instance, in experiments on a Bengali 6-class emotion dataset, the TinyBERT, pre-trained in English, achieves an accuracy of 33.42%. This accuracy drops to 24% if annotated data is reduced to 25%. So, TinyBERT requires training of the pre-trained model and suffers because of data scarcity. Whereas, for the proposed fusion model CNN + BiLST/LSTM + CNN, the initial accuracy (86.61) is almost retrievable (86.36) upon pruning and retraining (data shown in Table 7). Also, the model size reduces to around 5MB after pruning compared to the 16MB of the pre-trained TinyBERT.

5 Conclusion

Generally, the RNN and CNN models are computationally less intensive but compromise accuracy in textual classification. In contrast, BERT-variants and other advanced transformer-based implementations demonstrate improved performance but are computationally intensive. This study analyzed a few low-resource textual classification contexts to identify CPU-trainable and comparatively smaller deployable DNN models sufficiently accurate in textual classification tasks. These identified less-intensive DNN fusion models attained accuracy that frequently surpasses BERT performance in low-resource contexts. Interestingly, the efficacy of CNN + BiLSTM + CNN remains equally applicable in other alternative languages, tasks. This study also demonstrates that the fusion models are all CPU-trainable, making them easily accessible for communities suffering from an infrastructural deficiency. Moreover, low-resource languages always suffer from smaller corpus, infrequent research initiatives, and a lack of intensive computational facilities. These hinder the potential deployment of DNN models to monitor toxic and abusive elements in the ever-increasing social media platforms. Because of its relatively small size and acceptable classification accuracy, the fusion models are a suitable alternative to computationally intensive BERT variants for deployment in low-end devices.

Further improvement of the fusion models may consider a multichannel word-embedding technique, equipping the models better for out of vocabulary words now common in the era of social media platforms, POS-tagging to exploit the key phrases of the sentiment better. Such extensions, alone or in a cohort, can improve the fusion models to tackle the long-term dependencies analysis by forming phrases from the dependent and related words in longer sentences. Overall, this work provides sufficiently accurate, computationally less intensive CPU-trainable DNN models for NLP tasks for low-resource languages and may serve as the blueprint to identify the deployable NLP models for low-resource languages and environments.

Acknowledgements

We express our gratitude to Dr. Shafin Rahman, Department of Electrical and Computer Engineering at the North South University, Bangladesh and all the anonymous reviewers for their sincere comments, suggestions, and criticisms.

References

Amine Abdaoui, Camille Pradel, and Grégoire Sigel. 2020. Load what you need: Smaller versions of multilingual bert. *arXiv preprint arXiv:2010.05609.*

Mohammad Ehsan Basiri, Shahla Nemati, Moloud Abdar, Erik Cambria, and U Rajendra Acharya. 2021. Abcdm: An attention-based bidirectional cnn-rnn deep model for sentiment analysis. *Future Generation Computer Systems*, 115:279–294.

Luisa Bentivogli, Peter Clark, Ido Dagan, and Danilo Giampiccolo. 2009. The fifth pascal recognizing textual entailment challenge. In *TAC*.

Tom B Brown, Benjamin Mann, Nick Ryder, Melanie Subbiah, Jared Kaplan, Prafulla Dhariwal, Arvind Neelakantan, Pranav Shyam, Girish Sastry, Amanda Askell, et al. 2020. Language models are few-shot learners. *arXiv preprint arXiv:2005.14165.*

Zihan Chen, Hongbo Zhang, Xiaoji Zhang, and Leqi Zhao. 2018. Quora question pairs. *University of Waterloo*, pages 1–7.

Jason PC Chiu and Eric Nichols. 2016. Named entity recognition with bidirectional lstm-cnns. *Transactions of the Association for Computational Linguistics*, 4:357–370.

Kyunghyun Cho, Bart Van Merriënboer, Dzmitry Bahdanau, and Yoshua Bengio. 2014. On the properties of neural machine translation: Encoder-decoder approaches. *arXiv preprint arXiv:1409.1259.*

François Chollet et al. 2018. Keras: The python deep learning library. *Astrophysics source code library*, pages ascl–1806.

Avishek Das, Omar Sharif, Mohammed Moshiul Hoque, and Iqbal H Sarker. 2021. Emotion classification in a resource constrained language using transformer-based approach. *arXiv preprint arXiv:2104.08613.*

Jacob Devlin, Ming-Wei Chang, Kenton Lee, and Kristina Toutanova. 2018. Bert: Pre-training of deep bidirectional transformers for language understanding. *arXiv preprint arXiv:1810.04805.*

Jeffrey L Elman. 1990. Finding structure in time. *Cognitive science*, 14(2):179–211.

Daniel Grießhaber, Johannes Maucher, and Ngoc Thang Vu. 2020. Fine-tuning bert for low-resource natural language understanding via active learning. *arXiv preprint arXiv:2012.02462.*

Song Han, Huizi Mao, and William J Dally. 2015a. Deep compression: Compressing deep neural networks with pruning, trained quantization and huffman coding. *arXiv preprint arXiv:1510.00149.*

Song Han, Jeff Pool, John Tran, and William J Dally. 2015b. Learning both weights and connections for efficient neural networks. *arXiv preprint arXiv:1506.02626.*

Vong Anh Ho, Duong Huynh-Cong Nguyen, Danh Hoang Nguyen, Linh Thi-Van Pham, Duc-Vu Nguyen, Kiet Van Nguyen, and Ngan Luu-Thuy Nguyen. 2019. Emotion recognition for vietnamese social media text. In *International Conference of the Pacific Association for Computational Linguistics*, pages 319–333. Springer.

Sepp Hochreiter and Jürgen Schmidhuber. 1997. Long short-term memory. *Neural computation*, 9(8):1735–1780.

Zhiheng Huang, Wei Xu, and Kai Yu. 2015. Bidirectional lstm-crf models for sequence tagging. *arXiv preprint arXiv:1508.01991.*

Xiaoqi Jiao, Yichun Yin, Lifeng Shang, Xin Jiang, Xiao Chen, Linlin Li, Fang Wang, and Qun Liu. 2019. Tinybert: Distilling bert for natural language understanding. *arXiv preprint arXiv:1909.10351.*

Pratik Joshi, Sebastin Santy, Amar Budhiraja, Kalika Bali, and Monojit Choudhury. 2020. The state and fate of linguistic diversity and inclusion in the nlp world. *arXiv preprint arXiv:2004.09095.*

Armand Joulin, Edouard Grave, Piotr Bojanowski, and Tomas Mikolov. 2016. Bag of tricks for efficient text classification. *arXiv preprint arXiv:1607.01759.*

Nal Kalchbrenner, Edward Grefenstette, and Phil Blunsom. 2014. A convolutional neural network for modelling sentences. *arXiv preprint arXiv:1404.2188.*

Md Karim, Sumon Kanti Dey, Bharathi Raja Chakravarthi, et al. 2020. Deephateexplainer: Explainable hate speech detection in under-resourced bengali language. *arXiv preprint arXiv:2012.14353.*

Stefan Larson, Anish Mahendran, Joseph J Peper, Christopher Clarke, Andrew Lee, Parker Hill, Jonathan K Kummerfeld, Kevin Leach, Michael A Laurenzano, Lingjia Tang, et al. 2019. An evaluation dataset for intent classification and out-of-scope prediction. *arXiv preprint arXiv:1909.02027.*

Yann LeCun, Léon Bottou, Yoshua Bengio, and Patrick Haffner. 1998. Gradient-based learning applied to document recognition. *Proceedings of the IEEE*, 86(11):2278–2324.

Andrew Maas, Raymond E Daly, Peter T Pham, Dan Huang, Andrew Y Ng, and Christopher Potts. 2011. Learning word vectors for sentiment analysis. In *Proceedings of the 49th annual meeting of the association for computational linguistics: Human language technologies*, pages 142–150.

Tomas Mikolov, Ilya Sutskever, Kai Chen, Greg S Corrado, and Jeff Dean. 2013. Distributed representations of words and phrases and their compositionality. In *Advances in neural information processing systems*, pages 3111–3119.

Shervin Minaee, Nal Kalchbrenner, Erik Cambria, Narjes Nikzad, Meysam Chenaghlu, and Jianfeng Gao. 2021. Deep learning–based text classification: A comprehensive review. *ACM Computing Surveys (CSUR)*, 54(3):1–40.

Telmo Pires, Eva Schlinger, and Dan Garrette. 2019. How multilingual is multilingual bert? *arXiv preprint arXiv:1906.01502*.

Daniel Quang and Xiaohui Xie. 2016. Danq: a hybrid convolutional and recurrent deep neural network for quantifying the function of dna sequences. *Nucleic acids research*, 44(11):e107–e107.

Pranav Rajpurkar, Jian Zhang, Konstantin Lopyrev, and Percy Liang. 2016. Squad: 100,000+ questions for machine comprehension of text. *arXiv preprint arXiv:1606.05250*.

Nauros Romim, Mosahed Ahmed, Hriteshwar Talukder, and Md Saiful Islam. 2021. Hate speech detection in the bengali language: A dataset and its baseline evaluation. In *Proceedings of International Joint Conference on Advances in Computational Intelligence*, pages 457–468. Springer.

Victor Sanh, Lysandre Debut, Julien Chaumond, and Thomas Wolf. 2019. Distilbert, a distilled version of bert: smaller, faster, cheaper and lighter. *arXiv preprint arXiv:1910.01108*.

Mei Silviana Saputri, Rahmad Mahendra, and Mirna Adriani. 2018. Emotion classification on indonesian twitter dataset. In *2018 International Conference on Asian Language Processing (IALP)*, pages 90–95. IEEE.

Elvis Saravia, Hsien-Chi Toby Liu, Yen-Hao Huang, Junlin Wu, and Yi-Shin Chen. 2018. Carer: Contextualized affect representations for emotion recognition. In *Proceedings of the 2018 Conference on Empirical Methods in Natural Language Processing*, pages 3687–3697.

Richard Socher, Alex Perelygin, Jean Wu, Jason Chuang, Christopher D Manning, Andrew Y Ng, and Christopher Potts. 2013. Recursive deep models for semantic compositionality over a sentiment treebank. In *Proceedings of the 2013 conference on empirical methods in natural language processing*, pages 1631–1642.

Emma Strubell, Ananya Ganesh, and Andrew McCallum. 2019. Energy and policy considerations for deep learning in nlp. *arXiv preprint arXiv:1906.02243*.

Zhiqing Sun, Hongkun Yu, Xiaodan Song, Renjie Liu, Yiming Yang, and Denny Zhou. 2020. Mobilebert: a compact task-agnostic bert for resource-limited devices. *arXiv preprint arXiv:2004.02984*.

Alex Wang, Amanpreet Singh, Julian Michael, Felix Hill, Omer Levy, and Samuel R Bowman. 2018. Glue: A multi-task benchmark and analysis platform for natural language understanding. *arXiv preprint arXiv:1804.07461*.

Alex Warstadt, Amanpreet Singh, and Samuel R Bowman. 2019. Neural network acceptability judgments. *Transactions of the Association for Computational Linguistics*, 7:625–641.

Moshe Wasserblat, Oren Pereg, and Peter Izsak. 2020. Exploring the boundaries of low-resource bert distillation. In *Proceedings of SustaiNLP: Workshop on Simple and Efficient Natural Language Processing*, pages 35–40.

Wenpeng Yin, Katharina Kann, Mo Yu, and Hinrich Schütze. 2017. Comparative study of cnn and rnn for natural language processing. *arXiv preprint arXiv:1702.01923*.

Wenpeng Yin, Hinrich Schütze, Bing Xiang, and Bowen Zhou. 2016. Abcnn: Attention-based convolutional neural network for modeling sentence pairs. *Transactions of the Association for Computational Linguistics*, 4:259–272.

Rui Zhang, Honglak Lee, and Dragomir Radev. 2016. Dependency sensitive convolutional neural networks for modeling sentences and documents. *arXiv preprint arXiv:1611.02361*.

Chunting Zhou, Chonglin Sun, Zhiyuan Liu, and Francis Lau. 2015. A c-lstm neural network for text classification. *arXiv preprint arXiv:1511.08630*.

Xiaodan Zhu, Parinaz Sobihani, and Hongyu Guo. 2015. Long short-term memory over recursive structures. In *International Conference on Machine Learning*, pages 1604–1612. PMLR.

Generating Complement Data for Aspect Term Extraction with GPT-2

Amir Pouran Ben Veyseh[1], Franck Dernoncourt[2], Bonan Min[3] and Thien Huu Nguyen[1]
[1]Department of Computer Science,
University of Oregon, Eugene, Oregon, USA
[2]Adobe Research, San Jose, CA, USA
[3]Raytheon BBN Technologies, USA
{apouranb, thien}@cs.uoregon.edu
franck.dernoncourt@adobe.com, bonan.min@raytheon.com

Abstract

Aspect Term Extraction (ATE) is the task of identifying the word(s) in a review text toward which the author express an opinion. A major challenges for ATE involve data scarcity that hinder the training of deep sequence taggers to identify rare targets. To overcome these issues, we propose a novel method to better exploit the available labeled data for ATE by computing effective complement sentences to augment the input data and facilitate the aspect term prediction. In particular, we introduce a multi-step training procedure that first obtains optimal complement representations and sentences for training data with respect to a deep ATE model. Afterward, we fine-tune the generative language model GPT-2 to allow complement sentence generation at test data. The REINFORCE algorithm is employed to incorporate different expected properties into the reward function to perform the fine-tuning. We perform extensive experiments on the benchmark datasets to demonstrate the benefits of the proposed method that achieve the state-of-the-art performance on different datasets.

1 Introduction

Aspect Term Extraction (ATE) is one of the fundamental tasks in Aspect-based Sentiment Analysis (ABSA). Its goal is to recognize the terms upon which a sentiment opinion is expressed in text. For instance, in the sentence "*The staff of the restaurant were good but the quality of the food was terrible*", an ATE system should recognize the two aspect terms (targets) "*staff*" and "*quality of food*". ATE finds its applications in ABSA systems to identify targets toward which sentiment analysis is done.

A major challenge for ATE is the lack of enough training data. For instance, the widely-used SemEval datasets, e.g., Res15 (Pontiki et al., 2015) or Res16 (Pontiki et al., 2016), contain less than 2,000 training samples with only 20% of the words appearing more than five times (Chen and Qian, 2020a). This small size of training data hinders the deep sequence taggers to achieve optimal performance, especially for the tail targets (i.e., targets with few examples in the dataset) (He et al., 2018; Chen and Qian, 2019). In order to alleviate this issue, prior work has resorted to data augmentation techniques to exploit additional training signals from different sources, including data from related tasks, e.g., ABSA (performing multi-tasking learning (Luo et al., 2020; Chen and Qian, 2020b)), new labeled data for ATE produced by pre-trained sequence-to-sequence models (Li et al., 2020), and soft prompts that are generated by pre-trained language models (Chen and Qian, 2020a). As such, the critical requirements for such prior methods involve annotation for related tasks of ATE (e.g., ABSA), or large in-domain corpora to train the sequence-to-sequence/language models for data generation (called external data). Unfortunately, these requirements might be unavailable or very expensive to obtain in different domains, making it less applicable for various scenarios in practice.

To this end, this work aims to solve the issue of data scarcity for ATE without relying on annotated data for related tasks and large in-domain corpora. In particular, our main proposal is to fine-tune existing large-scale language models so they can generate complement sentences for input sentences in existing labeled datasets for ATE (i.e., not using external data as in prior works). Here, the motivation is that data scarcity might present a challenge for ATE models, especially on tail examples with rare aspect terms and context patterns (Chen and Qian, 2020a). The complement sentence thus aims to provide supporting evidence and facilitate the recognition of aspect terms for the input sentences.

As such, our method first seeks to obtain complement sentences for all the sentences in a given ATE dataset via a multi-step training procedure. In the first step, we train a base ATE model on a labeled training dataset to encode the available

Proceedings of the Third Workshop on Deep Learning for Low-Resource Natural Language Processing, pages 203 - 213
July 14, 2022

knowledge about aspect terms in the dataset. However, due to data scarcity, the base model might not be exposed sufficiently to aspect term patterns, thus limiting the ability of the produced representations for the input sentences to fully capture relevant information/features for ATE. To achieve complement sentences for ATE datasets, in the second step, we thus propose to learn optimal representation vectors/word embeddings that can be combined (e.g., via adding) to improve the representation vectors from the base model for ATE (called complement representations). Our motivation is that the insufficient coverage of aspect term patterns in the representations would cause the base model to exhibit poor performance (i.e., high loss) on the validation dataset. To this end, we propose to infer the complement representations for each validation sentence by incorporating them into the base model as additional parameters and minimizing the loss of the augmented model on the validation data. In the implementation, we divide the training data for an ATE dataset into k folds. By choosing one fold as validation data and treating the $k-1$ remaining folds as training data, the aforementioned procedure can return the optimal complement representations for each sentence in the validation fold. As such, we repeat this process for k possible choices of the validation fold that in all produce complement representations for each sentence in the training data.

To employ the complement representations for training data, we can introduce them into the base model for retraining. However, this will cause a mismatch in the test time where labels for sentences are not available and the complement representations cannot be obtained. To this end, instead of directly using the learned complement representations, we propose to first transform them into complement sentences based on the GloVe word embeddings (Pennington et al., 2014). This is done by introducing constraints to encourage the learned representation vectors to belong to the same space with GloVe word embeddings. The complement representations can then be mapped into complement sentences by finding the words whose GloVe embeddings are closest to the complement representations. In this way, each original training sentence for ATE can be associated with a complement sentence. Using pairs of original and complement sentences as training data, in the next step, we propose to train a generative model that can transform the original sentences into their complement versions. As such, in the test time, we can apply the generative model to generate complement sentences for test data and use GloVe embeddings to produce complement representation vectors for data augmentation.

In this work, we propose to fine-tune the language model GPT-2 (Radford et al., 2019) on the original and complement sentence pairs to obtain the generative model. Our motivation stems from the small number of the pairs for the original and complement sentences (due to the small size of ATE datasets) that might not be sufficient to train a generative model well. By leveraging the pre-trained GPT-2 model, we expect that its language priors can compensate for the data scarcity issue and bootstrap the learning process from complement data. Finally, we use REINFORCE (Williams, 1992) to fine-tune GPT-2 to facilitate the enforcement of expected properties for the generated sentences (i.e, the similarity or the length comparability with respect to the complement sentences produced in prior step). We perform extensive evaluations for the proposed method on different benchmark datasets for ATE. Our experiments reveal the superior performance and demonstrate the effectiveness of the proposed method.

2 Model

Problem Definition: ATE is formulated as a sequence labeling problem. Formally, given the input sentence $S = [w_1, w_2, \ldots, w_n]$, the goal is to predict the gold label sequence $Y = [y_1, y_2, \ldots, y_n]$ where $y_i \in \{B, I, O\}$, B stands for the "Beginning of a target", I stands for "Inside a target", and O stands for "Other". Our proposed model consists of a four-step procedure: (I) Training a base model for ATE using the available labeled data, (II) Finding the word representations of the optimal complement sentences for training data, (III) Fine-tuning a the language model GPT-2 to produce complement sentences for input sentences, and (IV) Training a final ATE model on the training data augmented with complement sentences.

2.1 Training a Base ATE Model (Step I)

For the first step, we train a base model on an available labeled ATE dataset. The trained model will serve as a base to find the optimal complement representations for input sentences of the ATE dataset in the next step. To this end, we employ a Bi-LSTM base model. In particular, the input sentence S is first fed into the pre-trained BERT model (Devlin et al., 2019) to obtain the contextualized word embeddings $X = [x_1, x_2, \ldots, x_n]$ (x_i is the average of the representation vectors for the wordpieces of w_i in the last layer of BERT). As such, to further abstract the word embeddings X for ATE, we feed X into a Bidirectional LSTM (Bi-LSTM) network to obtain the hidden states $H = [h_1, h_2, \ldots, h_n]$. Afterward, the vectors in H are sent into a two-layer feed-forward layer FF to generate the label probability distribution $P(\cdot|S, w_i)$ for i-th word: $P(\cdot|S, w_i) = FF(h_i)$. Finally, to train the base model, we use negative log-likelihood loss: $\mathcal{L}_b = -\frac{1}{n}\sum_{i=1}^{n} \log P(y_i|S, w_i)$.

2.2 Finding Complement Representations (Step II)

As mentioned in the introduction, the limited size of the ATE datasets might prevent the base model from being imposed sufficiently to training samples to learn necessary aspect term patterns in the representations, potentially leading to inferior performance (i.e., high loss on validation data), especially on tail targets. As such, it is necessary to enhance the representation learning capability of the base model by imposing it to further information. To achieve this goal, prior work has resorted to data augmentation (Li et al., 2020) or soft-prompts (Chen and Qian, 2020a) in which the training data is augmented with new sentences (e.g., generated by a pre-trained language model) to provide more evidences for aspect terms. However, the limitation of the prior work is that the generated sentences to augment ATE data is either ignorant of the ATE task (Chen and Qian, 2020a) or constrained on some heuristics (i.e., replacing non-aspect terms with other words generated by a language model) (Li et al., 2020). As such, we argue that these data augmentation methods might not achieve the optimal augmentation for the available ATE data. We thus posit that the optimal augmentation for an input sentence is the one whose combination with the sentence could directly reduce the objective loss on validation data. Concretely, to find the optimal augmentation for a sentence S in the validation data, we search for the sentence S' whose combination with S (i.e., by adding their word representations) could further reduce the objective loss $\mathcal{L}_b$ computed on validation data. Since this augmentation is optimized over validation data and not bound to any heuristics-based constraints, we expect it to be the optimal augmentation for the input sentence. Note that the optimality of the sentence S' is with respect to the objective loss $\mathcal{L}_b$ and changing the criteria could lead to a different sentence S'.

To find the optimal complement sentence S' for S in the validation data, since this is a discrete variable, we first attempt to find the representation vectors X' for its words w_i. That is, S' is parameterized by a set of learnable vectors X' which are combined with the word embeddings X and are updated with the objective loss $\mathcal{L}_b$ over validation data. In this work, the combination of X and X' is defended as the sum of their corresponding vectors x_i and x'_i. As such, the number of tokens of X' should be equal to the number of tokens of X, i.e., $X' = [x'_1, x'_2, \ldots, x'_n]$. In addition, the dimension of the vectors should also match, i.e., $|x_i| = |x'_i| = D$, where D is the dimensionality of the word embedding vectors. Hence, the total number of parameters defined for all representation vectors is $N \times n \times D$, where N is the total number of sentences in the validation set.

In the next step, we seek to optimize the representation parameters complement sentences by reducing the objective loss $\mathcal{L}_b$ over validation data. In particular, for the sentence S with embeddings X and the complement sentence S' with parameters (i.e., embeddings) X', we compute the sum of the corresponding vectors for the i-th token: $\hat{x}_i = x_i + \lambda x'_i$ where λ is a trade-off parameter (i.e., the data augmentation in this work). The vectors $\hat{X} = [\hat{x}_1, \hat{x}_2, \ldots, \hat{x}_n]$ will be sent to the base model architecture (i.e., BiLSTM followed by a feed-forward layer) to obtain the label distribution $P(\cdot|S, S', w_i)$. As such, the objective loss for this training step, i.e., $\mathcal{L}_f$, is defined similar to $\mathcal{L}_b$: $\mathcal{L}_f = -\frac{1}{n}\sum_{i=1}^{n} \log P(y_i|S, S', w_i)$ (computed over validation data). Note that in this training step, the original parameters of the trained base model is fixed so the only parameters to be updated are the parameters for the complement sentences S', i.e., the vectors X'.

Embedding Regularization: To further improve the complement embeddings and facilitate the mapping to complement sentences S' later, we introduce two additional regularization terms for the learning objective of complement embeddings. The first regularization seeks to encourage the complement embeddings X' to capture different (i.e., complementary) information from those for the embeddings X of the input sentence S, thus enhancing the contribution of complement embeddings. In particular, we compute the representation vectors R_S and $R_{S'}$ for the original and complement sentences using the max-pooling operation: $R_S = MAX\_POOL(x_1, x_2, \ldots, x_n)$ and $R_{S'} = MAX\_POOL(x'_1, x'_2, \ldots, x'_n)$. Afterward, the complementary nature of embeddings is enforced by introducing the dot product $\mathcal{L}_{reg}$ between R_S and $R_{S'}$ into the loss function for minimization (i.e., minimizing the similarity between R_S and $R_{S'}$): $\mathcal{L}_{reg} = R_S \odot R_{S'}$.

For the second regularization, we aim to align the complement embeddings X' to the space of the GloVe embeddings (Pennington et al., 2014) to facilitate the transformation to complement sentences in the next step. Here, we use the GloVe embeddings for convenience and leave other possible pre-trained embeddings for future work. In particular, for each vector $x'_i \in X'$, we use a feed-forward network F to transform x'_i into the vector $F(x'_i)$ of the same dimension with Glove embeddings. Afterward, we find the vector e_i in the GloVe embedding table that is closest to $F(x'_i)$ based on the Euclidean distance. The Euclidean distance between $F(x'_i)$ and e_i is then incorporated into the loss function to promote the alignment of complement and GloVe embeddings: $\mathcal{L}_{GloVe} = \frac{1}{n}\sum_{i=1}^{n} \|F(x'_i) - e_i\|_2^2$. Finally, the overall loss function to learn the complement representations X' is: $\mathcal{L}_{emb} = \mathcal{L}_f + \alpha_{reg}\mathcal{L}_{reg} + \alpha_{GloVe}\mathcal{L}_{GloVe}$ where α_{reg} and α_{GloVe} are the trade-off parameters. Note that the parameters for F are also optimized in this process.

As such, this training step produces the complement embedding X' for each sentence in the validation data. To maximize the use of data, we implement this training step in a 10-fold validation fashion described in the introduction. In particular, we train the base model on 9 folds of the training data (i.e., Section 2.1) and use the remaining fold for the validation data in the complement representation optimization. By alternating the choice of validation fold, we can obtain a complement representation sequence X' for each sentence in the original training data.

2.3 Generating Complement Sentences (Step III)

As mentioned in the introduction, the complement embeddings X' can be used directly to augment training data and train a model for ATE. However, as the optimization for complement embeddings cannot be done in the test time (due to the unavailability of labels for data), the direct augmentation will cause a mismatch between the training and test phases. To enable the generation of complement embeddings in the test time, we thus propose to first transform the complement embeddings X' into a complement sentence $S' = [w'_1, w'_2, \ldots, w'_n]$ where w'_i is the word whose Glove embedding is closest to the transformed complement vector $F(x'_i)$ for w_i. The set of every pair (S, S') for sentences S in training data is then employed to train a generative language model that seeks to consume S and produce its complement sentence S'. In this way, we can apply the generative model in the test time to generate complement sentences for test data, that, in turn, can be transformed into complement embeddings by mapping words into Glove embedding vectors for data augmentation.

One potential issue is that the number of original and complement sentence pairs (S, S') might be small due to the limited size of ATE datasets, thus hindering the training of effective generative models for our complement sentence goal. As such, we propose to leverage the language priors in the pre-trained generative model GPT-2 (Radford et al., 2019) as the bootstrap knowledge for the complement generation. In particular, we propose to fine-tune the GPT-2 model on the sentence pairs (S, S') in this step. The policy-gradient method REINFORCE (Williams, 1992) is utilized for the fine-tuning process to facilitate the incorporation of different expected properties for complement sentences. Concretely, the input to GPT-2 consists of the S sentence "$w_1 w_2 \ldots w_n SEP$" from which GPT-2 will generate the sentence S''. To compute the reward for the generated sentence S'', we propose three objectives: (1) **Similarity with Complement Sentence**: The generated sentence S'' should be similar to the actual complement sentence S'. To compute the similarity of the two sentences, we employ the CIDEr score (Vedantam et al., 2015) for S'': $R_{sim} = CIDEr(S'')$; (2) **Length Penalty**: As discussed earlier, since we use sum of the corresponding word embeddings of the original and complement sentences for data augmentation, it is intuitive to encourage the generated sentences S'' to have the same length as the original sentence S. Thus, we introduce the length penalty as a part of the reward: $R_{len} = ||S| - |S''||$;

(3) **Difference with Original Sentence**: Similar to embedding regularization $\mathcal{L}_{reg}$ presented earlier for complement embeddings, here we also aim to promote the semantic difference between the generated sentence S'' and the original sentence S (for complementary information). To this end, we represent each sentence using the max-pooled representation of their word embeddings obtained from the GloVe embedding table, i.e., $\hat{R}_S$ and $\hat{R}_{S''}$. Next, their dot-product is employed for the difference reward $R_{diff} = \hat{R}_S \odot \hat{R}_{S''}$. Consequently, the overall reward to train the generative model is computes as $R(S'') = R_{sim} - \beta R_{len} - \gamma R_{diff}$. With REINFORCE, we seek to minimize the negative expected reward $R(S'')$ over the possible choices of S'': $\mathcal{L}_{tune} = -\mathbb{E}_{\hat{S}'' \sim P(\hat{S}''|S)}[R(\hat{S}'')]$. The policy gradient is then estimated by: $\nabla \mathcal{L}_{tune} = -\mathbb{E}_{\hat{S}'' \sim P(\hat{S}''|S)}[(R(\hat{S}'') - b)\nabla \log P(\hat{S}''|S)]$. Using one roll-out sample, we further estimate $\nabla \mathcal{L}_{tune}$ via the generated sentence S'': $\nabla \mathcal{L}_{tune} = -(R(S'') - b)\nabla \log P(\hat{S}''|S)$ where b is the baseline to reduce variance. In this work, we obtain the baseline b via: $b = \frac{1}{|B|}\sum_{i=1}^{|B|} R(S''_i)$, where $|B|$ is the mini-batch size and S''_i is the generated sentence for the i-th sample in the mini-batch.

2.4 Training a Final ATE Model (Step IV)

To achieve a consistency in the training and testing phase, we use the generated sentences from the fine-tuned GPT-2 model as the complement sentences for data augmentation in both phases. In particular, for the training data, similar to the complement embedding optimization Section 2.2, the fine-tuning of GPT-2 is performed with 10-fold cross validation. In particular, the GPT-2 model is fine-tuned on the (S, S') pairs of 9 folds and then employed to generate S'' for each sentence in the remaining fold. To this end, each sentence S in the training data is associated with a generated sentence S''. For test data, we simply apply the fine-tuned GPT-2 model directly to generate a complement sentence for each sentence in that data.

As such, for each sentence S (in the training or test data), its complement sentence from GPT-2 $S'' = [w''_1, w''_2, \ldots, w''_n]$ is first transformed into a representation vector sequence $X'' = [x''_1, x''_2, \ldots, x''_n]$ based on the mappings for their words w''_i from GloVe embeddings[1]. Next, the augmented representation $\bar{X} = [\bar{x}_1, \bar{x}_2, \ldots, \bar{x}_n]$ from the two sentences is computed by the sum of their corresponding word representations: $\bar{x}_i = x_i + \lambda G(x''_i)$, where G is a feed-forward network to match the dimensions of the GloVe embedding $G(x''_i)$ and x_i. Finally, following the base ATE architecture, the resulting vectors $\bar{X}$ are sent to a BiLSTM network followed by a feed-forward layer to obtain the label distribution $P(\cdot|S, S'', w_i)$ for the i-th word. This distribution is used for prediction in the test phase while the training phase employs the negative log-likelihood (over training data) to train the final ATE model: $\mathcal{L}_{final} = -\frac{1}{n}\sum_{i=1}^{n} \log P(y_i|S, S'', w_i)$.

[1]Note that the generated sentence S'' might have a different length from the original sentence S. For these cases, we pad (with zero vectors) or truncate the vector sequence X'' to have the same length as S.

Datasets	Lap14		Res14		Res15		Res16	
Type	Train	Test	Train	Test	Train	Test	Train	Test
Sentences	3045	800	3041	800	1315	685	2000	676
Aspects	2342	650	3686	1134	1209	547	1757	622

Table 1: Statistics of the SemEval datasets

3 Experiments

Datasets & Parameters: To evaluate the effectiveness of the proposed method, we employ the commonly used SemEval datasets for ATE. Specifically, we use the datasets of SemEval 2014 Task 4 (Pontiki et al., 2014), i.e., Lap14 and Res14 reviews for laptops and restaurants, and SemEval 2015 Task 12 (Pontiki et al., 2015) and SemEval 2016 Task 5 (Pontiki et al., 2016), i.e., Res15 and Res16 with reviews for restaurants. Following prior work (Chen and Qian, 2020a), we employ the official train/test splits and randomly select 150 samples from training data as validation data for those datasets. Table 1 shows the statistics for the datasets.

In our experiments, we use the development set of the Lap14 dataset to tune the hyper-parameters. Based on our experiments, the following values are selected: 200 dimensions for the BiLSTM layer and the feed-forward layers; 1 layer for BiLSTM and 2 layers for the feed-forward networks; the BERT$_{base}$ version for the encoding layer with fixed parameters; GPT-2 small for sentence generation; 0.3 for the λ in the word vector augmentation; 0.1 for the trade-off parameters α_{reg} and α_{GloVe} in the complement embedding optimization; 0.1 and 0.05 for the trade-off parameters β and γ in the reward for GPT-2 fine-tuning; 0.3 for the learning rate for the Adam optimizer; and 50 for batch-size.

Baselines: Following prior work, we compare our model with: (1) the winners of the SemEval tasks:

IHS-RD	74.55	79.62	-	-
DLIREC	73.78	84.01	-	-
EliXa	-	-	70.04	-
NLANGP	-	-	67.12	72.34
RNCRF	78.42	84.93	67.74	69.72
MIN	77.58	-	-	73.44
CMLA	77.80	85.29	70.73	72.77
HAST	79.52	85.61	71.46	73.61
RACL-BERT	81.99	85.37	72.82	-
Dual-MRC	82.51	86.60	75.08	-
BiLSTM-CRF	74.28	-	-	71.44
Seq2Seq	78.68	-	-	74.01
BERT	81.14	-	-	75.89
DE-CNN	81.58	-	-	75.19
BERT-PT	85.33	-	-	80.29
SoftProto	83.19	87.39	73.27	76.98
CL-BERT	85.61	-	-	81.14
ATEOA (ours)	**86.71**	**88.99**	**75.41**	**82.58**

Table 2: F1 scores on the test sets of the SemEval datasets. The proposed model ATEOE is significantly better than prior work ($p < 0.05$).

IHS-RD (Chernyshevich, 2014), **DLIREC** (Toh and Wang, 2014), **EliXa** (San Vicente et al., 2015), **NLANGP** (Toh and Su, 2016); (2) Deep joint models, i.e., jointly train ATE with Opinion Term Extraction (OTE) or Aspect-Based Sentiment Analysis (ABSA): **RNCRF** (Wang et al., 2016), **MIN** (Li and Lam, 2017), **CMLA** (Mao et al., 2021), **HAST** (Li et al., 2018), **RACL** (Chen and Qian, 2020b), **Dual-MRC** (Mao et al., 2021); (3) Deep models trained on ATE datasets augmented with external in-domain corpora and resources: **BiLSTM-CRF** (Li et al., 2020), **Seq2Seq** (Ma et al., 2019), **BERT** (Li et al., 2020), **DE-CNN** (Xu et al., 2018), **BERT-PT** (Li et al., 2020), **SoftProto** (Chen and Qian, 2020a). We also compare with **CL-BERT** (Yang et al., 2020) which employs constituency trees for ATE. For the evaluation metric, following prior work, we report the F1 score for aspect term prediction. A prediction is counted as correct if its boundaries match the gold aspect term. We name our model ATEOA which stands for Aspect Term Extraction with Optimal Augmentation.

Results: The main results are shown in Table 2. This table shows that the proposed model can effectively improve the performance compared to existing joint inference and data augmentation methods. This achievement is significant as the proposed model does not utilize any external in-domain data nor extra supervision from other related tasks. This is important for domains with limited data where collecting large-scale in-domain data or supervision from related tasks could be prohibitively expensive. Moreover, as the proposed model employs pre-trained language models (i.e., GPT-2) to generate effective augmentation sentences for training/test data, it can directly benefit from growing advances in pre-trained language models.

Ablation Study: The proposed ATEOA model is trained in four major training steps. In this section, we study the role of those proposed steps for the performance of the ATE model. For each training step, we aim to answer two questions: (i) Whether the proposed step is beneficial for ATEOA? and (ii) Is the current configuration for the step optimal? To this end, we consider the following ablated models: (1) **- Base Model Training (Step I)**: This model ignores step I to train a base ATE model in Section 2.1. In particular, step II for finding complement embeddings will only employ an ATE base model with randomly initialized parameters. Here, the parameters for the base model are not fixed; they are jointly updated with the complement embeddings in step II of the training; (2) **- Complement Representation Finding (Step II)**: This model excludes step II of the training procedure that makes the optimized complement representations unavailable for the fine-tuning of GPT-2 in step III. As such, to achieve a fair access to the trained base model in step I in this model, we change step III by fine-tuning the GPT-2 model with the reward of F1 score of the trained base model (from step I) on the validation data. Here, the base model is applied on the representation combinations of the original and GPT-generated sentences (also using GloVe embeddings for the words in the generated sentences); (3) **- Embedding Regularization $\mathcal{L}_{reg}$**: This model removes the regularization loss $\mathcal{L}_{reg}$ in step II of the training process; (4) **- GloVe Alignment $\mathcal{L}_{GloVe}$**: This model excludes the regularization $\mathcal{L}_{GloVe}$ for representation alignment with GloVe in step II; (5) **- Language Model (Step III)**: This ablated models does not utilize step III, thus eliminating the GPT-2 model trained over the original and complement sentence pairs (S, S'). As such, in step IV, we directly retrain the base model on the augmented data with the complement representations X' (i.e., $x_i + \lambda x'_i$) and do not apply data augmentation for test data (i.e., applying the train model on x_i directly); (6) **- Language Model + FForward**: This model is similar to (5) (i.e., excluding GPT-2 in step III). However, to allow the augmentation on test data, a feed-forward network is trained on pairs (x_i, x_i') to directly transform the representation vectors x_i of the original sentence S into the complement representations for data augmentation in both training and test phases of step IV; (7) **- Similarity Reward**: For this model, we do not use the similarity reward R_{sim} in the reward function to fine-tune GPT-2 in step III; (8) **- Length Penalty**: This model does not employ the length penalty R_{len} in the reward for tuning GPT-2; (9) **- Difference Reward**: For this baseline, the reward based on difference with original sentence, i.e., R_{diff}, is ablated from the reward for GPT-2 fine-tuning; (10) **- Final Training (Step IV)**: This baseline skips the last step of the proposed training procedure. As such, the combined representations of the original sentence S and the complement sentence S'' generated by GPT-2 (i.e., $x_i + \lambda G(x_i''))$ are directly sent into the base ATE model (trained over the entire training data) from step I for prediction; and (11) **- Generated Data in Final Training**: Finally, to demonstrate the benefit of augmenting training data with generated sentences from the fine-tuned GPT-2 model in step IV, we report the performance of the base model that is instead trained on the combination of the word representations X and the optimized complement representations X', i.e., $x_i + \lambda x_i'$ in step II (as in (5)). The fine-tuned GPT-2 model is still used to generate complement sentences for data augmentation in the test phase for this model.

The performance of the models on the test sets of the SemEval datasets is reported in Table 3. This table clearly shows that all training steps in the proposed procedure are necessary as skipping any of these steps will hurt the performance. In particular, among the four steps, removing step III has the most negative impact as the ablated model "*- Language Model*" has the lowest performance across datasets. We attribute the importance of step III to its ability to enable augmentation consistency for training and test data (i.e., the fine-tuned GPT-2 can generate complement sentences for both training and test data). This is further highlighted by the worse performance of the "**- Generated Data in Final Training**" model where the training data is augmented with X', but GPT-generated data is used to augment test data. Table 3 also shows that among the three awards for GPT-2 fine-tuning, the similarity reward is most important. This is expected as the primary goal of fine-tuning is to generate sentences that are similar to the complement sentences S'.

Model	Lap14	Res14	Res15	Res16
ATEOA (Full)	**86.71**	**88.99**	**75.41**	**82.58**
- Base Model Training (Step I)	84.39	86.91	74.18	78.91
- Comp. Rep. Finding (Step II)	84.96	86.18	74.22	79.65
- Embedding Regularization $\mathcal{L}_{reg}$	85.04	87.93	74.31	80.32
- Glove Alignment $\mathcal{L}_{GloVe}$	86.02	88.12	75.31	81.95
- Language Model (Step III)	84.22	85.91	73.17	78.91
- Language Model + FForward	84.13	86.94	73.22	80.51
- Similarity Reward	83.33	85.98	73.54	79.05
- Length Penalty	85.10	87.99	73.91	81.18
- Difference Reward	85.11	88.02	73.88	80.04
- Final Training (Step IV)	84.40	87.12	74.09	80.01
- Generated Data in Final Train.	84.01	86.92	73.81	79.88

Table 3: Performance of the ablated models on test sets.

4 Analysis

Generative Language Models: As it is evident in the ablation study, exploiting a pre-trained generative model (i.e., GPT-2) for ATEOA is preferable since it can provide language priors to support the sentence generation learning from limited ATE datasets. In this section, we study how the performance of the model changes if we alter the generative language model used in step III of ATEOA. Concretely, we compare the performance of three different models: (1) **GPT-2** (Radford et al., 2019): This transformer-based model is pre-trained on WebText corpus. We examine its small version with 117 million parameters; (2) **T5** (Raffel et al., 2019): This language model employs the encoder-decoder architecture in Transformer for sequence-to-sequence tasks. We explore its base version with 220 million parameters. We use the input sentence S as the source sequence and the complement sentence S' as the target sequence to fine-tune the T5 model; and (3) **BART** (Lewis et al., 2019): This model is a transformer-based auto-encoder language model. We also utilize its base version with 139 million parameters. Similar to T5, this is a sequence-to-sequence generative model that is fine-tuned by treating S and S' as the source and target sequences respectively.

To compare the performance of the three language models, we use them in the training step III of the final ATE model and report the corresponding performance. Furthermore, we compare the language models on their capability to generate sentences that are similar to the complement sentences S'. In particular, using the Lap14 dataset, we seek to find a complement sentence S' for each sentence in the test data portion with the proposed method.

Language Model	Lap14	Res14	Res15	Res16
GPT-2	**86.71**	**88.99**	**75.41**	**82.58**
BART	84.32	88.05	74.91	79.49
T5	84.18	86.95	73.16	79.15

Table 4: Performance of the final ATE model on test sets with different language models in step III.

Language Model	BLUE-4	METEOR	ROUGE-1	ROUGE-2
GPT-2	12.05	12.25	31.89	10.33
BART	9.39	10.14	29.05	9.06
T5	13.10	11.92	30.33	8.95

Table 5: Similarity between the generated sentences from the language models and the "ground-truth" complement sentences on test data of Lap14.

To this end, a base model is first trained on the training data portion using step I; the complement representations X' are then computed for each sentence in the test data portion using step II; each X' is then mapped into the complement sentence S' with the GloVe embeddings. Here, S' serves as the "ground-truth" complement sentence for the test sentences in our approach. Next, we use the fine-tuned language model to generate the complement sentence S'' for each test sentence (i.e., prompting the language model with test data). Finally, we evaluate the similarity of the generated sentence S'' and the "ground-truth" complement sentence S' (for the test data) using ROUGE-1, ROUGE-2, METEOR (Banerjee and Lavie, 2005) and BLUE4 as the similarity metrics. The results for this experiment are shown in Tables 4 and 5. Both tables clearly demonstrate the capacity of GPT-2 to generate better complement sentences to augment ATE data (i.e., yielding better performance for ATE in Table 4 and generating more similar sentences to the obtained complement sentences S' in Table 5).

Tail Aspect Term Analysis: Following prior work (Chen and Qian, 2020a), we evaluate the performance for our model on the tail aspect terms in test data (i.e., aspect terms occurring less than 5 times in the training sets). As such, we compare our model with prior work that reports their performance in this analysis, i.e., **DE-CNN** (Xu et al., 2018) and **SoftProto** (Chen and Qian, 2020a). Note that we replace the contextualized BERT representations (i.e., X) in our model with the GloVe embeddings to achieve a fair comparison with prior work in this section. The results are provided in Table 6 that clearly shows the superiority of ATEOA to recognize tail aspect terms and further highlights the benefits of the proposed method.

Model	Lap14	Res14	Res15	Res16
DE-CNN	74.37	77.61	70.00	70.68
SoftProto	79.85	82.22	76.80	70.93
ATEOA (ours)	**81.92**	**83.69**	**77.39**	**73.49**

Table 6: Performance for tail aspect terms on test data.

Case Study: To provide more insight into the quality of the complement sentences generated by the pre-trained GPT-2 model, Table 7 showcases some examples from the laptop and restaurant domains whose aspect terms can only be correctly predicted by our proposed method (i.e., prior work fails to recognize aspect terms in these cases). The table suggests that although the generated sentences might not look natural, they clearly provide more evidence and emphasis on the aspect terms which makes the task easier for the ATE model. Specifically, in the first example, the generated complement sentence emphasizes the target word "*touchpad*" in the original sentence by replicating it and including the related word "*mouse*". The same pattern of emphasis can be seen in the second example where the model excludes the word "*money*" and includes the related word "*Food*" (that are more related to the target word "*meal*") in the generated sentence.

5 Related Work

ATE has been first approached with rule-based (Hu and Liu, 2004; Wu et al., 2009) or feature-based (Li et al., 2010; Chen et al., 2014; Toh and Su, 2016) methods. Recently, ATE methods have focused on neural networks such as LSTM (Liu et al., 2015), CNN (Xu et al., 2018) or Transformer (Li et al., 2020). An ATE system can be used in downstream applications such as sentiment analysis (Wang et al., 2019; Pouran Ben Veyseh et al., 2020b; Orbach et al., 2021) or opinion term extraction (Pouran Ben Veyseh et al., 2020a). One of the challenges for this task is the scarcity of training data which hinders the training of large neural networks. To alleviate this issue, two major directions have been explored in the literature: (I) Joint Training, i.e., jointly solving ATE task with another related task such as ABSA (Wang et al., 2016; Mao et al., 2021; Chen and Qian, 2020b) or Opinion Term Extraction (OTE) (Li and Lam, 2017; Dai and Song, 2019); and (II) Data Augmentation, i.e., augmenting ATE models with in-domain unlabeled data (Xu et al., 2018; Li et al., 2020; Chen and Qian,

Input Sentences	Generated Complement Sentences	Targets
however , there are major issues with the touchpad which render the device nearly useless .	Although , exist some problems with the touchpad and mouse makes touchpad useless and touchpad useless	touchpad
way too much money for such a terrible meal .	Food costs so much for such a bad meal .	meal

Table 7: Generated complement sentences by GPT-2.

2020a). In this work, we also propose a method to augment the training data for ATE. However, unlike prior work that requires large in-domain corpus, our approach employs an existing large-scale language model (i.e., GPT-2) to facilitate the generation of complement sentences for the available ATE datasets. Using GPT-2 to address data scarcity has been shown to be effective in other domains and tasks (Papanikolaou and Pierleoni, 2020; Pouran Ben Veyseh et al., 2021; Peng et al., 2020). In this work, we demonstrate the viability of this technique for aspect term extraction.

6 Conclusion

We introduce a new training procedure for Aspect Term Extraction. In the proposed procedure, the available ATE dataset is employed to train a deep model which is further used to find complement representations for input sentences in training data. Later, to obtain the complement sentences at the inference time, we tine-tune the pre-trained language model GPT-2 to generate sentences similar to the complement sentences found in the previous steps (with GloVe mapping). Our extensive experiments on benchmark datasets reveal the superiority of the proposed model, leading to the state-of-the-art performance for the datasets. Moreover, our analysis show that all steps of the proposed procedure are necessary and effective for the ATE task. In future, we will explore the application of this procedure in other related task such as OTE and ABSA.

Acknowledgement

This research has been supported by the Army Research Office (ARO) grant W911NF-21-1-0112 and the NSF grant CNS-1747798 to the IUCRC Center for Big Learning. This research is also based upon work supported by the Office of the Director of National Intelligence (ODNI), Intelligence Advanced Research Projects Activity (IARPA), via IARPA Contract No. 2019-19051600006 under the Better Extraction from Text Towards Enhanced Retrieval (BETTER) Program. The views and conclusions contained herein are those of the authors and should not be interpreted as necessarily representing the official policies, either expressed or implied, of ARO, ODNI, IARPA, the Department of Defense, or the U.S. Government. The U.S. Government is authorized to reproduce and distribute reprints for governmental purposes notwithstanding any copyright annotation therein. This document does not contain technology or technical data controlled under either the U.S. International Traffic in Arms Regulations or the U.S. Export Administration Regulations.

References

Satanjeev Banerjee and Alon Lavie. 2005. Meteor: An automatic metric for mt evaluation with improved correlation with human judgments. In *Proceedings of the acl workshop on intrinsic and extrinsic evaluation measures for machine translation and/or summarization*, pages 65–72.

Zhiyuan Chen, Arjun Mukherjee, and Bing Liu. 2014. Aspect extraction with automated prior knowledge learning. In *Proceedings of the 52nd Annual Meeting of the Association for Computational Linguistics (Volume 1: Long Papers)*, pages 347–358, Baltimore, Maryland. Association for Computational Linguistics.

Zhuang Chen and Tieyun Qian. 2019. Transfer capsule network for aspect level sentiment classification. In *Proceedings of the 57th Annual Meeting of the Association for Computational Linguistics*, pages 547–556, Florence, Italy. Association for Computational Linguistics.

Zhuang Chen and Tieyun Qian. 2020a. Enhancing aspect term extraction with soft prototypes. In *Proceedings of the 2020 Conference on Empirical Methods in Natural Language Processing (EMNLP)*, pages 2107–2117, Online. Association for Computational Linguistics.

Zhuang Chen and Tieyun Qian. 2020b. Relation-aware collaborative learning for unified aspect-based sentiment analysis. In *Proceedings of the 58th Annual Meeting of the Association for Computational Linguistics*, pages 3685–3694, Online. Association for Computational Linguistics.

Maryna Chernyshevich. 2014. IHS R&D Belarus: Cross-domain extraction of product features using CRF. In *Proceedings of the 8th International Workshop on Semantic Evaluation (SemEval 2014)*, pages

309–313, Dublin, Ireland. Association for Computational Linguistics.

Hongliang Dai and Yangqiu Song. 2019. Neural aspect and opinion term extraction with mined rules as weak supervision. In *Proceedings of the 57th Annual Meeting of the Association for Computational Linguistics*, pages 5268–5277, Florence, Italy. Association for Computational Linguistics.

Jacob Devlin, Ming-Wei Chang, Kenton Lee, and Kristina Toutanova. 2019. BERT: Pre-training of deep bidirectional transformers for language understanding. In *Proceedings of the 2019 Conference of the North American Chapter of the Association for Computational Linguistics: Human Language Technologies, Volume 1 (Long and Short Papers)*, pages 4171–4186, Minneapolis, Minnesota. Association for Computational Linguistics.

Ruidan He, Wee Sun Lee, Hwee Tou Ng, and Daniel Dahlmeier. 2018. Exploiting document knowledge for aspect-level sentiment classification. In *Proceedings of the 56th Annual Meeting of the Association for Computational Linguistics (Volume 2: Short Papers)*, pages 579–585, Melbourne, Australia. Association for Computational Linguistics.

Minqing Hu and Bing Liu. 2004. Mining and summarizing customer reviews. In *Proceedings of the tenth ACM SIGKDD international conference on Knowledge discovery and data mining*, pages 168–177.

Mike Lewis, Yinhan Liu, Naman Goyal, Marjan Ghazvininejad, Abdelrahman Mohamed, Omer Levy, Ves Stoyanov, and Luke Zettlemoyer. 2019. Bart: Denoising sequence-to-sequence pre-training for natural language generation, translation, and comprehension. *arXiv preprint arXiv:1910.13461*.

Fangtao Li, Chao Han, Minlie Huang, Xiaoyan Zhu, Ying-Ju Xia, Shu Zhang, and Hao Yu. 2010. Structure-aware review mining and summarization. In *Proceedings of the 23rd International Conference on Computational Linguistics (Coling 2010)*, pages 653–661, Beijing, China. Coling 2010 Organizing Committee.

Kun Li, Chengbo Chen, Xiaojun Quan, Qing Ling, and Yan Song. 2020. Conditional augmentation for aspect term extraction via masked sequence-to-sequence generation. In *Proceedings of the 58th Annual Meeting of the Association for Computational Linguistics*, pages 7056–7066, Online. Association for Computational Linguistics.

Xin Li, Lidong Bing, Piji Li, Wai Lam, and Zhimou Yang. 2018. Aspect term extraction with history attention and selective transformation. In *IJCAI*.

Xin Li and Wai Lam. 2017. Deep multi-task learning for aspect term extraction with memory interaction. In *Proceedings of the 2017 Conference on Empirical Methods in Natural Language Processing*, Copenhagen, Denmark. Association for Computational Linguistics.

Pengfei Liu, Shafiq Joty, and Helen Meng. 2015. Fine-grained opinion mining with recurrent neural networks and word embeddings. In *Proceedings of the 2015 conference on empirical methods in natural language processing*, pages 1433–1443.

Huaishao Luo, Lei Ji, Tianrui Li, Daxin Jiang, and Nan Duan. 2020. GRACE: Gradient harmonized and cascaded labeling for aspect-based sentiment analysis. In *Findings of the Association for Computational Linguistics: EMNLP 2020*, pages 54–64, Online. Association for Computational Linguistics.

Dehong Ma, Sujian Li, Fangzhao Wu, Xing Xie, and Houfeng Wang. 2019. Exploring sequence-to-sequence learning in aspect term extraction. In *Proceedings of the 57th Annual Meeting of the Association for Computational Linguistics*, pages 3538–3547, Florence, Italy. Association for Computational Linguistics.

Yue Mao, Yi Shen, Chao Yu, and Longjun Cai. 2021. A joint training dual-mrc framework for aspect based sentiment analysis. In *AAAI*.

Matan Orbach, Orith Toledo-Ronen, Artem Spector, Ranit Aharonov, Yoav Katz, and Noam Slonim. 2021. YASO: A targeted sentiment analysis evaluation dataset for open-domain reviews. In *Proceedings of the 2021 Conference on Empirical Methods in Natural Language Processing*, pages 9154–9173, Online and Punta Cana, Dominican Republic. Association for Computational Linguistics.

Yannis Papanikolaou and Andrea Pierleoni. 2020. Dare: Data augmented relation extraction with gpt-2. In *SciNLP workshop at the Conference on Automated Knowledge Base Construction (AKBC)*.

Baolin Peng, Chenguang Zhu, Michael Zeng, and Jianfeng Gao. 2020. Data augmentation for spoken language understanding via pretrained language models. *arXiv preprint arXiv:2004.13952*.

Jeffrey Pennington, Richard Socher, and Christopher D Manning. 2014. Glove: Global vectors for word representation. In *Proceedings of the 2014 conference on empirical methods in natural language processing (EMNLP)*, pages 1532–1543.

Maria Pontiki, Dimitris Galanis, Haris Papageorgiou, Ion Androutsopoulos, Suresh Manandhar, Mohammad AL-Smadi, Mahmoud Al-Ayyoub, Yanyan Zhao, Bing Qin, Orphée De Clercq, Véronique Hoste, Marianna Apidianaki, Xavier Tannier, Natalia Loukachevitch, Evgeniy Kotelnikov, Nuria Bel, Salud María Jiménez-Zafra, and Gülşen Eryiğit. 2016. SemEval-2016 task 5: Aspect based sentiment analysis. In *Proceedings of the 10th International Workshop on Semantic Evaluation (SemEval-2016)*, pages 19–30, San Diego, California. Association for Computational Linguistics.

Maria Pontiki, Dimitris Galanis, Haris Papageorgiou, Suresh Manandhar, and Ion Androutsopoulos. 2015.

SemEval-2015 task 12: Aspect based sentiment analysis. In *Proceedings of the 9th International Workshop on Semantic Evaluation (SemEval 2015)*, pages 486–495, Denver, Colorado. Association for Computational Linguistics.

Maria Pontiki, Dimitris Galanis, John Pavlopoulos, Harris Papageorgiou, Ion Androutsopoulos, and Suresh Manandhar. 2014. SemEval-2014 task 4: Aspect based sentiment analysis. In *Proceedings of the 8th International Workshop on Semantic Evaluation (SemEval 2014)*, pages 27–35, Dublin, Ireland. Association for Computational Linguistics.

Amir Pouran Ben Veyseh, Viet Lai, Franck Dernoncourt, and Thien Huu Nguyen. 2021. Unleash GPT-2 power for event detection. In *Proceedings of the 59th Annual Meeting of the Association for Computational Linguistics and the 11th International Joint Conference on Natural Language Processing (Volume 1: Long Papers)*, pages 6271–6282, Online. Association for Computational Linguistics.

Amir Pouran Ben Veyseh, Nasim Nouri, Franck Dernoncourt, Dejing Dou, and Thien Huu Nguyen. 2020a. Introducing syntactic structures into target opinion word extraction with deep learning. In *Proceedings of the 2020 Conference on Empirical Methods in Natural Language Processing (EMNLP)*, pages 8947–8956, Online. Association for Computational Linguistics.

Amir Pouran Ben Veyseh, Nasim Nouri, Franck Dernoncourt, Quan Hung Tran, Dejing Dou, and Thien Huu Nguyen. 2020b. Improving aspect-based sentiment analysis with gated graph convolutional networks and syntax-based regulation. In *Findings of the Association for Computational Linguistics: EMNLP 2020*, pages 4543–4548, Online. Association for Computational Linguistics.

Alec Radford, Jeffrey Wu, Rewon Child, David Luan, Dario Amodei, and Ilya Sutskever. 2019. Language models are unsupervised multitask learners. *OpenAI blog*, 1(8):9.

Colin Raffel, Noam Shazeer, Adam Roberts, Katherine Lee, Sharan Narang, Michael Matena, Yanqi Zhou, Wei Li, and Peter J Liu. 2019. Exploring the limits of transfer learning with a unified text-to-text transformer. *arXiv preprint arXiv:1910.10683*.

Iñaki San Vicente, Xabier Saralegi, and Rodrigo Agerri. 2015. EliXa: A modular and flexible ABSA platform. In *Proceedings of the 9th International Workshop on Semantic Evaluation (SemEval 2015)*, pages 748–752, Denver, Colorado. Association for Computational Linguistics.

Zhiqiang Toh and Jian Su. 2016. NLANGP at SemEval-2016 task 5: Improving aspect based sentiment analysis using neural network features. In *Proceedings of the 10th International Workshop on Semantic Evaluation (SemEval-2016)*, pages 282–288, San Diego, California. Association for Computational Linguistics.

Zhiqiang Toh and Wenting Wang. 2014. DLIREC: Aspect term extraction and term polarity classification system. In *Proceedings of the 8th International Workshop on Semantic Evaluation (SemEval 2014)*, pages 235–240, Dublin, Ireland. Association for Computational Linguistics.

Ramakrishna Vedantam, C Lawrence Zitnick, and Devi Parikh. 2015. Cider: Consensus-based image description evaluation. In *Proceedings of the IEEE conference on computer vision and pattern recognition*, pages 4566–4575.

Jingjing Wang, Changlong Sun, Shoushan Li, Jiancheng Wang, Luo Si, Min Zhang, Xiaozhong Liu, and Guodong Zhou. 2019. Human-like decision making: Document-level aspect sentiment classification via hierarchical reinforcement learning. In *Proceedings of the 2019 Conference on Empirical Methods in Natural Language Processing and the 9th International Joint Conference on Natural Language Processing (EMNLP-IJCNLP)*, pages 5581–5590, Hong Kong, China. Association for Computational Linguistics.

Wenya Wang, Sinno Jialin Pan, Daniel Dahlmeier, and Xiaokui Xiao. 2016. Recursive neural conditional random fields for aspect-based sentiment analysis. In *Proceedings of the 2016 Conference on Empirical Methods in Natural Language Processing*, pages 616–626, Austin, Texas. Association for Computational Linguistics.

Ronald J. Williams. 1992. Simple statistical gradient-following algorithms for connectionist reinforcement learning. In *Kluwer Academic*.

Yuanbin Wu, Qi Zhang, Xuanjing Huang, and Lide Wu. 2009. Phrase dependency parsing for opinion mining. In *Proceedings of the 2009 Conference on Empirical Methods in Natural Language Processing*, pages 1533–1541, Singapore. Association for Computational Linguistics.

Hu Xu, Bing Liu, Lei Shu, and Philip S. Yu. 2018. Double embeddings and CNN-based sequence labeling for aspect extraction. In *Proceedings of the 56th Annual Meeting of the Association for Computational Linguistics (Volume 2: Short Papers)*, pages 592–598, Melbourne, Australia. Association for Computational Linguistics.

Yunyi Yang, Kun Li, Xiaojun Quan, Weizhou Shen, and Qinliang Su. 2020. Constituency lattice encoding for aspect term extraction. In *Proceedings of the 28th International Conference on Computational Linguistics*, pages 844–855, Barcelona, Spain (Online). International Committee on Computational Linguistics.

Introducing QuBERT: A Large Monolingual Corpus and BERT Model for Southern Quechua

Rodolfo Zevallos[◇] **John E. Ortega**[§] **William Chen**[▽] **Richard Castro**[Ω] **Nuria Bel**[◇]
Cesar Yoshikawa[ψ] **Renzo Ventura**[ψ] **Hilario Aradiel**[ψ] **Nelsi Melgarejo**[α]
[◇]Universitat Pompeu Fabra [§]Universidade de Santiago de Compostela (CITIUS)
[▽]University of Central Florida [Ω]Universidad Nacional de San Antonio Abad
[ψ]Universidad Nacional del Callao [α]Pontificia Universidad Católica del Perú
{rodolfojoel.zevallos, nuria.bel}@upf.edu, john.ortega@usc.gal, wchen6255@knights.ucf.edu,
rcastro@hinant.in, {ctyoshikawaa, rventuras, haradielc}@unac.edu.pe, nelsi.melgarejo@pucp.edu.pe

Abstract

The lack of resources for languages in the Americas has proven to be a problem for the creation of digital systems such as machine translation, search engines, chat bots, and more. The scarceness of digital resources for a language causes a higher impact on populations where the language is spoken by millions of people. We introduce the first official large combined corpus for deep learning of an indigenous South American low-resource language spoken by millions called *Quechua*. Specifically, our curated corpus is created from text gathered from the southern region of Peru where a dialect of Quechua is spoken that has not traditionally been used for digital systems as a target dialect in the past. In order to make our work repeatable by others, we also offer a public, pre-trained, BERT model called *QuBERT* which is the largest linguistic model ever trained for any Quechua type, not just the southern region dialect. We furthermore test our corpus and its corresponding BERT model on two major tasks: (1) named-entity recognition (NER) and (2) part-of-speech (POS) tagging by using state-of-the-art techniques where we achieve results comparable to other work on higher-resource languages. In this article, we describe the methodology, challenges, and results from the creation of QuBERT which is on on par with other state-of-the-art multilingual models for natural language processing achieving between 71 and 74% F1 score on NER and 84–87% on POS tasks.

1 Introduction

With the availability of online digital resources for computation and data storage, the capability for executing natural language processing (NLP) tasks such as named-entity recognition (NER), part-of-speech (POS) tagging, and machine translation (MT) on low-resource languages, languages with few digital resources available, has increased. The processing power and data available for experimentation are unsurpassed in history and research (Edwards, 2021) has shown that in the current decade we are on track to overcome previous methods, such as Moore's law (Schaller, 1997), for predicting computing time of experiments. This finding is better observed on high-resources languages like English and French where the amount of data that exists is more than enough to take advantage of the latest computing architectures. Unfortunately, for other low-resource languages like Quechua, an indigenous language spoken by millions in Peru, South America, it is more difficult to create statistically significant NLP models due to the amount of data needed (typically on the order of millions of sentences). Therefore, it is critical to create public-facing mechanisms for low-resource languages like Quechua to help provide research collaboration which will improve the quality for low-resource language NLP systems. We aim to improve the digital resources available for Quechua by curating a large monolingual corpus for southern Quechua, a dialect of Quechua spoken in the southern region of Peru not commonly found in most literature.

The initiative we present in this article can be considered a major contribution and advancement as means to improve the quality of NLP tasks for the Quechua language. We outline the multiple innovations and contributions provided below.

1. A considerably large, curated, monolingual corpus of southern Quechua consisting of nearly 450K segments.

2. A normalization technique applied to the corpus based on finite-state transducers (FSTs) (Rios, 2015; Rios and Göhring, 2016; Ortega et al., 2020a).

Proceedings of the Third Workshop on Deep Learning for Low-Resource Natural Language Processing, pages 214 - 226
July 14, 2022 ©2022 Association for Computational Linguistics

3. Several tokenization techniques applied to the corpus, each made available for download, including byte-pair encoding (BPE) (Sennrich et al., 2015), BPE-Guided (Ortega et al., 2020a), and Prefix-Root-Postfix-Encoding (PRPE) (Chen and Fazio, 2021; Zuters et al., 2018).

4. A pre-trained transformer model based on RoBERTa (Liu et al., 2019) called *QuBERT* that uses the corpus along with the best performing normalization and tokenization techniques from items 2 and 3 above.

5. A comparison of the performance of the techniques introduced in items 2 and 3 above on a NER classification task.

6. A comparison of the performance of the techniques introduced in items 2 and 3 above on a POS classification task.

In order to cover our innovations and contributions, we highlight the details in several sections. First, in Section 2, we describe the latest work on Quechua and other techniques related to low-resource NLP tasks such as the ones we introduce on NER and POS. Next in Section 3, we provide more background on the Quechua language by covering morphological, phonological, and other important grammatical details. Then, we describe how we curated our corpus in Section 4. In Section 5, we provide details on the parameters and configuration for our models and tokenization techniques which leads way to the experimental evaluation and results from the NER and POS tasks in Section 6. Finally, we wrap up with a few proposed lines of future work and a conclusion in Section 7.

2 Related work

In this section we present several works that can be considered state-of-the-art at this time for Quechua. Since we are introducing several new contributions, we briefly cover the most recent work and how it related to each contribution mentioned.

First, concerning the introduction of the corpus, we discuss work where corpora have been introduced for public use. Like many low-resource NLP projects, one of the several corpora that is often used is the Opus[1] (Tiedemann, 2012) corpus. It contains text similar to ours in southern Quechua (Quechua II, see more details on Quechua variants in Section 3); however, it contains biblical text only. Other work (Ortega et al., 2020a) introduced the JW300 corpus (Agić and Vulić, 2019); their corpus was for one domain also. The corpus we present contains entries from several diverse sources while at the same time including Opus and the JW300. Ortega et. al (Ortega et al., 2020a) also presented a magazine selection known as *Hinantin* which contained 250 non-biblical Quechua—Spanish sentences found on-line[2]. While the Hinantin magazine was a more diverse domain than other Quechua corpora previously introduced, our corpus is the largest and most diverse compiled currently available.

Our second contribution consists of a normalization technique used in previous work (Rios, 2015; Rios and Göhring, 2016; Ortega et al., 2020a). The work presented in this article uses the same normalization technique (described further in Section 5) but, to our knowledge, this is the first time that the normalization technique has been used on a corpus of this size for southern Quechua.

Thirdly, for Quechua, there has not been a tokenization comparison similar to the one presented here. There are two works (Chen and Fazio, 2021; Ortega et al., 2020a) that present approaches called *BPE-Guided* and *PRPE* separately but their work did not compare on such a varied corpus for named-entity recognition or part-of-speech tasks, both of their works for the machine translation task only.

The fourth, fifth, and sixth contributions are all related to the first-time presentation of a deep learning transformer model for Quechua that is used for NER and POS classification tasks. One of the works that presented deep learning approaches for Quechua is a shared task (Mager et al., 2021a) from the first workshop on NLP for indigenous languages of the America (Mager et al., 2021b). Another work called *indt5* (Nagoudi et al., 2021) used an encoder-decoder model transformers based on T5 (Raffel et al., 2020). Both models were mainly used for translation and the data did not contain nearly as much Quechua–Spanish text as ours. (Ortega et al., 2020a) applied a deep learning approach where quality was low due to the use of the Opus corpus for training and Hinantin for test – their deep learning approach was for machine translation also. Other work (Zheng et al., 2021; Liu et al., 2020) has presented large corpora with trans-

[1] http://opus.nlpl.eu

[2] http://hinant.in

former architectures but did not include Quechua as one of the low-resource languages. The one work that can be considered closest to ours in size and technique is the work by Wongso et. al (Wongso et al., 2021), they pre-trained mono-lingual models on GPT-2 (Radford et al., 2019), BERT (Devlin et al., 2019), and RoBERTa (Liu et al., 2019). Like our work, they used a monolingual corpus which consisted of a variety of text and evaluated the models on a sentiment classification task for Sudanese. The main difference between their work and our work is that our tasks are slightly different and are based on Quechua. In order to better understand why NLP tasks for Quechua can be more complex than for other languages, we present more details in the next section on the language.

3 Quechua language

Quechua is an indigenous language native to several regions in South America, mainly Peru, Ecuador, and Bolivia, and is spoken by nearly 8 million people. It is known (Pinnis et al., 2017; Kann, 2019; Karakanta et al., 2018) to be a highly inflective language based on its suffixes which agglutinate. Due to its morphology, Quechua has been found to be similar to other languages like Finnish (Ortega et al., 2021, 2020b; Ortega and Pillaipakkamnatt, 2018).

Linguistically, Quechua can be considered a unique and even complex language due to the highly polysynthetic nature and phonology. Slight changes in morphemes (small sub-word units) can modify a word's meaning drastically. Since Quechua is the South American language with the highest amount of native speakers and those speakers tend to introduce diverse accentuated tones on different words depending on the locality, one can assume that the combination of morphological and tonal rules that cause inflection can make tasks like the ones presented in this article (NER and POS) difficult due to the high likelihood of non-common meanings for sub-words and letters. For example, by adding an accent to the letter 'o' in Quechua, words become plural.

Quechua synthesis, or the *synthetic index* (Greenberg, 1963) – the average number of morphemes per word, is about two times larger than English. English typically has around 1.5 morphemes per word and Quechua has about 3 morphemes per word. This high morphological complexity has been described in detail in the past (Muysken, 1988); few have been able to overcome the challenges that low-resource languages like Quechua present for digital processing. Quechua's phonology uses three vowels for the most part: *a*, *i*, and *u*. Consonants, on the other hand, are numerous and depending on the region where it is spoken, Quechua can have up to 14 constants (Ortega et al., 2020a). Generally speaking, lexemes are monosyllabic or bi-syllabic having two vowels (VV) or two consonants (CC) that do not concur in the same syllable. From a phonological perspective, the scheme of any Quechua root is: (C)V(C)-CV(C) (Cerrón-Palomino, 1994).

The region where Quechua is spoken can be considered important. Alfredo Torero (Torero, 1964) reported that there are two main divisions of the language (Quechua I and Quechua II). Quechua II is mostly spoken in regions such as Ayacucho, Peru and is considered a "southern" language. There are several more dialects spoken and others (Adelaar, 2004) report several divisions for Quechua II; but, in this article we focus specifically on the southern version at a high-level.

A lot of the Quechua morphology has been documented in previous works (Rios et al., 2008; Rios, 2015; Muysken, 1988; Monson et al., 2006; Torero, 1964); however, there is not a clear consensus to resolve all morphology issues that may arise. In order to statistically determine which branch of morphemes a verb phrases falls under can be difficult with Quechua since there are so few resources. A short example sentence of how complex morpheme determination can be is depicted in Table 1. In some cases, there are hundreds of options to choose from when choosing which suffix to use for a given Quechua word.

4 Corpus details

4.1 Monolingual

We consider the introduction of our monolingual corpus on southern Quechua the largest corpus of its kind to date. Table 4 gives a precise overview of all of the corpora that we have combined in October 2021 in order to present our corpus publicly online[3]. We have created the corpus from several sources. The majority of corpora combined to create the final corpus is a compilation of 50 monolingual corpora from different sources on the web including OSCAR (Suárez et al., 2019), JW300 (Agić and

[3] https://huggingface.co/datasets/Llamacha/monolingual-quechua-iic

Test sentence: Chantapis **Bibli**anejta **qotucha**kuynejta **ima yanapalla**wanchejtaj

Stemmed Morpheme	Potential Suffixes
Chanta	–pis –s
Biblia	–niq –ta
qutachu	–ku –y –niq –ta
ima	
yanapa	–lla –wa –nchik –ta
yanapalla	–wa –nchik –ta

Table 1: The sub-segment suffix choices of a short sentence for a Quechua sentence. (Ortega et al., 2020a)

Vulić, 2019), and CC-100 (Conneau et al., 2020; Wenzek et al., 2020). To our knowledge, these corpora have not yet been introduced as one southern Quechua corpus to the wider research community. Additionally, our corpus contains other corpora mentioned below (see Table 4 for a complete list) that are not easily found on-line.

The introduction of our corpus is part of a larger project called *Llamacha*[4] focused on helping underresourced communities . In Llamacha, the authors have begun to use the corpus directly as a form of creating software tools able to help teachers in regions of southern Peru where Quechua II is spoken. Llamacha tools cover several use cases such as government documents, children's internet tools, and more. This demand constitutes the main reason we distribute this corpus for public use – it is our hope that others from the research community will get involved to help develop more tools that can use our corpus.

With such a high demand for diverse performance, we compiled our corpus to cover the domains mentioned and more. Our compilation spans across several domains including religion, economics, health, social, political, justice and culture. We consulted several sources such as books and stories from Andean narratives and the Peruvian Ministry of Education[5] to collect data. Table 4 illustrates the entire data set which consists of 4,408,953 tokens and 384,184 sentences, including what are known as "Chanka" and "Collao" variants, variants specific to the Quechua II branch. In effect, we have created a corpus that is nearly ten times larger than most widely used Quechua corpus (Rios, 2015) until now which has eight combined corpora, 47,547 tokens, and 3,614 sentences.

4.2 Named-entity recognition and part-of-speech

Both the NER and POS corpora were created using the corpus introduced and are made publicly available online[6]. There are slight differences, nonetheless, between the amount of examples used that we note in this section.

In order to create the NER and POS corpora a team of ten annotators were selected. The annotators were university students and 7 of 10 of them were native Quechua speakers. Nonetheless, they were all students of what is known as a "Intercultural Bilingual Education" in Peru where students are taught coursework in both Quechua and Spanish. Annotation was performed using Label-Studio[7] to annotate sentences for NER and POS.

The NER corpus was built using 5,450 sentences using the CoNLL2003 (Sang and De Meulder, 2003) format. Work was reviewed to ensure that annotations were standardized and using an BIO format annotating only the following tags: Person (PER), Location (LOC) and Organization (ORG). The POS corpus was built using 4,229 sentences and annotated identical to previous work on POS Rios (2015) for Quechua. Additionally, as a way of having a more precise tagging strategy, we used official dictionaries of "Chanka" and "Collao" Quechua from the Peruvian Ministry of Education to identify POS tag correctness.

5 Experimental settings

5.1 Tokenization

Our tokenization strategy is to include the state-of-the-art techniques currently being used for Quechua, regardless if it is Quechua I or II (Torero, 1964). We do this as a mechanism to show that

[4]https://llamacha.pe
[5]http://www.minedu.gob.pe/
[6]https://github.com/Llamacha/QuBERT
[7]https://labelstud.io

Text	Ismael Montes Hatun Yachay Wasi Yachachiqkunap
BPE	Ismael Montes H@@atun Yachay Wasi Yachachiqkuna@@p
PRPE	Ismael Monte@@s Hatun Ya@@chay Wasi Yach@@achiq@@kuna@@p
BPE-Guided	Is@@m@@a@@el Mon@@t@@es Hatun Yachay Wasi Yach@@achiq@@kunap

Table 2: The use of four word-tokenization techniques for Quechua.

the corpus presented in Section 4 can be used to achieve high performance (around 80–90% accuracy) for tasks similar to high-resource languages as a recent survey (Li et al., 2020) has shown.

We use the latest tokenization techniques which focus on sub-word segmentation. (Haddow et al., 2021; Chen and Fazio, 2021; Ortega et al., 2020a; Sennrich et al., 2015) Byte-pair encoding (BPE) (Sennrich et al., 2015) can be considered one of the most widely-used approaches and a fundamental technique that has served as a baseline for previous research (Ortega et al., 2021, 2020a,b) on Quechua. The BPE approach is considered the de-facto standard tokenization algorithm for agglutinative languages (Chimalamarri and Sitaram, 2021). BPE represents text at the character-level and then merges the most frequent pairs iteratively until a pre-determined number of merge operations have been reached. Our BPE tokenizer was trained on the entire collective corpus from Section 4 with a vocabulary size of 52,000.

Alternatively, we additionally experiment with a popular extension of the BPE technique called *BPE-Guided* (Ortega et al., 2020a), used for increasing performance on Quechua machine translation. BPE-Guided is similar to the BPE approach in that it iteratively "discovers" sub-word segmentation by jointly learning a vocabulary and character-level segmentation. The extension offered by BPE-Guided is that it introduces Quechua knowledge in a *a-priori* manner by using the BPE algorithm for excluding common suffixes found on Wikimedia[8] before learning a vocabulary or segmentation. In our experiments, we use the list of Quechua suffixes introduced previously (Ortega et al., 2020a).

Another tokenization technique that has been shown to perform better than BPE and BPE-Guided on Quechua texts (Chen and Fazio, 2021) is known as the Prefix-Root-Postfix-Encoding (PRPE) (Zuters et al., 2018) technique. The PRPE algorithm separates words into three main divisions: (1) a prefix, (2) a root, and (3) a postfix. It completes this separation by first learning a sub-word vocabulary through detecting potential prefixes and post-fixes based on a heuristic. It then aligns the prefixes and post-fixes into sub-strings of a word to find potential roots. Once the roots have been located, the text is segmented into sub-words according to their statistical probability. Table 2 shows an example southern Quechua sentence tokenized by the three approaches mentioned.

Lastly, all text with exception of one experiment (Text and BPE in Table 3) is normalized with the Quechua toolkit (Rios, 2015) that uses finite-state transducers (Mohri, 1997) to determine if words belong to the same category and can be merged into one. Rios (2015)[Section 2.5] describe their normalization methodology which contains four models that are based on morphology, the "normalization" technique used in our experiments follows their work which includes all four models.

5.2 Model Architecture

We call our model **QuBERT** because it is a transformer model based on BERT (Devlin et al., 2019). More specifically, our model has been trained using the RoBERTa (Devlin et al., 2018) enhancement to BERT which can be considered higher-performing for NER and POS tasks (Li et al., 2020). An example of the model architecture is shown in Figure 1 which shows how our model produces NER classifications given a Quechua sentence.

Our model has been first pre-trained with southern Quechua text on 384,184 sentences. Then, we fine tuned the model with 4,360 sentences for the NER task and 3,383 sentences for the POS task. For the training process, we used 6 hidden layers. Each layer was 768 dimensions, giving us a total of 84 million parameters. For optimization, we used the Adam optimizer with hyper-parameter values of β_1=0.9 and β_2 = 0.99 along with a learning rate of 2.7e-06. Lastly, we incorporated a weight

[8]https://en.wiktionary.org/wiki/Category:Quechua_suffixes

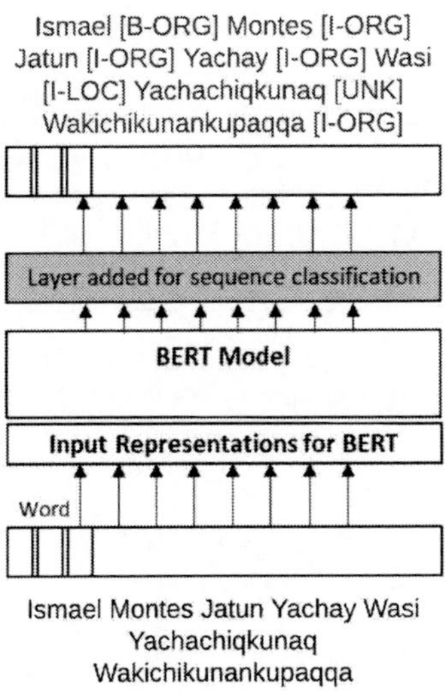

Figure 1: Model architecture based on Bert (Devlin et al., 2019).

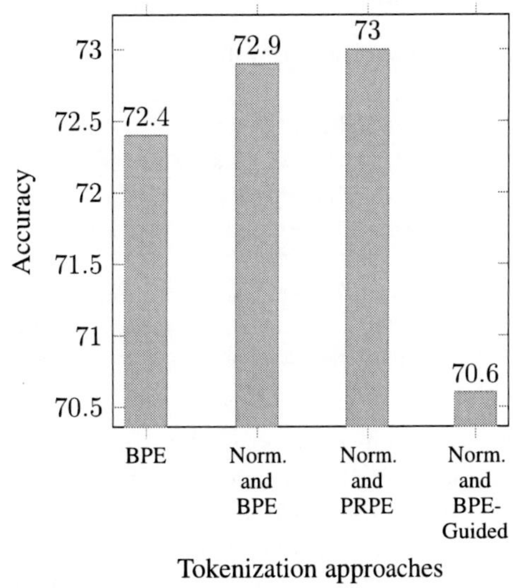

Figure 2: An accuracy comparison of tokenization techniques on southern Quechua (Quechua II) using a RoBERTa (Liu et al., 2019) model for named-entity recognition (NER).

decay factor of 0.1 to prevent overfitting. The pre-training was for two epochs and a batch size of 64 with 12k iterations, before being fine-tuned on the downstream task for 10 epochs and a batch size of 32. Initial development was done on a Google Colab[9] notebook, while models used for final testing were pre-trained and fine-tuned on a single 16GB NVIDIA Tesla V100 GPU.

6 Results

The results presented in this section show how well **QuBERT** performs on two main tasks: NER and POS. We feel that the contributions presented in Section 1 are sufficient to warrant wider use of our work; however, it is our intention to show that the corpus, model, and experiments could provide easy access for future work. We cover each task (NER and POS) as separate sections below in order to provide better insight into how the model performs in different scenarios, specifically for the different tokenization and normalization (called "norm." in Table 3) techniques mentioned in Section 5. Nonetheless, we provide precision, recall, and F1 scores in Table 3 for both tasks as an aggregate to get an overall sense of how well our base model performs on both tasks.

6.1 Named Entity Recognition

Figure 2 illustrates the accuracy from our model on the NER task. We note that the accuracy scores are somewhat lower than the state-of-the-art for high-resource languages on the NER task (Li et al., 2020). However, our F1 scores seems to be inline with other newly published work on low resources (Bouabdallaoui et al., 2022) (69–70%) for various deep learning models). In future work, we plan on adapting our model to more complex architectures such as those found in SemEval-2022 Task 11 (Malmasi et al., 2022).

To further investigate the findings we report the following findings[10] based on these NER tags: B-LOC, B-ORG, B-PER, I-LOC, I-ORG, I-PER, O. When text was normalized and then tokenized with BPE we noticed that I-ORG and I-PER were the highest amount of true positives (227 and 196 respectively) when compared to other tokenization techniques. However, BPE without normalization performed worse than other techniques on I-PER classification, mainly classifying them as B-LOC. BPE-Guided generally scored similar to BPE on NER with a trend of being slightly lower than BPE. PRPE scored better on I-LOC and I-ORG (306 and 227 respectively) than other techniques and was able to achieve the highest accuracy of all techniques.

From the illustration in Figure 2, we believe that

[9]https://colab.research.google.com

[10]For a complete confusion matrix, please refer to Appendix Table 5.

Tokenization Approach	NER			POS		
	F1	Prec	Recall	F1	Prec	Recall
Text and BPE	0.736	0.749	0.724	0.860	0.859	0.862
Text with norm. and BPE	0.741	0.753	0.729	0.861	0.861	0.862
Text with norm. and PRPE	0.741	0.753	0.730	0.867	0.866	0.868
Text with norm. and BPE-Guided	0.716	0.726	0.707	0.843	0.843	0.843

Table 3: A comparison of tokenization techniques on southern Quechua (Quechua II) using a RoBERTa (Liu et al., 2019) model for classification. Normalization (norm.) is applied using the Quechua toolkit (Rios, 2015). Scores are calculated at the token level and weighted-averaged by class.

the different techniques are closely related but it is clear that the BPE-Guided approach was not as successful for the NER task as it has been in the past for machine translation (Ortega et al., 2020a). We feel that this is probably due to the amount of data introduced in our corpus which did not contain as many matching suffixes as was done in the previous work (Ortega et al., 2020a). Since this is a first-time introduction of a deep learning model for NER in Quechua, we believe that this can serve as a baseline for future work.

6.2 POS tagging

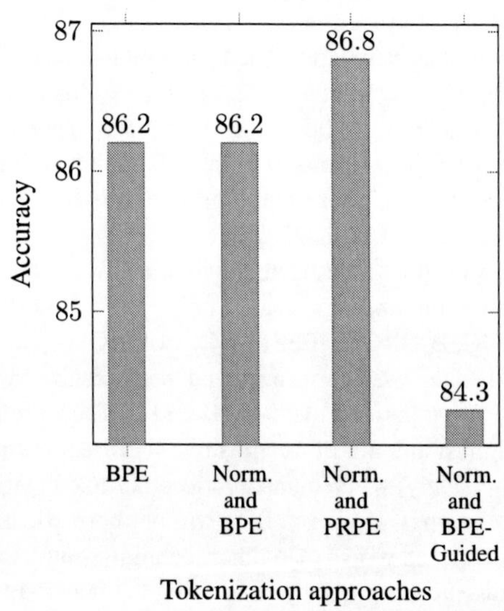

Figure 3: An accuracy comparison of tokenization techniques on southern Quechua (Quechua II) using a RoBERTa (Liu et al., 2019) model for part-of-speech (POS) tagging.

The part-of-speech task seems to be more fitted for our model since we are able to achieve accuracy in the high 80% range as shown in Figure 3, similar to other high-resource tasks(Li et al., 2020). We feel that for POS tagging our model is optimal given the current state-of-the-art. Also, our annotations, while completed by a near-native speaker were somewhat easier to complete due to the more rigid classification of vocabulary-based words in Quechua, essentially the annotator could look up words and parts of speech when there was doubt. In the future, as with the NER task, we fill that we can achieve higher quality with professional translators/annotators.

For POS tagging, unlike the NER task, we were able to discern performance from our analysis based on terms that could be found in a dictionary.[11] Adjectives, verbs and adverbs were mostly correct by all tokenization techniques. Particularly, PRPE outperformed other techniques with the correct classification of 262 adjectives when compared to BPE (259) and BPE-Guided (235). PRPE also performed slightly better on POS verb identification than other techniques. BPE-Guided, on the other hand, performed better with determinant detection finding 43 true positives as opposed to 39 by PRPE and BPE.

7 Conclusion and future work

In this article, we have introduced a novel monolingual corpus, curated and compiled for southern Quechua. We have shown that the corpus can be used for downstream tasks such as NER and POS tagging by creating and releasing a deep learning model based on BERT (Devlin et al., 2019) called **QuBERT**. Additionally, we experimented with the state-of-the-art tokenization techniques for preprocessing and normalization in order to achieve results similar to those found on high-resource languages.

[11] For a complete confusion matrix, please refer to Appendix Table 6.

In the future, we would like to experiment with other model architectures for more complex NER tasks such as those presented at SemEval-2022 (Malmasi et al., 2022), of particular interest is the work from Wang et al. (2022). We would like to include more native Quechua speaking annotators in order to improve the data set even more. The introduction of two or more annotators will allows us to introduce models for tasks such as machine translation, question-answering, and topic modeling where the reference data is even more important. We believe that our work can serve as a baseline for future work and invite other researchers to use the contributions presented here for further investigative lines such as the ones we are considering: online tools for native Quechua speakers and human interaction.

Acknowledgments

This work was partially funded by Project PID2019-104512GB-I00 of the Spanish Ministerio de Ciencia, Innovación and Universidades and Agencia Estatal de Investigación.

References

Willem FH Adelaar. 2004. *The languages of the Andes*. Cambridge University Press.

Željko Agić and Ivan Vulić. 2019. JW300: A wide-coverage parallel corpus for low-resource languages. In *Proceedings of the 57th Annual Meeting of the Association for Computational Linguistics*, pages 3204–3210, Florence, Italy. Association for Computational Linguistics.

Ibrahim Bouabdallaoui, Fatima Guerouate, Samya Bouhaddour, Chaimae Saadi, and Mohamed Sbihi. 2022. Named entity recognition applied on moroccan tourism corpus. *Procedia Computer Science*, 198:373–378.

Rodolfo Cerrón-Palomino. 1994. Quechua sureño. diccionario unificado. *Biblioteca Básica Perúana, Biblioteca Nacionál del Peru.*

William Chen and Brett Fazio. 2021. Morphologically-guided segmentation for translation of agglutinative low-resource languages. In *Proceedings of the 4th Workshop on Technologies for MT of Low Resource Languages (LoResMT2021)*, pages 20–31.

Santwana Chimalamarri and Dinkar Sitaram. 2021. Linguistically enhanced word segmentation for better neural machine translation of low resource agglutinative languages. *International Journal of Speech Technology*, pages 1–7.

Alexis Conneau, Kartikay Khandelwal, Naman Goyal, Vishrav Chaudhary, Guillaume Wenzek, Francisco Guzmán, Edouard Grave, Myle Ott, Luke Zettlemoyer, and Veselin Stoyanov. 2020. Unsupervised cross-lingual representation learning at scale. In *Proceedings of the 58th Annual Meeting of the Association for Computational Linguistics*, pages 8440–8451, Online. Association for Computational Linguistics.

Jacob Devlin, Ming-Wei Chang, Kenton Lee, and Kristina Toutanova. 2018. BERT: pre-training of deep bidirectional transformers for language understanding. *CoRR*, abs/1810.04805.

Jacob Devlin, Ming-Wei Chang, Kenton Lee, and Kristina Toutanova. 2019. BERT: Pre-training of deep bidirectional transformers for language understanding. In *Proceedings of the 2019 Conference of the North American Chapter of the Association for Computational Linguistics: Human Language Technologies, Volume 1 (Long and Short Papers)*, pages 4171–4186, Minneapolis, Minnesota. Association for Computational Linguistics.

Chris Edwards. 2021. Moore's law: what comes next? *Communications of the ACM*, 64(2):12–14.

Joseph Harold Greenberg. 1963. Universals of language.

Barry Haddow, Rachel Bawden, Antonio Valerio Miceli Barone, Jindřich Helcl, and Alexandra Birch. 2021. Survey of low-resource machine translation. *arXiv preprint arXiv:2109.00486.*

Katharina Kann. 2019. Acquisition of inflectional morphology in artificial neural networks with prior knowledge. *arXiv preprint arXiv:1910.05456.*

Alina Karakanta, Jon Dehdari, and Josef van Genabith. 2018. Neural machine translation for low-resource languages without parallel corpora. *Machine Translation*, 32(1-2):167–189.

Jing Li, Aixin Sun, Jianglei Han, and Chenliang Li. 2020. A survey on deep learning for named entity recognition. *IEEE Transactions on Knowledge and Data Engineering*, 34(1):50–70.

Yinhan Liu, Jiatao Gu, Naman Goyal, Xian Li, Sergey Edunov, Marjan Ghazvininejad, Mike Lewis, and Luke Zettlemoyer. 2020. Multilingual denoising pre-training for neural machine translation. *Trans. Assoc. Comput. Linguistics*, 8:726–742.

Yinhan Liu, Myle Ott, Naman Goyal, Jingfei Du, Mandar Joshi, Danqi Chen, Omer Levy, Mike Lewis, Luke Zettlemoyer, and Veselin Stoyanov. 2019. Roberta: A robustly optimized bert pretraining approach. *arXiv preprint arXiv:1907.11692.*

Manuel Mager, Arturo Oncevay, Abteen Ebrahimi, John Ortega, Annette Rios Gonzales, Angela Fan, Ximena Gutierrez-Vasques, Luis Chiruzzo, Gustavo Giménez-Lugo, Ricardo Ramos, et al. 2021a. Findings of the americasnlp 2021 shared task on open machine translation for indigenous languages of the americas. In *Proceedings of the First Workshop on Natural Language Processing for Indigenous Languages of the Americas*, pages 202–217.

Manuel Mager, Arturo Oncevay, Annette Rios, Ivan Vladimir Meza Ruiz, Alexis Palmer, Graham Neubig, and Katharina Kann. 2021b. Proceedings of the first workshop on natural language processing for indigenous languages of the americas. Association for Computational Linguistics.

Shervin Malmasi, Anjie Fang, Besnik Fetahu, Sudipta Kar, and Oleg Rokhlenko. 2022. Semeval-2022 task 11: Multilingual complex named entity recognition (multiconer). In *Proceedings of the 16th International Workshop on Semantic Evaluation (SemEval-2022). Association for Computational Linguistics.*

Mehryar Mohri. 1997. Finite-state transducers in language and speech processing. *Computational linguistics*, 23(2):269–311.

Christian Monson, Ariadna Font Llitjós, Roberto Aranovich, Lori Levin, Ralf Brown, Eric Peterson, Jaime Carbonell, and Alon Lavie. 2006. Building nlp systems for two resource-scarce indigenous languages: mapudungun and quechua. *Strategies for developing machine translation for minority languages*, page 15.

PC Muysken. 1988. Affix order and interpretation: Quechua.

El Moatez Billah Nagoudi, Wei-Rui Chen, Muhammad Abdul-Mageed, and Hasan Cavusoglu. 2021. IndT5: A text-to-text transformer for 10 indigenous languages. In *Proceedings of the First Workshop on Natural Language Processing for Indigenous Languages of the Americas*, pages 265–271, Online. Association for Computational Linguistics.

John Ortega and Krishnan Pillaipakkamnatt. 2018. Using morphemes from agglutinative languages like quechua and finnish to aid in low-resource translation. In *Proceedings of the AMTA 2018 Workshop on Technologies for MT of Low Resource Languages (LoResMT 2018)*, pages 1–11.

John E Ortega, Richard Castro Mamani, and Kyunghyun Cho. 2020a. Neural machine translation with a polysynthetic low resource language. *Machine Translation*, 34(4):325–346.

John E Ortega, Richard Alexander Castro-Mamani, and Jaime Rafael Montoya Samame. 2021. Love thy neighbor: Combining two neighboring low-resource languages for translation. In *Proceedings of the 4th Workshop on Technologies for MT of Low Resource Languages (LoResMT2021)*, pages 44–51.

John E Ortega, Richard Alexander Castro Mamani, and Jaime Rafael Montoya Samame. 2020b. Overcoming resistance: The normalization of an amazonian tribal language. In *Proceedings of the 3rd Workshop on Technologies for MT of Low Resource Languages*, pages 1–13.

Mārcis Pinnis, Rihards Krišlauks, Daiga Deksne, and Toms Miks. 2017. Neural machine translation for morphologically rich languages with improved subword units and synthetic data. In *International Conference on Text, Speech, and Dialogue*, pages 237–245. Springer.

Alec Radford, Jeffrey Wu, Rewon Child, David Luan, Dario Amodei, Ilya Sutskever, et al. 2019. Language models are unsupervised multitask learners. *OpenAI blog*, 1(8):9.

Colin Raffel, Noam Shazeer, Adam Roberts, Katherine Lee, Sharan Narang, Michael Matena, Yanqi Zhou, Wei Li, and Peter J. Liu. 2020. Exploring the limits of transfer learning with a unified text-to-text transformer. *Journal of Machine Learning Research*, 21(140):1–67.

Annette Rios. 2015. *A basic language technology toolkit for Quechua*. Ph.D. thesis, University of Zurich.

Annette Rios and Anne Göhring. 2016. Machine learning applied to rule-based machine translation. In *Hybrid Approaches to Machine Translation*, pages 111–129. Springer.

Annette Rios, Anne Göhring, and Martin Volk. 2008. A quechua-spanish parallel treebank. *LOT Occasional Series*, 12:53–64.

Erik F Sang and Fien De Meulder. 2003. Introduction to the conll-2003 shared task: Language-independent named entity recognition. *arXiv preprint cs/0306050*.

Robert R Schaller. 1997. Moore's law: past, present and future. *IEEE spectrum*, 34(6):52–59.

Rico Sennrich, Barry Haddow, and Alexandra Birch. 2015. Neural machine translation of rare words with subword units. *arXiv preprint arXiv:1508.07909*.

Pedro Javier Ortiz Suárez, Benoît Sagot, and Laurent Romary. 2019. Asynchronous pipeline for processing huge corpora on medium to low resource infrastructures. In *7th Workshop on the Challenges in the Management of Large Corpora (CMLC-7)*. Leibniz-Institut für Deutsche Sprache.

Jörg Tiedemann. 2012. Parallel data, tools and interfaces in opus. In *Lrec*, volume 2012, pages 2214–2218.

Alfredo Torero. 1964. *Los dialectos quechuas*. Univ. Agraria.

Xinyu Wang, Yongliang Shen, Jiong Cai, Tao Wang, Xiaobin Wang, Pengjun Xie, Fei Huang, Weiming Lu, Yueting Zhuang, Kewei Tu, et al. 2022. Damo-nlp at semeval-2022 task 11: A knowledge-based system for multilingual named entity recognition. *arXiv preprint arXiv:2203.00545*.

Guillaume Wenzek, Marie-Anne Lachaux, Alexis Conneau, Vishrav Chaudhary, Francisco Guzmán, Armand Joulin, and Edouard Grave. 2020. CCNet: Extracting high quality monolingual datasets from web crawl data. In *Proceedings of the 12th Language Resources and Evaluation Conference*, pages 4003–4012, Marseille, France. European Language Resources Association.

Wilson Wongso, Henry Lucky, and Derwin Suhartono. 2021. Pre-trained transformer-based language models for sundanese.

Francis Zheng, Machel Reid, Edison Marrese-Taylor, and Yutaka Matsuo. 2021. Low-resource machine translation using cross-lingual language model pretraining. In *Proceedings of the First Workshop on Natural Language Processing for Indigenous Languages of the Americas*, pages 234–240, Online. Association for Computational Linguistics.

Jānis Zuters, Gus Strazds, and Kārlis Immers. 2018. Semi-automatic quasi-morphological word segmentation for neural machine translation. In *International Baltic conference on databases and information systems*, pages 289–301. Springer.

A Appendix

The figures below represent several of the individual differences between corpora and their corresponding language in Table 4 and tokenization approaches for NER and POS in Tables 5 and 6 respectively.

Corpus	# Sentences	# Tokens	Dialect	Year	Dominio
jw300_2013	124,038	1,465,494	Chanka	2013	Religion
wikipedia_2021	96,560	1,009,631	Collao	2021	Miscellaneous
cc100-quechua	86,250	1,206,770	Collao	2018	Miscellaneous
jw300_2017	25,585	294,473	Collao	2017	Religion
microsoft	5,018	60,847	Collao	2021	Norma
que_community_2017	21,139	38,570	Collao	2017	Miscellaneous
tribunal_constitucional	1,148	32,974	Chanka	2021	Justice
tierra_vive	4,731	27,768	Collao	2013	Religion
conectamef	433	20,683	Collao	2016	Economy
unesco	937	16,933	Collao	2020	Program
oscar_quz	491	12,717	Collao	2020	Miscellaneous
constitucion_simplified_quz	999	12,217	Collao	1993	Norma
libro_quechua	781	11,476	Chanka	2002	Agreement
handbook_quy	2,297	11,350	Chanka	2019	Education
dw_quz	325	11,079	Collao	2009	Social
yaku_unumanta	283	10,787	Chanka	2013	Norma
uywaymanta	683	9,231	Collao	2015	Education
maria_mamani	987	9,179	Chanka	2011	Education
anta	451	8,839	Collao	2010	Education
Agreement _nacional_2014	356	8,355	Chanka	2014	Agreement
omnilife	336	8,184	Collao	2017	Health
pasado_violencia	373	8,001	Chanka	2008	Social
cosude_2009-2011_qu	536	7,959	Collao	2011	Social
fondo_monetario_internacional	291	7,227	Collao	2010	Economy
peru_suyupi	449	6,420	Chanka	2014	Education
fundacion_quz	440	5,776	Collao	2008	Social
greg_quz	185	5,505	Collao	2010	Narrative
imayna	250	5,425	Chanka	2008	Social
ahk_1968-2008_quz	391	5,186	Collao	2008	Economy
directiva	355	4,988	Chanka	2014	Resolution
achka	256	4,844	Chanka	2015	Education
cartillas	870	4,674	Chanka	2006	Education
lectura-favorita-chanka-2019	781	4,363	Chanka	2019	Education
lectura-favorita-cusco-2019	769	4,351	Collao	2019	Education
amerindia	321	4,280	Chanka	2000	Education
yachay_qipikuna	464	4,174	Collao	2009	Education
reglamento_simplified_quz	287	4,053	Collao	2008	Norma
focus_2008_quz	243	3,797	Collao	2008	Narrative
poder_judicial	154	3,347	Chanka	2021	Justice
focus_2007_quz	220	3,238	Collao	2007	Narrative
literatura	190	2,930	Chanka	1999	Culture
guia_collao	288	2,824	Collao	2015	Education
wikimedia	163	2,712	Collao	2021	Miscellaneous
docente	286	2,550	Chanka	2015	Education
convencion	115	2,548	Collao	1994	Agreement
yupaychaqa_ley	129	2,484	Chanka	2014	Norma
mikhunanchiskunamanta	127	1,925	Collao	2013	Social
tatoeba	428	1,778	Collao	2021	Miscellaneous
nanoquechua	92	1,431	Collao	2016	Culture
kallpa_qu	100	968	Collao	2019	Narrative
defensoria	60	882	Chanka	2021	Justice
yachay	62	756	Collao	2015	Culture
Total	**384,184**	**4,408,953**	-	-	-

Table 4: Details of each corpus included in the Southern Quechua corpus introduced.

Tokenization Approach		NER Class						
		B-LOC	B-ORG	B-PER	I-LOC	I-ORG	I-PER	O
BPE	True Positive	453	81	189	300	226	162	477
	False Positive	319	11	150	71	51	87	31
	False Negative	64	37	79	171	80	207	82
Norm. and BPE	True Positive	451	70	187	302	227	196	470
	False Positive	299	8	138	83	51	94	32
	False Negative	66	48	81	169	79	173	89
Norm. and PRPE	True Positive	449	79	187	306	227	186	471
	False Positive	304	14	135	95	53	74	28
	False Negative	68	39	81	165	79	183	88
Norm. and BPE-Guided	True Positive	453	71	176	299	222	156	466
	False Positive	294	16	164	93	57	113	28
	False Negative	64	47	92	172	84	213	93

Table 5: Breakdown of prediction results used to calculate weighted precision, recall, and F1 for the NER task .

POS Class		Algorithm			
		BPE	Norm. and BPE	Norm. and PRPE	Norm. and BPE-Guided
adj.	True Positive	253	259	262	235
	False Positive	98	106	92	96
	False Negative	143	137	134	160
verb	True Positive	764	760	761	744
	False Positive	77	86	72	98
	False Negative	78	82	81	72
pron.	True Positive	36	36	37	34
	False Positive	14	13	13	18
	False Negative	7	7	6	9
prep.	True Positive	0	0	0	0
	False Positive	0	1	0	0
	False Negative	1	1	1	1
adv.	True Positive	183	184	188	161
	False Positive	57	53	56	51
	False Negative	50	49	46	73
pron. indef.	True Positive	0	1	1	1
	False Positive	0	0	0	0
	False Negative	2	1	1	1
adv. interr.	True Positive	1	1	1	1
	False Positive	0	0	0	0
	False Negative	0	0	0	0
pron. interrog.	True Positive	8	7	8	7
	False Positive	5	2	5	2
	False Negative	2	3	2	3
num.	True Positive	0	0	0	0
	False Positive	0	0	2	3
	False Negative	5	5	5	5
conj.	True Positive	7	8	8	8
	False Positive	6	6	6	8
	False Negative	5	4	4	4
det.	True Positive	39	39	39	43
	False Positive	33	36	33	38
	False Negative	20	20	20	16
subj.	True Positive	1380	1376	1386	1380
	False Positive	138	124	131	193
	False Negative	112	115	107	113
interj.	True Positive	0	0	0	0
	False Positive	0	0	0	5
	False Negative	3	3	3	3

Table 6: Breakdown of prediction results used to calculate weighted precision, recall, and F1 for the POS task .

Unified NMT models for the Indian subcontinent, transcending script-barriers

Gokul NC
Devnagri AI
gokulnc@devnagri.com

Abstract

Highly accurate machine translation systems are very important in societies and countries where multilinguality is very common, and where English often does not suffice. The Indian subcontinent (or South Asia) is such a region, with all the Indic languages currently being under-represented in the NLP ecosystem. It is essential to thoroughly explore various techniques to improve the performance of such low-resource languages at least using the data available in open-source, which itself is something not very explored in the Indic ecosystem. In our work, we perform a study with a focus on improving the performance of very-low-resource South Asian languages, especially of countries in addition to India. Specifically, we propose how unified models can be built that can exploit the data from comparatively resource-rich languages of the same region. We propose strategies to unify different types of unexplored scripts, especially Perso–Arabic scripts and Indic scripts to build multilingual models for all the South Asian languages despite the script barrier. We also study how augmentation techniques like back-translation can be made use-of to build unified models just using openly available raw data, to understand what levels of improvements can be expected for these Indic languages.

1 Introduction

The Indian subcontinent is a well-studied linguistic area (Emeneau, 1956), known as South Asian sprachbund. The region is home to around a quarter of the world's population, with a total which is projected to reach more than 2 billion in a decade. Despite this, the progress in natural language processing is significantly lacking for South Asian languages (or Indic languages). Especially, machine translation is of core importance since South Asia is largely a multilingual society, with more than 25 languages recognized officially across the subcontinent and more than 100s attested and spoken. Although there are quite a few number of works which have released datasets for languages of India (Siripragada et al., 2020) and studied multilingual models for the same (Philip et al., 2019), they are not exhaustively studied. In particular, the Indic languages of other South Asian countries like Pakistan, Nepal and Sri Lanka are almost never studied together with the languages of India and Bangladesh.

In this work, we aim to study all the available Indic languages (of Indo-Aryan and Dravidian families) of all the above countries together, precisely 15 South Asian languages (listed in appendix A). Especially, we propose a simple strategy to unify digraphic languages like Hindi–Urdu, Sindhi and Punjabi which are written in Indic scripts in India and Perso–Arabic scripts in Pakistan. We propose how one can build a script-agnostic encoder which can generalize well across different types of translation models, like code-mixed, roman (social media) and formal texts. We study for the first time in literature backtranslation-based NMT for all script-unified Indic languages together, which provides significantly better performance than models trained only on parallel data, by using only freely available monolingual data. We finally provide brief recommendations for researchers working in this Indic-NMT domain, and finally mention how this work can be extended and its future scope.

2 Related works

Training multilingual models for neural machine translation currently the go-to approach for significantly improving the performance of low-resource languages (Ngo et al., 2020). Especially sharing of sub-word vocabulary among related languages (of the same or similar families) is of more importance to exploit the inter-relationships between the languages (Khemchandani et al., 2021), so that resource sharing from high-resource languages to

Proceedings of the Third Workshop on Deep Learning for Low-Resource Natural Language Processing, pages 227 - 236
July 14, 2022 ©2022 Association for Computational Linguistics

Dataset	as	bn	gu	hi	kn	ml	mr	ne	or	pa	sd	si	ta	te	ur
Samanantar	0.14	8.52	3.05	8.57	4.08	5.85	3.32		1.00	2.42			5.17	4.84	
CVIT-PIB	0.04														0.20
Anuvaad*	.003								0.02						0.02
PMI*															0.01
OPUS	0.03							2.25	0.12		1.89	8.53			8.69
U.Kathmandu								0.02							
Charles Univ															0.01
MTurks 2012															0.03
Total	0.21	8.52	3.05	8.57	4.07	5.85	3.32	2.28	1.14	2.42	1.89	8.53	5.17	4.84	8.97

Table 1: Open-source parallel Indic corpora (in millions), totalling around 69M sentence-pairs

low-resource languages is achieved. Recent works (Ramesh et al., 2021) have explored strategies to train multilingual NMT for 11 languages of India, both with and without shared vocabulary across languages, demonstrating that vocabulary sharing by script unification is significantly beneficial. It is also common to convert all the text across all languages to IPA (International Phonetic Alphabet) or any common script, especially in speech-to-text (Javed et al., 2021) and text-to-speech (Zhang et al., 2021) to obtain a universal representation of text across any language/script. In the case of South Asian languages, it is more convenient to map all scripts to a common Indic script (like Devanagari) which is capable of representing all phonemes used in the Indic families (Khare et al., 2021).

3 Background

This section sets provides the background required for the subsequent sections.

3.1 Datasets

As mentioned earlier, our work only focuses on open-source datasets inorder to explore how performance can be improved for low-resource languages just using openly available data. Overall, the datasets used in this work are mostly from the general domain, and hyperlinks are provided to access all the datasets. The next sub-section mentions the list of all aligned datasets used in this work and further, the we mention the list of all available monolingual data sources which we exploit in this work for improving performance.

3.1.1 Parallel datasets

Table 1 shows the list of all parallel datasets used for training our models. It is to be noted that the Samanantar (Ramesh et al., 2021) is the major source of data, for languages of India. To explore more languages as well as to study how the above data is useful for other similar Indic languages, especially focusing on other related South Asian countries, we gather more data from different sources shown in the same table. Specifically, we aim at increasing the amount of data obtainable for Indo-Aryan languages not covered in Samanantar, viz. Nepali, Sinhala, Sindhi and Urdu which are predominantly spoken in Nepal, Sri Lanka and Pakistan respectively. In addition, we also manually add new sources of data (marked *) from Anuvaad corpus and PM India corpus which were not covered in the latest Samanantar v0.2 for Assamese and Odia, although relatively very small in size.

3.1.2 Benchmark dataset

For test set, we use the FLoRes101 benchmark (Goyal et al., 2021) which has data for 14 Indic languages, manually translated from various domains of English Wikipedia. Since this new benchmark does not have data for Sinhala, we evaluate it on the initial FLoRes benchmark (Guzmán et al., 2019). Note that we do not use the WAT 2021 MultiIndicMT testset (Nakazawa et al., 2021) for benchmarking, since we find the data quite very close to the distribution of the corresponding training data, as also observed by IndicBART (Dabre et al., 2021). All BLEU scores reported in this paper are computed using sacreBLEU (Post, 2018) after generating translations with a beam decoding size of 4. Note that we compare our scores only against IndicBART (and experiment only with same architecture), as they already demonstrate superior scores over fine-tuned models like mBART and the chosen model is lighter than pretrained models like mT5 or mBART50.

3.1.3 Monolingual data

Table 2 shows list of all monolingual corpora used in this work. It is to be noted again that the AI4Bharat IndicCorp is the major source of data (row 1), for languages of India. For Indo-Aryan languages of other South Asian countries, we consolidate most of the available open-source corpora from different sources as shown in other rows of the table. We also try to consolidate more data for very-low-resource languages of India like Assamese and Odia.

3.2 Script Unification

As explained earlier, script unification is essential for sub-word vocabulary sharing between related languages. It is essential for the unification to be lossless so that the resultant dataset quality is not affected. In literature, it is common to use Devanagari as the common script to unify all the Brahmic scripts of India, although any script (like IPA) can be used as the pivot. For example, for models trained only for Dravidian languages, we use the Malayalam script as the common representation for the 4 languages: Kannada, Malayalam, Tamil and Telugu. But Devanagari is predominantly chosen since it is used for many languages like Hindi, Nepali, Marathi, etc. as well as due to the fact that it is one of the few Indic scripts which supports almost all phonemes required for both the Indic language families, not just Indo-Aryan for which the script is predominantly used. One important aspect of Devanagari is a diacritic called nuqta, which is essentially a dot mark placed below the main consonants to represent non-native phonemes. Its primary use is to represent consonants of other languages, including from different families like Dravidian, Iranic (for Persian), Semitic (for Arabic). Hence, using Devanagari for all Indic languages as a common script is preferable, including languages like Urdu, Sindhi and Kashmiri which are written in Perso–Arabic scripts. In the subsequent section, we explain how the latter is achieved, which is an unexplored track in research.

3.2.1 Mapping Devanagari and Perso–Arabic

The Perso–Arabic script is an abjad, meaning that it is based on a writing system which mostly has only consonants (in its purest form). In addition, in Perso–Arabic, two of the same consonants (w & y) are used to indicate few long-vowels (respectively: /u/, /o/ and /i/, /e/). So the reader of the script mentally fills-in / interprets most of the vowels as they read, based on their knowledge of the language and context. Devanagari is an abugida, meaning that it is an alphasyllabary system where the script is generally expected to be almost phonetic with all consonants and vowels represented. This makes a direct mapping of Perso–Arabic consonants to Devanagari slightly illegible for readers of usual Devanagari due to lack of any vowels. Figure 1 below shows an example of raw mapping for the Hindostani language.

Urdu	پلس نے چور کو پکڑ کے جیل مے ڈال دیا
Raw-Devanagari	पलस ने चवर कव पकड़ के जयल मे डाल दया
Hindi	पुलिस ने चोर को पकड के जेल मे डाल दिया
English	The police caught the thief and put him in jail

Figure 1: Row-1: Perso–Arabic, Row-2: Devanagari-transliteration, Row-3: Actual Hindi spelling, Row-4: Translation

Despite this, we propose that NMT models are capable of learning both abjad and abugida forms, with a deeper understanding of the underlying language. That is, we directly use the raw mapping of Perso–Arabic consonants to Devanagari (without any phonetic transcription) to train an unified model. It is to be noted that there are some consonants in Perso–Arabic for which, although the phonemes are different, they represent the same phone. Those consonants usually are mapped to a single Devanagari phoneme. In our work, especially to generate Perso–Arabic texts, we require lossless mapping of each character from Perso–Arabic. Hence we propose to map them uniquely by creating new Devanagari consonants using nuqta.We also open-source our transliterator implementation as a python library[1].

Upon training using the above unification, we see that our model is capable of understanding that the standard registers of Hindi & Urdu have the same underlying language, with only differences being in writing form and formal vocabulary. This was verified by swapping the scripts used for Hindi & Urdu to see if still produces legitimate outputs. As later described in Section 5.1, while training, we explicitly specify what is the expected output script-type and language that is to be produced by the model. Upon specifying Arabic as script for Hindi and Devanagari as script for Urdu to the

[1]Indic-PersoArabic Script Converter

Dataset	as	bn	gu	hi	kn	ml	mr	ne	or	pa	pnb	sd	si	ta	te	ur
IndicCorp	2.38	77.7	46.6	77.3	56.5	67.9	41.6		10.1	35.3				47.8	60.5	
University[a]				45				3.2								5.5
CC100	0.5							12.7	2.2		0.02	1.4	12.6			28
Wikipedia	0.3							0.4	0.3		1.2	0.4	0.6			1.3
Leipzig	0.06							4.2	0.04		0.06	0.007	0.4			1.1
Crawled[b]								2					4.8			
Total	3.24	77.7	46.6	122.3	56.5	67.9	41.6	22.5	12.64	35.3	1.28	1.807	18.4	47.8	60.5	35.9

Table 2: Open-source monolingual Indic corpora (in millions), totalling 650M sentences

[a] hi: IIT-B Corpus, ne: JNU Corpus, ur: Charles University

[b] ne: GitHub sources, si: FacebookDecade, News sources, SinMin

trained model, we found that the model still produced Urdu and Hindi sentences respectively. Now we generate augmented data for Devanagari-Urdu and Arabic-Hindi by transliterating 1M Hindi parallel data to PersoArabic (later unified again to abjadi-Devanagari) and by transcribing 1M Urdu parallel data to Devanagari using Sangam transliterator (Lehal and Saini, 2012). We fine-tune the model for few epochs using this synthetic data. We observe that even using such small fraction of data, the model was able to easily generate translations for Urdu in proper Devanagari and for Hindi in proper-Arabic for unseen data, hence qualitatively proving the hypothesis that the script-unified model can also learn writing-system-agnostic features.

Furthermore, we perform something similar for Sindhi language – Sindhi is majorly spoken in Pakistan by 30M people & written in Perso–Arabic script; in India, it is spoken by around 2M people & officially mandated to be written in Parivardhit-Devanagari, an extended version of Devanagari. Since all the Sindhi datasets available are in Perso–Arabic, we use the same Sangam transliteration API as mentioned above to generate Sindhi datasets in Devanagari. We use data this as well to train the models in Section 5, and find that the model now was also able to produce (almost) same Sindhi outputs for both the scripts. Note that we implement a similar but separate converter for Sindhi script-unification, as the Perso–Arabic script for Sindhi has significant difference from that of Urdu. Also, since the amount of Sindhi corpus is very low, we augment the dataset while training with the following synthetic data – since Gujarati is a closely-related language to Sindhi, we sample 2M random Gujarati translation-pairs and create Arabic-Gujarati dataset and train for this artifical language–script combination as well in the training described in Section 5.1.

We would also like to point out that we do not perform this for the Punjabi language, which is written in an Indic script called Gurmukhi in India, and using a Perso–Arabic alphabet called Shahmukhi in Pakistan. This is because all available Punjabi datasets are in Gurmukhi, an almost phonetic script (similar to Devanagari). Hence we directly use our transliterator to convert from Gurmukhi to Shahmukhi and return the translation if required. But it was observed that due to the formal nature of the Punjabi datasets, the generated translations were of Eastern-Punjabi literary standard, hence the outputs may not always be mutually-intelligible to speakers who are used to Western-Punjabi literary standard. We do not find this issue significant in the case of Sindhi, as the formal Sindhi standards of both the countries do not differ much.

3.2.2 Mapping Sinhala and Devanagari

Sinhala alphabet (of Sri Lanka) is mostly similar in phonetics to most other alphabets of India, except a couple of minor differences. Sinhala has separate unicode points for representing 6 prenasal consonants, whereas in Devanagari, they are represented as ligature of a nasal consonant with another consonant, as shown in Figure 2. In addition, Sinhala also has short and long forms of the vowel /æ/ which we also map to Devanagari uniquely, for both dependent & independent vowels. The publicly available transliterators (like the transliterate sub-package in Indic-NLP-Library) are lossy, and do not handle all these cases.

Sinhala	ඟ	ජ	ඦ	ඬ	ඳ	ඹ
Devanagari	ङ्ग	ञ्ज	ज्ञ	ण्ड	न्द	म्ब

Figure 2: Example mapping of pre-nasal consonants between Sinhala and Devanagari

3.2.3 Mapping between Indic scripts

For all the remaining scripts in this work, the mapping is mostly straightforward due to the fact that they follow the ISCII encoding scheme in which equivalent phonemes are mapped at same offsets in the unicode blocks. We use the AksharaMukha[2] tool to perform lossless transliteration between these Indic scripts.

3.3 Romanization of Indic languages

We also experiment with romanized models for all Indic languages in our work to translate to English. In this sub-section, we briefly explain the different ways using which we perform the romanization. Generally, there is no standard way to perform romanization for Indic languages, since the way one types it colloquially is quite personal in style. Hence we perform romanization using multiple ways. This includes machine learning-based romanization as well as rule-based romanization techniques which covers different possible ways of romanizing, which will be open-sourced[3].

In brief, for each language, we first generate 4 variants of romanization:

1. Raw & case-insensitive ASCII transliteration of the script (a readable lossy variant of the Velthuis scheme). For example, vowel diacritics are dropped (like ī→i, ū→u, etc.).
2. Approximate colloquial transcription of the script (taking into consideration phonological mapping to English, schwa deletion, etc.), and also involving language-specific random substitutions of related roman representations of consonants (like ph→f, v→w, etc.) and vowels (like ī→ee, ū→oo, etc.)
3. Consonant-only romanization (including initial vowels), to simulate (extreme) social media short-hand typing (not done for Urdu & Sindhi, as the roman variant-1 already does the same for languages that use Perso–Arabic scripts).
4. ML-based romanization using the python-library: LibIndicTrans[4].

We further generate generate 2 batches of the full dataset by mixing different variants of the above 4 romanizations at the word-level.

4 Indic to English MT

In this section, we explore different models for Indic to English translation using datasets mentioned in section 3.1.1. Note that before training, we perform text normalization of all datasets using the Indic-NLP-Library.

4.1 Experimental settings

The input sentence to the models is prepended with the language-tag token, "__*langcode*__ ", inorder to explicitly provides cues to the model about what the source language is. All the models experimented above are transformer-based, with the same network and hyperparameter configurations as in *transformer-big* (Vaswani et al., 2017), which has 6 encoder layers and 6 decoder layers inorder to be consistent with the scores comparison against the previous work (Dabre et al., 2021). For all experiments, we use the sentence-piece tokenizer (Kudo and Richardson, 2018) to build our sub-word vocabulary, with vocabulary sizes for input and output sides respectively 32000 (Indic side) and 16000 (English side). We use Marian-NMT toolkit (Junczys-Dowmunt et al., 2018) to train all our models, with mean cross-entropy as the loss function. Note that all models are trained from scratch.

4.2 Unified models

First, we build models from English specific to Indo-Aryan (ia2en) and Dravidian (dr2en) languages to compare how these models perform with respect to a model which is trained for both the Indic language families (in2en). As explained in section 3.2, we use Malayalam as the common script for Dravidian model and Devanagari for Indo-Aryan and Indic models.

Table 3 presents the performance across languages (ia2en and dr2en models are shown in same row for simplicity). We see that the Indic model trained on both the families outperform the scores

[2] https://github.com/virtualvinodh/aksharamukha

[3] https://github.com/GokulNC/Indic-Romanizer

[4] https://github.com/libindic/indic-trans

Model	as	bn	gu	hi	kn	ml	mr	ne	or	pa	sd	si	ta	te	ur
	Indic-En														
IndicBART	-	30.7	33.6	36.0	27.4	30.4	30.0	-	28.6	34.2	-	8.5	27.7	32.7	-
ia2en, dr2en	21.4	30.2	32.8	36.1	25.3	27.7	28.9	35.1	28.4	34.2	24.1	12.8	22.5	29.6	24.9
in2en	23.9	31.8	33.9	36.8	28.1	30.7	30.7	36.2	31.3	35.3	24.1	15.1	27.7	33.0	25.1
rom_in2en	**24.1**	**31.9**	**34.0**	**37.3**	**28.4**	**30.9**	**30.7**	**36.3**	**31.5**	**35.3**	**24.7**	**15.3**	**28.3**	**33.0**	**25.8**
	En-Indic														
IndicBART	-	17.3	22.6	31.3	16.7	14.2	14.7	-	10.1	21.9	-	-	14.9	20.4	-
en2ia, en2dr	6.3	17.4	22.6	31.4	16.1	14.1	14.8	10.5	10.1	21.7	18.9	8.8	14.4	20.5	20.2
en2in	6.3	17.2	21.9	31.0	16.2	13.7	14.7	10.4	9.9	21.5	18.1	8.9	14.5	20.5	19.8
bt_en2in	9.9	18.9	23.1	34.2	18.7	16.2	16.1	17.1	14.3	23.9	23.7	14.1	17.2	22.3	22.3
bt_en2ia, bt_en2dr	**10.8**	**19.8**	**23.7**	**36.1**	20.0	17.3	**16.8**	**17.6**	**16.7**	**24.3**	**24.2**	**14.1**	17.2	**22.9**	**23.6**
t_bt_en2dr	-	-	-	-	**20.1**	**17.5**	-	-	-	-	-	-	**18.1**	22.8	-

Table 3: Comparison of BLEU scores of different trained models of same network architecture on FLoRes101 benchmark (Goyal et al., 2021) along with the scores of the existing best open-source model trained on Samanantar, taken from IndicBART paper (Dabre et al., 2021)

of family-specific models. This observation is consistent with the results for many other languages, where we see significant gains in accuracy with a shared encoder, in-cases like many-to-one NMT (Arivazhagan et al., 2019).

4.3 Script-agnostic model

We generate a romanized version of the parallel dataset available as explained in Section 3.3, which is typically 6x large in size due to different ways of romanization the **same** data, and train a Roman-Indic-to-English model (rom_in2en). Table 3 shows the performance of this romanized model. We see that the model is slightly better (on the romanized benchmark) than the *in2en* model. This can be attributed to the significant reduction in alphabet size of the model: Devanagari usually requires more than 80 characters (on average) to represent all Indic languages; whereas in the roman model, only 26 characters (though a bit lossy). Based on manual analysis, we infer that romanized models are slightly more robust to noise in inputs, owing to the varied nature of the romanized data. We also note that owing to increased amount of data in abjad form (due to romanization variant-3, shown in section 3.3), the performance of Sindhi and Urdu (which use Arabic scripts) have significantly improved.

In addition, to study how our model performs with real-world code-switched (roman) data, we attempt the Microsoft GLUECoS (Khanuja et al., 2020) Machine Translation task[5]. We fine-tune our model on the training set of the above dataset, and measure a validation BLEU score of 27.36. Unfortuanately, the leaderboard of the task is not yet out. Upon manually checking the validation results, we see that our model has performed reasonably good despite the fact that the dataset is code-mixed and romanization styles were somewhat different. Although this is not a comparable result, we hope that this is helpful in advancing further Indic-NMT research on this benchmark.

5 English to Indic MT

In this section, we explore one-to-many NMT models for training English to Indic translator. We initially train models using the parallel data, then train few more models using synthetic data from monolingual corpora to understand the level of improvement achievable using raw data.

5.1 Experimental settings

The input sentences to all the models is prepended with a novel type of language-tag token, "*__lang-code____script-type__* ", inorder to explicitly provide cues to the model about what script-type is to be produced (in-addition for the given language). The possible script types are: 1. *'a'* to denote Perso–Arabic writing system; 2. *'i'* to denote Indic writing system; 3. *'t'* to denote Tamil alphabet, which is a small subset of the Indic set.[6]

[5]`https://github.com/microsoft/GLUECoS#code-mixed-machine-translation-task`

[6]Tamil script is a lossy Indic alphabet, which has same phonemes for unvoiced and voiced consonants (like 'k' and 'g'), in-addition to a few other features (like aspirated consonants) that are not explicitly supported in the script. In

All the trained models follow the same network configuration (transformer-big) as in the previous experiments; see section 4.1. The sub-word vocabulary sizes for input and output sides respectively 16000 (English side) and 32000 (Indic side).

5.2 Models trained only on parallel data

We initially train 3 different models (from English) just using the parallel data: Dravidian (en2dr), Indo-Aryan (en2ia) and Indic (en2in). The results are shown in Table 3. We see that the performance does not vary much between the family-specific models and the common model. This observation is consistent with the results for many other languages, where we see trivial to almost-no gains in accuracy with a shared decoder, in-cases like one-to-many NMT (Arivazhagan et al., 2019).

We experiment in the next subsection to understand if a common model could be more beneficial than family-specific models when a huge backtranslated data is augmented with the (upsampled) original data.

5.3 Models trained on parallel and back-translated data

Using all the Indic monolingual data listed in Section 3.1.3, we generate English sentences using the *rom_in2en* model with a beam-search width of 6. We then train 4 models (from English) after upsampling the parallel data and concatenating with the backtranslated dataset: 1. *bt_en2in*: To all Indic languages after 5× upsampling; 2. *bt_en2ia*: To Indo-Aryan languages after 6× upsampling; 3. *bt_en2dr*: To Dravidian languages after 10× upsampling; 4. *t_bt_en2dr*: To Dravidian languages after 7× normal upsampling, and 3× Tamilized-augmented upsampling (by converting other Dravidian alphabets to Tamil subset and marking their script_type as '*t*' when prepending language token). The upsampling scale is decided such that the amount of original parallel data and backtranslated data are in ratio 1:2.

Table 3 shows the performance of all the 4 models. We see that, family-specific models perform notably better than a common model (given a fixed model size). Moreover, for the *t_bt_en2dr* model, we observe a significant boost in accuracy for Tamil after the Tamilized-data is augmented, and a trivial improvement for Malayalam and Kannada compared to *bt_en2dr*.

Section 5.3, we further clarify on how treating Tamil as a special case could be helpful to improve its performance.

It is also seen that, our model easily outperforms models which are fine-tuned from language models like IndicBART (Dabre et al., 2021). This is because we use the same entire monolingual data (Kakwani et al., 2020) which was used to pretrain IndicBART, but along with supervised translation signals in the form of backtranslated data.

For very-low resource languages (like Sindhi and Sinhala), we notice very significant improvements with back-translation, even with relatively lesser amount of monolingul data.

6 Discussions and Conclusion

We demonstrate in this paper various methods to achieve improvement in performance, especially across South Asian languages which were not previously explored along with the languages of India. We believe our presented contributions are more of exploratory nature, and make fundamental proposals (like always building romanized models when the source side is Indic). Although the fact that a unified model results in better performance in low-resource scenarios has been discovered by many prior work and hence not surprising, our work merely focuses on quantitatively studying the improvement in the case of Indic languages. In this section, we provide general suggestions for research groups working on NMT for Indic languages.

In general, to train model for any low-resource Indic language to English, we recommend that data from all the languages is used to train a multilingual model.[7] Especially, training a romanized model would be more beneficial, since it would be a script-agnostic model, and hence easily generalize for code-mixed and social media texts.

For training English to any low-resource Indic language, it maybe be preferable to train family-specific models when working under resource-contrained settings. Especially for languages of the countries Pakistan, Bangladesh, Nepal and Sri Lanka, we highly recommend and encourage them to exploit the datasets made available by researchers of India. If possible, it is highly recommended to exploit the abundant monolingual data and train models using backtranslated data.

[7]Works like (Dabre et al., 2021) have already shown why multilingual models are more preferable for Indic languages, so we do not redemonstrate it in our work.

6.1 Limitations

As generally known, bigger models could push the improvements even further than what we have seen in our results. In fact, the recent work by (Ramesh et al., 2022) show better results on the FLoRes101 benchmark by using a transformer-4x model even without using back-translated data. We only benchmark on transformer-2x in this work for consistent comparison, and to be more practical during training and inference (as well as due to our unaffordability of large infrastructure for such experimentations). Also, we only perform one round of back-translation to study English to Indic models in Section 5.3. We encourage researchers to study multiple rounds of back-translations (which is out of scope for this paper).

Thorough anlaysis of the performance on code-mixed (not code-switched) data using benchmarks like PHINC (Srivastava and Singh, 2020) is required for the *rom_in2en* model in Section 4.3, which is one of the on-going works in our research.

References

Naveen Arivazhagan, Ankur Bapna, Orhan Firat, Dmitry Lepikhin, Melvin Johnson, Maxim Krikun, Mia Xu Chen, Yuan Cao, George Foster, Colin Cherry, Wolfgang Macherey, Zhifeng Chen, and Yonghui Wu. 2019. Massively multilingual neural machine translation in the wild: Findings and challenges.

Raj Dabre, Himani Shrotriya, Anoop Kunchukuttan, Ratish Puduppully, Mitesh M. Khapra, and Pratyush Kumar. 2021. Indicbart: A pre-trained model for natural language generation of indic languages.

M. B. Emeneau. 1956. India as a lingustic area. *Language*, 32(1):3–16.

Naman Goyal, Cynthia Gao, Vishrav Chaudhary, Peng-Jen Chen, Guillaume Wenzek, Da Ju, Sanjana Krishnan, Marc'Aurelio Ranzato, Francisco Guzman, and Angela Fan. 2021. The flores-101 evaluation benchmark for low-resource and multilingual machine translation.

Francisco Guzmán, Peng-Jen Chen, Myle Ott, Juan Pino, Guillaume Lample, Philipp Koehn, Vishrav Chaudhary, and Marc'Aurelio Ranzato. 2019. Two new evaluation datasets for low-resource machine translation: Nepali-english and sinhala-english.

Tahir Javed, Sumanth Doddapaneni, Abhigyan Raman, Kaushal Santosh Bhogale, Gowtham Ramesh, Anoop Kunchukuttan, Pratyush Kumar, and Mitesh M. Khapra. 2021. Towards building asr systems for the next billion users.

Marcin Junczys-Dowmunt, Roman Grundkiewicz, Tomasz Dwojak, Hieu Hoang, Kenneth Heafield, Tom Neckermann, Frank Seide, Ulrich Germann, Alham Fikri Aji, Nikolay Bogoychev, André F. T. Martins, and Alexandra Birch. 2018. Marian: Fast neural machine translation in c++.

Divyanshu Kakwani, Anoop Kunchukuttan, Satish Golla, Gokul N.C., Avik Bhattacharyya, Mitesh M. Khapra, and Pratyush Kumar. 2020. IndicNLPSuite: Monolingual Corpora, Evaluation Benchmarks and Pre-trained Multilingual Language Models for Indian Languages. In *Findings of EMNLP*.

Simran Khanuja, Sandipan Dandapat, Anirudh Srinivasan, Sunayana Sitaram, and Monojit Choudhury. 2020. GLUECoS: An evaluation benchmark for code-switched NLP. In *Proceedings of the 58th Annual Meeting of the Association for Computational Linguistics*, pages 3575–3585, Online. Association for Computational Linguistics.

Shreya Khare, Ashish Mittal, Anuj Diwan, Sunita Sarawagi, Preethi Jyothi, and Samarth Bharadwaj. 2021. Low Resource ASR: The Surprising Effectiveness of High Resource Transliteration. In *Proc. Interspeech 2021*, pages 1529–1533.

Yash Khemchandani, Sarvesh Mehtani, Vaidehi Patil, Abhijeet Awasthi, Partha Talukdar, and Sunita Sarawagi. 2021. Exploiting language relatedness for low web-resource language model adaptation: An Indic languages study. In *Proceedings of the 59th Annual Meeting of the Association for Computational Linguistics and the 11th International Joint Conference on Natural Language Processing (Volume 1: Long Papers)*, pages 1312–1323, Online. Association for Computational Linguistics.

Taku Kudo and John Richardson. 2018. Sentencepiece: A simple and language independent subword tokenizer and detokenizer for neural text processing.

Gurpreet Singh Lehal and Tejinder Singh Saini. 2012. Development of a complete Urdu-Hindi transliteration system. In *Proceedings of COLING 2012: Posters*, pages 643–652, Mumbai, India. The COLING 2012 Organizing Committee.

Toshiaki Nakazawa, Hideki Nakayama, Chenchen Ding, Raj Dabre, Shohei Higashiyama, Hideya Mino, Isao Goto, Win Pa Pa, Anoop Kunchukuttan, Shantipriya Parida, Ondřej Bojar, Chenhui Chu, Akiko Eriguchi, Kaori Abe, Yusuke Oda, and Sadao Kurohashi. 2021. Overview of the 8th workshop on Asian translation. In *Proceedings of the 8th Workshop on Asian Translation (WAT2021)*, pages 1–45, Online. Association for Computational Linguistics.

Thi-Vinh Ngo, Phuong-Thai Nguyen, Thanh-Le Ha, Khac-Quy Dinh, and Le-Minh Nguyen. 2020. Improving multilingual neural machine translation for low-resource languages: French, English - Vietnamese. In *Proceedings of the 3rd Workshop on Technologies for MT of Low Resource Languages*, pages 55–61, Suzhou, China. Association for Computational Linguistics.

Jerin Philip, Vinay P. Namboodiri, and C. V. Jawahar. 2019. A baseline neural machine translation system for indian languages.

Matt Post. 2018. A call for clarity in reporting BLEU scores. In *Proceedings of the Third Conference on Machine Translation: Research Papers*, pages 186–191, Belgium, Brussels. Association for Computational Linguistics.

Gowtham Ramesh, Sumanth Doddapaneni, Aravinth Bheemaraj, Mayank Jobanputra, Raghavan AK, Ajitesh Sharma, Sujit Sahoo, Harshita Diddee, Mahalakshmi J, Divyanshu Kakwani, Navneet Kumar, Aswin Pradeep, Kumar Deepak, Vivek Raghavan, Anoop Kunchukuttan, Pratyush Kumar, and Mitesh Shantadevi Khapra. 2021. Samanantar: The largest publicly available parallel corpora collection for 11 indic languages.

Gowtham Ramesh, Sumanth Doddapaneni, Aravinth Bheemaraj, Mayank Jobanputra, Raghavan AK, Ajitesh Sharma, Sujit Sahoo, Harshita Diddee, Mahalakshmi J, Divyanshu Kakwani, Navneet Kumar, Aswin Pradeep, Srihari Nagaraj, Kumar Deepak, Vivek Raghavan, Anoop Kunchukuttan, Pratyush Kumar, and Mitesh Shantadevi Khapra. 2022. Samanantar: The Largest Publicly Available Parallel Corpora Collection for 11 Indic Languages. *Transactions of the Association for Computational Linguistics*, 10:145–162.

Shashank Siripragada, Jerin Philip, Vinay P. Namboodiri, and C V Jawahar. 2020. A multilingual parallel corpora collection effort for Indian languages. In *Proceedings of the 12th Language Resources and Evaluation Conference*, pages 3743–3751, Marseille, France. European Language Resources Association.

Vivek Srivastava and Mayank Kumar Singh. 2020. Phinc: A parallel hinglish social media code-mixed corpus for machine translation. In *WNUT*.

Ashish Vaswani, Noam Shazeer, Niki Parmar, Jakob Uszkoreit, Llion Jones, Aidan N. Gomez, Lukasz Kaiser, and Illia Polosukhin. 2017. Attention is all you need.

Haitong Zhang, Haoyue Zhan, Yang Zhang, Xinyuan Yu, and Yue Lin. 2021. Revisiting ipa-based cross-lingual text-to-speech.

APPENDIX

A Indic languages

Language (& family)	ISO code	Script(s)	Countries
Assamese (Indo-Aryan)	as	Eastern Nagari	India
Bengali (Indo-Aryan)	bn	Eastern Nagari	Bangladesh, India
Gujrati (Indo-Aryan)	gu	Gujarati	India
Hindostani (Indo-Aryan)			
→ Hindi	hi	Devanagari	India
→ Urdu	ur	Perso–Arabic	Pakistan, India
Kannada (Dravidian)	kn	Kannada–Telugu	India
Malayalam (Dravidian)	ml	Malayalam	India
Marathi (Indo-Aryan)	mr	Marathi	India
Nepali (Indo-Aryan)	ne	Devanagari	Nepal
Oriya (Indo-Aryan)	or	Odia	India
Panjabi (Indo-Aryan)	pa	Gurmukhi Shahmukhi	India Pakistan
Sindhi (Indo-Aryan)	sd	Perso–Arabic Parivardhita Devanagari	Pakistan India
Sinhala (Indo-Aryan)	si	Sinhala	Sri Lanka
Tamil (Dravidian)	ta	Tamil	India, Sri Lanka
Telugu (Dravidian)	te	Telugu	India

Figure 3: List of all 15 South Asian languages studied in this work

Author Index

Association for Computational Linguistics
209 N. Eighth Street
Stroudsburg, Pennsylvania 18360

ISBN 978-1-7138-5628-3

CURRAN ASSOCIATES INC.
proceedings.com